T0339873

BUDDHISM AFTER MAO

BUDDHISM AFTER MAO

Negotiations, Continuities, and Reinventions

Edited by Ji Zhe, Gareth Fisher, and
André Laliberté

UNIVERSITY OF HAWAI'I PRESS
HONOLULU

© 2019 University of Hawai'i Press
All rights reserved
Paperback edition 2020

Printed in the United States of America

25 24 23 22 21 20   6 5 4 3 2 1

Library of Congress Cataloging-in-Publication Data

Names: Ji, Zhe (Researcher), editor. | Fisher, Gareth, editor. |
  Laliberté, André, editor.
Title: Buddhism after Mao : negotiations, continuities, and reinventions /
  edited by Ji Zhe, Gareth Fisher, and André Laliberté.
Description: Honolulu, Hawai'i : University of Hawai'i Press, [2019] |
  Includes bibliographical references and index.
Identifiers: LCCN 2018061665 | ISBN 9780824877347 (cloth ; alk. paper)
Subjects: LCSH: Buddhism—China—History—1949-
Classification: LCC BQ647 .B83 2019 | DDC 294.30951/09045—dc23
LC record available at https://lccn.loc.gov/2018061665

ISBN 978-0-8248-8834-3 (pbk.)

University of Hawai'i Press books are printed on acid-free paper and meet the guidelines for
permanence and durability of the Council on Library Resources.

Cover art: Jing'an Temple on West Nanjing Road, Shanghai. Summer 2013.
Photo by Huang Weishan.

CONTENTS

Acknowledgments   *vii*

Introduction: Exploring Buddhism in Post-Mao China   1
JI ZHE, GARETH FISHER, AND ANDRÉ LALIBERTÉ

Part I. Negotiating Legitimacy: Making Buddhism with the State

1. Buddhism under Jiang, Hu, and Xi: The Politics of Incorporation   21
ANDRÉ LALIBERTÉ

2. Administering Bodhisattva Guanyin's Island: *The Monasteries, Political Entities, and Power Holders* of Putuoshan   45
CLAIRE VIDAL

3. Spiritual Technologies and the Politics of Buddhist Charity   77
SUSAN K. MCCARTHY

4. Tourist Temples and Places of Practice: Charting Multiple Paths in the Revival of Monasteries   97
BRIAN J. NICHOLS

Part II. Revival and Continuity: The Monastic Tradition and Beyond

5. Bridging the Gap: Chan and Tiantai Dharma Lineages from Republican to Post-Mao China   123
DANIELA CAMPO

6. "Transmitting the Precepts in Conformity with the Dharma": Restoration, Adaptation, and Standardization of Ordination Procedures   152
ESTER BIANCHI

7. Schooling Dharma Teachers: The Buddhist Academy System and Sangha Education 171
JI ZHE

8. A Study of Laynuns in Minnan, 1920s–2010s: Buddhism, State Institutions, and Popular Culture 210
ASHIWA YOSHIKO AND DAVID L. WANK

Part III. Reinventing the Dharma: Buddhism in a Changing Society

9. Urban Restructuring and Temple Agency—a Case Study of the Jing'an Temple 251
HUANG WEISHAN

10. Places of Their Own: Exploring the Dynamics of Religious Diversity in Public Buddhist Temple Space 271
GARETH FISHER

11. Cyberactivities and "Civilized" Worship: Assessing Contexts and Modalities of Online Ritual Practices 290
STEFANIA TRAVAGNIN

References 313

About the Contributors 343

Index 347

ACKNOWLEDGMENTS

This book originated from a conference held in Paris in October 2014 as a part of the international research project "Buddhism after Mao: Religion, Power, and Society in China since 1980." We are extremely grateful to the "Emergence(s)" program of the City of Paris for its funding of this conference and the Sheng Yen Education Foundation for its publication grant. We would like to thank all participants and discussants of the conference, especially Vincent Goossaert, Adam Yuet Chau, Nicolas Sihlé, and Vincent Durand-Dastès, for their insightful comments. We thank also the anonymous manuscript reviewers whose remarks helped us to greatly improve our work. Finally, we would like to express our gratitude to the Institut National des Langues et Civilisations Orientales (INALCO); the Groupe Sociétés, Religions, Laïcités (GSRL); and the Centre d'Etudes Interdisciplinaires sur le Bouddhisme (CEIB) for their administrative support during different stages of the production of this book and the editors of the University of Hawai'i Press for their efficiency and professionalism.

INTRODUCTION

Exploring Buddhism in Post-Mao China

JI ZHE, GARETH FISHER, AND ANDRÉ LALIBERTÉ

In China resides the largest community of people on the planet who identify Buddhism as an important source of meaning in their lives. Surveys on religious attitudes conducted by both scholars and opinion research firms in the 2000s indicate that self-identified Buddhists represent the largest religious group in China, making up more than 10 percent of the adult population (Ji 2012). This percentage is far greater than that found in other officially recognized religions in China (i.e., Taoism, Catholicism, Protestantism, and Islam).[1] Since the beginning of the twenty-first century, Han (Mahayana) Buddhism alone (not including Vajrayana [Tibetan] or Theravada forms) is the largest institutionalized religion in China, with at least fifteen thousand sites and one hundred thousand clerics (Ji 2012, 14). At the time of this writing, Buddhism is also a more visible social and cultural phenomenon than at any time since 1949: Numerous temples and monasteries have received official permission and even encouragement to rebuild and expand, and the party-state has directly engaged Buddhist groups in activities to promote social welfare, national unity, and the PRC's soft power.[2] Buddhist actors and institutions also warrant increasing mention in the country's media.[3] This greater public visibility does not shield Buddhist leaders from critical stories, however. For example, one of the most shocking news stories in 2018 was that Xuecheng, the chair of the Buddhist Association of China (BAC; Zhongguo Fojiao Xiehui 中国佛教协会; see chapters 1 and 3 by Laliberté and McCarthy, respectively), faced accusations of corruption and sexual harassment. There are also aspects of Buddhism in China today that are less visible but just as important, such as the mobilization of Buddhist ideas and practices as moral resources in people's rapidly changing lives. Nevertheless, in spite of its size and influence, Buddhism (particularly Han Buddhism) has received relatively little scholarly attention. This volume aims to remedy this gap.[4]

The present regrowth of Buddhism in China has followed more than a century of tumultuous change. Beginning in the late nineteenth century, modernist reformers such as Kang Youwei 康有为 (1858–1927) and Zhang Zhidong 张之洞 (1837–1909) presented challenges to traditional forms of temple-based Buddhist religiosity by introducing campaigns to "build schools with temple property" (*miaochan xingxue* 庙产兴学), which were taken up in various forms throughout the Republican period (Duara 1991; Goossaert 2006; Poon 2011; Katz 2014). The neologism "religion" (*zongjiao* 宗教) was imported from the West through Japan. This concept brought with it the burden of Christian-inspired normative understanding, which placed religiosity as a special, isolated category of human thought and social life opposed to the secular. This, in turn, led political and intellectual elites of the Republic of China (Zhonghua Minguo 中华民国, 1912–) to favor highly institutionalized forms of Buddhism (Goossaert and Palmer 2011, 73–83). As a consequence, Buddhist leaders scrambled to fit their temples and practices into forms acceptable to the new nation-state and avoid the label of "superstition" (*mixin* 迷信), which would lead their activities to be banned (Goossaert 2008, 216–218). While many new forms of Buddhism developed during this period and Buddhists played a pivotal role in the construction of a new modern society (Chan 1953; Welch 1967, 1968; Ashiwa and Wank 2009; Katz 2014; Kiely and Jessup 2016; Ji, Campo, and Wang 2016; Ji 2017), precedent was established for intervention in Buddhist institutions and practices by a centralized state with a further reach into everyday society than its imperial predecessor's. This also set the stage for the greater control of Buddhism by the state during the subsequent People's Republic of China (PRC; Zhonghua Renmin Gongheguo 中华人民共和国, 1949–), which thoroughly co-opted Buddhist institutions by setting up a national association under its own control (Ji 2008a; chapter 7 by Ji Zhe in this volume). Expressions of Buddhist-based religiosity that fell outside of the association's control were marked as superstition or part of the evil legacy of feudalism and were restricted in a more aggressive and systematic manner than had been the case under the Republican regime (Welch 1972; Hou 2012; Jessup 2012; Xue 2015). During the Cultural Revolution (Wenhua Da Geming 文化大革命, 1966–1976), all forms of religion were denounced under the category of China's "four olds" (*sijiu* 四旧)[5] as obstacles to a modern Communist society: Mobs of Red Guards (Hongweibing 红卫兵) were allowed to ransack temples, destroy images and scriptures, and humiliate monastics. While recent studies have shown that a very small number of monastics continued to carry out religious activities in secret (see Qin 2000, 143; chapter 8 by Ashiwa and Wank in this volume), the overwhelming majority were forced to return to lay life. It is no exaggeration to say that, during this period, Buddhism experienced the worst destruction in its whole history in China.[6]

However, the death of Mao and the rise to power of Communist China's second paramount leader, Deng Xiaoping 邓小平 (1904–1997), brought with them a certain relaxation of control on religious activities. Document no. 19, issued by the party in 1982, established the legality of certain religious practices and even the restoration of religious sites destroyed during the Cultural Revolution (MacInnis 1989; Leung 2005). In the wake of this policy change, a variety of religious activities have reemerged in mainland China. In the case of Buddhism, this revival started slowly in the 1980s: At that time, few Buddhist temples were open to active worship, and access to Buddhist scriptures was limited. In the 1990s, 2000s, and 2010s, however, Buddhism has begun to grow at a rapid rate: Old temples are being restored and thousands of new ones opened all over the country; younger monastics are taking the place of older clergy who took the tonsure before the Communist revolution; and, with the help of both overseas and domestic Chinese Buddhists, a significant amount of religious literature is now available at temples and online. All of this has contributed to the remarkably robust reemergence of Buddhist institutions and practices we see today.

The rapid growth of Buddhism in the past few decades and its continued survival into the future has depended on the maintenance of a careful balance between varying interests and demands. On the one hand, Buddhist actors have to negotiate with the post-Mao authoritarian state, which is always officially atheist, to maintain or expand legal spaces for Buddhist practice. On the other hand, they must strive (or appear to strive) to rebuild or maintain continuity with the past, so that current doctrines, authorities, and organizations will be recognized as legitimate by fellow practitioners, as well as the state and society at large. In the process of negotiating Buddhist reconstruction, however, innovations have also emerged, by both design and necessity, on both discursive and practical levels. To gain legitimacy, innovations have also entailed reinventions of Buddhist history. Moreover, while change has been commonplace throughout Chinese Buddhist history, the challenges of both emerging from the greatest period of devastation in its history and adapting to a period of staggering economic and cultural change during the last forty years have increased the need for both continuities and reinventions.

Providing a comprehensive picture of the negotiations, continuities, and reinventions entailed in the making of Buddhism in post-Mao mainland China in a single volume presents a significant challenge. In order to make this into a manageable task, we focus in this volume mainly on the evolution of Buddhist institutions such as temples and monasteries, as places of worship and learning, as tourist sites, and as providers of philanthropy from the beginnings of Buddhist revival in the early 1980s through the middle 2010s. In this way, we follow the approach of Holmes Welch (1967, 1968, 1972) in his trilogy on modern Chinese Buddhism from the end of the Qing dynasty to the early Cultural Revolution, which explored how Buddhist institutions such as temples, academies, and lay associations responded to the challenges and opportunities of modernity. Institutions, however, are more than physical spaces and organizations: They also constitute norms, rules, and memories. It is to his last work, *Buddhism under Mao* (Welch 1972), that the title of our book pays homage. Thus, many chapters of this book also examine Buddhist institutions such as lineages, ordination procedures and training of clerics, and the relationship between Buddhist institutions and non-Buddhist actors. Contributors to this book are also aware of the changing nature of institutions, and so our chapters focus on the changed classification of nuns and lay practitioners, nonelite lay practitioners' role in restoring temples, and changing modalities of ritual practices. This book also explores the relationship between Buddhist institutions and the state and market and examines how the former act as active agents in the creation of the latter, just as they have throughout Chinese history. In this respect, our volume also continues the work of Ashiwa and Wank (2009), Goossaert and Palmer (2011), and Kiely and Jessup (2016) in exploring the importance of religion in general and Buddhism specifically in the making of state and society in modern China.

Besides providing a more manageable focus for a single volume, concentrating on an institutional approach is also necessitated by the availability of existing research. At present, studies on popular Buddhist practices and movements in post-Mao China, especially those led by the laity, are comparatively less developed. However, chapters 10 and 11, by Fisher and Travagnin, respectively, which examine the relationships between Buddhist institutions and lay and devotional movements, provide an important bridge to what we hope will be more detailed future research on noninstitutionalized Buddhist forms (see also Jones 2010; Sun 2010; Fisher 2014). Given the social scientific background of the contributors, we have also focused less on the intellectual and doctrinal history of Buddhism since 1978. We have also not focused much on the relations between Buddhism and the revival of non-Buddhist forms of religiosity. However, through its examination of Buddhist institutional revival, our volume does provide a fruitful place from which to begin to explore larger issues concerning the revival of religion in post-Mao China more broadly, such as the influence of social change on the role of the state, the impact of religious-themed media on social discourse, the relationship between pilgrimage and economic development (see in particular chapter 2 by Vidal), and the role of gender in navigating religious revival (see in particular chapter 8 on laynuns by Ashiwa and Wank).

With these considerations, this book addresses the gap in scholarship on lived Buddhism in the contemporary PRC by focusing comprehensively on its development in the post-Mao era. We outline below our theoretical framework and the main themes with which we seek to engage.

THEORETICAL FRAMEWORK AND GENERAL PROBLEMATIC

In recent decades, both Western and Chinese scholars have sought to move beyond early secularization theory and its simplistic statements about the disappearance of religion. As a result, a plurality of approaches to the study of religion in China has emerged.

The American approach of religious economy in the sociology of religion (Stark and Bainbridge 1987) is used by some scholars as a scientific rebuttal to secularization theory. Starting from rational choice theory and using the analogy of the market, this approach sees religious practice as consumption guided by a utilitarian calculation of costs and rewards, and religious institutions as firms providing religious goods. Accordingly, the analysis focuses on the mechanisms and impact of state regulation or deregulation of the market, the specificities of the religious "goods" offered by various "firms," and the preferences of various groups of religious consumers, which should determine together the levels of vitality of a certain religion. This theory has been most notably applied to the study of contemporary Chinese religion by Yang Fenggang (2006, 2011). Based on the assumption that "markets" for religion emerge when other spiritual substitutes, such as socialist idealism, are in retreat, the theory has provided some interesting insights about the role of the state as the key actor shaping the organizational dimension of religion in post-Mao China. However, we raise the critique that this approach is too mechanistic and that it minimizes the role of agency; its ahistorical assumption of *Homo religiosus*—the idea that being religious in a definite manner is a constant for people across space and time—leads to methodological biases that inflate the number of religious believers; and most important, it tends to reduce *Homo religiosus* to the classical liberal version of *Homo economicus*, which neglects the complex motives of religious practice and multiple motivations behind religious change. It leaves out some important drivers behind the religious beliefs and attitudes of individual adherents, such as the unique ways in which individuals living in contemporary China (or, indeed, any society) combine religion with any other number of culturally constructed elements to create particular moral repertoires (see Fisher 2012), which cannot be captured by the logics of market exchange.[7]

Another interesting approach we acknowledge, which has been applied to both Buddhism and Christianity in contemporary China, is the perspective of religious ecology developed by Sun Yanfei (2010, 2011), among others. We look at this approach as a corrective of the religious economy model because it takes into account the complex relations among religions and among different groups in the same religion, not only between religions and individuals or between religion and the state. In comparison with the religious economy model, which tends to interpret the religious landscape as an intentional consequence of the competition between religious groups, the analogy of ecology specifically sheds light on the equilibrium and complementarities between religious groups, who together form an (ideally) stable system. In this way, the religious ecology as a whole can be largely understood as the unintentional result of the practices of social actors. However, in some cases in the Chinese context (Mu 2006, 2012; Chen 2010; Li 2010; Wang and Gao 2012), the discourse of religious ecology implies the ideology of an "ecological balance," which is a euphemism that mirrors the state's ambition to "manage" religion and its opposition to the expansion of "foreign" or "new" religions. Although this is probably not the intent of its authors, the concept requires a more careful definition to free itself from this use. Moreover, the approach still relies on the assumption that religion is a "special" social category rather than a category that is mostly created and shaped by the state and that may be less relevant to ordinary actors as they pick and choose from among a variety of cultural frameworks to order their worldviews and social interactions. Following Goossaert and Palmer (2011, 13), we therefore prefer to emphasize the inclusion of Buddhist actors and institutions within a larger "social ecology" that includes both Buddhist and non-Buddhist forces. In sum, the approaches of religious economy and religious ecology have, despite their differences, heavy ideological burdens.

A third approach, developed by Adam Yuet Chau (2011b), which tries to capture the practical character of religion in general, appears more promising for understanding Chinese religion in particular. Chau suggests that there are five "modalities of doing religion" that people can adopt and combine to deal with different concerns in life. They are the discursive or scriptural, personal-cultivational, liturgical, immediate-practical, and relational. Understood from this perspective, the religious landscape can be seen as a result of competition both between and within these modalities (Chau 2011b, 2011c). This concept of "doing religion" is quite inspiring, especially in the way that it provides a means to liberate the study of religion from the substantivist and ideological view—or, to use Chau's (2011c, 550) term, the "conceptual fetishes" of the category of religion.

In our specific considerations of Buddhist religiosity in post-Mao China, we propose to build on Chau's model, particularly with respect to the way that it shifts the focus of analysis from a disproportionate emphasis on religion as a cognitive process to an action that one "does," which carries social force. This emphasis on action also leaves space for the wide variety of motivations that religious agents bring to the process of "doing" religion without the need to categorize those motivations as "sacred" or "worldly" in a way that implies a normative understanding of what religion is or ought to be. In exploring Buddhism in contemporary China, we see each of Chau's modalities at work. Using this model enables us to avoid the normative biases of singling out certain modalities of Buddhist religiosity (e.g., the discursive or scriptural) as somehow more authentic or better connected to a religious "tradition" than the others. We propose to extend Chau's model by examining the larger social processes and institutions that both inform and are created by the person-centered religious actions that Chau intensively examines. In doing so, however, we do not limit our analysis to "religious subjects" (Chau 2013) but also, and first of all, examine how Buddhism in China today is made by a variety of social institutions and forces. Indeed, it is desirable to take into account the agency of individual Buddhists and Buddhist institutions to foster social changes and macrohistorical factors that, in turn, shape Buddhist practice today; to examine both official Buddhist institutions (whether shaped by politics or the demands of religious practice) and their popular representations and local constructions; and to study both the efforts of Buddhist groups at self-preservation and their interactions with non-Buddhist social forces.

With these considerations, in this book we focus our attention on solving the following puzzle: How has Buddhism re-embedded itself into the Chinese political framework and the social fabric, which themselves have been in full transformation since the beginning of the 1980s? How have monastics and lay Buddhists overcome the significant historical discontinuities caused by Mao's three-decade rule? What new modes and strategies have they developed for social mobilization and identity construction? What does it mean for different social groups to be Buddhist or practice Buddhism in China today?

First, we look at the functioning and effects of Chinese religious policies and governmental modalities at both the national and local levels. Here our approach differs from any dichotomous model that would presume a zero-sum game between state and religion. Rather, we consider the reconfiguration of this relationship as a series of processes full of negotiations. During this production of new rules and norms, the form and content of Buddhism are reinvented, and links and borders between the religious and the secular are constantly remodeled.

Second, while focusing our study on the post-Mao era, we locate the ongoing evolution of Buddhism in a wider historical horizon, dating back to the Republican era and, in some cases, even earlier, so as to determine the dialectic between continuity and discontinuity, between the past and the present. We are building on recent research that looks into the recovering of Buddhism since the Republican period (Kiely and Jessup 2016). In fact, the remarkable ability of Buddhists to reinvent their own tradition explains to a certain extent how Buddhism has been able to rise from near extinction and thrive these last forty years. Having adapted to the vicissitudes of successive changes of dynasties, foreign influence, and warfare over two millennia, Buddhism in China has developed its own models of revitalization, some of which are still relevant to today's situation. The current political circumstances, important as they are, cannot fully explain religious change in China. In other words, Buddhists do not respond only to political constraints. Monastics in particular have elaborate strategies to deal with a wide variety of issues on the perpetuation of tradition, such as maintaining the performance of religious services, managing monastic communities, constructing temples, ensuring the transmission of precepts, and training young monastics as well as forming relations with Buddhists in other Asian countries and farther afield.

Third, Buddhists revitalize the resources they recover from their long history but also create new modes of cultural expression and new standards of morality through their participation in contemporary Buddhist institutions and activities. The dynamics that bring about these reinventions are produced not only by postreform politico-economic orders, but also by other movers of social change such as greater social stratification, the depoliticization of individual identity, a rise in social mobility, and the development of information and communication technologies. These reinventions are, of course, also due to the religious actors' creative capacities to mobilize both traditional and novel resources to recompose Buddhist doctrines, rituals, and organizations. By trying to explore these dynamics of Buddhism, our book deals with the diversification of modes of Buddhist sociability, which are also linked inseparably to general changes in the ways in which forces of globalization impact China.

In sum, what our contributors propose collectively in this book is to look at the multiple ways in which both the state and the market, both the religious and the nonreligious, and both collective and individual actors interact in the (re)production of Buddhism, with a particular focus on Buddhist institutions. We examine how these various forces and actors mobilize a variety of resources and means—from political ideologies to moral discourses, from monasticism to the Internet—so that Buddhism can persist, be justified, and be publicized. In fact, religious production and political, economic, and social production are all interwoven. While Buddhist practitioners' lives are influenced by political, economic, and social structures, the latter are also being transformed by the collective actions of Buddhist individuals. Although the lives and actions of these practitioners do not attract the attention of the world outside to the same extent as cases of social unrest, economic progress, or environmental crises, they do influence people's lives. From individuals who see in Buddhist ideas a response to their existential questions to participants in the World Buddhist Forum (Shijie Fojiao Luntan 世界佛教论坛), which mobilizes a considerable amount of resources in the sphere of the media, commerce, the security apparatus, the tourism industry, and diplomacy, Buddhism is becoming an increasingly significant component of contemporary Chinese society.

OVERVIEW OF CHAPTERS

The studies of contemporary Buddhism presented in this book are divided into sections that correspond to elements in our subtitle: "negotiations," "continuities," and "reinventions." The first section explores how Buddhist institutions have emerged and reemerged since the 1980s through a process of dynamic negotiation between state entities and religious agents. The second section focuses on the attempts of Buddhist persons and institutions to continue a range of monastic practices that were discontinued, often brutally, under Mao's reign. The third section focuses on the dynamic process by which Buddhist structures, practices, and institutions have been mobilized toward a wide range of political, economic, moral, and devotional agendas on the part of government officials, resident monastics, lay practitioners, and devotees.[8] While each section deals primarily with one of the main subthemes, all three subthemes intersect, to some degree, in each of our chapters: For instance, as many of the chapters in the third section reveal, "negotiation" is not only a process that occurs between the Buddhist leadership and government authorities but also one that occurs on an everyday level between a variety of Buddhist and non-Buddhist actors. Similarly, while the monastic institutions in the second section of the book mine Buddhist traditions to create continuities with past forms of Buddhist teachings, they inevitably reinvent certain aspects of monastic training to adapt to the circumstances and requirements of the post-Mao period.

Negotiating Legitimacy: Making Buddhism with the State

This first section of the book begins with André Laliberté's overview (chapter 1) of the relationship between several of the Chinese Communist Party's (CCP) political agendas and the expansion of Buddhist organizations in the post-Mao period, with particular attention to the more recent regimes of Presidents Hu Jintao 胡锦涛 and Xi Jinping 习近平. Just as Welch (1972, 169–230) noted several areas where the relationship between the early Mao-era state and organized Buddhism could be cooperative rather than adversarial, Laliberté sees several key areas where Buddhism and the post-Mao state share common interests. These are the ways in which a growing sangha can foster the perception overseas that the CCP is respectful of the freedom of religious belief; the potential philanthropic role that Buddhist groups can play to ease pressure on the state as a provider of social services; and the role that collaborative activities and events between mainland and Taiwanese-based Buddhists, such as the World Buddhist Forum, can play in easing cross-strait tensions. However, Laliberté stresses that these areas of common interest, particularly the latter two, have yet to develop to the extent that they can significantly advance the CCP's political agendas: Buddhist charitable groups are still relatively underdeveloped and most Taiwanese are not much influenced by the opinions of pro-mainland Buddhist leaders. Laliberté also stresses that just because areas of Buddhist development coincide with the state's interests, it does not mean that they have developed as a result of state policies: Local governments, ambitious clerics, and the support of lay practitioners are the real engines of Buddhism's growth in the post-Mao period. However, Laliberté's chapter sheds light on several reasons why the CCP does not oppose certain forms of Buddhist growth.

The next three chapters move us from a general view of the relationship between Buddhism and the national political scene to grounded local studies of how Buddhism is created with the state. Claire Vidal's chapter (chapter 2) examines Putuoshan 普陀山, one of the four sacred Buddhist mountain sites (si da ming shan 四大名山) in China. Putuoshan, an island off the coast of China's southeastern province of Zhejiang 浙江, has been designated by the state as a special tourist zone. Eschewing the popular notion that the development of Buddhist religiosity and tourism as a means of economic development are necessarily at odds with each other, Vidal explores how government agencies work with Buddhist leaders to develop religion and the economy together. This collusion is facilitated by the fact that the same persons often take on different official positions in the government bureaucracy and that local authorities and religious leaders can share close working relationships. Crucially, Vidal's findings challenge a commonly held perception that Buddhist leaders cannot or should not enter into collaboration with agents of tourist development because "true" Buddhism should be otherworldly in orientation. Citing the findings of historian Jacques Gernet, Vidal notes that Buddhist monasticism has been involved in the accumulation and circulation of money for most of its two-thousand-year history in China. The only difference in the contemporary period is that this circulation of money occurs in connection with state structures for religious governance.

While Vidal's chapter shows how monastic actors and the state make Buddhism through collaboration in the economic sphere, Susan McCarthy's chapter (chapter 3) explores the moral dimensions of state-sangha collaboration. McCarthy focuses on the figure of Xuecheng 学诚, from 2015 to 2018 chair of the BAC and abbot of the Longquan Temple (Longquan Si 龙泉寺) in Beijing. Xuecheng's moral visions for Buddhist development, which were based on the early twentieth-century reformist monk Taixu's 太虚 (1890–1947) notion of "Buddhism for the human realm" (*renjian fojiao* 人间佛教), were centered on philanthropy. The Ren'ai Charity Foundation (Ren'ai Cishan Jijinhui 仁爱慈善基金会), which is housed in the Longquan Temple and staffed by students close to Xuecheng, is dedicated to the provision of charitable services such as disaster relief, orphan care, and clothing for the needy, but also less typical charitable activities like providing rice congee to passersby in busy Beijing districts regardless of their economic need. McCarthy argues that activities like the congee distribution function less to directly provide social services (a potential area of common ground with the state that Laliberté's chapter identifies for Buddhists) and more to cultivate an ethic of civic-mindedness among Chinese citizens. Nevertheless, in this respect, it is also compatible with state goals, and state icons of selflessness such as Lei Feng are frequently invoked by Ren'ai participants. McCarthy also notes that, although it is based in a Buddhist temple, Ren'ai plays down its Buddhist connections while, at the same time, offering an outlet for Buddhist charitable giving that contrasts with more "religiously" oriented forms of Buddhist-based social activism that present problems for the state's development of an environmentally conscious, civically minded, and publicly secular citizenry, such as the purchasing of animals from the market for release in the wild (*fangsheng* 放生), which is popular among many lay Buddhists.[9]

The final chapter in this section, by Brian Nichols (chapter 4), focuses on the often intense negotiations and conflicts that occur between secular authorities and monastic leaders over the degree to which temples should exist as tourist sites instead of or in addition to serving as sites for Buddhist religious practice. Concentrating first on the problems of tourism and religious development more broadly, Nichols categorizes reviving Buddhist temples into three types: those operated by "curators," that is, those committed to restoring and maintaining the temples as heritage sites of cultural value, sometimes for the purposes of tourism, but not necessarily as active spaces for the practice of contemporary religiosity; those operated by "revivalists," who are committed to the renewal of religious practice, particularly monastic spiritual cultivation; and those that feature a combination of the two. After providing several examples of temples that fit into the first two types, Nichols devotes most of his analysis to examining the Kaiyuan Temple (Kaiyuan Si 开元寺) in Quanzhou 泉州, Fujian 福建, which exemplifies the third. His detailed examination of the temple's history in recent decades explores how the resident monastics have used a combination of resilience, growing economic power, and brute force to remove vendors and "curatorial" agencies of the local state from many parts of the temple, enabling it to function as a monastery even if it also still remains a tourist site. While Nichols acknowledges that curatorial and revivalist forces can coexist at a single temple site, his chapter mostly paints a picture of the relationship between the state and Buddhist monastics as an adversarial one. Nichols also places government authorities mostly in the curatorial camp and monastics in the revivalist one. In this way, his study contrasts with Vidal's earlier chapter on the development of Putuoshan, where monastic and state leaders appear mostly to have cooperative relations and share curatorial and revivalist aims.

Revival and Continuity: The Monastic Tradition and Beyond

The next set of chapters explores efforts of both Buddhist leaders and rank-and-file monastics, both nationally and locally, to revive monastic lineages and transmissions, the strategies they have used to carry out these revivals, and the challenges they have faced.

Daniela Campo (chapter 5) explores how monastic lineages have been revived in the post-Mao period in the Chan 禅 and Tiantai 天台 traditions. Campo traces the foundations for this revival to two eminent monks from the Republican period—Xuyun 虚云 in the Chan tradition and Dixian 谛闲 in the Tiantai tradition. First, both monks re-created certain defunct lineages within their traditions to revitalize them. Second, both emphasized the importance of spreading the Dharma as widely as possible, leading to the traveling of their disciples and the establishment of lineages outside of mainland China. In Dixian's case, this was primarily in Hong Kong; Xuyun's disciples worked to spread the Dharma in the United States. While many Chan and Tiantai temples were destroyed during the Mao era, they have been able to reestablish their lineages and re-fund the reconstruction of their temples with support from the overseas branches that Xuyun and Dixian helped to establish. Xuyun's and Dixian's Dharma heirs now also hold significant positions of authority within the BAC. Campo notes how the present-day state shares with its counterparts from previous eras support for monastics and monastic institutions that represent orthodox lineages and therefore can assert order over potentially heterodox forms of Buddhism that are more socially disruptive and less easy for the state to control.

Ester Bianchi's chapter (chapter 6) also addresses the efforts of Buddhist monastics to reestablish orthodox lineages, focusing on the standardization of procedures for monastic ordinations including the practice of "triple platform ordination" (*santan dajie* 三坛大戒) for monks and "dual ordination" (*erbuseng jie* 二部僧戒) for nuns. Bianchi traces concerns with establishing correct procedures as a means of ensuring the moral purity of the sangha at periods in Chinese history when it faced dwindling numbers and argues that the present-day sangha is motivated by similar concerns. Nevertheless, while the concerns for establishing correct ordination procedures are motivated by a desire for continuity, that is, to maintain correct procedures for ordination in spite of the disruption to the sangha created by the Cultural Revolution, they also constitute a kind of reinvention in that, as Bianchi points out, Chinese Buddhists did not always observe triple platform and dual ordination practices in the past. The adoption of these ordination procedures, however, does continue the projects of reform-minded monastics from the Republican period who were motivated to place the ordination procedures of the contemporary Chinese sangha more in line with those from other countries, which they hoped would strengthen its legitimacy at home.

The chapter by Ji Zhe (chapter 7) addresses the revival of Buddhist academies for the training of monastics. As with the revival of Dharma lineages and ordination procedures, the revival of Buddhist academies represents a continuation of the concerns of monastic reformers in the early twentieth century. However, while Dharma lineages and ordination procedures were merely modified during this time, Buddhist academies were introduced as a completely novel form of sangha education. Modeling the academies on Western secular schools and seminaries, their architects aimed to use them to replace traditional forms of sangha education that centered mostly on the training of monastics in ritual duties within regionally specific Dharma lineages with a national system of Dharma education centered on training in Buddhist doctrine and history along with secular subjects. While the establishment of these modern Buddhist academies met with mixed results in the Republican period and encountered dwindling numbers in the negative political environment of the Mao era, Ji's chapter shows that they have reemerged robustly in the post-Mao period. However, in contrast to the visions of Republican-era reformers, Buddhist academies in the PRC have been significantly controlled by the state and include courses on political education. Ji's chapter discusses in detail how BAC leaders have worked to try to centralize a national curriculum for sangha education focused on the Buddhist Academy of China (Zhongguo Foxueyuan 中国佛学院) in Beijing as the central (and sometimes only) institution of higher learning for monastics. These efforts at centralization, however, occasionally have been subverted by the growing financial independence of powerful regional academies and the interventions of increasingly powerful local governments.

While the chapters by Campo, Bianchi, and Ji focus on elements of sangha revival on a national level, chapter 8 by Ashiwa Yoshiko and David Wank focuses on a local phenomenon from the Minnan 闽南 region of Fujian, that of laynuns (*caigu* 菜姑), women who have not been ordained as nuns and do not shave their heads but, like nuns, do not marry, practice a vegetarian diet, and leave home to live communally. While the laynun tradition received support in the Republican period and laynuns were less apt than ordained monastics to be the targets of Mao-era political campaigns, this tradition has met with a number of challenges in the present post-Mao period. One of these is the passing of an elder generation of laynuns from before the Cultural Revolution who were unable to train disciples to replace them. Another is the difficulty since the 1990s that laynuns have experienced in receiving education at regional Buddhist academies that, in following national regulations, will enroll only fully ordained nuns (for part or all of their programs). While state authorities in Minnan have now recognized the laynun as an appropriate category of religious professional, it is still not recognized as a religious category within the practice of Buddhism. Here we see how the motivation to centralize on the part of both Buddhist leaders and the state, which, as demonstrated in the first three chapters of this section, is a driving force of national monastic revival, can threaten local forms of monasticism.

Reinventing the Dharma: Buddhism in a Changing Society

While the first two sections of our volume focus mostly on the process by which Buddhist institutions have been revived or refashioned by monastic leaders under the close concern and direction of the state, our third and final section explores how local religiosities as well as other forms of local economic and cultural development have been set in motion through the restoration and growth of Buddhist institutions such as monasteries. As the chapters make clear, both the BAC and the state have a strong influence even on these localized religious forms, but that influence is often more indirect, and popular religiosities that emerge, even in state-sanctioned temples, do not often conform to centralized visions of Buddhist revival.

Moreover, local governments often interpret religious regulations in very different ways from the central party-state. These differences in interpretation can present both opportunities and challenges to specific localized monasteries and Buddhist groups.

The first chapter in this section, by Huang Weishan (chapter 9), explores how the charismatic and entrepreneurial abbot Huiming 慧明 negotiates with state actors to promote his own vision of Buddhist religious development at the Jing'an Temple (Jing'an Si 静安寺). The temple has presented a particular challenge for restoration as a functioning religious site because it is located in the heart of Shanghai in one of the most expensive areas for commercial real estate in the country. After reclaiming a small area for temple use following the Cultural Revolution, Huiming succeeded in reclaiming a larger area by buying out local businesses and persuading them to relocate. The abbot's visions for religious revival sometimes still clash with those of local authorities, who prefer to view the temple as a "cultural" rather than a "religious" site, though both sides seem willing to use the interests of the other to further their own aims. Like Nichols, Huang stresses the importance of a strong-willed and well-connected abbot in ensuring that, to use Nichols's terms, a temple is dominated by "revivalist" forces committed to strengthening Buddhist religiosity rather than "curatorial" forces that see temples largely as cultural sites to be appreciated by tourists.

The final two chapters, by Gareth Fisher and Stefania Travagnin (chapters 10 and 11, respectively), switch the focus to lay and devotional practices. Rather than exploring cooperation or conflict between the state and monastics, Fisher's chapter examines the wide variety of popular "Buddhisms" that have accompanied the revival of institutional Buddhism in the post-Mao period. Through case studies of two prominent temples, the Guangji Temple (Guangji Si 广济寺) in Beijing and the Bailin Temple (Bailin Si 柏林寺) near Shijiazhuang 石家庄 in Hebei 河北, Fisher's chapter focuses on the large open spaces that exist within these temples for the legal practice of religion and how they are filled not merely by tourists but also by lay practitioners and devotees seeking everything from magical cures for health ailments to moral reorientation within a country where social roles and expectations are frequently upset. Fisher argues counterintuitively that important Buddhist sites like the Guangji and Bailin Temples, whose restoration has been spearheaded by leading monastic figures in close connection with central state authorities, actually facilitate a greater diversity of popular religious practices and moralistic discourses than smaller, more private religious sites constructed by grassroots lay practitioners that have relatively few dealings with the state. Fisher makes this argument through a comparison between the Guangji and Bailin Temples on the one hand and a small Buddha hall in the northeast province of Jilin 吉林 on the other. Fisher observes that, while the Buddha hall was constructed around the teachings and visions of a single lay Buddhist leader for her own followers, large portions of the Guangji and

Bailin Temples exist largely as public religious sites. Though the temple monastics and the state have the ability to control the religiosities that form in the public parts of their temples, they tend not to do so, leaving those spaces open for a variety of religious practices and discourses. This contrasts with the case of the Buddha hall, where all activities and speech are closely controlled by a central leader.

Travagnin's chapter provides insight into a rapidly emerging arena of Chinese religiosity about which scholarly studies are only just beginning to emerge (see Smyer Yü 2012; Travagnin 2016a)—that of religious practice online. Travagnin specifically focuses on online worship halls, such as those found on the website of the Nanputuo Temple 南普陀寺 in Xiamen 厦门, Fujian, where lay practitioners and devotees can enter into merit-making activities in a virtual setting that are traditionally performed in temple halls. Examples of these online worship activities include making offerings to buddhas and bodhisattvas, participating in the recitation of virtual liturgies, and copying characters from sutras by typing instead of writing. While one still sees many devotees engaged in "real-life" devotional activities at temples, Travagnin speculates that online versions, which are thought to be more appealing to younger practitioners, may become more popular so that, in the future, temple-based sociality may be eroded or at least transformed.

Taken together, the chapters present a picture of Buddhist religiosity in post-Mao China that is highly diverse and that defies easy reduction into categories like "revival," "erosion," or "co-option." Buddhism in China today appeals to a broad range of contemporary persons, from middle-class practitioners seeking deritualized forms of Buddhism to employ as a social ethic (chapter 3) to working-class practitioners seeking forms of moral direction and ritual cures (chapter 10); from nonelite monastics working to preserve a tiny localized tradition (chapter 8) to entrepreneurial monks who work to shape the cultural direction of large urban communities (chapter 9). Both monastics and laypersons sometimes engage in serious projects of personal religious cultivation and moral improvement, and they are sometimes supported in these endeavors by sympathetic officials (chapter 2). Conversely, social actors as diverse as government officials (chapter 4) and petty entrepreneurs (chapter 10) along with certain monastics (chapter 2) may use Buddhism as a means of local economic development, just like their counterparts in previous historical periods. In all of these areas, the influence of the state is strong, but it is by no means uniform and, as our studies show, individual practitioners, whether monastic or lay, and working through or around Buddhist institutions, adapt to its influence in diverse and sometimes unpredictable ways (chapter 1). Our close study of Buddhist institutions in post-Mao China and those who function within them aims to open up a wide range of new inquiries within the field of modern Chinese religion, one that is still in its infancy.

NOTES

1. Even though surveys about lay Buddhist numbers could be debated from a methodological point of view, more recent surveys are moving numbers upward from 200 to 300 million Chinese who say they are more or less sensitive to (some elements of) the Buddhist cosmology and at least occasionally participate in festivals and rituals of Buddhism. See Johnson and Grim 2013; Laliberté 2011a; and chapter 1 by Laliberté in this volume.

2. In Chinese, the character *si* 寺 is used to refer to what in English can be rendered as either "temple" or "monastery." The terms "temple" and "monastery" are often used interchangeably in English translations of *si*.

3. Even in media reports that focus critically on, for instance, the commodification of temples for the sake of tourism and in controversies in the media about the wealth of monasteries, it becomes clear that Buddhist institutions constitute important actors relevant to China's economy and society.

4. There exists, however, a growing body of work on topics that relate to the subject of this volume. Hence, there is scholarship on the revival of the Tibetan Buddhist tradition (Shakya 1999; Bianchi 2001; Tuttle 2005; Makley 2007; Smyer Yü 2012; Caple 2015) and on contemporary Chinese Buddhist practices in Taiwan and in the Chinese diaspora (Jones 1999; Chandler 2004; Laliberté 2003, 2004, 2008, 2013; Madsen 2007; Huang 2009; Yü 2013). Research on Buddhism of the Chinese tradition (Han Buddhism) includes studies on the role of the Buddhist Association of China in orchestrating Buddhist revival (Magnin 1989; Wang-Toutain 1997; Birnbaum 2003a; Jingyin 2006; Ji 2008a); the social lives of monasteries and lay groups (Qin 2000; Bianchi 2001; Jones 2010; Sun 2010; Nichols 2011; Fisher 2014); the emergence of new monastic economies (Ji 2004, 2016b, 2016c; Gildow 2014) and forms of education (Gildow 2016); Buddhist engagement in philanthropic causes (Laliberté 2009, 2012; Weller et al. 2017); interaction between monasteries and the state (Ji 2004, 2011a; Ashiwa and Wank 2006; Krause 2008; Fisher 2008; Laliberté 2011a); and the global spread of Chinese Buddhism (Ashiwa and Wank 2005; Ji 2014). Recently, several edited volumes, while not exclusively focusing on Buddhism in contemporary China, have brought new data and in-depth analyses to the topic (Yang 2008; Ji and Goossaert 2011; Palmer, Shive, and Wickeri 2011; Chau 2011a; Kiely and Jessup 2016; Ownby, Goossaert, and Ji 2017). However, only one monograph has been published that focuses exclusively on Han Chinese Buddhist revival (Fisher 2014), and no single book provides a general synthesis of the phenomenon with attention to both monastic and lay practices, Buddhism's evolving relationship to the state, and the tensions between touristic consumption and religiosity in the way that this volume does.

5. Old customs, old culture, old habits, and old ideas.

6. What are recorded as "Dharma disasters" in medieval China all lasted only a few years and were limited to certain regions in the Middle Kingdom's vast land. Only the impact of the Taiping Rebellion on Buddhism from 1850 to 1864 is comparable with Mao's persecution in magnitude and violent scope (Ji, Campo, and Wang 2016).

7. For more criticisms on the validity of the religious economy model in the Chinese context, see Ji 2008b; Fan 2008; Lu 2008; and Klein and Meyer 2011.

8. In this volume, we use the term "lay practitioners" or "laypersons" to refer to persons who have "taken the refuges" (*guiyi* 皈依) and formally converted as Buddhists but remain "inside the family" (*zaijia* 在家) and are not monastics. (One may also refer to this group as householders.) Lay practitioners have generally made an exclusive commitment to

Buddhist teachings and a Buddhist religious path. We use the term "devotees" to describe nonmonastics who take part in devotional rituals and worship activities in Buddhist temple spaces. Some of these devotees may also be lay practitioners, but many are not. Conversely, lay practitioners may also take part in many devotional activities, but their practice is generally not confined to those activities. For these reasons, it is important to keep the terms "lay practitioners" and "devotees" separate.

    9.   For a critique on the environmental damage caused by life rescue activities, see Shiu and Stokes 2008. For more on the phenomenon of life rescue in post-Mao China, see Jones 2010, 173, 187, 196–197; Fisher 2014, 127, 206; and D. Yang 2015.

PART I

Negotiating Legitimacy

Making Buddhism with the State

1

BUDDHISM UNDER JIANG, HU, AND XI

The Politics of Incorporation

ANDRÉ LALIBERTÉ

This chapter provides an overview of the close relationship between the CCP and the Buddhist Association of China (BAC) during the Hu Jintao era and at the beginning of the Xi Jinping administration. This relationship can be best described as a process of incorporation, whereby the state has sought to bestow the BAC with the monopoly of governance to control and monitor Buddhist temples, lay associations (*jushilin* 居士林), academies (*foxueyuan* 佛学院), philanthropic foundations (*cishan jijinhui* 慈善基金会), and other Buddhist-related institutions and groups and represent them in their demands to the political institutions of party and state. In doing so, it provides background on the national political context relevant to the other chapters in this book. The relationship between the state and Chinese Buddhism[1] in the PRC is an issue seldom examined in comparison to the significant literature on interactions between the state and other forms of religion in China.[2] The existing social science literature on the subject of relations between state and religions in China has long devoted most of its attention to Christianity, whether Protestant (Wickeri 1989; Covell 2001; Cheng 2003; Kindopp 2004; Schak 2011) or Catholic (Madsen 2003; Reardon 2011), and often from the perspectives of adversarial relations between religion and state (Bays 2003). Islam in China has attracted some attention from social scientists, and mostly from anthropologists, who have tended to focus on either descriptions of ethnic histories or everyday social relations, without examining in a significant way the relations between Islamic institutions and the state (Gladney 1996; Gillette 2000; Allès 2000). Among the new religions originating in China, groups such as Falungong 法轮功 have received considerable attention (Palmer 2007; Tong 2009; Ownby 2010), out of a concern for human rights following the persecutions of adherents of that religion.

However, there are very few studies in Western languages and in Japanese about relations between state and religion in post-Mao China that focus on

Taoism and Buddhism, the other two of the five institutionalized religions recognized by the CCP.[3] Research on Taoism and popular religions has looked at relations between government officials and local religions in the disciplines of history (Robinet 1997; Goossaert and Palmer 2011), anthropology (Dean 1993; Schipper 1994; Chau 2006; Palmer and Liu 2012), and sociology (Fan 2005) in ways that are not that different from those used by political scientists, but the latter have been reticent to study this issue. The same is true for Buddhism, which is the object of many studies in anthropology, sociology, and history in Western languages (Yang and Wei 2005; Wu 2009; Yang 2006; Fisher 2008, 2011a, 2011b, 2012, 2014; Ji 2008a, 2011a, 2011b, 2011c, 2012, 2016a, 2016b, 2017; Jones 2010, 2011). There are studies on the relationship between the state and Tibetan Buddhism (Barnett 1994; Terrone 2003; Tuttle 2005), on the relations between the state and Buddhism in Taiwan (Jones 1996, 1999; Laliberté 2005; Madsen 2007), on Buddhism in cross-strait relations (Laliberté 2003, 2013), and on Buddhist political thought and ethics (Chang 1971; Chan 1985; Xue 2012). The relations between Chinese Buddhism and the state before the Cultural Revolution have been covered by one of the main references in the study of Buddhism in China (Welch 1972) as well as Xue Yu's history of Buddhist associations' emergence between 1949 and the 1980s (Xue 2015). For the contemporary period, a few case studies examine relations between local governments in China and important temples, such as those of Ashiwa and Wank on the revival of Nanputuo Temple in Fujian (Ashiwa and Wank 2006; Ashiwa 2009) and Wank on the structure of authority over Chinese Buddhist institutions (Wank 2009), as well as Fisher's work on state-sangha relations, mostly from the perspective of the state's potential impact on popular lay practices (Fisher 2014). Among the few exceptions among political scientists, McCarthy has looked at the use of Buddhist resources in the promotion of tourism (McCarthy 2010, 2013), and Laliberté has looked at Buddhist philanthropic societies as social service providers that complement state social policy (Laliberté 2008, 2009, 2012). Buddhism deserves more attention than it has received so far among Western scholars because of its importance in contemporary China relative to other religions, and because of its increasing visibility in the public sphere under Hu and Xi. This is also the case because the scholarship written in Chinese about the relevance of Buddhism to different aspects of politics in that country is expanding significantly and deserves to be better known in the West (Deng 1994; Lai 1999; Li 2002; Liu 2002, 2006; Xue 2012; Wang Jia 2014).[4]

Buddhism has come a long way since the Cultural Revolution. The religion with the largest number of adherents in China according to official statistics, Buddhism has expanded steadily under Jiang Zemin 江泽民 (1989–2002), Hu Jintao (2002–2012), and Xi Jinping (2012–).[5] While the growth of the Protestant churches represents one of the most dramatic developments regarding religion in China, the expansion of Buddhism is interesting in its own right. If human rights organizations that focus on religious persecution in China are to be believed, followers of Buddhism are seldom targeted by government interference, in contrast to followers of Christianity.[6] Buddhism represents one of the pillars of the Chinese tradition, which the CCP claims to preserve. Party leaders since Jiang Zemin have openly supported the development of Buddhism over the years by making public appearances alongside temple abbots. This was part of Jiang's endorsement of a new line that emphasized the compatibility between religion and socialism[7] in 1993, and the recognition of the endurance (*changqixing* 长期性) of religion in socialist China (Laliberté 2015). Hu Jintao not only endorsed the policy of his predecessor but also gave it an additional impetus by approving the organization of the World Buddhist Forums in 2006, 2009, and 2012. Xi Jinping, who promoted the first forum while he was party secretary of Zhejiang, has reinforced these precedents under his tenure as PRC president, welcoming to Baoji the first ever meeting of the World Fellowship of Buddhists (WFB) on Chinese soil in 2014, after China's half century of exclusion from that international organization. Local governments, often with financial assistance from overseas Chinese, Hong Kong–based, or Taiwanese businesses, have promoted the repairing of temples and even the building of new ones. This climate of public support for Buddhism has unfolded in the midst of persecution against Falungong under Jiang's orders, and during the campaign against Protestant churches in Zhejiang after Xi assumed power. Why is the CCP more lenient toward Buddhism compared to other religions? What are the policy objectives being served by Buddhist institutions?

The chapter considers four policy domains of importance for the CCP and looks at the extent to which the growth of Buddhism could be helpful, presumably providing a rationale for state support. It identifies the four domains—local economic development; diplomacy; internal security; and relations with Taiwan—and takes into account changes within them through the three successive regimes of Jiang, Hu, and Xi as general secretaries of the CCP Central Committee.[8]

In the area of development, local governments have promoted the preservation of Buddhist heritage in the hope that it would develop the economy through revenues from tourism and pilgrimage, and encouraged the growth of philanthropy to assist the state in the delivery of social services. In the realm of diplomacy, the development of Buddhism helped the administrations of Jiang and Hu promote the images of "peaceful rise" and "peaceful development," respectively. Under Xi, the emphasis has shifted to "independence from foreign influence," and this new approach has coincided with a greater affirmation of Chinese Buddhism on the international stage. In the realm of internal security, the official support to Buddhism under Jiang meant enlisting the help of Buddhist clerics to "combat evil cults"; under Hu it signified building a "harmonious society" (*hexie shehui* 和谐社会) or "stability maintenance" (*weihu wending* 维护稳定); and under Xi it fits with the themes of "China dream" (Zhongguo *meng* 中国梦) and "cultural confidence" (*wenhua zixin* 文化自信).

Finally, Jiang and his successors have all looked at Buddhism as a component of the CCP United Front Work they could rely on to facilitate the improvement of relations across the Taiwan Strait.

These four kinds of objectives relate to one another. I argue that the official Chinese Buddhist Association at the national level may be of limited value in influencing Buddhist citizens in foreign countries, but local temples, devotee associations, and philanthropic societies can use their foreign contacts to develop activities that can buttress the legitimacy of local governments and CCP cadres. In particular, Buddhist institutions take advantage of their value as cultural resources to attract foreign investment and use part of their wealth to deliver social services, two achievements that local cadres support. Within the context of these activities, central and local Chinese Buddhist associations' opportunities for cooperation with Taiwanese Buddhist associations have increased, and they can presumably contribute to the improvement of the climate in cross-strait relations, an important objective for the CCP. Even though the actual achievements of Buddhist institutions may fall short of directly helping the CCP in the goals of projecting China's image as a benign emerging power, maintaining domestic security, and ameliorating relations with Taiwan, it is not so much the direct intervention of Buddhist associations in the realization of these objectives that matter to the CCP, but their capacity to act with actors that would not naturally cooperate with the CCP but are willing to work with fellow coreligionists: Buddhists in foreign countries, in China itself, and in Taiwan. Under the last three CCP leaders, these policies have gone through different iterations, reflecting difficulties in achieving success. In this context of changes in strategies, however, certain goals have remained constant: promoting development; reassuring the international community; ensuring domestic stability; and preventing Taiwanese independence.

THE BUDDHIST ECONOMY AND MARKET-ORIENTED REFORM

Field research and participant observations by many scholars have shown that the expansion of Buddhism results primarily from the initiatives of entrepreneurial monks and energetic lay practitioners, as well as their good relations with local governments (Deng 1994; Li 2002; Liu 2002; Yang and Wei 2005; Fisher 2008; Ji 2008b). Even if it delivers limited results on the diplomatic front, as I discuss later in this chapter, a policy of tolerance toward Buddhism in China can nonetheless provide to the CCP two positive outcomes: It makes it easier to mobilize the resources of Buddhist philanthropy to help address social and economic issues within China, and it is more likely to generate goodwill toward China among Taiwanese Buddhists, an important proportion of the Taiwanese population who oppose independence for Taiwan.[9]

Buddhism, in its institutional and informal dimensions, is too important an actor for the CCP to ignore. State statistics have mentioned since 1978 that

China has 100 million Buddhists.[10] Liu Zhongyu from the Research Center for Religious Culture, East China Normal University, estimated the number at 300 million in 2005 (Zhang 2009). Even if we accept the more modest estimates by Johnson and Grim for 2010, we find that China stands out as the country with the largest group of Buddhists in the world, with 207 million (Johnson and Grim 2013, 35–36).[11] More specific data for 2012 provided by the BAC indicated thirty-three thousand temples, out of which twenty-eight thousand are counted as Chinese (*hanchuan* 汉传), and more than 240,000 monks and nuns, of whom 100,000 only are Han Chinese. The BAC also counted thirty-eight Buddhist schools and colleges, with more than one hundred journals and more than two hundred Internet sites (Zhongguo Fojiao Xiehui 2012).[12] Numbers for laypeople, however, whose degree of commitment can vary considerably, tell us too little, because their source is not clear, and the methodology used to arrive at these figures is not specified.[13] What can be ascertained more confidently, however, is the growth of Buddhism as measured by the increase in the number of new temples built or old temples restored, which is recorded in data from the National Bureau of Statistics, which has tracked the history of temples and includes, among a vast array of information, the date of their founding or reopening (ACMRC 2010).[14] Moreover, in addition to this kind of evidence, research by contributors to this book has shown that Buddhist associations have successfully developed a wide variety of activities within the very strict parameters of the corporatist institutions supported by the state. They have emerged in all provinces and autonomous regions of China, and many have been created at the level of prefectures and cities.

As suggested previously, many local governments make use of the resources of Buddhism to support their legitimacy, banking on its value as a touristic attraction to generate wealth. As an aspect of China's cultural heritage, Buddhism indeed represents a major economic asset. Five out of the forty Chinese UNESCO World Heritage Sites are Buddhist: Wutaishan, the Longmen Grottoes, the Potala Palace in Lhasa (Tibet), the Mogao Caves, and the Yungang Grottoes (UNESCO 2011). The government's tacit approval of the revival of Buddhist institutions since the beginning of the reforms has sent a signal to coreligionists in Hong Kong, Taiwan, and Singapore and to overseas Chinese that pilgrimage to historical temples and monasteries is welcome. This religious tourism represents an important source of economic activities. It not only leads to greater prosperity for Buddhist temples and associations but also helps local economies. As Dong Wang demonstrated in her study of Longmen's inclusion in the World Heritage list in 2000, that Buddhist site has, among other benefits, brought considerable revenue to the city of Luoyang thanks to the growth of tourism linked to the site's new status (Wang 2010, 132). Moreover, the wealth some Buddhist temples have gained from pilgrimages and donations has allowed them to fund charitable activities and provide a number of social services. For some local governments, Buddhist institutions constitute economic resources that generate wealth and provide some degree of relief. In so doing, they can, at least to a certain degree, soften the impact of social inequalities that are generating so much discontent.

The development of religious tourism is visible all over China and is encouraged by the government (Oakes and Sutton 2010; Shepherd 2013).[15] The benefits from these activities for the state and Buddhist institutions are manifold. Religious tourism benefits local economies through the expenses of pilgrims, but also through the foreign direct investments that Buddhist institutions can attract. For local governments, it represents a convenient way to improve economic performance at a relatively low cost. Guo Shusen and Shi Chunyi, however, noted that the rebuilding of temples after the Cultural Revolution has brought a host of new problems. They lamented that "monks have forgotten the meaning of Buddhism" and that they focus on economic activities (Guo and Shi 2009, 75). Ji Zhe noted as early as 2004 that the relationships between local government and monasteries are full of tensions around the religious tourist industry (Ji 2004, 2016a). These tensions notwithstanding, many local governments are determined to take advantage of Buddhist cultural capital.

Also, China is emerging as an international pilgrimage tourism destination for foreign lay practitioners who want to visit the Buddhist historical sites from which the religion was introduced to their country, as well as for overseas Chinese interested to know more about their heritage (see chapters 2, 4, and 10 in this volume, by Vidal, Nichols, and Fisher, respectively). The effort to rebuild temples in that context could be read as a return to a policy adopted before the Cultural Revolution, when the CCP believed in showcasing the flourishing of Buddhism in China to convince fellow Buddhists outside China that religion was alive and well under socialism, and therefore that the country's policies on religion deserved support (Welch 1972; Xue 2015). The commercially successful branding of the Shaolin Temple, but also the activities at the sites of Putuoshan, described by Vidal in chapter 2, as well as the temples of Nanputuo, analyzed by Ashiwa and Wank in chapter 8, and Longquan, on which McCarthy focuses in chapter 3, illustrate this trend. This approach by the CCP is risky: Not all Buddhist devotees approve of this mixing between wealth and religion. The Shaolin Temple, which has long attracted foreign tourists and finally gained the status of World Heritage Site from UNESCO in 2010, stood out as an example where an entrepreneurial abbot's initiative stimulated the local economy and built the temple into a conglomerate with activities in martial arts performances, publishing, and cultural exchanges. However, many Buddhist practitioners have criticized the activities of organizations like Shaolin because of the latter's emphasis on such nonreligious activities, but others appreciate the fact that the temples are wealthy.[16] While a few laypersons Gareth Fisher talked with about the matter seemed to disapprove of the temple's activities, many others have complained that the Shaolin Temple situation has been misrepresented by the media.[17]

Charitable deeds represent a way in which Buddhist temples can avoid criticism from non-Buddhists. The accumulated wealth generated by tourism revenue and the sale of religious paraphernalia offers many temples the possibility to respond to demands by local governments to offer some services to vulnerable groups such as orphans, victims of natural disasters, and people suffering from AIDS. Under Hu Jintao, many Buddhist associations established foundations to raise money for the supply of social services, such as helping special schools for children with disabilities or providing emergency relief after natural disasters. These activities—which were unthinkable during the first few decades after the founding of the PRC—became accepted in the Jiang Zemin years and increasingly commonplace under his successor's tenure. The most remarkable aspect of this development is that it responds to requests from state officials. This expansion has not yet reached the scope of Taiwanese Buddhist philanthropy, but its existence nevertheless represents a significant trend. The philanthropic activities by individual temples or lay associations, which have been expanding every year (Fojiao tiandi 2011), have another benefit from the perspective of local governments: They are bringing in money and volunteers from Taiwan, Hong Kong, and overseas Chinese communities. This particular aspect of the Buddhist political economy is discussed in greater detail in the following section.

THE USE OF BUDDHISM IN CHINESE DIPLOMACY

In recent years, Buddhism has represented an important resource for the PRC in its attempt to project "soft power" in its diplomacy (Angelskar 2013; Ji 2012). This approach revives the strategy briefly employed by the CCP before the Cultural Revolution. In his study, Holmes Welch wrote that for Mao, Buddhism between 1952 and 1964 was useful in foreign relations (1972, 169–230). The CCP sought to persuade foreigners that Buddhism thrives under communism, hoping that Buddhist circles in foreign countries could influence public opinion and sway it to push governments to adopt a pro-China foreign policy (Welch 1972, 169). That approach became unsustainable on the eve of the Cultural Revolution because the government realized that the contradiction between the suppression of religious activities and deceptive attempts to convince foreigners otherwise was undermining its authority. In any case, foreigners were indifferent to Buddhism or, if they supported Chinese policy, it was not due to Buddhism's prosperity (Welch 1972, 229). Since the CCP has now abandoned its policy of actively suppressing religion, however, it is worth revisiting this issue. We need to ask whether the demonstration that Buddhism thrives in China is used by the state today to support its policies to foreign audiences that care about religious freedom, whether they are Buddhists or not. To what extent does the development of Buddhism under Hu Jintao give substance to the image of the PRC as a rising power focusing on "peaceful development" or, more recently, how much can the prosperity of Buddhism under Xi Jinping give credence to the view that China is inclusive of foreign religions (MOFA 2014)?

The Buddhist constituency in Asia is important, and it is reasonable to assume that the flourishing of Buddhism in China could influence a significant number of Buddhists elsewhere in Asia to adopt the view that their coreligionists thrive in China, and therefore that what is good for China is good for Buddhism. Buddhists constitute the majority of the population in Thailand, Myanmar, Sri Lanka, Cambodia, Laos, and Bhutan and represent a significant proportion of the population in Japan, Vietnam, Korea, Taiwan, and Nepal. And although they represent just a small proportion of the Indian population, they constitute a large number. Moreover, many overseas Chinese identify with Buddhism.[18] In Thailand, Cambodia, and Bhutan, the religion is part of the national identity, and the Buddhist sangha represents an important institutional actor in each country. In Japan, a number of Liberal Democratic Party governments have ruled through the support of a Buddhist political party. In democratic societies like Japan, South Korea, and Taiwan, Buddhists represent an important pressure group. Whether the CCP believes that it can sway public opinion through religious networks or not, it acts as if it believes in the usefulness of these international Buddhist networks.

The value of this form of diplomacy varies from country to country. Hence, Buddhism plays a minor role in promoting positive relations between China and other authoritarian states such as Vietnam, Myanmar, North Korea, and Laos. The CCP's use of the BAC to impress the national Buddhist associations of these countries has little value because these associations have little clout within the political systems of their own countries. On the other hand, encouraging the development of Buddhist institutions in China could presumably influence Buddhists in Japan, South Korea, and other democracies in the region, where they constitute a significant part of the electorate, to support China's goals. However, these connections should not be overemphasized. Japanese Buddhists are divided into a number of different sects that disagree among themselves on a wide range of issues. In South Korea, Buddhists represent less than half the population and remain bitterly divided over property and monastic regulations.

Not only did the BAC sponsor the organization of four China-based global Buddhist forums with the help of United Front Work organizations, but as we saw earlier, in 2012 it convened in China the WFB's twenty-seventh general conference. Although it is not clear to what extent the initiative came from the CCP or the BAC, the event was held under the theme of "Public benefit–charity," which mirrored the CCP position that religion can serve the Chinese public interest through charitable activities. The convening of that international congress was significant because it provided tacit consent to the admission of the BAC as a full-fledged member of the WFB.

The admission of the BAC to the WFB has removed a major obstacle to its international influence. Since its founding, the WFB has enforced its own "one China" policy, which forbade concurrent representation of organizations from the PRC and the Republic of China (ROC) in Taiwan.[19] As long as the United Nations recognized the ROC as the sole legitimate government of China, the WFB followed the same policy and ignored the nascent BAC between its inception in 1953 and its closure in 1966.[20] Whether the WFB was willing to change this policy or not after the PRC's admission to the United Nations, it could not do so, because the BAC was unable to function until 1980. The BAC was also excluded from the other major international Buddhist associations, such as the World Youth Buddhist Society and the World Buddhist Sangha Council, on the same grounds. For two and a half decades the BAC remained marginalized on the international stage, depriving the CCP of an additional channel of influence that could have complemented its other resources in trade, academia, and diplomacy. As is made clear in the following paragraphs, this does not mean that the BAC was inactive or that the CCP was indifferent to Buddhism during that period. Quite the contrary, the state was laying the groundwork for the international emergence of the BAC, a process that came to fruition with the World Buddhist Forum convened in 2006.

Perhaps the greatest impediment to the use of Buddhism in international forums to promote the PRC's foreign policy is the fact that few Chinese Buddhist leaders are known in the West, except perhaps leaders from Taiwan. North Americans and Europeans know much less about any of the BAC leaders than about the Dalai Lama, the spiritual leader of Tibetan Buddhists, even though BAC leaders can claim to lead a community that is at least ten times larger. The leadership of the BAC, from Yuanying 圆瑛 (whose term began in 1953) to Xuecheng 学诚 (2015–2018), never had the international prestige that the Tibetan leader enjoyed. Yuanying passed away within a year of his nomination as leader of the BAC, and during the tenure of his successor, Sherap Gyatso (1953–1966), a representative of the Tibetan branch of Buddhism, the Tibet Autonomous Region was invaded by the People's Liberation Army. From 1980 to 2000, Zhao Puchu 赵朴初, a lay Buddhist, led the organization. In this role, Ji Zhe reveals in his account of Zhao's career, he achieved much for Chinese diplomacy and enjoyed a good reputation within Japanese and Korean Buddhist circles (Ji 2017). The accession in 2014 of Xuecheng, a young Han Chinese monk, to head the BAC, signaled a new age of greater visibility for Chinese Buddhism. As the abbot of Longquan Temple in Beijing, Xuecheng actively promoted the internationalization of the BAC and Chinese Buddhism in general (see Susan McCarthy's chapter 3 in this volume). His presiding over the WFB Congress in Baoji in the same year offered him the opportunity to generate unprecedented international attention for the BAC. Moreover, Xuecheng and other Buddhist leaders expressed the view that their religious tradition is uniquely well placed to facilitate intercultural and international dialogue in

Asia and thereby give substance to Xi Jinping's signature foreign policy initiative in the region: "one belt, one road," the ambitious attempt to create a twenty-first-century equivalent to the ancient Silk Road in international trade.[21]

There is one key aspect of China's foreign policy in which Chinese Buddhism has proved useful to all CCP administrations since Jiang, and which is likely to be reinforced by the "one belt, one road" initiative: the encouragement of the religious tourism industry. The development of a mass tourism infrastructure has made it easier for pilgrims from other Asian countries to visit historical Buddhist sites (Oakes 2005). This religious tourism, in turn, has drawn attention to the financial needs of Chinese Buddhist institutions. For Japanese, Korean, Taiwanese, and overseas Chinese Buddhists, many Buddhist temples and monasteries in China represent sacred sites of historical value with deep meaning because they are the points of origin from which Buddhism was transmitted to their countries. The historical and spiritual value attached to Buddhist sites in China by outsiders, in other words, represents an asset to the CCP because it attracts money from foreign investors and philanthropic associations, two key actors that can help local governments deal with poverty and the possibility of social unrest.

FROM "HARMONIOUS SOCIETY" TO "CHINA DREAM"

The expansion of Buddhism is facilitated by the fact that the CCP and Buddhist institutions have many shared interests—that is, the party looks toward the BAC to implement some of its policies, and the latter, in turn, willingly obliges because it grants its leaders a measure of authority and influence over Buddhists. Intellectuals such as the late Fang Litian, a well-known scholar of Buddhism, wrote about the compatibility between Buddhism and the China dream (Fang 2013). Beyond the rhetoric, however, there is also substance. For example, the party and the BAC share an interest in clearly defining Buddhism, that is, in determining what they view as the correct practice of the religion. The CCP fears the proliferation of independent religious movements that could challenge its oligopolistic framework of five official religions, while the BAC is concerned with its own ability to control all activities in the Buddhist field (Ji 2008a, 256). This convergence of interests was already clear in the 1990s when *qigong* 气功 groups became popular, thereby prompting Buddhist scholars to criticize the Falungong as a threat to the BAC's monopoly over Buddhism three years before the clampdown by the CCP (Ji 2008a, 257, 362n14). In addition, both the CCP and the BAC seek to ensure the latter's authority over the different schools of the religion and to promote unity among the different ethnic groups where Buddhism is influential, most particularly the Tibetans. However, in such endeavors, the BAC has had difficulty maintaining control. Hence, the BAC could not prevent the emergence in the 1980s of groups that claim a loose affiliation to Buddhism, such as the Dajiang Foguo 大江佛国 and Fo

Shengmen 佛圣门, which ignored its authority (Munro 1989). As we saw earlier, it also was initially taken off guard by the Falungong, which borrowed symbols and aspects of doctrines from Buddhist symbols and early on even translated into English its name as the "Buddha Law" (Lu 2005). Finally, and more recently, it has not found a way to dissuade Tibetan Buddhist monks from waging self-immolation protests since 2009 (Shakya 2012).

To what extent could the development of Buddhism also help the party's effort to achieve a "harmonious society," the "hot phrase" (*reci* 热词) used by Hu Jintao in the promotion of his domestic policies,[22] and to what extent does this continue under Xi? The scholarship produced by Chinese researchers on the theme of "Buddhism and harmonious society" suggests that a lot happened under Hu (Juexing 2007; Guo and Shi 2009; Xue 2012),[23] in particular in the area of charity and the public interest (Yinshun and Wang 2014).[24] High-ranking Buddhist officials promote the state objectives, and their actions are duly assessed and investigated by researchers of the leaders of the State Administration for Religious Affairs (SARA), which provides guidance. These initiatives reflect a new turn in CCP thinking on religion that has evolved since Jiang, which stresses the compatibility between religion and socialism (Feng 2009; Guojia Zongjiao Shiwuju Zongjiao Yanjiu Zhongxin 2013) and the compatibility between Buddhist philosophy and socialism in particular. Both official literature and research on official policies are important because they are indicative of the state's political will and the policies it wants to implement. But they cannot tell us to what extent these policies meet the expectations of people who self-identify as Buddhists and whom the state targets.

In other words, an analysis of CCP United Front work cannot be limited to the study of party cadres' relations with BAC officials. In order to present a full picture, relations between local officials, on the one side, and Buddhist monks and lay practitioners, on the other, must be examined. Therefore, to better understand the substance of CCP relations with Buddhists, it helps to look at local institutions, ranging from county-level associations of devotees to philanthropic associations. Doing so reveals the gap between policy prescriptions and policy implementation, which is bound to exist in a vast country like China. As Ji Zhe notes in his discussion on the institutionalization of Buddhism, the complexity of the religion is reaching an extent that the task of imposing uniformity from above is becoming increasingly difficult (Ji 2008b, 256–257).

The expansion of charities run by Buddhist institutions represented during the Hu Jintao era one of the most dramatic forms of institutional change for Buddhism since the beginning of the reform period. The movement has become more institutionalized and there have been attempts to centralize the activities of Buddhist philanthropy. In 2010 the BAC established a nationwide Buddhist charity (Zhongguo Fojiao Xiehui Cishan Gongyi Weiyuanhui 2012a, 45; 2018), though the development of provincial Buddhist charities was uneven. The Hebei Buddhist Philanthropic Merit Society (Hebei Fojiao

Cishan Gongdehui 河北佛教慈善功德会), which was established in 1995 and after that offered relief to schools for children with special needs and to areas affected by natural disasters, was a case in point. At the time of this writing, it seems to have stopped activities.[25] In a previous account on this issue, I mentioned the findings from a 2006 report presented by the chair of the Shanxi Buddhist Association, Gentong 根通, during the First World Buddhist Forum (Laliberté 2011a). The fate of provincial charities he discussed in his report says a lot about uncertainties in the growth of Buddhist philanthropy. He discussed then the case of three Buddhist charities, but more recent evidence from the BAC suggests that their activities were not accurately reported (Zhongguo Fojiao Xiehui Cishan Gongyi Weiyuanhui 2012a, 2012b, 2012c). Gentong reported that in 2000, building on two decades of experience in fund-raising for disaster relief work by Buddhists in the province, the Hunan Buddhist Association had set up a province-wide foundation to finance elementary schools and offered scholarships to children in need (Gentong 2006, 269). There were records of these activities until 2012 (Zhongguo Fojiao Xiehui Cishan Gongyi Weiyuanhui 2012c, 921–957), but there was no online presence from then until 2016. However, things have changed dramatically since then.[26] Gentong also mentioned that, from 2004 to 2005, the Shanxi Provincial Association worked to set up its own merit society, the Wutaishan Buddhist Philanthropic Merit Association (Shanxi Wutaishan Fojiao Cishan Gongde Zonghui 山西五台山佛教慈善功德总会), to help people in poor households and offer scholarships (Gentong 2006, 269). The nationwide BAC charity mentioned activities until 2012 (Zhongguo Fojiao Xiehui Cishan Gongyi Weiyuanhui 2012b, 515–548), but there are no longer any traces online of this institution at the time of this writing.[27] The third charity discussed by Gentong, the Guangdong Provincial Buddhist Association, had more success. It set up six foundations between 1993 and 2002 for various tasks ranging from elderly care to maternity wards (Gentong 2006, 269), and in 2004 it established a network of clinics offering traditional Chinese medicine to the poor (Guangdongsheng Fojiao Xiehui Cishan Zhongyi Zhensuo 广东省佛教协会慈善中医诊所). The clinics were still running in 2010 when I visited the Dezheng 德政 branch, and the website documenting their activities reported activities up to 2017.[28] Moreover, the Guangdong Provincial Buddhist Association founded in 2013 a charity foundation (Guangdongsheng Fojiao Xiehui Cishan Jijinhui 广东省佛教协会慈善基金会).[29] The three provincial charities described by Gentong have succeeded to varying degrees, but they all faced a similar problem of scale: Province-wide charities represent ambitious ventures for Buddhist associations covering the needs of devotees in large populations. A look at the special municipality-level Buddhist associations that have also created their own charities reveals a more complex picture of institutionalization. The Shanghai Municipal Buddhist Association, for example, a wealthy association responsible for important locations such as the Yufo Temple (Yufo Si 玉佛寺)

and the Longhua Temple (Longhua Si 龙华寺), built on the strength of twenty years of experience and created its own charity foundation, the Shanghai Municipal Charity Foundation (Shanghaishi Cishan Jijinhui 上海市慈善基金会) to help children in need and sponsor elementary schools. Meanwhile, the Jade Buddha Temple set up its own charity, the Universal Awakening Compassionate Society (Juequn Ci'ai Gongdehui 觉群慈爱功德会), which remains very active at the time of this writing.[30] The two kinds of charities coexist, but the website of the Shanghai Municipal Charity Foundation, despite its origins, downplays the contribution of Buddhist institutions to philanthropy to the point of invisibility.[31]

The Tianjin Municipal Buddhist Association has also set up its own charity, the Tianjin Buddhist Philanthropic Merit Foundation (Tianjin Fojiao Cishan Gongde Jijinhui 天津佛教慈善功德基金会), which still operates at the time of this writing. The Ren'ai Charity Foundation (see McCarthy's chapter 3 in this volume) is another philanthropic association with a Buddhist background, founded in 2004 near the Longquan Temple in Beijing, with the sponsorship of the previous chair of the BAC, Xuecheng. This important patronage was meant to make its existence more secure, but as the success of the Tianjin association suggests, it is not necessary. Beyond these observations, it is hard to predict whether these associations will fare better than the charity established by the Chongqing Municipal Buddhist Association. Founded in 1993, it set up the Project Hope (Xiwang Gongcheng 希望工程) committee and sponsored the building of classes for elementary schools. More than ten years later, it established the Chongqing Buddhist Philanthropic Merit Society (Chongqing Foxie Cishan Gongdehui 重庆佛协慈善功德会), but its existence proved ephemeral, with no evidence of its activities after 2007.

As Raoul Birnbaum mentioned in an earlier survey (Birnbaum 2003a), the reach of these Buddhist associations has long been hampered by the limitations of their own resources—which are devoted to the rebuilding of their temples and the training of a new generation of monks—and by the immensity of the needs to address. There is little reason to believe that the circumstances are any different under Xi. Moreover, the spatial disparity of Buddhism's presence in China ensures that access to resources of different provinces varies from one to another. For example, although the Shanxi Buddhist Association can expect to benefit from alms and donations from pilgrims and tourists to the well-known site of Wutaishan, one of China's four sacred mountains, not all provinces are endowed with such an advantage. And even provinces with such assets do not necessarily choose to use them for charitable enterprises. Hence, the Buddhist Association of Anhui, which is home to another major site, Jiuhuashan 九华山, has yet to capitalize on this opportunity. People in Jiangsu have received relief from Hong Kong–based charities, but the Buddhist provincial association has not yet established its own provincial-level charity association. Such associations, however, support local organizations at the level of prefectures or counties.

Hence, the Jiangsu Buddhist Association has sponsored the development of Buddhist merit societies in Taixing 泰兴 Prefecture. The Liaoning Buddhist Association has done likewise with the Jinzhou 锦州 Prefecture Merit Society (Zhonghua Fojiao Xinxiwang 2005).

Buddhist associations at lower levels of administration, such as the prefecture and county levels, have also established their own charities. I am aware of such associations in the prefectures of Huaibei 淮北 (Anhui Province), Taizhou 台州 (Zhejiang Province), Nanting 南宁 (Guangxi Province), Shanwei 汕尾 (Guangdong Province), Putian 莆田 (Fujian Province), Xuzhou 徐州 (Jiangsu Province), Chenzhou 郴州 (Hunan Province), and Hunchun 珲春 (Liaoning Province). The Buddhist associations of cities such as Nanjing, Chengde 承德, and Quanzhou 泉州 have done likewise. Finally, even county-level associations have launched their own charities. Despite their limited resources, some, such as the Lingchuan 陵川 Buddhist Charity Foundation in Shanxi Province, have managed to set up their own websites. Buddhist charities are sprouting up in every region of the country, regardless of socioeconomic level or relations with other provinces or even other countries. Some of the temples have been able early on to capitalize on their history to attract support and afford philanthropic activities. Raoul Birnbaum mentions the example of the Nanputuo Temple in Xiamen, which has been able to use its renown as a temple where Taixu served as an abbot to establish a charity. Its success has been so considerable, he reports, that the Xiamen Nanputuo Temple Charity Foundation (Nanputuo Si Cishan Shiye Jijinhui 南普陀寺慈善事业基金会) has inspired a convent with which it has close links in order to do the same, and which eventually set up its own charity in 2000 (Birnbaum 2003a, 444).

The CCP attitude is ambiguous: On the one hand, it has encouraged the growth of Buddhist institutions because of their ability to generate growth and their performance in the delivery of social services, but at the same time it seeks to constrain their influence. But as Fisher demonstrates in the conclusion to his ethnography (Fisher 2014, 201–214), the performance of philanthropic activities by the Buddhist temples has been limited by the state's reluctance to let religious institutions gain too much capital through such activities. Chinese scholars researching Buddhist philanthropy who were interviewed in Shanghai, Nanjing, and Wuxi have all noted that the governments still impose too many constraints. Others elaborated that Buddhism is still too young and underresourced to affect social policy. Observations on different websites highlight many promises and much potential, but the reality of achievements falls far below. One of the major difficulties faced by the Buddhist organizations is the lack of resources to undertake sustained relief operations.[32] The BAC did not appear supportive of these initiatives under the Hu administration.[33] This remains an open question under Xi, who oversaw in rapid succession the promotion of Xuecheng as chair of the BAC followed by his resignation in 2018, with unclear consequences for the visibility of the Ren'ai Charity Foundation

Xuecheng had supported. Other associations already advertise such activities, however. The website Buddhism Online (Fojiao Zaixian 佛教在线), headquartered in Beijing, which claims to be the largest of its kind, advertises philanthropic activities by Buddhists throughout the country and reveals quite extensive activity (Fojiao Zaixian 2018).[34] Other local websites such as Contemporary Buddhist Charity Net (Dangdai Fojiao Cishan Wang 当代佛教慈善网) link to fund-raising for specific projects (Dangdai Fojiao Cishan Wang 2018).

In sum, through these philanthropic activities, local temples and Buddhist associations, by contributing to the alleviation of suffering with the support of authorities, have often buttressed the legitimacy of local governments and party cadres. Moreover, to fund these activities, Buddhist temples and monasteries have taken advantage of their value as cultural resources to attract foreign investment. Both local governments and CCP cadres support this situation as long as it bestows legitimacy on the party-state. This mutually beneficial arrangement, however, faces limits when Chinese Buddhists seek help from abroad. Foreign and overseas Chinese Buddhists may help bring investments to the PRC, but they cannot operate charitable activities, at least directly, lest this appear as foreign interference and contradict CCP policy. There exists one important exception, however, for Taiwanese Buddhists, who have achieved considerable success in the development of philanthropic associations on the island. They are bound to play a privileged role because of the party's objective of achieving reunification with Taiwan.

BUDDHISM AND THE ISSUE OF NATIONAL UNIFICATION

The issue of national unification, as far as Buddhism is concerned, has two dimensions. The first one relates to the constitutional framework of the PRC as a multinational state, which brings to mind accommodation to the specific Buddhist practices of nationalities living in Tibet and elsewhere within the country. The second dimension relates to the framework of a Chinese, or Han, ethnic nation that lives in the PRC, but also in Taiwan.[35] The issue of Tibetan Buddhism is a very complex one at the intersection of ethnic identity and historical memory that deserves a separate treatment, and I can only refer here to some of the best-known specialists on this issue (Kolås 1996; Goldstein and Kapstein 1998; Shakya 1999; Tuttle 2010). I therefore limit the discussion of national unification to the case of relations with Taiwan.

Taiwanese, Hong Kong, and mainland Chinese Buddhist associations have over the years found complementary interests in cooperation with one another. Taiwanese associations welcome the opportunity to grow and expand in China, and mainland Buddhists appreciate the financial support given them by enthusiastic Taiwanese practitioners. Although this cooperation was difficult to develop openly during the administration of Jiang Zemin because of tense cross-strait relations, it became possible under Hu Jintao, especially after the election to the presidency of Ma Ying-jeou (Ma Yingjiu) 马英九 (2008–2016), the CCP-favored candidate in Taiwan.[36] Buddhists provide in the special administrative region extensive amounts of services in social welfare and education, and nurture academic studies of the tradition in China as well. The convening of the World Buddhist Forums in Hangzhou in 2006, in Wuxi and Taibei in 2009, in Hong Kong in 2012, and in Wuxi in 2015 represents an example of that cooperation. Unfolding in the context of the rapprochement in cross-strait relations, the events received support at the highest level of government in China. But we should not infer from that that Buddhists can help the CCP achieve its objective of integrating Taiwan into the PRC; neither Buddhist associations in China nor those in Taiwan have the clout to influence public opinion or their respective governments. In the end, however, cooperation between the BAC and Taiwanese Buddhist associations serves the PRC government because the technical help that Taiwanese Buddhists can bring to the development of Buddhist charities in China contributes to local governments' goal of implementing the conditions for a "harmonious society" in the areas under their jurisdiction. The following paragraphs explore these issues.

Considering the importance for the CCP of the policy of "one country, two systems" directed at Taiwan, the role of Chinese Buddhist institutions in supporting that policy deserves consideration. Over recent years, the PRC leadership has acquired the ability to prevail militarily over Taiwan (Parameswaran 2009). It successfully deterred moves toward a proclamation of independence by previous president Chen Shui-bian (Chen Shuibian 陈水扁), and the 2008 presidential elections brought to power a government with which China shared some interests in increasing economic cooperation and easing military tension, without the People's Liberation Army having used intimidation in any ways comparable to the presidential elections of 1996 and 2000. Yet, despite the lessening of tension, the political dynamics in Taiwan prevented the former president, Ma Ying-jeou, from contemplating negotiations for an eventual unification with the PRC, which the CCP had wished to bring about. Political negotiation between the governments is impossible, and as long as PRC leaders do not recognize the legitimacy of their counterparts in the ROC, the impasse remains. At the time of this writing, the Democratic Progressive Party is likely to dominate the political landscape for at least one mandate of four years, an outcome the CCP dislikes. This makes United Front work all the more relevant to the CCP, for whom Buddhists could play a crucial role, especially thanks to key figures who are well-known on both sides of the Taiwan Strait.

Political dialogue between Hu Jintao, as general secretary of the CCP, and Lien Chan (Lian Zhan) 连战, as chair of the Kuomintang (KMT, Guomindang), in 2005, did not lead to significant change in the short term, even if it helped the resumption of meetings between the Straits Exchange Foundation (SEF) and the Association for Relations across the Taiwan Strait (ARATS), which were restarted in 2008 (Ko 2009). But as long as a majority of the electorate in Taiwan remains unconvinced that it is in its best interest to accept incorporation into the PRC, the goal of peaceful reunification is bound to be difficult to achieve (Romberg 2010). It is in this context that the CCP relies on civil society to convince Taiwanese of the benefits of reunification with China. The SEF-ARATS meetings, which were exchanges between business elites, did produce some agreements between the two sides but did not lead to a change of opinion in Taiwanese society (Mainland Affairs Council 2010). The CCP has to think of strategies to win the hearts of Taiwanese "compatriots." Hence, the idea that the two sides share the same culture and therefore that reunification is natural was often expressed under Hu (Xinhua News 2009) and has been reiterated under Xi (Hui 2015). Buddhism, as an institutional religion with deep roots in China and a vibrant development in Taiwan, represents an important resource to achieve that goal.

Buddhist institutions in the PRC have shown great interest in knowing more about the welfare of their counterparts in Taiwan since the beginning of the reform policy. After the Cultural Revolution almost destroyed the last remnants of their institutions on the mainland, Buddhist leaders and younger generations of monks and laypeople looked to Taiwan as a source of continuity for their tradition. After Taiwan embarked on its democratic transition and the regulations preventing the expansion of independent Buddhist associations were relaxed, large lay Buddhist associations expanded and started to establish branches overseas. In so doing, they became known to overseas Chinese, and from their locations in North America and Asia, the members of these Taiwanese associations could visit the PRC.

At the beginning, cooperation between Buddhist institutions on both sides of the Taiwan Strait was limited. Yet, high-profile visits by prominent monks based in Taiwan, such as Hsing Yun 星云, the founder of the Buddha's Light Mountain (Foguangshan 佛光山), who was a native of mainland China, generated high hopes from the leadership of the CCP that he could sway Taiwanese Buddhists to their side. For the leaders of the CCP, Hsing Yun has emerged as an important player among Taiwanese Buddhists and in Taiwanese society at large whom they can welcome in China. During the presidential election of 1996, Hsing Yun supported a candidate who opposed Taiwanese independence and won about 10 percent of the vote. Although this was not significant electorally, it demonstrated to the PRC where Hsing Yun and his organization stood. Lay Buddhists with important positions in the Buddha's Light Mountain were instrumental in facilitating some form of dialogue between the two sides of the Taiwan Strait. Hence Wu Po-hsiung 吴伯雄, chair of the Taiwan chapter of the Buddha's Light International Association (BLIA)—the organization founded by Hsing Yun after successfully developing the Buddha's Light Mountain—was also the chair of the KMT and became instrumental in maintaining channels of communication between the leadership of the KMT and the CCP. His visit to the PRC paved the way for the historic meeting between Lien Chan and Hu Jintao.

The Buddhist Compassion Relief Tzu Chi Foundation (Ciji Gongdehui 慈济功德会), the most important charity organization in Taiwan, is another Taiwanese Buddhist association that has received support from governments in China. The foundation finally received authorization from the central government to set up a branch in Beijing in the immediate aftermath of its rapid effort to provide relief to Sichuan after the earthquake of May 12, 2008. Tzu Chi has also established branches in other cities, with the help of Taiwanese businesses operating in the PRC. The information about the PRC government's acceptance of Tzu Chi's presence in China has been relayed relatively recently by the official site of China Corporate Social Responsibility. However, the organization has been active in the PRC since 1992, when it provided relief to victims of natural disasters in central China (Shi 1999; Laliberté 2013). Until 2008, Tzu Chi was welcome to provide relief, help establish schools in impoverished areas, and contribute to the reconstruction of communities affected by floods or earthquakes but could not set up a permanent presence. During those years, the foundation relied on the goodwill of local governments. Since Tzu Chi has received permission to operate in China, more local governments have approved, or have not opposed, its opening of new liaison bureaus, including a headquarters in Suzhou (Guojia Zongjiao Shiwuju 2010). Tzu Chi's activities are known to all members of the association overseas and in Taiwan. Leaders of the foundation's administrative board have also managed to leave their imprint on Chinese institutions. Wang Tuan-cheng, the brother of Tzu Chi's founder, Cheng Yen (Zhengyan 证严), was a member of the honorary board of China's National Philanthropic Association.

The crowning achievement of the CCP's religious diplomacy was the convening of the World Buddhist Forum. Its co-organizers included the BAC, the BLIA, the Hong Kong Buddhist Association (HKBA), and the China Religious Culture Communication Association (CRCCA, Zhonghua Zongjiao Wenhua Jiaoliu Xiehui 中华宗教文化交流协会). The BAC is presented as a national patriotic association for Buddhists of various nationalities, the BLIA as an international association, the HKBA as a leading organization in Hong Kong, and the CRCCA as a national organization founded voluntarily by residents of the Chinese mainland, Taiwan, Hong Kong, and Macau and overseas Chinese. After an initial event organized in Hangzhou in 2006, Buddhist leaders on both sides of the Taiwan Strait agreed to organize the event in Wuxi, Jiangsu Province, and to conclude it in Puli, in central Taiwan. Hsing Yun, as leader of the BLIA, contributed to the organization of the event in that capacity, and not as a member of the Buddhist Association of the Republic of China (BAROC), which claims legitimacy over all Buddhists in China. The CRCCA chairship was held by Ye Xiaowen 叶小文, general director of SARA. The event received the support of the very top leadership: Jia Qinglin 贾庆林, head of the constitutionally second-most important state organ, the Chinese People's Political Consultative Conference (CPPCC; Zhongguo Renmin Zhengzhi Xieshang Huiyi 中国人民政治协商会议), launched the forum in a widely broadcast ceremony in China.[37]

The close connection between Hsing Yun and people close to the political leadership of the PRC, however, has generated some outrage in Taiwan, and some of the members of his organization have expressed strong opposition to their spiritual leader. It is clear that the membership in the Buddha's Light Mountain does not always support Hsing Yun's rapprochement with the mainland government. A similar caveat needs to be made with respect to Tzu Chi: Many Taiwanese are uncomfortable with the work the association is performing in the PRC. Despite these limitations, however, the CCP has learned over the years that cooperation between Chinese and Taiwanese Buddhists does not present the kind of political risks that Christians, who have links with their coreligionists in the West, could represent. Buddhists tend to be apolitical. Taiwanese Buddhists proved to be so during the period of martial law in Taiwan, and they were absent from the movements in civil society pushing for democratization (Jones 1999). They were never proactive to the same extent as the Way of Unity (Yiguandao 一贯道) (Lin 1994) or the Presbyterian Church of Taiwan (Rubinstein 1991) in pushing for political reforms. In addition, the considerable number of charitable activities undertaken by lay Buddhist associations in Taiwan has not led to a questioning of state legitimacy and has never engendered an oppositional political movement. In short, Buddhist institutions, in Taiwan at least, have shown the leadership in China that it need not fear the empowerment of Buddhism within its borders. Although support for the development of Buddhist charities in China is not spelled out explicitly in CCP documents, it is tacitly expressed in the willingness of the Chinese government at all levels to allow the registration of Buddhist charities and foundations whose activities are similar to those of their counterparts in Taiwan. Buddhist monks and lay leaders in locations as diverse as Shijiazhuang, Tianjin, Taiyuan, and Xiamen have all confirmed in the course of interviews that Taiwanese Buddhist associations have provided the model they would like to emulate.

Under Xi Jinping, the calculus from Beijing has not changed. The changed nature of Taiwanese sentiments, however, already visible in the last two years of the second Ma administration, was made clear to Chinese leaders with the outbreak of the "Sunflower" student movement, which expressed its displeasure and anxiety over a hastily negotiated Economic Cooperation Framework Agreement between Taibei and Beijing, which appeared to the students as a loss of sovereignty for Taiwan. Faced with a public opinion in the island that does not accept the CCP's objective of annexation of Taiwan under the "one country, two systems" policy, the Chinese leadership may reconsider the usefulness of Buddhist organizations in its United Front work directed toward Taiwan. The evidence so far, however, suggests that the survival of Buddhism in China still serves the objective of presenting to the world a less threatening side of the country, and helping local governments allay some aspects of poverty.

The CCP sees the expansion of Buddhist institutions in the PRC favorably because it can serve three important and interrelated policy objectives at little cost. First, it can demonstrate to foreigners that Buddhism thrives in China and can foster a religious tourism that brings in revenues from pilgrims coming from countries where Buddhism matters. This is a rather different approach from the objective sought by the CCP in the first decade of the PRC's existence, when the new regime sought to convince foreign public opinion that Buddhism thrives under socialism and hoped that as a result foreign governments would improve their relations with China. Second, tourism and pilgrimages have generated wealth for Buddhist institutions that has made possible the development of philanthropic activities. The delivery of social services by Buddhist charities is appreciated by local governments because it dampens the worst effects of China's mode of development and contributes to the goal of social stability encapsulated in the slogan of "harmonious society." Finally, one additional benefit of that development that is invoked in official propaganda is the hope that the cooperation between Chinese and Taiwanese Buddhist associations puts in place conditions favoring détente between the two sides of the Taiwan Strait at the political level. So far, there are no signs that this approach to generate support for Taiwan's annexation to China has been successful in any meaningful way.[38] We cannot infer from the fact that the state looks favorably at the success of Buddhist tourism and the expansion of Buddhist philanthropy, however, that these developments result from deliberate CCP policies at the central level. The evidence discussed here suggests that the wealth of Buddhist associations and the activities of Buddhist charities result from initiatives on the part of these organizations rather than from state action. Moreover, as the ethnographic observations made by most contributors to this volume attest, most of the wealth of these associations does not come only from fund-raising activities: It also comes from merit-seeking devotees who thereby express their religiosity.

However, the achievements of Buddhist institutions in promoting China's diplomacy, fostering economic growth, delivering social services, and improving the climate of cross-strait relations should not be overstated. The BAC has not managed to convince the rest of the world that the Dalai Lama is an illegitimate leader or that Chinese in China enjoy total religious freedom. Although they have helped improve cross-strait relations and facilitated contacts between mainland Chinese and Taiwanese, Buddhist institutions cannot contribute to reunification, as long as most Taiwanese reject the policy of "one country, two systems" proposed by the PRC. With respect to investments by foreign and overseas Chinese tourists and devotees to help restore old temples or build new ones, the data available does not allow us to make generalizations valid for the entire country. It is clear that the recently acquired wealth of Buddhist temples allows them to operate charities that can complement the shortcomings of impoverished local governments, but there are wide variations throughout the country. Though temples with historical reputations such as Nanputuo in Xiamen and the Jade Buddha Temple in Shanghai are able to reach large numbers of destitute people, temples in interior provinces are often unable to maintain themselves, let alone succor others.

Buddhist institutions benefit from CCP tolerance of their activities to the extent that the party-state does not impose too many obstacles to their growth. But this tolerance does not mean total support for the expansion of their influence within and outside the country. Temples are being rebuilt, monastic orders are expanding, temple networks are becoming denser, publications are becoming more numerous, scholarship is increasing, and charitable activities are spreading thanks to the initiatives of Buddhist institutions and leaders; little of this depends on state patronage. All of the above should not be confused with a hands-off state policy of neutrality toward religion. The wider scope of these activities becomes permissible to the CCP as long as it can serve, among others things, to buttress its newfound claim to legitimacy as the promoter of Chinese tradition, help fill gaps in the provision of social services, and support the goal of national unification. The Chinese state is largely supportive of Buddhist activities in China today, but this support is qualified. The nature of the Chinese central government's support of Buddhist activities can be best described as merely a lack of opposition rather than an overt support of the kind Confucian Institutes receive for their expansion around the world. Local governments vary in their response to the growth of Buddhism. China being such a large, complex, and diverse country, it is impossible to provide a generalization about the relations between local governments and Buddhist institutions, but the available evidence, discussed in this chapter, has shown an enthusiasm across regions for the development of Buddhist tourism and philanthropy. The CCP's acceptance of Buddhism's growth in China is one of the most important aspects of its policy toward religion, even though it is not particularly well-known outside the country.

NOTES

An earlier version of this chapter, under the title "Buddhist Revival under State Watch," appeared in the *Journal of Current Chinese Affairs* (Laliberté 2011a). The author would like to express his gratitude to the editorial board of the journal for graciously accepting a revision of that paper in its current form; the Social Sciences and Humanities Research Council of Canada for its financial support for the research behind this chapter; and coeditors Gareth Fisher and Ji Zhe, along with two anonymous reviewers, for their very helpful suggestions. Any remaining omissions or mistakes are mine.

1. The question of the relationship between Tibetan Buddhism and the state has received greater coverage than Buddhism among Han Chinese (*hanchuan fojiao* 汉传佛教), which has many times more adherents. The relationship between the state and the latter constitutes the focus of this chapter.

2. There are noteworthy exceptions, such as those by Laliberté (2003, 2008, 2009, 2012); Ji (2004, 2008a, 2015, 2016c); Yang and Wei (2005); Wank (2009); Jones (2010); Sun (2011); Huang (2012); and Travagnin (2015, forthcoming).

3. The PRC also recognizes Protestant Christianity, Catholicism, and Islam. Some local governments have tolerated the activities of other religions, such as Eastern Orthodox Christianity and Judaism. Moreover, the State Administration for Religious Affairs (SARA) established in 2004 a fourth division (*yewu si si* 业务四司) for "other religions," which mostly oversees issues dealing with popular beliefs. I am grateful to Ji Zhe for pointing this out. There are excellent studies about the relationship between local governments and ancestral halls, lineage associations, and village temples, all expressions of popular beliefs (see Feuchtwang 2000; Eng and Lin 2002; Tsai 2002).

4. My apologies for any omission of sources in a rapidly expanding literature.

5. The dates refer to each individual's accession to the position of CCP Central Committee general secretary.

6. It is possible, however, that these human rights organizations may be unduly influenced by the perspectives of Western missionaries and Chinese Christians with good connections in the West who have effective channels to inform public opinion when they are targeted by Chinese authorities.

7. *Jiji yindao zongjiao yu shehuizhuyi xiang shiying* 积极引导宗教与社会主义相适应.

8. Although the framework of this book concerns Buddhism after Mao, not much can be written about CCP policy toward religion in general, let alone Buddhism. Although the revival of Buddhism started with the reform and opening policy of Deng Xiaoping, it was not an issue for which he cared much. His successors Hu Yaobang and Zhao Ziyang were liberals in economic matters and politically open, but their rule was too brief to affect the policy on religion, and they had more pressing concerns with which to deal.

9. An important nuance: Opposing Taiwanese independence does not mean support for China's annexation of Taiwan.

10. These numbers are still mentioned by the BAC on the opening page of its website. See Zhongguo Fojiao Xiehui 2012.

11. China does not figure in the top ten countries with the largest proportion of Buddhists, nor among those with the fastest growth in number of Buddhists.

12. The number of temples, monks, and nuns has increased since my last visit to this site, but not the estimates for lay practitioners. For an estimation of the evolution of the numbers of clerics and monasteries in post-Mao China, see Ji 2012.

13. From the layperson who works in a Buddhist charity and has taken the Bodhisattva Precepts to the occasional pilgrim who visits a temple once a year on a holiday, it is more difficult to count Buddhists than it is to estimate the numbers of members of congregational religions such as Christianity or Islam, who meet more regularly.

14. This source also underreports the number of institutions, but it is more fine-grained than the numbers for believers.

15. The National Administration of Tourism website (https://www.topchinatravel.com /china-guide/chinese-philosophy-religion/) offers very little information about religious tourism or pilgrimages. Its Chinese link is broken. It is more often local Buddhist associations or governments that promote the historical value of Buddhist sites.

16. For a more detailed study on the contemporary evolution of the Shaolin Temple's monastic life, see Ji 2016a. Most of my respondents, whether monastics, laypeople, or scholars, have expressed their disapproval of Shaolin's activities, saying that they did not consider them appropriate for Buddhists. Although I do not claim any scientific validity for that sample, it is interesting that the economic benefit of these activities was seen as part of the problem.

17. Gareth Fisher wonders if we should read the *media* attention to the alleged corruption of Buddhism's involvement in financial matters as a veiled attempt by the state to rein in too much economic development on the part of Buddhists. Fisher, personal e-mail communication with the author, July 2016.

18. For numbers on Buddhists in these countries, see Pew Research Center 2012.

19. I could not find evidence that this policy was imposed by others in the WFB.

20. These Buddhist organizations were also established in countries that were staunchly anti-Communist and therefore more inclined to support the claim of Taiwan to represent "free China."

21. The official China Tibet Online website quotes BAC chair Xuecheng and BAC vice-chairs Juexing and Zhanru's approving comments to that effect. The three of them are members of the CPPCC.

22. The *People's Daily,* the CCP's flagship newspaper, carried a story about Xi Jinping's twelve "hot phrases" that he uses to promote his own policies. None of them bears on the relation between the CCP and Buddhism, or even on religion. See Bandurski (2015) and Tiezzi (2015) for all of these phrases.

23. The three articles mentioned here were included in the proceedings of a conference on this issue that gathered more than forty scholars assembled by the BAC vice-chair Juexing.

24. Yinshun and Wang's recent compilation of papers was endorsed by another BAC vice-chair, Yinshun.

25. In 2004 and 2006, I visited the Bailin Temple, which sponsored the merit society. Its website, consulted October 11, 2018, did not show activities or news more recent than July 2014. See the society's website at http://www.hdjy.org/news/ShowInfo.aspx?ID=1161 (accessed October 11, 2018).

26. For reports of philanthropic activities since 2016, see the website Hong De Wang 弘德网 (Spreading Virtue Website), http://www.fjhnw.com/list.asp?classid=22 (accessed October 11, 2018).

27. The Wutaishan site does not mention charity at all, but Changshan 昌善, the chair of the Wutaishan Municipal Buddhist Association, is also deputy secretary general of the Buddhist Merit Charity Association (Fojiao Gongde Cishan Zonghui 佛教功德慈善总会), http://www.wutaishanfojiao.com/ (accessed October 11, 2018).

28. The site reports that as of 2016, the clinic provided a total of about 120,000 medicines for the destitute for free. This charity was also praised by the National Religious Affairs Bureau and the Chinese Buddhist Association. Guangdong Sheng Fojiao Xiehui 2017a.

29. Guangdong Sheng Fojiao Xiehui 2017b.

30. I visited the offices of the Universal Awakening Compassionate Society in the Jade Buddha Temple in 2009 and 2010, and more recently its new office in the summer of 2015. They are still operating a website: http://zt.pusa123.com/zt/15456.html (accessed October 11, 2018).

31. Buddhist references are absent from the website of the Shanghai Municipality Charity Association (see http://www.scf.org.cn/, accessed October 11, 2018).

32. This assertion was corroborated by observations on site in Hebei and Jiangsu during my fieldwork in 2004, 2006, and 2009.

33. The opening page of the organization's website lacks a tab marking anything along the lines of "charity" (Zhongguo Fojiao Xiehui 2018).

34. For July to October 2018 alone, it advertised more than forty activities. See Fojiao Zaixian website, http://www.fjnet.com/cssy/default_1.htm (accessed October 11, 2018).

35. Hong Kong before 1997 and Macau before 1999 would have been included along with Taiwan as territories that are not under the jurisdiction of the PRC. Now that they have become special administrative regions, they are entitled to a quasi-autonomous status, but as far as the central government in Beijing is concerned, they have returned to Chinese sovereignty. For the CCP, they are a matter of domestic politics.

36. With President Tsai Ying-wen in power since the beginning of 2016, the situation may become fluid again. The Democratic Progressive Party, which President Tsai leads, and which now dominates the legislature for the first time, favors independence, an option the PRC opposes.

37. The event was posted on the State Council website, in English. "Chinese Top Political Advisor Meets Delegates to World Buddhism Forum," March 28, 2009, www.gov.cn /english/2009-03/28/content_1271035.htm (accessed October 22, 2018).

38. The views expressed by Hsing Yun, the founding abbot of the Buddha's Light Mountain monastic order, in Taiwan during the second World Buddhist Forum that Taiwanese and Chinese "belong to one family" and that they "will naturally become unified" echoed the views of the CCP but generated rebuke from Taiwanese Buddhists who participated at the event (Loa 2009).

2

ADMINISTERING BODHISATTVA GUANYIN'S ISLAND

The Monasteries, Political Entities, and Power Holders of Putuoshan

CLAIRE VIDAL

Located in the Zhoushan 舟山 archipelago in Zhejiang Province, the island of Putuoshan (Mount Putuo) 普陀山 is a Buddhist pilgrimage site that each year welcomes many thousands of visitors from different Asian countries (in particular Korea and Japan) to worship Guanyin 观音, the bodhisattva of compassion. Many Asian Buddhists consider Putuoshan the Chinese version of the Potalaka (the original name in Chinese was Putuoluojia 普陀洛迦), the mythical Indian site where, according to tradition, Avalokiteśvara (Guanyin) resides. Putuoshan has been a pilgrimage site since the end of the ninth century; its history closely relates to the construction of regional pilgrimage networks during the formative period of Chinese Buddhism, when devotion to Avalokiteśvara was sinicized (Yü 1992, 2001).[1] Famous as a site for apparitions of the bodhisattva to those asking for blessings and hoping for miracles, Putuoshan is one of the four sacred mountains of Buddhism.[2]

In addition to incorporation into this network of Chinese Buddhist places of worship, Putuoshan also benefits from its strategic location between the South and East China Seas, at the nexus of ancient trade routes for North and South Asia, which early on made it a major center for the expansion of Buddhism at the regional level. It formed its reputation as a pilgrimage site open to all when tales from monks and pilgrims of miraculous events at key sites helped to trace pilgrimage routes between them. Today, books addressed to devotees, tourist guides, and journals about culture and Buddhism at Putuoshan connect the famous tales of monks and pilgrims from many different places throughout Asia with contemporary accounts of travelers from Asian countries.[3] This juxtaposition helps to spread the idea of a Putuoshan that is open to all. This interpretation of a highly regarded sacred site not only represents a conceptual elaboration by local monastic communities likely to have proselytizing goals. The daily rush of crowds of travelers who end up in Putuoshan's port, not only from China, but from all over Asia, also provides empirical evidence of contemporary Chinese Buddhism's prosperity and of the popularity of the worship of Guanyin and the pilgrimage devoted to her.[4]

Separated by a small body of water from the other Zhoushan islands,[5] the Putuoshan site is visited by travelers coming from Shanghai, via twice-daily boats in the daytime and nighttime, or from Ningbo 宁波, Shenjiamen 沈家门, or Zhujiajian 朱家尖, at the end of bus routes taken by those coming from elsewhere in China. It is a privileged year-round destination for certain travelers for whom other sites, such as the three other sacred mountains, are more difficult to reach, even for those who come from far away (Thailand, for instance). The travelers to Putuoshan are just as heterogeneous as the itineraries that reach it. Some come alone; some visit with friends, immediate relatives, or extended kin; others come accompanied by fellow lay practitioners affiliated with a temple; some come even as clients of a tour operator. Most visitors rush through the island within a day, visiting several sites in many monasteries and nunneries, while others prefer to stay longer, often in expensive hotels, at temples, or at local residences. Three times a year, on the nineteenth days of the second, sixth, and ninth months of the lunar year, the island's temples leave their doors open all night long for those who come, in great numbers, to worship Guanyin.[6] The popularity of her cult, caused by the spread of many stories of and literature on "the miraculous responses" (ganying 感应) of Guanyin,[7] also explains why many believers favor this destination. They come to pray to the bodhisattva, hoping that she will grant them their wish for a child, healing, or financial or professional success. Testimonies of bodhisattva sightings and miraculous responses during a family pilgrimage or a large religious gathering are common and contribute in shaping the strong reputation of Putuoshan as a Buddhist holy site.

Since the 1980s and through the 1990s, projects for reconstruction, development, and modernization, launched in the context of the opening and reform policies of Deng Xiaoping 邓小平, transformed the island's natural landscape and cultural settings. After the Cultural Revolution, when monastic communities were allowed to return to the island, the first stage of reconstruction began inside temples that had been partially destroyed; halls and rooms that had been abandoned were gradually renovated and decorated with new images and paintings. Caves in which the bodhisattva is believed to appear were also renovated. New roads were built across the island, running from its port to its northern edge. From the mid-1990s, reconstructions of earlier destroyed or derelict sites gave way to more ambitious projects that displayed the new prestige of the monastic communities of Putuoshan, such as an immense statue of the Guanyin of the South Sea (Nanhai Guanyin 南海观音), which became emblematic of the island. In the twenty years since the start of reform, official visits of politicians from China and around the world, as well as famous

Buddhist religious leaders or groups of foreign devotees, often signaled an opportunity to obtain new funds to launch new building projects, such as huge doors for the island's monasteries or stairs inside natural spaces (on Fodingshan 佛顶山, for example).[8]

Now delineated, the different spaces of Putuoshan—monasteries, nunneries, pavilions, forests, stones, gates, temples, grottoes, and beaches—are marked with directional and informational signposts. Translated into English, Korean, and Japanese, these signs mix scriptural references to mythical sites (such as the Purple Bamboo Forest or the Paradise of Western Bliss, also known as the Amitabha's Pure Land) with revised terminology approved by the tourist industry (such as "scenery areas," from the Chinese *fengjingqu* 风景区).[9] As is the case with other tourist locations in China, Putuoshan is at once a sacred mountain, a pilgrimage site, and a much-sought-after tourist site, which charges 160 RMB for an adult entrance fee. Its administrators also organize a yearly Tourism Day (Lüyou Jie 旅游节) and a regular Guanyin of the South Sea Day (Nanhai Guanyin Jie 南海观音节). These huge transformations, which have considerably accelerated since the beginning of the 2000s, have led to the emergence of a new landscape based on the delimitation of the island into eight "scenic spots." These include the first Buddhist hall, known as the Don't Want to Go Guanyin Temple (Bu Ken Qu Guanyin Yuan 不肯去观音院),[10] and the three historical temples of Fayu 法雨, Puji 普济, and Huiji 慧济. With the aim of developing Putuoshan's influence as a great Buddhist sacred site and an eminent center for the spreading of the Dharma, the monastic communities also launched their own initiatives, in agreement with local authorities' guidelines and expectations. An example of this is the building of the fourth great monastery on the island, the Baotuo Jiang Temple 宝陀讲寺, opened in May 2011, which since then has become a space for bimonthly Dharma assemblies for lectures on the sutras (*jiangjing fahui* 讲经法会).[11] The building of new structures and the growth of the local tourism industry have both inspired new means of going on pilgrimage in Putuoshan and introduced new practices to the island's environment. For instance, with the construction of a cable car, some pilgrims no longer climb on foot to Fodingshan (whose name means *uṣṇīṣa*, i.e., the protuberance on top of the Buddha's head); the ascent of this natural space of Putuoshan to reach one of the three historical major temples of Putuoshan is no longer a significant stage of their pilgrimage. Going on pilgrimage in this area of Putuoshan thus boils down to a simple visit to the temple, similar to visiting the Puji Temple or the Fayu Temple, except during the three annual festivals of Guanyin, when devotees climb the mountain by practicing the "three steps and one salutation" (*san bu yi bai* 三步一拜), an ascetic practice that consists of kowtowing every three steps to the top of the Fodingshan.

Today visiting Putuoshan involves going to the different scenic spots. Within the temples, pilgrims are used to burning large amounts of incense; greeting buddhas and bodhisattvas (by pressing their palms together and kowtowing);

and making offerings of fresh flowers, fruits, cookies, and money. Most pilgrims take the wood boardwalks built along the road to visit well-known spots on the island of Guanyin. While listening to the sound of a sweet melody in homage to Guanyin broadcast through artificial rocks placed at the edge of the well-traveled paths, they go to the Purple Bamboo Forest to admire the great "Image of Guanyin" in the Open Air (Lutian "Nanhai Guanyin Lixiang" 露天 "南海观音立像"). Others then cross the forest of the Paradise of Western Bliss (Xitian 西天), where they go into each nunnery and, for each visit, make the same gestures of offering incense and greeting buddhas. At the side of the road or in nearby monasteries, shops sell many "objects of the Dharma" (fa wu 法物), such as bracelets, necklaces, Guanyin images, small radios with recordings of sutra chants, and Guanyin cookies of Putuoshan. Many devotees buy these items, sometimes in large quantities, to bring home.

I observed during my fieldwork with pilgrims that very few of them talked about the merit that devotees gain when they make offerings or give money to build Buddhist images. They did not talk about the quest for enlightenment either. For Somkid,[12] a Thai Buddhist who visits Putuoshan every year with his family, there are four main reasons why people make the pilgrimage to Putuoshan: money, business, luck, and salvation; their request to the Guanyin images on the island follow on from these four motives. While these motives are quite common to those at temples throughout China, some pilgrims' experiences are particular to Putuoshan. For example, Xinxue from Shanghai went to Putuoshan accompanied by her daughters and their children in order to acquire knowledge of religious practices and to share her experience of Buddhist pilgrimage with her daughters. During their journey to Putuoshan, two events occurred: After she had offered them two ancestral tablets, Xinxue had a vision of both her deceased parents and parents-in-law while she slept; the day after, she had a vision of Guanyin in the Fanyin Cave 梵音洞; her daughters also claimed to have "seen [Guanyin]" (kan Guanyin 看观音) with their mother's guidance, thus experiencing Putuoshan as the central site to witness apparitions. Other pilgrims seek first of all to talk with monks and nuns about their existential problems, such as difficulties in getting married and starting a family. This is what Yang Jing, a thirty-year-old single woman, told me in confidence. From Shanghai, she went to Putuoshan for the first time with the desire to discover what Buddhism is and how to pray to the Buddha and Guanyin. Her wish to learn religious practices seemed to be incompatible with the tourist industry atmosphere that she had experienced during her trip to Putuoshan; in fact, when she returned to Shanghai with one of the Zhoushan bus companies, she was really displeased to have to visit a shopping mall called City of Regional Specialties of Zhoushan (Zhoushan Techan Cheng 舟山特产城). Like her friend Li Wenlei, with whom she traveled, she was surprised to find a disconnect between her idea of what a pilgrimage should be and the touristic atmosphere she actually encountered.[13]

From the point of view of the local residents, the insular world of Putuoshan relies on a social organization influenced by recent changes that has consolidated around an economy entirely based on pilgrimage and tourism. Since the beginning of the 1980s, all activities related to fishing have ceased. Local residents are employed in hotels, transportation, restaurants, and trade sectors and thereby contribute to the attempts of local governments to promote economic growth-generating initiatives and to support the projects of the monastic communities aimed at propagating "Putuoshan's Buddhism" (*Putuoshan fojiao* 普陀山佛教). The activities that promote heritage tourism, the diverse measures encouraging the expansion of religious communities, and the numerous innovations in the site's administration have in the end deeply transformed the local institutional field, multiplying and diversifying the actors who participate in local life and "produce the religious." These transformations involve as much laypeople and state officials as monks. The activities of each of these groups occur within the framework of the state and the religiously diverse organizations to which they belong. While the functions of these various groups seem clearly identifiable from the state perspective, in fact their behavior reveals the ambiguities of their statuses, as it often results from individual initiatives and ambitions rather than from official positions within the island's governance.

Putuoshan's religious field, though enmeshed in the logics of a national system for the management of religious affairs and of local politics, has been reshaped, in particular the modalities of administration for the pilgrimage site.[14] The processes used in administering Putuoshan and the mechanisms that have contributed to the reorganization of local governance demonstrate that the institutional environment of this Buddhist site creates interstices where some local personalities who own relatively well-developed social and cultural capital are able to innovate in the production of the religious and the functioning of politics. Their outlook on the institutional landscape to which they belong and their claims on the function they occupy reveal lively self-made institutions that reinvent themselves. They do so as much within the reality of social change in contemporary China (in relation to its global power ambitions) as in the discursive frameworks of official texts (albeit the discourses fostered by those texts contribute in their own way to these transformations).

Analysis of accounts from officials, lay practitioners, and monks, along with written excerpts taken from official documentation, in particular the annual *Gazetteer of the Putuoluojiashan* (*Putuoluojia shanzhi* 普陀洛迦山志), reveals the components of the religious field on the island of Guanyin. They interact in a back-and-forth movement between new initiatives and ancient organizational logics (namely, the principle of the "three unifiers," discussed further in the second part of the chapter), which are, in turn, influenced in part by individual agency. A high-ranking monk of the Buddhist Association of Putuoshan (Putuoshan Fojiao Xiehui 普陀山佛教协会) who was surprised both by my interest in the organizational logics of the Putuoshan site and by my knowledge of the "three unifiers" claimed that Putuoshan pilgrims are not concerned with these organizational changes, which affect only the inner world of the monasteries. He also claimed that pilgrims do not know everything about religious organizations.[15] Further research is needed to determine whether this statement is accurate from the pilgrims' point of view. Data on the modalities of administration was for the most part collected during fieldwork conducted in the summer of 2012. Hosted by the Buddhist Academy of Putuoshan (Putuoshan Foxueyuan 普陀山佛学院),[16] I met clerics involved in the management of the temple and lay employees working on projects related to the temple. It is from their accounts that I sought to gain a detailed overview of the operations of the multiple organizations involved in the management of Putuoshan, to which various written sources commenting on these initiatives for the island's development refer. Far from being comprehensive, this examination nonetheless provides an overview of the ways in which the people who establish, reproduce, and reinvent local institutions imagine Putuoshan as a major site of Chinese Buddhism.

ZHANG MINXI'S PATTERNS: A LOCAL PUBLIC SERVANT'S VIEW ON THE ADMINISTRATION OF BUDDHISM

The Buddhist Academy of Putuoshan, which has been located on the small neighboring island of Zhujiajian since 2010, counts among its members a public servant named Zhang Minxi. Installed in the office adjoining that of the academy's vice-rector, he describes himself as a simple teacher, native of the Zhoushan archipelago, and a recently retired public official from the municipal Religious Affairs Bureau, the Committee for the Ethnic and Religious Affairs of Zhoushan (Zhoushan Shi Minzu Zongjiao Shiwuju 舟山市民族宗教事务局), where Putuoshan is located. Although for some time he provided support to the president of the municipal office, he now claims to have retired from state affairs. However, his frequent travels to the academy, the fact he has obtained a workspace there, and the way that he is welcomed at the academy's guesthouse attest to his position at the peak of a hierarchy that contains different political and religious organizations. In August 2012, I met with Zhang Minxi on several occasions to clarify the operating modes of the temples about which I had read in the official literature and heard mentioned by both state authorities and monastics. At once interested in my work but also suspicious—he refused to let me record or take notes during our first meetings—he eventually agreed to guide me in the drawing up of diagrams to summarize and clarify the relationship among all actors engaged in the development of Buddhism in Putuoshan. Diagramming the complexity of these relationships was a difficult task: Zhang would frequently add marginal annotations as he drew a chart that revealed new connections between individuals and groups and attempted to specify the tangled nature of the relationships among them.

From China Down to Putuo: A System of Administrative Entities and Decision Makers

At the end of our interviews, the resulting schema—which I treat here as primary ethnographic material—revealed a system articulated around three organizations: the United Front Work Department (Tongzhanbu 统战部), the Religious Affairs Bureau (Zongjiao Shiwuju 宗教事务局), and the Buddhist Association (Fojiao Xiehui 佛教协会). These organizations are developed at different administrative levels: national, provincial (in this case Zhejiang Sheng 浙江省), municipal (in this case Zhoushan Shi 舟山市), and local (in this case Putuo Qu 普陀区). These three entities have structured the Buddhist religious field in China since their rehabilitation after the Cultural Revolution. Together, they make up a political system based on a sprawling network of administrative

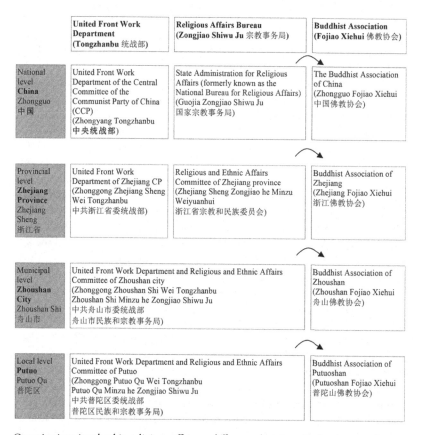

Organizations involved in religious affairs at different administrative levels, according to Zhang Minxi (in interviews with the author in the summer of 2012). Arrows show relations of control between religious affairs bureaus and Buddhist associations.

units that are diffused throughout the country and which cover fields of action related to organs of the Communist Party (*dang* 党), state administrative units (*zheng* 政), parts of the People's Liberation Army (*jun* 军), and organizations involved in the country's economic development. Their areas of action, missions, and relations, far from always being clearly defined, shape central, regional, and local authorities whose mandates are characterized by a degree of institutional confusion (Cabestan 1994, 2014).

Before analyzing Zhang Minxi's schema more specifically, I will provide a brief overview of the role the central state articulates for these organizations. The Buddhist Association of China (BAC) is one of five national religious organizations recognized by the state in China. Established in 1953, it links the leaders and members of the Buddhist clergy and serves to regulate religious practices.[17] Reestablished during the 1980s, the BAC's mission is to apply state guidelines on religion, administer monasteries, and account for the initiatives that are implemented in the various temples under its responsibility. The BAC is connected to the United Front Work Department, an organ of the CCP, and to the State Administration for Religious Affairs (SARA; Religious Affairs Bureau), a department of the state apparatus. Established during the 1920s, the United Front Work Department's founding principle is to unite all possible allies of the CCP in a common cause and neutralize non-Communist forces. Still today, it serves as a conduit to party policies and works toward increasing its influence in China and abroad (Cabestan 2014, 178). Since the 1990s, it has become a prolific space for the publication and diffusion of official documents that set the framework for the implementation of legislation and regulations (Groot 2004, 179–202), including in matters of religion. Its rehabilitation in 1978 accompanied the liberalization of the religious. It established measures to restore temple life and the activities of religious leaders and to promote good relations between government officials and clergy (Goossaert and Palmer 2011, 328–330). SARA is in charge of relations between the government and the five religious associations. Divided into different departments, it must fulfill three missions: helping monasteries to manage land and buildings, distributing the funds provided by the state for the reconstruction and upkeep of temples, and seeing to the application of the policies adopted by state authorities (Ashiwa and Wank 2006, 344).[18]

Two major aspects emerge from Zhang Minxi's schema and his explanation of it. On the one hand, the vertical relationship between the three national organizations and their local representatives was a crucial factor structuring the institutional landscape. On the other hand, these organizations were reproduced on the local level *for the sole purpose of* sustaining the integrity of the relations between their regional and national counterparts rather than because of local administrative needs. Zhang Minxi confided to me that Putuo's Religious and Ethnic Affairs Committee (Putuo Qu Minzu He Zongjiao Shiwu Ju 普陀区民族和宗教事务局) is in fact a small office with only two officials. However, he asserted that its existence is crucial since it contributes to the permanence of the overall system. Zhang Minxi seemed amused when I probed him on the day-to-day work of these two officials. He thought it more crucial to explain the back-and-forth movement between a given system, its structure and its origins, and the local reality of power as it has been formed in Zhoushan since the end of the 1970s and to which he has contributed significantly. The differences he explained between the independence of the United Front Work Department and the Religious Affairs Bureau at the national and provincial levels and the merging of these two authorities at the lowest levels in Zhoushan and Putuo came through very clearly. As a matter of fact, government officials on the archipelago who work for SARA are also those who are employed by the party, even though, in theory, there is supposed to be a distinction between government administrative and party units at the upper level of government (Cabestan 2014, 35). This conflation between the party and state authority is rendered visible even on business cards that display the name of the United Front Work Department, accompanied by the image of the hammer and sickle, and on the reverse a reference to the government administrative unit, that is, the Religious and Ethnic Affairs Committee of Zhoushan. According to Zhang Minxi, this sharing of roles is justified by an insufficient number of available government officials.[19] By providing a concrete reason (the reality of human resources), he avoids discussing the lack of independence of the state administrative and party organs, whether symbolically or in their actual day-to-day functions, especially with respect to the distribution of assignments to each of these two entities. Indeed, this is not unique to Zhoushan and Putuo. Goossaert and Palmer observe that "in practice, at lower levels of government the same official was often in charge of the United Front, religious affairs, and minority nationalities affairs" (Goossaert and Palmer 2011, 329). They also mention that we cannot describe the implementation of religious policies as a simple vertical relationship between national-level organizations and lower-level units. What they wrote about the policies established before 1978 remained true throughout the 1980s and 1990s: "This was not a centralized system, however: whereas lower-level Religious Affairs and United Front officials were supposed to follow directives and policies of the central government, they were appointed by the provincial and local government and Party committee, to which they remained accountable, not to the central RAB [Religious Affairs Bureau] and United Front. There were thus extreme variations in the application of religious policy at the local level" (Goossaert and Palmer 2011, 329).

While party interference in religious affairs is clearly evidenced, it should not be considered only from the organizations' standpoint. The Chinese political system often presents its institutions as administrative entities with clearly defined contours (which is probably why they seem so easy to schematize in the first place), but this can be misleading. In fact, the links that unite all these organizations cannot be determined solely by a bureaucratic arithmetic taken from the territorial zones they cover and their theoretical position within a bureaucratic hierarchy. Far from being disembodied, they are above all made up of government decision makers whose actions are motivated both by their own career ambitions and by the local interpersonal relationships within which they are embedded. This importance of local relationships is well illustrated in the case of Zhang Minxi: On many occasions, he justified the installation of his office at the Buddhist Association of Putuoshan as the result of his desire to be closer to the residences of Buddhist monastics, whom he claimed were his "friends" (*pengyou* 朋友). From the perspective of SARA, placing this retired public official near the monasteries is likely linked to a strategy to maintain an almost permanent control over religious affairs at Putuoshan. Nonetheless, my observation suggests that Zhang's placement also serves his genuine wish to take part in Putuoshan temple projects and help his "Buddhist friends" to "develop" (*fazhan* 发展) themselves.

By describing his relations with monks as "friendship" and in choosing to make that the reason for his presence, Zhang removed the need to describe bureaucratic details on how the bureau manages Putuoshan. A frequent interlocutor of the Putuoshan Buddhist Association's members, he plays a key role in exchanges and negotiations between monastic communities on the one hand and state and party on the other. His special relationship with the Buddhist Academy of Putuoshan, in which he has a workspace without any official functions, and his status as retired from the bureau (with which he continues to organize meetings) contribute to blurring boundaries between the religious sphere and the state's field. That is why the ideal models of hierarchical relationships that Zhang drew for me became invalidated by the reality of multiple exceptions; the arrows considered as symbols of hierarchy became less and less significant as he answered my questions about the practical functioning of these relationships.

Zhang Minxi's schema, far from being a simple summary of the administrative bodies involved in the management of the religious at different levels, highlights a local power holder's view on the system to which he contributes, that is, not only as an actor of institutional reproduction but also as a vector of local reinterpretations. In sum, he ensures the perpetuation of the bureaucratic system at the local level, thereby contributing to the diffusion of a certain conception of the state and of the relationship it maintains with individuals, while also participating in contemporary changes of institutions rooted in a local religious context with a singular history. In this way, Zhang Minxi embodies the bureaucracy in form as well as in action. Moreover, his view invites a reflection on the structures that underpin power in China and undergird both the reproductive and transformative capacities of the Chinese bureaucratic system and its officials.[20] From the national government of China to Putuo, the party, the state, and the bureaus, how in these various configurations is Putuoshan's Buddhism produced? To what extent do processes for innovating in religious matters at Putuoshan simultaneously participate in manufacturing politics?

On Power Relations at Putuoshan and on the Modalities of Buddhism's Control

During our conversations, Zhang Minxi made sure to clarify the full names of the authorities and their territorial—national, provincial, and local—positions but remained particularly vague on their relationships with one another, reducing them to a schema of hierarchical authority where Buddhist associations are subordinated to control by religious affairs bureaus and both are under the authority of administrative authorities at higher territorial levels. As pointed out in the schema, the Religious Affairs Committee of Zhoushan is placed under the responsibility of Zhejiang. The same applies to the Buddhist Association of Zhoushan (Zhoushanshi Fojiao Xiehui 舟山市佛教协会) with respect to Zhejiang's association. Yet how do these relations between religious associations and religious bureaus operate in reality? In response to this question, Zhang Minxi asserted that religious bureaus do not intervene in the associations' religious content. They do not give any instructions regarding rituals or scriptures. This assertion of noninterference was echoed by Zhong Jin, an employee of the Buddhist Association of Zhejiang (Zhejiangsheng Fojiao Xiehui 浙江省佛教协会), whom I met for the first time in 2012 during the opening ceremony of the Buddhist Academy of Putuoshan in the company of Zhang Minxi. A forty-year-old woman, Zhong holds a position with many responsibilities: She is in charge of relations with local Buddhist associations, Zhejiang monasteries, and administrative units' officials. Of course, the declarations by Zhang Minxi and Zhong Jin must be analyzed from the standpoint of their respective functions, each adhering to the policy pursued by his or her office. Regardless of whether these officials spoke truthfully according to the information available to them or consciously lied, their claims remain significant. It is recognized that the Religious Affairs Bureau has responsibility for controlling religious practice but also that that control does not always translate into the prohibition of certain practices (or at least prohibition is not so obvious that it would be vain to deny it). Then on what basis are power relations between the Religious Affairs Bureau of Zhoushan and the Buddhist Association of Putuoshan premised?

The modalities of control can be understood by looking at the characteristics of the religious field itself as it was reconstructed after the Cultural Revolution and as it is thought out and developed today. Several initiatives aimed at developing the pilgrimage site are the result of collaboration between political actors (organized in administrative entities) and monastic communities (under the auspices of the association). The short film *Putuoshan chaoxiang* 普陀山朝香 (Pilgrimage of Putuoshan), broadcast since April 2010 on the boat shuttles leading to Putuoshan Island, offers one such example. Jointly produced by the

Buddhist Association of Putuoshan, the Religious and Ethnic Affairs Committee of Zhoushan, and the Zhoushan Tourism Office, it explains to passengers how to participate in a "good" pilgrimage and what behavioral norms must be adopted in the monasteries and in the presence of Buddhist monks and nuns. It describes ways to kowtow before the Buddha and offer incense as well as ways to think about the presence of the bodhisattva Guanyin on the island. A collective discourse on correct pilgrimage practices not only is transmitted through this movie among clergy, laypeople, and devotees, but also connects Zhoushan's Religious Affairs Bureau and the Buddhist Association of Putuoshan as open collaborators in its creation (Vidal 2014).

Like many other local initiatives, *Putuoshan chaoxiang* was shaped by institutional relations that define the scope of action of religious actors and eliminate any components located outside the path outlined by national authorities if needed. Therefore, it is in the elaboration phase of these projects promoting Putuoshan's Buddhism that authorities' guidelines are incorporated into the ambitions of Buddhist communities.[21] The internal documents written for the employees of the tourism office and for SARA that explain and support the realization of these initiatives provide the contours of a framework for action. They take note of national policies toward religions partly by incorporating the ideological rhetoric of the state (such as the "harmonious society" under Hu Jintao's government) and partly by using arguments developed from the numerous local regulations and laws. Thus, the words used to establish a framework of religious practices (in order to control them) circulate from media to media and are found in various forms in the temples' posters, in local officials' speeches, and in books that spread the national propaganda. For instance, the use of only three incense sticks is strongly promoted in monasteries through many notices glued on temple walls. Buddhist monastics call this practice of the only-three-sticks gift "the civilized use of incense offering" (*wenming jingxiang* 文明敬香); they use the Chinese word *wenming* (civilized), which refers to the ideological rhetoric mobilized in the state project of "moral education" (Boutonnet 2009). The Putuoshan monastics' explanations also mix ecological and health-related explanations ("to keep clean and to freshen the environment") with religious explanations ("to purify of defiling illusion and for the peace and safety of the Buddha kingdom") to reinforce the message. The practice of using three incense sticks is also mentioned in the short film, but without any justifications; the voice-over only says, "The offering of incense must not be in excess. Do not abuse it, as it shows greed toward the Buddha" (*jingxiang bu zai duo, mo yi tanxin lifo* 敬香不在多, 莫以贪心礼佛). Many devotees, however, consider the offering of a larger number of incense sticks as a good propitiatory act and proof of their strong devotion.

Some of the initiatives that are the result of the collaboration between monastics and political authorities are not even related to devotees' practices, such as the First World Buddhist Forum, organized in Hangzhou in April 2006, by the BAC, with official administrative entities in charge of cultural exchanges with Asian countries. At the end of the ceremony, after three days of conferences and rituals, guests from mainland China, Taiwan, Hong Kong, and other Asian countries went to Putuoshan to attend the last sequence of the ceremony, the "Declaration of Putuoshan" (Putuoshan Xuanyan 普陀山宣言). In this short text, which was carved on a huge rock and has since been displayed next to the visitors' entrance port, six vows have been written on a model of a Buddhist litany: a call to peace and harmony for the individual, the family, the community, the country, and the whole world. No mention of Putuoshan, Guanyin's cult, or Buddhist doctrinal notions is made; instead, the references to the ideology of "harmony" make clear the support of Buddhist monastics for the Chinese state and its ideologies and policies. Even if this initiative did not directly relate to local-level organizations (although it took place on the Putuoshan site), it echoes various strategies used within the temples of Guanyin's island. It shows in written public texts monastics' actions in favor of state policies for religious regulation, just as one finds on posters on temple billboards entitled "Rules for Administering the Development of Harmony" (Guifan guanli, hexie fazhan 规范管理, 和谐发展). In a nutshell, the "Declaration of Putuoshan" reminds both Putuoshan monastics and visitors (who read the huge rock just as they used to look at popular calligraphy written on rocks by eminent monks and well-known scholars) that Buddhist communities give way to state projects, rather than being moral rivals to them. It also shows that Putuoshan's monastics play an important role in Buddhist geography, as is shown by the staging of part of the World Buddhist Forum and its permanent marking of the site as the "Declaration of Putuoshan" suggests.[22]

At Putuoshan, these modes of collaboration between SARA and the Buddhist Association are the product of the temples' recent history. Annihilated during the Cultural Revolution, they were reconstructed under the initiative of Zhang Jingfu 张静赴, an official who sought to restart the local economy during the early 1980s. He invited the religious specialists who had been forced out of

The "Declaration of Putuoshan," March 2011. Photo by the author.

the island to come back, including Miaoshan 妙善 (1909–2000), a significant force in the building up of Putuoshan.[23] In 1980, Miaoshan was made responsible for reestablishing and managing the Buddhist Association of Putuoshan. During his twenty years in that role, he founded the Buddhist Academy and launched major construction works, such as the statue of the Guanyin of the South Sea. The implementation of the site's administrative system that was set up during those years under the leadership of local officials and their relations with the reestablished monastic communities removed all elements that might have contradicted policies on religious development implemented throughout China and Zhejiang's coastal regions. Numerous inspections (*shicha* 视察) regularly conducted by the CCP and government officials as early as 1981 have closely guided the development of the pilgrimage site, paying special attention to its control. This reestablishment, in the wake of the Cultural Revolution, of the local institutional landscape and of the power relations it established led to the shaping of new processes (such as the recent short movie). It also increased the reach of the state in regulating Buddhism and the influence of the pilgrimage site by producing an official Buddhism aligned with the policies and conceptions of the state concerning the place of religion in Chinese society.

The religious field of Putuoshan thus has been constructed in a back-and-forth movement between an imposed and evolving system of administration, capable of taking notice of the transformations in Chinese society, and a local social organization whose specificities have been formed over time under the impact of local figures (officials, monks, and tourism business leaders). While the activities of these local figures are necessarily circumscribed by their need to comply with evolving policies on religion articulated by the central state, the institutional complexity inherent to the Chinese bureaucratic regime nonetheless creates gaps. Within these gaps, local figures with leadership skills and strong social capital act to redefine, through their actions, temple-state relations and to innovate both in the production of the religious and in the exercise of power itself. The reality of political control over the religious, and more globally the nature of the links among the organizations, is defined through configurations between national religious policies and the agentive actions of local operators of power.

The Circulation of Monks and Wealth: Cementing of the Local Religious Field

Buddhist associations constitute among themselves networks that are based on the circulation of human and financial resources. According to Zhong Jin, while the provincial Buddhist Associations of Zhejiang and the local Buddhist Association of Zhoushan are located at different levels of territorial power, their relations are "egalitarian" (*pingdeng* 平等) and also "good" (*hao* 好). During a second interview at the office of the Zhejiang association, located in its provincial capital, Hangzhou, Zhong explicitly asked me to reconsider the hierarchical links between Buddhist associations that I had developed from my conversations with Zhang Minxi. The descriptions she provided of the operations of the Zhejiang association suggested instead an organization of temples based on the distribution of administrative functions related to the movement of both monastics and capital within a larger system of economic transactions.

Buddhist associations are headed by an official chair (*huizhang* 会长) and a group of vice-chairs (*fuhuizhang* 副会长); however, the status of vice-chair is not exclusive. It is often combined with other responsibilities within associations at other levels. Among the eight leaders of the Buddhist Association of Zhejiang who serve as vice-chairs, two are also members of the Putuoshan association. Similarly, the vice-chair of the Buddhist Association of Putuoshan is also the chair of the Zhejiang association. This nonexclusivity of duties entails, even perhaps favors, the roaming behavior of the monastics inside the circle of Buddhist associations. Monks often move to attend, as guests, various temple meetings, events, and rituals (e.g., the consecration of Buddhist statues, eminent foreign monks' visits, huge donations, and the planning of buildings), thus increasing exchanges within the networks of temples that are partly constituted by the usual itinerant practices of individual monks (e.g., on pilgrimages in the mountains, studying, and seeking scriptures). It is reasonable to assume that these movements of monastics connect them within a tangle of relations between temples and associations (including those with laypeople) rather than among strictly separated networks with their own logics. In other words, monastics' movements should not be considered the result of modern ways to manage official positions within the confines of associations; instead, they should be analyzed, from a structural perspective, in relation to Buddhist modes of creating, managing, and perpetuating the sangha over time. To what extent, then, are the current modes of distributing positions within associations based on historically established, enduring structures of Chinese Buddhism or Chinese temples more generally, as opposed to purely modern bureaucratic structures? To what extent can we observe these structures in other historical and regional contexts such as the spread of Chinese Buddhism across Asia (Ashiwa and Wank 2005; chapter 5 by Daniela Campo in this volume) and in the creation of institutes of Buddhist studies during the nineteenth and twentieth centuries (Chau 2012)? In short, to what extent do these sorts of informal monastic links fuel the implementation and continuity of Chinese religion and Chinese Buddhism overall, of which their functioning in contemporary mainland China is but one example?

Financial flows constitute the glue that unites all religious entities in China, both administrative institutions that represent the state and are affiliated with the party and those linked to monastic communities. For example, the Buddhist Association of Zhejiang provides need-based funding to Buddhist associations of the cities in the province, such as Zhoushan, Hangzhou, and Ningbo. Part of this money is then redistributed among temples in these cities to finance their construction and renovation projects. As Tian Zhizu, a well-educated manager of the Buddhist Academy of Putuoshan, explained to me, at Putuoshan, the Buddhist Association raises capital from temples, which comes from both the donations of devotees—the "benevolent donors, believers of the ten directions" (*shi fang xinzhong shan juan* 十方信众善捐)—and the Religious Affairs Committee of Zhoushan. The Putuoshan Buddhist Association then gives money to the island's temples or to the academy to finance expenditures related to construction and renovation, education, and charity.[24] Questions concerning the structure of management of Buddhist institutions in post-Mao China are thus not only political but also economic.

The Institutional Environment of the Buddhist Site of Putuoshan: A Laboratory for Innovation?

The study of Zhang Minxi's schema—revised numerous times, supported by different arguments, discussed, and revised again by the employee of the

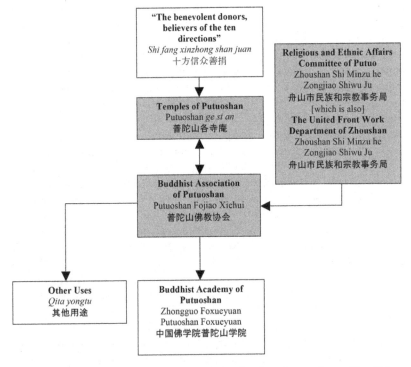

The flow of funds between organizations on Putuoshan Island, according to Tian Zhizu (in interviews with the author in August 2012).

Zhejiang Buddhist Association—has revealed that a network of politico-administrative institutions, whose boundaries are locally redefined, overlap with Buddhist organizations, whose modalities and spheres of action are also reorganized at the local level. These reconfigurations for the management of Buddhism at Putuoshan, and changes in the definition and implementation of local power, connect both the institutions and their finances and the authority figures who establish, shape, and transform them. As mentioned previously, this local system is defined according to two peculiarities linked to the history of the island from the time that many of its religious sites were restored at the beginning of the 1980s. First, the process of implementing development and Putuoshan's Buddhism-promotion projects unites the ambitions of political authorities, monastic communities, and tourism actors under a single banner. Second, the flow of wealth, like the sharing of administrative roles by the same individuals, contributes, among other factors, to the weakening of boundaries among state organizations, party organizations, and Buddhist associations.

The resulting institutional intertwinement opens spaces conducive to creation and innovation just as much in the production of Putuoshan's Buddhism as in the organization of local governance, by offering wiggle room to authorities to invest in vernacular categories of "religion" (*zongjiao* 宗教), "politics" (*zhengzhi* 政治), "tourism" (*lüyou* 旅游), and "culture" (*wenhua* 文化), which the regime committed itself to shaping, along with the entire administrative apparatus that is supposed to implement them. Indeed, while the whole Buddhist affairs bureaucratic management system substrate is seemingly based on a strict distinction between the scope of the religious and that of the political, the actors of different organizations, gifted with creative inventiveness, give new meaning to these categories.

As claimed by Ji Zhe (2011b), the social and political transformations experienced in China at the end of the nineteenth century and beginning of the twentieth century led to profound mutations in the organization of religion and a detachment of education from religion. The content of religions had to be defined, as did their place in a Chinese society engaged in a quest for modernity. Monastic communities and state authorities devised diverse strategies to rethink education and reconfigure public space. These included composing regulatory texts calling for religion to take on a patriotic role and implementing policies to confiscate monastic communities' assets to build schools. However, they also included attempts by monastics to emphasize the scholarly dimensions of religious practice in an effort to escape allegations of superstition. Since the twentieth century, the concept of *jiao* 教 (teachings)—henceforth broken down into three elements, "religion" (*zongjiao* 宗教), "politics" (*zhengzhi* 政治), and "education" (*jiaoyu* 教育)—has been continuously deconstructed, reconstructed, and redefined. Because of this variability, the category of *jiao* takes on a variety of meanings and can be invested in by local actors who will define it according to their interests and strategies, playing, for instance, on recent categories of "religious culture" (*zongjiao wenhua* 宗教文化) or "religious tourism" (*zongjiao lüyou* 宗教旅游). These strategies to rethink the "changing *jiao*" (Ji 2011b) are effective in the particular local context of Putuoshan. Examples of this effectiveness include its concerns with managing tourism sites, growing initiatives to promote Buddhism, and its complex institutional environment. For instance, the retired head of Putuoshan's government, Jiang Baohua 蒋宝华, cowrote in 2008 a book entitled *Putishu xia ren xiaoyao: Zhejiang zongjiao wenhua lüyou chuangxin* 菩提树下任逍遥: 浙江宗教文化旅游创新 (The Bodhi Tree Unfettered: Tourist Innovations in Zhejiang Religious Culture). Published on the model of a research study on Putuoshan's tourist modalities, it spreads positive views of the recent changes related to the growth of tourism. It simultaneously popularized the use of keywords, such as "the culture of religious tourism" (*zongjiao lüyou de wenhua* 宗教旅游的文化) or "traveling as a cloud in the Buddha's kingdom under sea and sky" (*yunyou haitian foguo* 云游海天佛国), which then were used in the regional literature of travel guides as well as in the religious speeches of eminent abbots.

These interests and strategies may seem at first glance to exist only on a rhetorical level; however, these ways of thinking about change, shaped by the actors of the institutional environment, have real impact on the ways that the religious is designated, categorized, and produced, which is not without consequences for devotees' practices. For instance, in his description of contemporary Buddhist practices, Jiang Baohua mixes all kinds of heterogeneous practices without distinguishing or ordering them: he juxtaposes worshipping the Buddha (*baifo* 拜佛), seeking the Dharma, studying religious texts, and visiting old monasteries and sacred mountains while also attaching great importance to tourism. To what extent does his book influence actual practices on Putuoshan by justifying the measures that aim to evolve Putuoshan into a model of a perfect combination of tourism and religion? Regarding the administrative system, it is not only a space for the reproduction of the bureaucracy, of its actors (officials), of the conceptions of power associated with it, and of the modalities of control of the religious. It is also a real laboratory where ideas and projects are thought up and manufactured to realize and promote a "Buddhism of Putuoshan" compatible with changing regimes, the various modernities they promote, and changes in the globalized world in which they operate. In sum, the local configurations of the administration of the religious ensure the maintenance of the Chinese bureaucracy while simultaneously adapting to change.

The institutional landscape described here is not exclusive to Putuoshan. The leading role of elites in the implementation of local governance peculiar to a place and its history and producers of new ways of producing the religious and of making society locally has been seen elsewhere in China, as Adam Chau (2011a) notes in his discussion of "local charismatic figures" (in Chinese often called "persons of high capability," *nengren* 能人). Drawing from his research in Shaanxi Province, Chau notes how these local charismatic figures possess a great ability to organize collective mobilizations (both within temples and in politics more broadly), adding that the presence of these figures in different localities significantly contributed at the beginning of the 1980s to the initiation of a national religious revival (Chau 2011a, 9). In view of the specific presence of the state in religious affairs, social actors create various strategies, such as "creative dissimulation which is to disguise one's religious activities as something else that is more palatable in official eyes" (Chau 2011a, 6). Celebrating cultural festivals, giving an academic credential to cults or promoting them as cultural heritage, participating in charitable work, connecting Communist heroes like Lei Feng within a Buddhist framework as bodhisattvas (see chapter 3 by Susan K. McCarthy in this volume), and describing religion from a patriotic perspective with the slogan "love [one's] country, love [one's] religion" (*aiguo aijiao* 爱国爱教), are examples of this strategy of "creative dissimulation."

However, the case of Putuoshan is unique in important respects: Changes since the 1980s have profoundly transformed the socioeconomic organization of the island. Instead of being a mixed economy, it is now one that is almost exclusively dedicated to pilgrimage activities and tourism, making Putuoshan a space entirely centered on Buddhism. This "Buddhist site" identity seems to give particular resonance to the administrative system for the religious and its features. It constitutes a focal point of what Prasenjit Duara (1993) refers to as a "cultural nexus of power," which I define in this case as a space rooted in a sacred territory for asserting the power of local elites and a diffusion of representations on which their authority is based. In the main, the administration of the religious takes on an additional dimension in Putuoshan's insular microcosm, that of bringing into play all facets of the local governance of a sanctified site. It is thus this feature of the site that encapsulates how the institutional confusion and the logics of cooperation and negotiation in development projects represent, in certain cases and in the eyes of unique local figures, opportunities to rethink Buddhism and its relationship with the state. As a Buddhist site, Putuoshan is thus a space in which to innovate. However, the extent to which modes of administering the sacred sites of Chinese Buddhism constitute in and of themselves engines to imagine new ways to produce and disseminate the religion of the Buddha still remains to be determined.[25]

THE PRINCIPLE OF THE "THREE UNIFIERS": A STRATEGY FOR REESTABLISHING BUDDHIST GOVERNANCE

The administrative system schematized by Zhang Minxi accounts for only part of the functioning of the island, bringing together local actors who are primarily represented by their institutional affiliation (on the Zhoushan committee or in the Buddhist Association). This schema is a totalizing representation embodied by the Buddhist Association of Putuoshan, and thus Buddhist temples do not appear in the schema. (Their existence is rendered visible only through financial flows.) Buddhist monastics use a unique system to rethink the modes of governance that administer Guanyin's island from their own perspective. How do they use the system of the "three unifiers" to reintegrate Putuoshan's temples within the core of relations between various local actors?

On the *San Tongyi* System: The Economics of Putuoshan's Temples

Relations between temples at Putuoshan are set according to the system of the "three unifiers" (*san tongyi* 三统一). This system was set up after 1979 by the then recently reestablished Buddhist Association of Putuoshan, which needed to determine new operating rules for the monks who were authorized to come back to Putuoshan's temples, thanks to the public official Zhang Jingfu's efforts.[26] It was designed as a means to centralize funds and labor and to launch reconstruction projects. At the beginning of the 1980s, the Organization for Construction (Xiujian Zu 修建组) of the association chose ten temples to be renovated. According to local historian Wang Liansheng 王连胜, author of the "Putuoluojiashan zhi" 普陀洛迦山志 (Gazetteer of Putuoluojiashan [1999] 2012), the policy of the three unifiers was first administered around that time. Since 1991, the date on which the association sent an official situation report concerning the adoption of this system to SARA, the *san tongyi* principle has been based on unity in three domains: human resources (*renshi tongyi diaopei* 人事统一调配), construction projects (*xiujian tongyi jihua* 修建统一计划), and economic management (*jingji tongyi guanli* 经济统一管理). First, a planned distribution of monks would prevent inequality between the island's great temples and those of a more modest size. As explained by the historian, "applying redistribution to all allows a constant balance and mutual support between people of each of the temples" (*shixing tongyi diaopei, ke suishi pingheng ge siyuan renshi, huxiang zhiyuan* 实行统一调配，可随时平衡各寺院人事，互相支援). Unity in planning of construction (e.g., of rooms, bedrooms, sculptures, and items of Buddhist material culture) was also presented as a necessity in light of the importance of the investments required for Buddhist temple buildings. As explained by Wang Liansheng, decisions are often made collaboratively within the Buddhist Association in order to determine temples' needs and set priorities. Last, economic management would have been unified, because, at the time the policy was made, "the income of each mountain temple was extremely unbalanced" (*quan shan ge siyuan shouru ji bu pingheng* 全山各寺院收入极不平衡), with the Puji Temple, which houses the offices of the association, bringing in almost half of the island's profits.

Wang concluded his brief presentation of the system's three main principles by praising its efficacy, which, in his view, is widely recognized: "The practice over the last twenty years proves that the administrative system of the 'three unifiers' has not only fitted the realities of Putuoshan, but has also been efficient. Results have been remarkable, and deeply supported by monks and nuns of the entire mountain. Moreover, they have received important praise from the world of Buddhism in China and abroad, and from brothers in sacred sites all over."

The success of the system is also linked to the famous monk Miaoshan, who embodied, for many, the revival of Buddhism at Putuoshan after the Maoist period. He mentioned on many occasions the importance of the three unifiers, seeing them as a "Dharma treasure" (*fabao* 法宝) of Putuoshan that "preserves the Buddha's kingdom under sea and sky" (*weihu haitian foguo* 维护海天佛国) (Wang [1999] 2012). The human and financial resources allocation system even appears in the six precepts Miaoshan left as a testament to his deeds on August 25, 1999, a few months before his death. He emphasized that it must be "preserved" (*jianchi* 坚持) and "should not be changed" (*buyao bian* 不要变; Jieren et al. 2009). Linking the three unifiers to the pioneering monk Miaoshan is a way to integrate this principle of temple administration with several other initiatives (such as building temples and the statue and founding the Buddhist academy) that, taken together, provide evidence of the development of Putuoshan since the end of the Cultural Revolution.[27]

However, Wang Liansheng suggests that the three unifiers cannot solely be understood as Miaoshan's creation during Deng Xiaoping's reforms. They are part of a much older mode of production within the monasteries of Putuoshan that Wang dates back to the Ming (1368–1644) and Qing (1644–1912) dynasties. Referring briefly to the ancient temple management modalities centered on the authority of the abbot and the innovations attempted during the Republican era, he dates the appearance of the first modern monastic revival on Putuoshan to 1959. He explains that previous conflicts had diminished the number of monastic residents so that there were only 265 clergy on the entire mountain by the beginning of the 1960s. Prior to the revival, these remaining monastics focused mostly on the study of scriptures, and many left their monasteries to travel throughout China or abroad. Finally, when only 178 monastics (monks and nuns) remained, they decided to combine their efforts by gathering in the island's "three great temples" (*san da si* 三大寺)—Puji Temple, Fayu Temple, and Huiji Temple—to constitute a "group of productive monks and nuns" (*sengni shengchan dadui* 僧尼生产大队), each staying attached to his or her home monastery and not traveling. The division of labor and the pooling of accounts transformed older operating rules. Later, however, Wang Liansheng concludes, the Cultural Revolution achieved the destruction of centuries-old habits and customs. However, he does not give more details on the concrete evolution of this system during the Mao era and after 1980 and thus does not clarify the links between the old modalities of administering the three great temples and the current realities of the three unifiers and their modes of operating.

In this short historical narrative, Wang traces the fiscal logics of the three unifiers to the economic modes of production of this early reform movement. In other words, this administrative system is understood both as a recent innovation contributing positively to the success of Buddhism at Putuoshan for more than thirty years and as a modernized and changed form of an earlier monastic system of wealth production that is partly linked to the management modes of Buddhist temples since the Ming dynasty. While these two interpretations may appear contradictory—is it an innovation or only a simple evolution?—they nonetheless are aimed at characterizing the modern system by which Putuoshan is administered as thoroughly Buddhist in nature. By that I mean that Wang discusses the concept of the three unifiers as if it concerned only an internal management system of monasteries. The role of the Committee for Ethnic and Religious Affairs of Zhoushan, especially the funding component mentioned by Tian Zhizu, is absent. Only the Buddhist Association and the temples of Putuoshan appear in this landscape, without explanation for the coexistence of a secular economic model based on the centralization of resources or each temple's claim to independence.[28]

Orchestrating the Circulation of Gifts, Reintroducing the Administration of Buddhism into Temples

Consequently, what is the place of the three unifiers in the institutional environment whose contours Zhang Minxi mapped on his schema? Should they be understood as a system developed in disconnection with this set of politico-administrative organizations and the rules they have established? The significant role of Buddhist associations within the religious affairs management system and the modes of capital flows would rather tend to question this hypothesis. Wang Liansheng's description of the three unifiers leaves no room for the members of the Religious Affairs Bureau who gravitate around the temples and the Buddhist Association of Putuoshan, but, in their discussions about management systems, my informants incorporated these institutions. For example, the employee of the Buddhist Association Tian Zhizu shared with me a definition of the administrative system of the three unifiers as a means to deal with income inequality between the island's monasteries.[29] However, as he explained (see the figure describing the flow of funds on Putuoshan), it also seems to represent a driving force of wealth circulation (particularly in the funding of construction, education, and charity) within a larger system that brings together several economic partners at different levels, rather than a closed system among an association and different temples. Conversely, considering the three unifiers as a principle for the operation of religious institutions that functions in opposition to a broader administrative system that incorporates state bureaus and actors into the administration of the island does not accurately explain how the local religious field operates. The system of the three unifiers does not belong solely to the domain of ideas. It is fully anchored in reality, as was shown by the redistribution of donations (under the auspices of the Buddhist Association) from the highest-income monasteries to those with the lowest incomes.[30] However, each of these politico-administrative organizations carries its own incommensurable ideologies. Neither of them exists in a subordinate hierarchical position to the other, yet neither does each system function in isolation, since, in reality, the local functioning of the religious is completely intertwined with the operation of state administrative units.

The system of the three unifiers is more a means to order the reality of political and economic governance that otherwise evades monasteries, by reintroducing the local modes of administration into one of the key structural components in the operation of Buddhist temples, that is, the circulation of wealth. This sort of Buddhist ordering of economic power is legitimized by ideological or doctrinal arguments; the three unifiers are the "Dharma of Putuoshan," as Wang Liansheng wrote. Because the three unifiers system incorporates the circulation of wealth into the concrete realities of the state-administrative entities, it avoids calling into question modes of doing and managing the religious dictated and imposed by Chinese authorities. Thus, it does not constitute a parallel system that could be considered a convoluted means of breaking the law and going against the might of the state. It is rather a superstructure within which a rearrangement of the dynamics linking all actors engaged in the production of Buddhism operates. This superstructure reconfigures relations between actors in a Buddhist economy, and it refocuses operations in a defined space—that of temples. In this view, the development of Putuoshan is no longer the business of society outside of temples, but the work of the religious community.

The question of what explains the ordering that takes place through the Buddhist economy remains open. An apparent contradiction exists between, on the one hand, Buddhism's fundamental doctrines extolling renunciation, and, on the other, monastic communities' taste for auspicious and ostentatious spending coupled with economic pragmatism. This religion calls for detachment from worldly things but at the same time takes part, sometimes actively, in social life, thereby taking a leading role in the exercise of economic and political power (albeit one that differs throughout history). In his study of economic aspects of Chinese Buddhism between the fifth and tenth centuries, the historian Jacques Gernet (1995) explains that wealth accumulation has long been a component of Buddhism in China. Some Chinese Buddhist models of wealth accumulation were inherited from India, while others were linked to the trade practices of Chinese laypeople. Gernet describes temples as economic powerhouses with multiple sources of income, some coming from market transactions and others being the fruits of offerings. Far from being contradictory, these two types of revenues complemented each other in a system of production and wealth circulation anchored in China's social and economic life. Land exploitation, usury, investments in the development of Buddhist art and luxury activities, religious services and rituals performed for laypersons, charity work for the poor and needy, and offerings: All of this generated capital that fueled the whole circuit of economic exchanges between monasteries and the wider society. These practices of accumulation were framed by Buddhist notions of gift exchange whose widespread institutional forms were facilitated by a network of temples and small sanctuaries. As Gernet explains, the role of Buddhist temples was no less than that of introducing

> a form of modern capitalism into China: consecrated property, constituted by an accumulation of offerings and commercial revenues, formed communal wealth, the communal management of which was more profitable than individual operations. But what is most remarkable about this conception it its *religious origin*. The Buddhist theory of giving already proceeded from a notion of productive capital; in concrete terms, we are dealing with a capitalization of offerings. . . . The increase of the assets and that of their religious effect go hand in hand, and charitable gifts, again a form of investment in the lay world, appear as one of the essential elements in this system. (Gernet 1995, 228)

Of course, the economy of Buddhist temples during this distant thriving era cannot be automatically compared with that of today's Chinese monasteries. However, many aspects also characterize the relationship that contemporary Chinese Buddhist institutions, such as those on Putuoshan, have with economics. That includes the doctrinal framework (specifically, the concepts of donations, renunciation, and asceticism) within which these economic practices took place. It also incorporates the representations associated with the temple as a space for wealth accumulation and production (for instance, in the accumulation of precious objects and in charitable work) and the porosity of the border between the circuit of monasteries' core funds and the circuit of economic transactions outside of temples. Incorporating the complex bureaucratic system that defines religious life in contemporary China into the superstructure of the three unifiers therefore means integrating the social relationships of multiple religious actors into a logic of giving and process of circulation understood in terms of networks of places of worship. In sum, it is redefining (economic and political) power in light of Buddhist conceptions and methods for being a community within society.

An event that took place on July 4, 2012, illuminates the previous argument. On that day, the *Renmin ribao* 人民日报 (People's Daily) devoted a page to what was argued was the commodification of the four famous mountains of Chinese Buddhism (Zhao and Tao 2012). Reporters provided accounts of a meeting organized at the end of May by the Putuoshan Tourism Development Company (Putuoshan Lüyou Fazhan Gufen Youxian Gongsi 普陀山旅游发展股

份有限公司), founded in 2008–2009, that proposed the capitalization of Putuoshan, and of the reactions news of the meeting elicited among the population at large.[31] They reported that, from the perspective of the public, Buddhist mountains, once "lands purified of defiling illusion" (*qingjing zhi di* 清净之地), are now stuck in a "sea tide of circulating money" (*quan qian dachao* 圈钱大潮), suggesting controversy. The proposed capitalization echoed projects to grow tourism that had been developed by similar firms at other mountains: Wutaishan had initiated the process a year before, Jiuhuashan had attempted to initiate the process but its demands had not been met, and Emeishan had been benefiting from capitalization for several years. Launched by those companies in charge of local development and with close ties to the local governments—such as the government of Putuoshan, which, according to the official website, shares responsibility with local authorities for "building" (*jianshe* 建设), "tourism" (*lüyou* 旅游), and the "production of quality goods" (*jingpin* 精品)—these attempts at capitalization were supported by political authorities. In the case of Putuoshan, the authorities focused their argument for allowing tourist companies to "develop" the island on the protection of culture and on a quick return on the investment that had led to Putuoshan's expansion. As a member of Xinzhou 忻州 city, where Wutaishan is located, maintained, "Pushing the tourism and culture industry into a capital-driven market enables it to spread more widely" (*ba lüyou wenhua chanye tui xiang ziben shichang, shi qi chuanbo geng yuan* 把旅游文化产业推向资本市场, 使其传播更远) (Zhao and Tao 2012). Without comparing points of view or giving more details on the political and economic contexts, the authors of the newspaper article concluded by explaining the necessity of setting limits on the growth of capitalism that are compatible with their views of Chinese society and the expectations of the population.

Under the cover of a touristic firm, the capitalization of Putuoshan initially was the result of a local government initiative that was taken without consulting monastic communities, as was mentioned to me by a well-educated and rather young monk (about forty years of age), who is vice-rector of the Buddhist Academy of Putuoshan and vice-chairman of the Buddhist Association of Putuoshan. His view on the decision did not seem favorable, even if he did not share much on the topic. Pointing to the contradiction between the ideal of a monastic life based on renunciation of the worldly and his daily duties, he compared himself to a "businessman," always traveling and being overwhelmed by work. His comments echoed those frequently made by a number of monastics, who claimed that temple responsibilities made them too busy to dedicate themselves to studies and meditation. More generally, these statements are connected to the commodification of Buddhism. They emphasize the tension between the economic features that are due to local policies (making Putuoshan a well-known tourist site) and the ambitions of clergy (making Putuoshan a highly influential site in Asian religious networks). They also reflect the monastics' reflexive outlook on the changes of Buddhism through a doctrinal and moral approach. Those issues are at the heart of their reflections on the relations between Buddhism and modernity (see also chapter 4 by Brian Nichols in this volume).

However, even if this apparent contradiction can explain the vice-rector's lack of enthusiasm, his reprobation also seems to be linked to changes from the traditional operation of the Buddhist economy. The capital produced by the marketing of Putuoshan would have been totally disconnected from the circulation of the monasteries' wealth. In addition, this initiative would have had the effect of decentering temple economic and political governance. This wealth-production system would have constituted a parallel circuit that competed with that of the three unifiers and functioned as an alternative to Buddhist propositions to recenter the process of wealth creation and circulation in monasteries. These projects of placing Putuoshan on the market are part of the various initiatives of the Chinese state to create a concurrent economic circuit to that of the monastics' by investing in temples; the entrance tickets offer one of the most visible examples of the state's actions. The majority of the entrance fees visitors pay are transferred to the local government. Most visitors assume incorrectly that entrance fees, as well as donations, provide income support to temples. From the clergy's point of view, this economy of entrance tickets establishes a parallel economic circulation of the economy of gifts. How the monastics' recent attempts to remove entrance fees, observed by Ji Zhe (2016a; see also Fisher 2011a), contributes to the various efforts of monasteries to reappropriate the management of their own economy remains an unanswered question.

In this chapter, I have provided a detailed account of the modes of administering Putuoshan by presenting the categories of actors involved in the organization of the site and the relations between them. This was done, notably, by taking into account the perspective of Zhang Minxi, a retired public official. I have also highlighted the means by which Buddhist temples reorganize some aspects of the island's religious life to reintegrate monasteries into their space and their conceptions of a production of the religious. The use of the three unifiers superstructure is a potential contributing factor in this reintegration process. It should be mentioned that however the system of the three unifiers has transformed practices in relation to the circulation of wealth among monasteries on an island-wide scale, the impact of the system on concrete aspects of monastic community life remains to be examined. This examination needs to occur from the perspective of individual practices of monks and nuns along with their relationship to other entities connected with this system. Also, to what extent does the system influence relations other than economic ones in Putuoshan temples, such as the ritual aspects of daily life? A second issue for future research is the impact of these changes within the Putuoshan religious field on the realities of pilgrimage. For instance, to what extent is there a connection between institutional transformation and the monastic communities' aim to promote orthodoxy and orthopraxy among pilgrims (through different initiatives such as the short movie *The Pilgrimage of Putuoshan*)? We can assume a link exists, seeing how normative discourses directed toward pilgrims incorporate authorities' guidelines for religious life. On the other hand, if we consider more precisely what Tian Zhizu's account seems to suggest, changes within the institutional framework are also a response to the transformations of the Putuoshan site and the pilgrimage activities that take place there (which, in turn, have been influenced by changes in contemporary Chinese society that undergird projects for religious revival, heritage, and globalization). In short, we should think more widely about the impacts of these institutional changes beyond the economic, especially on the realities of both clerics' rituals and pilgrims' practices. It is the future of Putuoshan in all its facets that we should further study.

In response to strong state control that has the power to delocalize the production of Buddhism, monks and nuns seek to implement processes that reincorporate Chinese Buddhist modes of economic and political governance into their ways of shaping local religion and developing the island of Guanyin. They do so through their decision-making body, the Buddhist Association of Putuoshan, without directly opposing the exercise of state power. By incorporating a vast state administrative system for the management of the religious into one of the structural dynamics of Buddhist temples—the flow of donations—Buddhist communities have aimed to reclaim tools for administering the island and founding a sacred site. The proposals of temples to produce "Putuoshan's Buddhism" reflect their ambitions for the construction of a pilgrimage experience whose influence in China and the rest of Asia would be unparalleled. These goals occur within the necessity to work within state administrative structures and deal with the realities of complex networks of local authority figures.

These remaining unanswered questions point to the need for a more general interrogation of the relationship between local governance as it is implemented, its territorial anchoring, and the special feature of Putuoshan as sacred site. I have followed the anthropologist Marcel Détienne (1990), who writes about the necessity of questioning, in a comparative perspective, the social modalities by which a "site" is shaped. The objective is to understand the many mechanisms that shape Putuoshan. It is an insular microcosm inhabited by monastic communities whose socioeconomic organization is oriented toward pilgrimage, a place submitted to the rules of central state authorities regarding religion, and a locality subjected to the ambition of the local government to make it a prime destination for the clients of tourist firms. It is also an area particularly renowned for apparitions of the bodhisattva Guanyin, crossed daily by thousands of travelers who come to worship her. This multifaceted sacred territory exemplifies much of the economic and political functioning of contemporary Chinese Buddhism.

NOTES

I warmly thank André Laliberté, Ji Zhe, and Gareth Fisher for their revisions and Philippe Martin for his English translation.

1. Very few studies in Western languages have been published on Putuoshan. Yü Chünfang wrote an article in 1992 on the island's ancient history and its evolution through successive dynasties (based on the study of local gazetteers and sutras). In a later book on Guanyin (Yü 2001), she analyzes how the Indian tradition of devotion to Avalokiteśvara became transformed in China by local societies and diffused abroad through the travels of pilgrims. See also Marcus Bingenheimer's (2016) historical study of Putuoshan through an analysis of gazetteers.

2. The sites of Wutaishan 五台山 (Shanxi 山西), Emeishan 峨眉山 (Sichuan 四川), and Jiuhuashan 九华山 (Anhui 安徽) are associated with the three other great bodhisattvas of Wenshu 文殊 (Manjusri), Puxian 普贤 (Samantabhadra), and Dizang 地藏 (Ksitigarbha), respectively. James Robson (2010) discusses how Chinese Buddhist sites emerged before the Tang dynasty (618–907) and argues that the diffusion of the Buddha's teachings in China was not merely a simple transposition of Indian concepts into the Chinese religious field, but rather the result of a number of strategies put in place by Chinese Buddhist communities, such as the constitution of multiple and interrelated places of worship.

3. A large amount of media circulates, free or for sale, at different locations on Putuoshan. There are two magazines—*Putuoshan fojiao* 普陀山佛教 (Putuoshan Buddhism), published by the Putuoshan Buddhist Association, and the more recent *Putuoshan wenhua* 普陀山文化 (Putuoshan Culture), published by the Putuoshan Institute for Cultural Studies. There are also famous masters' books, booklets of sutra excerpts, and monastics' lectures recorded on video CDs concerning tales of Guanyin's incarnations. This media is often collected by monks and laypersons and then displayed on desks in a temple's rooms or on shelves in particular rooms. As is the case in most Chinese temples, visitors can take away some of them (sometimes in exchange for donations) or give their own media (that they take away from other temples or that they write themselves). That is why visitors often see a mix of various media piled up in temples and, with the exception of the tourist guides, distributed freely. More generally, Putuoshan is a well-known center for the diffusion of Buddhist media. Hence, the Research Institute for Buddhist Culture of Putuoshan (headed by monks) purchases much Buddhist media from different Asian countries to give away at Putuoshan. For an analysis of the role of Buddhist media in the making of modern Chinese Buddhism, see Philip Clart and Gregory Scott (2015) on the modern history of religious print culture and Gareth Fisher (2011b; 2014, 136–168; 2016) on the publishing and distribution practices of contemporary laypeople.

4. The reputation of Putuoshan as a universal site has multiple origins. The development of tourist literature is a response to an increase in the number of pilgrims from the 1990s on. Concomitantly, the spread of this literature has "updated" the interpretations of what the island represents to its devotees.

5. They are connected to the east coast of Zhejiang Province by a series of bridges.

6. In the Buddhist calendar, the nineteenth day of the second lunar month celebrates the birthday (*shengdan ri* 圣诞日) of Guanyin; the nineteenth day of the sixth month commemorates the day when Guanyin attained enlightenment (*chengdao ri* 成道日); and the nineteenth day of the ninth lunar month celebrates her choice to "leave home" (*chujia* 出家), that is, to become a nun.

7. For an analysis of the miraculous tales of Guanyin, in addition to the previously mentioned studies by Yü Chün-fang and Marcus Bingenheimer, see Campany 1993, 1996.

8. On the second floor of the Putuoshan Tourist Center, a gallery of photos shows historical visits of famous official personalities (from Asian and Western countries) since Sun Yat-sen 孙中山 in 1916. They are on display alongside those that show the ruins of monasteries from the Republican era and the Cultural Revolution. This juxtaposition suggests an improvement of conditions for Putuoshan's monastics, who, as the photos show, work together with political authorities for the development of the island. Today the center's employees continue to exhibit official photos that are supposed to highlight Putuoshan's worldwide reputation as a great historical site of Buddhism.

9. On Putuoshan, the mix between religious terms and tourist language has helped to produce new terms and fueled the development of a local rhetoric, for example, with the three-character word compound "pilgrim-tourist-guest" (*xiang you ke* 香游客), a contraction of two words, *xiangke* 香客 (literally "the one who [offers] incense"), and *youke* 游客 (used to refer to tourists). It was created to designate anyone who visits Putuoshan without having to distinguish visitors according to their practices (e.g., praying, performing circumambulation, having fun on the beach, eating local specialties). This word is used only on certain advertisements (such as for Guanyin's cookies or Putuoshan's tea) and in local travel guides, published by the Putuoshan government, in order to legitimize some initiatives for tourist development that would otherwise be considered insufficiently related to the religious nature of pilgrimage.

10. The name Bu Ken Qu Guanyin Yuan comes from the miraculous tale of the Japanese monk Hui'e 慧锷 (Egaku), who wanted to return to Japan with a statue of Guanyin. Guanyin refused to leave, so the ship carrying Hui'e and the statue miraculously ceased moving forward and diverted itself to Putuoshan. As a result, Hui'e understood that Guanyin did not want to go to Japan, and thus he founded the first temple on Putuoshan. Different books narrate this tale with different versions (see, for instance, Yü 1992, 215–216).

11. Both laypeople and devotees from Zhoushan and Shanghai come to listen to the masters' teachings. As I observed (and a master told me), a few of Putuoshan's monks also attend these lectures on the sutras. Moreover, these lectures are not only for Batuo Jiang's monks; all Putuoshan monastics can attend if they wish.

12. The names of my interviewees have been changed to ensure the anonymity of their transcribed testimonies.

13. For more on the topic of tourism in Chinese religious sites, see Oakes and Sutton (2010) on the role of the state, as well as the more general work of Nyíri (2006, 2010) on the origins of tourism in China, its evolution, and the expansion of practices associated with it. On tourism at Chinese Buddhist sites specifically, see chapter 4 by Brian Nichols in this volume.

14. I use Pierre Bourdieu's (1971) sociological concept of "religious field" as a system of interrelations among several agents involved in the local production of religion.

15. My focus is on the views of officials, clerics, and laypersons rather than on the practices of the pilgrims.

16. In 2003, the name of the Buddhist Academy of Putuoshan was changed to the College of the Buddhist Academy of China (Zhongguo Foxueyuan Jiaoyu Xueyuan 中国佛学院教育学院). Since 2011, the new official name is the Buddhist Academy of China, Putuoshan College (Zhongguo Foxueyuan Putuoshan Xueyuan 中国佛学院普陀山学院), but monks, officials, and local people prefer using the original name, Buddhist Academy of Putuoshan.

17. The other four religions that are organized in the form of state associations are Taoism, Islam, Catholicism, and Protestantism.

18. The institutional landscape of the management of the religious in China has resulted in numerous publications. In particular, I have cited the seminal work of Yoshiko Ashiwa and David Wank (2006) on the shaping of Buddhist institutions in the post-Mao period and more recent work by Vincent Goossaert and David Palmer (2011), which has provided a more general overview of the institutionalization of religion throughout the twentieth and early twenty-first centuries. Another study that provides focused, site-specific descriptions on these administrative entities and their local anchorages is Kang Xiaofei's (2009) analysis of the reconstruction of two Taoist temples in Huanglong (Sichuan Province).

19. This conflation between state and party exists at all levels of government, but at the central level, there are attempts to institutionalize the separation between the two.

20. These problems have been examined from different angles. For example, see the work of Philip Kuhn (1999), who is interested in the question of the origins of the modern state in China and proposes the theory of the "constitutional agenda" in order to make sense of the historical upheavals that led to the transition between the late imperial and modern eras. The introduction to Kuhn's book by the historian Pierre-Étienne Will (in the French translation) provides an analytical framework with which to understand these questions of institutional reproduction. It would be interesting to apply this theory to contemporary China; Kuhn and Will's perspective leads us to consider, from an anthropological point of view, how power structures in China have significant historical influence while still being subject to a strong impact from social change.

21. However, not all projects entail collaboration between these different actors. As the internal documentation suggests, decisions are not always taken in consultation with the local Buddhist association. For example, the First International Exhibition of the Objects of Buddhism at Putuoshan (Shoujie Zhongguo Putuoshan Guoji Fojiao Yongpin Bolanhui 首届中国普陀山国际佛教用品博览会) was organized in 2008 by the municipality of Zhoushan, the Buddhist Association of Zhejiang, and American partners. At this exhibition, five great bronze statues representing Shancai followed by four pilgrims were installed. In addition, the World Youth Forest (Shijie Qingnian Lin 世界青年林) planting project, launched in 2010 by the Putuoshan Mountain Scenic Area Management Committee (Putuoshan Fengjing Mingsheng Qu Guanli Weiyuanhui 普陀山风景名胜区管理委员会), consisted of inviting students from twenty-six foreign countries to plant young shoots in order to celebrate peace.

22. Additional World Buddhist Forums were organized in 2009, 2012, and 2015. For more on the forums and their significance for understanding the relationship between Buddhism and the state, see Ji 2011a and chapter 1 by André Laliberté in this volume.

23. Miaoshan's important role in the rebuilding of Putuoshan Buddhism is detailed in the *Miaoshan laoheshang baisui danchen jinian tekan* 妙善老和尚百岁诞辰纪念特刊 (Special Edition of the Commemoration of the Century-Old Monk Miaoshan), edited in 2009 for the celebration of the centenary of the birth of Miaoshan. It includes passages from the *Miaoshan dashi nianpu* 妙善大师年谱 (Bibliographical Notes on the Venerable Master Miaoshan) prepared by Jieren 戒忍 (2002), who succeeded Miaoshan, serving as the head of the Putuoshan Buddhist Association until 2009.

24. My discussions with Tian were related only to the administrative organizations of Zhoushan and Putuo. Therefore, the figure describing the flow of funds on Putuoshan does

not aim to reflect the features of economic exchange of all organizations and entities across Zhejiang Province, let alone the whole of China (Zhong Jin's description of transactions with the Zhejiang association does not appear). It is a visual aid to summarize the exchanges of capital referred to in the chapter. In that, it is also different from the chart made with Zhang Minxi, shown earlier in the chapter, which I have analyzed as ethnographic material because it was based entirely on his conceptualizations.

25. Comparative work looking at the administrative systems of other sites, such as the three other sacred mountains (Wutaishan, Emeishan, and Jiuhuashan), could put into perspective what constitutes the local singularities of Putuoshan as opposed to specificities linked to the status of being a sacred site in general. This could constitute a first step in anthropological research on mainland China's great Buddhist centers. Few ethnological studies on these four mountains have been produced up to now, an exception being Pál Nyíri (2006)'s ethnography of Emeishan. For perspectives from the functioning of these sites in late imperial times, see Hargett's (2006) study of Emeishan and Charleux's (2015) research on Wutaishan.

26. In April 1979, Zhang Jingfu was appointed head of the Religious Affairs Bureau of Zhoushan. He called for the return of Putuoshan monastics who were forced to leave the island during the Cultural Revolution. In October of that year, some of the monastics were authorized to come back; Miaoshan was one of the first abbots to return. See Jieren et al. 2009.

27. Both in the narratives I gathered from some of my lay and monastic informants and in the locally disseminated texts I was able to access, Miaoshan personifies the monastic figure responsible for all the recent changes many of them considered positive. His involvement has taken on such a strong legitimating quality that it is sometimes difficult to determine whether he truly played a significant role in the decisions and achievements of certain projects or whether the planners of certain initiatives have merely evoked his name to gain approval for their plans. As such, he has become a symbol of the modernization of Putuoshan, the success of pilgrimage, and the development of monastic communities. That is one reason why, accompanied by Miaoshan's approval, the system of the three unifiers is recognized as a driving force for the economic success of Putuoshan's temples.

28. Wang Liansheng's text stipulates that while the system of the three unifiers establishes economic unity between temples, it does not necessarily involve the loss of their autonomy. The nature and degree of this independence, however, is not defined in precise terms. We also must consider that Wang's statements are intended to describe an abstract set of rules and not intended to consider concrete fiscal practices. Under the model Wang describes, what are the accounting channels through which finances circulate? Even if temples remain autonomous, would they have any recourse to oppose a decision made by the discretionary members of the association concerning the use of capitalized funds? At present, I do not have enough material to formulate a hypothesis that could begin to answer these questions.

29. One of the high-ranking monks of the Buddhist Association of Putuoshan with whom I spoke in September 2012 resorted to the same argument to explain the principle of the three unifiers.

30. Some temples are neglected by devotees, whereas others see a large number every day (e.g., the three great temples). As my interlocutors stressed to me on several occasions, redistributing gifts to the poorest temples of Putuoshan allows them to have sufficient income. While this system has a goal of equity, it is not clear in what proportion gifts are really redistributed. The inequalities of wealth are noticeable and, in some cases, visible in

even buildings' external appearance. This may be in relation to the logics of investment, wherein recovering costs is easier for temples with the highest income.

31. This information was also relayed in the international media: The British newspaper the *Guardian* featured an article entitled "Chinese Shrine Seeks Stock-Market Path to Financial Nirvana" (Branigan 2012) in which the author provides accounts, taken from various articles in Chinese, of the debate regarding the strategies of the commercialization of Putuoshan and the question of the ethics of these strategies.

3

SPIRITUAL TECHNOLOGIES AND THE POLITICS OF BUDDHIST CHARITY

SUSAN K. MCCARTHY

Charity is an increasingly popular modality through which Chinese people encounter and practice Buddhism. In recent decades scores of formal and informal Buddhist organizations have emerged that engage in a variety of charitable endeavors. Some of these are affiliated with prominent temples and clerics, including high-ranking monks within the Buddhist Association of China (BAC). Others are run by registered lay associations, which also conduct a range of religious programming. Still more are informal, ad hoc, and even virtual (i.e., online) endeavors that may or may not be connected to clerics or religious sites.

For Buddhists, both clerical and lay, charity serves a variety of spiritual and secular purposes. Charity can garner favorable media attention and improve a group's image among Chinese officialdom and the broader public, much of which remains skeptical about both religion and charity. Doing charity may allow prominent Buddhist sites to deflect attention from the tremendous wealth they have amassed in recent decades (Laliberté 2011a; Sun 2011). For abbots of large temples, establishing or advising philanthropic organizations can burnish their public profile and possibly facilitate their ascent through the ranks of the official Buddhist hierarchy. Charity also functions as a form of religious practice and expression (McCarthy 2013). Through philanthropy and social service, adherents cultivate compassion for all sentient beings, contemplate the nonduality of self and other, and acquire merit. Charity can also be a means of drawing outsiders to the faith, non-Buddhists attracted by the camaraderie, devotion, and sense of purpose they see among charity practitioners. Doing charity can also satisfy a desire to engage civically in one's local and national communities. Through charity, Buddhists serve society while walking the bodhi path.

Buddhist charity offers benefits to the party-state as well. Direct social service can relieve burdens on the party-state for the provision of public goods, potentially reducing sources of social discontent and bolstering regime legitimacy. Charity also models behaviors and attitudes the regime would like to see broadly inculcated, such as selflessness and public service. Faith-based charity appeals also because it is a somewhat "secularized" mode of religiosity, one that in theory focuses adherents' attention on the problems of this world rather than salvation in the next. Officials have long stressed the need for religions to "mutually adapt" (*xiang shiying* 相适应) to modern socialist society and exhorted them to use the resources they command to assist the needy rather than to "build big temples and restore big buddhas" (*jian damiao, xiu dafo* 建大庙, 修大佛) (Yu 2003). Despite its longtime aversion to allowing religion greater visibility in social life, in recent years the regime has acknowledged publicly the compatibility of Buddhist and other faith-based charity with its own goals and ideals. In February 2012 six central government agencies including the State Administration for Religious Affairs (SARA), the Ministry of Civil Affairs, and the Communist Party's United Front Work Department issued a joint opinion (*yijian* 意见) calling on religious groups to step up their charitable activities and instructing government officials to "enthusiastically support and encourage" (*jiji zhichi he guli* 积极支持和鼓励) these endeavors (Guojia Zongjiao Shiwuju 2012).

This chapter analyzes how Buddhist charity intersects with and complements the goals and interests of the party-state, while also facilitating religious aims and ideals. It does so by examining the case of the Beijing-based Ren'ai Charity Foundation (Ren'ai Cishan Jijinhui 仁爱慈善基金会), an independent lay charity affiliated with Master Xuecheng (Xuecheng fashi 学诚法师). Before he was removed from his posts in August 2018 following an investigation into sexual harassment allegations, Xuecheng served as the abbot of Dragon Spring Temple (Longquan Si 龙泉寺) in Beijing and chair of the BAC (Johnson 2018). The case of Ren'ai underscores the complex mix of strategic and spiritual purposes that Buddhist charity serves. Over the years the foundation's activities worked to enhance the public profile of Xuecheng and Longquan Temple while fostering the spiritual development of its many volunteers. Because of its endeavors and Xuecheng's prominence, Ren'ai won accolades from the regime and was promoted as a model charitable organization.

Yet not all Buddhist charity is as amenable to regime interests or acceptable as models for imitation. Ren'ai's civic-minded, partially secularized approach to Buddhist charity diverges from others that emphasize charity's merit-making effects over conventional service to society. In particular, the practice of life rescue (*fangsheng* 放生), in which captive animals such as birds and fish are released into the wild, causes consternation among officials and some Buddhist leaders because of its environmental and social consequences as well as its resistance to top-down control. The party-state has enlisted Buddhist leaders including Xuecheng to rein in life rescue by promoting conceptions of charity more conducive to its vision of a modern society. Whether these efforts will pay off remains to be seen. Many adherents believe life rescue to be a particularly efficacious "spiritual technology" (Jeavons 1998, 88), one that exemplifies Buddhist notions of charity and furthers their salvific aims. The popularity of the practice reveals how the spiritual dimensions of Buddhist charity can complicate and even undermine the goals and interests of the party-state.

THE REN'AI CHARITY FOUNDATION AND THE VENERABLE XUECHENG

On April 5, 2012, a group of workers from the Research Center of SARA paid a visit to Longquan Temple. The employees were there not so much as state workers but as members of the Research Center's Communist Party branch; the purpose of their visit was to strengthen branch cohesion by "learning" from Lei Feng 雷锋, a Mao-era icon of revolutionary dedication to the masses. Specifically, the outing was a chance for branch members to "study Lei Feng, offer compassion, and do charity" (Sun 2012). At Longquan Temple, branch members met with monks and representatives from the Ren'ai Charity Foundation, a private lay charity affiliated with the temple and its abbot, the aforementioned Xuecheng. Following a discussion of temple history, Ren'ai programs, and the ongoing work of SARA's Research Center, branch members toured the grounds and participated in team-building exercises led by Ren'ai volunteers. They also spent an hour or so sorting piles of secondhand clothing collected by Ren'ai's clothing-donation program, a task described in a follow-up report as "truly not relaxing" (Yuan 2012). Branch members themselves had brought clothes from home to contribute, and the group donated more than 5,000 RMB to Ren'ai's orphan assistance program. The temple outing appears to have been a success. Reflecting on their experience, participants shared that doing charity work with Ren'ai strengthened their awareness that cultivating the Lei Feng spirit requires practical action, not just empty speech. Members felt their compassion and their comprehension of the Lei Feng spirit had been enhanced, and they expressed the hope that in the future, branch leaders would organize similar activities for them to study Lei Feng, spread compassion, promote civic morality, and together build the socialist harmonious society.

How is it that a lay charity operating out of a one-thousand-year-old Buddhist temple[1] would be seen as an appropriate venue in which members of the CCP might learn from Lei Feng? This vignette illustrates the extent to which the regime's attitudes toward and treatment of religion have changed since the Mao period. In that era religion was deemed a product of exploitative class relations and consequently suppressed. Though it still curtails and controls much religious activity, today the government tries to mobilize religion to address social problems and enhance social stability. The branch visit to Ren'ai also alludes to regime anxiety regarding social and moral decay, including within the CCP itself, which it has sought to combat by fighting corruption, promoting public service, and strengthening grassroots party organization (Thornton 2012). It furthermore underscores the diversification of Chinese social life, as seen in the growth of nonstate organizations like

Ren'ai. While this diversification poses challenges to regime authority, the vignette described here suggests that nonstate organizations may buttress that authority by modeling a civility that, far from being "alternate," embodies norms, attitudes, and behaviors sanctioned by the party-state (Weller 2001; Laliberté 2012).

As incongruous as it may at first seem, the branch visit makes sense given some of the characteristics of Ren'ai and of the temple and abbot with which it is affiliated. First, as André Laliberté makes clear in chapter 1 in this volume, Xuecheng is no ordinary Buddhist monk. At the time of the party branch visit, Xuecheng was a vice-chair of the BAC and one of its most visible spokespersons; in early 2015 he was named chair of the association. Xuecheng advocated a version of "Buddhism for the human realm" (*renjian fojiao* 人间佛教) that complemented values and ideals supported by the regime. In particular, he promoted a civic-minded Buddhism that spoke to China's modernizing ambitions and increasingly sophisticated yet atomized and acquisitive society. Certain programs and organizational features of both Ren'ai and Longquan Temple manifest this embrace of modernity and the effort to marry Buddhist spirituality with concern for the public good. For instance, although grounded in Buddhist principles, Ren'ai also at times draws on socialist frames—including the rhetoric and symbolism surrounding Lei Feng—to legitimize and popularize its endeavors. The party-state's embrace of Ren'ai thus signaled its approval of a particular mode of Buddhist charity, a particular *model* that, like Lei Feng, deserves emulation.

Ren'ai is one of many Buddhist philanthropic groups established in the last several decades. Such groups are the product of two broad trends: the post-Mao religious revival and the emergence of the so-called third sector, the nonstate associational sphere. The relaxation of restrictions on religion, combined with the call for a "small government, big society," has resulted in the creation of a variety of charitable endeavors from hospitals and homes for the aged to soup kitchens, charity supermarkets, and disaster relief. Determining the number of Buddhist charities (and religious charities in general) is, however, difficult. The Chinese government strictly monitors religion and religious organizations, but it does not keep detailed statistics on the number of Buddhist and other faith-based NGOs. It keeps *some* statistics: The Ministry of Civil Affairs puts the number of registered Buddhist charities at around seventy (Ethnic and Religious Affairs 2014). However, this figure includes only registered foundations, merit societies, and other philanthropic entities (e.g., clinics and orphanages) established at or by state-approved Buddhist temples and lay associations. Much Buddhist charity is not recognized as such because it is not formally affiliated with a registered temple or because it is not "organized," that is, the product of stand-alone groups registered with the state.

Ren'ai illustrates the difficulty of figuring out what counts as a Buddhist charity. Established in 2006 as a private foundation and registered with the

Beijing Municipal Civil Affairs Bureau, at its inception Ren'ai was formally independent of any religious entity. The organization and its programs are managed by laypeople, not religious personnel. In its first few years its main office was housed in a luxury high-rise apartment building in Beijing's Haidian District, roughly forty kilometers from the mountainous nature park where Longquan Temple is located. In terms of most of its programs, Ren'ai looks like many other non-Buddhist, nonreligious charitable foundations and service groups. Initially it focused on providing scholarships and other aid to orphans and poor children, and in its first two years its efforts were expended primarily on identifying and contacting potential beneficiaries. Since then it has branched out into disaster relief, antipoverty work, and community development. Like many Chinese nonprofits, Ren'ai was active in and gained experience and media attention from the 2008 Wenchuan earthquake relief effort. It also contributed to relief efforts following the crippling 2008 snowstorm in southern China, as well as subsequent earthquakes in Qinghai, Sichuan, and Yunnan. As mentioned, Ren'ai also runs a clothing-donation program; donated items are sorted, packed, and delivered to impoverished communities throughout the country and to those suffering the effects of natural calamity. In addition, the organization operates an unusual and rapidly expanding program that serves free congee (i.e., porridge) every morning at sites in Beijing and around the country. Its programs have won it accolades: In 2011 the Capital Philanthropy Federation honored Ren'ai as an exemplary charity, naming then director Lin Qitai 林启泰 and deputy director Wang Lu 王璐 its model philanthropists of the year (Tang 2013).

Despite its formally private and nonreligious character, Ren'ai is deeply influenced by Buddhist ideas and institutions. From its inception the group has been closely connected with Xuecheng and Longquan Temple. Xuecheng did not personally direct Ren'ai's projects, but he was central to its existence, at times providing social capital and connections that enabled Ren'ai to thrive and expand. As stated, until August 2018 he held a number of high positions in China's Buddhist administrative hierarchy. In addition to serving as chair of the BAC and abbot of Longquan Temple, Xuecheng was abbot of Famen Temple (Famen Si 法门寺) in Shaanxi and Guanghua Temple (Guanghua Si 广化寺) in Fujian. He became abbot of Guanghua Temple in 1990 at the age of twenty-four, the youngest monk ever to achieve the position of abbot in a mainland Chinese Buddhist temple. Later that decade Xuecheng took over as director of the Fujian Buddhist Academy, was appointed head of the Fujian provincial Buddhist Association, and was named to the standing committee of the Eighth Chinese People's Political Consultative Conference of Fujian Province. In 2005 he assumed the directorship of the United Front Theory Research Association (Famen Temple 2011). Xuecheng also served as a director of the Chinese Buddhist Museum and Library. He was a member of the national Chinese People's Political Consultative Conference and delivered speeches at plenary sessions of its meetings. In 2012 he attended the Eighteenth CCP National Congress as a nonvoting member.

Though formally independent of Xuecheng and Longquan Temple, in the years since its creation Ren'ai's Buddhist underpinnings have become increasingly explicit. Its website states that it was created by Buddhist devotees inspired by Xuecheng's teachings, and some media reports describe Xuecheng as a "co-founder" of the organization (Tang 2013). In 2009 its headquarters and staff residence relocated to Longquan Temple. On relocation Ren'ai assumed formal responsibility for all of the temple's charitable endeavors, though a deputy director acknowledged in an October 2014 interview that Ren'ai had performed that function from the very beginning. Though it retains its name and status as a private foundation, Ren'ai now serves openly as the temple's philanthropic division.

At present, the foundation and its programs are managed by a group of approximately two dozen mostly full-time volunteer staff, none of whom receive a salary and most of whom reside at Longquan Temple when they are not working at program sites in other provinces. This core staff is composed of people from a variety of backgrounds, including a former telecommunications executive, a party member and former banking executive, a former journalist, and holders of degrees from some of China's top universities. Their commitment to Ren'ai and to Longquan Temple is long-term, and several have been with Xuecheng since before the temple reopened in 2005. A few who have left the organization have done so in order to take monastic vows. Like the cadre of dedicated, regular volunteers who carry out the programs of the Taiwanese-based Tzu Chi Foundation, these volunteers are referred to as *zhigong* 志工 rather than *yigong* 义工, the Chinese term typically used to denote volunteers. Whereas the latter can apply to volunteering of a more casual and intermittent variety, *zhigong* connotes seriousness and professionalism. As Richard Madsen explains regarding Tzu Chi's use of the term, the volunteerism of the *zhigong* "is seen not so much as an exercise of an individual's free choice as it is an enlightened acceptance of one's duties towards others" (Madsen 2007, 18).

Prior to Ren'ai's relocation to the temple, about a dozen of these volunteer staff lived in the apartment that housed the foundation's headquarters. Their living arrangements were communal, with women sharing one bunk-filled bedroom and men sharing another. The office/apartment contained a small altar along with wall hangings and other objects of a Buddhist nature. Meal preparation and other chores were shared, and the staff members ate vegetarian meals together in silence, in the meditative manner directed by Xuecheng and practiced at Longquan Temple. During the workday the office was a hive of activity, as staff fielded requests for scholarships, organized trips to poor rural areas to distribute materials, planned relief efforts, and so on. Staff members also engaged in group meditation and discussions of Buddhist scripture and Xuecheng's teachings. The relocation to Longquan allows Ren'ai staff to adhere even more closely to monastic discipline, rising before dawn, meditating, and sharing their morning meal with the monks and other temple volunteers prior to the start of the workday.

All this suggests that Ren'ai's core staff can be regarded as a Buddhist "intentional community," whose members integrate their faith into every aspect of their lives. They are quasi-renunciants; one staff member I spoke with used the term "semi-monastic" (*ban chujia* 半出家) to describe her situation. For some a stint with Ren'ai is a trial run, a chance to experience a life of Buddhist discipline before making a full commitment to the monastic existence. Since Longquan Temple accepts and ordains only male monastics, for the women in the organization their full-time involvement allowed them to live a quasi-monastic life without having to leave the temple and give up their close collaboration with Xuecheng. In other words, for these women and for the men in the organization who benefit from their contributions—including Xuecheng—Ren'ai ameliorated a dilemma arising out of the gendered division of labor in Chinese Buddhism. None of the full-time volunteers I interviewed indicated any plans to leave the organization and do something else, and several deflected my questions about future plans by pointing out the Buddhist emphasis on being present in the here and now. All cited Xuecheng as a powerful influence on them personally. For some, Xuecheng's focus on compassion drew them to him as a Buddhist teacher, and consequently to Longquan Temple. For others, volunteer activities at the temple were a stepping-stone to volunteering, either full- or part-time, with Ren'ai. Their efforts embody a core idea of *renjian fojiao,* to enter the world and attend to its concerns, but to do so in a spirit of world renunciation.

LOVING HEART CONGEE: MELDING BUDDHISM, PUBLIC SERVICE, AND A CULTURE OF CHARITY

Though its Buddhist origins are apparent, in much of its charity work Ren'ai does not emphasize its religious character, in great part because Chinese law forbids proselytizing in public and the use of charity as a means to win converts. Instead, it frequently draws on socialist and other nonreligious cultural and political frames to explain and legitimize its endeavors. Ren'ai has found creative ways of reaching out to a broad public through rhetorical and behavioral strategies that, while not exactly masking its Buddhist influences, stress the civic and cultural dimensions of its endeavors, even their compatibility with socialist norms. Though many volunteers are drawn to Ren'ai by the teachings of Xuecheng or their experiences at Longquan Temple, many others are attracted by its efforts to create a culture of charity and public service.

This marriage of the civic with the Buddhist is evident in Ren'ai's most unusual endeavor, the Loving Heart Congee (Aixin Zhou 爱心粥) program. This program began as an occasional happening at temple Dharma assemblies, where Ren'ai volunteers would serve free cups of porridge to attendees and any other visitors who happened to wander by. Loving Heart Congee became a daily event in early 2007 with the opening of a community center, the Benevolent Heart Inn (Ren'ai Xin Zhan 仁爱心栈), in a Beijing neighborhood. The center catered to neighborhood residents, especially elderly retirees, and served as an activity center as well as a place to get a warm cup of congee each morning. In early 2008 Ren'ai expanded the reach of the program with the purchase of motorized food carts to transport congee from the kitchen at Benevolent Heart Inn to busy locales such as Beijing's West Railway Station and the sidewalk in front of a nearby Walmart. On January 15, 2008, which coincided that year with the traditional Rice Porridge Festival (Laba Jie 腊八节), Ren'ai launched the 365 Days of Congee project with the goal of serving porridge every day for the next year. Though regarded by many as a Chinese cultural festival, for Buddhists the Rice Porridge Festival celebrates the enlightenment of Śākyamuni (Shijiamouni Fo 释迦牟尼佛); according to one legend, Śākyamuni achieved Buddhahood after years of asceticism during which he survived on just one meal of congee per day.

In recent years the program has grown tremendously. Although the original Benevolent Heart Inn is now closed, as of May 2017 there were "Heart Inns" (i.e., congee stands) in forty-seven locations around the country (Liu Xuanguo 2017). Beijing sites include a sidewalk on a busy thoroughfare adjacent to the West Railway Station, established in 2008; a stand near the Tsinghua University Science Park in Haidian District and another near the SOHO department store in Chaoyang District, both established in 2009; one each in the suburbs of Yizhuang and Tongzhou, set up in 2013 and 2014, respectively; and an additional Haidian site established in 2014. Outside of Beijing there are now congee programs in Guangzhou, Shenzhen, Shanghai, Tianjin, and Ya'an, Sichuan Province, where Ren'ai created a Benevolent Heart Inn community center as part of its relief efforts following the 2013 earthquake in Lushan County. Volunteers have served congee every day since the initiative began in 2008. The foundation estimates that six thousand volunteers hand out thirty thousand cups of congee every week.

Loving Heart Congee is an unusual charity endeavor. Anyone is welcome to have a cup; a demonstration of financial need is not required. Recipients include white-collar executives, tech entrepreneurs, government retirees, schoolchildren, shoppers, migrant workers, and the homeless. Congee sites are located in some of the most affluent neighborhoods in all of China; the Tsinghua site, for example, is in the heart of China's high-tech district, down the street from the Beijing headquarters of Google and Microsoft. Though congee is cheap to produce, Ren'ai has produced a lot of it since the program began, and the resources expended on the program are not insubstantial.

Yet for Ren'ai the primary goal of the program is not to feed those suffering from physical hunger. Instead, it aims to rouse the public's compassion and concern for others, eliminate barriers between people, and in doing so alleviate the estrangement that characterizes contemporary social existence. As explained in an English-language volunteer recruitment notice on a Ren'ai blog: "We believe in the magical effect of a small bowl of porridge in wakening up [*sic*] people's social concern and love. The Foundation offers free Ren Ai porridge in community everyday. . . . Through providing free porridges [*sic*] in communities, as well as carrying out 'the orphans, the disabled and the elderly' caring practices, family education, healthcare, community sanity and other public welfare volunteering activities, we aim to arouse people to love, care and to contribute" (Ren'ai Charity Foundation 2009).

Loving Heart Congee thus involves more than just handing out cups of warm, rice-based porridge to early-morning passersby. When distributing congee Ren'ai volunteers bow and offer recipients their good wishes, and they thank recipients for allowing the volunteers to serve them. For volunteers who are Buddhist, this practice demonstrates Buddhist equanimity and humility, as well as concern for sentient beings. Serving congee, in other words, is a form of Buddhist practice and self-cultivation. This is evident from postings on a daily blog kept by Ren'ai volunteers that detail their thoughts and experiences. Volunteers describe how participation in this relatively simple act of service has helped them break through the "small self"—the individual ego—in service of something larger. As one blog posting explained, serving congee "[demonstrates] concern for all sentient beings. It is an act of unselfish love that asks nothing in return" (Yang Jie 2012). Volunteers describe wrestling with emotions that arise in the course of their charity work, including resentment that some of those being served congee probably don't need it, given the affluence of the neighborhood. Such posts wax philosophical on the nature of "need," pointing out that a cup of porridge given to one freely by a stranger offers spiritual warmth, a rare commodity in China's materialistic and competitive society. Blog posts also address volunteers' struggles to maintain equanimity when dealing with an individual who cuts in line or comes back for a third cup before others have had any.

The Loving Heart Congee program is an example of a "spiritual technology," a tactic or resource for addressing problems the perceived efficacy of which is rooted in religious ideas and practices, not unlike prayer or the laying on of hands in Christian faith healing (Jeavons 1998, 88). As such it demonstrates how religious beliefs can shape both the perception of social problems and the methods used to address these. For Ren'ai core staff, one of the key problems in the world today is a lack of love and compassion, a dearth of concern for the suffering of others. They believe this absence is at the root of problems such as poverty, illness, and even natural disasters, which are often compounded or created by corruption, selfishness, and neglect. By handing out congee to random strangers, Ren'ai aims to increase good cheer and good feelings among people, and perhaps to inspire them to show more concern for others in their communities. In a sense, Ren'ai is seeking to bring about a kind of psychological and spiritual transformation of the individual in contemporary Chinese society, through simple, everyday interactions. If it can accomplish this, its founders and core volunteers believe many social problems might be avoided. Thus Ren'ai doesn't just address the aftereffects of tragedy, that is, the consequences of bad karma, but seeks to create good karma so that tragedies will not occur (McCarthy 2013, 67).

Although Loving Heart Congee is inspired by spiritual principles and pursues spiritual goals, many if not most program volunteers are not self-identifying Buddhists. Core Ren'ai volunteers were the main providers of congee in the first few years, but increasingly volunteers are drawn from members of the general public, including groups of schoolchildren and employees from local firms. This is by design: The program was meant to be a charitable project, a service activity that just about anyone could participate in simply by showing up to hand cups of porridge to passersby. Many volunteers are drawn to the program after having been given a cup themselves. Through endeavors like Loving Heart Congee, the Benevolent Heart Inn, and other volunteer-driven, bottom-up programs, Ren'ai seeks to nurture a culture of compassion and empower a broad spectrum of people to participate in public service.

For these reasons and because of the legal issues mentioned previously, in its outreach Ren'ai tends to play down the Buddhist principles and objectives that inform the Loving Heart Congee program. Volunteers are not supposed to hand out Buddhist tracts, engage congee recipients in discussions of Buddhism, or even play Buddhist music while handing out the porridge (or in the course of other charitable events not located on temple grounds). Consequently Ren'ai often draws on secular frames, values, and ideals in presenting itself to the public and rationalizing its endeavors, including socialist frames like the Lei Feng spirit mentioned at the outset of the chapter. In recent years Ren'ai has used the opportunity presented by Lei Feng Day, held every March 5, to promote charity and attract the attention of the public. In 2014 Ren'ai organized Lei Feng–related activities at each of its congee stands, putting up posters with images of the model worker and slogans alluding to his selfless devotion, such as "With whole heart and whole mind serve the people!" and "March 5th study Lei Feng, together we offer porridge." Contributors to that day's blog entry related the ways Lei Feng ("Uncle Lei Feng," *Lei Feng shushu* 雷锋叔叔, as one volunteer called him) inspired their service. As one Shenzhen volunteer wrote, "The leader of our [congee team] put it well: One who serves the people is a *bodhisattva*, however, one who does so with whole heart and mind is a great *bodhisattva* (*da pusa*). Lei Feng is one of those who served the people with his whole heart and mind. We should study this worthy predecessor, not to do just one or two good deeds, but to persevere in doing so our whole lives." The individual blog posts from March 5 are grouped together under the heading "With compassion in the heart, Lei Feng is by one's side" (Ren'ai zai xinjian, Lei Feng zai shenbian 仁爱在心间, 雷锋在身边) (Ren'ai Charity Foundation 2014).

Ren'ai is not the only practitioner of Buddhist charity to connect its endeavors to this icon of Maoist self-sacrifice and devotion. A similar connection was drawn by the Venerable Shenghui, director of the Hunan Province Buddhist Compassion Charity Foundation, in a 2012 speech titled "Devotion Is Practice: The Buddhist Spirit and the Lei Feng Spirit Are the Same" given at the Changsha conference the Meaning of the "Lei Feng Spirit Today." In his speech the former vice-chair of the BAC explained that the Lei Feng spirit is one of dedication, gratitude, and unceasing service to others. As Shenghui put it, the "Lei Feng spirit . . . embodies the idea of doing for others rather than for oneself. In life it is not hard to do good things for others; what is hard is to do so incessantly." Shenghui further likened the Lei Feng spirit to Buddhist self-cultivation: In his telling, doing good deeds for others is "a kind of practice, a method for improving oneself . . . from beginning to end we must engrave the words 'conscience, ethics, gratitude' in our hearts, and only in this way can we achieve a sublime state." Audience members were apparently deeply impressed with this Buddhist perspective on Lei Feng. According to an account posted on the website of the Beijing Ethnic and Religious Affairs Department, for some attendees, hearing Shenghui's "brilliant exposition" was akin to a "spiritual baptism" (Tao et al. 2012).

These evocations of Lei Feng in the context of Buddhist charity are perhaps not surprising given that both Shenghui and Xuecheng hold or have held high positions in the Buddhist administrative hierarchy. Both represent institutional Buddhism, which is promoted by the regime and which possesses an interest in maintaining official religious structures (Laliberté 2011b; Sun 2011). Allusions to socialist practice and ideals may help further this objective while legitimating Buddhism in the eyes of party-state officials. References to Lei Feng are not necessarily purely strategic or instrumental in nature, however. In an October 2014 interview with one of Ren'ai's deputy directors I inquired about the foundation's use of Lei Feng imagery and rhetoric, including rhetoric that portrays Lei Feng as a bodhisattva, an enlightened being dedicated to helping others achieve Buddhahood. "Some people say Lei Feng is a bodhisattva," I started to say, but before I could finish my query the deputy director interjected enthusiastically: "He is! Lei Feng is definitely a bodhisattva!" (*Ta jiushi! Lei Feng yiding shi yige da pusa!* 他就是! 雷锋一定是一个大菩萨!) She elaborated: "We Buddhists don't view Lei Feng so much as a revolutionary or soldier but as someone who dedicated himself to helping others his whole life." She explained that while each of us had the potential to be a bodhisattva by helping others, what distinguished Lei Feng as an icon worthy of emulation was the depth and constancy of his service.

These evocations of Lei Feng also reflect the fact that the model soldier retains cultural currency, though periodic resuscitations of his myth by the government engender a good deal of cynicism. For Buddhist charities, deploying that currency can transform acts of beneficence rooted in spiritual tradition into the acts of loyal Chinese citizens. At the same time, these appropriations of Lei Feng "repurpose" the icon in ways that alter its meanings, however subtly (McCarthy 2013). The myth of Lei Feng has become what Wu Ka-ming terms an "ex-socialist resource," one that communicates norms of collective devotion that transcend the myth's Maoist roots (Wu 2011). Lei Feng, the model of self-sacrifice to the revolutionary proletarian and peasant masses, has become Lei Feng, exemplar of public service and compassion. As I explain in the next section, the use of secular and socialist political frames and the effort to connect Buddhist practice with civic norms also reflected the goals and commitments of Xuecheng, Ren'ai's monastic patron. Such framing cohered with Xuecheng's efforts to promote modes of Buddhist charity—and Buddhist practice in general—attentive to the concerns of contemporary Chinese society.

XUECHENG: THE VERY MODEL OF A MODERNIZING MONASTIC

In many respects the emergence of Ren'ai and similar groups entails a revival of Buddhist tradition stretching back centuries. This is how contemporary Buddhist charity is often portrayed in Buddhist and academic writings, popular media, and official pronouncements. In funding and operating orphanages, clinics, and a variety of other programs, today's Buddhists carry on spiritually grounded traditions of service that were suppressed during the more radical periods of the Mao era. Yet one of the "traditions" being revived in organizations like Ren'ai and Longquan Temple is the religious embrace of the modern. Practitioners of Buddhist charity frequently cite the early-twentieth-century Buddhist reformer Taixu as inspiration for their endeavors (regardless of whether or not those endeavors accord with Taixu's ideas). Taixu is best known today for having developed and promoted "Buddhism for the human realm," a mode of Buddhism that stresses engagement with rather than renunciation of this world and its concerns. As Donald Pittman has argued, Taixu "emphasized what could actually be accomplished in this world through the self-sacrificial work of thousands of average bodhisattvas dedicated to building a pure land here and now" (Pittman 2001, 10). Taixu was also a modernizer: In reworking Buddhist understandings of the path to enlightenment and in his proposals to reform the sangha and monastic education, he sought to modernize Buddhism so that it might respond to the challenges of his era. Such challenges included philosophical ones posed by secularism, relativism, and modern science, against which many Buddhist practices appeared, to some, atavistic and irrelevant. Such criticisms and the responses to them were not unique to Buddhism. A good deal of Chinese religious philanthropy of the early twentieth century constituted a similar effort to reconcile normative understandings of what it meant to be Chinese, religious, and modern (Ashiwa 2009; Yang Mayfair Mei-Hui 2011; Nedostup 2009).

To an extent Taixu's reforms can be regarded as defensive, insofar as they sought to rescue Buddhism from charges of backwardness, superstition, and incompatibility with China's modernizing ambitions. In Pittman's words, Taixu "shaped his presentation of his Mahayana heritage so as to highlight the tradition as potentially, if not in actual practice, the most scientifically respectable and socially responsible religious force within human society" (Pittman 2001, 9). Subsequent advocates and innovators of Buddhism for the human realm have continued to emphasize the relevance of socially responsible Buddhism for a rapidly modernizing society. These include the Taiwan-based clerics Hsing Yun (Xingyun 星云), the founder of Taiwan's Buddha's Light Mountain, and Cheng Yen, founder of the Tzu Chi Foundation, both of whom meld practically oriented Buddhist teachings with Confucian reverence for family, community, and tradition. At the same time, these clerics' respective associations have employed advanced technology and modern organizational strategies to augment their founders' reputation and influence (Laliberté 2004; Madsen 2007; Huang 2009).

In the People's Republic of China (PRC), Buddhist clerics and laypeople continue to grapple with the meaning of post-Mao modernity and what it implies for this ancient spiritual tradition. Although charges of feudal backwardness are increasingly rare, many nonbelievers, including party-state officials, continue to view Buddhism and other religions as unsuited to contemporary life, even as a drag on China's ongoing developmental project. Buddhist charity seeks to counter these perceptions by demonstrating practitioners' concern for those who do not share their faith but do share membership in the Chinese nation-state. By modeling modern civic behavior and ideals alongside religious ones, Buddhist charities emphasize the continued relevance of their beliefs.

Xuecheng exemplified this enthusiastic embrace of the modern. Until his fall from power in August 2018, he was the very model of a modern Chinese monastic, a would-be Taixu of the twenty-first century. Born in 1966, Xuecheng and the temple he headed garnered media attention for initiatives aimed at updating monastic life and Buddhist practice. For instance, the temple administration includes an IT department staffed partly by monks who hold advanced degrees in STEM fields from some of China's top universities. So many Longquan monks possess advanced academic degrees that the temple has been dubbed a "branch school" (*fenxiao* 分校) of Beijing and Tsinghua Universities. Another temple initiative is an animation department that produces comic books and videos for children about the fictional adventures of a young monk named Xian'er trying to spread compassion and do good deeds. Xuecheng furthermore counted a number of prominent, wealthy tech entrepreneurs among his acolytes, including Zhang Xiaolong, the creator of WeChat, the mobile text- and voice-messaging service. Legend has it that Zhang came up with the idea for WeChat while talking with a monk during an extended retreat at Longquan Temple (He 2016).

Dough figurines of Xian'er, the Little Monk, on display in the animation department of Longquan Temple, November 2014. The figurines are used in stop-motion-animation videos produced for children. Photo by the author.

Although a modernizer, Xuecheng was not oblivious to the deleterious effects of rapid growth and technological change. During his tenure as abbot of Longquan Temple, Xuecheng spoke out against the commercialization of Buddhism, in particular plans to launch IPOs by state-run firms that manage tourist facilities at some of China's most sacred Buddhist sites (Li 2012). Cognizant of the threats growth poses to the environment, Xuecheng became an advocate of a "low-carbon lifestyle" (Xinhua wang 2010). The Internet environment was also the focus of his concern. In July 2014 the temple's animation department released an online public service video aimed at combating incivility, pornography, and violence on the web (Longquan zhi sheng 2014). The release of the video, which coincided with a broad government crackdown on Internet pornography and prostitution, was first announced on Xuecheng's microblog and Twitter feed.

As these initiatives demonstrate Xuecheng embraced social media, enabling him to reach an audience far beyond Beijing. He was the first prominent mainland Buddhist cleric to keep a blog, begun in 2006, an endeavor that earned him the moniker "mainland Chinese Buddhism's 'Number One Blogger'" (Han 2012). According to the English news weekly *Beijing Review,* Xuecheng maintained a "Chinese, English and Japanese website, a personal blog, a personal microblog, a temple blog, a temple microblog, a charity foundation blog, personal English Twitter, personal and temple instant messaging groups and microblogs on sina.com and QQ.com in eight different languages" (Liang 2011). Translation was carried out by dozens of volunteers in Longquan Temple's media department (Tang 2012). That department published more than one hundred volumes in both digital and paperback form containing Xuecheng's blog posts, also in multiple languages. Xuecheng regarded social media as beneficial to the mission of Longquan Temple and the development of Buddhism: "The advancement of information technology has given tremendous opportunities for the dissemination of Buddhism. . . . We must grasp this changing era and use technological means to spread the spirit of Buddhism and share the wisdom of Buddhist sutras with the general public" (quoted in Liang 2011). He acknowledged that although social media is not required for Buddhist practice, "the Internet is very significant in spreading Buddhism and bringing benefits to all human beings. Nowadays, it is not realistic for Buddhist followers, the general public and foreign friends to go to the temple for Buddhist lectures every day. However, they do use computers every day. . . . Buddhism should keep up with the times and embrace modern technology to promote Buddha's teachings in an innovative and recipient-friendly way" (Tang 2012).

Keeping up with the times has its pitfalls, however. In 2014 Longquan Temple was implicated, albeit indirectly, in an exposé detailing the use of public funds to pay tuition and fees for officials and managers of state-owned enterprises to attend Executive MBA and post-EMBA programs at top Chinese universities. Tuition for some programs can exceed US$140,000, depending on an official's rank or, for managers, their firm's annual revenue. Before new regulations were issued forbidding the practice, in some programs half or more of the students were party-state officials and state-owned enterprise managers whose tab was being picked up by the public. Program curricula included wine tasting, Western etiquette, foreign travel, and for those enrolled in programs at Beijing and Tsinghua Universities (which featured Xuecheng as a guest lecturer), overnight visits to Longquan Temple to learn Buddhist meditation and briefly experience the monastic lifestyle (Chen 2014). Furthermore, in the end Xuecheng's embrace of technology and especially social media contributed to his undoing. Among the most damning evidence for the sexual harassment allegations against him were salacious WeChat messages he sent to two nuns.

These initiatives suggest that Longquan Temple is a variation on the type of "hybrid" institutions analyzed by Brian Nichols in chapter 4 in this volume, in that it is "responsive to both a secularly interested public and a more religiously motivated clergy." On the one hand, the temple has attracted a pool of highly educated individuals pursuing monastic vocations rooted in traditional forms of Buddhist cultivation. Furthermore, many of its regular volunteers, especially women, are drawn by the quasi-monasticism of the temple's lay programs. On the other hand, the temple's outreach efforts, tech initiatives, and focus on contemporary social problems demonstrate its secular concerns. Like other hybrid temples Longquan draws a good number of tourists, in part because it is situated in a nature preserve on the outskirts of Beijing.[2] Nichols argues that the hybrid character of certain monasteries typically reflects "the competing interests and actions of clerical and nonclerical parties actively negotiating levels of authority and jurisdiction." In the case of Longquan Temple, however, it was not the interests of a nonclerical administrative committee driving this embrace of public, secular affairs, but the ambitions and commitments of an abbot who was both a religious leader and a representative of the party-state.

GUIDING GRASSROOTS CHARITY: THE CASE OF LIFE RESCUE

It is important to realize that while many of the temple and charitable endeavors discussed in this chapter were supported and blessed by Xuecheng, they resulted from the initiative, ideas, and efforts of laypeople in collaboration with the monks of Longquan Temple. Ren'ai exemplifies the decentralized, even grassroots character of the service activities of the temple; promoting grassroots initiative and connections is one of Ren'ai's chief aims. Temple and foundation activities are thus conducted in ways that (try to) avoid some of the problems of Chinese Buddhist charity regarding social capital, innovation, and civic engagement. Deng Zimei and Wang Jia have argued that much mainstream Chinese Buddhist charity conducted through temple-sponsored associations reinforces traditional, hierarchical relationships between clerics and laity (Deng and Wang 2008, 2012). Such groups may marshal impressive resources for worthwhile projects, but the way they mobilize funding and volunteers can dampen communication, innovation, and leadership among their lay members. Typically, members offer their time and money in response to a top-down request from an abbot; projects and participation are rarely the result of horizontal mobilization or self-directed cooperative action among lay volunteers. Of course, whether one considers this to be a problem depends on what one understands the purpose of Buddhist charity to be. For many believers the aim is not to nurture public service or stimulate social capital, but to adhere to the Dharma and acquire merit. Charity, good works, and the like are conducted in accord with religious teachings so as to achieve religious ends. That the pursuit of such ends might contravene secular understandings of the public good need not deter the faithful.

The contradiction between the pursuit of merit and the public good (as secularly construed) is perhaps most evident in the controversy surrounding life rescue, the practice of setting captive animals free. Despite the apocryphal nature of the texts on which this practice is ostensibly based, the ritual holds great appeal for adherents of Buddhism and Taoism. Practitioners believe that liberating animals, typically birds and fish, generates merit (*gongde* 功德), promotes the Dharma, and furthers them along the path to the Pure Land and, ultimately, nirvana (Shiu and Stokes 2008; Smith 2009, 15–42). Thus, much like the Loving Heart Congee served by Ren'ai, life rescue is a spiritual technology aimed at achieving a conception of "the good" informed by Buddhist beliefs and ideals. Though often carried out under the auspices of registered temples, increasingly events are staged by unofficial lay groups, some of which are devoted solely to practicing life rescue. Personal testimonies posted on microblogs and on the websites of prominent temple merit societies trumpet the benefits of life rescue in this life as well as the next. Such testimonies detail how personal fortunes turned around once an individual was introduced to the practice: jobs materialized, relationships healed, health improved, and bank accounts fattened, all following the liberation of birds and fish.

Though popular, the practice has provoked extensive criticism from various corners of society as well as the party-state. For good reason, life rescue is seen as enmeshed in a web (real and figurative) of rampant commercialization. As incomes have increased on the mainland, so too has participation in the ritual, generating a kind of life rescue industrial complex dedicated to profiting from the practice. Many people believe that the amount of merit earned is influenced by the quantities of money spent and animals released. Proprietors of companies that trap birds and fish to sell to practitioners frequently install nets in the vicinity of popular life rescue ritual sites so as to recapture and resell the "liberated" animals. Life rescue is lambasted also for being ecologically unsound and for demonstrating disregard rather than compassion for sentient beings. Each time events are held, some animals die or are injured before and during release. Because of their rarity, endangered species are more expensive (and thus more profitable), and some practitioners believe the release of such animals to be particularly meritorious. Animals have been set free far from their natural habitats, and fish have been released into waters too warm for them to survive, leading to massive kills (Gong 2011). In one case from January 2015, life rescue practitioners used a truck to dump tens of thousands of river snails into the Grand Canal, which subsequently washed up dead on the banks of the canal in Hangzhou (China Daily 2015).

Life rescue has also been criticized—including by other Buddhists—for diverting resources away from programs that aid vulnerable populations and the broader society. The practice is not inherently at odds with the provision of broader social benefits; one group that does both is the Donglin Charity Merit Association, based at Donglin Temple (Donglin Si 东林寺) in Jiangxi Province. The association funds and operates medical clinics, old-age homes, and other projects. Its lay volunteers, adherents of Pure Land Buddhism, also collectively engage in life rescue and other spiritual practices, such as the "blood writing" of sutras (Donglin Charity 2011; Kieschnick 2000). Yet many Buddhists believe merit is attainable solely through activities that are explicitly Buddhist in character and that promote Buddhism. However, for various reasons including legal issues previously discussed, many charitable endeavors include little or no Buddhist content in their programming. For instance, a Buddhist-run orphanage may not include overt religious messages or practices in the curriculum it provides to the children under its care. This "wall of separation" between religion and charity can depress support for such programs among devout lay Buddhists, precisely the demographic such charities would like to cultivate as donors and volunteers. In the words of Master Changhui, the monk who directs an orphanage established by the Hebei Provincial Buddhist Association, "many more Buddhist believers would rather spend money buying animals to set free than donate funds to [our orphanage]" (Feng 2008).

Changhui's complaint underscores the fact that although religion can be a powerful force for charitable action, it does not always inspire the kinds of public welfare activities typically considered philanthropic and can even be inhospitable to them. Beliefs may lead adherents to reject practical measures to alleviate social suffering as pointless or as a diversion from sacred obligations. This phenomenon is not unique to Buddhism. Cao Nanlai argues that among some evangelical Chinese Christians who believe in the doctrine of justification by faith, social problems are regarded as "a consequence of bad human-God relations [that] can only be resolved in the spiritual sphere, especially by continuous faithful prayers to God." These Christians consequently "reject the concept of religious philanthropy . . . understood in terms of a religious and moral duty to give or help others" (Cao 2013, 254).

Governments at the central, provincial, and municipal levels have pursued a number of strategies in response to the proliferation of life rescue and its attendant problems. One approach is to institutionalize the practice. Some municipalities have established life rescue holidays during which city officials, along with Buddhist and Taoist clerics, hold joint public ceremonies to liberate animals in an ostensibly environmentally appropriate manner (China News Net 2014). Local governments have also set up organizations to facilitate and manage the practice. For instance, in 2010 the government of Guangdong Province approved the creation of the Guangdong Fangsheng Association (Guangdong Fangsheng Xiehui 广东放生协会), a "grassroots" social organization established under the auspices of the Guangdong Ocean and Fisheries Administration, which serves as its supervisory unit. According to the association's chair, a former deputy head of the standing committee of the provincial People's Congress, the group's purpose is to "protect the earth, show concern for life, and to do good works and earn merit" (China News Net 2010). The leader of the provincial Buddhist Association expressed his conviction that the group would "promote correct ecological and ethical concepts" and help life rescue practitioners "gain a better understanding of and appreciation for life" (China News Net 2010). Municipal and district governments throughout the country have also established life rescue "small groups" (xiaozu 小组) to respond to growing interest in the practice and supervise its execution. Nevertheless private life rescue organizations—sometimes called "charity groups" (cishan zu 慈善组)—continue to proliferate via the Internet and social media applications like WeChat and QQ.

The government has also enlisted prominent Buddhist and Taoist clerics to help it rein in the practice. One of these was Xuecheng, who in his speeches and writings sought to broaden popular awareness of the ideas underlying life rescue, and what it truly means to show compassion for all sentient beings. Xuecheng played a leading role in the composition of new life rescue guidelines issued in July 2014 by the national Buddhist and Taoist Associations. These guidelines call on adherents to "release captive wildlife in a correct fashion," that is, in a manner that is "intelligent," "rational," and "scientific" (Zhongguo Fojiao Xiehui 2014). In a television news report Xuecheng was quoted as saying that "human beings must keep up with the pace of the current age and adjust their behaviors in terms of environmental protection and development. For example, we must not release freshwater animals in saltwater, and we must not release alpine animals on the plains" (Liu and Yang 2014). It remains to be seen what effect the guidelines will have. Life rescue remains popular, and for many believers it exemplifies Buddhist charity. To them life rescue *is* "charity" (*cishan* 慈善), an expression of compassion and mercy that is particularly efficacious for the acquisition of merit.

Increasingly the contemporary party-state regards religion and religious charity as resources that may help alleviate social problems it cannot or will not resolve. Whether faith-based charity can be deployed in this way, however, depends on the congruence between the charity objectives and beliefs of adherents and the interests of the party-state. In the case of Ren'ai, this congruence reflects the ideals, commitments, and status of the organization's founders and core members, including Xuecheng. It also reflects the fact that Ren'ai frames many of its activities in secular terms, partly in deference to political constraints on mixing religious expression with charitable endeavors. Harmonizing one's goals and practices with regime-sanctioned ideals can make a good deal of political sense for any religious group in China. For Ren'ai, doing so may also render its endeavors comprehensible to a broader Chinese public, much of which remains suspicious of both charity and religion. The appropriation and deployment of familiar national ideals and images, including socialist ones like Lei Feng, can augment the appeal of religious charity to a largely secular population.

The controversy over life rescue, however, reminds us that the religious dimensions of Buddhist charity cannot be overlooked. The motivations guiding charity can vary widely, but for many believers it is fundamentally a religious act. Through charity, adherents express beliefs, enact ritual, pursue the Dharma, acquire merit, and expand the community of believers, all while serving others and addressing social needs. These adherents may conceive of service, need, and the public good through a Buddhist lens, in ways that diverge from state-sanctioned norms and objectives. The primacy of the religious may confound efforts to make Buddhist charity serve either secular versions of the public good or the interests of the party-state.

NOTES

Research for this chapter was supported by grants from the Chiang Ching-kuo Foundation and the Providence College Committee on Aid to Faculty Research.

1. The temple was first built in AD 951 during the Liao dynasty. After decades of closure and neglect, it was reopened in 2005 under Xuecheng's leadership (Tang 2012).

2. Tourists must purchase a ticket to enter the nature preserve; entry to the temple complex itself, however, is free.

4

TOURIST TEMPLES AND PLACES OF PRACTICE

Charting Multiple Paths in the Revival of Monasteries

BRIAN J. NICHOLS

Visitors to Beijing often visit temples such as the Lama Temple (Yonghe Gong 雍和宫), the White Stupa Temple (Baita Si 白塔寺), and many others where one purchases entrance tickets and walks through a turnstile. In addition to tickets, tour groups, and turnstiles, a visit to such sites often involves passing rows of stalls selling souvenirs upon entering or exiting. Beyond Beijing there are many other popularly visited temples that also cater to tourists, such as Shanghai's Jade Buddha Temple (Yufo Si 玉佛寺), Famen Temple (Famen Si 法门寺) near Xi'an, and Shaolin Temple (Shaolin Si 少林寺) near Luoyang. Buddhist venues have been rebuilt and restored and marketed as sites of heritage, and many have been successful in attracting scores of tour groups.[1] Visitors to China who tour popular temples such as these would be forgiven for having an impression that Buddhist temples in China had yet to make an authentic recovery from the years of suppression under Mao, that they had been reopened not as sites propagating the Dharma, but as tourist sites and commercial enterprises.[2] There have indeed been economic and political motives behind the restoration of many Buddhist sites in China. This is part of the story of the revival of Buddhism in China, but only part and, increasingly, arguably, the smaller part. What is more common is the rebuilding of temples by clergy driven to reclaim sites for the sangha and the restoration of monastic Buddhism.

The clergy who wish to reclaim monastic lands and buildings and revive them as sites of practice typically work within legal frameworks with approval from the Buddhist Association of China (BAC; Zhongguo Fojiao Xiehui 中国佛教协会) and the local and provincial offices of the State Administration for Religious Affairs (SARA; Guojia Zongjiao Shiwuju 国家宗教事务局). If a temple is the site of cultural treasures, historic value, or natural beauty, it will also typically fall under the jurisdiction of other bureaus as well. When a temple becomes designated an Important National Cultural Heritage Protected Site (Quanguo Zhongdian Wenwu Baohu Danwei 全国重点文物保护单位) or an AAAA National Tourist Attraction (Guojia Dengji Lüyou Qu 国家等级旅游区), for example, certain government entities, in addition to SARA, become associated with the temple in various capacities of oversight, management, and exploitation. These include bureaus and committees that deal with tourism (*lüyou ju* 旅游局), culture (*wenhua ju* 文化局), heritage (*wenwu ju* 文物局), and nonmonastic temple administration (*guanli weiyuan hui* 管理委员会). In line with the Communist Party's ultimate view on religion, these secular entities seek to frame religion as an artifact of the past rather than a living phenomenon with a future. In order to capture this vision of treating religion as an artifact to be preserved, I refer to these organizational entities as "curators." Doing so enables us to distinguish these actors from the monastics, lay Buddhists, and worshippers who are eager to recover monastic spaces and restore them to religious use—these are the "revivalists." While the revival of monastic Buddhism in contemporary China is a complex and dynamic affair, it is critical, I argue, to be aware of the different roles played by these groups in charting three major paths in the revival: the path of the curators, driven by economic and political motivations; that of the revivalists, informed by religious concerns; and a third path forged through the necessary negotiations between the curators and revivalists.

Buddhist monasteries and temples are being rebuilt throughout China on a scale unmatched in recent centuries, if ever. The key questions examined by this chapter are: What kinds of institutions are being developed and what are the key factors determining what kinds of institutions are developed? This chapter proposes three basic paths in the revival of monastic Buddhism. One of the most visible paths is that of the site that serves as a tourist attraction with few or no monastics having limited or no opportunities for religious cultivation. Among these sites are those that have no clergy in residence and are fully operated by nonmonastic authorities. The administration of these sites is dominated by a group of people I refer to as curators. This group includes businesspeople, temple administrators, and government officials, who exercise various degrees of temple oversight through bureaus of culture, bureaus of tourism, and units known as Temple Administrative Commissions. These groups actively promote temples as sites of historic and cultural value rather than places of living religious practice. At their most extreme, such sites function as museums without clergy. Others have limited numbers of clergy or employ fake monks to tend halls during business hours. These sites are properly considered "tourist temples." Examples discussed in this chapter include the White Stupa Temple, the Hongluo Temple (Hongluo Si 红螺寺), and the "museumified" Yangzhou Tianning Temple (Yangzhou Tianning Si 扬州天宁寺).

At the other end of the spectrum is the monastery that serves as a home to a growing cohort of monks engaged in various forms of traditional Buddhist cultivation. These sites are supported by core groups of clergy and laypersons actively promoting the restoration of Buddhist sites, rituals, practice, and administration. Among the revivalists is an emerging clergy asserting itself across China against entities seeking to exploit monasteries. Monasteries in this category have regular morning (*zaoke* 早课) and evening services (*wanke* 晚课), which punctuate a monastic day that includes communal meals served in silence in a dining hall (*wuguan tang* 五观堂). In addition to this baseline of monastic cultivation, monasteries in this group offer other forms of religious practice such as Buddha recitation sessions (*nianfo* 念佛), communal sutra recitation (*nianjing* 念经), and communal meditation, as well as a variety of ritual services.[3] Examples of such sites discussed in this chapter include Mount Taimu's Pingxing Monastery (Taimu Shan Pingxing Si 太姥山平兴寺) and Jiangsu's Gaomin Monastery (Gaomin Si 高旻寺).

Between these two poles of tourist temple and place of practice is a third type of institution that both caters to tourists and tour groups and houses a body of monastics who engage in baseline forms of monastic practice. This third type of site is established through the competing interests and actions of clerical and nonclerical parties actively negotiating levels of authority and jurisdiction. This group creates hybrid institutions responsive to both a secularly interested public and a more religiously motivated clergy. Although these sites are less conducive to religious cultivation given the busyness that emerges from dealing with the public and other interested parties, hybrid institutions such as Famen Temple and Quanzhou Kaiyuan Temple (Quanzhou Kaiyuan Si 泉州开元寺) serve as training grounds for monastics, albeit less than ideal ones.

Driving these different paths are two distinct groups representing two different visions of what temples should be in contemporary China. When one group dominates, the result is a tourist temple or a place of practice; when both are actively involved in administration, the result is a hybrid institution that serves as both a tourist site and a functioning monastery. This typology can be used to distinguish three general types of religious sites that one finds in China and anticipate degrees of presence or absence of secular or clerical agents.

Among the various parties associated with temples in China, there is both cooperation and competition. The cooperation is expedient, motivated by economic needs and political realities. Competition exists over resources (e.g., entrance fees) and control (e.g., building plans, access); from the perspective of the sangha it may be characterized as a battle for greater autonomy. This competition can erupt in dramatic ways that reveal, I suggest, a growing assertiveness among the clergy in China. I begin by introducing four events that reveal the sangha's effort to gain greater control over Buddhist sites.

A GROWING ASSERTIVENESS AMONG CLERICS?

Bailin Chan Temple (Bailin Chan Si 柏林禅寺; hereafter Bailin Temple) in Hebei Province is well-known as a model monastery for the authentic revival of

Chan meditation.[4] Under the leadership of successive abbots Jinghui 净慧 (1933–2013) and Minghai 明海 (b. 1968), it has become a robust training and practice center. A physical symbol of its vitality is a magnificent Hall of 10,000 Buddhas. Its reputation has garnered it the respect of both Buddhists and the state and popularity among pilgrims and tourists. Locals seeking to capitalize on the temple's thousands of daily visitors have begun to sell incense and offer guide services; their entrepreneurship was tolerated until it turned violent. One day in February 2009, two visitors who complained to one of these vendors about the poor quality of their incense were assaulted by the vendor. Security guards were also assaulted when they tried to prevent hawkers from entering the temple; when the head of security responded, he, too, was attacked.[5] Minghai, the abbot, quickly posted a notice on the temple's website lamenting the disturbances, announcing the closure of the monastery to visitors, and expressing desire that local officials help regulate this problem. The monastery remained closed to the general public for two months while steps were taken to address the local residents' unruly behavior. The incense burner was moved outside the gate so that incense and incense sellers would remain outside and not disturb life inside the monastery grounds. The county government responded by creating training and licensing procedures for guides.

In the same year, another famous Buddhist monastery, Famen Monastery, outside of Xi'an, also closed its doors to the public. In this case the problem was with a state-sponsored plan to develop the Famen area into a tourist zone known as the Famen Temple Cultural Scenic Area (Famensi Wenhua Jingqu 法门寺文化景区). The plan involved construction of a vast concrete plaza and a space-age stupa, along with a shopping and dining street that connects the monastery to this new stupa, museum, and plaza. In March 2009, the developers began to build a wall to encircle the monastery. The monks had had enough; they immediately set about tearing down the wall. Images of this act of monk resistance were quickly uploaded to the web. The monks also posted an announcement on the temple's website declaring that the monastery would remain closed until grievances had been addressed. The monastery reopened the next morning; the immediate issue of the wall had been settled, as the developer withdrew plans for the wall. As in the case of Bailin Temple, the monks had asserted themselves and won concessions.

A third instance of monastic protest had occurred several years earlier in Southeast China at Quanzhou Kaiyuan Monastery in Fujian. From 2001 to 2002 a series of confrontations between monks and the Temple Administrative Commission ultimately led to a violent exchange led by the monks against the commission. Disputes between the abbot, Daoyuan 道元 (b. 1935), and members of the commission had been growing at least since the winter of 2001, when the abbot had monks attack the vice-director of the commission after an argument regarding New Year's decorations. By August of that year, the monks' relations with the front-gate security crew had reached a critical point. One of the security guards had parked his car in the Hall of Heavenly Kings (Tianwang Dian 天王殿) and refused to move it when the abbot asked him to do so. The abbot called together a group of more than ten monks, who threatened to damage the car if it was not promptly removed. It was then that the monks and their abbot vowed to have the Temple Administrative Commission and its employees removed from the temple within two years.

The next winter witnessed the culmination of tension between the monks and the administrative commission. One morning Daoyuan returned to his monastery after attending a meeting of the municipal people's congress. Upon arriving at the main gate of his monastery, Daoyuan, a man of diminutive stature then in his sixties, met a security guard with whom he had had disagreements in the past, and another argument broke out between them. The abbot repaired to the monks' living quarters and summoned the monks to attack the security guard. Some twenty or more monks, armed with sharp and blunt objects, did just that. Two of the unfortunate guard's coworkers came to his aid and were also assaulted. The monks then advanced to the office of the administrative commission, which employed the security guards, and proceeded to trash it. No one was seriously wounded in the fray, but the security guard was hospitalized for treatment and released. This event, witnessed by picture-taking tourists and devotees alike, was a manifestation of tensions between the clerics and the employees of the Temple Administration Commission that had been brewing for months.

Most recently the Panlong Temple (Panlong Si 盘龙寺) in Kunming closed its doors to the public on the morning of August 15, 2014, in protest against what it perceived as being prodded into "commercialization and corporatization" (*shangyehua he gongsihua* 商业化和公司化) by local government bureaus. It posted notices announcing this throughout the temple grounds. The acting mayor, He Qiyun 何其云, moved quickly to defuse the situation by asserting that it was simply a misunderstanding, and the abbot, Nengshou 能寿, reopened the doors before noon. The "misunderstanding" was between the monastics and the Temple Administrative Commission, which had begun to discuss plans for the updating of the antiquated Wanghai Building 望海楼, an important building at Panlong Temple (Tang 2014). They wanted to update the site to be more pleasing to tourists and promote it as a cultural attraction. These gestures angered the monks as an infringement on their autonomy and an attempt to "commercialize" their temple. When they protested, the acting mayor was able to intervene and defuse the situation. As in the case with Famen's protesting the building of a wall, and Bailin's protesting renegade incense sellers, this seems to be another win for the sangha against curatorial agents.

Conflict between temple clergy and curatorial forces represented by various bureaus and their employees is so widespread that SARA, together with the Ministry of Housing and Urban-Rural Development (Zhufang He Chengxiang Jianshe Bu 住房和城乡建设部), convened a special training seminar to educate clergy, staff, and leaders of departments and commissions in the management of sites and to cultivate cooperation between the parties I have dubbed curators and revivalists. Held in Beijing at the State Bureau of Religious Affairs Training Center in May 2014, it was attended by more than 160 religious and administrative leaders associated with Buddhist and Taoist sites all over China. The title of the meeting was the Conference on the Management of Buddhist Monasteries and Taoist Temples in National Scenic and Historic Areas (Quanguo Fengjing Mingsheng Qu Nei Fojiao, Daojiao Siguan Guanli Gongzuo Yantaoban 全国风景名胜区内佛教, 道教寺观管理工作研讨班) and the principal objective, according to Deputy Secretary of Religious Affairs Chen Zongrong 陈宗荣, was to promote harmonious relations and establish a foundation for mutual benefit and cooperation *between the two parties* (Huiyan 2014). The two parties are those managing famous scenic sites and the clergy in charge of sites of religious activity inside those scenic areas, corresponding to my fieldwork-based scheme of revivalists and curators.

What the four events and this training seminar indicate is the struggle faced by clergy reviving sites of practice in their inevitable confrontations with nonmonastic parties that are associated with their sites and pursuing their own agendas. In the case of the Bailin Temple, the nonmonastics were entrepreneurial incense vendors and tour guides; at the Famen Temple, the entity was a development agency; and at the Quanzhou Kaiyuan and Panlong Temples the nonmonastic party was their respective Temple Administrative Commissions. In all cases, the monks protested various kinds of incursions on monastic space, and in all cases, they won the concessions sought with state support, whether explicit or implicit. I want to emphasize a word I have used to characterize relations between revivalists and curators, namely, *inevitable.* This inevitability is the result of policy expressed in the training meeting as a need for cooperation between the *two parties* and in other discussions as a "two-track management model" (*shuanggui guanli moshi* 双轨管理模式). The "two tracks" are management by the government agencies and management by members of the religious order. Monks do not have a choice of not working with nonmonastic and governmental entities; it is part of the institutional structure (see chapter 2 by Claire Vidal in this volume). But as these events show, monks can and do say no, and as the economic power of the clergy grows, so does their ability to assert themselves. Huang Weishan's study of Jing'an Temple 静安寺 in chapter 9 in this volume suggests the struggles faced by sites that are not as wealthy as the temples in the four examples given here.[6] Buddhist temples in the post-Mao era enjoy a good deal of autonomy, but there are external, nonmonastic entities, which I have characterized as curators, that must be dealt with.

TOURIST TEMPLES AND PLACES OF PRACTICE

While it is true that curators, strictly speaking, support the cause of tourism over that of religious revival, one should recall that Buddhist monasteries have long hosted those in pursuit of leisure, culture, beauty, and history as well as those in search of religion. I suspect that the sentiment expressed in the popular saying used to describe travel in China—"tour temples during the day and sleep at night" (which rhymes in Mandarin: *baitian kanmiao, wanshang shuijiao* 白天看庙, 晚上睡觉)—is not one of modern invention. Monasteries are often located in mountains, often in places enjoying fine vistas.[7] In addition, temples and monasteries have long been some of the premier repositories of art in China. The combination of natural and human-wrought beauty along with the tranquil atmosphere that allows visitors to temporarily leave the noise and dust of the world has long made Buddhist monasteries in China and elsewhere a natural site for visitors, both those bearing incense (*xiangke* 香客) and tourists (*youke* 游客).

While the connection between what we may term tourism and temples can be traced back at least as far as the Tang dynasty, the notion that temples and monasteries may play a key role in planned economic development is an idea that has come to prominence only within the past thirty years under such mottoes as "culture sets the stage and the economy performs" (*wenhua datai, jingji changxi* 文化搭台, 经济唱戏; see Ji 2004). China's reform-era obsession with economic development wedded to the notion that culture sets the stage for such development has been a boon, in some sense, to monasteries with or without cultural artifacts; it has been the principal strategy used to secure the support of local officials for restoration projects.[8] The cultural turn that supports the restoration of Buddhism is also explored in chapters 2 and 9 by Vidal and Huang, respectively, in this volume. Party officials and monks alike regularly talk about the economic benefits that accrue to a community that restores a temple. When I have asked officials from Hebei and Fujian how temples benefit the economy, the answer is always tourism. The phrase used by an official in Quanzhou's Bureau of Cultural Heritage to describe temples such as Kaiyuan is colorful, yet forbidding: He described such sites as "smokeless factories" (*wuyan gongchang* 无烟工厂).[9] He was expressing a view repeated by government employees all over China that restoring places of historic or cultural interest is an integral part of economic development (*jingji fazhan* 经济发展) and that restored temples promote economic development (*cujin jingji fazhan* 促进经济发展). The connection between economic development, cultural preservation, and cultural revival, on the one hand, and the central place of religion in Chinese culture, on the other, has generated a great deal of cooperation between curators and revivalists in the restoration of temples in China since the 1980s (Flower and Leonard 1998; Flower 2004; Eng and Lin 2002, 1271–1273; Ashiwa and Wank 2006; Fisher 2008, 152; Ji 2011a).[10] Given the common ground between curators and revivalists, most of China's larger or more famous temples fall somewhere between the extremes of tourist temples and austere sites of devotion. Before examining Quanzhou Kaiyuan as an example of a temple that accommodates both tourism and monastic practice,

I first review examples of sites focused on tourism and those more dedicated to religious practice.

A spectrum of configurations can be found at Buddhist temples in mainland China, ranging from temples that are inhabited by no monastics and are managed by the local bureau of tourism or bureau of cultural heritage, such as Beijing's White Stupa Temple or Yangzhou's Tianning Temple, to temples that host more than a hundred monks and enjoy a high degree of autonomy, such as Mount Taimu's Pingxing Monastery in Fujian, which has no historic or cultural relics. Pingxing Monastery, associated with Vinaya practice, is among the monasteries respected by the clergy as places dedicated to Buddhist cultivation. When I began my fieldwork at Quanzhou Kaiyuan in 2005, one of the monks felt I was wasting time studying Kaiyuan and recommended I go to Pingxing Monastery in order to research a place dedicated to practice. I replied that I was interested in researching an average site, rather than an exemplary one. Also in Fujian is Putian's Guanghua Temple (Putian Guanghua Si) 莆田广化寺, a large temple with more than two hundred monks and home of the Fujian Buddhist Academy (Fujian Foxueyuan 福建佛学院); this temple neither encourages nor receives many tourists. When I visited in 2006 there were no tourists and I was prevented from entering a hall where sutra recitation was taking place. A third Fujian monastery of note is Xiamen's Nanputuo Temple (Nanputuo Si 南普陀寺). Although a popular tourist attraction, it abolished the sale and use of entry tickets on March 22, 2011, and is home to an important Buddhist seminary, the Minnan Institute for Buddhist Studies (Minnan Foxueyuan 闽南佛学院), an influential training ground of the monastic leadership.

Monasteries that have distinguished themselves in contemporary China as places dedicated to religious cultivation include Jiangsu's Gaomin Monastery. Highly respected during the Qing and Republican periods, the Gaomin Monastery revived its Chan Hall in 1989 and is a place of regular meditation and sutra recitation. When I visited the Gaomin Monastery with a group of students and scholars led by Venerable Yifa 依法 in 2009, the abbot at first refused us entry to the meditation hall since they were in the middle of a retreat. He eventually relented and led us to the hall after the monks had emptied out; austere decorum was observed in the hall. Other sites known as places of revived Chan training are Guangdong's Nanhua Monastery (Nanhua Si 南华寺) and Jiangxi's Yunjushan Zhenru Temple (Yunjushan Zhenru Si 云居山真如寺). In all cases, the efforts of members of the clergy have been key in guiding the restoration of clerical training and practice. These efforts represent the revivalists at their most successful.

In addition to these large sites, there are countless small temples that often house two or three monastics. These small temples serve as revived sites of Buddhist tradition where lay Buddhists may offer incense and make petitions to buddhas and bodhisattvas. I have visited more than a dozen of these sites in urban and rural settings, and although these temples are distinctly quiet, their residents are typically busy with the upkeep of their temples and the raising of funds, which leaves them with little time for religious cultivation. While they may not be models of religious cultivation, they are, nevertheless, temples that have been revived by and for the sangha and may therefore be considered places of practice in the most general sense of reviving traditional Buddhist ritual activities.

WHEN CURATORIAL FORCES GAIN THE UPPER HAND: "MUSEUMIFICATION"

While large famous temples of exceptional historic or cultural value have had an easier time with physical restoration and financial support for the sangha, their position as places of historic and cultural value typically ensures that they will attract tourists. Tourists may bring in income, but they destroy the tranquility that is most appropriate for regular, sustained religious practice. Beyond the influence of megaphone-bearing tour guides and their minions is the danger of "museumification." Museumification is the process by which a temple becomes directed toward display, spectacle, and secular education while, by degrees, being directed *away from* worship and religious cultivation.[11] Museumification is in evidence when shrine halls have been transformed from places of worship into display rooms for cultural and historic exhibits or souvenir shops. Such places are staffed, not by monks, but by workers, often young ladies in matching uniforms, who introduce visitors to products for sale.

Museumification is at its most vulgar when a temple falls under the management of a government bureau such as the bureaus of tourism or cultural heritage to the exclusion of monastic leadership. My experience suggests that this phenomenon is more prevalent the closer one is to Beijing, the political center, and perhaps provincial capitals (which serve as satellites of Beijing). Near Nanjing in the city of Yangzhou is an extreme version of a museumified site, namely, Yangzhou's Tianning Temple, otherwise known as the Yangzhou Buddhist Culture Museum (Yangzhou Fojiao Wenhua Bowuguan 扬州佛教文化博物馆).[12] Construction and restoration began in 2007, and when I visited in 2009, the first stage of the museum had been completed. The halls of the temple were filled with interpretive displays introducing aspects of Buddhism, such as an outline of Chinese Buddhist history, the various schools of Chinese Buddhism, Buddhist sites in India, and examples of Buddhist sculpture and architecture. Signage was posted in four languages guiding visitors to exhibits inside the halls. A highlight of the museum was a three-dimensional holographic talking Buddha head dispensing wisdom to visitors. There were no monastics or devotional activity anywhere to be seen, except as historical illustrations. This site serves as the model of a historical temple that has been fully museumified. More common are temples having museum characteristics shared with religious or devotional elements. Many such temples may be found in or near

Beijing; I have already mentioned the White Stupa Temple. In addition there are Hongluo Temple and Yunju Temple (Yunju Si 云居寺), both lying on the outskirts of Beijing, and Longxing Temple (Longxing Si 隆兴寺) in Hebei Province, just south of Beijing.[13]

Hongluo Temple is part temple, part park, in the mountains near the Mutianyu 慕田峪 section of the Great Wall. It has no resident monks and is directly managed by the local bureau of tourism and staffed by a team of young ladies in white shirts. Although it is more than one thousand years old,[14] the temple possesses no cultural relics and is almost entirely reconstructed. The tourism bureau, having no cultural properties to promote, has turned instead to the piety/leisure market. Buddhist hymns are played over loudspeakers throughout the temple, incense and other religious paraphernalia are sold throughout the grounds, and a steady stream of worshippers offer incense to statues of buddhas, bodhisattvas, and patriarchs as they tour the extensive grounds that rise to hilltops that afford panoramic views of the surrounding mountains and the smog of Beijing. At the time of my visit, no monastics lived at the temple, but there were monks, or rather employees with shaved heads dressed in robes, who reported to work in the morning, tended some of the halls, and returned home at five.

Beijing's Yunju Temple, which boasts the world's largest collection of stone-inscribed scriptures, is managed by a Temple Administrative Commission, that is, not by the sangha. In addition to the more than ten thousand stone sutras, it has Tang dynasty stupas and an attractive natural setting.[15] Most of the halls of this monastery have been converted into museum-like display halls presenting interpretive exhibits of cultural relics found at the temple such as ceramics and sutras written in blood. Employees in light-blue knit shirts tend the halls and sell items throughout the grounds; the products they sell are primarily religious in nature. When I entered the main hall a young lady who was a member of the staff accosted me, quickly introduced the figures enshrined, and immediately suggested I purchase what appeared to be a small plastic temple credit card. She explained that the cards entitled the bearer to the benefits of monks chanting in the hall for a full year. They were available in three grades, 50, 100, and 200 RMB; the 100 RMB (US$14) card would include a banner in the hall and a ritual service, while the 200 RMB card would include a scroll of calligraphy, an alms bowl in a tote bag, and two services. The cards and the benefits of each were also explained on large posters that were placed in multiple shrine rooms. At the bottom of these posters was written the name of the entity in charge: the Yunju Monastery Temple Administrative Commission (Yunju Si Simiao Guanli Weiyuanhui 云居寺寺庙管理委员会). This is commodification on top of museumification, two related but different processes.[16] The Yunju Temple, however, unlike the Hongluo Temple, did have a community of eleven monks. I spoke with one of them who had been there for three months and he simply reported that Yunju was not a Buddhist temple;

it was a tourist site. I asked what he meant. Expressing a common sentiment among members of the sangha, he said there weren't enough monks living there; a Buddhist temple, in other words, must be tended by the sangha—at this temple, management was in the hands of the Temple Administrative Commission. When the restoration of the Yunju Temple's South Pagoda was completed in September 2014, the China News Service reported that the project was overseen by the Temple Administrative Commission and approved by both the State Administration of Cultural Heritage (Guojia Wenwu Ju 国家文物局) and the State Council (Guowu Yuan 国务院). The completion was marked by a "pagoda construction completion viewing ceremony" (*nanta luocheng guanzhan yishi* 南塔落成观瞻仪式; Wang 2014). There was no mention of monastics or consecration of the pagoda or of any religious significance of the pagoda. Its completion was marked by the administrative commission and the state with a viewing ceremony; there was no Dharma ceremony (*fahui* 法会) or ritual organized by monastics. It is a site administered by curators, and the ceremonies marking the completion of a newly constructed pagoda were a cultural affair, not a religious one (see also Huang's discussion of the display of the Buddha relic at Shanghai's Jing'an Temple in chapter 9 in this volume).

Hebei's Longxing Temple, also known as Big Buddha Temple (Dafo Si 大佛寺), is about a three-hour drive from Beijing in the city of Zhengding 正定. Longxing is an urban temple that functions primarily as a museum, showcasing a fabulous collection of cultural properties from the tenth century onward, including paintings, statues, buildings, and the inevitable oversized Qianlong and Kangxi steles. The abbot of the nearby Linji Temple (Linji Si 临济寺) informed me that the sangha was working to reestablish itself there. What is likely to happen, however, is something analogous to the situation at Xi'an's Famen Temple, which is divided into two halves, one controlled by the Bureau of Tourism, the other by the monks.

These three temples near Beijing, while they all have their own characteristics, present one end of the spectrum of Buddhism in China today and one that would have dominated impressions of visitors throughout most of the Communist period, when only a handful of showcase monasteries were preserved to show foreign visitors. The impression of Buddhism as barely alive and in the hands of curators is one that we understandably held for decades of the People's Republic of China; the reality in China, however, has been changing since reforms were inaugurated at the end of 1978. But change has come at different paces to different parts of China. I have made the observation that the closer one is to Beijing (and other centers of political power such as provincial capitals), the more likely one is to find temples that are in the hands of secular authorities and deserve the moniker "tourist temple." One also finds monasteries free of such museumification, and still others, represented by the examples of Famen and Quanzhou Kaiyuan monasteries, struggling against curatorial forces and secular incursions.

CASE STUDY: KAIYUAN TEMPLE'S QUEST FOR GREATER AUTONOMY

The Quanzhou Kaiyuan Temple, which is far from Beijing, not in a provincial capital, and in Fujian, a province known for widespread religious participation, presents a different model of how a famous temple full of cultural treasures negotiates with the secular powers that be. While I know of no instance in which a historically important temple in possession of valuable cultural properties has fully escaped the attention of curatorial forces and tourists, the Kaiyuan Temple provides an example of how such a monastery may negotiate a degree of autonomy from such curatorial interest. Pressures from secular curatorial forces may be considered systemic for sites of historic and cultural value. Resistance to these pressures requires leadership from the revivalists. Similarly, behind efforts to establish traditions of training and education, we likewise find leadership. Adam Chau points out the importance of such local leaders in early revival efforts (Chau 2011a), as does Vidal in her study of Putuoshan in chapter 2 in this volume. In this chapter I have already alluded to the examples of the abbots of Bailin (Jinghui and Minghai). To these we might add Miaozhan 妙湛 (1910–1995), former abbot of Xiamen's Nanputuo Temple, and Delin 德林 (1914–2015), the abbot of the Gaomin Monastery in Jiangsu. While the Quanzhou Kaiyuan Temple's abbot has done little to revive a tradition of education or meditation, he has provided strong leadership in battling curatorial forces for greater autonomy and providing a space for devotional practice in the midst of a popular tourist site. His efforts are thus comparable to those examined by Huang in her study of Huiming in chapter 9 in this volume. In the absence of strong monastic leadership it is likely that curatorial forces would enjoy much greater influence at the Kaiyuan Temple than they do today. In addition, the sociopolitical conditions manifested by officials having jurisdiction over a site can help or hinder efforts to revive a religious site. Huang's chapter 9 discusses the challenges faced by Shanghai's Jing'an Temple to engage in explicitly religious activities and the pressures to reframe activities as cultural. The situation at the Quanzhou Kaiyuan Temple has not been as restricted.

Although the Kaiyuan Temple's recovery began soon after the death of Mao in 1976, throughout the 1980s the halls remained under the jurisdiction of the Cultural Heritage Management Committee and the Temple Administrative Commission. The heritage committee had been established in the 1950s to protect and maintain the temple properties; it went underground during the Cultural Revolution and reemerged after the death of Mao, asserting its jurisdiction over the Kaiyuan Temple's cultural properties. Tables staffed by employees of the heritage committee were set up in all the halls containing historic properties. The heritage committee also operated a research center and in 1982 opened a souvenir and stele rubbings shop located in one of the shrine halls, precisely the kind of shop that may detract from the religious atmosphere sought by some pilgrims.[17] This shop was a visible and prominent contributor to museumification and commodification at the Kaiyuan Temple; it was a classic case of a former shrine hall being converted to commercial uses and managed by nonmonastics, members of the curatorial forces. When I visited Shanghai's Jing'an Temple in 2009, there was a shop selling religious items set up in the front gate/Hall of Heavenly Kings, run by three women. The hall had been rearranged such that it was impossible to enter through the front and prostrate to the Dharma protectors; free movement was blocked by cabinets displaying items for sale. The hall had been transformed from a formal entrance into a hall selling religious items. Similarly, at the Kaiyuan Temple, this hall had lost its function as a shrine and was made to function as a souvenir shop rather than a place of commemoration and devotion.

The Cultural Heritage Management Committee, however, was not the only government entity with jurisdiction over the Kaiyuan Temple. As a tourist attraction and the home of dozens of monastics holding morning and evening devotions, the Kaiyuan Temple was seen to be fit, in the eyes of the government and SARA, to host a Temple Administrative Commission. The Temple Administrative Commission is a product of 1980s reform and opening policy, which loosened restrictions against religion and, at the same time, established means of oversight and control of the legally recognized religious groups. At the Kaiyuan Temple, the Temple Administrative Commission operates entry and exit gates, sees that the grounds are secure, and offers tour guide services; it is self-funded through the sale of entrance tickets and tour services. Members of this commission also operate two small kiosks. One of them sells photo supplies and drinks; in 2008 it began selling small souvenirs of Quanzhou and incense. The incense sold by this vendor is the same as the incense available to visitors for free in the main hall some thirty feet away. This demonstrates the different loyalties held by the nonmonastic commission and the monks. The curators seek to capitalize on visitors, while the revivalists at this site seek to facilitate worship by offering free incense and candles. The other kiosk is staffed by a man who writes poems using the characters of one's name—a common form of art found at tourist sites.

The combined effect of the administrative commission employees and the heritage committee's presence was to give the Kaiyuan Temple the touristic orientation that one finds at temples previously described as catering to tourists. Nonmonastic employees working as curators rather than religionists sold tickets, monitored the gates, the grounds, and the halls, and sold souvenir items, which generally had nothing to do with religion, inside one of the shrine halls. While a similar situation prevails today at the temples mentioned earlier (Yunju, Hongluo, and Longxing Temples) as well as many other temples, such as Beijing's famous Tanzhe Temple (Tanzhe Si 潭柘寺) and Jietai Temple (Jietai Si 戒台寺) or Shanghai's Jade Buddha Temple, the situation at the Kaiyuan Temple began to change in the late 1990s.

THE CULTURAL HERITAGE COMMITTEE AND THE TEMPLE ADMINISTRATIVE COMMISSION

The situation was able to progress under the leadership of the abbot Daoyuan, who was successful in removing dozens of individuals employed by as many as a dozen different entities occupying monastic space. Among the entities removed and relocated were a landscape and gardening office, private homes, a bank, and a puppeteers troupe. In 2004 Daoyuan was able to deal with the Cultural Heritage Management Committee in much the same way that he dealt with the other groups occupying space on temple property: He successfully argued to municipal authorities that the property belonged to the monastery and was therefore illegally occupied, and he offered sufficient financial compensation to the affected parties. Daoyuan negotiated that the Kaiyuan Temple would pay 70,000 RMB (about US$10,000), while the Bureau of Finance would pay 36,020 RMB.[18]

After more than twenty years of operating a souvenir shop in the Donor's Ancestral Hall (Tanyue Ci 檀越祠), the Cultural Heritage Management Committee shut down the shop and vacated the hall. The three small rooms and courtyard of this hall were cleaned up and returned to their state as an ancestral shrine to Huang Shougong 黄守恭, the temple's founding donor. In this way, the hall that had been used as a souvenir shop was restored to monastic control and now functions solely as a shrine. I was present when it was officially reopened in exceptionally grand style in September 2009. The three-day memorial celebration marked the 1,380th anniversary of Huang Shougong's birth and the 1,323rd anniversary of the founding of the Quanzhou Kaiyuan Monastery; it was attended by thousands of members of the Huang family from locations stretching from Shanghai to Singapore.[19]

In addition to the return of this shrine hall, the other divisions of the heritage committee, such as the research center, have been removed from the Kaiyuan Temple's property and placed in a newly formed Bureau of Cultural Heritage located in an office several miles from the Kaiyuan Temple. The transfer from curator to revivalist in the case of the heritage committee and their shrine hall souvenir shop has been complete—a true victory for the revivalists.

The situation with the post-Mao entity known as the Temple Administrative Commission, however, has not been so easily resolved. An ad hoc decision or buyout has not been possible because, unlike all the others, the commission is part of reform-era national policy as interpreted by SARA. Large, important temples designated as National Tourist Attractions or Important National Cultural Heritage Protected Sites typically have a Temple Administrative Commission on site charged with monitoring activities to make sure that the temple acts in accordance with the law. This system of oversight is a nationally recognized system of religious management sometimes referred to as a two-track management model.[20]

After the strong-arm tactics of 2002, the abbot has managed to win con-cessions and clearly gain the upper hand, though unable, nonetheless, to fully dislodge the administrative commission. A concession won by Daoyuan is that security guards are no longer stationed in the gates and no one is allowed to park in front of the main gate, including tour buses.[21] In addition, administra-tive commission employees have been effectively removed from all the temple buildings except for the ticket booths in the gates and two small offices; monks are now responsible for monitoring all of the halls. The monks have also begun to take on the task of watching the gates, especially in the evening, but the se-curity guards working for the administrative commission keep an eye on secur-ity camera monitors in one of their two offices. From the late 1990s to the present, the number of employees of the administrative commission has been reduced by half, from sixty to thirty. The temple has also been able to negotiate to receive 50 percent of the sales from entrance tickets, whereas previously they had received none of this money.[22] According to my informants, this brings in 4 million RMB to the temple per year. The abbot has said, however, that he would not sell tickets if he were able to abolish the administrative commission.[23] The abbot has effectively been able to force the commission to recognize him as their boss and has won back a significant level of autonomy on behalf of the sangha at this monastery. As a result, the Kaiyuan Temple is a monastery that attracts tourists, rather than a tourist site where a few monks live.

This last point is quite important because we may be inclined to place all temples that serve as tourist attractions together in the same category, a cat-egory that tends to devalue such places as "tourist temples." The reality is more nuanced. In this chapter we have surveyed a sample of the many temples in China that serve as tourist attractions, each with its own characteristics—at one extreme is the temple that has converted into a museum, like Yangzhou's Tianning Temple; at the other is the Pingxing Monastery, which has prac-tically no tourists and is dedicated to religious cultivation. Falling between these extremes is a spectrum along which many temples fall, exhibiting char-acteristics of both monastic and nonmonastic management. The three temples surveyed near Beijing are all managed by curators who have succeeded in pre-senting them more as museums than as living religious institutions. Quanzhou Kaiyuan offers a contrast to the museumified temples discussed earlier; the key difference is that it is managed not by agents of the state or curators, but rather by revivalists, by its monastic leadership, who have invested the Kaiyuan Temple with a distinctly religious atmosphere. This atmosphere includes regu-lar construction and burning of paper houses and gold paper (*jinzhi* 金纸) as offerings to the dead in a recently enlarged furnace. It also includes the evoca-tive pseudo-theatrical performance of the Release of Burning Mouths ritual (*fang yankou* 放焰口) on designated evenings throughout the year after the monastery has been closed to benefit hungry ghosts and earn merit to transfer to lay sponsors. Compare this with a site like Jing'an Temple, which Huang points out in chapter 9 was unable to display a visiting relic in a devotional manner but had to display it as a museum item. The Kaiyuan Temple has been able to establish a stronger religious identity under the leadership of its abbot.

The administrative commission at the Kaiyuan Temple is limited to staffing entrance and exit gates, selling tickets, staffing a small office, running a small tour office, and manning two small kiosks, all on temple property. In these activities—the selling and collecting of entry tickets, the offering of tour guide services from the grounds of the Kaiyuan Temple, and the operation of tourist-oriented kiosks—the Temple Administrative Commission is responsible for institutionalizing tourism as a feature of the Kaiyuan Temple. Without their presence, there would be thousands of tourists, but the temple clerics would not cater to the tourists in the same way that the nonmonastic administrative commission does. As previously stated, monks do not sell incense, but temple commission vendors do. In addition, commission employees charge for tours, whereas monks offer tours as needed for devotees without charge. One day, as I was visiting with the kiosk vendor, he helped a friend who came up catch one of the doves that had recently been freed in a life rescue ceremony. The monks at the back of the temple fed the doves, and these doves stayed at the temple for several months. This friend wanted to catch and eat the bird, but a monk saw what was going on and stopped them. This episode, along with the selling of incense and tour guide services, illustrates the difference between employees of the administrative commission and the monastics with respect to their contributions to the identity of the site. In all cases the monastics promote the religious and devotional goals of the temple while employees of the administrative commission seek to profit from the site, going so far as to cheat visitors, if mildly. The administrative commission is, nonetheless, interested in the survival and flourishing of the site as a place of tourism, in order to generate more income.

The two-track management system at the Kaiyuan Temple—management by the monastics and limited management by the Temple Administrative Commission—thus creates formal conditions for the dual institution that the Kaiyuan Temple is today: Buddhist monastery and tourist site. Eliminating problems associated with tourism does not seem to be a realistic option for famous tourist attractions like the Quanzhou Kaiyuan Temple, the Famen Temple, and many other sites. Realistically, it comes down to a question of mitigating harmful influences.

The Kaiyuan Temple has taken an active role in fashioning its identity in a way that promotes tourism, but not in the same manner that one finds at temples managed by secular authorities. The Kaiyuan Temple has successfully mitigated the problems associated with tourism by maintaining physical boundaries and limiting or eliminating the presence of vendors and tertiary industries. In addition, the Kaiyuan Temple maintains a religious identity by housing and feeding monks, holding daily services, conducting twice-weekly and monthly Buddha recitation sessions, and offering ritual services. A group of about three hundred laypersons attend twice-weekly *nianfo* services dressed in dark lay robes. Those who work the gates recognize these individuals or check their Buddhist conversion certificates (*guiyi zheng* 皈依证) and in either case allow them free entry. On the monthly Buddha recitation day, noodles are prepared the night before and served free of charge to devotees. The temple is open free to the public on this day, which brings in around two thousand devotees who collectively chant the Buddha's name and circumambulate the temple courtyard. This tradition, followed by most Buddhist temples in southern Fujian, is an important source of income for temples, as visitors tend to donate to the temples on these days.

PROBLEMS AND METHODS OF MITIGATION

Scholars studying the revival of folk (*minjian* 民间) and Taoist temples in China have noted behavior and strategies analogous to those found in business enterprises.[24] Adam Chau (2006, 122) writes that his field site, a Taoist temple in Shaanxi Province, may be considered "a petty capitalist enterprise" concerned with provisioning magical efficacy "increasingly in a manner resembling convenience stores and one-stop shopping malls."[25] Graeme Lang, Selina Chan, and Lars Ragvald (2005) have studied a group of popular Taoist temples built by entrepreneurs in Guangdong and Zhejiang and marketed according to business

Circumambulating the Main Courtyard at Quanzhou Kaiyuan Monastery on the monthly Buddha Recitation Day, 2009.

models.[26] These temples also hired Taoist priests and priestesses to work for them (Lang, Chan, and Ragvald 2005, 164). While the Kaiyuan Temple does promote itself as a tourist site as well as a spiritually responsive site, it has distinctly not engaged in the kind of market-based diversification seen at the folk or the Taoist temples mentioned earlier.

At some temples, monks or Taoist priests are hired to essentially serve as performers in the religious drama being marketed (Lang, Chan, and Ragvald 2005; Kang 2009). In some cases, monks take on such performative roles themselves in catering to tourists (Borchert 2005, 87–88). As monastics at a tourist site, the Kaiyuan Temple's monks are occasionally the object of the tourist gaze and they may be photographed, but they are not radically objectified like animals in a zoo or ethnic minorities in a cultural show. In particular, the morning and evening services are held, respectively, before tourists arrive and after most of them leave. The ceremonies are conducted near the back of the central axis in a nondescript hall with no valuable cultural properties. In other words, they are not intended as a spectacle for tourist consumption. Furthermore, a monk patrols and shoos away individuals who approach the main hall while the twice-weekly Buddha recitation service is occurring. In addition, photography is prohibited inside the halls. In short, neither the devotees nor their ceremonies are spectacles for the tourist gaze.

The monks' living quarters are located along the outer edges of the monastery, far from the route taken by tour groups. Individuals who wander into these areas are asked to turn back. The monks and their religious life, in other words, have not been commodified. The Kaiyuan Temple as a site of historic buildings and cultural treasures has been commodified—one gains access to it by purchasing a ticket. This form of commodification has been neither initiated nor managed by monks; it has been the work of the Temple Administrative Commission. The Kaiyuan Temple as a religious service provider may be seen to be involved in the commodification of religious goods (merits and blessings) and services (postmortem rituals and the like), but this is unrelated to tourism proper and is Chinese Buddhism's answer to the loss of landed wealth.[27]

Although tourism and administrative duties distract many of the Kaiyuan Temple's monks from religious cultivation, not all of the Kaiyuan Temple's eighty or so monks are burdened with such responsibilities. This monastery's sufficiently large number of monastics has enabled a core of twenty to thirty monks to remain free of duties that require dealing with the public. These monks are the backbone of communal monastic practice at the Kaiyuan Temple, which takes the form of daily morning and evening services, the defining communal practice at the Kaiyuan Temple and other monasteries. These monks are provided the opportunity to pursue religious cultivation somewhat like the elite monks in traditional training monasteries.[28] The difference is that they are not valorized; they are simply the monks without positions. Furthermore, what is missing is an educational system or meditation training system, but the option to develop such systems remains a possibility. The solution suggested by tradition is one of division of labor: Some monks sacrifice themselves by taking on more worldly responsibilities in order to enable others to dedicate themselves to devotional practice.

There remains a final consideration that escapes the notice of the average visitor: The noise and bustle of tour groups and visitors end every evening after five. Visitors and ticket sellers alike leave, and quiet reigns over the grounds until daybreak. The kind of atmosphere one expects of a monastery finally arrives, and it arrives every day. Self-motivated monks can practice after the evening meal, though no instruction or group opportunities are available. At the Kaiyuan Temple I met monks who took the time to engage in a number of different contemplative activities, including walking meditation around the grounds, calligraphy, playing the Chinese zither (*guqin* 古琴), and chanting sutras in their rooms.

On the one hand, the Kaiyuan Temple is a functioning Buddhist monastery housing more than eighty full-time monks and hosting hundreds of laypersons every day. On the other, it is a tourist attraction that appears at the top of every tourist's itinerary in Quanzhou and hosts dozens of groups that tour the grounds on a daily basis. As a site of valuable historic and cultural properties, the Kaiyuan Temple has had little choice but to accommodate tourists, but there are many directions such accommodations may have taken. One model gives freer rein to nonmonastic entities to sell souvenirs, post signboards and maps, and otherwise regulate the experience of visitors. The model negotiated by the Kaiyuan Temple's monks under the leadership of their abbot (the revivalists) has limited the role of the nonmonastics associated with the Temple Administrative Commission and cultural bureaus (the curators)—it has fought for greater autonomy. Daoyuan has succeeded in restricting the curatorial forces that cater to tourists to a handful of small spaces on the monastic grounds. By limiting the visibility of the nonmonastic forces catering to tourists and supporting a regular ritual calendar including twice-weekly and monthly recitation services, the abbot has succeeded in building an atmosphere of religious practice in the midst of a famous tourist attraction.

PROBLEMS ASSOCIATED WITH TOURISM AND THE QUESTION OF AUTHENTICITY

By way of conclusion I wish to explore some of the problems commonly associated with tourism and the question of authentic religious identity. Large-scale tourism at temples and monasteries generates disturbances for both monastic residents and lay visitors. Large tour groups (especially those led by megaphone-toting guides) destroy the quiet and contemplative atmosphere conducive to meditation, study, and most other forms of devotional and ritual practices. This kind of disturbance impacts lay visitors and monastics alike.

Monastics are further distracted from contemplative and educational pursuits by taking on responsibilities associated with tourism, such as monitoring gates and halls and otherwise dealing with the general public and their mundane concerns (e.g., "Where is the bathroom?" "How old is this statue?") for most of the day. Venerable Dr. Jingyin writes, "When monasteries become principally tourist attractions, the danger is that the energy of monks becomes devoted chiefly to receiving tourists, leaving no time for the sangha or to engage in Buddhist practice" (Jingyin 2006, 91–92). In addition, a temple's being open to the general public leads to problems such as the fighting between incense sellers, their customers, and security guards at Bailin Temple. Such events are a drain on the energy that clergy can put toward self-cultivation or ministering to the laity. Monastics are also distracted from traditional pursuits by their involvement in tertiary activities such as vegetarian restaurants or tourist shops (Jingyin 2006).

A third general problem affects the experience of lay visitors and sometimes monastics, namely, being hassled in various ways at entry gates or in shrine halls. This includes being asked or required to buy an entrance ticket or being accosted by salespersons. Venerable Jingyin, for example, lamented being asked to purchase a ticket to visit Shaolin Monastery, the ancestral home of Chan, in 1993 (Jingyin 2006, 91). Laypersons may encounter this problem if (1) they do not possess their "conversion certificates" (*guiyi zheng* 皈依证), (2) the temple in question is a tourist site (*lüyou jingdian* 旅游景点) without monastics, or (3) the temple is located in a larger scenic area that requires an entry ticket. In the latter two cases visitors are typically asked to purchase a ticket whether or not they have proof of being a Buddhist.[29] In addition, at the Kaiyuan Temple there are back doors that are accessible to lay volunteers and laity who have personal relationships with monks. These back doors provide hassle- and ticket-free entrance to laity and other visitors, allowing them to bypass the alienating and commercialized experience of the ticketed turnstile entrances.

Behind questions about the influence of tourism and the commodification of sites there lurks the often-raised question of authenticity. It may manifest as a suspicion that tourism corrupts. One point I hope to have made clear is that a commodified temple catering to tourists is often not the work of a corrupt clergy, but rather the influence of extraclerical forces, government bureaus, or private businesspeople. As for those sites managed by the clerics, I hope to have shifted the question from considerations of authenticity or corruption to one of degrees of conduciveness to practice: In what ways does a space encourage spiritual cultivation? In what sense might a space hinder and distract one from practice? As seen in this and other chapters in this volume, clergy are unable to extricate themselves from the oversight of secular authorities or the exigencies of financial needs, but clergy and managers of sites can and do make spaces more or less conducive to Buddhist practice while at the same time accommodating tourists and supporting their institutions.

Buddhist sites in China over the past two decades have been restored in tandem with China's phenomenal economic growth. These sites exist along a spectrum of identities described in this chapter. Beyond the ideals of tourist temples and (dedicated) places of practice are hybrid sites in which monastic communities (revivalists) negotiate with nonmonastic entities interested in tourism and economic development (curators) to establish degrees of autonomy and degrees of orientation toward religious goals. The typology presented here provides a means of clarifying the broad contours of Buddhist temple restoration that one finds in post-Mao China so that researchers may have a more informed starting point for analyzing the challenges and opportunities faced by Buddhists in China.

NOTES

1. Several scholars have begun to examine the relationship between tourism and religion in China. See Ryan and Gu 2009; Shi Fangfang 2009; Oakes and Sutton 2010; Fisher 2011a; Wong, McIntosh, and Ryan 2012; Shepherd 2013; Nichols forthcoming.

2. Such is the impression conveyed in a recent report in the *Economist:* "Monasteries throughout China have, in effect, been turned into tourist attractions" ("Making History" 2017, 37).

3. For more on the ritual activities of Buddhist monasteries in contemporary China, see Gildow 2014.

4. The best article in English is Yang and Wei 2005. In French there are two articles by Ji Zhe (2007, 2011c).

5. Details of this event were related by Sun Yanfei (2009) in a paper written for the Annual Meeting of the American Academy of Religion in Montreal.

6. See Huang Weishan's description of the monk Huiming in chapter 9 in this volume. Huiming had to borrow money to relocate the bank and, as a result, was not able to take full control of the temple as a religious site.

7. Urban monasteries achieve a similar effect by erecting lofty pagodas, which one can climb to have a view of the city, lakes and rivers, and mountains in the distance.

8. "Culture" certainly includes Taoism and certain folk deities (e.g., Tianhou/Mazu), and they, too, benefit from the notion that cultural revival promotes economic growth. An important group of Taoist and folk temples, for example, has been restored in downtown Suzhou as part of its economic/tourist development scheme. See also Lang, Chan, and Ragvald 2005.

9. Quanzhou Bureau of Cultural Heritage official, personal communication, Wenwu ju, Quanzhou, September 28, 2009.

10. The cooperation between curators and revivalists over time, however, has turned to competition and rivalry. See Kang 2009. Thomas Borchert (2009) examined the case of the building of a tourism-oriented temple for the Dai nationality in Southwest China in a paper delivered at the National Meeting of the American Academy of Religion in Montreal.

11. Gareth Fisher and I codeveloped the term "museumification." See also Fisher 2011a.

12. The museum site also includes the Chongning Temple 重宁寺, which had not been reconstructed when I visited in 2009.

13. To these one could add the Tanzhe and Jietai Temples, each lying just outside Beijing. I visited these temples, however, before I had identified the key role of the Temple Administrative Commission and therefore did not ask the appropriate questions or make the appropriate observations to determine how they fit into the scheme I present here.

14. It was founded in the fourth century.

15. Beginning in the seventh century at this site, Buddhist scriptures were inscribed on stone and interred in caves in an effort to preserve the Dharma from destruction and loss. Lothar Ledderose has studied stone sutras in Shandong (Ledderose and Wang 2014–2015).

16. Commodification is less dependent on the presence or absence of state functionaries in management; temples can become commodified without having any cultural properties to promote. Posting a schedule of fees for ritual services is a basic form of commodification that one finds in many, if not most, temples. See chapter 2 by Claire Vidal in this volume for a discussion of commodification at Putuoshan.

17. For example, Shi Fangfang interviewed visitors to Buddhist temples on Wutaishan, interested in their experiences of the site. He found levels of dissatisfaction regarding "lack of religious ambience and the apparent commercialization" (Shi Fangfang 2009, 206). At Kaiyuan, rubbings were made of the various stone steles that had been collected at the site during the Mao era and sold to visitors. Ink rubbings on rice paper of historic steles are relatively common souvenir items where steles have been collected, such as at the Forest of Steles (Beilin 碑林) in Xi'an.

18. Interestingly, the arguments offered for the recovery of this property under monastic control were framed in terms of cultural and historic integrity rather than religious integrity. It was argued that the Donor's Ancestral Hall dedicated to Huang Shougong was an important part of the Kaiyuan Monastery's history and an important institution to many overseas Chinese who are Huang family descendants. The city of Quanzhou was then applying to UNESCO for World Heritage Site status as the starting point of the maritime silk route; the return and restoration of the Donor's Ancestral Hall was seen as contributing to Quanzhou's UNESCO application.

19. The platform before the main hall served as a kind of stage where Daoyuan and other distinguished guests made speeches in front of members of the Huang family from the Quanzhou region, Shanghai, the Philippines, Malaysia, Singapore, and so on, who were arranged by point of origin in folding chairs set up throughout the monastery's expansive courtyard. Bands played, a small parade was held, and dozens of young ladies in uniform were on hand as greeters and tea servers. The culmination, perhaps, was the grand sacrifice offered to the ancestral tablets of Huang Shougong in the Donor's Ancestral Hall. The Huang family expected to make meat sacrifices, but the monastery insisted the offering be vegetarian; a characteristically Chinese compromise was reached by having animal forms made from vegetarian materials offered.

20. David Wank and Yoshiko Ashiwa have recorded a similar conflict between the monastic leadership and the administrative commission at Xiamen's Nanputuo Temple. Unlike Kaiyuan's, Nanputuo's commission profited from an array of tourist-related business it operated near the temple entrance. Zhao Puchu (1907–2000), then president of the Buddhist Association of China, helped reduce the power of the commission by having it redesignated a business post (*shiwu suo*) rather than a commission with administrative duties (Ashiwa and Wank 2006, 41–42).

21. The effect of this change has been so dramatic that businesses outside the main gate complain that they have lost lots of money since the change. Of five restaurants that were once there, only two remain.

22. During the last conversation I had with the abbot, at the end of 2009, he suggested that the monastery now controlled the money generated from gate tickets and paid out salaries to the members of the temple management group.

23. Daoyuan, personal communication with the author, Quanzhou, 2006.

24. My use of the term "Taoist" to indicate a type of site is in line with usage by David Palmer and Liu Xun (2012, 6–8) to designate self-identified Taoist and Taoist-affiliated institutions. The term "folk" (*minjian*) is used to designate local temples dedicated to spirits or deities that do not exclusively belong to one of the five officially recognized religions (Buddhism, Taoism, Islam, Protestant Christianity, and Catholicism). See Lang, Chan, and Ragvald 2005 and Tamney 2005, 1–3.

25. In his study of a large folk temple in Shaanxi Chau writes, "Different temples quite consciously compete with one another in promoting their own deity's magical power, and in the process different ways of provisioning *ling* are invented, modified, or expanded." Temples, Chau argues, develop "business models" and aim to increase convenience to increase market share. Chau points out that the Black Dragon King Temple has increased the convenience of receiving divination by having on hand a full-time reader/interpreter (previously not available), having divination slips that one can take home (previously they were in a book, not to be removed), providing bottles for divine water, prepackaging medicine (previously it was not), and adding a shrine to the Dragon Mother to attract people with problems related to fertility or reproduction who might otherwise go to a goddess temple (Chau 2006, 120–121). Robert Hymes (2002) looks at Taoists and others as competing in a religious market, rituals being the commodities they provide; they struggle for market share. Marc Moskowitz (2001) looks at religious consumerism related to dealing with fetus ghosts in contemporary Taiwan.

26. See, in particular, Lang, Chan, and Ragvald 2005, 163–165. One of the more successful temples had been improved with "unusual animal-shaped stones from Guangxi, gardens and trees, and most recently, a stage on a plaza immediately behind the temple for cultural performances" as well as craft shops and children's activities.

27. This trend was noticed by Welch in his study of monastic Buddhism in the first half of the twentieth century (Welch 1967, 240–243).

28. See Buswell's (1992) description of life in a modern Korean Zen monastery. See also descriptions of Tibetan monasticism by Goldstein (1998) and Dreyfus (2003).

29. Fisher describes accompanying a lay Buddhist with her ID (*guiyi zheng*) to Beijing's White Stupa Temple (Baita Si 白塔寺); she expected free entry but was required to pay (Fisher 2011a).

PART II

Revival and Continuity

The Monastic Tradition and Beyond

5

BRIDGING THE GAP

Chan and Tiantai Dharma Lineages from Republican to Post-Mao China

DANIELA CAMPO

More than twenty years separate the last ordination ceremonies of the Mao era, around 1957,[1] from the resumption of monastic ordinations in 1981.[2] How was this gap bridged? After the end of the Cultural Revolution, many formerly young representatives of the Buddhist clergy reemerged to lead Buddhist reconstruction, often responding to the calls of local governments. They engaged in the renovation of Buddhist sites and in the reestablishment of Buddhist training centers, while at the same time holding political positions within the Buddhist Association of China, at the local and/or national levels.[3] The majority of these men and women had already been monks and nuns prior to the beginning of Communist rule. Some of them had never really given up their religious vows in spite of the increasingly hostile, and then patently dangerous, climate of the Mao era. Many others had returned to lay life, started a family, and moved into other jobs, and yet resumed monastic life after the end of the Cultural Revolution and the partial opening of the country. Only a handful of these monks and nuns are still active today; it is now largely their disciples who are carrying out the tasks of revival and renewal.

How did the Buddhist legacy of the Republican era (1912–1949) make the transition to contemporary times? From where did the senior generation of monks and nuns draw the material and immaterial resources it needed to engage in the Buddhist reconstruction at the beginning of the post-Mao period?

In the 1960s, Holmes Welch identified the three key networks of Buddhist affiliation in mainland China as based on (1) religious kinship (including shared tonsure, ordination, and Dharma teachings);[4] (2) loyalty to charismatic monks; and (3) regionalism (Welch 1967, 403–407). Ashiwa and Wank (2016) have described many examples of how these networks operated transnationally.

The present chapter investigates one particular kind of religious kinship connecting the monastic leaders of the first half of the twentieth century to the senior generation of monks and nuns who first engaged in the Buddhist reconstruction of post-Mao China: Dharma lineages. Only Dharma lineages of the Chan and Tiantai schools of Buddhism, and only private Dharma lineages and not monastery lineages, are considered in this chapter. I first describe what Dharma lineages consist of and outline the history of major Chinese Buddhist lineages during the Republican era (1912–1949). I then focus more specifically on private Dharma transmissions accomplished by Chan master Xuyun 虚云 (ca. 1864–1959)[5] and Tiantai master Dixian 谛闲 (1858–1932).[6] Selected biographical overviews are provided that exemplify common patterns of religious careers and aspirations of these two masters' Dharma heirs in post-Mao China, as well as the propagation of Chan and Tiantai Dharma lineages to Hong Kong and the United States. These patterns allow me to analyze the social, political, and religious effects of private Dharma transmission and to investigate the role that this particular kind of religious kinship has played in Buddhist reconstruction domestically and abroad. In the appendix to this chapter, partial charts of Xuyun's and Dixian's Dharma transmissions are provided, as are the complete transmission stanzas mentioned in this chapter.

My aim is to show that the highly structured nature of this system has consistently favored the preservation of the Buddhist tradition beyond the Mao era, and that its long-standing authoritative stance has contributed to ensuring a connection between religious legitimacy and political power. This research is based on both textual evidence and fieldwork.

TRANSMISSION OF THE DHARMA AND DHARMA LINEAGES IN CHINESE BUDDHISM

In Chinese Buddhism, the "transmission of Dharma" (or Dharma transmission, *chuanfa* 传法) is a religious entrustment by which a master formally recognizes the spiritual accomplishments of a disciple, names him as his heir, and confers on him the authority to teach others. Besides being a private practice, Dharma transmission has also been used to seal or determine the handover of abbotship in Buddhist monasteries (Welch 1967, 156–165). A "Dharma lineage" (*famai* 法脉) is a line of spiritual descent claiming direct and uninterrupted filiation from a common ancestor through a succession of Dharma transmissions. The transmission of Dharma relies on Buddhist stanzas (*chuanfa ji* 传法偈, sets of Buddhist verses comparable to poems) that have been composed and handed down for this purpose;[7] characters are chosen in the same order as they appear in stanzas to compose Dharma names for the representatives of each successive Dharma generation.[8] In the course of history, Buddhist masters have composed and added supplementary stanzas to existing ones, either to extend one lineage and revive it, or to create a new sublineage within the same transmission. The practice of delivering a Dharma succession certificate (*sishu* 嗣书, *fasishu* 法嗣书) dates back to the Song dynasty (Schlütter 2008, 63–65) and is continued in modern times by Dharma scrolls (*fajuan* 法卷). These are paper scrolls where the Dharma genealogy is recorded in the form of a long list of names, beginning with the name of Śākyamuni and ending with the name of the Dharma heir to whom the scroll is destined.[9]

The notion of lineage arose inside different Buddhist groups (most notably Tiantai[10] and Chan,[11] but also Sanlun and Faxiang) in medieval and Tang China before becoming central to the Chan tradition, where it attained its fullest development. Starting from the late seventh and eighth centuries, Chan lineage claims and genealogies based on Dharma transmission became powerful ideological devices that served strategic and political purposes.[12] As T. Griffith Foulk has convincingly shown, the function of Chan genealogies is double: "The aura of immediacy and reality that surrounded the hagiographies of . . . relatively recent ancestors [in the line of Dharma transmission] lent a sense of historicity to the hagiographies of much more ancient figures in the lineage. At the same time, the hagiographies of the more recent ancestors gained sanctity and legitimacy by their association with those of the ancients" (Foulk 1993, 155–156).

The Qing document "The Ramification of all Branches' Lineages,"[13] included in the *Manji shinsan dainihon zokuzōkyō* (Revised Edition of the Supplement to the Manji Canon), lists transmission stanzas for the following lineages (and their sublineages) across Chinese Buddhist history: Linji, Weiyang, Dongshan, Yunmen, Fayan, Tianhuang[14] (these being all Chan lineages), Tiantai, Huayan Xianshou, and Nanshan lü (a Vinaya lineage).

There is no consensus on the fate of Huayan and Nanshan lü Dharma lineages in the twentieth century. According to Chen Bing and Deng Zimei (2000, 385–386, 399–405), the Nanshan lü lineage was carried on in association with the handover of abbotship of the Longchang Monastery of Baohuashan[15] in Jiangsu from the beginning of the Qing dynasty until the 1950s. As for the Huayan school, the fourth Huayan patriarch, Chengguan 澄观 (738–839), had already adopted Chan practice and, at the time of Chengguan's heir, Guifeng Zongmi 圭峰宗密 (780–841), Huayan lineages had partly merged with those of Chan. The school had a low degree of systematization and its fortunes varied in the following centuries. At the end of the Qing dynasty, while studies of Huayan doctrine and texts were thriving thanks to prominent lay and monastic figures such as Yang Wenhui 杨文会 (1837–1911), Zhang Taiyan 章太炎 (1868–1936), and Yuexia 月霞 (ca. 1858–1917), the school lacked its own places of practice and scarcely had any distinct religious rules, let alone Dharma lineages (Chen and Deng 2000, 383–385).

However, this is not the view upheld in Buddhist circles nowadays. According to at least two Chinese abbots whom I interviewed in the summer of 2017, the Dharma of a few Vinaya and Huayan lineages—including the Huayan Xianshou (also called Nianhua lineage),[16] mentioned in "The

Ramification of all Branches' Lineages"—is still being transmitted. The contradiction between the findings of Chen and Deng on the one hand and the interviewed abbots on the other is due, among other factors, to the intricate proliferation of Dharma sublineages and branches since the end of the Qing dynasty and to the somewhat arbitrary nature of the system (discussed in "A Legitimation Device and Its Ambiguities").

As for Chan and Tiantai Dharma transmissions, not only were they definitely conducted in the first half of the twentieth century, both as private practices and in association with the handover of abbotship (Welch 1963),[17] but they still undoubtedly are. If the long-standing centrality of genealogies in the Chan school and the historical fortunes of the school itself account for the longevity of its Dharma lineages, different factors may have favored the preservation of Tiantai lineages into the first half of the twentieth century. The Tiantai school very early developed a set of practices and norms in relation with Dharma transmission, such as ceremonies for the examination of candidates and for the delivery of Dharma scrolls. Moreover, the custom of Tiantai masters traveling near and far to espouse the scriptures was very convenient for seeking valuable candidates for the transmission among their audiences and fostering them, as well as for obtaining the support of wealthy lay patrons (Chen and Deng 2000, 383–384). Even though Tiantai studies did not flourish at the end of the Qing dynasty and the beginning of the Republican era, the school's lineages still spread out, especially thanks to Dixian.

XUYUN'S DHARMA LINEAGES AND STANZAS

Although Dharma lineages are particularly associated with the Chan school of Buddhism, not all Chan masters conducted Dharma transmissions in the Republican period. For example, the Buddhist activist Taixu was opposed to this custom and therefore did not comply with it. Other Republican Chan masters transmitted the Dharma to only a small number of disciples: For example, the former abbot of Putuoshan Miaoshan (*Miaoshan laoheshang baisui danchen jinian tekan* 2009, 2)[18] and the former abbot of the Gaomin Monastery Delin 德林 (1914–2015) number among the few Dharma heirs of master Laiguo 来果 (1881–1953).

The Chan master who accomplished the greatest number of Dharma transmissions in the first half of the twentieth century was Xuyun, a well-known Buddhist leader who led the restoration of six large Chan public monasteries in South China. The extended nature of Xuyun's Dharma lineages and their far-reaching scope are not haphazard, but appear to be the result of a systematic and programmatic approach on his part. I analyze the procedure conceived by Xuyun to conduct Dharma transmissions in all five branches of Chan before turning to their religious, social, and political effects in post-Mao China.

The Chinese Buddhist saying "one flower with five petals" (*yihua [kai] wuye* 一花 [开] 五叶) refers to the five branches and lineages that made the fortune of the Chan school during the Tang and Northern Song dynasties: Weiyang, Linji, Caodong, Fayan, and Yunmen. Three of these branches (Weiyang, Fayan, and Yunmen) disappeared in the period between the Five Dynasties and the Southern Song. Therefore, at the beginning of the twentieth century, only two Chan branches were still extant, the Linji and Caodong branches.

Xuyun's concern with Chan genealogies dates back to the mid-1930s, when he composed and/or edited at least three works devoted to this topic: *The Revised and Enlarged Edition of the Inscribed Portraits of the Buddhist Patriarchs* (Xuyun 1935), *The Amended Edition of the Starry Lamp Collection*,[19] and *The Amended and Enlarged Collection of the Exemplar Genealogy of Gushan Patriarchs* (Xuyun 1936b). At around the same time, Xuyun also undertook to reinstate one after another the three interrupted lineages of the Weiyang, Fayan, and Yunmen branches by resorting to one and the same procedure. He composed three new stanzas of fifty-six characters each, where the first character was drawn from the name of the last (known) patriarch of each branch and where the second character was drawn from one of his own monastic names, therefore appointing himself as the only, deferred receiver of the three interrupted transmissions. Xuyun would then symbolically associate to each Chan branch one of the monasteries that he was restoring, and in that monastery he would carry out most of the Dharma transmissions of that specific branch. To every disciple in each specific branch he would confer a Dharma name containing the third character of the relative stanza. According to Xuyun's Dharma heir Jinghui (1933–2013),[20] since the five branches had all stemmed from the same religious tradition of Chan, they accounted for one and the same spiritual filiation. Since Xuyun had received Linji and Caodong Dharma transmissions at the Yongquan Monastery of Mount Gu in Fujian[21] in 1892, this spiritual filiation still connected to its source allowed him to pass on the Dharma of any one of the five branches of Chan. In other words, the uninterrupted Dharma of the two surviving branches legitimized the three other transmissions.

I will show how the system works concretely through the example of the stanza that Xuyun composed for the Weiyang branch.[22] The first character, *ci* 词, appears in the name of its seventh and last known patriarch, Xingyang Ciduo 兴阳词铎, of the Tang dynasty. Xuyun drew the second character, *de* 德, from his own public name, Deqing 德清. To his Dharma heirs in the Weiyang branch, Xuyun would confer Dharma names containing the third character, *xuan* 宣:

词德宣衍道大兴　　戒鼎馨遍五分新
慧焰弥布周沙界　　香云普荫灿古今

慈悲济世原无尽　　　　光昭日月朗太清
振启拈花宏沩上　　　　圆相心灯永昌明[23]

This stanza would continue the Weiyang lineage: by a sort of "posthumous" reception of its Dharma, Xuyun therefore declared himself the eighth patriarch of the Weiyang branch. This master transmitted the Dharma Weiyang to about fifteen disciples, especially at the last monastery he restored in the 1950s, the Zhenru Monastery on Mount Yunju in Jiangxi.

By the same procedure, Xuyun appointed himself eighth patriarch of the Fayan branch and twelfth patriarch of the Yunmen branch. There are about thirty representatives of the thirteenth generation Yunmen, whose serial character is *miao* 妙. Xuyun accomplished most of the transmissions in the Yunmen lineage at the Yunmen Monastery in Guangdong, the site established by the very founder of the lineage that he revived in the 1940s. Xuyun's Dharma heirs in the ninth generation Fayan all bear a name containing the character *ben* 本.

Like other Chan masters of the Republican era, Xuyun also transmitted the Dharma of the two extant branches of the Chan school, the Linji branch and the Caodong branch.[24] To transmit the Dharma Linji, he relied on the stanza of the Linji "Longchi" lineage.[25] His own Dharma name in the Linji lineage was Xingche 性彻; he belonged to the forty-third generation. Therefore, his Dharma heirs in the Linji lineage all bear a name containing the character *ben* 本:

觉性本常寂　　　　心惟法界同

The Caodong stanza on which Xuyun relied to transmit the Dharma is one of the supplementary stanzas of the Caodong "Jiangxi Shouchang" lineage. Xuyun's Dharma name in the Caodong lineage was Guyan 古岩; he belonged to the forty-seventh generation. Therefore, Xuyun's Dharma heirs in the Caodong lineage all bear a name containing the character *fu* 复:

耀古复腾今　　　　今日禅宗振

The system Xuyun envisioned allowed him to accomplish a great number of diversified Dharma transmissions from the mid-1930s until his death in 1959. It would also appear that, starting from the mid-1940s, this master intensified Dharma transmissions in a sort of "Dharma fever," without relying on any apparent criteria for selecting his heirs and, on some occasions, even conferring Dharma transmissions by mail.[26]

I have shown the highly systematic nature of Xuyun's Dharma transmissions. I will now analyze some of their consequences and effects by considering the life paths of his Dharma heirs. A great number of them did in fact resume active religious lives after the political turmoil of the 1960s and 1970s, and their religious careers serve to illustrate the manifold significance that has come to be associated with Xuyun's Dharma lineages in post-Mao China.

XUYUN'S DHARMA HEIRS IN POST-MAO CHINA

To whom did Xuyun transmit the Dharma? What has become of these monks? While many of Xuyun's Dharma heirs have vanished without a trace, others have reappeared since the end of the Cultural Revolution to engage in the Buddhist reconstruction at various levels. Some of these monks have become Buddhist leaders in contemporary China, while others have chosen to stay away from the limelight, and their reputation has only spread among Chan practitioners.[27] Today, only a handful of them are still alive.[28]

The religious careers of a few of these monks can be retraced through textual sources and fieldwork, and at least three common patterns may be detected: first, the endeavor of Xuyun's Dharma heirs to restore the monasteries associated with their master and/or with the Chan tradition in general, and to perpetuate Chan Dharma lineages through further transmissions; second, their commitment to national and international Buddhist networks based on Xuyun's Dharma lineages; and third, the high-ranking positions that many of his heirs have held in the Buddhist Association of China in the last decades. Taken as a whole, these patterns illustrate the religious, political, and social meanings that have come to be associated with Xuyun's Dharma lineages in post-Mao China as well as their resulting effects.

The following selected biographical overviews exemplify these three main common patterns and assess the relevance of Xuyun's Dharma lineages in the Buddhist reconstruction of the post-Mao era.

THE RESTORATION OF (XUYUN'S) CHAN MONASTERIES

The religious career of Miaoxin Foyuan 妙心佛源 (1923–2009) has been entirely linked to the site founded by the ancestor of his Dharma lineage, Yunmen.[29] A native of Hunan Province, Foyuan received Dharma transmission from Xuyun at Yunmen Monastery in Guangdong in 1951 and became its abbot the next year. He was imprisoned in 1958, and his sentence was later commuted to eighteen years of penal labor. Rehabilitated in 1979, Foyuan was invited by the authorities of Ruyuan District to go back to Yunmen in 1982, again in the position of abbot, and lead the reconstruction of the site for more than ten years ("Yunmen shan Dajue chansi—zhuanji," 43–49; He 2000, 287b–290a). After having rebuilt two more Chan monasteries in his home province,[30] Foyuan decided to retire at Yunmen in the twilight of his life, and it is there that his ashes now rest. The case of Foyuan is one example of how the bond to Dharma Master Xuyun and to one's Dharma monastery appears in some cases to be stronger than tonsure or ordination kinship, and also transcends native regionalism.

The commitment to Dharma affiliation has not dissolved with the following Yunmen generation. A native of Guangdong, Mingkong Weisheng 明空惟升 (b. 1973) entered religious life in 1992, received Dharma transmission at Yunmen Monastery from Foyuan, and, in 1996, graduated from the Yunmen Institute of

Buddhist Studies. The following year, Weisheng undertook the reconstruction of the Yunqi Temple on Mount Jizu in Yunnan, a monastery that had been restored by Xuyun in the 1910s and then destroyed during the Cultural Revolution. In 2002, Weisheng became the abbot of a new temple that he built nearby and called the Chan Monastery of Xuyun (Xuyun Chansi 虚云禅寺). The Dharma disciples of Weisheng belong to the fifteenth Yunmen generation.

The examples of Foyuan and his disciple Weisheng are illustrative of a wider trend: Almost all the monasteries restored by Xuyun in the first half of the twentieth century have been rebuilt by his Dharma heirs since the 1980s. The restoration of the Nanhua Monastery in Guangdong, for example, was undertaken in 1982 by Xuyun's Dharma grandson Weiyin Jinguo 惟因今果 (1914–1992).[31] A native of Guangdong, Weiyin hardly ever left Nanhua Monastery after he first arrived there in 1939. In the 1940s, he served as guest prefect (*zhike* 知客) and head monk (*shouzuo* 首座) at Nanhua and accompanied Xuyun on the occasion of many religious assemblies he held in various places. In 1953, he received Dharma transmission in the Caodong lineage at Zhenru Monastery in Jiangxi from one of Xuyun's heirs, before graduating at the Institute of Buddhist Studies in Beijing. Weiyin went back to Nanhua right after his graduation and continued to attend to the site even when it became a labor camp in the 1960s. Persecuted during the Cultural Revolution, this master was finally invited to become the abbot of Nanhua in 1982 and undertook its restoration until he passed away in 1992 (He 2002, 1–35). It is at Nanhua that his ashes are enshrined.

Many other Dharma heirs of Xuyun have engaged in restoring sites of the Chan tradition since the partial opening of the country in the 1980s. I will mention one last example. A native of Hubei Province, Benhuan Chengmiao 本焕乘妙 (1907–2012)[32] entered religious life in 1930, then practiced with Master Laiguo at Gaomin Monastery for seven years before moving to Wutaishan. In 1948, he received Dharma transmission in the forty-fourth generation Linji at Nanhua right after its restoration by Xuyun and became its abbot the next year. It is at this monastery that Benhuan was arrested in 1958.[33] Having served his term for seventeen years, Benhuan went back to his prison as a free worker for a few more years, since his imprisonment and class status had made him unwelcome at both Nanhua and his home village. Finally rehabilitated in 1982, this master has successively built, rebuilt, and/or directed eight sites of the Chan tradition (five in Guangdong,[34] two in Hubei,[35] and one in Jiangxi[36]). Among these is the Guangxiao Monastery in Guangzhou, which Xuyun had unsuccessfully vowed to rebuild in the 1930s (see Cen 1995, 287–288). Benhuan was personally involved in restoring a few of these monasteries, while in other cases he "lent" his name and the prestige associated with his religious filiation to attract funds and donations.

As these few examples show, Xuyun's Dharma transmissions have aroused in his Dharma heirs not only a long-lasting bond to his person and memory, but also a sense of belonging to the different traditions of Chan and the concern to preserve their sacred sites. While the reconstruction of Buddhist monasteries in post-Mao China was also undertaken in small temples in the south that did not have Dharma lineages (see, for example, Wank 2009), Dharma filiation to a charismatic figure such as Xuyun has greatly contributed to this enterprise.

NATIONAL AND INTERNATIONAL NETWORKS

The last time I met her in 2015, Buddhist master Yinkong 印空 (b. 1921), the abbess of Jinshan and Dajinshan Monasteries in Jiangxi Province, was still an extraordinarily peppy ninety-four-year-old woman.[37] She received ordination (*shoujie* 受戒) from Xuyun at Zhenru Monastery in Jiangxi in 1955 and Dharma transmission in the Linji lineage from Xuyun's Dharma disciple Benhuan[38] sometime after the Cultural Revolution. From Yinkong's discourse and self-representation, it clearly emerges that the prestigious lineage to which she belongs is a founding theme of her religious identity. In her lodging, many portraits and statuettes of her Dharma "grandfather" Xuyun and of her Dharma master Benhuan stand out next to those of buddhas and bodhisattvas, and together with those of a few other of Xuyun's Dharma disciples who have recently passed away.[39] The Dharma lineage to which she belongs is also displayed at Dajinshan Monastery in a large poster featuring color photographs of Xuyun, Benhuan, and herself, as well as their respective Linji Dharma generations and the Linji Dharma transmission stanza.

Statuettes and pictures of Xuyun, Benhuan, and Jinghui in Yinkong's lodging.

Xuyun's lineage has also provided her with prestigious religious networks. In recent years, Yinkong has attended a number of highly symbolic events such as a ceremony held in 1999 to commemorate the forty years of Xuyun's passing away, as well as rites held for the passing away of her Dharma master Benhuan in 2012. Benhuan himself made a few trips to Jinshan Monastery on special occasions. In 2010, together with Yinkong, he personally transmitted the Dharma to a group of nuns in the forty-sixth generation of the Linji lineage— that is, to his Dharma granddaughters. Finally, Dajinshan has been one of the four monasteries to have received and enshrined a share of Benhuan's relics so far.

The religious legitimation associated with Yinkong's prestigious kinship has also complemented her personal charisma and determination to attract funds from Chinese and overseas donors. While many laypersons count among the "great Dharma protectors" (*dahufa* 大护法) of the Dajinshan Monastery, among whom is the Hong Kong layman Yang Zhao 杨钊 of the Glorisun Group (Xuri Jituan 旭日集团), its main monastic sponsors belong to Yinkong's Dharma family. Yinkong recalls how Xuyun's Dharma heir Shengyi 圣一 (1922–2010) of the Baolian Chansi in Hong Kong, has been among the main donors to the monastery since the beginning of its reconstruction in the early 1980s, offering a total of 33,000 RMB. Since that time and up until now, that is, even after his death in 2012, the most substantial funds have been provided, besides by Yinkong herself, by her Dharma master Benhuan. With a donation of 1 million RMB in 2015, Benhuan's Hongfa Monastery in Shenzhen is the main funder of Dajinshan's retirement home (*anyang yuan* 安养院).[40]

Networks based on Dharma affiliation are not confined to the national scale. A great number of Xuyun's Dharma heirs moved abroad before the beginning of Communist rule in 1949. Through lineage networks, they have been able to contribute from abroad to the Buddhist reconstruction on the mainland, both ritually and financially. One example is Xuanhua Dulun 宣化度轮 (1918–1995), a representative of the ninth generation Weiyang who approached Xuyun in the late 1940s at Nanhua Monastery. In 1956, Xuyun sent his Dharma scroll to Xuanhua in Hong Kong, where Xuanhua had taken refuge after the Communist takeover. After preaching the Dharma in Hong Kong for about a decade, Xuanhua traveled to San Francisco. In 1976, not far from this city, he founded one of the largest Buddhist temple complexes in the United States, the City of Ten Thousand Buddhas (Wanfocheng 万佛城; hereafter WFC). For almost two decades, Xuanhua led and sent delegations to Southeast Asia and Europe, founded Buddhist monasteries and academies in Taiwan and Canada, and gave lectures in many American universities.

From the end of the 1980s, he also established religious bridges with mainland China: He sent disciples to monasteries in China to help conduct ordination ceremonies, while Chinese masters traveled to WFC to take part in Buddhist rituals. In July 1987, for example, the abbot of the Longhua Temple,

Master Mingyang 明旸 (1916–2002),[41] led a massive delegation of monks from Shanghai's Longhua Temple and Beijing's Guangji Temple to WFC to attend a Ritual for the Release of the Souls of the Water, Land, and Air (*Shanghai tongzhi* 2005, vol. 14, chap. 2, pt. 4). In May 1990, a few American monks from WFC helped administer the first ordination ceremony held in Shanghai since 1949. The ceremony, presided over by Master Mingyang at the Longhua Temple, included two eminent Tiantai monks from Hong Kong in the most important ritual roles. Political bridges were also established with mainland China and Taiwan: Xuanhua received the visit of political representatives of the Judicial Yuan, the Legislative Yuan, and the Executive Yuan, as well as two advisers to the president of the People's Republic of China. The tradition of the Weiyang branch is still perpetuated in North America by Xuanhua's Dharma disciples.[42]

A few of Xuyun's Dharma disciples have related how their master pushed them to leave the continent against their will before the beginning of Communist rule in 1949. One example is Benmiao Zhiding 本妙知定 (Jy Din, 1917–2003).[43] A Dharma representative of the Linji lineage, Zhiding received ordination in 1937 at the Nanhua Monastery. He then became the director of the primary school and the deputy director of the Institute of Buddhist Studies, both established at Nanhua by Xuyun, and was also in charge of the Qujiang branch of the Buddhist Association. By enjoining him to leave, Xuyun was therefore losing a presumably valuable collaborator. After spending a few years in Hong Kong, Zhiding went to Honolulu, Hawai'i, in 1956 and there completed over ten years the construction of the Hsu Yun Temple. In 1997, he established the Zen Buddhist Order of Hsu Yun.[44] Besides being the first monk to spread Mahayana Buddhism in North America, Zhiding was among the main donors who gathered funds abroad for Weiyin's restoration of the Nanhua Monastery in the 1980s.[45]

It appears, then, that, since the end of the Mao era, religious identity based on Xuyun's Dharma lineages has favored the creation of national and transnational networks. These networks have not only reinforced the cohesion and the religious power of Xuyun's Dharma family; they have also contributed both to reintroducing ritual expertise and to generating funds for the material reconstruction of their ancient monastic sites on the mainland.

THE BUDDHIST ASSOCIATION OF CHINA

In addition to the fact that all the above-mentioned monks and nuns have occupied different positions in the Buddhist Association of China (BAC) at the local and provincial levels, at least three Dharma heirs of Xuyun have risen to the highest institutional positions for Buddhists in contemporary China. Yanxin Yicheng 衍心一诚 (1927–2017) was president of the BAC from 2002 to 2010. He was a representative of the tenth generation Weiyang and thus a

Dharma grandson of Xuyun. He received Dharma transmission in 1957 from the first abbot of Zhenru Monastery on Mount Yunju in Jiangxi during its restoration accomplished by Xuyun.[46] In 1985, Yicheng was also invited to lead the restoration of his lineage temple, the Zhenru Monastery, and he remained its abbot until 2005. His disciples have already passed the Dharma to the next generation Weiyang, the twelfth.

Another Dharma heir of Xuyun succeeded Yicheng in the position of president of the BAC in 2010: Xuanchuan Yuechuan 宣传月川 (b. 1927), better known under his other name, Chuanyin 传印 (see also chapter 7 by Ji Zhe in this volume). Chuanyin entered religious life at the Zhenru Monastery in 1954 and there received Dharma transmission from Xuyun the following year. After graduating from the Institute of Buddhist Studies in Beijing, in the 1970s and 1980s he divided his time between Mount Yunju; the *Bukkyō* University in Kyoto, where he perfected his studies; and Mount Tiantai in Zhejiang. He concurrently held positions at the Buddhist Association in Beijing and at its Institute of Buddhist Studies. In 1994, he became the abbot of the Pure Land Donglin Monastery on Mount Lu in Jiangxi. In 2010, he was elected chair and president of the BAC, a position he maintained until April 2015.

For twenty years—that is, from 1993 until his death in 2013—the position of vice-chair of the BAC was occupied by another Dharma disciple of Xuyun: Jinghui, a well-known public figure of institutional Buddhism. Born in Hubei in 1933, Jinghui was conferred the tonsure at the Sanfo Monastery in Wuchang and met Xuyun in 1951, when he arrived at Yunmen to attend the ordination ceremony. He affirmed having received Dharma transmission in all five Chan lineages from Xuyun in 1952.[47] Starting from the end of the Cultural Revolution, Jinghui built or rebuilt at least three Chan monastic sites, among them the Bailin Monastery near Shijiazhuang, the capital of Hebei Province (see also chapter 10 by Gareth Fisher in this volume).[48] As Ji Zhe has convincingly shown (Ji 2007, 2016d), Xuyun's memory and the continuity of his tradition are founding themes in the legitimacy of this newly rebuilt temple. Jinghui is one of the main promoters of Xuyun's legendary authority in contemporary China, a task he was able to ensure, among other things, by editing the *Supplement to Master Xuyun's Dharma Collection* (Jinghui 1990).

Besides being a springboard for acceding to the highest positions within the BAC, affiliation to a prestigious Dharma lineage such as Xuyun's also represents a religious and political credential for the abbotship of important public monasteries. As I have mentioned, in many instances, Xuyun's Dharma heirs have been invited by the local government or BAC authorities to rebuild their ancient monasteries on the mainland—just as, whenever available, Dharma disciples of other eminent Republican masters have been so asked.[49] From 2015 until he was deposed in 2018, Master Xuecheng (see chapter 3 by Susan K. McCarthy in this volume), born in Fujian Province in 1966, was chairman of the BAC. His fall from grace notwithstanding, Xuecheng's recent tenure at the top is a telling sign that, at least from an institutional point of view, the monastic generation trained since the end of the Cultural Revolution is taking over: The gap caused by almost twenty-five years of ordination vacuum has been bridged.

It is well-known that the strongest bond within Chinese Buddhism ties a monk to his tonsure master. Although none of the monks mentioned previously had received tonsure from Xuyun,[50] it is to this master and to his memory that they felt the deepest commitment, and it is with this master that their names are associated today. If this fact can be explained by Xuyun's charisma, and by his great renown and influence both at a religious and an institutional level, Dharma transmission represented the means through which these monks' connection to their master could be formalized and legitimated.

Consequently, Xuyun's Dharma lineages have been instrumental in the reassertion of Buddhism in post-Mao China thanks to the religious, social, and political meanings associated with them. Some of Xuyun's Dharma heirs have maintained an unwavering commitment to the monasteries of their religious tradition, while some others have also succeeded in fulfilling the long-standing political ambitions of the school. National and international networks based on Xuyun's lineages have been instrumental in both cases. If it is true that the fecundity of the five Chan lineages once ensured the school's prosperity during the Tang and Northern Song dynasties—many lineages producing many heirs, and many heirs soon monopolizing the richest and most powerful monasteries and positions—Xuyun's Dharma legacy continues to represent today a powerful device that serves well the school's continued ambition to religious and political supremacy in mainland China and beyond. Tiantai Dharma lineages have also played a major role in bridging the religious gap of the Mao era, especially thanks to their preservation and growth in Hong Kong since the 1940s.

THE TIANTAI DHARMA LINEAGE OF MASTER DIXIAN

The transition of Tiantai lineages from the Qing dynasty to twentieth-century China was chiefly, although not exclusively, ensured by Master Dixian. Dixian, whose Dharma name was Guxu 古虚, was a representative of the fifteenth generation (*shi* 世) of the Tiantai Lingfeng lineage and an heir of the forty-third generation (*dai* 代) counting from the first Tiantai patriarch Huiwen of the Northern Qi (550–577).[51] The Lingfeng lineage[52] dates back to Master Baisong Zhenjue's 百松真觉 (1537–1589) restoration of Gaoming Monastery on Mount Tiantai. The stanza initiated by Baisong can be found in "The Ramification of all Branches' Lineages":[53]

真传正受　　灵岳心宗　　一乘顿观　　印定古今　　念起寂然[54]

Besides managing to make its way into modern times, the Tiantai Lingfeng lineage also succeeded in bridging the religious gap of the 1960s and 1970s and is currently thriving in China and Hong Kong. The survival of the transmission brought about by Dixian appears to be mainly due to one fundamental factor: the high mobility of his Dharma heirs. After conquering northern China in the 1920s and 1930s, the Tiantai Lingfeng lineage reached British Hong Kong in the 1940s and soon found itself a relevant place in the religious panorama of the island. Contemporary Tiantai Dharma representatives are effectively contributing to the prosperity of the school in Hong Kong and, especially since the handover of Hong Kong to the People's Republic in 1997, to the reassertion of Buddhism in post-Mao China.

TANXU, BAOJING, AND THE INTRODUCTION OF THE LINGFENG LINEAGE TO HONG KONG

I have mentioned that mobility is a time-honored characteristic of the Tiantai school and one that ensured the survival of its Dharma lineages in the past. In the first half of the twentieth century, two main factors strengthened Tiantai masters' predisposition to travel near and far: first, the stance taken by Dixian's Dharma heir Tanxu 倓虛 (Jinxian 金銜, 1875–1963)[55] against the transmission of the Dharma in association with the abbotship; and second, the migration of a few representatives of the Lingfeng lineage to Hong Kong since at least one decade before the start of Communist rule in 1949.

Tanxu was a well-known Buddhist leader of the Republican era and the promoter of a major innovation in discourse and practice about Dharma transmission. This master strongly opposed the custom of transmitting the Dharma in association with the position of abbot and devoted to this issue one long essay, "Transmitting the Dharma without Transmitting the Abbotship" ("Chuanfa bu chuanzuo" 傳法不傳座; Tanxu 1998, *vol. 2*, 226–236).[56]

According to Tanxu, in the majority of public monasteries in China, choice of the abbots was determined well ahead of time by transmitting the Dharma to many virtual candidates to the position rather than by selecting the worthiest candidate when the need arose. Tanxu attributed the decline of many old monasteries to this custom, chiefly because of three malpractices (*liubi* 流弊) that were commonly associated with it. First, abbots in charge usually chose Dharma/abbotship heirs not on the basis of merit, but on the basis of personal feelings. Second, the fact that the many Dharma heirs (and therefore virtual candidates) competed for the abbotship led to serious disputes that disgraced Buddhism. Third, the standard criteria guiding an abbot in his choice of heirs caused each generation of abbots to fall off in virtue from the one before.[57]

According to Tanxu, another major problem related to this custom was that Dharma heirs would stick to one monastery in the expectation of acceding to the position of abbot, instead of traveling around to practice, study, and spread the Buddhist law as they were supposed to. In this master's view, the transmission of Dharma belongs to the sphere of "self-interest" (*zili* 自利), while the transmission of abbotship belongs to the sphere of benefiting others, and even if in some cases the two spheres can coincide, in principle they are not alike. The abbot must be able to guide the monastic community: This is his duty and his role and therefore the most important qualification he is required to have.[58] The qualifications of a Dharma heir pertain instead to the realm of individual attainments, since he is a "vessel of the Buddhist Law" (*faqi* 法器): "As for he who receives the Dharma, whenever the time of his causes and conditions is ripe, he can rely on his virtue and observance of the practice and precepts to spread [the Dharma] in the four directions, and teach and instruct according to circumstances; whenever people in the ten directions invite him, he can go to temples here and there, perform duties, be an abbot, be a Dharma master, establish monasteries, revive places of practice, and write books advancing his theories. This all depends on his own causes and conditions" (Tanxu 1998, vol. 2, 232).

Tanxu practiced what he preached: starting in the 1920s, he established or rebuilt at least six Tiantai public monasteries in Jilin, Tianjin, Heilongjiang, Liaoning, and Shandong,[59] among which was the Zhanshan Temple that he built in Qingdao in 1933. Through Tanxu's enterprising actions, the Lingfeng lineage was able to play a pioneering role in the Buddhist conquest of new territories: Whereas other foreign institutional religions were already well diffused and entrenched in northern China, Buddhism was altogether absent in many of these regions before Tanxu's arrival. The establishment of Tanxu's Buddhist monasteries in northern cities pervaded by foreign culture and landmarks also carried a strong political and nationalistic meaning, since traditional Buddhist architecture was perceived as an emblem of Chinese identity (Carter 2011).

Besides being a conscious choice, the mobility of Dixian's Dharma heirs in the first half of the twentieth century was also due to historical factors. In 1949, toward the end of the civil war between Nationalist and Communist forces (1945–1949), Tanxu moved to Hong Kong. There, he continued his work by playing a leading role in the restoration of the Buddhist monastic community in the colony, which "had declined almost to the vanishing point by 1949" (Welch 1961, 99). Nevertheless, Tanxu was not the very first monk to have introduced Tiantai Buddhism to Hong Kong, since another Dharma heir of Dixian had already ferried the Lingfeng lineage there. This was Baojing 宝静 (Jinde 全德, 1899–1940), who paved the way for the creation of a few Buddhist sites on the island through successive trips between 1927 and 1939.[60]

The "migration" of the Tiantai tradition to British Hong Kong was all the more valuable as it would seem that the third most prominent Dharma disciple of Dixian (out of ten)—Master Jingquan 静权 (1881–1960)—did not carry on the lineage on the mainland beyond the Maoist period.[61] Starting from the

1950s, Tanxu's and Baojing's Dharma heirs have carried on the task initiated by their masters while reinforcing the manifold meanings associated with the transmissions they received.

DIXIAN'S DHARMA HEIRS IN POST-MAO CHINA AND HONG KONG

If many of the Buddhist monks seeking refuge in Hong Kong in the early 1950s later on moved to other countries—as was the case for Xuyun's Dharma heirs Xuanhua, Zhiding, and Fayun—at least two of Dixian's Dharma heirs have permanently settled on the island. These are Baojing's Dharma grandson Jueguang 觉光 (Qiben 起本, Sik Kok Kwong, 1919–2014) and Tanxu's Dharma disciple Yongxing 永惺 (Niangen 念根, Wing Sing, 1926–2016). From the beginning of the 1940s until now, these two representatives of the Lingfeng lineage have committed to planting Tiantai Buddhism in Hong Kong and, since the handover of Hong Kong in 1997, they have also contributed to reasserting it in mainland China. They have been able to do so principally by capitalizing on the social, religious, and political meanings associated with Tiantai Dharma transmission.

Jueguang arrived in Hong Kong in 1939 together with Baojing and there received Dharma transmission in the forty-sixth generation Tiantai.[62] In 1945, Jueguang was among the founders of the Hong Kong Buddhist Association (Xianggang Fojiao Lianhehui 香港佛教联合会, hereafter HKBA)[63] and was its president from 1966 until his death in November 2014—that is, for almost fifty years. Already in the 1960s, Holmes Welch described him as one of the leaders of the Buddhist community in Hong Kong (Welch 1963, 117–119). Besides being president of the HKBA, Jueguang was the president of the board of its monthly magazine, *Xianggang fojiao* 香港佛教 (Buddhism in Hong Kong), which he had contributed to founding in 1960.[64] These two concurrent positions provided him, first of all, with high visibility. A survey of the magazine's issues from 1999 to 2009 is revealing in this sense: Jueguang appeared on more than half of the 132 covers of this period. From the end of 2011, the magazine also has devoted a special monthly column to memories and stories recounted by this old master.[65]

In one of these editorials, Jueguang recounts the circumstances that led him to be received by Deng Xiaoping on the occasion of the celebrations for National Day in 1984 (Jueguang 2014). As this example illustrates, in addition to providing him with high visibility, Jueguang's institutional positions also allowed him to play an increasingly active political role. In 1972, he was chosen as president of the Hong Kong and Macau Regional Center of the World Fellowship of Buddhists,[66] an organization in charge of Buddhist foreign relations strictly linked to the HKBA.[67] Starting in the 1980s, Jueguang was also engaged in preparatory work for the transfer of sovereignty of Hong Kong from Britain to China, as a member of the Committee for Drafting the Basic

Law of the Hong Kong Special Administrative Region[68] and other related committees (Chen and Deng 2000, 388).

Curiously enough, the current vice president of the HKBA, Yongxing, is also an heir of Dixian's Dharma: In 1949, he followed Tanxu to Hong Kong and received Dharma transmission from him there. After the handover of Hong Kong in 1997, Jueguang and Yongxing—the two men at the highest level in charge in the HKBA, both representatives of the Tiantai Lingfeng lineage—have made the point that the association enables dialogue to occur between the sangha on the one hand and the national and local Hong Kong governments on the other. As a survey of *Xianggang fojiao* issues of the last fifteen years shows, the pair of Dharma relatives Jueguang and Yongxing have represented Hong Kong Buddhists in an endless series of official ceremonies and political celebrations of a very diverse nature. I will just mention a few examples.

In May 1999, they presided over the huge celebrations for the "return" of the Buddha's tooth relic to Hong Kong. This was to celebrate the declaration from the Hong Kong Special Administrative Region Government of a national holiday on the day of the Buddha's birthday, the result of years of lobbying on the part of Buddhists in Hong Kong ("Daibiao tuan fu Jing Hu fangwen" 1999). In winter 2000, Jueguang and Yongxing paid official visits to a few national political leaders in Beijing and Shanghai to discuss issues related to the education of the sangha ("Xianggang fojiao jie qingzhu Fodan yingqing Foya sheli zhanli dahui" 1999, n487). In spring 2001, they welcomed to Hong Kong five representatives of the United Front Work Department ("You cong yuanfang lai buyilehu" 2001). In autumn that same year, it was the turn of the chief of the State Administration for Religious Affairs, Ye Xiaowen, to honor the HKBA with his visit. This was in addition to the annual official celebrations held by the HKBA for the anniversary of the founding of the PRC.

Thus, both Xuyun's and Dixian's Dharma lineages are nowadays strongly associated with a certain institutional prestige that has facilitated the access of their representatives to the highest official positions. Nevertheless, political diplomacy is not the only contribution of Tiantai Dharma representatives in Hong Kong to the reassertion of Buddhism in the post-Mao era, as, just like Xuyun's Chan Dharma lineages, the Tiantai Lingfeng lineage also carries a certain religious meaning.

In Hong Kong, Jueguang established a temple of the same name as the one Dixian had directed in Ningbo and where he himself had studied, the Guanzong Temple. A few elements point to the role that this lineage temple played in Jueguang's religious identity. First, from the 1980s, this master relied on his political relationships to advocate for the reopening of his ancient monastery in Ningbo, which finally started to be restored in 1993. Moreover, since at least 1992, Jueguang transmitted the Dharma to many disciples at a time during several public ceremonies at his Guanzong Monastery in Hong Kong, in a seemingly programmatic effort to expand the school's otherwise limited lineage. Monks from Korea, Indonesia, Singapore, Taiwan, and the mainland received the Tiantai Dharma from Jueguang on the occasion of these ceremonies and are now transmitting it abroad.[69]

Yongxing has extended the spread of Tiantai Buddhism even farther than his master, Tanxu. Besides founding a temple (the Xifang Temple; Xifang Si 西方寺) in Hong Kong, Yongxing has established or coestablished several temples in Malaysia (such as the Putuo Temple; Putuo Si 普陀寺) and in the United States.[70] His work in spreading Buddhism in the United States led him to establish the Texas Buddhist Association, which has a Jade Buddha Temple and an American Bodhi Center associated with it.[71]

Besides bringing the Tiantai tradition to North America, both Jueguang and Yongxing have contributed to bringing back ritual expertise to the mainland. For example, in 1990, they directed together with Master Mingyang the first ordination ceremony held in Shanghai after 1949 (*Shanghai tongzhi*, 2005, vol. 14, chap. 2, pt. 4). The fact that they had continued to perform ordinations in Hong Kong in the 1960s and 1970s and were thus able to ensure a certain ritual continuity may help explain the invitation of these two Tiantai Dharma heirs to Shanghai. The location of the ceremony provides further clarification: Longhua Temple is the monastery where Dixian received the Dharma transmission and of which he was the abbot in the 1910s, and where Jueguang himself served as prior (*jianyuan* 監院) in the 1940s.[72] Monks from the Chan WFC were also present at the ceremony. From this example, we can see how networks linking Hong Kong with mainland China have also been created on the basis of Tiantai Dharma affiliation. The creation of networks has been favored not only by a sense of religious identity, but also by the desire of monastic representatives in Hong Kong to renew old bonds with monasteries and fellow disciples on the mainland.[73]

Moreover, the Tiantai Lingfeng lineage itself has been partially reintroduced to the mainland from Hong Kong since the end of the Cultural Revolution. At least three Dharma heirs of Tanxu have actively contributed to Buddhist reconstruction, and they have done so in the very stronghold of their eminent predecessor, the northern regions. These are Nengchan 能闡 (1922–2009), who rebuilt a conspicuous number of temples in Shandong; Yuanshan 圓山 (b. 1919), who has been (and still is, despite his great age) active in Liaoning; and the well-known master Mingzhe 明哲 (1925–2012). Having resumed monastic life after the end of the Cultural Revolution, in the 1980s, Mingzhe worked in Beijing for the Institute of Buddhist Studies and the BAC and in the Meditation Hall of the Guangji Temple. In 1988, he became the abbot of the newly rebuilt Zhanshan Monastery in Qingdao that Tanxu had established in the 1930s, and it is here that his relics are enshrined. Only Nengchan, however, received direct Dharma transmission from Tanxu: Yuanshan and Mingzhe received the Dharma of Tanxu posthumously from a monk who traveled from

Hong Kong for this end (see "A Legitimation Device and Its Ambiguities"). Just like Jueguang and Yongxing, they all have transmitted the Tiantai Dharma to many disciples on the mainland.

Networks linking Chan and Tiantai Dharma representatives have also been established. A long-lasting bond tied Benhuan and Jueguang, as the many articles in *Xianggang fojiao* devoted to this Dharma heir of Xuyun show. In 1987, Mingzhe was appointed deputy head of the delegation led by Mingyang to participate in the Buddhist ritual at Xuanhua's WFC. Despite the fact that he mainly practices Pure Land Buddhism just like many contemporary Tiantai monks, Yongxing has also established in Hong Kong a memorial hall for Master Xuyun (Xuyun Heshang Jiniantang 虚云和尚纪念堂).

A LEGITIMATION DEVICE AND ITS AMBIGUITIES

Let us consider some ambiguities of Dharma transmission, starting from what Holmes Welch called its "toleration of proxy" (Welch 1963, 127). The case of Mingzhe is a recent example of proxy within the Tiantai transmission of Dharma. Unlike Nengchan, who received direct Dharma transmission from him, Mingzhe was never a disciple of Tanxu; in fact, he most probably never met him in his youth. However, when Mingzhe became the abbot of the Zhanshan Temple in Qingdao in 1988, the need was felt that he be symbolically linked to the eminent Republican Tiantai master who had established this monastery, that is, that he be inscribed in Tanxu's Dharma lineage. Baodeng 宝灯 (d. 1997), a direct Dharma disciple of Tanxu in the forty-fifth generation who had established a Zhanshan Temple in Hong Kong in 1964, fit the bill. However, it was inappropriate for Baodeng to become the Dharma master of Mingzhe: Not only were the two masters about the same age, but Mingzhe was much more renowned than Baodeng by this time. Therefore, in 1991 when Baodeng traveled to the mainland to transmit the Dharma of the Lingfeng lineage to Mingzhe, he did so by acting as a proxy for the long-since-deceased Tanxu, and Mingzhe became a Dharma heir of Tanxu in the forty-fifth generation—and a Dharma brother of Baodeng.[74]

Another obvious case of proxy is Xuyun's deferred reception of the Dharma of the three Chan lineages that had been interrupted for almost eight centuries. The proliferation of Dharma transmissions at particular times in history, of which Xuyun's case is also an illustration, represents another of the ambiguities of the system, as it raises questions about, on the one hand, the criteria guiding the choice of candidates for the transmission, and, on the other hand, the authenticity of the transmissions themselves.

Jinghui, one of Xuyun's Dharma disciples, replicated in the post-Mao period his master's systematic and programmatic approach in transmitting the Dharma. From 1999 to his death in 2013, Jinghui alone transmitted the Linji Dharma to 123 recipients including, in 2009, Willigis Junger, a German

Chan practitioner and the director of the Benediktushof Zen Center, and the Caodong Dharma to 55 recipients. In 2014, the year after Jinghui's death, Chuanyin acted as a proxy for him and transmitted the Weiyang, Fayan, and Yunmen Dharma to 22 more recipients—as Jinghui had apparently received Dharma transmission in all five Chan lineages from Xuyun.

Given the great number of Dharma transmissions accomplished in Republican and post-Mao China, it is reasonable to wonder which criteria have guided the choice of Dharma recipients. When, in the 1960s, Holmes Welch interviewed Jueguang in Hong Kong on the reasons why he had never transmitted the Dharma up to that moment, Jueguang replied that he had so far found no one who was qualified: "As he explains it, a qualified disciple must know the T'ian-t'ai doctrine, be competent to spread the Dharma, and be a person with real promise" (Welch 1963, 119). However, as we have seen, from at least the 1990s until his death, Jueguang transmitted the Dharma on many occasions. This suggests that his criteria for the selection of recipients had probably become more flexible, and that, as in the Song (Shinohara 1999), one of the purposes underlying these transmissions might have been the expansion of Tiantai lineages in response to the challenge represented by the great number of Chan Dharma transmissions in the post-Mao period.

If the number of Jinghui's Dharma heirs (two hundred overall) and their identities are so well ascertained, it is because his closest disciples have drawn a detailed outline of all his transmissions (each accompanied by the date of the transmission, the Dharma name of the recipient, and a poem composed by Jinghui for each recipient) and published it in *Chan* magazine (Minghai et al. 2016), a periodical published and widely distributed by the Bailin Temple. According to Jinghui's disciples, two main reasons motivated this enterprise: first, the impossibility of ascertaining the exact number and identity of Xuyun's Dharma heirs after the end of the Cultural Revolution; and, second, the growing circulation, after Jinghui's passing away, of fake Dharma scrolls by monks claiming to have received transmission from him.

The preoccupation of clearly determining genealogies of Dharma families and the problem of the falsification of Dharma scrolls of eminent masters attest to the importance of Dharma lineages in contemporary China. While Dharma transmission is not the only or the most important factor granting a monk a high-ranking status and access to material and immaterial resources in contemporary China, the position of a monk within a Dharma lineage represents a very important credential and is consistently emphasized in biographies contained in both electronic and print materials of the temples he has restored.

This is because Dharma transmission not only bears a high symbolic value, but also entails concrete privileges. Unlike tonsure and ordination, which mostly create a direct master-disciple relationship and "horizontal" networks of brothers, Dharma transmission allows for the creation of extended "vertical" lineages that connect monastics to eminent figures of the past, offering a kind of a posteriori legitimation. Moreover, far from having only symbolic value, Dharma transmission also entails concrete privileges within the contemporary sangha. Suffice it to say that, as in the Republican period, private Dharma transmissions are frequently linked to the transmission of abbotship. In many public monasteries today, the current abbot is often a Dharma disciple of the previous one, and possessing Dharma transmission from the previous abbot is a necessary prerequisite for all candidates to abbotships.

Of course, the very nature of the lineage has changed since the early twentieth century. While it used to be a corporate entity owning material (temples) and intangible (monopolies, rights) assets, this has been entirely abolished, thus changing the very meaning and role of lineage in transmitting Buddhism. However, belonging to an exclusive and powerful Dharma family still is a valuable asset in contemporary China, where monastic competition has become fierce.

The Mao era, and especially the 1960s and 1970s, marked an interruption in the transmission of religious knowledge and in monastic ordinations, as well as a long period of temples' closure, destruction, or reallocation. The Buddhist reconstruction of the post-Mao period has been led chiefly by a senior generation of religious specialists who had been trained by the Buddhist leadership of the first half of the twentieth century. The Dharma lineages of Chan and Tiantai traditions represent one solid thread linking the Buddhist legacy of the Republican era to contemporary China. Besides sharing a considerable mobility, Chan and Tiantai Dharma lineages also carry strong religious, social, and political meanings, a combination of features that has allowed this special kind of Buddhist affiliation to play an instrumental role in the transition of Buddhist authority, expertise, and legitimacy beyond the Mao era.

The dissemination of Dharma lineages abroad in the 1940s—of Tiantai lineages principally in Hong Kong and of Chan lineages principally in the United States—has allowed the propagation of Chinese Buddhism and the preservation of its ritual expertise. Starting from the 1980s, it has also facilitated the flow of financial contributions and the reintroduction of religious expertise on the mainland. Through extensive religious networks based on Dharma kinship, material and immaterial resources have been provided to monks engaged in Buddhist reconstruction.

Besides inducing the creation of horizontal and vertical networks that have extended well beyond the Chinese borders, Chan and Tiantai Dharma lineages also bear intrinsic religious and political meanings. Dharma transmissions have in many cases tied senior monastic representatives to temples of their lineage and, after the end of the Mao era, provided them not only with the determination but also with the religious authority and legitimacy to restore them. In the last decades, the same religious authority and legitimacy associated with Dharma lineages has also favored the access of Dharma representatives to leading positions within Buddhist associations on both a regional and a national scale. In the twentieth century, Dharma lineages appear in fact to be the prerogative of a monastic elite belonging to the institutional form of Buddhism, with its public monasteries, institutes of studies, and associations.

This phenomenon has its roots in past Buddhist history. Since the establishment of the school's patriarchal lineage during the Tang and Song dynasties, Chan Dharma genealogies have often ensured the connection between religious legitimacy and political power, thus highly contributing to the fortunes of the school. One major reason is that genealogies based on Dharma transmission have long been considered as a token of orthodoxy from both an internal, religious perspective and an external, political point of view. In this sense, Dharma lineages also represent one way to define a boundary between Buddhist religious orthodoxy and other forms of Buddhist practices with a potentially ambiguous status. Given the enduring preoccupations of the Chinese state with religious orthodoxy throughout the twentieth century and beyond, it is therefore not surprising that the religious legitimacy associated with prestigious Dharma affiliation led the state to favor certain lineages of masters connected to private Dharma transmissions from well-known masters of the Republican period.

Notwithstanding their mythical origin and old-fashioned aura, Chan and Tiantai Dharma lineages are still alive and well in the twenty-first century. Genealogies dating back to a mythicized glorious past are one of the factors that have ensured the survival of the Chan and Tiantai schools of Buddhism across the centuries. Thanks to their long-standing prestige and systematic nature, they still represent a powerful device for the preservation and propagation of Chinese Buddhism in modern times.

APPENDIX 5.1: LINEAGE STANZAS AND PARTIAL CHARTS OF DHARMA TRANSMISSIONS

Xuyun's Dharma Transmissions (Chan School)

1. Weiyang branch (Xuyun's lineage)

7th generation: Patriarch Xingyang Ciduo 兴阳词铎
8th generation: Xuyun (public name Deqing 德清):

<u>词</u>德<u>宣</u>衍道大兴　　戒鼎馨遍五分新
慧焰弥布周沙界　　香云普荫灿古今
慈悲济世愿无尽　　光昭日月朗太清
振启拈花宏沩上　　圆相心灯永昌明[75]

9th generation Weiyang:

Xuanhua Dulun 宣化度轮 (1918–1995)	USA
Xuanyang Xingfu 宣扬性福 (1893–1966)	PRC

Xuanming Haideng 宣明海灯 (1902–1989)   PRC
Xuande Shaoyun 宣德绍云 (b. 1938)   PRC
Xuanchuan Yuechuan 宣传月传 (Chuanyin 传印, b. 1927)   PRC
Xuandao Jinghui 宣道净慧 (1933–2013)   PRC
Xuanyun Manjue 宣云满觉 (1907–1995)   PRC
Xuanxuan Shengyi 宣玄圣一 (1922–2010)   HK

2. Yunmen branch (Xuyun's lineage)

11th generation: Patriarch Yi'an Shenjing 已庵深淨
12th generation: Xuyun (tonsure name Yanche 演彻):

深演妙明耀乾坤   湛寂虚怀海印容
清净觉圆悬智镜   慧鉴精真道德融
慈悲喜舍昌普化   宏开拈花续传灯
继振云门关一旨   惠泽苍生法雨隆[76]

13th generation Yunmen:

Miaoxin Foyuan 妙心佛源 (1923–2009)   PRC
Miaoyun Fobao 妙云佛宝 (1911–1951)   PRC
Miaoci Fayun 妙慈法云 (d. 2003)   USA
Miaozong Jinghui 妙宗净慧 (1933–2013)   PRC
Miaodao Langyao 妙道朗耀 (d. 1987)   PRC
Miaoxu Fowei 妙虚佛纬 (Kuanneng 宽能 biqiuni, 1895–1989)   PRC

3. Fayan branch (Xuyun's lineage)

7th generation: Patriarch Xiangfu Liangqing 祥符良庆
8th generation: Xuyun (public name Xuyun 虚云):

良虚本寂体无量   法界通融广含藏
遍印森罗圆自在   塞空情器总真常
惟斯胜德昭日月   慧灯普照洞阴阳
传宗法眼大相义   光辉地久固天长[77]

9th generation Fayan:

Benxing Jinghui 本性净慧 (1933–2013)   PRC
Lingyi Jizhao 灵意寂照 (b. 1926)   PRC

4. Linji branch ("Longchi" 龙池 lineage)

42nd generation: Miaolian Dihua 妙莲地华 (ca. 1846–1907);
   Dharma name: Juehua 觉华
43rd generation: Xuyun Xingche 性彻

觉性本常寂   心惟法界同
如缘宏圣教   正法永昌隆[78]

44th generation Linji:

Benzong Jinghui 本宗净慧 (1933–2013)	PRC
Benhuan Chengmiao 本焕乘妙 (1907–2012)	PRC
Benda Yinxuan 本达印玄 (Tiguang 体光, 1924–2005)	PRC
Benzhao Shengkong 本昭圣空 (Yichao 意超, 1927–2013)	HK
Benmiao Zhiding 本妙知定 (Jy Din, 1917–2003)	USA
Zhenxin Benru 贞心本如 (Zhenxun Xiuyuan 贞训修圆, 1900–1959)	PRC

5. Caodong branch ("Jiangxi Shouchang" 江西寿昌 lineage)

46th generation: Dingfeng Yaocheng 鼎峰耀成 (1858–?)
47th generation: Xuyun Guyan 古岩

慧元道大兴	法界一鼎新
通天兼彻地	耀古复腾今
今日禅宗振	宏开洞上传
正中妙挟旨	虚融照独圆[79]

48th generation Caodong:

Fuxing Jinghui 复性净慧 (1933–2013)	PRC
Furen Fazong 复仁法宗 (1889–1973)	HK
Fuben Chandao 复本禅道 (b. 1934)	PRC

Dixian's Dharma Transmissions (Tiantai School)

Tiantai (Baisong's "Lingfeng" 灵峰 lineage)

42nd generation: Jiduan Dingrong 迹端定融
43rd generation: Dixian Guxu 谛闲古虚 (1858–1932)

真传正受	灵岳心宗	一乘顿观	印定古今
念起寂然	修性朗照	如是智德	体本玄妙
因缘生法	理事即空	等名为有	中道圆融
清净普遍	感通应常	果慧大用	实相永芳[80]

44th generation: Tanxu Jinxian 倓虚今衔 (1875–1963)	PRC/HK
45th generation: Yongxing Niangen 永惺念根 (1926–2016)	HK
45th generation: Baodeng 宝灯 (d. 1997)	HK
45th generation: Nengchan 能阐 (1922–2009)	PRC
45th generation: Yuanshan 圆山 (b.1919)	PRC
45th generation: Mingzhe Nianjing 明哲念晶 (1925–2012)	PRC
44th generation: Jingquan 静权 (1881–1960)	PRC
44th generation: Baojing Jinde 宝静今德 (1899–1940)	PRC/HK
45th generation: Xianming Nianfa 显明念法 (1917–2007)	PRC/HK/ TW/USA
46th generation: Jueguang Qiben 觉光起本 (1919–2014)	HK

NOTES

1. On the ordination ceremonies of the years 1955–1957, see Welch 1972, 121–123.

2. At the Beijing Guangji Temple from December 31, 1980, to January 1, 1981; see Jan 1984, 41–42.

3. For a sociological perspective on Buddhist revival since the end of the 1970s, see Ji and Goossaert 2011; Ji 2011a, 2012.

4. Tonsure (*tidu* 剃度)—having one's head shaved by a Buddhist master—is the preliminary act by which a layperson enters the Buddhist monastic community and becomes a "novice" (*shami* 沙弥 for men, *shamini* 沙弥尼 for women); in Chinese, tonsure is also called "leaving home" (*chujia* 出家). Ordination (*shoujie* 受戒, "accepting the precepts/prohibitions") is the ceremony by which a novice formally becomes a monk (*bhikṣu*) or a nun (*bhikṣuṇī*); nowadays in East Asia, Buddhist monasteries comply with the procedure known as "great precepts of the triple platform" (*santan dajie* 三坛大戒) where the ordinand successively accepts the Three Refuges of the laity, the ten prohibitions of the novitiate, the 250 prohibitions of the monk (348 for the nuns), and the fifty-eight vows of the bodhisattva. On ordination, see Ester Bianchi's chapter 6 in this volume.

5. On Xuyun, see Campo 2013, 2017.

6. On Dixian, see Yu 1995, 26–28; Ruan and Gao 1992, 219–221.

7. On Chan transmission stanzas as a literary genre, see Lai 1983.

8. The same procedure is observed in Chinese Buddhism for conferring the tonsure.

9. On the way religious clans based on Dharma have shaped the organization of modern Chinese Buddhism, see Zhang 2015.

10. On lineage in early Tiantai (and for a bibliography), see Penkower 2000. On Tiantai lineage in the Sung, see Shinohara 1999.

11. On Chan lineages, see Wu 1998. On the development and meanings of Chan lineages in the school's formation period, see, for example, Morrison 2010; Adamek 2007.

12. See, on this, Foulk 1999.

13. "Zongjiaolü zhuzong yanpai" 宗教律诸宗演派, compiled by Shouyi 守一, X88n1667. CBETA version, accessed January 2018, http://tripitaka.cbeta.org/X88n1667.

14. This is the lineage of the Tang dynasty Chan Master Tianhuang Daowu 天皇道悟.

15. Baohuashan (near Nanjing) was the model monastery for ordinations in China in the first half of the twentieth century; see Welch 1967.

16. On this lineage, see Zhang 2015, 57.

17. Private Dharma transmissions are also recorded in the Sino-Tibetan tradition of Master Nenghai 能海 (1886–1967); see Bianchi 2017c.

18. On Miaoshan and the revival of Putuoshan after the Mao era, see chapter 2 by Claire Vidal in this volume.

19. *Jiaozheng xingdengji* 校正星燈集, a work devoted to the lineages of the Linji branch. For a few extracts, see *Xuyun laoheshang fahui* 2005 (238–242); the 1932 preface was published in 1936 in the Buddhist magazine *Foxue ban yuekan* (Xuyun 1936a).

20. Jinghui, interview with the author, Beijing Guangji Temple, 2001.

21. At the end of the Qing dynasty and the beginning of the Republican era, the collective transmission of the Caodong Dharma was used at the Yongquan Monastery in Fujian in association with the handover of the abbotship; see Campo 2017b.

22. For all complete stanzas and references, see the appendix to this chapter (translation of stanzas is not provided).

23. Xuyun relates the conditions having led him to resume the three interrupted lineages in his essay "Chanzong wupai yuanliu" 禅宗五派源流 (Origin and Development of the Five Schools of Chan). This essay, annexed to the revised and enlarged edition of *The Inscribed Portraits of the Buddhist Patriarchs* (Xuyun 1935), is included in *Xuyun laoheshang fahui* (243–245), where the three complete stanzas can also be found.

24. The most important stanzas of the Linji and Caodong schools are also included in the last section (*zongpai* 宗派) of the breviary *Chanmen risong* 禅门日诵, here cited as Lan 2004, vol. 97, *Zaji bu shisi* 杂集部十四.

25. As for tonsure, Xuyun belonged to the fifty-fourth generation Linji; his tonsure master was Shangci Changkai 善慈常开. The character *yan* 演 of Xuyun's tonsure name Yanche 演彻 was taken from the "Wutai Emei Putuo" stanza of the Linji lineage. The Linji "Wutai Emei Putuo" stanza is the most widely used in modern times for conferring tonsure names (*ming* 名); for this stanza, see *Manji shinsan dainihon zokuzōkyō* (X88n1667, 0560a08); Lan 2004, vol. 97, 625–626. Xuyun also composed a series of supplementary verses to continue the "Wutai Emei Putuo" stanza, which by his time was approaching its end; he also composed one separate stanza for conferring public names (*zi* 字) for tonsure: *Xuyun laoheshang fahui* (240–242, annexed to the amended edition of *The Starry Lamp Collection*). On Xuyun's monastic names, see also Campo 2017b.

26. See, for example, "Fu Yunnan Yuantong Si Zixing, Hongjing er heshang" 复云南圆通寺自性宏净二和尚, *Xuyun laoheshang fahui,* 180.

27. One example is Benda Yinxuan 本达印玄 (Tiguang 体光, 1924–2005). His religious instructions (delivered in his last years to his community of the Jingju Monastery of Mount Qingyuan in Jiangxi) have been published in a volume that is well-known by Chan practitioners, the *Tiguang laoheshang kaishi lu* (2006).

28. For example: Xuande Shaoyun 宣德绍云 (b. 1938) in Anhui; Qixian 齐贤 (b. 1939) in Hebei; Fuben Chandao 复本禅道 (b. 1934) in Hunan; Lingyi Jizhao 灵意寂照 (b. 1926) in Inner Mongolia.

29. I conducted fieldwork and interviews with Foyuan at Yunmen Monastery in 2006.

30. The Bailu Temple (Bailu Si 白鹿寺) and the Zhusheng Temple (Zhusheng Si 祝圣寺) in Hunan.

31. I conducted fieldwork at the Nanhua Monastery and interviews with its abbot Chuanzheng 传正 in 2006.

32. I interviewed Benhuan at Hongfa Temple (Hongfa Si 弘法寺) in Shenzhen in 2006.

33. A few articles appeared in the journal *Xiandai foxue* on Benhuan's arrest: "Nanhua si zhuchi Benhuan yuanlai shi ge fangeming fenzi" 1958; "Nanhua si quanti sengtu yonghu zhengfu daibu Benhuan" 1958; "Guangzhou shi fodao jiaotu jihui shengtao fangeming fenzi Benhuan" 1958; "Manasi xian dafo si fojiaotu yonghu zhengfu daibu Benhuan" 1958; see also Welch 1972, 239–247, 261–263.

34. The Biechuan Temple (Biechuan Si 别传寺), the Guangxiao Temple (Guangxiao Si 光孝寺), the Hongfa Temple, the Kaijing Nunnery (Kaijing Si 开净寺), and the Daxiong Chan Temple (Daxiong Chan Si 大雄禅寺).

35. The Bao'en Temple (Bao'en Si 报恩寺) and the monastery of the Fourth Chan Patriarch at Huangmei (Sizu Zhengjue Daochang 四祖正觉道场).

36. The Baizhang Chan Temple (Baizhang Chan Si 百丈禅寺).

37. I conducted fieldwork and interviews with Yinkong at the Dajinshan Monastery in 2006 and 2015, as well as in 2013 with sinologist and emeritus professor Catherine Despeux.

38. Her Dharma name is Changzhen 當真; she belongs to the forty-fifth Linji Dharma generation.

39. Among these were her Dharma "uncles" Foyuan and Jinghui.

40. On the Buddhist Academy of Hongfa Temple, see chapter 7 by Ji Zhe in this volume.

41. Mingyang was a disciple of Chan master Yuanying 圓瑛 (1878–1953) and is the compiler of his official biography (Mingyang 1996).

42. On Xuanhua, see *In Memory of the Venerable Master Hsuan Hua* (1996, vol. 2; see p. 40 for a photograph of his Dharma scroll). The website of the City of Ten Thousand Buddhas is http://www.cttbusa.org (accessed January 2018).

43. Shi Zhiding 釋知定, "Daonian Yungong laoren" 悼念云公老人 (*Xuyun laoheshang nianpu fahui zengding ben* 1997, 983); on Zhiding, see also Ashiwa and Wank 2016. Benzhao Shengkong 本昭聖空 (Yichao 意超, 1927–2013), a Dharma disciple of Xuyun in the Guiyang lineage, also recounted how Xuyun had literally forced him to move to Hong Kong one week before the Communist takeover. (I am grateful to Bill Porter for discovering this information during an interview with Yichao in 2006.) A native of Hong Kong, where he was conferred the tonsure, Yichao left the city and received ordination at the Nanhua Monastery in 1944. For a few years, he accompanied Xuyun on the occasion of his journeys to Hong Kong and served as an interpreter. Eventually Yichao returned to Hong Kong, becoming abbot of the Zhulin Chan Monastery 竹林禪院, where he passed away in 2013; on the Zhulin Chan Monastery in the 1950s, see Welch 1961.

44. The Zen Buddhist Order of Hsu Yun website is http://hsuyun.org (accessed January 2018).

45. The Yunmen lineage, too, has reached the United States, through Xuyun's Dharma heir in the thirteenth generation and former personal attendant Miaoci Fayun 妙慈法雲 (1933–2003). Fayun approached Xuyun at the Nanhua Monastery and followed him to Yunmen. After assuming the office of guest prefect at the Liurong Monastery in 1953, he left the continent in 1958 and moved to Hong Kong; then, in 1969, he went to New York, where he established a Buddhist temple (Meiguo Niuyue Fo'en Si 美国纽约佛恩寺). After Fayun's death in 2003, his disciples followed his written wishes and brought his ashes back to Yunmen. His great stupa now occupies a place of honor in the hill behind the monastery.

46. Xuanyang Xingfu 宣扬性福 (1893–1966). The second abbot of the Zhenru Monastery, Xuanming Haideng 宣明海灯 (1902–1989), also received the Guiyang Dharma from Xuyun in 1956 and was a representative of the ninth generation; on Haideng, see "Haideng fashi zhuchi Yunju Shan Zhenru Si" 1957; Fan 1991. Xuyun never occupied the position of abbot of the Zhenru Monastery.

47. Jinghui, interview with the author, Beijing Guangji Monastery, 2001.

48. On summer camps organized by Jinghui at the Bailin Temple, see Ji 2011c.

49. This is, for example, the case for Delin, who was abbot of the Gaomin Monastery (the monastery of his Dharma master Laiguo) from 1984 to 2005.

50. With the possible exception of Zhiding. It should be noted that a few of these monks had been ordained by Xuyun.

51. Dixian received Dharma transmission from Jiduan Dingrong 迹端定融 (fl. 1800), the abbot of the Longhua Monastery in Shanghai (Tanxu 1998, 231). See also Ma 2015, 31–48.

52. The lineage derives its name from its third representative, Lingfeng Ouyi 灵峰蕅益 (1599–1655).

53. X88n1667, 0565b24.

54. For the complete stanza, see the appendix to this chapter.

55. Tanxu's autobiography is Tanxu 1998; on Tanxu (and for a bibliography), see Carter 2011.

56. For a partial English translation, see Welch 1967, 173–176.

57. They had to be younger than him; their virtue, prestige, and qualifications had to be inferior to his own; they had to comply with his directions in every matter. See Tanxu 1998, *vol. 2,* 228.

58. Tanxu gave prescriptions for the transmission of abbotship in his code for the Zhanshan Monastery ("Qingdao Zhanshan Si gongzhu guiyue" 青岛湛山寺共住规约: Tanxu 1998, *vol. 2,* 174–178) and composed separate rules focusing on the abbot's responsibilities and obligations as leader of the monastic community ("Zhanshan Si zhuchi jiandan lingzhong kecheng guize" 湛山寺住持简单领众课程规则: Tanxu 1998, *vol. 2,* 219). See also Campo 2017c.

59. For a chart, see Tanxu 1998, *vol. 2,* 222. In these northern provinces Tanxu also established thirteen modern institutes of Buddhist studies and Buddhist schools.

60. On Baojing, see Chen and Deng 2000, 388.

61. On Jingquan, see Chen and Deng 2000, 391–392.

62. From Baojing's Dharma disciple Xianming 显明 (Nianfa 念法, 1917–2007); see Welch 1963, 118–119. Many videos are available on the Internet of Xianming expounding on the sutras.

63. The Hong Kong Buddhist Association has always been strongly engaged in welfare activities. These included four schools, a cemetery, and two clinics at its beginning (Welch 1961, 109–110); the association's website and magazine today list forty enterprises including primary and middle schools, kindergartens, hospitals and medical services, services for young and elderly people, and a cemetery ("Hui shu danwei yu xuexiao" 会属单位与学校, Hong Kong Buddhist Association, accessed January 2018, http://www.hkbuddhist.org/).

64. The sixty-page magazine's issue number 655 (December 2014) is entirely devoted to Jueguang, who had just passed away.

65. "Ting zhanglao shuo gushi" 听长老说故事 (The Elder Tells a Story).

66. Shijie Fojiao Youyihui Gang Ao Diqu Fenhui 世界佛教友谊会港澳地区分会.

67. On the beginnings of this organization, see Welch 1961, 110–111.

68. Xianggang Tebie Xingzhengqu Zhengfu Jibenfa qicao Weiyuanhui Fenhui 香港特别行政区政府基本法起草委员会分会.

69. Accounts of these ceremonies can be found in many issues of HKBA's magazine *Xianggang fojiao* (see, for example, "Tiantaizong chuanfa dadian" 2009; "Hongyang jiaoguan, zhongxing Tiantai" 2007).

70. The Jade Buddha Temple (Yufo Si 玉佛寺) and the Buddha Light Temple (Foguang Si 佛光寺) in Houston; the Qianfo Temple (Qianfo Si 千佛寺) in Boston.

71. The website for the Texas Buddhist Association is http://www.jadebuddha.org/?index=en. For the association's organization chart, see http://jadebuddha.org/pdf/tba-organization.pdf, accessed October 2018.

72. Jueguang has offered to the Longhua Monastery a Buddha statue that is now displayed in the main hall, as well as a few calligraphies and inscriptions (fieldwork observations at the Longhua Monastery in Shanghai, 2013).

73. See the case of Miaozhan and Hongchuan in chapter 8 by Ashiwa and Wank in this volume.

74. Mingzhe's Dharma scroll is displayed in his memorial hall at Zhanshan Monastery in Qingdao (fieldwork conducted in July 2017).

75. *Xuyun laoheshang fahui* 2005, 244.

76. Ibid., 245.

77. Ibid.

78. *Manji shinsan dainihon zokuzōkyō*, 1975–1989 (X88n1667, 0559c06); Lan 2004, vol. 97, 624.

79. This supplementary stanza of the "Jiangxi Shouchang" stanza of the Caodong lineage is not included in the *Manji shinsan dainihon zokuzōkyō* (X88n1667) but can be found in Lan 2004, vol. 97, 641–642.

80. *Manji shinsan dainihon zokuzōkyō* (X88n1667, 0565b24).

6

"TRANSMITTING THE PRECEPTS IN CONFORMITY WITH THE DHARMA"

Restoration, Adaptation, and Standardization of Ordination Procedures

ESTER BIANCHI

In contemporary Chinese Buddhism, there seems to be a precise will aimed at revitalizing discipline and at restoring ancient—thus reputed to be "correct"—ordination procedures and rules.[1] More precisely, the "triple platform ordination" (*santan dajie* 三坛大戒), which dates back to the early seventeenth century and was already a widespread ordination criterion during the Republic of China, was recently selected as the normative procedure to be followed in the PRC for both monks and nuns. There is also a movement to confer ordinations to nuns according to "dual ordination" (*erbuseng jie* 二部僧戒), a model that was first introduced in China during the fifth century but that was long disregarded and never the standard procedure.

My starting assumption is that ordination procedures have been restored after a long ban in the Mao era in order to revive the monastic community according to what are perceived as elevated and "proper" criteria. This is clearly suggested by a saying that recurs frequently in both monastic and official documents: "to transmit the precepts in conformity with the Dharma" (*rufa chuanjie* 如法传戒), that is, according to "proper and correct" monastic protocol and rules. However, this restoration and adaptation of ancient rituals and rules has further involved a process of standardization and unification. The objective of the present chapter is to provide a general overview and a tentative evaluation of this contemporary phenomenon, taking into account the positions and perspectives of the various actors involved (the monastic establishment and individual monks and nuns), as well as external factors such as the role of governmental authorities and international interlocutors.

REESTABLISHING ORDINATION PROCEDURES FROM TRADITIONAL MODELS

The contemporary proponents of a Vinaya resurgence (*jielü fuxing* 戒律复兴) can refer to some very authoritative forerunners, who were also involved with the ordination issue. For instance, Daoxuan 道宣 (596–667), the well-known Sui and Tang master who is traditionally viewed as the founder of the Southern Monastery (Nanshan 南山) Vinaya lineage,[2] believed that the crisis of the Buddhist community of his time was caused by shortcomings in the ascetic and ritual practices of monks and nuns, and this was the reason for his reformation of the ordination system through the "ordination platform" (*jietan* 戒坛).[3] Similarly, a rejuvenation of ordination ceremonies also occurred during the late Ming and early Qing, following the ban on Buddhist ordinations of the Jiajing reign (1526); it was set in motion by the works and efforts of a number of masters acknowledged as late imperial China's revivers of the monastic discipline.[4] These and other examples reveal that a regeneration of the monastic community from its very basis and beginning (i.e., the entrance into the monastic order) has been often deemed indispensable to cope with an alleged moral decline of Buddhism. This seems also to be the case for the ordination reforms carried out in the PRC.

Particularly relevant for the contemporary situation is the Vinaya resurgence, which occurred between the end of the Ming and the beginning of the Qing dynasties. Guxin Ruxin 古心如馨 (1541–1615), who declared himself to have received the true transmission of the "orthodox lineage of the Southern Monastery" (Nanshan Zhengzong 南山正宗), thus reconnecting himself with Daoxuan (Wu Jiang 2008, 30), created the triple platform ordination, which was destined to become the only ordination criterion in the contemporary PRC. This system was thus elaborated within the Nanshan tradition at a time of Buddhist resurgence and in reaction to a previous ban on Buddhist ordinations.[5] It was later promulgated by Hanyue Fazang 汉月法藏 (1573–1635) in his *Chuanshou santan hongjie fayi* 传授三坛弘戒法仪 (Ritual for the Conferment of the Triple Platform Great Ordination; X 1127). In the year 1660, during the first phase of the Qing dynasty, Duti Jianyue 读体见月 (1601–1679), a second-generation disciple of Guxin, published the *Chuanjie zhenfan* 传戒正范 (Rules for Ceremonies of the Transmission of the Precepts; X 1128), which further detailed ritual procedures and were destined to become the standard guidelines in modern times.

According to this system, a monk or nun must participate in three different ordination ceremonies (novice, complete, and bodhisattva), which are held together in one place and within a specific period of time, generally between twenty and sixty days. Every ceremony is preceded by a study period of one to three weeks and a purification and confession ritual the night before. As the ordination procedures and the number of precepts to be accepted differ, monks and nuns are ordained separately.[6] In the case of novice ordination, the ritual is identical for male and female ordinands, who are requested to recite the Three Refuges (in the Buddha, Dharma, and sangha) formula and to accept the Ten Precepts.[7] On the other hand, "complete ordination" (Ch. *juzujie* 具足戒, Skt. *upasampadā*) differs for monks and nuns and implies a much more elaborate ceremony, since it involves the conferment of all *prātimokṣa* prohibitions, that is, the full set of precepts that *bhikṣus* and *bhikṣuṇīs* have to follow.[8] The ritual is headed by a "principal master" (*heshang* 和尚), a "master of the ritual," or *karmācārya* (*jiemo* 羯磨), an "instructor" (*jiaoshou* 教授), and seven other monastic "witnesses" (*qi zheng shi* 七证师).[9] Finally, in addition to these two ordinations, which are prescribed in the *Vinayapiṭaka*, in East Asia, monks and nuns also receive the very Mahayanic Bodhisattva Precepts of the *Brahmā's Net Sutra*, which are the same for nuns and monks, as well as for those laypeople who choose to take them.[10]

As for the particular case of nuns' ordination, it is stated in the *Vinayapiṭaka* that "after a woman has been trained as a probationer [*śikṣamāṇā*] for two years, the ordination ceremony must be carried out in both [nuns' and monks'] orders."[11] According to this rule, female novices first shall receive and respect the *śikṣamāṇā* six rules for a period of two years.[12] Only after this period of time should female novices be conferred complete ordination, a ritual to be performed according to the dual ordination system (*erbuseng jie*, literally "ordination by the two sangha orders"); nuns receive the precepts first by ten *bhikṣuṇīs* acting as nun masters, and then by ten ordained monks, representing the *bhikṣu* community.[13]

The figure of the *śikṣamāṇā* never really developed in imperial China. Dual ordination procedures, on the other hand, were transmitted to China from Sri Lanka in 433–434,[14] but they were mostly discarded afterward. We know from historical sources that dual ordinations were sometimes held during the Song, at the end of the Ming and during the Qing dynasty, but these cases were most probably exceptional:[15] In imperial times, full ordination was usually conferred to the nuns by ten *bhikṣu* masters alone, a procedure that in Chinese Buddhism—differently than other Buddhist traditions—was reputed to be fully legitimate.[16] It is noteworthy that Shuyu 书玉, author of the principal reference text for the "Dual Ordination Procedures" (Erbuseng shoujie yishi 二部僧受戒仪式, X 1134), was a direct disciple of the above-mentioned Vinaya master Duti Jianyue, and his book was written on the basis of a *bhikṣuṇī* ordination performed by Duti Jianyue in 1667. This reconnects dual ordinations with the Vinaya resurgence that occurred in late imperial times and also brought the establishment of the triple platform system.

Following the reopening of many temples and monasteries in the early 1980s, China witnessed an immediate increase in monastic ordinations, after a ban that had lasted for more than two decades.[17] The first *bhikṣu* ordination took place at Beijing's Guangji Temple between December 31, 1980, and

January 1, 1981 (Jan 1984, 41–42; Mingshan 2002, 125); one year after, on January 1982, the first *bhikṣuṇī* ordination was held in Chengdu's Tiexiang Temple 铁像寺. Both of these occasions can be regarded as Chinese Buddhists' first attempts to stand up again. Even if they involved only small groups of new ordinands, they hold a very great symbolic importance and are thus often recollected and celebrated both by contemporary monastics and by most of the relevant sources.[18]

The Guangji Temple ordination was held for the forty-seven monk students of the newly founded Buddhist Academy of China (Zhongguo Foxueyuan 中国佛学院; see chapter 7 by Ji Zhe in this volume). According to Xuecheng, chair of the Buddhist Association of China (BAC) from 2015 to 2018, "complete ordination was conferred to the monks following the Vinaya of the (Mūla-)sarvāstivāda tradition, and this was something that had not occurred in China for centuries" (Xuecheng 1997, 11); on the other hand, though celebrated as a triple platform ordination, the ceremony lasted only two days, whereas twenty to sixty days are usually required.[19] In order to celebrate the event, Zhao Puchu himself, at that time chair of the BAC, presented "vegetarian offerings" to the newly ordained monks. That same year, the Fujian branch of the BAC organized a triple platform ordination in the Yongquan Temple 涌泉寺 (Gushan 鼓山) in accordance with the Nanshan lü 南山律, thus referring to the Vinaya of the Dharmaguptaka;[20] afterward new ordinations were held in succession in Shanxi, Sichuan, Guangdong, and Zhejiang (Wen 2010, 3).

The first *bhikṣuṇī* ordination in twenty-five years took place in 1982 in Chengdu. Since ordination was conferred to the nuns according to the dual ordination system, it was celebrated first in the Tiexiang Temple, a nunnery headed by Longlian 隆莲 (1909–2006), and subsequently inside the most prominent male Buddhist monastery in Chengdu, the Wenshuyuan 文殊院.[21] On this occasion, only nine ordinands participated in the ceremony; in March 1987 it was the turn of twenty more nuns, new graduates from the Sichuan Buddhist Academy for Nuns in the Tiexiang Temple.[22] Meanwhile, another dual ordination had been celebrated in 1984 in the Chongfu Temple 崇福寺, in Fuzhou (Chen 2011, 24–25).

After these first significant events, male and female ordinations increased rapidly and steadily: The scope of the phenomenon is quite impressive, judging from the fact that, as observed by Ji Zhe, during the 1990s and 2000s the number of newly ordained monastics regularly exceeded the limits imposed by the BAC (Ji 2012, 14–15). Moreover, not only was there an increasing demand to have greater numbers of ordinations (quantitative factor); there was also an interest that ordinations be restored according to what were believed to be "correct" standards and "proper" models (qualitative factor), thus causing the widespread affirmation and, finally, standardization of the triple platform ordination and, within this system, of dual ordinations for nuns.

STANDARDIZATION AND UNIFICATION OF RULES AND PROCEDURES

Standardization of ordination procedures in the PRC actually began in the early 1980s, but its origins can be traced back to the beginning of the 1950s. Consider that already at the first meeting of the BAC in 1953, the question of the sangha system (*sengqie zhidu* 僧伽制度) was regarded as one of the two key problems facing Chinese Buddhism, together with doctrinal issues. In 1957, at the second meeting of the national congress of the BAC, the newly elected chair, Sherab Gyatso (Ch. Xirao Jiacuo 喜饶嘉措), declared:

> As for ordinations in Chinese Buddhist monasteries . . . a committee has been established . . . in order to carry out research on ordination procedures and on methods for Vinaya studies and to raise plans and suggestions. It is our hope that all Han Chinese delegates, once they have returned to their original areas, shall pass on to the monasteries and the believers of their respective places the spirit of "transmitting the precepts according to the Dharma" that was sustained by this meeting of the congress, with the hope that no more flawed transmissions will occur.[23]
>
> 其中大家最关心的汉族地区的传戒问题，已由大会决定，在理事会下设立一个委员会，并推定了委员的筹备人，这个委员会的任务，主要是对传戒、学戒办法进行研究，提出方案。 希望汉族各位代表回到各地后将这次会议重视如法传戒的精神向各地寺庙和教徒，广泛传达，务期滥传现象不再发。 (Xirao Jiacuo 1957, 29)

This statement should not come as a surprise: In the 1950s Buddhist leaders were carrying on "traditions" that had been consolidating during the first half of the twentieth century. Triple platform ordination ceremonies were already a widespread practice during the Republican era, though they were often carried out in an "inaccurate and oversimplified manner," as pointed out by Daniela Campo (2017b, 133); at the same time, these were not the only possible criteria, as other ordination typologies (notably, complete ordinations separated from novice ordination, and/or not including bodhisattva ordination) also continued to be practiced (Bianchi 2017b, 116, 118; Welch 1967, 285–296; Xuecheng 1997, 8–11). On the other hand, Longlian, principal promoter of dual ordinations in modern China, had already been instructed in what she believed to be the "correct procedures" for nuns' ordinations in 1949[24] but was not able to resurrect them before 1982. Accordingly, Xiaoyun 晓云 (Hiuwan in Cantonese), one of the most influential Buddhist nuns in Hong Kong and Taiwan, who met Longlian during her years in Sichuan in the 1940s,[25] was also an advocate for the introduction of the dual ordination system.[26] This suggests that *bhikṣuṇī* ordination rules were a typical topic of discussion among Buddhist circles in China during the first half of the century, at least in Sichuan.

Whatever the case, the resolutions taken by the BAC in the 1950s were to be abandoned very soon, considering that, from 1957, no more ordinations took place in China; still, the initiatives of these early-twentieth-century monastic leaders can be regarded as significant antecedents of the more recent movement.

As proved by the monks' ordination at the Yongquan Temple (1981) and by the nuns' ordination at the Chongfu Temple, the Fujian Buddhist Association played a major role in establishing the ordination system for the new era. Indeed, in the early 1980s, while first ordinations were already taking place, the BAC created at the Fujian Institute of Buddhist Studies a "team for the study of the Vinaya" composed by the monks Jiequan 界诠 (a very authoritative contemporary Vinaya master), Xingguang 性光, Yiran 毅然, Yanlian 演莲, and Jiqun 济群, a sign that the need was felt to establish proper disciplinary standards. Instructed by Yuanzhuo 圆拙 (1909–1997), who had been a direct disciple of the renowned Vinaya master Hongyi 弘一 (1880–1942),[27] the "five *bhikṣus*" (*wu biqiu* 五比丘)—a name that also refers to the first five disciples of Śākyamuni—took on the task of revitalizing the Nanshan tradition in the contemporary era.[28]

The definitive standardization of triple platform ordinations occurred in the 1990s. A first "standard ordination ceremony" (*guifan chuanjie* 规范传戒) was held at Putian Guanghua Temple (Fujian) between October 1996 and January 1997; based on this exemplary model and other previous experiences, final rules were set in three official documents promulgated in September 2000.[29] The whole operation was conducted on the basis of the alleged "Chinese Buddhist tradition." For instance, we read in ordination announcements that "following the inherited tradition of the Chinese Buddhist world, those willing to take the Buddhist vows ought to receive all three ordination levels [novice, complete, and bodhisattva] in order to be unanimously recognized as legitimate Mahayana monks or nuns" (*hege zhi dasheng chujiaren* 合格之大乘出家人).[30]

Contemporary official regulations also state clearly that nuns' ordinations must follow the dual ordination procedures.[31] The dual ordination system, after being introduced by Longlian in the 1980s, was chosen as the ordination criterion for the mass *bhikṣuṇī* ordination that took place in 1993 in Baima Temple 白马寺 (Luoyang) and was consequently followed in most subsequent nuns' ordinations. Finally, at the century's turn, it became the rule.[32] As for the *śikṣamāṇā*s, according to a recent study by Ann Heirman and Chiu Tzu-Lung, they are now less uncommon in China than before, probably thanks to Longlian's influence and despite her belief that she had partially failed in this regard.[33] As a matter of fact, official rules state that nuns' complete ordination can take place only after a two-year period following entrance into the Buddhist order (while for male novices only one year is requested in the official regulations); furthermore, some nuns' ordination announcements explicitly refer to female novices and *śikṣamāṇā*s, thus officially recognizing the existence and legitimacy of this status.[34]

Unlike in Taiwan (where different ordination criteria still coexist),[35] this clear and evident standardization coincides with a process of unification of ordination rules and criteria, even down to the last details. A tendency toward strict uniformity is revealed by the comparison of ordination announcements of the first four years of the 2010s. General details, requirements, and rules, which one finds in the ordination announcements, include the following:[36]

- Most ordination ceremonies last one month (from twenty-eight to thirty or thirty-one days).[37]
- Most ceremonies take place on a national scale, even if in some cases priority is granted to local ordinands (only a few are regional).
- When data is available, participants' maximum quota is usually 300 to 350 male and/or 300 to 350 female ordinands for each ceremony. Registration is generally closed once the maximum quota has been reached.
- Ordinands should have been tonsured in a Han Chinese Buddhist monastery for at least one year (male) or two years (female).
- Ordinands must submit the following documents: recommendation letters from the tonsure master and from the local Buddhist association or, if there is none in the area, from the local Religious Affairs Bureau (Zongjiao Shiwu Ju 宗教事务局); identity card; tonsure certificate; health certificate; marital status certificate (or divorce certificate).
- General requirements include the following: age between twenty and fifty-nine;[38] junior middle school degree; unmarried status at the moment of ordination; healthy condition.[39]
- Ordinands must have a firm faith, be patriotic, observe discipline and law, and have never been involved in criminal activities.
- Ordinands have to know by heart basic texts such as the "Morning and Evening Chanting Services" (Zhaomu gongke 朝暮功课), the "Ten Novice Precepts" (Shami shijie 沙弥十戒) or "Rules and Ceremonies for Novices" (Shami lüyi 沙弥律仪), and the "Daily Vinaya" (Pini riyong 毗尼日用).

RELIGIOUS AND POLITICAL MEANINGS OF THE STANDARDIZATION

My hypothesis is that the process of Vinaya resurgence taking place in the PRC serves as an effort to guarantee "purity" and "orthodoxy" for the monastic community on a moral-disciplinary basis, considering that Vinaya is traditionally understood as the very foundation of the Buddhist Dharma.

In the Buddhist scriptures one finds unmistakable sentences supporting this hypothesis, which are often cited in current discourses: "if the Vinaya dwells in the world then the Dharma will dwell in the world" (毗尼住世佛法则住; X 41, 732, 875); "thanks to the permanence of the Vinaya in the world, the Dharma will dwell long as well" (毗尼住世则正法久住; X 40, 720, 489); and so on. These and similar passages were quoted, for instance, by Chuanyin 传印, former chair of the BAC, and by other Buddhist delegates participating at the Workshop on Standard Ordinations in Chinese Buddhism (Quanguo Hanchuan Fojiao Guifan Chuanjie Yantaoban 全国汉传佛教规范传戒研讨班) that was held at Putuoshan 普陀山 Buddhist Academy in July 2011 (Chen 2011, 22, 27). As a consequence, these same quotations are also often reported in blogs and on web pages by prominent Buddhist masters, as in the case of Jiqun and Chongrou 崇柔 (see Chongrou 2013 and Jiqun 2013).[40]

Interestingly, in his speech delivered at the Sixth Meeting of the Congress of the Hunan Buddhist Association (November 2013), Shenghui 圣辉, abbot of the Nanputuo Temple 南普陀寺 and presently vice-chair of the BAC, quoted the same canonical passages and further declared:

> The Vinaya serves to help monastics to control their bodies and minds, it is the foundation of Buddhism and its lifeblood. It is necessary to keep it always in mind and to constantly put it into practice. . . . The monastic community must persist in abiding to monastic discipline and must behave in a dignified manner; sangha members have to speak in terms of human dignity, monastic dignity and national dignity; they ought to be exemplary persons worthy of their name, they cannot become the "false monks" or "Buddhist cheaters" so much detested by the people. . . . Only in this way Buddhism may be able to complete its mission of spreading the Dharma and benefitting living beings, only then Buddhism may really realize the "China dream."
>
> 戒律作为约束僧众身心的准则, 是佛教的根本, 是佛教的命脉所在, 必须时刻牢记, 常抓不懈。...僧人必须坚持持戒、修行、具足威仪, 必须讲人格、僧格、国格, 成为名符其实的天人师, 而不能成为人所非议的 "假和尚"、"附佛骗子" ... 也只有这样, 佛教才会具足弘法利生的资粮, 才能真正地实现 "中国梦." (Shenghui 2013)

The contemporary Vinaya resurgence is thus presented not only as an important aspect of the so-called Buddhist revival (*fojiao fuxing* 佛教复兴), but moreover as its innermost foundation,[41] and the reaffirmation of a disciplinary strictness seems to be deemed necessary for the subsequent regeneration of the monastic community and of Chinese Buddhism as a whole. This not only aims at elevating virtues and qualities of the sangha, but also enables its members to act as adequate spiritual guides for the increasingly demanding laity and as authoritative interlocutors for political institutions. This was a primary objective for the monastic establishment, which was also pursued via means of Dharma transmission and the creation of Dharma lineages, as pointed out by Daniela Campo in chapter 5.

In this light, it seems reasonable for Buddhist authorities to consider the restoration of "orthodox" rules for entrance into monastic orders as a priority. In the words of William B. Bodiford, the process of ordination—in the Christian tradition understood as "the conferral of priestly status"—when applied to the Buddhist tradition "overlaps with aspects of ceremonies that in other religions are not necessarily associated with ordination, such as Baptism (a ritual purification and a rite for joining a religious community), christening (a ritual for assigning a religious name), consecration (as a ritual anointment that confirms a religious status), or initiation (as a ritual admission to the secret traditions or knowledge of a religious order)" (Bodiford 2005, 16). This process serves to define monks and nuns as the heirs of the religious authority of the Buddha, as the sole actors who can assure the maintenance of the Buddhist Dharma in the world. But this is true only as long as the ordination ceremonies "are performed properly (by a qualified preceptor and applicant, before the appropriate witness)," because if a ritual is performed incorrectly, "the essence of the precepts (*jieti* 戒体) will be lacking and the applicant's membership rendered invalid" (Bodiford 2005, 2–3).

Judging from official statements made by high-ranking representatives of the Buddhist establishment, reform and revival of monastic ordinations need to be implemented in the modern era in order to cope with a state of decline in the Buddhist community, echoing the concerns of Daoxuan, Guxin Ruxin, and other previous leaders, including those during the Republican era.[42] Consider that, at the foundation ceremony of the BAC in 1953, Zhao Puchu gave a speech on the development of the "fine Buddhist tradition" and stated:

> Finding ways to counter malpractices inherited from the past and facing the complex situation of the contemporary monastic community, solving some of the existing problems on the basis of Vinaya principles, and enabling the monastic community to recover the "six harmonies" [*liu he* 六和],[43] are really important actions to be undertaken.
>
> 怎样针对过去的弊病和现在僧团内的复杂情况，依照戒律的原则，实际解决目前存在着的一些问题，使今后的僧伽得以恢复六和的意义，这实在是一件重要的事 (Zhao 1953, 6).

More recently, Shenghui, at the celebration of the fiftieth anniversary of the association, reported that

> monastic discipline has become lax and Buddhist customs are not upright. . . . These bad customs have already seriously corrupted the sangha, ruining the image and prestige of Buddhism; if they continue to

develop, they will certainly endanger the future destiny of Chinese Buddhism. All nuns and monks must have a firm faith, regard monastic discipline as their master [*yijie wei shi* 以戒为师], practice diligently the three learnings [discipline, meditation, and wisdom], and adopt solemn Buddhist customs. . . . As for those who violate Vinaya rules and ruin Buddhist customs, Han Chinese Buddhist monastics ought to take disciplinary actions such as confiscating their ordination certificates, discharging them from monasteries, expelling them from the sangha, canceling them from the monastic registers, and so on.

年来, 伴随商品经济的发展, 产生了拜金戒律松弛, 道风不正. . . . 这种不良风气已经严重腐蚀到僧人队伍, 败坏了佛教的形象和声誉, 如果任其发展下去, 势必危及中国佛教的前途与命运。出家二众要坚定信仰, 以戒为师, 勤修三学, 严肃道风。汉传佛教僧人要. . . . 对于违犯戒律, 败坏道风者, 应视不同况, 给予收回戒牒, 迁单离寺, 摒出僧团, 撤销僧籍等处分。(Wen 2010, 5–6, quoting Shenghui 2005, 612)

Other than the narrative about an alleged moral decline in Buddhism, which was a concern before the 1960s, as it is nowadays, it should also be considered that at the beginning of the 1980s Buddhists had to face a desolate situation emerging from the material destruction of texts, images, and institutions and from the resignation of almost all clerics in the Buddhist community during the previous decade. In this regard, the term *fuxing* 复兴 *strictu sensu* refers to the restoration of the concrete circumstances that preceded the iconoclastic and destructive wave of the Cultural Revolution.[44] In other words, ordinations were soon restored primarily because there was a growing and pressing demand for them. While it has to be acknowledged that, as pointed out by Ji Zhe, the number of regularly ordained Buddhist monastics has not yet reached the size it had attained prior to 1949,[45] its recent growth—an average 8 percent annual increase between 1994 and 2006—is still impressive.[46] As far as members of the sangha are concerned, the general resurgence of monastic discipline and the search for the most proper ritual procedures for ordination ceremonies is right and necessary, after the recent ordination vacuum, similar to the way it was at the end of the Ming dynasty.

On the other hand, in the early 1990s, alongside the standardization and unification of ordination procedures that we have seen previously in this chapter, a process of state monopolization of monastic ordinations also took place.[47] The "Administrative Measures of Han Buddhist Temples' Ordination," promulgated in 1993, clearly stated that ordination ceremonies could be organized only by the BAC and its affiliated institutions (local branches and qualified monasteries) and that each ordination had to be approved by the local branch of the Religious Affairs Bureau and by the national BAC.[48] Numbers of ordinations and ordinands were also pre-defined, even if there has been a consistent increase both in the number of ceremonies (from five to eight a year in 1993–2000 to the ambiguous "about ten" in 2011) and in the maximum number of ordinands admitted for each ceremony (from 200 to 350).[49] Among the new rules, in 1993 it was decided that ordination certificates should be printed and issued only by the BAC,[50] which was presented as a necessary step to counter "the many irregular ordinations being held in the country (such as the ordination of the 500 arhats, that of the 800 arhats, or the ordination of the thousand buddhas)."[51] As in the case of sangha education (see chapter 7 by Ji Zhe in this volume), which in contemporary times still keeps its basic post-1949 orientation toward forms of statalization, rules on monastic ordinations are also unequivocally measures of state control over the sangha.[52]

State control over religious matters and religious actors is nothing new in China. The Chinese government has been using ordination platforms as "a new mechanism for controlling the Buddhist clergy" and restricting the Buddhist cleric population, distinguishing "between orthodox monks who had ascended the platforms for ordination and false monks [*weilan seng* 伪滥僧] who had not," since Daoxuan's reform of the ordination procedures and the establishment of special monasteries for official ordinations (Bodiford 2005, 8). The novelty, in contemporary China, lies in the fact that there seems to be no space left for unauthorized clerics anymore (i.e., men and women who have not taken the complete set of vows and have either only taken novice vows or simply shaved their heads regardless of Vinaya rules). While in imperial times these unauthorized Buddhists were somehow tolerated, even if not admitted in state-sponsored monasteries, in contemporary China they are labeled as illegal figures, and as chapter 8 by Ashiwa and Wank demonstrates in regard to laynuns in Fujian, they are probably destined to disappear within a few generations' time.

THE INTERNATIONAL DIMENSION OF THE ORDINATION ISSUE

The "ordination issue" can also be regarded as a sign of the impact of the transnational arena on the development of Chinese Buddhism, even if relations are not immediately evident and seldom declared. Suffice it to note that some ordination ceremonies held in China also attract foreign participants;[53] that information about Taiwanese, Singaporean, and Hong Kong ordinations are posted on mainland China's monastic websites; and that the BAC seems interested in collaborating with foreign Buddhist institutions for the organization of triple platform ordinations abroad, as can be inferred from a recent case in Nepal.[54]

The international dimension of the ordination issue, an interesting topic that I believe deserves to be further investigated, is well represented by the case of the dual ordination.

To begin with, it should be clarified that the first dual ordination of the modern era was not the Tiexiang Temple ceremony in 1982, as is usually maintained in the PRC, but a ceremony held in Taibei in 1970. Dual ordination became a widespread criterion in Taiwan after 1976, thus six years before it was introduced in mainland China. Both in Taiwan and in the PRC, the dual ordination issue was soon linked with an active involvement in the international restoration of the *bhikṣuṇī* lineage.[55] As for mainland China, it was only after Longlian went to Beijing in 1981 to meet the minister of culture from Sri Lanka that the decision was taken to hold a dual ordination the following year. Since the Sinhalese *bhikṣuṇī* sangha had disappeared, authorities from both countries decided that it should be reestablished by Chinese nuns.[56] Unfortunately, the Sinhalese nuns did not attend, most probably because of political and diplomatic reasons, as suggested to me by a disciple of Longlian.[57] Some years later, the renowned American Buddhist activist nun Karma Tsomo Lekshe, whose name is linked with the Sakyadhita International Association of Buddhist Women,[58] also showed an interest in Longlian's deeds and went to Chengdu to discuss with her the possibility of collaborating with an international "dual ordination ceremony."[59] Finally, however, Sinhalese nuns, as well as nuns in other Theravada countries and in the Tibetan tradition, turned to the "politically easier" Taiwanese way.[60]

Even if it might be true that "Shi Longlian's endeavours [to reestablish the dual ordination procedures] were much less global than the issues debated today" (Chiu and Heirman 2014, 267),[61] one still should not disregard the fact that the first and most important reason for the Tiexiang Temple ceremony in 1982 was the restoration of the *bhikṣuṇī* lineage in the Theravada tradition. This connects the Chinese dual ordination issue with an international arena and with "global" (because not only Chinese-oriented) discourses, in line with a Pan-Asian Buddhist perspective that was so much in vogue during the first part of the twentieth century (when these procedures were first discussed),[62] as well as with more recent trends to use religions in soft power strategies.[63]

Xuecheng, until recently chair of the BAC, was a fine connoisseur of Vinaya matters; he not only engaged himself in deep Vinaya studies[64] but also constantly reported on the necessity for monks and nuns "to value, study, and enhance monastic discipline" (必须重视戒律, 学习戒律, 弘扬戒律, quoted in Chen 2011, 27). In July 2011, he presided over the above-mentioned Workshop on Standard Ordinations in Chinese Buddhism,[65] which aimed at "standardizing ordination ceremonies in Chinese Buddhist monasteries on a national scale, and at ensuring that ordinations shall be bestowed according to the Dharma and to Vinaya rules, in order to further elevate the comprehensive quality of monks and nuns and to safeguard purity and dignity of the monastic order" (规范全国汉传佛教寺院传戒活动, 确保传戒法会如法如律进行, 不断提升出家僧众的整体素质, 维护僧团的清净庄严; Chen 2011, 21). In the words of Xuecheng, the workshop served the purpose of "laying steady foundations for the further implementation and development of standard ordinations" (我们应当把本次研讨班的心得与收获继续发扬开去, 为下一步规范传戒的实施与开展打下扎实的基础; Chen 2011, 27).

Meanings and implications of the promotion of standardized and "correct" ordination procedures are many and different. In this chapter, I have provided a tentative evaluation of the phenomenon, pointing to a few significant issues ranging from the position of the Buddhist establishment and that of common sangha members to the role of governmental institutions and possible international interlocutors. As this chapter has demonstrated, adopting rigorous ordination procedures is considered a priority in order to cope with an alleged decline of Buddhism, a perspective that mirrors other similar phenomena from earlier in the history of Chinese Buddhism. The reestablishment of clear and "orthodox" criteria is also deemed a necessary measure to guarantee correct and valid entrance into the monastic community for growing numbers of aspirants. Other than internal concerns with restoring the purity and strength of the sangha, the measures of unification and monopolization of ordinations further reveal a clear will by the state to control monastic communities and institutions. Finally, the "ordination issue" has proved to have an international dimension and is liable to be used in the development of relationships with other Buddhist traditions and Buddhist countries.

In any case, the above-mentioned words by Xuecheng clearly imply that the process of defining procedures to enter the monastic community is not yet completed. The range of topics and issues that were discussed at the 2011 Workshop on Ordinations (e.g., lack of control of ordinands' backgrounds, many monasteries' ignorance of the official regulations, excessively relaxed attitude in ordinands' training) reveal the persistence of a certain dissatisfaction of the Chinese Buddhist leadership about the status of ordination criteria, as well as a tendency toward even stricter uniformity.

NOTES

1. This study is part of a broader research project I am directing with Daniela Campo on the "Vinaya Revival in 20th Century China and Taiwan" (CCKF Research Grant, 2015–2018). On the restoration of monastic discipline in China during the Republic and in contemporary times, see Bianchi 2017b; Bianchi forthcoming; Campo 2017b, 2017c.

2. Daoxuan believed that "precepts are the foundation of the practice of all sages and the live root of the three learnings" (戒为众圣之行本，又是三法之命根, *T* no. 1892, 45: 807a18, translated by Chen 2007, 93). Daoxuan lived in a period when Buddhism in China was thought to be in decline and was regarded by later generations as reviving it through his learning and practice of Buddhist monastic discipline. On Daoxuan, see in particular Chen 2007.

3. The ordination platform for full ordination is reputed to be "one of Daoxuan's greatest contributions to Chinese Buddhism. Daoxuan's ordination platform mixes both traditional Indian Buddhist ideas with his own creation. Its three-level design creates a new form of ordination ritual in East Asian Buddhism. On his three-level platform, buddhas, bodhisattvas, and senior masters play a crucial role in leading the ceremony" (Chen 2007, 8, 93–131); on the same issue, also see McRae 2005.

4. On the movement of Vinaya resurgence of the late Ming and early Qing, see in particular Sheng-Yen 1991 and Wu Jiang 2008, 28–31; see also Liu 2008; Wang Hsuan-Li 2014, 105–128; and Yü 1981.

5. On the topic of Ming politics controlling the monastic community and for the ban on Buddhist ordinations that occurred during the Jiajing reign (1526), see Wu Jiang 2008, 28; and Yü 1981, 157–158.

6. On the triple platform ordination, see Wu Jiang 2008, 28–31; and Wang Hsuan-Li 2014, 94. For the first half of the twentieth century, see Welch 1967, 285–296; and Campo 2017b. For a general outline and a historical reconstruction, particularly see Xuecheng 1997.

7. The Ten Precepts are: (1) not to kill, (2) not to steal, (3) not to have sexual intercourse, (4) not to lie, (5) not to take intoxicating substances, (6) not to take part in singing, dancing, and other amusements, (7) not to use garlands or perfumes, (8) not to sleep on high or broad beds, (9) not to handle silver or gold, (10) not to eat food out of regulated hours. In China, female novices often took the Ten Precepts from a monk master; instead, according to Vinaya rules, and more precisely according to the *Bhikṣuṇīskandhaka,* they should receive the Ten Precepts from a nun master (*upādhyāyinī*), a habit that has been recently reestablished. See Heirman 1997, 43–44 (referring to the *Bhikṣuṇīskandhaka* of the Vinaya of the Dharmaguptaka: *T* no. 1428, 22).

8. The number of rules varies depending on the Vinaya tradition; the Vinaya of the Dharmaguptaka (*Sifenlü* 四分律: *T* no. 1428, 22), which is adopted by Chinese Buddhists, has 250 vows for monks and 348 for nuns.

9. Officiating masters are ten in number for monks' ordinations and twenty for nuns' ordinations (ten male and ten female). More precisely, the three masters (*san shi* 三师) include the teacher who grants the precepts (*jie heshang* 戒和尚 or *jie asheli* 戒阿阇黎), the *karmācārya* who recites the announcement and texts of the precepts (*jiemo shi* 羯磨师 or *jiemo asheli* 羯磨阿阇黎), and the instructional preceptor who teaches ritual to ordinands (*jiaoshoushi* 教授师 or *jiaoshou asheli* 教授阿阇黎).

10. The main feature of this ritual is the combination of the Indian Vinaya with the Mahayanic altruistic attitude. The Bodhisattva Precepts can be divided into three groups according to their significance: (1) precepts to avoid performing negative actions; (2) precepts to "liberate good essences," that is to do good; and (3) precepts for the liberation of all sentient beings. The ten major and forty-eight minor Bodhisattva Precepts are outlined in the *Brahmā's Net Sutra* (*Fanwang jing* 梵网经), an apocryphal scripture of the fifth century. See Bodiford 2005; Chu 2006; Demiéville 1930; Getz 2005; Longlian 1989; and Yamabe 2005.

11. This is the fourth of the eight "fundamental rules" (Ch. *ba jingfa* 八敬法, Skt. *gurudharma*) as they are exposed in the Vinaya of the Dharmaguptaka (*T* no. 1428, 22: 923a26–b21, translated in Heirman 2011, 606–607).

12. The figure of the *śikṣamāṇā*, an intermediate step between a female novice and a fully ordained nun, is prescribed by the Vinaya texts but was never very common in China. It refers to a young female practitioner accepting six precepts to be followed for a probationary period of two years. These six precepts prescribe abstinence from (1) sex, (2) stealing, (3) killing, (4) lying, (5) consumption of alcohol, and (6) eating at improper times. According to Huimin, "the śikṣamāṇā precepts are due to the possibility of pregnancy in female candidates. This training period lasts two years and ensures that the female candidate is not pregnant. Also, this time is used . . . for evaluation of the candidate's suitability for full ordination" (Huimin 2007, 16); pregnancy related to the *śikṣamāṇā* is mentioned only in the

Vinaya of the Sarvāstivāda (Heirman 2008, 108). For an analysis of other possible reasons for the creation of this figure and of its understanding in China, see Heirman 2008, 119–124. On *śikṣamāṇās* in Chinese history and in contemporary China and Taiwan, see Heirman 2008; Heirman and Chiu 2012; and Chiu and Heirman 2014.

13. On nuns' ordination procedures according to the Vinaya of the Dharmaguptaka, see in particular Heirman 2002, vol. 2; see also Heirman 2011; Li Yuzhen 2007a, 2008. For a critical analysis of historical sources, see Huimin 2007. For nuns' ordination rules and rituals in general, also see Horner (1930) 1989, 138–158.

14. According to the biography of the nun Sengguo 僧果, as reported in the *Biqiuni zhuan* 比丘尼传 (*T* no. 2063, 22: 939c07–940a05), in 433 a mercantile ship arrived in China with a group of *bhikṣuṇī*s from Sri Lanka on board. They thus permitted the transmission of the Buddhist nuns' order to China in the fifth century. As a matter of fact, nuns' ordination had already occurred during the fourth century, but it was conferred by monk masters alone, since no ordained nuns were available in China. On this issue, see in particular Heirman 2001, 275–304; and Zheng 2010.

15. Historical chronicles reveal that dual ordination procedures were sometimes followed around the twelfth century, were forbidden by law for a while, and then resumed in the thirteenth century. Afterward they seem not to have been implemented until the end of the Ming and the beginning of the Qing dynasty; also at that time most rituals continued to be held by monk masters alone. See Huimin 2007.

16. While neither the Tibetan nor the Theravada monastic establishments consider such ordination legitimate, in the Chinese tradition ordination conducted by monks alone was considered valid. On this issue, see, for instance, Heirman 2011, 603–631.

17. The last monastic ordination before the Cultural Revolution was held in 1957 at Baohuashan 宝华山 (430 nuns and 373 monks received complete monastic ordination; Welch 1972, 121–123). On the role played by Dharma lineages, particularly Chan and Tiantai, in "bridging this gap," see chapter 5 by Daniela Campo in this volume.

18. It should be noted, however, that neither Wen 2010 nor Chen 2011 mentions the Tiexiang Temple ordination.

19. Mingshan 茗山, who was one of the masters of the ceremony, reported in his diary that the practice was "very irregular" (*hen bu rufa* 很不如法). See Mingshan 2002, 125, 129 (reported to me by Ji Zhe, personal communication, June 2015).

20. This is the Vinaya tradition that became the standard reference in China from the seventh century, thanks to the works and deeds of Daoxuan.

21. On Longlian, who is reputed to be "the most outstanding *bhikṣuṇī*" in modern China" and on these events in her life, see Bianchi 2017a, 293–295; also see Qiu 1997, 239–243.

22. Founded in 1983 inside the Tiexiang Temple, this was the first institution of higher education for nuns in mainland China. See Bianchi 2001, 103–119; and Qiu 1997, 205–227; and chapter 7 by Ji in this volume.

23. Sherab Gyatso mentions "abuses in the [precepts'] transmission" (*lan chuan* 滥传), without referring to the specific irregularities involved; this term generically refers to any kind of abuse in ordination procedures (deficiencies in the training of ordinands, disrespect of transmission rules, etc.). See Wen 2010, 2–3.

24. This happened on the eve of the founding of the PRC inside the Tiexiang Temple, where Longlian attended some lessons given by the Vinaya master Guanyi 贯一 (1875–1954), abbot of the Baoguang Temple (Baoguang Si 宝光寺).

25. Xiaoyun met Longlian during the years she spent in Chengdu (1941–1945), when she took the refuges from Master Changyuan 昌源 (Longlian's own tonsure master), who *predicted* that she would eventually become a Buddhist nun. At that time, she was known by her lay name You Yunshan 游韵珊 and was already a famous painter in China. On Xiaoyun's encounter with Longlian, see Bianchi 2017a, 285; and Li 2007b, 20.

26. Li Yuzhen, personal communication, May 2014.

27. Hongyi, the most prominent Vinaya master of the first half of the twentieth century, is obviously the closest model for the contemporary Vinaya resurgence. On Hongyi, see Birnbaum 2003b, 2017.

28. See Bianchi 2017b, 120–121. I thank Ji Zhe for sharing this information with me (personal communication, December 2013).

29. The following three documents were promulgated on September 19, 2000: "Methods for the Management of the Triple Platform Ordination in Han Chinese Buddhist Monasteries" (Quanguo hanchuan fojiao siyuan chuanshou santan dajie guanli banfa 全国汉传佛教寺院传授三坛大戒管理办法), "Regulations Concerning Offices and Positions in Han Chinese Buddhist Monasteries" (Quanguo hanchuan fojiao siyuan zhuchi renzhi tuizhi de guiding 全国汉传佛教寺院住持任职退职的规定), and "Methods for Implementing the System of Monastic Registers and of Government-Issued Monastic Ordination Certificates in Han Chinese Buddhist Monasteries" (Quanguo hanchuan fojiao shixing dudie sengji zhidu de banfa 全国汉传佛教实行度牒僧籍制度的办法). The three documents were published in *Fayin* 9 (2000): 3–6.

30. This explanation is often included in ordination announcements. See, for instance, the Zen Monk website, accessed October 26, 2018, http://zenmonk.cn/stdj.htm.

31. The degree of importance attached to the recognition of these rules as the only possible and only "correct" ones is clearly stated in a wide range of books and materials produced for monastic milieus. See, for instance, Juedeng 2005 (a brief but clear explanation that was also reposted on Hangzhou's Lingyin Temple 灵隐寺 website at the time of the ordination ceremony that was held between September 25 and October 23, 2013; see Lingyin Temple website, accessed October 26, 2018, http://www.lingyinsi.com/).

32. Their introduction is regarded as one of Longlian's main contributions to modern Chinese Buddhism. Longlian was also the principal nun master in the *bhikṣuṇī* ordination at the White Horse Temple (Baima Si) in 1983.

33. Longlian did her best to restore this tradition; she conferred *śikṣamāṇā* precepts for the last time in 2005, one year before passing away, but by then she had long accepted her failure in this regard. See also Chiu and Heirman 2014.

34. For example, in the announcement for the ordination to be held at the Fajingjiang Temple (Fajingjiang Si 法镜讲寺) it was stated clearly that novices and *śikṣamāṇā*s would be accepted. See "Hangzhou Lingyinsi ji Fajingjiangsi chuanshou huguo xingsheng erbuseng jie santan dajie fahui tonggao" 杭州灵隐暨法镜讲寺传授护国兴圣二部僧三坛大戒法会通告, Lingyin Temple, June 2013, accessed October 26, 2018, http://www.fjnet.com/kuaixun/201306/t20130630_210484.htm.

35. Most Taiwanese ordination ceremonies contain triple platform ordinations (often also including dual ordinations), but other typologies are still practiced. In the 1950s, also the newly founded Buddhist Association of the Republic of China established the triple platform ordination system in order to "resume the orthodox status of Chinese Buddhism over Japanese Buddhism" (Li 2014). But though highly recommended, this is not the only possible procedure allowed, as is the case in the PRC. Moreover, in Taiwan "refuge

ceremonies and Five Precept ordinations" (*sangui wujie* 三皈五戒) for laypeople and "bodhisattva ordinations for laypeople" (*zaijia pusa jie* 在家菩萨戒) are also bestowed during the same period as monastic ordinations, whereas monastic and lay ceremonies are held separately in the PRC.

36. Lists with ordination venues and other information are edited by Buddhist monks and are available on Buddhist websites (e.g., the Zen Monk website, accessed February 17, 2018, http://zenmonk.cn/stdj.htm).

37. Governmental regulations establish that ordination ceremonies shall last from thirty to forty days. In the years 2011–2014 there was an exception of fifty-three days. On the other hand, many Taiwanese ceremonies last for longer periods.

38. In Taiwan the maximum age reported in the consulted material is sixty-five.

39. Candidates must have all "six roots" (the six sense organs: eye, ear, nose, tongue, body, and mind) "complete" and have no physiological or intellectual defects, no contagious diseases, nor any other physical disabilities.

40. Jiqun resides in the Xiyuan Jiezhuang Vinaya Temple (Xiyuan Jiechuang Lü Si 西园戒幢律寺) in Suzhou; Chongrou is a renowned scholar-monk who is studying for his PhD in Singapore.

41. On this issue, see also Bianchi 2017b.

42. For instance, in treating precept transmission, Xuyun is reported to have declared, "I have often said that the defeat of the Law of the Buddha is due to unorthodox precept transmission" (*chuanjie bu rufa* 传戒不如法; Campo 2017b, 146).

43. These "six harmonies" point to six ways to live in harmony within the monastic community: (1) to be unified in respectful deportment; (2) to be unified in chanting; (3) to be unified in purpose; (4) to be unified in practices of purity; (5) to be unified in views; (6) to be unified in benefits. See "Essay on the System of *Mahāyāna*" (大乘义章) by Huiyuan 慧远 (*T* no. 1851, 44: 712c26–713a25).

44. For analogies between the Buddhist renaissance after the Taiping Rebellion and that which occurred after the Cultural Revolution, see Ji 2016b.

45. In the 1930s there were, in China, 738,000 monks and nuns; in the period between 1949 and 1966 there was a rapid and dramatic decline, from about 500,000 to just a few thousand Buddhist monastics. "After sixty years of Communist government rule, China's population has more than doubled, but the number of Han Buddhist clerics has been reduced by four-fifths" (Ji 2012, 13).

46. In 1997, according to the white paper "Freedom of Religious Belief in China," the number of Han Chinese Buddhist clergy was around seventy thousand; in 2009, according to "incomplete statistics" referred to by Chen Xingqiao (reported by Ji 2012, 13), Han Chinese monastics numbered about eighty thousand. For a detailed analysis, see Ji 2012, 12–15.

47. On October 6, 1994, the BAC approved a pilot project in the Zhenru Temple (Zhenru Si 真如寺, Yunjushan 云居山, Jiangxi). The ceremony was a triple platform ordination and it lasted one month. Beginning with this ordination, all ordinations in Han Chinese monasteries have been carried out under the strict and sole supervision of the BAC. See Wen 2010, 4.

48. "Quanguo hanchuan fojiao siyuan guanli banfa" 全国汉传佛教寺院管理办法 (Administrative Measures of Han Buddhist Temples' Ordination) adopted by the Sixth National Congress of the BAC in 1993. See Ji 2012, 13–14; and Wen 2010, 3–4.

49. In 1993, regulations established that only five ordination ceremonies with a maximum of two hundred new ordinands could take place every year in China, thus determining

that each year only one thousand newly ordained monks and nuns could be admitted. A first revision was introduced in 2000, establishing that the number of ordination ceremonies could be five to eight, with a maximum quota of three hundred participants each time; in this way, every year twenty-four hundred newly ordained monks and nuns could be admitted. However, the number regularly exceeded these quotas. Therefore, following a modification introduced in 2011, ordination ceremonies are limited to "about ten times" each year and the maximum quota of participants for each ceremony is 350 people (Ji 2012, 14–15). See also Wen 2010, 4–6.

50. The mind immediately turns to the sale of ordination certificates during imperial China or to "the far greater struggle on the part of the state to regulate the numbers of Chinese entering the Buddhist clergy" (Barrett 2005, 104). On the state selling of tonsure/ordination certificates during the late Ming, see Wang Qifeng 2014, 105–106. For earlier times, see Yifa 2002, 76.

51. Ch. *wubai luohan jie* 五百罗汉戒, *babai luohan jie* 八百罗汉戒, and *qianfo dajie* 千佛大戒 (Wen 2010, 4). These terms refer to irregular ordinations disregarding rules of transmission of the precepts by a definite number of fully ordained monastics. Instead, precepts are believed to be conferred by arhats and buddhas themselves. Note that, according to Daoxuan's understanding of the ordination platform, buddhas and bodhisattvas are expected to gather at the platform and take part in the ritual together with the sangha (Chen 2007, 107) and that bodhisattva ordination conferred by buddhas and bodhisattvas alone is considered valid (Groner 2012, 140–142).

52. As suggested to me by Gareth Fisher (personal communication, June 2015), the Republican- and Mao-era states had similarly taken "a strong interest in the rationalization and greater institutionalization of religion, and put pressure on religious organizations to develop and follow set guidelines and procedures." See also chapter 7 by Ji Zhe in this volume.

53. For instance, at the Shaolin 少林 large ordination of 2005, foreign visitors from Malaysia, Germany, Italy, and Denmark also participated. See Wen 2010, 7–8.

54. The news about the Nepalese triple platform ordination (2013) was posted on many Chinese websites. See, for instance, "Zhongguo fojiao jie shouci zai Nipoer chuanshou santan dajie" 中国佛教界将首次在尼泊尔传授三坛大戒 (The First Triple Platform Ordination Bestowed by the Chinese Buddhist World in Nepal), Phoenix New Media, accessed October 2018, https://fo.ifeng.com/news/detail_2013_12/16/32158559_0.shtml. The same websites that give the list of monasteries organizing monastic ordinations in the PRC also include information on ordinations held in Taiwan (2011–2014), Singapore (2011), and Hong Kong (2014).

55. For the Taiwanese case, see Li 2014.

56. For this purpose, Longlian also translated the *erbuseng jie* ritual procedures into English.

57. On the same issue, also see Qiu 1997, 241.

58. On this association, see Ashiwa 2015. Also see Tsomo 1988.

59. Karma Tsomo Lekshe, personal communication with the author, December 1997 and March 2017.

60. The first Sinhalese nuns were fully ordained at the Sakyadhita conference in Bodh Gaya in 1998; back in Sri Lanka, they held the first *bhikkuni* ordination in centuries at a temple in Dambulla in March 1998. See Ashiwa 2015, 19, 30–31. On the revival of the nuns' monastic order in the Theravada tradition, also see Anālayo 2013.

61. Here, Chiu and Heirman refer to the global movement aiming at restoring nuns' ordination in those Buddhist traditions that never had or no longer have a *bhikṣuṇisaṃgha* (namely, Theravada and Tibetan Buddhism). For the history and background of this modern phenomenon, see Ashiwa 2015, 30–35. Also see the online proceedings of the "E-Learning Course on Bhikkhuni/Bhikshuni Ordination," Numata Center for Buddhist Studies, Universität Hamburg, 2014, accessed October 26, 2018, https://www.buddhismuskunde.uni -hamburg.de/en.html.

62. The idea of Pan-Asian Buddhism, that is, of Buddhism understood as a unique religion spread throughout Asia, dating back to the end of the nineteenth and the first part of the twentieth centuries, favored the development of common issues and objectives among representatives of the different Buddhist traditions, as is the case with the nuns' ordination issue. On the rise and development of the modern conception of Buddhism as a Pan-Asian religion, with reference to the Tibetan and Chinese traditions, see Tuttle 2005, 68–102 (particularly 74–76); and, with reference to the Vinaya resurgence, Bianchi forthcoming.

63. Despite the failure of the Sinhalese nuns' ordination plan to go through, this case shows that religious issues might be used by the state to develop its relationships with Buddhist countries in Asia. For the Chinese government's attempts to use Chinese Buddhism (and religion in general) in soft power strategies, see Laliberté 2011a, 2011b; and chapter 1 by Laliberté in this volume.

64. Xuecheng began his Vinaya studies under the guidance of Yuanzhuo at Fujian Guanghua Temple, before taking on the abbotship there in 1988.

65. For a detailed account of Putuoshan's workshop on ordinations, see Chen 2011. Xuecheng, in his capacity as vice-chair of the BAC, gave the closing speech.

7

SCHOOLING DHARMA TEACHERS
The Buddhist Academy System and Sangha Education

JI ZHE

Since 1980, more than fifty academies of Han Buddhism (*hanchuan fojiao* 汉传佛教 or *hanyuxi fojiao* 汉语系佛教) have opened in different parts of China. Today, thousands of monks and nuns are trained in those Buddhist academies, which have become one of the most important reproduction mechanisms of the contemporary sangha elite. Based on both fieldwork conducted from 2010 to 2014 and archival analysis, this chapter provides an overview of the evolution of the Buddhist academy system in the PRC in the post-Mao period; presents a case study of the students, curriculum, and pedagogy of the Buddhist Academy of China (Zhongguo Foxueyuan 中国佛学院) in Beijing; and explores the implications of ongoing debates on sangha education.

The Buddhist Academy (also translated as "Institute of Buddhist Studies" for those founded before 1949) is an institutional invention that first appeared in early-twentieth-century China (Ji 2016a) in a context where modern educational reform profoundly affected relationships between Buddhism, power, and knowledge. First, the political program of "building schools with temple property," launched by some local governors in 1898 and renewed several times later, was intended to establish a modern secular public education system with religious material resources, meaning a part of the estate and income of temples. It resulted in the unification of Buddhist monastics, for the first time in Chinese history, in the common aim of protecting temple property. Some monks took the initiative by introducing modern schooling into monasteries and even began to invest in public education, so that temple property could remain in the hands of the clergy. This situation not only stimulated the emergence of Buddhists as an interest group in the modern sense by the alliances they formed across temples, but also enlarged the social functions of monastic orders through participation in community affairs and even nation building. In this way, monastic schools (*seng xuetang* 僧学堂) as institutions began to be transplanted into some monasteries. They offered supplementary basic education in reading to newly ordained monks in addition to their traditional training in ritual matters.

Second, the intellectual elite, represented by Yang Wenhui 杨文会 (1837–1911) and Ouyang Jian 欧阳渐 (1871–1943), who worked to establish Buddhology, or Buddhist studies (*foxue* 佛学), a discipline with modern, rationalist philology as its basic content, not only laid the cultural basis for a Buddhism seriously wrecked under the Taiping Rebellion, but also created a modern lay Buddhism religiously independent of clergy, which revolved around institutions of scholarship, publication, and research (Goldfuss 2001; Ji 2009). Yang Wenhui established the Jetavana Hermitage (Qihuan Jingshe 祇洹精舍),[1] a Buddhist seminary in Nanjing, during the years 1908–1909. It was a small boarding school bearing a resemblance to traditional Confucian private schools (*sishu* 私塾) but one where, for the first time in Chinese history, monks studied Buddhist texts under a lay teacher outside of monasteries (Welch 1968, 9). More important, for Yang and his successors, the building of a modern sangha education was not a temporary expedient for protecting temple property, but a thoughtful project to rescue Buddhism from what he saw as ignorance and decline.

Third, reformist monks under the leadership of Taixu 太虚 (1890–1947) attempted to put in place an even more comprehensive program for building a socially engaged and well-educated sangha. Taixu, who once attended Yang Wenhui's Jetavana Hermitage, attempted, with the establishment of institutes for Buddhist studies, to train and mobilize a new generation of monastics. In 1922, he founded the Wuchang 武昌 Institute for Buddhist Studies, the first educational institution in China's history with the name *foxueyuan*. This designation was widely imitated: From then on, up to 1949, the dozens of newly created Buddhist seminaries were mostly called *foxueyuan* (Welch 1968, 107). Compared with earlier monastic seminaries, the Wuchang Institute for Buddhist Studies introduced modern, secular schooling in the most systematic way and hence served as a model for later academies. Both the Wuchang Institute for Buddhist Studies and later the Minnan 闽南 Institute for Buddhist Studies, founded by Taixu in 1925 in Fujian, adopted a rigorous system of examination and evaluation as well as a degree-granting curriculum. As a result, institutes for Buddhist studies, as unique institutions, became more clearly distinguished from monasteries: The central content of the curriculum was no longer monastic discipline or practices of religious services, but Buddhist philosophy and theory, supplemented by nonreligious courses such as history, geography, and foreign languages. The aim of the education was no longer to uphold the tradition of a particular monastery or locality, but rather to reform Buddhism under changed social conditions and to expand its influence. Master-disciple relations were no longer constrained by affiliation to a monastery or a lineage but were reconstructed via the bidirectional choice of teachers and students through the learning of a standard curriculum. The breadth of Taixu's reforms has led some scholars to argue that his institutes for Buddhist studies triggered a paradigm shift in Buddhist education by constructing a new type of identity, that of student-monastics (*xueseng* 学僧; Lai 2013), and creating a new relationship between the Buddhist community and a China under social and political transformation (Chan 1953; Welch 1968; Chen and Deng 2000; Pittman 2001).

These modern movements of Buddhist education in the first part of the twentieth century have witnessed different destinies and maintain their content and structure to different degrees in today's China. Since the communist takeover in 1949, the means for organized religions to invest in public education are no more; the participation of Buddhism in public life is strictly limited. However, some of the reforms in methods of monastic education that were introduced in the early twentieth century survived into the Mao era and now the post-Mao period. In short-term sangha training classes, which have largely appeared in monasteries since the 1980s, we can see the shades of "monastic schools." Buddhist studies, for thirty years swept into the "dung heap of history," now have been recycled by the secular university system as a dereligionized subordinate discipline and continue to contribute to the growth of Buddhist education. However, they are deeply secularized and no longer able to regain their centrality in the development of Buddhist religiosity (Ji 2011a).[2] Institutes for Buddhist studies, on the other hand, have continued to play a significant role throughout the history of the PRC with the exception of the period of the Cultural Revolution and shortly after. In 1956, the Buddhist Association of China (BAC; Zhongguo Fojiao Xiehui 中国佛教协会) as the official representative body of Buddhism in China founded the Buddhist Academy of China.[3] Since 1980, the number of Buddhist academies has risen steadily nationwide. These academies have strongly influenced the way monastics are educated and trained.

However, to a degree, this continuity is merely formal. During the latter half of the twentieth century, the nature and function of Buddhist academies underwent a profound transformation in comparison to the earlier models envisioned by reformers like Yang Wenhui and Taixu. Compared with the Republican era, sangha education since 1949 has been much more constrained by the political regime, in form as well as in content.

THE ETATIZATION OF SANGHA EDUCATION (1949–1966)

In his book *The Buddhist Revival in China*, Holmes Welch (1968, app. 2) enumerated the seventy-one Buddhist seminaries within his knowledge that had opened in China in the 1912–1950 period.[4] Among the forty-two institutions with documented dates of opening and closing, more than fourteen were closed between 1946 and 1949, that is to say, during the civil war period.

For instance, the Tianning 天宁 Institute for Buddhist Studies and the Han-Tibetan Buddhist Institute (Hanzang Jiaoli Yuan 汉藏教理院), both influential seminaries, terminated their activities in 1949. In fact, where the Communist troops arrived, monastics either fled in disarray or ceased their religious activities. I have failed to find any information indicating that any Buddhist educational institution founded by monks before 1949 was still able to function following the beginning of Communist rule.[5]

In 1953, the BAC was founded under the Communist regime. A few years later it became the only legal nationwide Buddhist organization that could exist; it incorporated as a symbolic gesture Republican-era Buddhist leaders who stayed in mainland China and cooperated with Communist power, but its real leadership was composed of party members and pro-Communist Buddhists.[6] In 1955, the BAC decided to create the Buddhist Academy of China, for which it obtained permission from the CCP government. On September 28, 1956, the Buddhist Academy of China was opened at the Fayuan Temple (Fayuan Si 法源寺) in Beijing, thus ending the seven-year-long absence of Buddhist seminaries in China. In its first year, there were more than one hundred student-monks, who came from twenty-four provinces. They were divided into two programs: thirty-six entered the A class (*jia ban* 甲班) with a four-year curriculum (also called *benkeban* 本科班, the bachelor's degree class), while the rest entered the B class (*yi ban* 乙班), with a two-year curriculum (called *yukeban* 预科班, the preparatory class). Chinese language, the PRC's constitution, "History of Buddhism," and "Introduction to Buddhist Classics" figured among the courses taught in both programs, while the bachelor's curriculum taught further courses in Buddhist philosophy (Xirao Jiacuo [Sherab Gyatso] 1956). In reality, however, bachelor's degree students graduated after a mere two and a half years, so their curriculum was not much more developed than that of the preparatory class. Some of the bachelor's degree graduates entered a postgraduate program that opened in 1959. In 1962, a Tibetan-language class was opened with twenty-six new students.

The opening of the postgraduate program and the Tibetan-language program did little to ameliorate the difficulties the Buddhist Academy encountered in its development. In *Xiandai foxue* 现代佛学 (Modern Buddhist Studies), the bulletin of the BAC, I failed to find any information indicating that the Buddhist Academy recruited another class either in the bachelor's degree or associate's degree program before its discontinuation in 1966, in marked contrast to the optimism expressed in the cheerful 1957 report on its inauguration. One article in *People's Daily* from 1986 (Mao 1986) mentioned obscurely that there were "five classes in various forms such as associate-degree, Bachelor-degree, and postgraduate programs" before the Cultural Revolution. In 1996, Zhao Puchu, then chair of the BAC, in his speech commemorating the fortieth anniversary of the Buddhist Academy of China, also mentioned that before 1966 there were "a total of six classes," including the associate's degree and bachelor's degree classes, an associate's degree class for Tibetan-language Buddhism, and two six-month short-term "study classes" (*xuexiban* 学习班) held after 1959 (Zhao 1996, 3). Apparently, except for the study class, every program enrolled students only once. At any rate, according to a statement of the current BAC, the Buddhist Academy trained 410 monk-students in total, of whom 384 belonged to Han Buddhism (Wen 2006).[7]

Compared with institutes for Buddhist studies before 1949, the Mao-era Buddhist Academy of China did not make a spectacular contribution in teaching and research. However, it did contribute to the preservation of Republican-era Buddhism under radically transformed historical conditions. First, a number of important teachers in the Buddhist Academy had been educated in the institutes for Buddhist studies operated by Taixu, such as Fazun 法尊 (1902–1980), Zhengguo 正果 (1913–1987), Guankong 观空 (1903–1989), Yuyu 虞愚 (1909–1989), and Ye Jun 叶均 (1916–1985). In this way, although Taixu himself was consigned to *damnatio memoriae* after 1949 due to his close links with the Nationalist government, his disciples were able to retain some portion of influence in the Buddhist Academy. Second, it provided a place of refuge for persons from Buddhist groups by then closed or operating under difficult conditions. For example, the famous lay scholar Lü Cheng, whose Chinese Inner Studies Institute was closed in 1952, and Wang Enyang 王恩洋 (1897–1964), whose Research Institute for Oriental Culture and Education (Dongfang Wenjiao Yanjiuyuan 东方文教研究院), founded in 1947, was closed by the local government in 1952, were both appointed professors. Among the thirty-six student-monks in the bachelor's degree class, eight came from the Three Times Study Society in Beijing (which ceased activities in 1956), and two came from the Diamond Bodhimaṇḍa (Jingang Daochang 金刚道场) in Shanghai (ordered by the government to dissolve itself in 1957; Zhiyan and Zongdao 2014). Third, the Buddhist Academy recruited talented young monks from all over China and gave them the chance to study under monks or Buddhist scholars already prominent before 1949. Part of this student body would later become the backbone of the post-Mao Buddhist revival. Typical examples are Cizhou 慈舟 (1915–2003), Mingxue 明学 (1923–2016), Mingzhe 明哲 (1925–2012), Songchun 松纯 (1927–2017), Jinghui 净慧 (1933–2013), and Wuxiang 无相 (1927–2018).

However, the Buddhist Academy of China was still different from any institute for Buddhist studies of the Republican period. In fact, it could be regarded as the first *national* institute for Buddhist studies. More specifically, it was both the result and the instrument of the etatization of Buddhism. In one of my previous studies (Ji 2008a), I noted that for Buddhism in the PRC, secularization was not primarily manifested as the separation of religion and state, but essentially meant etatization. That is to say, the human, material, and spiritual resources of Buddhism were controlled, appropriated, and used by the secular party-state according to its ideology and for its own political purposes.

The BAC, the association with a legal monopoly on representation, was the means by which the etatization of Buddhism was carried out by the CCP under a state-corporatist structure. The Buddhist Academy of China, a subsidiary body of the BAC, doubtlessly incarnated this nature of the BAC.

Even though the Republican Nationalist state was also very interventionist (or occasionally tried to be) in deciding what religion was acceptable and in regulating what went on in religious sites, compared to the Communist regime it permitted religion (especially institutionalized religions like Buddhism) far more space and respected much more formally a Western-style separation between politics and religion. Hence Republican-era institutes for Buddhist studies could develop but only as private institutions. According to a recent investigation of historical archives (Gong and Lai 2014, 129–153), Taixu, whose closeness to the Nationalist government was widely known, on multiple occasions in the 1930s and 1940s sought to incorporate sangha education into the state education system in order to receive government approval and funding. These proposals, however, were rejected firmly by the contemporary education administration. In this respect, pro-Communist monks did tell the truth when, on the occasion of the inauguration of the Buddhist Academy of China, they said that "past reactionary governments never supported institutes for Buddhist studies operated by us Buddhists" (Shengyin 1956, 10). On the contrary, the Buddhist Academy of China was, from its very beginning, an institution operated by the official BAC under the support but also the control of the government.

Although I have not yet found any specific evidence of economic state support before 1966, it is certain that, as the director of the Bureau of Religious Affairs of the State Council[8] stated in the inauguration ceremony, the Buddhist Academy was founded "by the Buddhist Association of China, under government auspices, with great human and material investment" (He 1956, 6). In fact, around 1956, after land reform and the implementation of the policy of joint public-private management of private enterprises, the Communist government controlled almost all economic resources in the country. Under such a situation, it was impossible, in both financial and political terms, to create a school without government investment. For example, we can confirm that the China Islamic Institute (Zhongguo Yisilanjiao Jingxueyuan 中国伊斯兰教经学院), inaugurated in the same period, was built with government funding. Also, the funding of the BAC was provided from the very beginning by the government. It was in fact a state organ under the guise of a civic organization, a situation that has persisted to a certain degree until today. Since 1980, the Buddhist Academy of China has received government money every year, though of an amount that has risen only a little (Zhongguo Foxueyuan 2003).[9] These facts give us sufficient ground to believe that the Buddhist Academy of China was, from its beginning, a state-run, state-funded Buddhist school.

It was obviously impossible for state generosity to expect nothing in return. According to the basic logic of state corporatism, in order to reduce the cost of state control, it is necessary to reduce the number of its representatives as social forces as much as possible. Hence, just as there was only one monopolistic BAC, the state permitted the existence of one and only one Buddhist academy (a situation, as we will later see, that changed only in 1980). The Republican-period free competition of private institutes of Buddhist studies no longer existed. The state managed both to maintain the facade of religious freedom and to abolish the market of sangha education at the cost of investing in only one state-run Buddhist seminary.

The sole Buddhist Academy—like its parent organization, the BAC—also played a role in symbolizing the unity of the multiethnic nation and strengthening the bonds between the PRC and other Asian countries influenced by Buddhism. The first dean of the Buddhist Academy was a Tibetan—Sherab Gyatso (Ch: Xirao Jiacuo 喜饶嘉措; 1884–1968), also chair of the BAC—even though all student-monks at that time belonged to the Han tradition. Present at the inauguration ceremony were a Tibetan visiting delegation, a Visiting Delegation of National Minorities from the Nomadic Regions of Gansu Province, and a Visiting Delegation of International Buddhist Monks made up of monks from India, Vietnam, and other countries. Afterward, the academy undertook the task of receiving foreign guests multiple times.

At the same time, however, in order to minimize the possible threats from Buddhist education to the hegemony of official, atheistic ideology, teaching in the Buddhist Academy was necessarily politicized. This politicization was not just limited to the course on the constitution. In fact, all "work units" (*danwei* 单位) at that time, including Buddhist groups, were required to conduct "political studies" based on the teachings of historical materialism, on Marxism-Leninism-Maoism, and on the policies and documents of the CCP (Welch 1972; Xue 2015). The Buddhist Academy of China was no exception. Despite a shortage of materials, we can gauge the contradictions implied in such a politicization with the following fact: In the beginning of 1961, the Buddhist Academy had to dedicate thirteen days to discussion and rectification, as ultraleftist politics "caused confusions in major issues of the Academy, such as its mission, its guiding principles of teaching, the duration of its programs, its curriculum, and its teaching management" (Zhongguo Foxueyuan 2006). Also, teachers and students of the Buddhist Academy were mobilized to participate in political activities like the May First demonstrations to celebrate the proletariat's victory and the denunciation of the "Dalai clique" after the 1959 Tibet rebellion and the exile of the Dalai Lama from Tibet to India in the same year. The short-term study classes that opened in 1959 were in fact a response to the Great Leap Forward (Da Yuejin 大跃进, 1958–1961) campaign,[10] in the name of greater efficiency.

In the discussion of 1961 mentioned previously, it was proposed that there should not be an "excessive" emphasis on politics and that Marxist criticism of religions should not be imposed on religious seminaries. However, these visions could not rival the coming torrents of "revolution." Circumscribed tolerance and the utilitarian appropriation of religion were soon replaced by a policy of eradication. In 1964–1965, the teaching activities of the Buddhist Academy of China were forced to come to a halt amid the general chaos on the eve of the Cultural Revolution. The academy was formally closed in August 1966.

THE RENEWAL AND BREAKUP OF THE CENTRALLY
PLANNED SYSTEM (SINCE 1980)

The establishment of the Buddhist Academy was a result of the "socialist transformation" of the whole economy, society, and culture of China and one stage in the building of a centrally planned system in Buddhism. As the unique legal institution of monastic training, the national Buddhist Academy once entertained the ambition of extending itself to the education of all the ethnolinguistic traditions of Buddhism. In his 1956 inauguration discourse, Sherab Gyatso declared that a branch for nuns' training, a research institute of Mongolian and Tibetan Buddhism, and a research institute of ethnic Dai Buddhism of the Pali tradition would be opened, and also that the Sanskrit and Pali languages would be taught in the academy. All these came to nothing. The conception of a centrally planned sangha education, however, was maintained for a time by the BAC after 1980, even through its constant adjustment during reform-era mutations of political, economic, and social conditions. However, in the last decade, due to the growth of local Buddhist resources, the strengthening of local authorities' power, and the will of the latter to intervene in religious matters, this centralized system started to be dismantled, resulting in new tendencies of localization, specialization, and pluralism.

Some Buddhist temples were gradually reopened after the end of the 1970s. One of the main reasons for the reopening was to receive an increased flow of overseas Buddhist visitors, both ethnically Chinese and other Asian peoples. At that time, the temples were mostly administered by public garden or cultural relics administrations, whose agents, of course, could not conduct religious services (see chapter 4 by Brian Nichols in this volume). This provided Buddhists with a legitimate reason for the restoration of the sangha, a reason that, at that time, stood on more practical grounds than the notion of "freedom of religious belief." Under their efforts, monastics that had been forced to return to secular life were called back into temples; those who had stayed in temples as peasants were allowed to don their monks' robes again and restart their religious activities. The number of monastics started to increase slowly, and, after a short while, new Buddhists, including monks, nuns, and lay practitioners, emerged. However, being a monk or nun was not considered a respectable occupation with a future at that time. The few new monastics often came from poor families with low levels of education. If Buddhism was to be rebuilt, the urgent task was to offer them systematic training both in religious doctrines and in basic secular education.

In view of this situation, the BAC decided, as one of its matters of priority, to reopen the Buddhist Academy and obtained the relevant government permission. In September 1980, the Buddhist Academy of China restarted its operation after fourteen years of closure. On December 19, the United Front Work Department of the Central Committee of the CCP gave its assent to the "Suggestions about the Restoration of Religious Schools" (Guanyu huifu zongjiao xueyuan de yijian 关于恢复宗教学院的意见) of the State Bureau of Religious Affairs (Luo 2001, 284–285). Four days later, the Buddhist Academy held the opening ceremony of the new academic year, when forty-one people were recruited into a two-year preparatory program.

After the nightmare of the Cultural Revolution, Buddhist leaders did see a gleam of hope for the revival of their religion and held great enthusiasm for the prospect of the sangha's restoration, notwithstanding the still stigmatized and marginalized state of religion. Under the encouragement and support of Zhao Puchu, the Lingyanshan Temple (Lingyanshan Si 灵岩山寺) in Suzhou, Jiangsu, reopened in 1979, directed by Mingxue, a graduate of the Buddhist Academy of China who had entered the school in 1956. One year later, in December 1980, the Buddhist Academy of China, Mount Lingyan Branch (*fenyuan* 分院) was founded with forty-three students. In 1982, after two years of preparation, the Qixia Temple (Qixia Si 栖霞寺) in Nanjing, Jiangsu, founded a "sangha training class" (*sengqie peixunban* 僧伽培训班),[11] directed by Mingshan 茗山 (1914–2001), who had studied in several Republican-period institutes for Buddhist studies. The first recruitment of the class brought in more than 180 student-monks from all over China. One year later, the class changed its name to the Buddhist Academy of China, Mount Qixia Branch. It is important to note that the two "branches" were relatively independent of the Buddhist Academy of China from a pedagogical point of view, even though they could be seen as preparatory schools for the latter, since they were at a less advanced level. However, they kept the name "Buddhist Academy of China" for two reasons: First, keeping the same name enabled them to circumvent the policy barriers for creating new names, since at the time only the "restoration" of earlier existing religious schools was permitted in the official discourse. Second, as local Buddhist organizations had not been completely resurrected yet, and local governments had a conservative attitude on religious affairs, the naming showed that they worked on behalf of a national organization and facilitated its operation, especially in its efforts to recruit acceptable students from all over the country. That the "branches" both opened in Jiangsu was probably related to the fact that Zhao Puchu worked in Shanghai and was familiar with Buddhism in the Lower Yangtze Region. At any rate, despite the nominal connection with the Buddhist Academy of China, the appearance of these two "branches" marked the de facto end of its monopoly on monastic education.

In March 1982, the Central Committee of the CCP issued Document no. 19, which, in addition to establishing the legal grounds for post-Mao religious revival, rendered explicit the legal status and political task of religious seminaries: "It is decisively important for the outlook of religious organizations in our country to train and educate a younger generation of patriotic religious professionals in a planned manner. We should not only continue to win over, show solidarity with, and educate current religious figures, but also help religious organizations to run religious schools and cultivate new religious professionals well. The task of religious schools is to create a group of young religious professionals who love the motherland, support the party's leadership and the socialist regime, and possess a considerable level of religious scholarship" (Zhongguo Gongchandang Zhongyang Weiyuanhui 1982).

On September 10, the State Council Office gave its consent to the "Request for Instructions on the Establishment of Religious Schools" (Guanyu kaiban zongjiao yuanxiao de qingshi 关于开办宗教院校的请示) from the Bureau of Religious Affairs, the first document that granted permission for the opening of new religious schools (Luo 2001, 312–313). In April 1983, the State Council agreed to the reopening of 142 Chinese Han Buddhist temples of historical significance. These policies stimulated the development of local Buddhism and created space for the establishment of regional Buddhist academies. In the single year of 1983, the Sichuan Buddhist Academy for Nuns was founded in Tiexiang Temple (Tiexiang Si 铁像寺) in Chengdu, the Shanghai Buddhist Academy in the Yufo Chan Temple (Yufo Chan Si 玉佛禅寺), the Fujian Buddhist Academy in the Guanghua Temple in Putian, and the Caoxi 曹溪 Buddhist Academy in the Nanhua Chan Temple (Nanhua Chan Si 南华禅寺) in Shaoguan, Guangdong. Notably, except for the Sichuan Buddhist Academy for Nuns, all three were "restorations" of Republican-era institutes for Buddhist studies. In addition, in the same year, a sangha training class was opened in Zhongfeng Chan Temple (Zhongfeng Chan Si 中峰禅寺) on Mount Emei 峨眉 in Sichuan (renamed in 1991 as the Sichuan Emei Buddhist Academy) and a Research Institute in Buddhist Studies at the Guoqing Temple (Guoqing Si 国清寺) on Mount Tiantai 天台 in Zhejiang (renamed in 1999 as the Mount Tiantai Buddhist Academy).

The number of Buddhist academies has gradually increased since then. In 2003, according to BAC statistics, there were thirty-four Buddhist academies in total, of which twenty-six were of the Han tradition, six were of the Tibetan tradition, and two were of the Pali tradition (Wen 2006). In 2011, Zhanru 湛如 (b. 1968), then executive vice-dean of the Buddhist Academy of China and director of the Education Committee of the BAC, stated that, according to incomplete statistics, there were forty-five Buddhist academies of the Han tradition, five higher Buddhist academies of the Tibetan tradition, and four academies of the Pali tradition (Zhanru 2011). However, neither the BAC nor the State Administration for Religious Affairs (SARA) (formerly the State Bureau of Religious Affairs) has given an official list of Buddhist academies. According to my surveys from the period 2009–2014, by the mid-2010s there were fifty-eight Buddhist academies of the Han tradition (see Appendix 7.1).

Although the number of Buddhist academies increased, the BAC still attempted to manage this sector with its methods of central planning. In August 1986 in Beijing, the BAC held the National Work Forum of Han Buddhist Schools, a meeting attended by the BAC leaders, leaders of seven Buddhist academies and one sangha training class, and a representative from the State Bureau of Religious Affairs. The main purpose of the meeting was "unified planning and hierarchicalization" (*tongyi guihua, fenqing cengci* 统一规化, 分清 层次). It refers to arranging then disconnected regional academies under the guidance and supervision of the BAC so as to build a national unified system of sangha education at three levels: primary, secondary, and tertiary. According to the minutes from the meeting (Zhongguo Fojiao Xiehui 1986):

> Primary-level Buddhist education mainly designates sangha training programs and study classes. They are to be held by key temples, and may vary in size, duration and focus of the curriculum. Provincial Buddhist associations may also commission key temples to hold primary-level education. Also, secondary-level Buddhist academies may hold primary-level classes. The aim of education is to train general temple staff and provide a source of students for secondary-level institutes.
>
> Secondary-level Buddhist education mainly designates branches of the Buddhist Academy of China and regional Buddhist academies run by provincial Buddhist associations. These Buddhist academies should recruit morally sound young monastics either with primary-level Buddhist education or [secular] junior middle school education and should have a two-year curriculum. Graduates should have the level of [secular] high school graduates in the liberal arts [*wenke* 文科] track, and are, in particular, expected to master Classical Chinese and a foreign language to a high level. The aim of the education is to train mid-level temple managers and provide a source of students for the higher-level academy.
>
> Higher-level Buddhist education is provided by the Buddhist Academy of China. Students should be selected from morally sound young monastics who have graduated from secondary-level Buddhist academies or [secular] high schools and have been ordained for at least two years. The higher-level Buddhist academy should have a four-year curriculum. The aim of its education is to train academic researchers of Buddhism, people capable of international exchange in Buddhist studies, teaching personnel in Buddhist studies and high-level temple managers.

When conditions permit, the Buddhist Academy of China will open postgraduate programs (currently present in a small-scale trial). For now, its students are to be selected from among Bachelor-degree graduates of the Buddhist Academy of China. The aim of its education is to train high-level Buddhist intellectuals with a deep level of scholarship on par with that of international researchers.

The minutes also stated that the clear hierarchicalization serves "comprehensiveness, focus and coordination" (*quanmian guihua, baozheng zhongdian, xietiao fazhan* 全面规划, 保证重点, 协调发展). Obviously, the main focus of sangha education was still on the Buddhist Academy of China. The meeting even required that local resources be concentrated in existing seminaries and that no new schools of secondary grade should be opened. Additionally, the meeting proposed a list of basic textbooks for Buddhist academies at all three levels and suggested that larger temples reserve a certain percentage of their yearly income as a fund for Buddhist education to be allocated by the BAC for Buddhist seminaries.

In the official discourse of the BAC, this meeting fixed the direction of the contemporary development of sangha education. In fact, however, almost none of the plans proposed in the meeting were later implemented. According to my own statistics, the period between 1986 and 2000, in spite of the recommendations at the meeting, not only was not a period that saw no new academies formed, but was in fact the period of fastest growth of Buddhist academies, with one to six academies founded every year, mostly at the secondary level. Furthermore, the teaching in these local academies was mostly autonomous from the central academy and the BAC: The BAC's textbook recommendation had no actual binding force. The centralized allocation of funds for education also did not materialize.

In January 1992, the BAC once more convened a national work forum of Han Buddhist academies. It was admitted in the meeting that "the higher, secondary, and primary levels of Buddhist seminaries have failed to attain standardization, normalization and serialization in their curricula, syllabi, and textbooks, causing pedagogical overlaps and lacunae between the three levels of schools, thus impeding the regularization of Buddhist schools" (Zhongguo Fojiao Xiehui 1992, 10). Hence, it was proposed in the meeting that the BAC set up a committee for textbook compilation and approval. A standard for three grades of Buddhist seminaries would be made, with deadlines assigned to requirements and measures for upgrading and downgrading. Also proposed in the meeting were the "Interim Measures on the Qualification of Teaching Personnel in Han Buddhist Schools" (Hanyuxi fojiao yuanxiao jiaoxue renyuan zhicheng pingding shixing banfa 汉语系佛教院校教学人员职称评定试行办法) and a renewed proposal to set up a fund for sangha education. In order to strengthen the influence of the Buddhist Association on the system of

Buddhist academies, it was proposed in the meeting that the creation of a secondary-grade Buddhist academy or the upgrading of a primary-grade academy to a secondary-grade one had to be approved by the provincial Buddhist Association and put on record by the BAC. Also, the upgrading of a secondary-grade academy or the setting up of a higher-grade program in a secondary-grade academy had to be authorized by the provincial Buddhist Association and then submitted to the BAC for approval.

In short, the mentality of the 1992 meeting was still to strengthen the central planning of sangha education, with the BAC playing the role of the government of the Buddhist community, keeping to itself the powers of approval, management, and funding. At the time of this writing, the resolution of this meeting and the resolution of the 1986 meeting are still theoretically guiding principles for the educational activities of the BAC. However, in the past thirty years, according to my observations, the central planning system of sangha education not only has not been achieved, but has gradually eroded. This has to do with a double decentralization in resource control. On the one hand, local monasteries and regional Buddhist associations have increased in power compared to the BAC. On the other hand, local authorities have increased in power in comparison to the central government.

In the 1980s, newly reopened temples faced serious economic difficulties and frequent hostility from local authorities. In contrast, the BAC held political legitimacy from the central government and a limited but important amount of economic resources. In consequence, local temples were highly dependent on the BAC for their restoration. After the mid-1990s, however, with an increase in the economic power of Chinese Buddhists and a strengthening of their interaction with temples, the economic power of local temples increased considerably. At the same time, local authorities began to make conscious use of Buddhist historical and cultural resources to develop the tourist industry (Ji 2004, 2011). In regions where Buddhism enjoys a high popularity, local authorities have been very enthusiastic in building religious sites and attending to the quantitative and qualitative growth of religious service personnel. Hence, temples in those areas, along with some prominent temples in other areas, have developed sufficient economic power and political support to create Buddhist academies according to their own will and do not need the sanction or support of the BAC.

Since the beginning of the twenty-first century, the central state's main modality of religion management has become "territorial management" (*shudi guanli* 属地管理), which endows provincial governments with more legal and administrative responsibilities and has further increased the autonomy of local authorities and temples. In March 2005, the State Council issued "Regulations on Religious Affairs" (Zongjiao shiwu tiaoli 宗教事务条例), a basic legal document on religious affairs. Article 8 of the regulations stipulates: "When the creation of a religious school is to be proposed, national-level religious associations should submit their application to the authorities on religious affairs of the State Council. Or in other cases, religious associations on the level of provinces, autonomous regions, or municipalities should submit their application to the provincial, regional, or municipal authorities on religious affairs of the eventual locality of the school. The authorities on religious affairs should give their opinion within thirty days. If the authorities wish to give consent, they should report to the authorities on religious affairs of the State Council to get approval."

In other words, since the passing of the regulations, provincial Buddhist associations (often under the control of regional Buddhist leaders and a few large monasteries), with consent from provincial Religious Affairs Bureaus, are able to open legal Buddhist academies, even though, in principle, the central government still has the last word.[12] In practice the application procedures are very flexible. Certain Buddhist academies even operate only with the consent of local authorities other than the Religious Affairs Bureau, such as the United Front Work Department and the local branch of the political consultative conference. This constitutes an effective rejection of the measures of approval proposed by the BAC in 1992 for centralizing the authority for approving the construction of new seminaries. The BAC is not completely out of the game, however. Some regional Buddhist leaders still seek the BAC's official recognition of their academies for more political legitimacy and greater attractiveness to potential students, and this is not difficult because very often they themselves have positions in the BAC. Nevertheless, this recognition is no longer indispensable.

Under this context, the national coordination of Buddhist education, an edifice not yet fully completed, has started to be dismantled. Even to this day, the BAC recognizes only one "higher-level" (*gaoji* 高级) Buddhist academy, namely, the Buddhist Academy of China,[13] but this distinction is now of little meaning, as all sorts of regional Buddhist schools have raced to open associate's degree, bachelor's degree, and even postgraduate programs. For example, the Minnan Institute for Buddhist Studies, which reopened in 1984, since as early as 1997 has become a large Buddhist institution with male and female sections, enrolling students for a two-year preparatory program, a four-year bachelor's degree program, and a three-year postgraduate program. The Jiechuang Research Institute of Buddhist Studies (Jiechuang Foxue Yanjiusuo 戒幢佛学研究所), built in the Jiechuang Lü Temple (Jiechuang Lü Si 戒幢律寺) in Suzhou, Jiangsu, started to recruit three-year postgraduate students in 2000. The Henan Buddhist College, upon its creation in 2005, was already permitted by SARA to offer a full-time bachelor's degree program in four years and started its first enrollment in 2009. On May 17, 2014, the Zhejiang Buddhist Academy was officially opened in the Xuedou Temple (Xuedou Si 雪窦寺) in Fenghua. The Maitreya Buddhist Academy of Mount Xuedou 雪窦, the Wenzhou Buddhist Academy, and the Tiantai Buddhist Academy, all three subsidiary to the

Zhejiang Buddhist Academy, officially opened on the same day as four-year bachelor's program schools, after a prior de facto existence.

To some extent, sangha education is once again marketized as in the Republican era. In order to attract student-monastics, some Buddhist academies started to emphasize their local or lineage characteristics. For example, the Nanhua Chan Temple, famous for preserving the body of the sixth patriarch Huineng 慧能 (638–713), sports a Caoxi[14] Buddhist Academy that claims to specialize in Chan school training. The Jianzhen Buddhist University (named after the Tang dynasty monk Jianzhen 鉴真 [688–763], who contributed to the propagation of Buddhism to Japan), founded in 2005 in Yangzhou, Jiangsu, aiming to emphasize foreign language studies, set up two four-year bachelor's degree specializations—English for Buddhism and Japanese for Buddhism. Other Buddhist seminaries have cooperated with secular universities in order to increase the value of their degrees. For example, the Xianqing 显庆 Buddhist Academy in Baoshan Temple (Baoshan Si 包山寺) in Yangzhou, Jiangsu, has held together with Yangzhou University a training base for research in Buddhist history. After taking the required courses and passing examinations, student-monastics receive diplomas jointly sealed by the Jiangsu Council for Self-Taught Higher Education Examinations and Yangzhou University (Li Shangquan 2008). The Jiangsu Buddhist Academy for Nuns has cooperated with Nanjing University to open three programs spanning from associate's degree to master's degree. The Buddhist Academy of Hongfa Temple (Hongfa Si 弘法寺) in Shenzhen has collaborated with Peking University in four specializations—Chan, Pure Land, Buddhist art, and Buddhist communication studies—and has proposed short-term programs for lay Buddhists.[15] In addition, some regional academies are not content with their local impact and have begun to pursue formal recognition on a national level. The Buddhist Academy of Hongfa Temple, for example, claims that it "belongs directly" (*zhishu* 直属) to the BAC. The Buddhist Academy of Putuoshan, founded in 1988, changed its name to the Buddhist Academy of China, Putuoshan College in 2011. However, both in financing and in teaching, these Buddhist academies are completely independent of the national BAC and the Buddhist Academy of China. The BAC does not object to this rise of local academies, because regional leaders are themselves leaders of the BAC. In fact, after the death of its prestigious ex-chair Zhao Puchu in 2000,[16] the BAC has become a central venue for balancing the interests of regional Buddhist leaders.

SCALE, OPERATION, AND IMPACT OF BUDDHIST ACADEMIES

It should be noted that this trend of diversification and competition is a fairly new phenomenon. In fact, most Buddhist academies still operate on a limited scale. Deficiencies in funds, teaching staff, and the educational level of student-monastics have put some Buddhist academies in an unsustainable position, sometimes even causing a halt in student recruitment (Li 2013). Early established and renowned Buddhist academies, like the Buddhist Academy of China and the Minnan Institute for Buddhist Studies, are still in an advantaged position. Their entrance examinations are very competitive. It is still unknown what the new type of Buddhist academies, such as the Jianzhen Buddhist University and the Hongfa Temple Buddhist Academy, which place more emphasis on nonreligious practical skills and collaboration with secular universities, will contribute to Buddhist education in China.

In the following pages, I give a general description of the scale and curriculum of Buddhist academies, as well as their influence on the Buddhist field. The Buddhist Academy of China is taken as the primary example, but other regional Buddhist academies are also surveyed.

Scale

Most Buddhist academies are small in scale. Biennial enrollment brings in, on average, twenty to forty new students. Only a few academies enroll students every year, such as the Guangdong Buddhist Academy for Nuns (since 1998) and the Buddhist Academy of Hongfa Temple (since 2011). In 2016, the Buddhist Academy of China and its Putuoshan College joined in.[17] However, this is still far from the norm.

I mentioned earlier that the sangha training class of Qixia Temple brought in 184 student-monks from all over China for its first enrollment when it was founded in 1982.[18] This, however, is an exceptional case where the numbers were inflated because of pent-up demand from a long period of time when monastic education was not available. Two years later, this institution, now the Buddhist Academy of China, Mount Qixia Branch, reduced its enrollment to 87 entering students (Mingshan 2002, 387). In fact, during the whole period from 1982 to 2012, the total number of graduates was only 718 (Jiangsu Sheng Fojiao Xiehui 2012), with a biennial average of 48. Since 1990, there have been between 30 and 40 graduates every other year. In 2014, only 20 students were enrolled. Of course, there are Buddhist academies that have both male and female sections and enroll student-monastics under different categories, such as preparatory programs and various kinds of short-term training programs. Those schools are relatively large-scale. In Fujian Province, for example, where Buddhism is highly popular, the Minnan Institute for Buddhist Studies and Fujian Buddhist Academy have each brought in more than 100 entering students during each new enrollment period.

Among the fifty-eight Buddhist educational institutions I have surveyed, eleven are specialized institutions for women. Fifteen other Buddhist academies accept both men and women. The Sichuan Buddhist Academy for Nuns, the oldest and most renowned women-only institution, takes around forty nuns for its bachelor's program each biennial enrollment. Mount Wutai

Buddhist Academy for Nuns is considered the largest Buddhist academy for nuns, but this fame comes mainly from the academy's many short-term training programs, each with a duration of only a few months. The size of its bachelor's program enrollment in 2012 was a mere forty-eight students. In general, women's education is on a smaller scale than men's education, a situation that corresponds to the greater proportion of men overall in the Chinese sangha.[19]

According to a cadre of SARA in charge of managing religious schools, there were thirty-two Buddhist academies throughout China in 2005; the number of student-monastics approached 4,600 (Sangji zhaxi [Sangye Tashi] 2005). These numbers included the academies of Tibetan and Pali traditions and probably also counted more numerous student-monastics in short-term primary-grade classes. According to this piece of data, there are 140 students on average in a Buddhist academy. Extrapolating from these statistics to ten years later, I would infer, at the time of this writing, that the size of the student body of Han Buddhist academies is approximately 8,000, which is 4–5 percent of the total population of Han monastics.[20] However, my own field experience suggests that the actual number is lower, because in many Han Buddhist academies, the number of student-monastics does not reach 100.

The Buddhist Academy of China, though the oldest and the only "higher-level" Buddhist academy recognized by the BAC, has a scale that matches the national average. From 1980 on, the revived Buddhist Academy of China enrolled students once every other year (every three years during the period 1994–2001). The first enrollment took in 41 people in a two-year preparatory program. In 1982, 39 students graduated among the 41 when the preparatory program was stopped. Sixty students were recruited into the bachelor's degree program (including the 39 fresh preparatory program graduates). However, in the 1980s, student-monks showed a relatively high rate of dropout during a time when the social and political environment was less favorable to Buddhism. In the three decades that followed 1986, the number of graduates stayed at the level of 26–45, with the single outlier of 2003, when there were 64 graduates.

From 1986, the Buddhist Academy of China started enrolling postgraduate students in a three-year program. The first twelve classes of postgraduates were recruited from the freshly graduated students of the school's bachelor's program. Since 2011, the academy has admitted students with a bachelor's degree from Buddhist academies and temples all over China, as well as former graduates of the academy.

In recent years, the Buddhist Academy of China has persistently sought to build new campus housing. In 2014, it obtained a land-use permit to build a new campus in the Haidian District of Beijing. In the same year, for the first time in its history, the academy recruited five doctoral students from the younger portion of its faculty. These signs are suggestive of a desire for expansion in the future.

Graduates of Buddhist Academy of China Undergraduate Programs (1982–2009)

Year	1982	1984	1986	1988	1990	1992	1994	1997	1998	2001	2003	2005	2007	2009	Total
Graduates	39	19	27	31	35	26	40	29	31	41	64	36	44	45	507

Graduates of Buddhist Academy of China Postgraduate Program (1989–2014)

Year	1989	1991	1993	1995	1997	2000	2001	2004	2006	2008	2010	2012	2014	Total
Graduates	2	2	6	1	8	3	3	9	6	6	13	6	3	68

Enrollment

In the early 1980s, the enrollment of Buddhist academies came under the strict control of the Bureau of Religious Affairs as well as the United Front Work Department of the CCP. The quota for the first enrollment of the Buddhist Academy of China was distributed from the top down by party and governmental sections in charge of religious affairs. Jiequan 界诠 (b. 1959), one of the first class of student-monks, wrote in a memoir (2010) that his region of Ningde in Fujian, a place where Buddhism is very popular, had a quota of two people. The director of the CCP's county-level United Front Work Department personally gave him the notice that he was selected to participate in the examination. In 1982, the sangha training class of Qixia Temple planned to recruit two hundred students. The State Bureau of Religious Affairs determined the following quota for each province: thirty-five each for Jiangsu and Zhejiang, thirty each for Anhui and Guangdong, twenty each for Shaanxi, Shanxi, and Jiangxi, and ten for Henan (Mingshan 2002, 259). The principle guiding the distribution is unknown, though it was probably related to the number of temples reopened at that time.

Nevertheless, territorial constraints were soon canceled. Registration, however, remained controlled, especially for those who wished to enter the Buddhist Academy of China. According to the academy's regulations, registrants should be recommended by their local Buddhist academy, temple, or association to their local Religious Affairs Bureau, which then would give the assent for registration. This regulation is still in force at the time of this writing. At least in the 1990s, letters of acceptance were not delivered to the admitted student-monastics themselves, but to the student-monastics' provincial Religious Affairs Bureaus. An admitted student could be accepted only with a letter of introduction from the provincial Religious Affairs Bureau (Zhongguo Foxueyuan Zhaosheng Bangongshi 1994), a practice that has continued into the twenty-first century. However, relatively speaking, regional Buddhist academies today are not as strictly constrained as they were in the 1990s: They often enjoy a greater sphere of liberty in their choices of enrollees in short-term and low-level classes.

The requirement of consent by the State Bureau of Religious Affairs serves mainly to curb any potential political threat posed by an applicant. Political collaboration, labeled "support towards the party's leadership and the socialist regime" or "love toward the country and the religion," is almost always the first requirement in the enrollment brochures of any Buddhist academy. Otherwise, the substantive requirements of Buddhist academies to applicants usually refer to age, duration of ordainment, previous degrees obtained, marital status, and health. According to the eight enrollment brochures I collected for the years 1990, 1994, 2003, 2005, 2007, 2009, 2011, and 2013, there have been no major changes to these requirements in the past twenty years: They require that applicants be under the age of twenty-eight, have graduated from a secondary-grade Buddhist academy or senior middle school, have been tonsured as monks for a "suitable time" (*yiding shijian* 一定时间),[21] have no marital or romantic relationships, have an "upright appearance,"[22] be in good health, and be free of psychological illnesses and infectious diseases. Beginning in 2011, a new requirement of no criminal record was added (see Appendix 7.2). Other Buddhist academies have similar requirements.

Student-monastics who succeed in their registration also need to pass a written examination. In 1980, the entrance examination of the Buddhist Academy of China included three subjects: Chinese language, Buddhism, and politics. The Buddhism examination question was to write an essay about the "significance of the cultivation of discipline, concentration, and wisdom in Buddhism" (Jiequan 2010). In 1990, the number of subjects on the exam swelled to six, containing a mix that has stayed valid to this day: Buddhism, current events and policies, Chinese language, history-geography, foreign language (English or Japanese), and daily recitation. The entrance examination for the higher-level or bachelor's degree program of other Buddhist academies is similar, but some of them do not require foreign languages. Primary- and secondary-level programs often recruit students without an examination or require only a recommendation letter or essay that reflects the applicant's understanding of Buddhism. Not surprisingly, highly renowned Buddhist academies like the Buddhist Academy of China and the Minnan Institute for Buddhist Studies have the most selective entrance examinations. In 2011, the Buddhist Academy of China recruited 42 new student-monks from among 180 applicants.

Curriculum and Teaching

The curriculum of Buddhist academies usually includes Buddhist knowledge (classics and history of individual sects), general culture (Chinese history and literature, philosophy, and foreign languages), knowledge of politics (laws and policies concerning religious affairs), and supplementary courses linked to personal cultivation such as calligraphy, music, and so on. According to a survey by Jingyin and Zhang Qi (2008) of sixty-one Buddhist academies and other sangha training programs (fifty-one of which belong to Han Buddhism), in the curriculum of these institutions, knowledge of Buddhism makes up 65.06 percent, culture and liberal arts 12.8 percent, and education on "patriotism and legality" 6.11 percent (see Appendix 7.3). This proportion corresponds to the double objective of Buddhist academies to conduct both religious education and supplementary general education; it also reflects their constraint by state policies that mandate a degree of political awareness in the education of religious professionals. Even though there were no explicit regulations regarding the curriculum in the "Measures for Establishing Religious Schools"

(Zongjiao yuanxiao sheli banfa 宗教院校设立办法) implemented in 2007, the "Request for Instructions about Opening Religious Schools" (Guanyu kaiban zongjiao yuanxiao de qingshi 关于开办宗教院校的请示), approved by the central government in 1982, set explicit provisions that "the proportion of courses taught is generally 70 percent religious courses, 20 percent cultural courses, and 10 percent political courses" (Luo 2001, 313), provisions that have remained consistent throughout the past three decades. However, it is important to note that the degree to which "political courses" seek to inculcate particular ideological views differs by school and teacher. Under the heading of "political courses," Buddhist academies can teach about laws, policies concerning religion, management systems of temples, and documents of the BAC.

As far as the religious portion of the curriculum is concerned, the Buddhist Academy of China, in particular, has inherited the ecumenical idea first proposed by Taixu to "promote all the eight sects" (*bazong binghong* 八宗并弘), namely, to teach a comprehensive curriculum of Chinese Buddhist doctrines from each of the Mahayana schools of Madhyamaka, Consciousness-Only, Huayan, Tiantai, Pure Land, Chan, Vinaya, and Abhidharmakośa, as well as knowledge about Buddhism's roots in India.

Let us take the curriculum for the 2009 class as an example. For the first year, an overall comprehension of Buddhist history and sects was emphasized, with courses not only on Vinaya, the Three Treatise school, and Chan, but also an introduction to the history of Indian Buddhism and Theravada Buddhism. For the second year, the main content was the classics and history of the sects of Vinayapiṭaka, Consciousness-Only, Tiantai, Huayan, and Abhidharmakośa. For the third year, the texts studied were the *Lotus Sutra*, *Dharmaguptavinaya*, the *Awakening of Faith in the Mahāyāna*, the *Mūlamadhyamakakārikā*, the *Mahāyānasamgraha*, and the texts and histories of Huayan, Chan, and Pure Land. The fourth year partially continues the contents of the third year, with the Bodhisattva Vows, the *Saṃdhinirmocana Sūtra*, the *Vimalakīrti Sūtra*, methods of contemplation in the Huayan school, and extracts from *Zangyao* 藏要 (The Essentials of the Buddhist Canon, composed by Ouyang Jian and Lü Cheng at the Chinese Inner Studies Institute) added to the curriculum.

In the 1990s, Republican-era compositions were used as textbooks, such as the *Fojiao gezong dayi* 佛教各宗大意 (Essential Ideas of Different Sects of Buddhism) and the *Zhongguo fojiao shi* 中国佛教史 (History of Chinese Buddhism) by Huang Chanhua 黄忏华 (1890–1977), a student of Yang Wenhui and friend of Taixu. The current scope of textbooks and teaching materials is considerably wider, including books by Shengyan 圣严 (Sheng-Yen, 1931–2009), a Chan master who has lived in Taiwan since 1949,[23] such as *Yindu fojiao shi* 印度佛教史 (The History of Indian Buddhism) and *Jielü xue gangyao* 戒律学纲要 (Outline of Precept Studies). The curriculum also includes the *Nanchuan fojiao shi* 南传佛教史 (History of Southern [Theravada] Buddhism) by Jinghai 净海 (b. 1931), a monk who lived in Taiwan after 1949 and later propagated Buddhism in the United States.

In the first period after the restoration of 1980, some teachers of the original Buddhist Academy survived to teach in the restored academy, including Zhengguo, Juzan 巨贊 (1908–1984), Mingzhen 明真 (1902–1989), and Guankong. But several years later they all passed away. The task of education then fell on the first cohort of graduates from before the Cultural Revolution, including Mingzhe, Chuanyin 传印 (b. 1927), and Liu Feng 刘峰 (1923–2003), who earlier had been a monk and was now a layman. The current faculty of the Buddhist Academy is composed mainly of graduates of the academy's own post-graduate program since 1980. According to my surveys, among the fifty-two teachers (including temporary lay teachers hired from secular institutions) of the 2014 Buddhist Academy of China, at least twenty-six fall into this category. Since between 1989 and 2014 only sixty-eight students in total graduated from the post-graduate program, this means that more than one-third of graduates from the academy's postgraduate program have gone on to teach at the academy. Indeed, as the lack of faculty members is persistently the greatest difficulty Buddhist academies encounter, especially small, regional ones, retaining graduates of the same academy in teaching positions is a very common strategy nationwide.

Impact

Although Buddhist academies have educated tens of thousands of monastics in the past three decades, most of their programs are primary-grade, secondary-grade, or short-term. According to a survey conducted around 2006 by SARA concerning the education of Buddhist clergy in thirty provincial-level regions, only 1.5 percent have a higher-education degree from a Buddhist academy (Liu 2007). Under these circumstances, obtaining a degree from a Buddhist academy, especially one of the most renowned ones, provides the degree holder with a significant amount of symbolic capital.

According to my field experience, the younger generation of abbots of major temples have often been trained in Buddhist academies. According to an early 2000s survey by Christian Cochini (2008), among 157 Buddhist temples of the Han tradition of important historical and cultural status (the list includes the 142 "Buddhist temples of historical significance in Han regions" nominated by the central government in 1983), at least 46 temples have abbots who graduated from various Buddhist academies, and at least 30 temples operate Buddhist academies or branches themselves.

The same is true for the BAC leaders. Among members of the Eighth Governing Council of the BAC (2010–2015), the chair, Chuanyin, studied in 1960 in the Buddhist Academy of China. After 1984, he was successively director of pedagogic affairs and vice-dean of the academy, assumed responsibility for its teaching activities, and became dean in 2010. There are fifteen monks and one nun of the Han tradition among the twenty-five vice-chairs of the

Schooling Dharma Teachers   **193**

Eighth Governing Council. As far as I can ascertain, thirteen of them have studied in Buddhist academies; seven graduated from the Buddhist Academy of China (six of which studied after 1980); and eleven direct or have directed at least one Buddhist academy.

Han Monastic Vice-Chairs of the BAC Eighth Governing Council (2010–2015)

Religious Name	Institute of Most Recent Graduation	Date of Matriculation	Final Diploma	Post in the System of Buddhist Academies
Shenghui 圣辉 (b. 1951)	Buddhist Academy of China	1982	Postgraduate	Vice-dean, Buddhist Academy of China (1993–2007); dean, Minnan Institute for Buddhist Studies (1996–2015), the Hunan Buddhist Academy (1998–), and the Mount Jiuhua Buddhist Academy (2001–2007)
Jinghui 净慧 (1933–2013)	Buddhist Academy of China	1956	Postgraduate	Dean, Hebei Buddhist Academy (2000–2013)
Xuecheng 学诚 (b. 1966)	Buddhist Academy of China	1984	Postgraduate	Vice-dean (2007–2015) and dean (2015–2018), the Buddhist Academy of China; dean, Fujian Buddhist Academy (1995–2018) and Famen Temple Buddhist Academy (2010–2018)
Yongshou 永寿 (b. 1963)	Buddhist Academy of China, Mount Qixia Branch		No specific degree	Dean, Mount Emei Buddhist Academy (2003–)
Yongxin 永信 (b. 1965)	No training in a Buddhist academy			Dean, Henan Buddhist College (2005–)
Mingsheng 明生 (b. 1960)	Buddhist Academy of China	1986	Bachelor's	Dean, Guandong Buddhist Academy (2012–)
Juexing 觉醒 (b. 1970)	Shanghai Buddhist Academy	1985	No specific degree	

(Continued)

(Continued)

Religious Name	Institute of Most Recent Graduation	Date of Matriculation	Final Diploma	Post in the System of Buddhist Academies
Rurui 如瑞 (nun, b. 1957)	Sichuan Buddhist Academy for Nuns	1981	No specific degree	Dean, Mount Wutai Buddhist Academy for Nuns (1992–)
Zhanru 湛如 (b. 1968)	Buddhist Academy of China	1984	Bachelor's	Vice-dean, Chinese Buddhist Academy (2010–2015)
Miaojiang 妙江 (b. 1952)	Buddhist Academy of China, Mount Qixia Branch	1982	No specific degree	
Xincheng 心澄 (b. 1963)	Buddhist Academy of China	1986	Postgraduate	Dean, Jinshan Buddhist Academy (2003–)
Daoci 道慈 (b. 1953)	Buddhist Academy of China, Mount Qixia Branch	1982	No specific degree	Dean, Chinese Buddhist Academy, Putuoshan College (2012–)
Chunyi 纯一 (b. 1964)	Buddhist Academy of China, Mount Qixia Branch	1984		
Zhengci 正慈 (b. 1971)	Buddhist Academy of China	1990	Postgraduate	Vice-dean, Wuchang Institute for Buddhist Studies (2008?–)
Yinshun 印顺 (b. 1974)	No training in a Buddhist academy			Dean, Hongfa Temple Buddhist Academy (2012–)
Zengqin 增勤 (b. 1962)	No training in a Buddhist academy			

The position of a monastic within Buddhist institutions is determined by multiple factors, such as reputation, lineage, and networks. However, Buddhist academies of national renown have become an important part of the internal elite production of the sangha. Even smaller, regional Buddhist academies provide opportunities for social mobility for young monastics. Buddhist academies command great investment and require complex management; they can only be run in places where the power and resources of the Buddhist community are well concentrated. Entering a Buddhist academy is in fact approaching the center of power and resources. This is vital for young monastics who are ordained in small, provincial temples under unknown masters, and who, as a result, lack cultural and social capital.

TENSION BETWEEN STUDY AND PRACTICE

In the nearly four decades since 1980, academies have made a great contribution to the Buddhist revival and have enjoyed an increasing influence on the evolution of the landscape of Buddhism. However, within Buddhist circles, there has been persistent criticism of Buddhist academies. Observers do not need much effort to find a great number of monks, including Buddhist leaders, who think that current Buddhist academies are not able to cultivate qualified Dharma teachers. One of the most critical Buddhist leaders is Miaozhan 妙湛 (1910–1995), who served as dean of the Minnan Institute for Buddhist Studies from 1985 to 1995. In an unpublished 1992 report to the BAC national work forum of Han Buddhist academies, he stated that "many Buddhist academies have appeared in different regions [of the PRC] in the last ten years or so. Only a handful of sufficiently capable people have come out of them. What is that if not drawing water with a sieve—[something of] the utmost futility?" (quoted in Wang 2001, 9).

This dissatisfaction on the part of some Buddhist leaders is not without its reasons. Miaozhan pointed out on different occasions (Xuecheng 2010) that many young graduates of Buddhist academies are marked by a narrow focus on certain Buddhist sutras, or worse, only the studies of these sutras as history or literature. Other critics focus on the informal and unorganized features of some academies' curriculum because of their lack of capable teachers. However, the most debated topic is the "loss of a sacred resource" (Wang 2001), that is to say, a declining emphasis on the importance of religious faith in academy training. This is certainly a subjective judgment, but it is true that some Buddhists doubt that the current Buddhist academies can teach their students what they see as the real purpose of sangha education, namely, the training of Dharma teachers to develop strong moral character and deep "faith" (*xinyang* 信仰) in Buddhist teachings and practices.

This distrust has generated a discourse that contrasts "study" (*xue* 学) with "practice" (*xiu* 修) and academy (*xueyuan* 学院) with monastery (*conglin* 丛林, which literally means "forest"). According to this discourse, the real failing of Buddhist academies is that the study of knowledge is emphasized at the expense of the religious practice and that the academies are not organized and run according to the monastic tradition.[24] Here "study" basically means the learning of Buddhist history and doctrines, while "practice" suggests personal commitment to the following of a religious way, which, in the Buddhist case, can refer to committing to an ascetic path that follows the Vinaya, engaging devoutly in monastic duties, attaining practical competence to correctly perform ritual services, and cultivating dignified bearing as a sign of religious belief. Critics of the academy model do acknowledge the importance of mastering religious history and conceptions but argue that, due to the limited level of student-monastics and teachers in academies, their graduates can neither reach the requirements of scholarly research to a level comparable with secular religious studies programs nor apply their knowledge of Buddhist history and doctrine in the performance of religious duties. The critics also complain that monastics trained at academies are not willing to participate in the labor and religious practice of temples and lack the ability to handle "Dharma affairs" (*fawu* 法务) such as temple management and ritual organization.[25]

Sensitive to these criticisms, the BAC work forum of 1992 proposed "integrating study and practice" (*xue xiu yitihua* 学修一体化) and "giving a monastic spirit to student-monastic life" (*xuesheng shenghuo conglinhua* 学僧生活丛林化). These are now slogans vaunted by every Buddhist academy. However, it remains unclear how these concepts are applied. Certain monks have proposed detailed measures to fit Buddhist academies into more traditional ideals of sangha education. For example, Jiqun 济群 (b. 1962) holds that Buddhist academies should enjoy the guidance of famous masters and that students should not be satisfied with superficial and unsystematic studies of the history and concepts of Buddhism but should spend sufficient time meditating on basic questions of human life. Miaozhan proposes that, in teaching and assessment, the proportion of study to practice should be fifty-fifty, where "practice" signifies the mastery of meditative and ritual skills and participation in collective monastic activities. Some Buddhist academies require not only participation in morning and evening devotions from student-monastics, but also the added content of meditation and labor. A few sangha educational organs are not named "Buddhist academies" anymore, but "Vinaya institutes" (*lüxueyuan* 律学院) or related names in order to show their concern with teaching the mastery of monastic precepts. To a certain degree, this anti-intellectualist tendency is a reaction to the Buddhist secularization that originally stems from early-twentieth-century reforms. It has raised the question about what is the very foundation of Buddhist religious virtue.

From a sociological point of view, the contradiction between study and practice is a reflection of the tension between the roles of academy and monastery as two different kinds of institutions. A monastery is above all a site for religious practice (*daochang* 道场), a place where everyday rituals are organized, routine administrative business is carried out, and religious service is provided to lay Buddhists and other devotees.[26] Neither of these is an objective of a Buddhist academy, which dispenses diplomas to young monastics based on their ability to master testable areas of knowledge following the model of modern Western schools. In general, student-monastics are relieved of most of their duties to the hosting monastery so that they can focus on mastering this testable knowledge. Buddhist academies, however, are usually housed and funded by monasteries. This often causes a tension between resident monastics (*changzhu* 常住), who belong to the temple and fulfill its everyday duties, and student-monastics, who belong to the Buddhist academy. The former sometimes complain about the latter's absence or unwillingness to fulfill the traditional ritual duties and labor required of a monastic, while the latter hold that participation in ritual and service to laypersons and other devotees, as well as sometimes to the local authorities and the requirements of tourists, unnecessarily dissipates time and energy that is more properly used for study. Some temples also pay heftier stipends to resident monastics than to student-monastics (not to mention the possible supplementary income they receive from the performance of religious services), which arouses discontent among student-monastics (Lijing 2006).

Moreover, it is not only a matter of lack of consensus on matters concerning the division of labor, duty, and rights. Buddhist academies have a vastly different internal organization from monasteries, and a different relationship to the secular world. The abbot of a monastery often holds a traditional master-disciple relationship with the resident monastics. The resident monastics are always free to leave the temple, but they are expected to stay indefinitely. Monastics in middle and lower positions in the hierarchy are constrained by the rules of the temple to which they belong and live a way of life that, with the exception of ritual service, is mostly closed off to the outside world. They are not allowed to foster close personal relationships with laypeople. Due to this commitment of indefinite duration and the regular, stable nature of their lifestyle, resident monastics form a closed community.

In contrast, Buddhist academies are modeled after the bureaucratic hierarchy of secular schools. In principle, student-monastics do not enter a Buddhist academy due to a private relationship between themselves and the abbot or monastic teachers. In fact, most student-monastics leave the Buddhist academy after one to four years of study. They either return to their original monastery or try to fend for themselves. Also, the power of decision making in Buddhist academies is sometimes not vested in the hosting monastery alone. Although some Buddhist academies are located in temples, their leadership partly belongs to the Bureau of Religious Affairs, the local Buddhist association if there is an affiliation between it and the concerned academy, or powerful local Buddhist leaders. Also, Buddhist academies often invite laypeople to teach courses, and provide tools like libraries and computers. For this reason, student-monastics have more time and opportunity to acquire knowledge about the secular world. At the same time, the institution of Buddhist academies encourages mobility in pursuit of a higher diploma and better chances of education (entering a better academy or a secular university, or even studying abroad). Hence, from the point of view of monasteries, Buddhist academies are a highly unstable hetero-geneous element.

With these considerations, it seems to me that the so-called contradic-tion between study and practice is first of all the ideological translation of the institutional tension between monasteries and academies. This discourse implicitly refutes the religious validity of textual learning on Buddhist history and concepts and assumes that student-monastics are therefore lack-ing in ritual skills or even in moral character. In fact, however, there is no reliable evidence that student-monastics practice "worse" or "less" than monastics in general. In terms of "practices" such as the propagation of Buddhism or the following of an ascetic path, the most respected monks are often graduates of Buddhist academies, for example, Jiqun, who devotes himself to Buddhist mass education, and Jiequan, who is famous for his mastery and respect of Vinaya. Therefore, it is probably more interesting to put the question this way: Why are monasteries so motivated to run Buddhist academies, despite the tensions between these two institutions? Why are young monastics willing to attend Buddhist academies, even though the lat-ter suffer criticisms?

Apart from the problem that monastics commonly have a low level of education, a situation that needs remedying so that they may better manage temples in a fast-changing society, there are still two other factors that deserve attention. First, through the recruitment of teachers and student-monastics, Buddhist academies are able to collect human resources for mon-asteries. Although temples frequently complain that their graduates "went to who knows where," there will still be student-monastics who will maintain a good relationship with their hosting monasteries and the resident monastics. Sometimes, monasteries can even select and retain satisfactory talent from their exogenous pool of teachers and student-monastics. Also, it improves the public image of a temple for a batch of young monastics busy in their studies to live in the monastery: It reinforces the idea that Buddhism is neither outdated nor superstitious. This creates a potential basis for positive interaction between the monastery and secular society, where education is highly valued.

Moreover, the tradition of Chinese Buddhism has lacked a formal means to obtain social recognition for the knowledge level of monastics. Besides the division of labor inside monasteries, no titles were traditionally available to certify the level of a monk's scholarship. In the imperial period, a dwindling number of monastics were awarded commendation by the emperor. The major-ity could accumulate social prestige only by directing disciples, socializing with the secular elite, engaging in some extraordinary ascetic practices, or showing supernatural abilities. The diploma system of Buddhist academies has provided the majority of young monastics with a system of evaluation and certification and given them the chance to gradually accumulate graded and calculable symbolic capital. To some extent, Buddhist academies embody the democratization of Buddhist knowledge and authority in a modern society and are the result of a credentialism that originates from both the century-long modern bureaucratization of education and the recent marketization of labor.

TOWARD A "NORMALIZATION"?

The dualistic view of "study" and "practice" in sangha education reveals that the legitimacy of the Buddhist academy system is constrained by its interdependent and conflicting relationship with monasticism. At the same time, the functioning of the whole system depends mainly on the evolution of the relationship between various actors, namely, the state (central government and local authorities), monasteries, and the Buddhist associations.

On November 5, 2012, SARA published its *Zongjiao yuanxiao jiaoshi zige rending he zhicheng pingshen pinren banfa [shixing]* 宗教院校教师资格认定和职称评审聘任办法 [试行] (Interim Measures for Qualification, Accreditation, and Appointment of Teachers in Religious Schools) and *Zongjiao yuanxiao xuewei shouyu banfa [shixing]* 宗教院校学位授予办法 [试行] (Interim Measures for Awarding of Diplomas in Religious Schools), with the intention of "normalizing" (*guifanhua* 规范化) institutions for religious education. These laws could transform these relationships again. According to these measures, the diplomas of religious schools are to be classified into three grades: bachelor's, master's, and doctorate; the hierarchy of teaching staff is to be composed of assistant professors, lecturers, associate professors, and professors. This is a model that closely mirrors that of the secular education system, even if the laws stipulate that these diplomas would be valid only inside the religious community. Still more important is the fact that the final power of review and assessment and printing of diplomas and certificates all resides in the education committee of the national-level official religious associations. If these policies are effectively enforced, in the case of Buddhism, the power of the BAC would be increased relative to the power of regional Buddhist academies. The bureaucratic and hierarchical nature of the management of Buddhist academies would be more marked. On July 19, 2014, as a unit where the two interim laws were experimentally implemented, the Buddhist Academy of China issued, for the first time, accreditation certificates to twenty-eight teachers and awarded master's degree certificates to three newly graduated students (earlier graduate students did not have the title of "master"). According to the working plan of SARA, these two measures should be applied throughout the country in the coming years. If the measures represent an exploration toward a "way of running religious schools with Chinese characteristics" (Guojia Zongjiaoju Di Si Si 2014), the "way" still keeps its basic post-1949 orientation, which leads to state-corporatism, or the statist institutionalization of religion (Ji 2008a).

APPENDIX 7.1: SANGHA EDUCATIONAL ORGANS OF THE HAN TRADITION IN THE PRC (2014)

Name	Founding Date(s) (reopening or first enrollment)	Location(s)
1 Buddhist Academy of China 中国佛学院	Created in 1956, closed in 1966, reopened in 1980	Fayuan Temple 法源寺 (Beijing)
2 Buddhist Academy of China, Mount Lingyan Branch 中国佛学院灵岩山分院	1980	Lingyanshan Temple 灵岩山寺 (Suzhou, Jiangsu)
3 Buddhist Academy of China, Mount Qixia Branch 中国佛学院栖霞山分院	Created in 1982 as a sangha training class, formally established in 1983	Qixia Temple 栖霞寺 (Nanjing, Jiangsu)
4 Sichuan Buddhist Academy for Nuns 四川尼众佛学院	1983	Tiexiang Temple 铁像寺 (Chengdu, Sichuan), moved to Qifu Temple 祈福寺 (Pengzhou, Sichuan) in 2008
5 Sichuan Mount Emei Buddhist Academy 四川峨眉山佛学院	1983	Originally in Zhongfeng Temple 中峰寺, moved to Dafo Chan Temple 大佛禅院 in 2007 (Mount Emei, Sichuan)
6 Shanghai Buddhist Academy 上海佛学院	1983	Yufo Chan Temple 玉佛禅寺 (Shanghai)
7 Fujian Buddhist Academy 福建佛学院	1983	Guanghua Temple 广化寺 (Putian, Fujian)
8 Mount Tiantai Buddhist Academy 天台山佛学院	Created in 1983 as Society for Buddhist Studies 佛学研究社, renamed in 1999	Guoqing Temple 国清寺 (Mount Tiantai, Zhejiang)
9 Caoxi Buddhist Academy 曹溪佛学院	Opened in 1983, closed in 1993, reopened in 2000, affiliated to Guangdong Buddhist Academy 广东佛学院 in 2012	Nanhua Temple 南华寺 (Shaoguan, Guangdong)
10 Minnan Institute for Buddhist Studies 闽南佛学院	Registered in 1984, first enrollment in 1986	Nanputuo Temple 南普陀寺 for monks and Wanshilian Temple 万石莲寺 for nuns (Xiamen, Fujian)
11 Mindong Buddhist Academy for Nuns 闽东尼众佛学院	1986	Guanzong Temple 观宗庵 (Fu'an, Fujian)

Name	Founding Date(s) (reopening or first enrollment)	Location(s)
12 Quanzhou Buddhist Academy 泉州佛学苑 (for nuns and laynuns)	1987	Qinglian Jing Temple 庆莲净寺 (Quanzhou, Fujian)
13 Buddhist Academy of China, Putuoshan College 中国佛学院 普陀山学院	Created in 1988 as Putuoshan Buddhist Academy, renamed in 2011	Originally in Fuquan Chan Temple 福泉禅林, moved to Zhoujiajian Island in 2011 (Putuoshan, Zhejiang)
14 Yilan Buddhist Academy for Nuns 依兰尼众佛学院	1988	Ciyun Temple 慈云寺 (Yilan, Heilongjiang)
15 Guangde Buddhist Academy 广德佛学院	1989	Guangde Temple 广德寺 for monks, Jingye Chan Temple 净业禅院 for nuns (Suining, Sichuan)
16 Konglin Buddhist Academy 空林佛学院	Opened in 1989, officially established in 2002	Wenshu Temple 文殊院 for monks, Aidao Hall 爱道堂 for nuns (Chengdu, Sichuan)
17 Ciyun Buddhist Academy 慈云佛学院	1989	Ciyun Temple 慈云庵 (Ninghai, Zhejiang)
18 Jile Temple Buddhist Academy 极乐寺佛 学院	1990	Jile Temple 极乐寺 (Harbin, Heilongjiang)
19 Mount Jiuhua Buddhist Academy 九华山佛学院	1990–2007, reopened in 2016	Ganlu Temple 甘露寺 (Qingyang, Anhui)
20 Lingdong Buddhist Academy 岭东佛学院	Reopened in 1991, affiliated to Guangdong Buddhist Academy in 2012	Kaiyuan Temple 开元寺 (Chaozhou, Guangdong)
21 Mindong Buddhist Academy 闽东佛学院	1992	Ziguo Temple 资国寺 (Fuding, Fujian)
22 Chongqing Buddhist Academy 重庆佛学院	1992	Originally in Luohan Temple 罗汉寺, then moved to Huayan Temple 华岩寺 (Chongqing)
23 Yunmen Buddhist Academy 云门佛学院	Created in 1992, affiliated to Guangdong Buddhist Academy in 2012	Yunmen Temple 云门寺 (Ruyuan Yao Autonomous County, Guangdong)

(Continued)

Name	Founding Date(s) (reopening or first enrollment)	Location(s)
24 Jiangxi Province Buddhist Academy 江西省佛学院	1992	Baofeng Chan Temple 宝峰禅寺 (Jing'an, Jiangxi)
25 Mount Wutai Buddhist Academy for Nuns 五台山尼众佛学院	1992	Pushou Temple 普寿寺 (Mount Wutai, Shanxi) and Dacheng Temple 大乘寺 (Yuci, Shanxi)
26 Puyin Hall 普隐堂	1992	Pingxing Temple 平兴寺 (Mount Taimu, Fuding, Fujiang)
27 Zhongde Buddhist Academy for Nuns 种德尼众佛学院	1993	Zhongde Temple 种德寺 (Fu'an, Fujian)
28 Jiangxi Buddhist Academy for Nuns 江西尼众佛学院	1994	Jinshan Chan Temple 金山禅寺 (Linchuan, Jiangxi)
29 Wuchang Institute for Buddhist Studies 武昌佛学院	1994	Baotong Temple 宝通寺 for monks, Lianxi Temple 莲溪寺 for nuns (Wuhan, Hubei)
30 Jinshan Buddhist Academy 金山佛学院	1995	Jiangtian Chan Temple 江天禅寺 (Zhenjiang, Jiangsu)
31 Tianning Institute for Buddhist Studies 天宁佛学院	1995	Tianning Chan Temple 天宁禅寺 (Changzhou, Jiangsu)
32 Guangdong Buddhist Academy for Nuns 广东尼众佛学院	Created in 1995, affiliated to Guangdong Buddhist Academy in 2012	Dingguang Chan Temple 定光禅寺 (Lufeng, Guangdong)
33 Maitreya Buddhist Academy of Mount Xuedou 雪窦山弥勒佛学院	Created in 1995 as a sangha training class, affiliated to Zhejiang Buddhist Academy 浙江佛学院 in 2014	Zisheng Chan Temple 资圣禅寺 for monks, Daci Chan Temple 大慈禅寺 for nuns (Fenghua, Zhejiang)
34 Wenzhou Buddhist Academy 温州佛学院	Created in 1995 as Taiping Buddhist Academy (for Nuns) 太平佛学院 (女众), affiliated to Zhejiang Buddhist Academy in 2014	Taiping Temple 太平寺 for nuns, Anfu Temple 安福寺 for monks (Wenzhou, Zhejiang)

APPENDIX 7.1 (Continued)

Name	Founding Date(s) (reopening or first enrollment)	Location(s)
35 Jiechuang Institute for Buddhist Studies 戒幢佛学研究所	1996	Xiyuan Jiechuang Lü Temple 西园戒幢律寺 (Suzhou, Jiangsu)
36 Nongchan Buddhist Academy 农禅佛学院	1996	Longquan Temple 龙泉寺 (Changle, Fujian)
37 Hualin Buddhist Academy 华林佛学院	1997	Longhua Temple 龙华寺 (Shanghai)
38 Xianqing Buddhist Academy 显庆佛学院	Created in 1997 as Baoshan Study Society 包山学社, renamed in 2005	Baoshan Chan Temple 包山禅寺 (Yangzhou, Jiangsu)
39 Liaoning Buddhist Academy 辽宁佛学院	1998	Sanxue Temple 三学寺 (Haicheng, Liaoning)
40 Mount Baohua Vinaya Institute 宝华山律学院	1998	Longchang Temple 隆昌寺 (Mount Baohua, Nanjing, Jiangsu)
41 Hunan Province Buddhist Academy 湖南省佛学院	1998	Lushan Temple 麓山寺 for monks, Kaifu Temple 开福寺 for nuns (Changsha, Hunan)
42 Hangzhou Buddhist Academy 杭州佛学院	Created in 1998 as a sangha training class, formally established in 2005	Zhong Tianzhu Fajing Temple 中天竺法净寺, moved to Lingyin scenic area in 2010 (Hangzhou, Zhejiang)
43 Mount Wutai/ Zhulin Temple Buddhist Academy (for Monks) 五台山/竹林寺(男众)佛学院	Created in 1999, without government approval or open enrollment	Dasheng Zhulin Temple 大圣竹林寺 (Mount Wutai, Shanxi)
44 Hebei Province Buddhist Academy 河北省佛学院	2000	Bailin Chan Temple 柏林禅寺 (Zhao County, Hebei)
45 Jinxian Buddhist Academy 金仙佛学院	2000	Jinxian Temple 金仙寺 (Ningbo, Zhejiang)
46 Hanshan Academy 寒山书院	2003	Originally in Hanshan Temple 寒山寺, moved to Chongyuan Temple 重元寺 in 2008 (Suzhou, Jiangsu)

(*Continued*)

Name	Founding Date(s) (reopening or first enrollment)	Location(s)
47	Jiangsu Buddhist Academy for Nuns 江苏尼众佛学院	2003	Jiming Temple 鸡鸣寺 (Nanjing, Jiangsu)
48	Xingfu Temple Vinaya Institute for Nuns 兴福寺尼律学苑	Created in 2003 as a Vinaya study class 律学班	Xingfu Temple 兴福寺 (Taizhou, Zhejiang)
49	Yunnan Buddhist Academy 云南佛学院	2004	Anning, Kunming, Yunnan (the only Buddhist Academy where the teaching of Han [Mahayana], Tibetan [Vajrayana], and Theravada traditions coexist)
50	Zhanshan Buddhist Academy 湛山佛学院	2004	Zhanshan Temple 湛山寺 (Qingdao, Shandong)
51	Wujin Buddhist Academy 武进佛学院	2004	Dalin Temple 大林寺 (Changzhou, Jiangsu)
52	Famen Temple Buddhist Academy 法门寺佛学院	Created in 2004 as a sangha training class, officially established in 2010	Famen Temple 法门寺 for monks (Xi'an, Shaanxi), Huayan Temple 华严寺 for nuns (Fufeng, Shaanxi)
53	Henan Buddhist College 河南佛教学院	Established in 2005, first enrollment in 2009	Mount Tongbai 桐柏山, Tongbai County, Henan
54	Jianzhen Buddhist University 鉴真佛教学院	2006	Slender West Lake spot, (Yangzhou, Jiangsu)
55	Hongfa Temple Buddhist Academy 弘法寺佛学院	2011	Hongfa Temple 弘法寺 (Shenzhen, Guangdong)
56	Buddhist Academy of Tiantai School 天台宗佛学院	2014, affiliated to Zhejiang Buddhist Academy	Wannian Chan Temple 万年禅寺 (Tiantai, Zhejiang)
57	Chengtian Buddhist Academy for Nuns 承天尼众佛学苑	no data available	Chengtian Temple 承天寺 (Quanzhou, Fujian)
58	Zhiti Vinaya Institute 支提律学院	no data available	Huayan Temple 华严寺 (Mount Zhiti, Ningde, Fujian)

APPENDIX 7.2: REQUIREMENTS FOR STUDENT-MONK APPLICANTS BY THE BUDDHIST ACADEMY OF CHINA

	1990	1994	2003	2005	2007	2009	2011	2013
Age	20–28	20–28	19–25 Up to 28 tolerated for those with university education	19–25 Up to 28 tolerated for those with university education	19–25 Up to 28 tolerated for those with university education	19–28	19–28	19–28
Educational background	Senior middle school or equivalent	Graduation from secondary-grade Buddhist academy; senior middle school or equivalent	Graduation from secondary-grade Buddhist academy; senior middle school or equivalent	Graduation from secondary-grade Buddhist academy; senior middle school or equivalent	Graduation from secondary-grade Buddhist academy; senior middle school or equivalent	Graduation from secondary-grade Buddhist academy or equivalent	Graduation from secondary-grade Buddhist academy; senior middle school or equivalent	Graduation from secondary-grade Buddhist academy; senior middle school or equivalent
Time since becoming a monk	"Considerable time" (*xiangdang shijian* 相当时间)	"Suitable time" (*yiding shijian* 一定时间)	Suitable time	No specific requirement	No specific requirement	No specific requirement	No specific requirement	Suitable time
Marital status	No specific requirement	No marital or romantic relationship	No marital or romantic relationship	No marital or romantic relationship	No marital or romantic relationship	No marital or romantic relationship	No marital or romantic relationship	No marital or romantic relationship

(*Continued*)

APPENDIX 7.2 (Continued)

	1990	1994	2003	2005	2007	2009	2011	2013
Health		Good physical health, no history of mental illness, infectious diseases (including HBsAg+), or disability	Good physical health, no history of mental illness, infectious diseases (including HBsAg+), or disability	Regular facial features, good physical health, no history of mental illness, infectious diseases (including HBsAg+), or disability	Regular facial features, good physical health, no history of mental illness, infectious diseases (including HBsAg+), or disability	Regular facial features, good physical health, no history of mental illness, infectious diseases (including HBsAg+), or disability	Regular facial features, good physical health, no history of mental illness, infectious diseases, or disability	Regular facial features, good physical health, no history of mental illness, infectious diseases, or disability
Misc							No criminal record	No criminal record

APPENDIX 7.3: 1,883 COURSES TAUGHT IN 61 SANGHA EDUCATIONAL ORGANS

Category	Number of Courses	Proportion (%)
Patriotism and legality (*aiguo fazhi jiaoyu* 爱国法制教育)	115	6.11
Education for all-round development (*suzhi jiaoyu* 素质教育)	14	0.74
Basic monastic skills (*jiben jineng* 基本技能)	50	2.66
Religious practice (*xiuchi* 修持)	5	0.27
Faith and karma (*faxin, ming yinguo* 发心, 明因果)	42	2.23
Culture (*wenhua jiaoyu* 文化教育)	192	10.20
Liberal arts (*tongshi jiaoyu* 通识教育)	49	2.60
Knowledge of Buddhism (*fojiao zhishi* 佛教知识)	1,225	65.06
Professional education (*zhiye jiaoyu* 职业教育)	14	0.74
Applied studies (*yingyong xueke* 应用学科)	29	1.54
Hygiene (*weishengxue* 卫生学)	22	1.17
Public relations (*shehui gongguan* 社会公关)	23	1.22
Traditional culture (*chuantong wenhua* 传统文化)	14	0.74
Literature (*wenxue* 文学)	14	0.74
Arts (*yishu* 艺术)	75	3.98

Source: Jingyin and Zhang (2008, 152).

NOTES

I am very grateful to Gareth Fisher, André Laliberté, and Douglas Gildow for their comments, suggestions, and corrections. I owe many of my surveys to the help of Master Jieyu 戒毓 at the Buddhist Academy of China.

1. Jetavana was an ancient city in India where the Buddha gave his teachings.

2. Scholars today in China, in contrast to their predecessors before 1949, such as Yang Wenhui and Ouyang Jian, have never engaged in either transforming intellectualized research into religious merit or forming an "association of conviction" in the Weberian sense (*Gesinnungsverein*). For the history of academic Buddhist studies in the PRC and the tensions between Buddhists and academia, see Gildow 2016, chaps. 4 and 5.

3. This is the official English name of the institution, widely imitated by institutes for Buddhist studies founded later. Hereafter, when institutes for Buddhist studies founded in the PRC after 1949 are referred to, I apply the translation "Buddhist academy" except when the relevant institute has its own official English title.

4. For a concise summary of the development of Buddhist seminaries during the Republican era, see Gildow 2016, app. 11.

5. Buddhist research institutes directed by laymen experienced a somewhat better fate, relatively speaking. One example is the famous Chinese Inner Studies Institute (Zhina

Neixueyuan 支那内学院), founded by Ouyang Jian in Nanjing in 1922. Ouyang's successor, Lü Cheng 吕澂 (1896–1989), who became the institute's director in 1943, strove to exhibit a cooperative attitude to the new regime at the time of the beginning of Communist rule. In 1950, Lü even proposed an ambitious working plan in order to greet "the cultural upsurge of the new era" (Lü 1950). In 1952, however, he was forced to declare that the difficulties encountered by the institute could only be solved by the "end of activities" (Lü 1952). The Three Times Study Society (Sanshi Xuehui 三时学会), founded in Beijing in 1927 by Han Qingjing 韩清净 (1884–1949) and other lay Buddhist scholars, managed to maintain its existence for a longer period but still stopped its activities in 1956.

6. See Ji 2008a, 2012, on Communist manipulation and control of the BAC.

7. Inferring from the logic of the 1996 speech by Zhao Puchu, the number of 410 also included students from short-term study classes. Due to archival loss, the Buddhist Academy of China can provide only an approximately 200-person list of students from before the Cultural Revolution, including 90 students who attended study classes (Zhongguo Foxueyuan 2012).

8. This organ was renamed the State Administration of Religious Affairs (SARA) in 1998.

9. The Sichuan Buddhist Academy for Nuns, the first and the most famous modern institution for nuns' training, founded in 1983, is also sponsored by the state and officially identified as a "public work unit" (*shiye danwei* 事业单位) affiliated with the Religious Affairs Bureau of Sichuan Province. It should be noted that Buddhist academies in post-Mao China are not prohibited from accepting private donations, especially those coming from overseas Chinese Buddhists.

10. The Great Leap Forward was launched by Mao, who believed it was possible to rapidly industrialize China through a nationwide mobilization, under the general line of "building socialism with greater, faster, better and more economic results." This unrealistic project caused both economic and social disasters, most particularly the Great Famine (1959–1961), which resulted from the rapid diversion of agricultural processing to industrial work. The number of victims of the famine is estimated at between 30 and 45 million (Dikötter 2010; Yang Jisheng 2012).

11. From then on, the "sangha training class" (a similar organization under the same name having already appeared at the beginning of the twentieth century) has become a generally followed model by monasteries to create a preparatory and informal Buddhist academy before getting governmental approval. Sometimes it can also designate a short-term training program conducted in a monastery or an academy.

12. In the new version of the regulations promulgated in 2017, there is no substantial change in this respect.

13. For example, Zhanru, in an interview with a Chinese journalist (2011), stated that there is one higher-level (i.e., the Buddhist Academy of China), twenty-seven secondary-level, and seventeen primary-level Buddhist academies.

14. Caoxi is the place where Huineng was active for about forty years. The name is usually used to label the southern school of Chan Buddhism.

15. Even when they are connected with secular universities, as with other Buddhist academies, the formal training programs for diplomas are strictly reserved for monastics. However, monasteries can organize different kinds of short-term training programs (from one to several weeks) for laypeople, either outside of or within the framework of their academy.

16. Zhao was very concerned with Buddhism in the Lower Yangtze Region, where he was born and worked before moving to Beijing in 1954. However, as a servant of the CCP and a lay Buddhist without special affiliation to a monastery or a lineage, his faction color was not obvious during his half-century-long leadership (1953–2000) of the BAC. On Zhao's life and his role under the PRC's regime, see Ji 2017.

17. At the same time, for the Buddhist Academy of China, the number of students in each enrollment has been reduced from forty (2015) to thirty (2016).

18. Due to the dropping out of a dozen student-monks (Minshan 2002, 277), it was sometimes claimed that the first enrollment brought in a little more than 160 freshmen.

19. According to the BAC's statistics on ordinations, the current proportion of males to females in the Han sangha is about two to one (see Ji 2009, 12).

20. According to my estimate, there were about 100,000 Han Buddhist monastics altogether around 2007 (Ji 2012). This number could rise to 250,000 by the end of the 2010s if it maintains the annual growth rate of 8 percent as during the period 1994–2006. In 2014, SARA's estimation is 72,000 (2014), which should include only registered monastics, while some Buddhist insiders' estimation for the same period is 200,000.

21. The brochures do not specify an exact length, but some other academies require more than one or two years. The five monks I know who graduated from the Buddhist Academy of China in the 2000s all were tonsured for more than three years before being admitted into the academy. According to an informant, in practice the requirement is at least one year. In the 1980s this requirement was less stringent, and some students were tonsured for less than one year before being admitted.

22. In Chinese *xiangmao duanzheng* 相貌端正. Here it means without physical disability or deformity. The same requirement is also generally applied for tonsure, as a long-standing code rooted in the primary Buddhist Vinaya.

23. On Shengyan and his Dharma Drum Mountain, see Madsen 2007, chap. 4.

24. For a summary of different viewpoints on the relationship between study and practice, see Zongshun 2012; Gildow 2016, chap. 4.

25. Yang Der-Ruey (2010, 2011) studies how the modern curriculum in Taoist academies introduced a new epistemology privileging discursive knowledge and therefore resulted in a revolutionary change in monastic organization and practice. His research on the tensions between textual knowledge, monastic codes, and ritual services in Taoist education offers a very interesting point for comparison.

26. Buddhist temples provide many services to people who are not necessarily committed lay Buddhists who have taken the refuges, such as the worship of popular cults and funerary activities.

8

A STUDY OF LAYNUNS IN MINNAN, 1920s–2010s

Buddhism, State Institutions, and Popular Culture

ASHIWA YOSHIKO AND DAVID L. WANK

Caigu 菜姑, literally "vegetarian women," are a special group of lay Buddhist women in southeastern China, hereafter referred to as "laynuns."[1] They live mainly in Quanzhou 泉州, Zhangzhou 漳州, and Xiamen 厦门 Prefectures, which are located in the coastal region of Fujian Province 福建省 known as Minnan 闽南.[2] They lead a communal, celibate, vegetarian lifestyle centered on worship of the Buddha and the bodhisattva Guanyin (Guanyin *pusa* 观音菩萨, hereafter called "Guanyin") but are not ordained as nuns, do not shave their heads, and can work in regular jobs to support themselves. In Buddhist societies, there are various styles of these women, such as *dasasilmatha* in Sri Lanka (Ashiwa 2015; Bartholomeusz 1994), *thila shin* in Myanmar (Kawanami 2013), and *mae chi* in Thailand (Collins and McDaniel 2010), who are neither ordained nuns nor ordinary female lay practitioners living with their families. Within Buddhism their position has been ambiguous and a focus of demarcation between Buddhism as formally defined in texts and Buddhism as adjusted to local and historical conditions (Ashiwa 1998; Levine and Gellner 2005).[3] This chapter is about the modern recognition of laynuns in China.

In 2012, laynuns were classified as a form of "religious professional" (*zongjiao jiaozhi renyuan* 宗教教职人员) by the local Xiamen government. Within the Buddhist community this institutional classification in the state religious policy had previously applied only to nuns and monks, including novices, but not to lay practitioners. However, in 2012 the Xiamen government officially included laynuns in the category of religious professional. It did so by calling the laynun a "person who left their family" (*chujiaren* 出家人), a term that throughout the history of Buddhism has exclusively referred to ordained nuns and monks who renounce lay life. This shows that the government recognizes laynuns, which are a Minnan custom, as equivalent to nuns and monks, and therefore qualified for incorporation into the state category of religious professional.

However, within the orthodox Buddhist classification of the community that constitutes Buddhism, there is no acknowledgment of a person such as the laynun.[4] According to the teachings of Buddha, there are four major groups (*sibuzhong* 四部众). They are ordained monks (*biqiu* 比丘, Skt. *bhikṣu*), ordained nuns (*biqiuni* 比丘尼, Skt. *bhikṣuṇī*), male lay practitioners (*youposai* 优婆塞, Skt. *upāsaka*), and female lay practitioners (*youpoyi* 优婆夷, Skt. *upāsikā*). In addition, there are two subgroups, male novices (*shami* 沙弥, Skt. *śrāmaṇer*) and female novices (*shamini* 沙弥尼, Skt. *śrāmaṇeri*). In the case of females there is the additional status called *shichamona* 式叉摩那 (Skt. *śikuṣamānā*), which is a two-year transitional position for studying the Dharma that lies between the positions of female novice and ordained nun. In Chinese, it is also called "Dharma studying female" (*zhengxuenü* 正学女). While the religious position of the laynun might seem equivalent to *shichamona,* it does not easily fit, because the laynun position is for an entire lifetime, not just for two years as a *shichamona.*

Therefore, laynuns are newly included in the institutional category of "religious professional," which already includes nuns and monks, but this has not changed the religious categories in orthodox Buddhism, and laynuns are still not considered as clergy in Buddhism. This is because the intention of the Xiamen government is not to change the four major groups in Buddhism, but rather to accommodate a local situation in Minnan within the state religious policy. Yet it is undeniable that institutional recognition has opened up new possible directions for religious activities by laynuns and their religious recognition in Buddhism, although many Buddhist clerics are ambivalent about this.

The roots of recognition of laynuns as religious professionals can be traced back to the Buddhist modern reform movement from the 1920s. A key aspect of this movement was "Buddhicization" (*fohua* 佛化), a term used by modernist clerics and lay practioners to refer to the transformation of popular religions into "rightful belief Buddhism" (*zhengxin fojiao* 正信佛教). This consisted largely of educating people in Buddhism in order to filter out aspects of popular religions from their practice (Ashiwa 2009). During this process, the eminent cleric Hongyi 弘一[5] named laynuns as "ascetic and pious women" (*fanxing qingxinnü* 梵行清信女).[6] This recognition of laynuns as a special category of Buddhists in Minnan has deeply affected their situation in Xiamen. It enabled some of them to survive the first three decades of political turmoil after the founding of the People's Republic of China (PRC) in 1949, then recover from the Cultural Revolution (1966–1976), and, most recently, be officially designated as "religious professionals" in the 2010s.

The chapter first examines various explanations of the premodern origins of the laynuns, including neo-Confucianism, sectarian religions, and local customs of women's communities. The second section focuses on the century-long modern history of the laynuns, which the Xiamen government now emphasizes. The third section describes cases of transformation among laynuns since the 1920s. The fourth section recounts the efforts of two laynuns after the Cultural Revolution to maintain the laynun tradition, revealing its respect by society and government in Minnan. The fifth section examines the local government recognition of the laynun as religious professional and its implications for the problems that laynuns now face. Finally, we explain the persistence of the laynuns as a sociocultural force through the legend of Miaoshan 妙善 that links people's image of laynuns to Guanyin. The data comes from fieldwork in Xiamen and Minnan between 1989 and 2017 and documentary sources.[7] All English translations of interviews and documents from Chinese are our own.

EXPLANATIONS OF THE CULTURAL AND HISTORICAL ROOTS OF LAYNUNS

The laynun tradition has deep historical roots in Minnan culture and society. Several explanations of these roots have been put forth by the government and by scholars who focus on religious or sociocultural factors. A summary of these explanations serves not to adjudicate among them, but rather to provide fuller historical contexts to our focus on the modern situation of the laynuns from the 1920s.

First is the official explanation by the state that links the laynun tradition to Neo-Confucianism (Lixue 理学), which spread from the tenth century, becoming especially strong in Fujian Province. According to this explanation, Neo-Confucianism criticized Buddhism and discouraged people from becoming nuns and monks (Chen 2000; Goto 1991). It imposed strict rules on women, such as prohibiting widows from remarrying, while the Qing dynasty (1644–1912) stipulated that only women above the age of forty could be nuns (Jiang 2000). This meant that women who wanted to reside separately because of widowhood or marriage refusal were unable to do so by becoming Buddhist nuns. Therefore, some wealthy families who wanted to support these women built small cultivation places for widows and marriage-refusing daughters to dwell separately. Located on or off the family property, these places enabled women in similar circumstances to live together. They enabled pious Buddhist women who did not shave their heads and therefore did not appear to be Buddhist nuns to leave their families and reside communally almost as Buddhist nuns without violating Qing restrictions on women and Confucian standards of family reputation. This explanation also implies that the women were actually Buddhist but hid their religion due to the pressure of Neo-Confucianism.

Like the current state discourse, this explanation sees the origins of the laynuns as residing in the gender oppression of the Confucian society that was overthrown by the CCP with the establishment of the PRC in 1949. Studies of this phenomenon have appeared in official publications, including *Fayin* 法音 (Voice of Dharma), the journal of the Buddhist Association of China (BAC; Chen 2000; Zheng 1998),[8] and *Xiamen fojiao zhi* 厦门佛教志 (Gazetteer of Xiamen Buddhism; Xiamenshi Fojiao Xiehui 2006, 121–122), the official history of Buddhism in Xiamen compiled by the Xiamen Buddhist Association (XBA; Xiamenshi Fojiao Xiehui 厦门市佛教协会).[9]

The second explanation links the origins of laynuns with the spread of a sectarian religion[10] called Zhaijiao 斋教, which combined aspects of Buddhism, Taoism, and Confucianism.[11] It spread in southern China and Taiwan in the late Ming and early Qing dynasties, becoming part of a revival of the White Lotus sect (Bailianjiao 白莲教), which the Qing dynasty labeled heterodox. Zhaijiao prohibited its followers from eating meat, scallions, and garlic, as well as consuming alcohol, tobacco, and opium. Female devotees were called "zhai women" (*zhaigu* 斋姑). Some were married and lived with their families, while others, both unmarried and married, as well as widows, left their families to dwell communally with other female Zhaijiao followers in *zhai* halls (*zhaitang* 斋堂).[12] Women who were not wealthy could also stay in laynun halls and pursue a religious life (Tainaka 2000, 52–53). These women were much respected by the local society for their piety, hard work, and devotion to social welfare activities, including taking care of old people, orphans, and widows.

The cosmology of Zhaijiao was fused with Buddhism (Tam 2007). In *zhai* halls, Buddhist images, such as that of Śākyamuni and Guanyin, were often placed alongside statues of gods from popular religions and Taoism, such as Mazu 妈祖 and Guandi 关帝. Followers chanted the *Amitabha Sutra* (*Amituo jing* 阿弥陀经) and *Vijra Sutra* (*Jin'gang jing* 金刚经), two of the most popular Buddhist sutras in China. Due to these similarities, some scholars see the origins of the laynuns as lying in the three Zhaijiao sects that became prominent in Minnan in the nineteenth century—the Dragon Flower Teachings (Longhuajiao 龙华教), the Way of the Former Heaven (Xiantiandao 先天道), and the Golden Pennant Teachings (Jinchuangjiao 金幢教; Chang 2007; Lin and Li 2014). When the Qing dynasty declared Zhaijiao to be heterodox (Sato 2006), women followers placed greater emphasis on their Buddhist aspects to avoid state repression (Seiwert and Ma 2003, 476–484).

However, laynuns' link to Zhaijiao is excised in the official state explanation of their origins. Even though the *Gazetteer of Xiamen Buddhism* prominently mentions laynuns, it does not mention Zhaijiao. It only observes the similar pronunciation between the words *zhai* and *cai* in Minnan dialect; the terms for "observing *zhai*" (*chi zhai* 持斋) and "being vegetarian" (*chi su* 吃素) are homonyms in Minnan dialect, as are the terms "*zhai* woman" (*zhaigu* 斋姑) and "laynun" (*caigu*; Xiamenshi Fojiao Xiehui 2006, 212). The failure to mention Zhaijiao as one of the phenomena for the origins of the laynuns is due to the local government's need to justify the preservation of the laynun tradition in the context of the CCP's religious policy. This policy distinguishes between religions, including Buddhism, which the state permits, and "superstition" (*mixin* 迷信) and non–"normal religion" (*bu zhengchang zongjiao* 不正常宗教), which are banned by the CCP as causing crime and anti-state activity. The CCP's strong concern about links between Buddhism and anti-state cults was reignited by the emergence of the Falungong in the 1990s. For these reasons, we assume that the *Gazetteer of Xiamen Buddhism* erases Zhaijiao from the historical background of laynuns and only mentions *zhai* as a phonetic issue concerning vegetarianism.[13] Although the laynun tradition in Minnan was undeniably linked to sectarian religion, the local government reformatted it to enhance the religious legitimacy of acknowledging the laynuns as part of Buddhism. This fits with the aforementioned explanation that sees laynuns as hidden Buddhists under the "feudal" oppression of Neo-Confucianism.

Additionally, a consideration of the situations of Zhaijiao in Minnan and Taiwan underscores the importance of local history and specific state regimes in the position of laynuns. Lin Meirong and Li Jiakai (2014), who have done extensive research on laynuns in Taiwan as well as some in Minnan, take for granted that the laynuns in both places are more or less the same custom. Therefore, they refer to them all as *zhaigu,* considering the term *caigu* to simply be one of the colloquial terms in Minnan for laynuns, and discuss *zhaigu* as a broader phenomenon in both Taiwan and Minnan. This ignores the diverging modern histories of the laynuns over the past century due to differences in political regimes. After Taiwan became a Japanese colony (1895–1945), the Japanese colonial government recognized Zhaijiao as a religion and laynuns continued to be called *zhaigu.* In contrast, in Minnan during the early twentieth century, modernist clerics who recognized laynuns as Buddhists called them *caigu,* not *zhaigu,* in order to de-emphasize their ties to Zhaijiao, which the central authorities had long stigmatized as heterodoxy. Thus, in Taiwan, the term *zhaigu* was legitimated during colonization, while in Minnan it was delegitimized and replaced by *caigu* through the Buddhicization process.

A third explanation is found in anthropological studies of local customs and traditions regarding women who lived communally that have been undertaken by Lin Huixiang 林惠祥and others. One custom is marriage practices in Hui'an Prefecture (Hui'an Xian 惠安县) in Quanzhou, home to the largest numbers of laynuns (Lin 1981; see also Shi Yilong 2009; Wei 2014). Its residents have distinct customs, almost as an ethnic minority, even though they are considered to be Han ethnicity. One of these customs is called "not leaving the parental home" (*chang zhu niangjia* 长住娘家). After marriage, a woman continues to reside in her parental home, visiting her husband's house a few times a year. She will start to reside with her husband only after bearing their first child.[14] According to Chen Zhenzhen 陈珍珍 (2000), a laywoman and scholar, this practice was difficult for women because they could not live with their husbands until they bore a child. Therefore, some avoided marriage by becoming laynuns.[15]

There is another custom, called "sister bonds" (*jiemei ban* 姐妹伴), practiced in Hui'an Prefecture in Quanzhou, whereby girls from different families live together when they reach puberty (Chen and Cai 1990). This is similar to the custom of communal living and activities of the "girls' houses" (*nüzai wu* 女仔屋) described by Stockard (1992) in the Pearl River Delta of Guangdong Province. About half a dozen young women who are neighbors or relatives live as a group and do such activities as learning housekeeping skills from older women; they develop lifelong bonds of mutual support. According to Kuwana (1994, 41), "this custom of girls' houses is inseparable from the marriage custom of 'not leaving the parental home.' . . . Stockard's research shows that 'not leaving the parental home' spread to areas that already included the custom of girls' houses. This custom is always accompanied by the tradition of 'girls' houses.'" In this way, the sister bonds might have constituted local traditions of women's communal dwelling that are very similar to the laynun tradition.

While each of these three explanations suggests possible origins of the laynuns, we posit a sociocultural understanding based on our fieldwork. It is related to the popular consciousness of the people as represented in the story of Miaoshan. The heroine Miaoshan, who is the human form of Guanyin that is the center of worship in laynun halls, projects the image of the laynun. This explanation helps us to understand ongoing projects by Buddhists to define and accommodate the laynuns as a local form of Buddhism over the course of the political turmoil and conflicts of the past century.

THE MODERN HISTORY OF LAYNUNS IN XIAMEN

The recognition of laynuns as Buddhists occurred during the movement for the modernization of Buddhism in Minnan. The historical background of this movement was linked to Xiamen's position as among the earliest treaty ports open to the West in 1842.[16] The new transnational interactions that flourished made Xiamen a spearhead for the modern reform movement.[17] In the mid-nineteenth century, the city experienced a large influx of Christian missionaries, giving it the first Christian church in China that preached to Chinese.[18] The growing attraction of Chinese followers to Christianity was a challenge to the survival of Buddhism. By the early twentieth century this had stimulated the formation of a movement of monks and lay practitioners in the treaty ports inspired by the Buddhist reformer Yang Wenhui 杨文会 (1837–1911) to advocate for the modernization of Buddhism in response to the Christian challenge. This included adopting such practices of Christianity as educating clerics in seminaries, training them to preach to the people, providing social services in hospitals and clinics, and emphasizing spiritual cultivation.

In the 1920s, Xiamen became a center of the Buddhist modernization movement in China. A major event was the ecumenization in 1924 of the city's major temple, Nanputuo Temple 南普陀寺, to make it open to all Buddhist denominations. The following year the Buddhist College of Minnan (Minnan Foxueyuan 闽南佛学院) opened with the famous modernist monk Taixu as rector.[19] It was one of the first Buddhist academies to educate monks in the modern educational style of classroom lectures and with a curriculum that combined Buddhist education with secular courses, such as foreign languages, history, psychology, literature, accounting, and music. The college and the presence of Taixu attracted notable and talented clerics from around China to study and lecture, including Hongyi, who first visited in 1928 and became one of the eminent monks to support laynuns.

The other major modernizing initiative was led by well-educated wealthy sons of Xiamen business families who were concerned about the decline of Chinese tradition and growth of Christianity. In 1924 they founded the Minnan Buddhist Propagation Youth Society (Minnan Fohua Qingnianhui 闽南佛化青年会), which started the monthly journal *Foyin yuekan* 佛音月刊 (Sound of the Buddha Monthly) and organized the New Youth World Buddhicization Propagation Troupe (Fohua Xinqingnian Shijie Xuanchuandui 佛化新青年世界宣传队). Their goal was to "actively propagate Buddhist philosophy, transmit Buddhist thought, promote 'rightful belief Buddhism,' and oppose superstition" (Xiamenshi Fojiao Xiehui 2006, 120). Through this movement, laynuns gained prominent masters among the monks who acknowledged them as Buddhists and encouraged educational efforts to deepen their understanding of Buddhism.

Laynuns and Buddhicization, 1920s–1950s

In the 1920s, the laynun community in Xiamen grew rapidly. This was a time of Xiamen's flourishing international trade with Southeast Asia and a large inflow of migrants from rural Minnan seeking work and opportunities. By the early 1930s, Xiamen had twenty-one laynuns in eight laynun halls.[20] By 1939 this number had grown to eighty laynuns in nineteen laynun halls (Xiamenshi Fojiao Xiehui 2006, 124). These women included widows, married women escaping abusive in-laws, and young women refusing marriage. More than half came from Hui'an Prefecture, the center of the marriage custom of "not leaving the parental home" in the Minnan region (Xiamenshi Fojiao Xiehui 2006, 122), which, as described in the previous section, created difficulties for women.

A hall typically began when a woman made a room for self-cultivation in her house. This attracted worshippers, some of whom moved into the house, where they resided communally, worshipped Guanyin, and kept vegetarian and celibate. The women in a hall considered themselves a family. They adopted female orphans to care for them in old age and succeed them as heads of their laynun halls. They maintained self-sufficiency, earning money by growing and selling vegetables, washing clothes, making handicrafts, and collecting alms for performing Buddhist rituals at funerals and salvation rites (*chaodu* 超度). Such activities gave laynuns closer ties to and respect from local people.

The fact that laynuns worshipped Guanyin and led communal lives similar to ordained nuns was viewed positively by monks and lay practitioners in the Buddhist modernization movement, including Hongyi, who often lectured at laynun halls after coming to the Minnan region in 1928. He was greatly impressed by the simple and pious life of these women, who chanted daily and advanced in their cultivation while living together and doing domestic and agricultural labor to support themselves. He called them "ascetic and pious women" and wrote an appreciation of them entitled "An Introduction for Ascetic and Pious Women" (Fanxing qingxinnü jiangxihui yuanqi 梵行清信女讲习会缘起):

> In the Minnan region there are no nuns. Most people say that this is regrettable. However, don't they know that this is the Buddha's will? The Vinaya says that fundamentally the Buddha did not let women become clerics. Were he to do so, the rightful Dharma would be split into two. However, even after he said this, women started to shave their heads. So Ananda [Anan Zunzhe 阿难尊者], one of Buddha's highest disciples, asked him three times to accept them. Thereupon, he admitted them as clergy but only after imposing the Eight Respected Rules [Bajingfa 八敬法; Pali, Aṭṭhagarudhammā].[21] However, we have rarely heard of a nun obeying the Eight Respected Rules. This does not accord with the Buddha's regulations and completely breaks down the Great Dharma. Therefore, it is not regrettable that there are no nuns in Minnan.
>
> In Minnan there is a group of women who study Buddhism. They have accepted the Three Refuges and Five Precepts [*sangui wujie* 三皈五戒][22] and become pious vegetarian women [*qingxinnü* 清信女]. Among them are people called laynuns [*caigu*] who are completely celibate and live separately in hermitages, colloquially called vegetarian halls [*caitang*], that are something like a temple for clergy. They work long at their cultivation and assiduously chant devotions. Compared to nuns they are excellent. (Hongyi 2010a, 626)

Hongyi was critical of nuns for not following the Eight Respected Rules and some of the Buddha's other teachings. Therefore, he was not concerned by their absence in Minnan. Instead he saw the strong commitment of laynuns to Buddhist practice and named them ascetic and pious women.[23] However, he did not advocate converting laynuns into nuns but rather accepted them as a special form of Buddhism in Minnan.

Hongyi saw potential for laynuns to propagate Buddhism among the people. His view is suggested in a talk he gave in 1933 in which he argued that the subordinate position of nuns to monks in Buddhism reflected the social context of Indian society at the time when Siddhartha Guatama lived (Hongyi 2010b, 191). For example, a nun had to follow almost one hundred more precepts than a monk.[24] Hongyi said that while the Buddha ordered nuns to follow the Eight Respected Rules by showing respect and obedience to monks, in modern society the position of women was becoming equal to that of men. Therefore, in modern society the Eight Respected Rules were no longer practical but rather constituted an obstacle for the equal position of the nun in Buddhism and a hindrance to their initiative and activity. In light of Hongyi's views on the Eight Respected Rules, it is likely that he considered laynuns as standing apart from the subordinate position of nuns and, therefore, better fitting into modern society. Laynuns could work alongside people, unlike ordained nuns, who were prohibited from working in society. This daily contact in the secular world enabled laynuns to better understand the problems and sorrows of the people and provide them with such services as teaching and nursing. Hongyi saw laynuns as performing the same functions as nuns in Christianity, who served as nurses and teachers and ran orphanages, hospitals, and mission schools.

In this context, Hongyi advocated the education of laynuns to address their lack of knowledge of Buddhism and widespread illiteracy.[25] In 1932 Hongyi and his lay followers proposed establishing a school in Xiamen to be called the Minnan Women's Buddhist Institute (Minnan Nüzi Foxueyuan 闽南女子佛学院) in order to teach Buddhism and literacy to women and laynuns. However, the school did not open at that time due to the lack of suitable female teachers. It was not until 1948 that Hongyi's fellow monk Xingyuan 性愿 opened the first such school, called the Juehua Women's Buddhist Institute (Juehua Nüzi Foxueyuan 觉华女子佛学院), with Chen Zhenzhen serving as principal. Its mission was to teach illiterate laynuns and girls to read and to offer basic courses on Buddhism (Xiamenshi Fojiao Xiehui 2006, 223). After graduation some laynuns remained in Xiamen, while others emigrated abroad to Hong Kong, the Philippines, and the United States, where they established laynun halls, medical clinics, and other charitable activities.

Another undertaking to Buddhicize laynuns was transmitting Buddhist precepts to them. For example, in 1948, the monk Xingyuan held a large cere-mony of the "triple platform ordination" (also known as "The Transmission of the Three Great Precepts"; Chuanshou Santan Dajie 傳授三坛大戒) at the Nanputuo Temple for members of the Buddhist community. It is said that laynuns made up almost half of the one thousand attendees (Chen 2000). In general, after taking their precepts, laynuns belonged to the same Buddhist sects as the monks who were their masters. In this way, many of the laynuns became part of the Linji 临济 and Yunmen 云门 sects, which were common among monks in Xiamen.[26]

These efforts spurred the growth of the laynun population in Xiamen to its high point in the early 1950s of 159 laynuns in thirty-one halls (Xiamenshi

Fojiao Xiehui 2006, 124). This growth during the first years of the PRC was aided by the recognition of laynuns as Buddhists, which helped shield them from state efforts to eliminate sectarian religions during the "Withdraw from the Sects" campaign (Tui Dao Yundong 退道运动, 1951–1953). Some laynuns gained further protection from state attacks on religion by establishing textile factories in their halls to generate income to offset the decline in funds from alms and rituals. By laboring in the factories, laynuns also could gain recognition as members of the working class, shielding them from the CCP critique of religion as parasitically living off society.

Nevertheless, by the mid-1950s, the number of laynuns and laynun halls in Xiamen declined sharply as the CCP attack on religion diffused into people's lives and fewer women wanted to become laynuns. The decline was hastened by new state residency restrictions in urban areas that prevented women from the Minnan hinterland from moving to Xiamen to join laynun halls, while a number of laynuns in Xiamen migrated abroad to Southeast Asia. Another factor in the decline was the loss of Buddhist educational opportunities for laynuns in Xiamen when the Juehua Women's Buddhist Institute, in order to escape persecution, moved to Quanzhou and then a rural area, eventually disbanding during the Cultural Revolution (Chen 2000). Then, in the late 1950s, district governments in Xiamen began taking over some laynun halls for public residences and factories, which drove laynuns out of these halls. Although spared from the forced laicization experienced by clerics, the remaining laynuns were abused during the Cultural Revolution. Their halls were ransacked, they were forced to violate Buddhist precepts, such as being made to serve meat in cafeterias, and younger laynuns were pressured to marry.

Revival of Laynuns and Buddhism, 1980s–2010s

The revival of the laynun tradition in Xiamen after the Cultural Revolution began with the economic liberalization starting in 1979. The first laynun hall reopened in 1982, and within a decade there were sixty-five laynuns in eleven laynun halls. All the halls were in bad condition, requiring restoration and rebuilding. For those halls that had been confiscated, the first step was to negotiate with the local government to reclaim ownership. Funding for all these efforts came from laynuns and clerics who had emigrated abroad.

The revived laynun population was overwhelmingly elderly. According to a 1992 survey conducted by the XBA of the sixty-five laynuns living in Xiamen at that time, forty-one were over sixty years of age (Xiamenshi Fojiao Xiehui 1992, 155). They consisted almost entirely of laynuns driven out of their halls during the 1950s and the Cultural Revolution who had returned to their reclaimed halls. The 1992 survey also noted much variation by age in the formal educational level of the laynun population in Xiamen. The elderly laynuns were mostly illiterate or semiliterate, while the twenty-four younger laynuns had a much better formal education, including three high school, sixteen middle school, and five primary school graduates (Xiamenshi Fojiao Xiehui 2006, 123). Additionally, there was a generational difference in the visual appearance of the laynuns. In the late 1980s we observed that older laynuns wore their hair in buns at the back of their heads, whereas younger ones had loose hanging hair down to their jawlines. However, all laynuns wore similar unadorned white or gray blouses with mandarin collars, loose black pants, black cloth shoes, and no accessories.

This rebuilding of the laynun tradition after the Cultural Revolution was strongly supported by prominent Buddhist monks. This reflected the respect of Buddhist clerics for the Minnan laynuns that began with the Buddhist modernization movement in the 1920s. It also reflected the clerics' practical effort after the Cultural Revolution to find capable and pious Buddhists to manage the temples that were being recovered and rebuilt and to handle administrative tasks.[27] For these reasons, they let laynuns study in the main Buddhist academies in Fujian Province, which were also reviving and starting to promote the education of nuns. Both the Buddhist College of Minnan, which began to reopen in 1982,[28] and the women's section of the Fujian Buddhist Academy (Fujian Foxueyuan 福建佛学院), which reopened in 1983 at the Chongfu Temple (Chongfu Si 崇福寺) in a suburb of the provincial capital Fuzhou 福州, permitted laynuns to study together with nuns in their four-year Buddhist studies programs.[29]

Some of the first laynuns to graduate were assigned important administrative positions in temples and Buddhist associations and played a large role in the revival of orthodox Buddhism in Xiamen. For example, Miaozhan 妙湛, the first abbot of the Nanputuo Temple after the Cultural Revolution, who strongly supported laynuns, recruited a laynun from the 1987 graduating class of the Fujian Buddhist Academy, the first since the Cultural Revolution, to supervise the nuns in the Buddhist College of Minnan. Another laynun, who graduated in 1989 from the Buddhist College of Minnan, the first graduating class of its four-year program, went to work in the XBA. Because they could work outside temples and alongside laypersons, these first laynun graduates of the academies were very much needed to rebuild the administration of Buddhist temples and associations, which demanded personnel able to do such things as record keeping and negotiating with government officials.

The number of laynuns in Xiamen peaked in 2000 with 113 laynuns living in twenty-six halls (Xiamenshi Fojiao Xiehui 2006, 124) but then shrank dramatically as elderly laynuns passed away without young laynun disciples to replace them. By 2012 there were only about 25 laynuns, including 13 under the age of thirty, who lived in five laynun halls.[30] An especially significant factor in this decline was the introduction of the nun tradition in the early 1980s into Fujian Province, where it had not previously existed (DeVido 2015). This introduction occurred when the Buddhist College of Minnan and the

Fujian Buddhist Academy started sections for the education of nuns. Initially, the academies accepted laynuns to study alongside nuns in the four-year programs because the academies were headed by elderly clerics who respected the laynun tradition. The heads of laynun halls began sending their young disciples who were being groomed as successors to study in the academies, with the expectation that they would return as laynuns. However, upon entering the academy, the disciples saw that nuns had higher formal status in the religious tradition of Buddhism, and many were ordained as nuns.

Then, in the late 1990s, opportunities for laynuns to study Buddhism in Xiamen were severely curtailed when the Buddhist College of Minnan stopped admitting them. This reflected the view of Shenghui 圣辉, the second abbot (1997–2003) of the Nanputuo Temple after the Cultural Revolution, who was sent by the national BAC to succeed Miaozhan as abbot of the Nanputuo Temple and rector of the Buddhist College of Minnan. His appointment by the national association was part of an effort to standardize practices among the dozens of Buddhist academies that had opened since 1980 (see chapter 7 by Ji in this volume). Shenghui saw the purpose of the college as educating nuns and monks, not nurturing such local traditions of Buddhism as laynuns. Therefore, he banned their study in the Buddhist College of Minnan. The other major educational opportunity for laynuns ended when the Fujian Buddhist Academy stopped admitting them to its four-year program. While laynuns could still study in its two-year preparatory program, they had to shave their heads and become novices or nuns to study further.

From the late 1990s, the only other possibility for laynuns to get a Buddhist education was at the Quanzhou Buddhist Institute (Quanzhou Foxueyuan 泉州佛学院), which was founded in 1986 with support from Buddhist believers in Singapore. Chen Zhenzhen, principal of the earlier Juehua Women's Buddhist Academy, was its rector. It offered a tuition-free education to laynuns and novices in a curriculum of Buddhist and secular topics. It had two programs: The preparatory program was the equivalent of middle school, while the foundational program was high school level. The instructors of Buddhism were nuns who had graduated from Buddhist academies, while the secular courses were taught by professors from local colleges and high school instructors of foreign languages. All but one of the sixty-four women in the first entering class came from the Minnan region, and their numbers were divided between young laynuns and novices. For further education in Buddhism after graduating, a laynun had to shave her head to become a novice or be ordained as a nun in order to enter a Buddhist academy, such as the Buddhist College of Minnan or the Fujian Buddhist Academy.

The declining number of laynuns, especially in Xiamen, created a succession crisis in laynun halls. Many elderly laynuns lacked young disciples to inherit their halls and succeed them as head laynuns. In some cases, disciples sent by elderly laynuns to a Buddhist academy to study who decided to become or-dained nuns did not return to their halls as expected. The XBA offered to help solve this problem by sending ordained nuns who had graduated from the Bud-dhist College of Minnan to reside at the halls. The understanding was that, once all the laynuns in a hall had passed away, it would become a Buddhist temple for nuns.

Laynuns initially resisted this offer because the XBA required them to turn over legal ownership of the hall to the XBA to receive support. The XBA demanded this because the local government legally classified the halls as private residences rather than religious sites. Therefore, sending nuns to live in the halls would be a violation of the state religious policy stipulation that ordained clerics—"religious professionals"—reside in religious sites, which could not be privately owned but rather belonged to the XBA or, in the case of a large temple such as Nanputuo Temple, were the collective property of the monks in residence. However, the elderly laynuns, who had seen their halls occupied as factories, recreation halls, and family residences during the Cultural Revolution, were loath to relinquish the ownership that they had struggled to regain. Their will was to pass on ownership to laynuns whom they could trust to keep their halls as sites of communal Buddhist worship and not use them for secular purposes. However, by the late 1990s most had to agree to the XBA demand for ownership because they lacked successors, and so nuns began to move into the halls.

This introduction of young nuns caused problems in the strict seniority system in laynun halls. Normally, lay Buddhists accepted the religious su-periority of ordained clerics, which meant that an ordained nun, even one who was formerly the laynun disciple of an elderly laynun, was now her reli-gious superior. During religious rituals, the seniority of a young nun in terms of religious status made elderly laynuns her followers in chanting and other rituals. For example, it was a New Year's custom for disciples to bow to the head laynun of the hall as a show of respect. However, as an ordained nun was in a religiously higher position, she could not bow to a laynun. One elderly laynun described the situation as follows: "A laynun hall does not welcome nuns. They take the nuns' precepts and are ordained, but laynuns only take Five Precepts. So, the nuns' [religious] status is higher and they cannot get along with laynuns. . . . A nun who has been ordained only one year thinks that she has more authority to chant than a laynun with over twenty years of experience. So, she will ask the laynun to stand to the side. It is difficult for the two to be happy together."[31]

The discomfort was increased by the fact that most of the nuns came from outside Minnan. They were unable to speak the local dialect, while many elderly laynuns spoke only the Minnan dialect. This often created a communication gap between those living in the same hall. Additionally, some non-Minnan nuns did not understand and respect the laynun tradition. They expected the elderly laynuns to provide services, such as cooking, laundry, and cleaning, for them, even though the laynuns had originally expected the nuns to look after them.

In these ways, the introduction of the nun tradition into the Minnan region in the 1980s had the effect of marginalizing the laynuns from Buddhism. By the 1990s, the growing number of nuns in laynun halls had placed the laynuns in secondary roles in their halls. Laynuns who had survived the Cultural Revolution and worked hard to reclaim and revive their halls now had to work for the growing number of nuns, who were focused on their own religious cultivation. By the 2000s, most elderly laynuns had passed away without young laynun successors and many halls became recognized by the XBA as Buddhist temples for nuns.

ADAPTATIONS AND INCORPORATIONS: CASES OF LAYNUN HALLS

In various ways, laynuns and their halls in Xiamen have been affected by and have adapted to changing circumstances since the early twentieth century when Hongyi first recognized them as Buddhists. These effects and adaptations include a laynun hall that, after surviving decades of political vicissitudes, became a Buddhist temple for nuns in the 2000s; laynuns' perceptions and adaptations to the broader religious and political contexts before 1949 and then after the Cultural Revolution when their halls became Buddhist temples; and, unusually, a laynun hall's being preserved even after its laynun head became an ordained Buddhist nun. Together these cases illustrate how laynuns' various strategies to survive in modern circumstances have furthered their incorporation into orthodox Buddhism and the state system.

A Laynun Hall Becomes a Nun Temple

Miaoqing Temple 妙清寺 shows the development from a laynun hall guided by a Buddhist monk to a Buddhist temple for nuns.[32] Its origins lie in a prayer hall devoted to Guanyin that was established by a laynun in downtown Xiamen. Then, in 1942, the laynun, a disciple of Juebin 觉斌 (1897–1942), a prominent monk at the Nanputuo Temple, rebuilt the hall.[33] She named it Miaoqing Temple, most likely including the character for "temple" (*si* 寺) in its name to enhance its status in Buddhism. The hall had five laynuns in residence. In the 1950s, they established the Lotus Friend Cotton Mill (Lian you Mianfangchang 莲友棉纺厂) in the hall to manufacture burlap bags, which they sold to the state during the Korean War (1950–1953). During the Cultural Revolution, laynuns continued to reside at Miaoqing Temple, even as it fell into disrepair.

The restoration of the laynun hall after the Cultural Revolution began in 1986. The process is described in its commemorative stele, erected the following year.

Madam Jinghua [a laynun formerly residing at the hall who had emigrated abroad] returned from America and was greatly moved when she saw the temple collapsing in disrepair and the country implementing a new policy of religious freedom. She willingly used money earned in America by doing rituals to repair the temple to provide Buddhists with a place for cultivation. Fortunately, other domestic and overseas believers gave financial support so the restoration was successful. The huge merit of this undertaking is limitless. To make the temple a place to propagate Buddhism, only those of high talent and cultivation can reside here, purity must be kept, and mixing of customs is not allowed [*buxu xisu hu za* 不许习俗糊杂]. (Stele entitled *Miaoqing si yuanqi beiji* 妙清寺缘起碑记 [The Origins of Miaoqing Temple]), 1987

The stele highlights the role of overseas Buddhists in reviving the halls, which was typical for halls that were reclaimed and restored in the 1980s and 1990s. It also shows the desire of laynuns to distinguish Buddhism from the customs of popular religions, which reflects the influence of the Buddhicization movement earlier in the twentieth century.

The rebuilt laynun hall was a three-story modern building occupying 253 square meters of land with a floor space of 680 square meters. The first floor contained a wooden statue of Guanyin, the second floor was the Great Shrine Hall (Daxiong Baodian 大雄宝殿), and the third floor was for worshipping the Western Pure Land Trinity (Xifang Sansheng 西方三圣). When we visited in 1999 there were ten laynuns and four nuns in residence. The laynuns, all in their seventies and eighties, held daily morning and evening rituals that were attended by neighbors and ran a clinic dispensing free medicine. For income, they relied on the pensions of the laynuns who had once worked at the Lotus Friend Cotton Mill. In the late 1990s, the XBA began sending nuns to live at the hall. In the early 2000s the XBA recognized the hall as a Buddhist temple for nuns. In this way, a laynun hall became a temple for nuns.

Changes to Inheritance in a Laynun Hall

The story of the Jinglian Hall (Jinglian Tang 净莲堂) shows the changing contexts that shaped the views of laynuns regarding ownership and succession in their halls.[34] The hall, founded in 1932, was located in a downtown residential alley next to another laynun hall. The two founding laynuns, disciples of an eminent monk at Nanputuo Temple, were of the Huangpi 黄檗 sect. In an unusual decision, they downplayed the importance of sect by proclaiming Jinglian Hall to be ecumenical. This important matter was inscribed on the stele placed in the hall in 1933. It declared the hall to be owned by all resident laynuns; this differed from the typical practice of a laynun hall being the private property of the head laynun. The stele also declared that the head laynun of Jinglian Hall was chosen by election, which broke from the usual practice of a head laynun designating a disciple as successor. Based on these rules, Jinglian Hall then underwent several changes of head laynuns who had different masters.

Occupied during the Cultural Revolution by a factory, Jinglian Hall was reclaimed by laynuns in 1983. Rebuilding was funded by a laynun who had formerly lived at the hall and then emigrated overseas. Its head laynun at this time declared that inheritance of the hall was limited to members of the Huangpi sect, contradicting the earlier 1933 declaration of ecumenicism. This new view of inheritance was expressed in an inscription carved in the hall in 1992 titled *Jingliantangfangdichan jichengquan ji tongzhu gongyue* 净莲堂房地产继承权及同住公约 (Jinglian Hall Property Inheritance and Cohabitation Convention).

Regarding ownership, it declared, "This restoration was entirely completed by the masters and disciples of our sect so that our disciples can live here together for Buddhist cultivation. We will not let other sects invade and occupy. The right of ownership and residence will always belong to us." In regard to succession, it stated that the head laynun should be of the Huangpi sect.

These contradictory inscriptions, carved opposite each other on the walls of the hall, reflect the different historical contexts that laynuns experienced. The 1933 inscription was adopted during the height of the movement for the modern reform of Buddhism. The strong ties of the laynuns to clerics who had instituted collective ownership and abbot election at Nanputuo Temple without regard to sect no doubt influenced the laynuns to do likewise in the Jinglian Hall. The 1992 inscription reflected the strong will of the head laynun, who had suffered by having her hall occupied during the Cultural Revolution, to keep the restored hall a Buddhist site. Her concern was that a successor might marry and turn the hall into her private family residence. Should this happen, the inscription authorized other members of the sect to transfer inheritance of the hall to someone who could be trusted to maintain it for communal worship.

When we visited Jinglian Hall in 1999, the elderly head laynun, lacking a successor, had finally been persuaded to turn over ownership of her hall to the XBA. At that time, there were six elderly laynuns and seven ordained nuns in residence. In the early 2000s the head laynun passed away and a young nun became the head. She rebuilt the hall as a five-story building several times larger than the original one. Then it was renamed Jinglian Temple and recognized by the XBA as a Buddhist temple for nuns. This illustrates the complicated issues of inheritance facing laynun halls.

The Closeness of a Laynun Hall to Local Society

The close ties of laynuns to local society can be seen in the relationship of Miaofalin Hall (Miaofalin Tang 妙法林堂) with the CCP.[35] Miaofalin Hall was founded in 1934 as a laynun hall on a quiet street in a residential neighborhood, with eight laynuns in residence. Its founder was an overseas Chinese lay practitioner who was a disciple of a leading monk at Nanputuo Temple. In 1938, the hall became a base of the local CCP underground resistance to the Japanese army during its occupation of Xiamen; in 1946 it became the center of the underground CCP in Xiamen during the civil war (1945–1949) in the fight against the Nationalist government. In 1959, the hall was taken over by the city government for residential housing. In 1982, laynuns regained ownership of the hall. A laynun living in Singapore who had resided in the hall in the 1940s sent funds for restoration and a white jade Buddha statue carved in Thailand for the main shrine hall.

However, the political history of the laynun hall complicated its recovery for Buddhist worship. In 1982, the Xiamen government designated it a municipal-level Revolutionary Cultural Relics Protection Unit (Geming Wenwu Baohu Danwei 革命文物保护单位). Many officials came to pay respects, frightening away the laynuns. Then local residents moved in to occupy the empty buildings and land. In 1985 the CCP in Xiamen sent an elderly woman named Hubing 胡冰 to live at Miaofalin Hall to supervise its revival. When we visited in 1998, Hubing complained of the stream of visitors, especially during the Qingming Festival (Qingming Jie 清明节) to venerate ancestors, when large tours of schoolchildren came. This disrupted the daily ritual life of the hall and kept worshippers away, depriving the hall of revenue. Its meager income came from Hubing's salary and occasional donations. At that time, there were ten elderly laynuns and four young ordained nuns at the hall.

Hubing's personal history was intertwined with that of Miaofalin Hall. In 1937, she became a CCP member and organized its underground activities that were based there. After her husband was arrested by the Nationalist Party and died in prison during the civil war, the CCP sent her to Singapore for her safety. She returned to China in 1950, worked first in the United Front Work Department in Beijing, and then in 1955 returned to Xiamen to work in the local branch of the department. She told us that she managed Miaofalin as a public servant rather than as a Buddhist. In fact, she said she was not a Buddhist but only kept Buddhist practices such as vegetarianism. This reluctance to say that she was Buddhist was no doubt due to the CCP regulation that party members could not believe in religion. However, she is described as a prominent laynun in the *Gazetteer of Xiamen Buddhism* (Xiamenshi Fojiao Xiehui 2006, 326–327).

In 2003 Hubing passed away, and Miaofalin Hall was subsequently recognized by the XBA as a Buddhist temple for nuns with the new name of Miaofalin Temple. In 2010 it was officially recognized by the local government as an open religious site. The following year, on the ninetieth anniversary of the founding of the CCP, it was nationally recognized as one of the first national Patriotic Religious Education Bases (Zongjiaojie Aiguozhuyi Jiaoyu Jidi 宗教界爱国主义教育基地) by the State Administration for Religious Affairs (SARA). By then there were eight nuns and two laynuns in residence. Its head was an ordained nun who had graduated from the two-year program of the Fujian Buddhist Academy and the four-year program at the Buddhist College of Minnan. These developments illustrate its ties to both the state and the Buddhist establishment.

A Laynun Ordains as a Nun to Preserve a Laynun Hall

Qingfu Hall (Qingfu Tang 庆福堂) is an unusual case of a laynun hall that came to be headed by an ordained nun but was committed to remaining a place of Buddhist worship for laynuns. It was founded by a laynun in 1925 on what was the edge of the urban district at that time and close to the harbor neighborhood where many fisherman and their families lived.[36] During the Cultural Revolution its courtyard was occupied by the city district government for a factory even as laynuns continued to inhabit its building. In 1987, the elderly head laynun sent her twenty-four-year-old disciple to study in the four-year course of the Buddhist College of Minnan. Upon the disciple's graduation in 1991, the head laynun and her disciple decided to rebuild the hall with funds from local believers, overseas Chinese in Singapore, a private loan, and the savings of the head laynun.

In 1993 the rebuilt hall was consecrated, affiliated with the Linji sect, and renamed Qingfu Temple (Qingfu Si 庆福寺). It was a modern building on 436 square meters of land next to the factory that still occupied its courtyard. The first floor contained the main shrine hall, the second floor had a Buddha hall (*fotang* 佛堂) to worship the Paradise of Western Bliss and residential quarters, the third floor was a secluded abode for meditation (*jingshe chanfang* 精舍禅房), and the fourth floor was a sutra library. In 1993, the disciple founded a salon at the Qingfu Temple for artists and intellectuals called the Buddha Calligraphy and Painting Society (Foguang Shuhua 佛光书画). Its honorary president was Nanputuo Temple abbot Miaozhan, who strongly supported the laynuns. It was a site for intellectuals and artists to interact and hold exhibitions of artwork. The money raised from the exhibitions was used to support a free medical clinic.

These various changes from 1993 strengthened the ties of the laynun hall to the Buddhist temples and the local community in Xiamen. In 1998, the local government officially recognized the laynun hall as an open religious activity site, which made it easier for it to hold large art exhibitions and interact with foreign artists. When we visited the hall in 1999, the disciple had become the head laynun. She said that the hall emphasized self-cultivation and propagated moral education for correct behavior and positive perception of Buddhism, and a spirit of dedication to serve the public.[37] It held worship services on the first of each month and every Saturday, regularly attended by about forty worshippers.

Then, in the early 2000s, the head laynun was ordained as a nun. As we interviewed her before this, we do not know her motivation. But she has remained committed to preserving the laynun hall, despite the fact that she renamed it a temple and ordained as a nun. In 2005, five laynuns and three lay practitioners resided at the hall. In 2007, the factory that had occupied its courtyard during the Cultural Revolution moved out. In an interview with the XBA in 2015 we learned that the XBA and the local government continue to recognize it as a laynun hall even though it is headed by an ordained nun and its name changed to include the character for "temple."

Each of these case studies illustrates the actions that laynuns in Xiamen took to survive amid great changes and turmoil in China. A century after their recognition as ascetic and pious women, and having survived decades of political vicissitudes, many laynuns have seen their halls become temples for nuns, while younger laynuns have become nuns. These actions have resulted in the further incorporation of the Minnan laynun tradition into the nun tradition of Buddhism. However, there is an exceptional case of laynuns who have been actively adapting to changing circumstances while maintaining their laynun hall and position as laynuns.

MAKING A NEW LAYNUN HALL

Several exemplary laynuns are creating an innovative kind of laynun hall in Xiamen. They graduated from Buddhist academies in the 1980s and command much respect from Buddhists and society. One such laynun is Puguang 普光, whom we first met in 1989 when she was thirty-four years old.[38] We have since met this intelligent and energetic laynun repeatedly and heard her life story, which is presented in the following paragraphs. Especially striking is the success of Puguang and her Dharma sister Puci 普慈 in building Ciguang Temple (Ciguang Si 慈光寺), a laynun hall that is the size and structure of a large Buddhist temple. She has worked hard to start a program to educate laynuns in cooperation with the Buddhist College of Minnan. In 2015, there were thirteen laynuns living at the laynun hall, constituting half of all laynuns in Xiamen at this time, including most of the younger ones. Additionally, they had adopted several orphan girls who lived in the laynun hall.

The accomplishments of Puguang and Puci stand in contrast to the incorporation into the nun tradition seen in the four cases described previously. Their efforts are a remarkable testimony to the respect, local ties, piousness, and entrepreneurship of the laynuns in rebuilding the laynun tradition, as well as the constraints they are facing in the early twenty-first century.

Story of an Exemplary Laynun

Let us now describe the background of the laynuns. Puguang was born in 1955 in downtown Xiamen. Her father was a sales clerk in a government-run vegetable store and her mother was a housewife. Both parents were Buddhists. Next to their home resided an elderly widow in a laynun hall called Lianguang Hall (Lianguang Tang 莲光堂), which she had established in the 1940s. Puguang's parents often sent her to keep the old laynun company. At the age of thirteen she left her family to reside with the laynun at Lianguang Hall, taking Puguang as her Dharma name. This occurred in 1968, at the height of the Cultural Revolution, so her parents were questioned by the local government about permitting their daughter to go to the laynun hall.

> During the Cultural Revolution, the laynuns persevered in worship. People came every day [during the Cultural Revolution] to worship because we were in the city center. As the old laynun was very acute in predicting the future, the hall was well-known even though it was small. We burned incense brought to us by neighbors who hid it under their clothes. We never stopped morning and evening rituals. . . . We worshipped with believers hiding under mosquito nets so that we could not be seen. But we were discovered by the residents' committee.[39] That is why we were searched so many times. They confiscated our two copies of the *Fojiao xiuxue yaodian* 佛教修学要典 [Buddhist Cultivation Handbook]. It was a crime to have it. But the old laynun had memorized the sutras written in the book and so we could continue our chanting.

Altogether, Red Guards ransacked the hall eight times to uncover statues and ritual items, but the head laynun had sent them secretly to Nanputuo Temple for safekeeping.

In 1972, when Puguang turned seventeen, she was assigned by the government to work in a factory. This prevented her from participating in daily rituals at her hall, but she said that she had little choice.

> If I hadn't gone I would have been labeled a member of the exploiting class . . . someone who was a parasite who did not work but depended on others for their livelihood. The policy said that middle school graduates had to go down to the countryside but a family could keep one child to stay with parents.[40] So I was not sent down and continued to live in the hall. The government assigned me a job [in a factory that made cable wire]. I often felt tired because, as a vegetarian, there was nothing that I could eat in the factory cafeteria. But my thinking was calm and the political situation was peaceful. We were young girls at the factory, seventeen- and eighteen-year-olds. . . . We had a lot of fun. Our thinking was simple and we all got along. We were like sisters. Nobody looked down on me because I was a vegetarian. I had to bring my lunch from home. My friends put my food from home beside the stove in the factory kitchen so it could be hot like everyone else's lunch from the cafeteria.[41]

At the factory, she met Puci, one of her fellow workers, who would become her Dharma sister and partner in efforts to build their hall.

Lianguang Hall suffered its severest political attack during a violent political campaign in 1975 at the end of the Cultural Revolution.

> It was quite fierce. A work team came to the hall to "smash the four olds"[42] and change our thinking. They organized us to study for forty-five days to cleanse our minds. They changed the name of the hall to the Sun Facing Court [Xiangyang Yuan 向阳院]. They said that by 1980 I would get married and came often to persuade me. I was eighteen years old. My emotions were quite complicated. The old laynun was labeled a cow ghost and snake spirit.[43] If I criticized her I could be considered a red person.[44] But I didn't and got labeled a small cow and snake spirit. Yes, I didn't understand things very much then. All I knew was that to be an upright person you had to depend on your conscience.[45]

Despite all these hardships, the laynuns were able to remain in Lianguang Hall throughout the Cultural Revolution.

Lianguang Hall resumed worship services in 1982, the first hall to do so after the Cultural Revolution. The elderly laynun's master, a prominent monk named Guang'an 广安, encouraged Puguang to attend the Fujian Buddhist Academy when it reopened its four-year program in 1983.[46] Her thirty classmates at the academy came from all over China. While at the academy studying alongside the nuns and novices, she contemplated ordaining as a nun but then rejected the idea.

> Yes, I gave it some thought. I had studied many Buddhist texts and thought that shaving my head [becoming a nun] was somewhat better. But the Buddhist College of Minnan did not require this. . . . Those with hair [laynuns] and those with shaved heads [nuns] studied together without any distinction. Everyone received the same ten-yuan monthly stipend. This respected the Minnan tradition, although women from outside Minnan had to cut their hair to study at the academy. Also, my master, Guang'an, did not want me to shave my head because then I would not be able to stay at laynun halls, as they were for women who kept their hair as they cultivated [*dai fa xiuxing* 带发修行].[47] After this predestined relationship, I thought no more of it.[48]

Upon graduating in 1987, she was recruited by Nanputuo Temple abbot Miaozhan to supervise the nuns' section of the Buddhist College of Minnan. She did this for several years but had a difficult time because the young nuns did not sufficiently respect her authority as a laynun. In 1989, she transferred to a position as manager of the guesthouse for visiting clerics at the

Nanputuo Temple. That year, her Dharma sister Puci graduated from the Buddhist College of Minnan. As Puci had been a talented student, she was first assigned to the XBA to work on compiling the *Gazetteer of Nanputuo Temple* (*Nanputuo Si Zhi* 南普陀寺志) and then joined Puguang to manage the guesthouse.[49]

In 1989, their master, Guang'an, gave the laynuns money to buy a condominium for a worship hall to commemorate his master, Zhuanfeng 转逢, the monk who had ecumenicized Nanputuo Temple in 1925. The consecration ceremony of the hall, called the Ciguang Hermitage (Ciguang Jingshe 慈光精舍), occurred the following year. It was attended by significant clerics who had supported the laynuns, including the Nanputuo Temple abbot, along with lay disciples from Southeast Asia. Their presence symbolically showed the support given to the laynuns by monks and the historical tradition of popular respect and recognition of the laynuns in Minnan. However, in 1992 the city government requisitioned the land to make a shopping center. It compensated the laynuns with several apartments in a commercial housing complex built by the government. Puguang and Puci considered it disrespectful to place a Buddha statue in an ordinary apartment, so they decided to build a large hall that could be a Buddhist temple. They sold the apartments to raise money, resigned their positions at Nanputuo Temple, and set to work.

Building the New Laynun Hall

The construction of the Ciguang Temple was enabled by strong local support. As in many urban areas, the Xiamen government sought to prevent the proliferation of religious sites in order to control religion in society.[50] It only permitted the rebuilding and renovation of a temple on the site of a historically existing one. However, Ciguang Temple was built on land with no history of a Buddhist temple.[51] The fact that it could be constructed reflected the great respect of local people for laynuns in Minnan.

This respect was manifested in the support of government officials and Buddhist clerics in Xiamen. The officials were mostly from Minnan and respected the laynun tradition. When the laynuns visited government bureaus they were treated with respect and understanding.[52] Additionally, prominent overseas and domestic clerics supported them. Nanputuo Temple abbot Miaozhan and the laynuns' master, Guang'an, paid special attention to the laynuns' careers and greatly encouraged them. More recently, Zewu 则悟, the third abbot (2005–present) of the Nanputuo Temple after the Cultural Revolution, visited their hall to discuss their plans. The clerics respected Puguang and Puci as model laynuns who had worked hard to support the revival of Buddhism in Xiamen by working at the Nanputuo Temple and the XBA in the 1980s and early 1990s. Their education in the regular four-year program of Buddhist academies assured Buddhists clerics and government officials that they would establish a temple for proper Buddhist worship. Another form of support was their network of family, school, and work. In particular, their fellow women workers during the Cultural Revolution had since found jobs in the city government or married men who were officials and could provide administrative support and introductions. These former workers participated in the rituals at their hall and introduced relatives who were successful businesspersons in Xiamen to give large contributions.

These forms of support were visible in every step of the building of Ciguang Temple. To help them obtain land from the city government, a friend in the Public Security Bureau introduced them to an official in the Demolition Office, which was in charge of razing buildings for new construction. This official wrote a letter on their behalf to the City Planning Bureau requesting allocation of land. The letter noted that their master was a prominent overseas cleric, and so the request deserved special consideration.[53] The director of the Xiamen Municipal Land Planning Bureau was a Buddhist and a friend of Puci's brother-in-law. He designated a ridge in a new part of the city for the laynuns to select a piece of land. The laynuns invited Nanputuo abbot Miaozhan to inspect their choice. He brought a Tibetan expert in geomancy, who deemed it exemplary. Thereupon, the Xiamen Municipal Land Planning Bureau allocated 338 square meters of land for the Ciguang Temple, with additional land for a garden and entrance.

Obtaining the construction permits required many visits to multiple bureaus, but things went smoothly. As Puci said, "When we went to each bureau there was always someone whom we knew who could help us. They were sympathetic to us. They said, 'It is really something for you women to be coming out to do this.'"[54] A city vice-mayor designated the Ciguang Temple as a public facility, thereby waiving 400,000 RMB in fees for construction and other permits. To draft the blueprint, the laynuns selected a city government design institute rather than the more experienced Nanputuo Temple Construction Unit because the institute was the city agency that approved blueprints.[55] The laynuns garnered further local government support by hiring a private construction firm recommended by the design institute to build the compound. The firm lacked experience in building temples but, fortunately, the Nanputuo Temple Construction Unit agreed to advise it. It lent the firm its blueprints for building the roof and its craftsmen to supervise construction. This cooperation was possible because of the laynuns' ties to Nanputuo Temple abbot Miaozhan. Completed in 1996, the Ciguang Temple was a four-story building, with each story covering two hundred square meters, including a great shrine hall, meditation hall, and sutra hall. It was inhabited by six laynuns and four female lay practitioners.

The laynuns wanted to use Ciguang Temple as a multipurpose space, including a school for educating laynuns, and so expansion soon got under way. A Great Compassion Hall (Dabei Dian 大悲殿) was built on the ridge behind the great shrine hall to house a statue of Guanyin of the Thousand Hands and Thousand Eyes (Qianshou [Qianyan] Guanyin 千手 (千眼) 观音).[56] Then five-story buildings were built on both sides. By the time of our last visit in 2017, all of this construction had been completed. For future development, the laynuns planned to build a new great shrine hall of better quality.

The Issue of a School for Laynuns

However, there is one issue that has still not been resolved at the time of this writing. In 2013 Puguang and Puci proposed starting a school for the Buddhist education of laynuns and lay practitioners at the Ciguang Temple, with the classrooms in one wing and a dormitory in the other. This would compensate for the 1997 ban instituted on laynuns studying in the Buddhist College of Minnan. Their plan called for the establishment of a separate department for the education of laynuns within the Buddhist College of Minnan. However, the plan was suspended in 2015 because of lack of consensus among the clerics and the XBA. Some clerics felt that the purpose of the Buddhist College of Minnan was to educate monks and nuns, and therefore it had no responsibility to educate laynuns. They said that those who wanted to study Buddhism could simply become nuns. Some were also concerned that creating a section for laynuns in the Buddhist College of Minnan would damage the college's reputation as providing authentic Buddhist education for nuns and monks without any adaptation to local culture.

This ambivalence showed that even as the laynuns' position and contributions were recognized and respected by the local government and society, their position in Buddhism remained ambiguous. Despite Puguang and Puci's resources and efforts, they were unable to get consensus on their plan to create a school for educating laynuns due to clerics' strong belief in maintaining orthodox Buddhism. This raises the question of how the situation of the laynun in Buddhism has been affected by the Xiamen government's recognition of laynuns as religious professionals.

INSTITUTIONAL RECOGNITION AS RELIGIOUS PROFESSIONALS

In 2012, the modern history of laynuns developed further with their recognition by the local government in Xiamen as "religious professionals." Almost a century after being incorporated into Buddhism as a special group of Buddhists, the "pious and ascetic women" now came to be incorporated into the institutional structure of the state as the equivalent of clerics. The XBA officer we interviewed in 2014 told us with pride and excitement that this was the first case in Minnan and probably in China.[57] He said that this reflected the high regard of the Buddhist clerics and the Xiamen government toward laynuns for their contributions to preserving Buddhism during the Cultural

Revolution and restoring Buddhist temples afterward. He also noted the need to enhance the status of laynuns in order to stem their declining numbers. This concern reflected the new view of laynuns as an important form of the Minnan region's "cultural heritage." By 2017, on our most recent research trip to Xiamen, we heard that other local governments in Minnan, such as Quanzhou and Zhangzhou, had also implemented similar recognition of the laynuns.

Impetus for recognition began in 2007 with the central state's initiative to have local governments register all clerics in China. It began with SARA's issuance of a document entitled "Zongjiao jiaozhi renyuan bei'an banfa" 宗教教职人员备案办法 (Method for the Recording of Religious Professionals). According to the document, the reason for the effort was "to protect the legitimate rights and interests of religious personnel, and regulate religious personnel records and record management" (Guojia Zongjiao Shiwuju 2007). Needless to say, this would strengthen state control over religion by enabling local governments to better determine who was a religious professional and therefore authorized to reside in an "open" (*kaifang* 开放) temple.[58]

This state policy was then adopted by each national religious association, including the BAC, which issued its own version of the policy in 2009, adapted for Buddhism. It stipulates that persons to be recognized as religious professionals should be ordained clerics. Article 2 states, "The term of Chinese Buddhist professional . . . refers to Chinese Buddhist monks and nuns" (Zhongguo Fojiao Xiehui 2009). Article 3 lists the necessary conditions to become a nun or monk, including being "a tonsured man who has resided in a temple for more than one year, or a tonsured woman who has lived in a temple for more than two years" (Zhongguo Fojiao Xiehui 2009). Similar wording was then included in a document subsequently approved by the Buddhist Association of Fujian Province (Fujian Sheng Fojiao Xiehui 2010) to apply inside the province.

This stipulation of national and provincial Buddhist associations that only ordained clerics could be recognized as religious professionals pushed local governments in Minnan to consider the status of laynuns. In October 2011, a meeting was convened in Xiamen at the Ciguang Temple, in order to "properly solve the work of determining the qualification as religious professional of Minnan women who have renounced lay life" (Xiamen Fojiao Zaixian 2011). In attendance were leading officials from the provincial and local governments in charge of religious affairs, the four clerics who headed the XBA, including the abbot of Nanputuo Temple, Zewu, who was the XBA chair, and laynuns from Xiamen's five remaining halls.

> At the forum, the laynuns expressed their appreciation to the leaders from the provincial and city religious affairs bureaus and the leaders of the XBA for their concern and support and, moreover, introduced the

positive contribution and other aspects of the Minnan laynuns' formation and impact on Buddhism. Through this exchange, the high-ranking officials deepened their understanding and indicated that they would attach much importance to the work of determining the qualifications of the laynuns as religious professionals in order to actively find a solution to protect the special characteristics of Minnan Buddhism. (Xiamen Fojiao Zaixian 2011)

This meeting convinced officials from the provincial and city governments to let laynuns be recognized as religious professionals. Thereupon, in June 2012, the XBA issued its own document titled "Xiamen shi fojiao fanxing qingxinnü (caigu) jiaozhi renyuan zige rending banfa" 厦门市佛教梵行清信女（菜姑）教职人员资格认定办法 (Xiamen City's Method for Determining the Qualification of Ascetic and Pious Women to be Religious Professionals).

Justifications and Criteria

The justification for recognition as religious professional and the criteria for a laynun to qualify as one are outlined in the six articles of the aforementioned two-page document issued by the XBA in June 2012. Article 1 states the justification for recognizing laynuns as religious professionals.

Ascetic and pious women (commonly called *caigu*) are a unique phenomenon of a group of women who renounce laylife to live in temples [halls], are single, vegetarian, and wear distinctive laynun clothing. They formed during the process of the development of Han Buddhism in the Minnan region. Because they are a regional characteristic of the historical development of Buddhism in Minnan, Master Hongyi gave them this name [ascetic and pious women]. For the purpose of the good handling of the issue to determine the qualifications of the ascetic and pious women, regularize the management of the ascetic and pious women's temples [halls], and protect the legal rights and interests of ascetic and pious women, this approach was developed based on the opinion of a specialized investigation . . . with reference to the "Regulations for Implementing 'Methods for Ascertaining the Qualifications of Han Buddhist Religious Professionals' (Draft)" [Hanchuan fojiao jiaozhi renyuan zige rending banfa shishi xize (shixing cao'an) 汉传佛教教职人员资格认定办法实施细则 (试行草案)] issued by the Fujian Provincial Ethnic and Religious Affairs Office and suiting the actual conditions of Xiamen Buddhism. (Xiamenshi Fojiao Xiehui 2012)

This article justifies the recognition of laynuns as religious professionals by the criterion of "leaving the family" (*chujia* 出家), a term in Buddhism that represents clerics and distinguishes them from devotees and laypersons by the criterion of having renounced lay life—leaving their family. Therefore, Article 1 establishes the equivalency of laynuns and clerics on the basis that they have both renounced lay life. Furthermore, it extends government control over laynuns as a matter of protecting their "legal rights and interests." Finally, the phrase "opinion of a specialized investigation" indicates that the local government policy is an adaptation of state policy to the specific local conditions of Buddhism in Xiamen.

The criteria for eligibility to be a laynun are specified in Article 2.

[Article 2] All Buddhist temples that have been approved, established, and registered by Xiamen City can apply for the recognition of the qualifications of the ascetic and pious women living there as religious professionals. Applicants seeking recognition must be female Buddhist followers born in Xiamen, Zhangzhou, Quanzhou, or Putian 莆田,[59] have unshaven heads, have left their family, live in temples [halls], worship the Buddha, are single, vegetarian, wear laynun clothing, and have taken the Three Refuges, Five Precepts, and the Bodhisattva Precepts. (Xiamenshi Fojiao Xiehui 2012)

It is especially significant that this article strictly limits eligibility to only those women who are born in the Minnan region, as well as adjacent Putian. Those born outside Minnan who then come to the region and live as laynuns are not eligible to be recognized as religious professionals. This limitation both precludes the introduction of a category into locales all over China and prevents women from elsewhere in China coming to Minnan to be laynuns and register as religious professionals.

Additionally, Article 2 stipulates that taking the Three Refuges and Five Precepts and the Bodhisattva Precepts (pusajie 菩萨戒) is a condition for eligibility.[60] This is noteworthy because the Bodhisattva Precepts were previously not a condition to be a laynun, although those who voluntarily take them are respected as very pious lay practitioners. The imposition of the Bodhisattva Precepts is possibly an effort by the local government to more clearly distinguish laynuns from other lay practitioners, thereby bolstering their status as religious professionals. However, in an interview the XBA secretary said that this condition would not be rigidly imposed, and so elderly laynuns who have not taken the Bodhisattva Precepts would not be denied recognition as religious professionals.[61] The local government intent is not to define and enforce a new religious category in Buddhism, but rather to create a new institutional frame in the state religion policy for a local phenomenon of Minnan Buddhism.

Article 3 outlines the criteria for being a laynun so as to be eligible for recognition as a religious professional.

[Article 3] Ascetic and pious women seeking recognition as religious professionals must meet the following basic qualifications:

(1) love country, love religion [aiguo aijiao 爱国爱教], and be law abiding;

(2) be of pure faith, assiduously cultivate the Three Studies—discipline, meditation, and wisdom, comply with the teachings of the sutras, and be of upright character;

(3) be at least eighteen years old, and of sound body (no handicap) and mind;

(4) be women from the Minnan region, who have cultivated the Three Refuges, Five Precepts, and Bodhisattva Precepts and have stayed in a temple [hall] for at least two years;

(5) have standard Buddhist knowledge, ability to complete the daily Buddhist chanting on their own, and basic ability to conduct Buddhist services;

(6) have the four elements of "living in a temple [hall], being single, vegetarian, and wearing laynun clothes." (Xiamenshi Fojiao Xiehui 2012)

The first criterion is patriotism, expressed in the phrase "love country, love religion," which puts loyalty to country, including upholding the CCP religion policy, before religion. This is a common criterion in the national religion policy for clerics in all recognized religions in China. The qualifications in criteria 2 and 3 are the same as for a nun except in regard to age. A woman can become a laynun at eighteen years old, whereas a woman wanting to be a nun must be age eighteen to become a novice and then twenty-one to be ordained as a nun. Furthermore, criterion 4 enables a woman who wants to be a laynun to leave her family as early as age sixteen to reside in a laynun hall. This age of family leaving is two years earlier than for a woman who wants to become a novice in a Buddhist temple in order to be a nun.

Article 6 is entitled "Rights and Duties." It reaffirms that laynuns who meet the aforementioned criteria are incorporated into the state policy as religious professionals. Article 6 declares, "Ascetic and pious women who have undergone the procedure for being recognized as a Buddhist religious professional enjoy the rights and duties of religious professionals as stipulated in China's religious policies and regulations. These rights and duties include upholding the Buddhist order" (Xiamenshi Fojiao Xiehui 2012). This places laynuns in the same institutional category as clerics, who now share a common relationship to the state as religious professionals.

This analysis of the local document reveals its careful crafting to avoid two conflicts that would undermine its legitimacy. One is preventing a contradiction with the state criterion of ordainment as the key qualification for a religious professional. As laynuns are not ordained, the XBA has created an alternative criterion, which is renunciation of lay life, which applies only for women born in Minnan and Putian who live in laynun halls in Xiamen. In this way, the XBA policy is represented as a local exception that does not conflict with the policies of SARA and national and provincial Buddhist associations. Second, the XBA document avoids intervening in religious teachings and the rules of the Vinaya. The recognition of laynuns as "religious professionals" is an institutional category in local government policy but not a religious category of Buddhism itself. Even though the XBA document recognizes laynuns as persons who "leave the family," this differs from the religious meaning of the term whereby a person who "leaves the family" refers only to ordained clergy. In this way, direct conflict between the institutional recognition by the state and religious recognition by Buddhism is avoided by multiple meanings in the term "leave the family."

Implications and Effects

The XBA document let the Xiamen government resolve the contradiction between its local practice of allowing laynuns to reside in laynun halls and the state's tightened enforcement of rules requiring that residents of religious sites be registered as religious professionals. While this contradiction had existed from the beginning of the implementation of the new religious policy in 1979, the lack of systematic enforcement had created a space for local governments in the Minnan region to let laynuns live together in laynun halls without being certified as religious professionals.[62] Then the national effort that began in 2007 to register all clerics by their local governments compelled the Xiamen government to harmonize its local practice with the state religious policy. By 2013, all laynuns in Xiamen were registered as religious professionals just as the national effort was ending.[63]

While the recognition of the laynuns as religious professionals no doubt had positive implications for the Xiamen government, its effects on the laynuns themselves have been less so. Recognition has let laynuns remain in their halls without violating state religious policy. However, it has not changed the circumstances that were contributing to their declining number. By not touching the position of the laynuns in Buddhism, it has done nothing to encourage their reproduction. Recognition as religious professionals did not enable laynuns to once again study in Buddhist academies, which would have encouraged talented women to remain as laynuns rather than ordain as nuns. Therefore, recognition of laynuns as religious professionals appears to us as a short-term measure that only seeks harmonization within the state administration of religion rather than a solution addressing the existential problems facing the laynuns.

This was the most recent way in which the laynun tradition has been affected by modern recognition. The first occurred in the 1920s: As waves of modern Buddhism and its propagation spread into and influenced Minnan culture, Buddhicization reached the laynuns. They were named "ascetic and pious women" by the monk Hongyi, positioning them in modern Buddhism. Then, almost a century later, the equivalency of laynuns with clerics as persons who "left their family" was asserted by a local government in Minnan. Yet the status of laynuns remains difficult to ascertain. First, their recognition as religious professionals is only by a single local government and limited to women in Minnan. This constrains them as a local production of Minnan culture. Second, recognition as religious professionals is only an institutional status in the state but does not help to constitute religious status in orthodox Buddhism. Laynuns are never religiously recognized within the doctrinal category of a cleric who has been ordained as a nun or a monk. Therefore, they remain in an ambiguous religious position as a unique tradition of local Buddhist culture in the Minnan region.

Nevertheless, it is noteworthy that great efforts were expended in the 2010s to fit the laynuns into the state religion policy to give institutional legitimacy to their existence. This required the coordination of multiple actors, including national, provincial, and local levels of the Buddhist Association and state agencies of religious control.[64] It is remarkable that this local effort was successful despite skepticism within the Buddhist establishment toward measures to improve the situation of laynuns that enabled their continued existence. Skepticism was seen in the opposition of the XBA and some non-Minnan clerics in Xiamen to expand educational opportunities for laynuns. Therefore, the effort highlights the power that maintains the position of the laynuns as a Minnan cultural tradition in spite of opposition by orthodox Buddhism.

LAYNUNS AND THE STORY OF MIAOSHAN

The historical origins of the laynuns are fused into layers of the cultural foundation of the Minnan region. As explained earlier in this chapter, some scholars suggest various customs and phenomena that appear as historically or culturally related to the tradition of laynuns, but none can be ascertained as its sole origin. Therefore, it would be more accurate to say that the phenomena of laynuns and related customs based on women's social groups have hybridized and fused in history conventions and beliefs that have contributed to the common image of certain kinds of women. There has long existed in Minnan a widespread and popular image of women who leave their families without shaving their heads for a communal life of celibacy, piety, independence, vegetarianism, helping the weak, and worshipping Guanyin, the Buddha, and possibly other deities. It has appeared in various styles and shapes as local customs and beliefs at different times and in different regions and sociocultural contexts. Some of these Minnan customs are called "girls' houses," "not leaving the parents' home," "Zhai women," and "laynuns." By focusing our conclusion on the long existence of this image in the Minnan region, we end this chapter by raising further questions concerning the mass consciousness of the image of the Minnan laynun.

This image of a woman who is celibate, pious, and devout overlaps considerably with the stories of Miaoshan 妙善 and Guanyin 观音, especially Guanyin of the Thousand Hands and Thousand Eyes.[65] These stories have been shared by ordinary people through allegories in the form of legends and local histories that have appeared in various styles from time to time. We argue that these powerful stories and their manifestations in customs and practices in Minnan constitute an underlying current of sociocultural consciousness and emotion in the popular belief of Buddhism. We further argue that the persistence of the laynuns is linked to this current. Similar to Ken Dean's concept of the "preexisting sociocultural force" (2009) of folk religions, this deep current is not easily affected by actions and efforts to disrupt or halt it, and therefore it persists over time.[66] To understand this deep current and its persistence, it is necessary to dwell on stories and practices regarding Guanyin and, especially, Miaoshan.

The worship of Guanyin has been very popular since the tenth century, when it first began to spread in South China, and became established in various places, most famously Putuoshan 普陀山 in Zhejiang Province. In her landmark study, Yü Chün-fang (2001) shows the historical process of the sinicization of Buddhism by focusing on the transformation of the original nongendered image of Guanyin into a female Guanyin linked to local deities and legends in China. In the laynun halls, Guanyin is the central figure of worship and is also worshipped by social groups of women such as those who belonged to "girls' houses" and "Zhai women." Even the Nanputuo Temple, the major Buddhist temple in Xiamen, mentioned repeatedly in this chapter, is devoted to Guanyin.[67] The large number of people (in the tens of thousands) who come to the temple's Guanyin Birthday Festival, held three times a year, to worship at its magnificent statue of Guanyin of the Thousand Hands and Thousand Eyes reveals the depth of people's passion for Guanyin; this passion is both constituted by and reflective of its sociocultural power.

People's belief and passion for Guanyin, especially Guanyin of the Thousand Hands and Thousand Eyes, is very much affirmed by the well-known popular legend of Miaoshan, who is the human incarnation of Guanyin. The legend of Miaoshan has been passed down orally. Laynuns and others whom we interviewed had all heard this story from the older generations in their families. Similarly, in her book on Guanyin, Yü (2001, 293) describes how she learned the Miaoshan story from her grandmother. The legend has been the basis of novels and stage plays for a millennium.[68] Due to its widespread manifestations in the family and popular culture, the Miaoshan legend can be considered a vehicle for the transmission of societal values and norms.[69]

The basic plot and themes of the well-known legend of Miaoshan are relatively consistent over the many versions analyzed by Dudbridge ([1978]

2004). Here is the story as Yü heard it from her grandmother (2001, 293–294; see also Dudbridge [1978] 2004, 24–34): The third daughter of a king, Miaoshan, was drawn to Buddhism at a young age and kept celibate and vegetarian, read scriptures, and meditated. The king had no sons and wanted to choose a successor from among his sons-in-law. But unlike her sisters, Miaoshan refused an arranged marriage and only wanted to be a nun. To get Miaoshan to change her mind, the angry king inflicted hardships on her. But the gods helped her bear them and she did not budge. Then the king confined her to a nunnery, ordering the nuns to give her hard work to make her give up the idea of becoming a nun, but she overcame the hard duties by the help of gods and animals and again persevered. So he had her executed for unfilial behavior, and burned down the nunnery, killing its five hundred nuns. However, Miaoshan's body was preserved by a mountain spirit and she embarked on a tour of hell, where she saved demons by preaching to them. Upon returning to the world, she meditated for nine years at the Fragrant Mountain (Xiangshan 香山) by herself. One day, she heard that her father was deathly ill. She visited him disguised as a mendicant monk, telling him that he could only be cured with the eyes and hands of someone who had never felt anger and informing him where to find this person. When his messengers called on her, she offered her eyes and hands. The king took the medicine and was cured. Upon visiting her to offer thanks, he recognized that the eyeless and handless ascetic was his daughter. Overwhelmed with remorse, he and the royal family converted to Buddhism. Miaoshan died but was transformed into Guanyin of the Thousand Hands and Thousand Eyes. Her father, the king, then built a temple at Fragrant Mountain and preserved her ashes there.

The Miaoshan legend represents the story of the origin of the Guanyin of the Thousand Hands and Thousand Eyes. Miaoshan metamorphosed into Guanyin after her self-sacrifice of giving her hands and eyes to her father. Miaoshan's devotion to her father takes the shape of the compassion of Guanyin, who sees people in trouble with her thousand eyes and reaches out to help them with her thousand hands. The two extreme opposing images, one being Miaoshan, who has no eyes and no hands, and the other being Guanyin of the Thousand Eyes and Thousand Hands, constitute a single strong message of devotion and compassion. Yü argues that the Miaoshan story was the basis for the sinicization of Buddhism when Guanyin was born in human incarnation as a Chinese princess. Subsequently, the special worship of Guanyin became central to devotee movements that began to spread to the Minnan area in the twelfth century through the White Lotus and other groups with links to Zhaijiao, as noted previously (Yü 2001, 305–307). The story of Miaoshan is, in fact, the story of Guanyin. It is a story of compassion, self-sacrifice, independence, and supremacy over clerics and secular power by figures who lack eyes and hands. They also share the same dates of birth, enlightenment, and death, further indicating that Miaoshan is Guanyin.[70]

Additionally, Miaoshan and the laynuns share so many similar characteristics that, in the popular consciousness, Miaoshan undoubtedly evokes the
image of the laynun. First, both share the same attributes of piety, celibacy,
marriage refusal, renunciation of lay life, vegetarianism, hard work (although
Miaoshan had some help from gods), self-training, and self-cultivation (Yü
2001, 333–338). Second, both distinguish themselves from nuns. Miaoshan
never became a nun despite her original desire to do so. To the contrary,
following her banishment to a convent, she became critical of the nuns there
for obeying the order of the king to torment her rather than following the true
teachings of the Buddha. Pointing out the luxurious and extravagant life of the
nuns, she said that they did not follow the precepts (Yü 2001, 305; Dudbridge
[1978] 2004, 28). She practiced meditation by herself without guidance from a
master monk, did not join any religious establishment, and attained enlightenment by her own training as a hermit (Yü 2001, 337; Dudbridge [1978] 2004,
28–29). Similarly, laynuns seek to lead an independent existence. They see
their work to support themselves as a major distinction from nuns, who rely
economically on patrons for support. Laynuns cultivate themselves through
their own daily practice and perform small rituals by themselves, although
monks are occasionally invited to give guidance. Third, both Miaoshan and
laynuns did such daily chores as collecting wood and watering plants in order
to maintain self-sufficiency in their lives. Fourth, both showed compassion to
the sick and the weak. Just as Miaoshan saved her sick father, so do the laynuns
engage in social welfare work to help those in need. Therefore, until she became
reborn as Guanyin, Miaoshan lived the life of a model laynun.

Furthermore, it is crucial to understand that in the legend, Miaoshan's
execution, rebirth, and metamorphosis into the bodhisattva Guanyin shows
that her position as layperson is superior to that of an ordained nun, and even
to that of monks in Buddhism and the secular authority of the king, because
ultimately, she is the bodhisattva Guanyin. Miaoshan showed that rightful
belief and devotion are superior to the orthodox, clergy-centered Buddhism
and the secular authority of a king by emphasizing the supreme position of
Guanyin. However, even though Miaoshan evokes laynuns in people's minds,
those laynuns whom they meet in their neighborhoods are not challenging the
authority of Buddhism or the state in a confrontational manner. Instead, they
are doing the best they can to survive, supported by local people, including
officials and monks. People visit laynun halls to worship Guanyin, and attend
the Guanyin Birthday Festival held three times a year at temples, including
Nanputuo Temple, to obtain the compassion of Guanyin for their problems in
daily life. It is undeniable that the metamorphosis of Miaoshan into Guanyin,
and the overlapping images of Miaoshan and laynuns are naturally woven
together in people's imaginations, consciousness, and emotions. These bonds
are replicated and renewed in daily practice and at the Guanyin Birthday Festival.
This power drives the people who worship Guanyin to support laynuns,

enabling them to exist and influence the institutional and politico-religious world.

Now, in the early twenty-first century, there is much interest in Buddhism among the growing middle class, state officials, and even Buddhist clergy, not just as religion but as Chinese culture. This new tendency to see Buddhism as Chinese culture is an example of the sinicization of Buddhism in the modern context. It shows that, in the three decades since the Cultural Revolution, Buddhism has gone beyond the stage of reviving and is now moving into a new stage of interaction with the broad masses in their daily lives as "Buddhist culture" (*fojiao wenhua* 佛教文化). This most likely influenced the Xiamen government to support the decision in 2012 to institutionally acknowledge laynuns as religious professionals in order to help ensure their existence as a unique example of Minnan cultural heritage.

During our last visit to Xiamen in fall 2017, the issue of establishing a school at the Ciguang Temple to educate laynuns and women lay practitioners was still on hold, but other local governments in Minnan, including those in Quanzhou and Zhangzhou, had followed Xiamen's lead to recognize laynuns as religious professionals. This recognition has two aspects. One is the Buddhicization of local cultural tradition, as occurred in the early twentieth century through the efforts of Hongyi and other eminent clerics. The other aspect is the localization of Buddhism through the efforts in the early twenty-first century of local governments to institutionally recognize the laynuns in the national state religion policy. However, looking beyond these national trends to the Buddhicization of local culture and the sinicization of Buddhism as Chinese culture, it is remarkable that the localization of Buddhism was triggered by efforts to institutionally legitimate aspects of local culture, namely, that of laynuns. This official acknowledgment by the local governments of the deep current of sociocultural consciousness and emotion of the local people is reformulating Buddhism in the lay world, and possibly transforming Buddhism by creating it as culture.

NOTES

1. While some scholars writing in English refer to these women as "vegetarian nuns" (i.e., Chang 2007), we prefer the term "laynuns," first used by the anthropologist Marjorie Topley (1956, 126). This is because these women are not simply vegetarian but lead a life-style similar to that of Buddhist nuns, except that they are not ordained and do not shave their heads. The seemingly contradictory term "laynun" expresses their ambiguous situation between layperson and ordained nun. In this essay, we use the term *caigu* rather than *zhaigu* to refer to laynuns in Minnan.

2. Quanzhou, Zhangzhou, and Xiamen are the prefectures that constitute Minnan, a region of 18 million persons. Minnan has a distinct dialect and culture also found in Taiwan and overseas Chinese communities in Malaysia, Singapore, and the Philippines. Each prefecture has a central city, with the same name as its prefecture, surrounded by towns and

rural areas. Xiamen Prefecture is the smallest and most urban prefecture, with a population of 4 million, half of whom live in Xiamen City. For more than a century Xiamen has been one of the most prosperous cities in China.

3. There are several studies of laynuns as a Minnan local tradition (Chen and Cai 1990; Faqing 1992; Zhou 2000; Lin and Li 2014; Serizawa 2012; Li 2014; Wei 2014).

4. The term "orthodox Buddhism" in this chapter refers to Han Buddhism in the People's Republic of China, which is recognized by the Buddhist Association of China.

5. Hongyi (1880–1942) was born as Li Shutong 李叔同 in Zhejiang Province (Zhejiang Sheng 浙江省). He studied art in Shanghai and Tokyo and then was ordained as a monk in 1918. He devoted himself to restoring the study of the Nanshan Vinaya (Nanshan Lüxue 南山律學) and propagating Buddhism. From 1928, he lived in Minnan, teaching in the Buddhist College of Minnan and giving Dharma talks throughout the region. He is well-known for his aesthetic contributions to Buddhism, especially calligraphy (Birnbaum 2017). For his collected writings and art, see Hongyi 2010c.

6. The term *fanxing* 梵行 (Skt. *brahmacharya*) implies virtuous living through asceticism. The term *qing* 清 means pure, which connotes vegetarianism and celibacy. The term *xinnü* 信女 means pious woman, or female devotee. Hongyi combined these terms into the expression "ascetic and pious woman."

7. This chapter focuses on laynuns in Xiamen. We do not mention laynuns in Taiwan and overseas Chinese communities because our argument concerns the changing position and situation of laynuns under CCP religious policy. A broader overview of the laynun phenomenon as seen in their links to China is the subject of our further study.

8. The Buddhist Association of China is the national organization approved by the CCP that represents Buddhism in interacting with the state. It is staffed by clerics and lay practitioners who are vetted by the United Front Work Department, the branch of the CCP that manages non-CCP groups and parties. The BAC is supervised by the State Administration for Religious Affairs (SARA). Its function is to adapt and implement the state religious policy to Buddhism (Wank 2009).

9. The Xiamen Buddhist Association (XBA) is a local version of the BAC that supervises Buddhism in Xiamen.

10. Sectarianism refers to organized folk religious movements that are salvationist and millenarian, as distinct from ancestral lineage worship, local deities, and Buddhism and Taoism.

11. The term *zhai* has numerous meanings depending on context. In religion, it means "purification," as well as the place were rituals are performed. In Buddhism it refers to pure food in temples, which is "vegetarian cuisine" (*zhaishi* 齋食), although in colloquial Chinese, vegetarian food is called "vegetable food" (*caishi* 菜食). The meaning of *zhai* 齋 is purity in a religious sense, while *cai* 菜 refers to vegetables as material objects without any religious connotation. Due to its emphasis on vegetarian food practices, Zhaijiao is usually translated into English as "vegetarian religion" and "fasting religion" (see Seiwert 1992).

12. The term *zhaitang* 齋堂 also refers to the dining room of a Buddhist temple.

13. The links of laynuns to Zhaijiao in the nineteenth and early twentieth centuries are mentioned in the 1993 draft of the *Gazetteer of Xiamen Buddhism* but not in the published version in 2006.

14. The custom of "not leaving the parental home" is similar to those of "not living in the husband's home" (*bu luojia / bu luo fujia* 不落家 / 不落夫家) and "girls' houses" (*nüzai wu* 女仔屋) among minorities and Chinese in Guangdong Province's Pearl River Delta,

studied by, respectively, Topley (1954, 1975) and Stockard (1992). Topley argues that the custom of "not living in the husband's home" started when women who gained independent economic power as silk weavers spurned marriage to stay in their homes. Stockard infers that similar customs among ethnic minorities all along China's eastern coast originated in the delta.

15. Chen Zhenzhen, interview with the authors, Quanzhou, October 2015. Chen Zhenzhen is a woman scholar from a prominent intellectual family in Quanzhou. Well-educated in Chinese studies (Guoxue 国学) from a Christian missionary school, she became a disciple of Hongyi. Since the 1940s, she has been a leader for educating laynuns in Minnan. When we met her in 2015 she was still active at ninety-five years of age. Her life story, which we recorded but do not include in this chapter, spans eight decades of the modern history of laynuns. However, she said that she is not a laynun because she never left her family but is a woman lay practitioner (*nü jushi* 女居士).

16. Xiamen was among the first treaty ports opened to Western trade following China's defeat in the Opium War (1839–1842).

17. For transnational movements of Buddhist clerics and devotees between Xiamen and overseas Chinese communities in Southeast Asia and North America, see Ashiwa and Wank 2005.

18. The New Street Church (Xin Jie Libaitang 新街礼拜堂) opened in 1848.

19. Taixu was a leading advocate of Buddhist modernization in the first half of the twentieth century. He sought to move Buddhism away from its traditional concern with otherworldly detachment toward engagement with society and living people. For this, he developed his understanding of "Buddhism for the human realm" (Pittman 2001; see also chapter 3 by McCarthy in this volume).

20. The size of laynun halls was much larger in Quanzhou, the oldest city in the Minnan region, where up to fifty women resided in a single hall (Chen 2000).

21. The Eight Respected Rules are additional precepts for nuns beyond those required for monks. For example, one rule is that a nun has to obey a monk, even if she was ordained many years before the monk. Today the Eight Respected Rules are seen as an obstacle for nuns to obtain a position equal to that of monks in modern Buddhism.

22. To be recognized in Buddhism as a lay practitioner, a person participates in a ceremony to take the Three Refuges and Five Precepts. The Three Refuges are the Buddha, the Dharma, and the sangha. The Five Precepts are commitments to abstain from harming sentient beings, stealing, sexual misconduct, lying, and intoxication.

23. As Zhaijiao spread in Taiwan, it is possible that Hongyi, who studied in Japan, knew of and was influenced by the phenomenon in the Japanese colony of Taiwan (1895–1945). In Taiwan, laynuns forged ties with prominent clerics without becoming ordained nuns and sought protection for their halls by joining Japanese Buddhist lineages (Jones 1999, 34–94).

24. A female takes 348 precepts for ordination as a nun, while a male takes 250 precepts to be ordained as a monk (see also chapter 6 by Bianchi in this volume).

25. According to a 1955 survey of the 147 laynuns in Xiamen, 125 were illiterate or semiliterate, while only 9 had graduated from middle school (Xiamenshi Fojiao Xiehui 2006, 123).

26. For a related discussion of Dharma lineage among clerics, see chapter 5 by Campo in this volume.

27. Few clerics were ordained from the 1950s until the end of the Cultural Revolution. Consequently, when temples reopened in 1979, there were only a few elderly clerics in their

sixties and seventies. Although there soon emerged a growing number of young clerics in their twenties and thirties, middle-aged, experienced clerics who usually led temple administrations were lacking (see also chapter 7 by Ji in this volume).

28. In 1982, Nanputuo Temple resumed the education of clerics, culminating in the 1985 reopening of the Buddhist College of Minnan.

29. DeVido (2015, 84) notes that the Sichuan Buddhist Academy for Nuns, which opened in 1983 at the Tiexiang Temple 铁像寺, was also among the first Buddhist academies for nuns in the PRC.

30. XBA secretary, interview with the authors, Xiamen, September 2014.

31. Elderly laynun in Miaofalin Hall, interview with the authors, September 1998.

32. Data for the Miaoqing Temple comes from interviews in 1999 and 2000 and from the *Gazetteer of Xiamen Buddhism* (Xiamenshi Fojiao Xiehui 2006, p. 57).

33. In 1927, Taixu appointed Juebin as dean of education in the newly founded Buddhist College of Minnan (Xiamenshi Fojiao Xiehui 2006, 104–105).

34. Data for Jinglian Hall comes from interviews in 1999 and 2000 and from the *Gazetteer of Xiamen Buddhism* (Xiamenshi Fojiao Xiehui 2006, 94).

35. Data for Miaofalin Hall comes from interviews in 1999 and 2000 and from the *Gazetteer of Xiamen Buddhism* (Xiamenshi Fojiao Xiehui 2006, 94–95).

36. Data for Qingfu Temple comes from interviews in 1999 and 2000 and from the *Gazetteer of Xiamen Buddhism* (Xiamenshi Fojiao Xiehui 2006, 93).

37. Head laynun at Qingfu Temple, interview with the authors, August 1999.

38. The names of the laynuns and their hall are not real.

39. Residents' committees (*jumin weiyuanhui* 居民委员会) were created in the 1950s to assist local governments in grassroots policy implementation and policing.

40. It was a national policy from 1962 to 1979 to send urban high school graduates to live in rural villages.

41. Puguang, interview with the authors, Xiamen, August 1999.

42. A political campaign during the Cultural Revolution that mobilized people to "destroy the four olds" (*po si jiu* 破四旧)—customs, culture, habits, and ideas—caused the destruction of many cultural and historical artifacts.

43. These are terms from the popular belief in evil minor spirits.

44. This refers to a person who upholds the political ideas of Chairman Mao.

45. Puguang interview.

46. Guang'an was born in 1924 and served as proctor and prior at the Nanputuo Temple in the 1950s. In 1981, he became vice-chair of the Quanzhou Buddhist Association and prior of Kaiyuan Temple (Kaiyuan Si 开元寺) in Quanzhou before moving to Singapore (Xiamenshi Fojiao Xiehui 2006, 300). He supported the Quanzhou Women's Buddhist College.

47. In the strict laynun tradition observed in the 1980s, laynun halls did not permit nuns to reside in them. In the 1990s, succession problems led laynun halls to accept nuns, as described earlier.

48. Puguang interview.

49. The *Gazetteer of Nanputuo Temple* was published in 2011.

50. The construction of new temples, common in rural areas, was rare in cities at that time.

51. Local governments sometimes made exceptions for a temple whose land had been requisitioned and developed in such a way that it could not be returned to Buddhists. In such cases, the city government assigned a new piece of land to Buddhists to reconstruct the

temple. However, this situation evolved in historically existing temples. It did not apply to the Ciguang Temple because it was a new one with no history.

52. The laynuns could talk with government officials in Minnan dialect, something most clerics in Xiamen could not do, as they were from outside the Minnan region.

53. Local governments in Minnan sought to attract investment from overseas Chinese during the 1980s to stimulate the economy. This made officials especially solicitous to requests from overseas Chinese, including those from clerics.

54. Puci, interview with the authors, Xiamen, August 1999.

55. The Nanputuo Temple Construction Unit was created in the 1980s to restore the temple. It hired rural craftsmen who specialized in carpentry, painting, and masonry from families in Putian and Hui'an Prefectures that had practiced these crafts for generations.

56. The statue of Guanyin has multiple arms, each with an open hand with an eye in the center of the palm.

57. XBA secretary, interview with the authors, September 2014.

58. In China, a temple, church, or mosque is recognized as "open" by a local government when it meets the requirements of the state religious policy for a "religious activity site" (*zongjiao huodong changsuo* 宗教活动场所). One requirement is for religious professionals to be in residence. An open temple can hold religious services for the general public. Places that are not open can have small gatherings, such as Christian house churches.

59. Putian is a prefecture just north of the Minnan region.

60. In Chinese Buddhism, the Bodhisattva Precepts are an additional fifty-eight precepts a Buddhist can take to advance his or her cultivation.

61. XBA secretary, interview with the authors, September 2014.

62. A practice in Xiamen during the 1980s and 1990s was to register a monk to whom the laynuns had a strong tie as the legal owner of the hall. The monk did not reside at the hall but lent his status as a religious professional to satisfy the religious policy requirement that residents of religious sites be religious professionals. A similar practice in Zhangzhou is described by Lin and Li (2014).

63. The registration of religious professionals was completed nationally in 2013, with 316,299 of 322,717 clerics ascertained as religious professionals (Xinhua wang 2013).

64. For our argument that religions can be examined and explained through the interactions of multiple actors in the state and religions, see Ashiwa and Wank 2009.

65. Topley (1975) also describes overlaps in the images of Miaoshan and Guanyin among women marriage resisters (i.e., "not living in the husband's home"), whom she studied in the Pearl River Delta.

66. In his study of popular religious rituals in Fujian, Dean posits the concept of a "preexisting sociocultural force" to explain how rituals condemned by the state persist. He describes how government officials attend popular religious events to give speeches warning against "superstition" and "abnormal religion." While people ignore the speeches, the presence of the officials legitimates the performance of the ritual. Dean writes, "The entire event seemed to swallow them [officials] up in a prearranged ritual of government authorization of a preexisting sociocultural force" (Dean 2009, 197).

67. The name "Nanputuo," literally "South Putuo," refers to Putuoshan, the center of the Guanyin pilgrimage in China, lying several hundred kilometers north of Xiamen.

68. The first documented instance of the Miaoshan story is a stele from 1099 titled *Chronicle of the Bodhisattva of Great Compassion from Fragrance Mountain* (Xiangshan Dabei Pusa Zhuan 香山大悲菩萨传), followed by the *Precious Scroll of Fragrance Mountain*

(Xiangshan Baojuan 香山宝卷), which is dated 1103 (see Dudbridge [1978] 2004, 14–23). In imperial times, these formed the basis for such novels as *The Complete Chronicles of Guanyin of the South Seas* (*Nanhai Guanyin Quanzhuan* 南海观音全传) and such regional operas as *The Emperor's Third Daughter Leaves Home* (*Sanhuang Gu Chujia* 三皇姑出家) and *Guanyin Attains Enlightenment* (*Guanyin De Dao* 观音得道). The legend has also been popularized in modern media as, for example, a 1930s recording of the Minnan opera (*minju* 闽剧) called *The Sad History of Miaoshan* (*Miaoshan Aishi* 妙善哀史) (Shanghai Yiwen Shuju 上海益闻书局), the 1967 movie *The Goddess of Mercy* (*Guanshiyin* 观世音) (Shaw Brothers Pictures International Limited), the 1998 television drama *The Reincarnated Princess* (Guanshiyin 观世音) (Xianggang Dianshi Guangbo Youxian Gongsi 香港電視廣播有限公司), and a 2014 comic book adaptation with the same title as the original 1099 stele (Wenwu Chubanshe 文物出版社).

69. There is a field of study of popular culture and traditional stories related to Miaoshan. See, for example, Sawada 1975 and Dudbridge (1978) 2004.

70. Another name for Miaoshan is "Master of Three Significances" (San Gong Zhu 三公主), which refers to the significant events of her birth, enlightenment, and home leaving. The dates of these three events, based on the lunar calendar, are the same as Guanyin's birthday (February 19), enlightenment (June 19), and home leaving (Guanyin *chujiari* 观音出家日; September 19; see also chapter 2 by Vidal in this volume). This further indicates that Miaoshan is Guanyin.

PART III

Reinventing the Dharma

Buddhism in a Changing Society

9

URBAN RESTRUCTURING AND TEMPLE AGENCY—A CASE STUDY OF THE JING'AN TEMPLE

HUANG WEISHAN

In March 2013, I was a daily guest at the Jing'an Temple (Jing'an Si 静安寺) in Shanghai.[1] After many casual lunch conversations with the abbot, Huiming, and his staff, a semiformal sit-down chat was arranged with the abbot—an event all of my informants had anticipated for weeks. One morning at nine o'clock, with colorful candies and tangerines placed on the conference room table, the abbot entered with his usual efficiency. Within a few minutes, however, an outburst of flashy and sensational pop music came blaring from Jiuguang 九光 Square, which is right outside the west wing of the temple. The music was so loud that we had to stop or repeat our conversation a few times. I took the opportunity to ask about the relationship between the Jing'an Temple and its neighbor, the luxurious Jiuguang Department Store. Abbot Huiming 慧明 replied, "Even in the old times, there were always markets surrounding the temple. This noise could be a tofu vendor trying to sell tofu." Jing'an monastics have accommodated street commercial dances and music day and night for years as Nanjing Road West has further developed into a more affluent street in Shanghai proper. As the abbot pointed out to me, resting at the heart of an urban neighborhood has brought challenges to the temple for centuries, no less so now that it finds itself at the center of a global megacity. But with these challenges for the temple have also come opportunities.

This chapter examines the process of urban temple revival since the 1980s by focusing on the example of the Jing'an Temple, which was first constructed in 247, and its interaction with state-planned urbanization since the 1980s, when it was returned to religious use after being partially destroyed during the Cultural Revolution. A reopened Buddhist temple is compelled to find new niches when it encounters changed patterns of religious and urban identity brought on by neighborhood changes. It is challenged to find new ways of cooperating in its neighborhood and in the wider city. Under these circumstances, Buddhist temple revival is chiefly dependent on three key factors: the ability of religious agents to engage cooperatively with local state forces; productive collaboration between religious leaders and commercial interests; and, most crucially, the vision and determination of the temple's abbot.

JING'AN TEMPLE BEFORE REOPENING

The Jing'an Temple has been renovated numerous times, becoming one of the main local attractions in its area. Historically, renovation of the temple was costly and relied on governors, the local gentry (*shishen* 士绅), and the business class in general.[2] During the years 1862 to 1874, however, most of the temple was destroyed in the Taiping Rebellion, with only one hall remaining. In 1877, several gentry and local businessmen donated funds for its restoration, and on the eighth day of the fourth lunar month in 1880, the temple was reopened for a grand celebration of the Buddha's birthday. An epigraph on the present-day temple wall still marks this event. By the end of the nineteenth century, the spectacle of large crowds of worshippers and busy traffic flows had become commonplace at the temple's annual festival, giving birth to the saying "appreciating the peaches at Longhua [Temple] on the third day of the third lunar month and strolling the temple fair at the Jing'an [Temple] on the eighth day of the fourth lunar month." In 1884, however, the temple faced another challenge when it was forced to relocate its tombs when colonial powers carved up sections of the city. The temple monks and Dongyao Wendong, a member of the gentry, used the proceeds from these increased donations to rebuild the temple.

In the early twentieth century the temple benefited from the urbanization of the local area, which was rapidly developing into an important transportation and communications hub in the growing commercial city. In 1902, a British company set up a telephone exchange center on Jing'an Road. In 1908, another British company built a light rail running though the temple to the bund, a symbol of Shanghai's modernity. In 1919, the street in front of the temple was renamed Jing'an Temple Road by the Shanghai International Settlement. In 1921, the gentrification of the nearby neighborhood of Shanghai West provided the temple with more affluent contributors. In 1934, the temple's gate was extended because the booming growth of shops had overshadowed the temple's visibility.[3] In general, even as the expanding city grew around it, the ancient temple played a vital role in its community by continuing to host regular temple festivals.

After World War II, the relationship between the temple and its neighborhood was further strengthened by the temple's civil missions, which included the provision of secular education and medical services. In this way, the temple was not just like another landlord in the neighborhood. In responding to the problem of orphans in the Jing'an District, the temple established the Jing'an Elementary School on Huashan Road, adjacent to it. It also set up a Buddhist Nanxiang Rural Experimental School in Nanxiang, where the Jing'an Temple's branch temple, Nanxiang Temple (Nanxiang Si 南翔寺), was located. Both of the schools were established and managed by the Jing'an Temple, yet remained secular institutions.[4] In 1948, the temple launched a clinic that contained internal medicine, surgical, and dental departments, among others, on its own real estate. Master Chisong and Master Baisheng, two of the temple's monks, were in charge of clinic management and fund-raising. They successfully raised funds for the clinic by receiving donations of artworks from both domestic and overseas artists.

In the early years of Communist rule, the temple received financial assistance from the city government on two occasions for renovation.[5] In 1950, the whole district around the temple was named after it, a designation that continues today.[6] The temple also continued to play an active role in its local community. During the three-day Buddha Birthday Festival in 1954, there were more than 1,100 booth vendors, mostly homegrown craftspeople; there were more than 210,000 visitors, most of them workers, women, and peasants; and more than 2.2 million RMB was exchanged (Shanghai Jing'an Si 1954, 18).[7] The location of the temple was originally in the most remote part of the west side of the city, but during the growth of the city proper, the neighborhood surrounding it was gentrified. Not only did the value of the land increase and the temple market expand, but the location itself became a major factor in attracting more visitors.

The ancient temple also played a critical leadership role in the Buddhist communities that formed in the Republic of China and the early People's Republic: In 1912, the very first national Buddhist organization, the Headquarters of the General Association of Chinese Buddhism (Zonghua Fojiao Zong Hui 中华佛教总会), was established at the temple, which reflected the temple's political significance at that time. When the Jing'an Buddhist Academy was established in 1946, the well-known master Taixu served as its president. More than one hundred student-monks (xueseng 学僧) graduated from the academy that year. In 1947, the student-monks of the academy began to publish the magazine *Student Monastics' World* (*Xueseng Tiandi* 学僧天地), which contributed to the growing number of Buddhist publications available in Shanghai.

By 1963, however, the temple festival was halted. During the Cultural Revolution, temple statues were destroyed and the monks were forced to leave. Temple buildings were put under the control of the state's Housing Management Bureau (Fangguan Bumen 房管部门) and turned into spaces for manufacturing and storage.[8] In 1972, the main hall was occupied by a dye factory, which caught fire and completely destroyed the main building.

JING'AN TEMPLE IN THE POST-MAO PERIOD: A RECOVERY BASED ON POLITICAL INITIATIVE

Beginning in 1979, a limited number of Protestant and Catholic churches, Buddhist and Taoist temples, and Islamic mosques opened or reopened for religious services (Potter 2003).[9] This included the Jing'an Temple, whose important historical status as a key Han Buddhist temple, recognized by the central state in 1983, made it easier for it to gain assistance from the municipal government for restoration. As with religious revival elsewhere in China (Yang Der-Ruey 2012; Wang Zongyu 2014), the local government, particularly the district government, played a critical role in the temple's initial revival by assisting in the return of some of the temple's land. With the approval of the Shanghai municipal government, the Jing'an Temple Restoration Committee was established in 1984 under the rehabilitated Shanghai Buddhist Association (Shanghai Fojiao Xiehui 上海佛教协会), an arm of the national Buddhist Association of China (BAC).[10] The temple was reopened in 1985. In 1986, 5.17 acres were returned to the temple along with 30,000 RMB from the municipal government.[11] The municipal authorities also officially authorized the temple's registration for their site, which ended the monastery's status of being an unlicensed occupier of its own property.[12] As with many other temples throughout China (see chapter 8 by Ashiwa and Wank and chapter 10 by Fisher in this volume), much of the reclaimed temple property was in disrepair, requiring considerable restoration. In 1988, the main hall was rebuilt. In 1995, a new fifteen-year renovation was started. The current temple looks completely different from the old one, in spite of the fact that it is supposed to be its restoration: After thirty years of restoration, there is not a single roof tile or pillar that has been preserved from the pre-Communist temple. However, the temple crew has claimed this whole process as "renovation" (*gaijian* 改建) rather than "rebuilding" (*chongjian* 重建).

NEIGHBORHOOD CHANGES

The alteration of religious policy has created political opportunities for many religious groups to redevelop or regain growth. However, urban religious organizations also face a new challenge: the transformation of the traditional population. In the 1950s and earlier, the temple performed important religious, social, and economic functions within the local community. These ties were initially severed when the temple was closed during the Cultural Revolution. When the temple reopened in the post-Mao period, the residents could not resume these earlier ties because, as the district played an increasingly important role in Shanghai's rapid urbanization and economic growth, 70 percent of its land was rezoned for commercial use and many of the residents were relocated out of the city center.[13] In the fifteen years between 1998 and 2013 alone, more than fifty thousand residential units in Jing'an District were expropriated, a total of more than sixty-five hundred units for every square kilometer.[14] Seventy percent of what was once a mostly residential district has now been reallocated for commercial use.[15] Various older former residents I interviewed had not visited the temple since its reopening: One informant, who used to live one block away, reported that he only remembered the decayed temple gate and manufacturing sites within the temple during the Cultural Revolution and had never been there since its reopening. He had moved to Xujiahui District after the city-planned urban restructuring. Various older informants reported their memory of the vivacious Buddha Birthday Festival before the Cultural Revolution but had not visited the temple since its recovery.[16] Simply put, whereas during the Cultural Revolution the Jing'an District had been a neighborhood without a temple, since the 1990s it has become a temple without a neighborhood. However, the temple has readjusted to the restructuring of its neighborhood in innovative ways.

THE ABBOT AND TEMPLE GOVERNANCE

The succession of abbots at the Jing'an Temple has had a long and complicated history. Records from the early twentieth century suggest that the appointment of abbots often embroiled the temple, secular authorities, and local gentry patrons in controversy. Fighting between rival Buddhist schools was often played out through succession controversies, and one abbot was even imprisoned for a time.[17] Two features of the national BAC's Regulation for the Governance of Han Chinese Buddhist Temples (Zhongguo Hanchuan Fojiao Guanli Banfa 中国汉传佛教管理办法), established at its Sixth Annual National Meeting in 1993, have significantly influenced the structure of authority at Jing'an Temple in modern times. The first, established in the committee's Article 2, is the establishment of the organizational structure and ownership of the temple's monastic hierarchy as that of the Ten Directions Forest school (Shifang Conglin 十方丛林), and the second, established in Article 3, is the introduction of a Committee for Temple Affairs (Siwu Weiyuanhui 寺务委员会; hereafter the committee).[18] Based on my observations, the committee's revisions cannot prevent a strong centralization of power in the position of the abbot, whose personal agency ends up representing the agency of the temple as a whole.

The temple's most recent abbot, Huiming, has reacted to political and economic opportunities to carve out an agentive role for the temple. Huiming was born in 1968 in Jiangsu Province. In addition to being abbot of the Jing'an Temple, he is also deputy secretary-general of the Buddhist Association of China, chair of the Shanghai Buddhist Association, and principal of the Shanghai Buddhist Academy (Shanghai Foxueyuan 上海佛学院). He was first ordained as a monk at the Yufo Temple in Shanghai in 1983. He then studied at the Shanghai Buddhist Academy from 1983 to 1989. In 1988, he was hired as the guest prefect (zhike 知客) in the Yufo Temple and appointed as the prior-in-training (jianxue 监学) at the Shanghai Buddhist Academy.[19] He graduated from the graduate program at the academy in 1989 and taught there before serving as its vice-provost from 1993 to 2003. In 1995, he was appointed as the prior (jianyuan 监院) at the Jing'an Temple. In 1998, he was elected vice-chair of the Shanghai Buddhist Association. In 2000, he was promoted to abbot of the Jing'an Temple. In 2003, he became the principal of the Shanghai Buddhist Academy. In 2015, he was elected as chair of the Shanghai Buddhist Association. Huiming's achievements have also extended into the secular sphere: In 2008, he became a member in the standing committee of the Shanghai Municipal People's Congress. He received a PhD in history from Fudan University in 2009. Huiming's long experience in positions of power within different groups and associations surrounding Buddhism in Shanghai has made it easier for the abbot to mobilize different people and resources in regrowing the temple.

THE ORGANIZATIONAL STRUCTURE

The modern Jing'an Temple followed the teaching of the Caodong school (Caodong zong 曹洞宗) until 1947.[20] In 1947, the temple was transformed into a Ten Directions Forest school monastery. In terms of the function assumed among the temple monastics, the temple abbot (zhuchi 住持) is the main person in charge. The provost (dujian 都监) is the second in charge, to assist the abbot. The prior is in the third position. The provost is in charge of the monastics, while the prior presides over temple affairs. The temple provost and prior both have to host visitors from various political sections nationwide. The guest prefect is responsible for the reception of guests, while the precentor (weinuo 維那) is in charge of discipline among temple clergy. Most of the monks at Jing'an were hired after they graduated from the Shanghai Buddhist Academy, whereas the abbot, Huiming, is the current principal, so he has a lot of influence among them. The committee is composed of the abbot, the provost, the prior, the head of the Cultural Relics Department (Wenwu Bumen 文物部门), who is also the head of the Fuhui Foundation (Fuhui Jijinhui 福慧基金会, a philanthropic foundation), the head of the Renovation Department (Gaijian Bumen 改建部门), and one member of the administrative staff.[21] Both the head of the Cultural Relics Department and the head of the Renovation Department are retirees from former government sectors. They regard themselves as non-Buddhists. The management of the temple is dually run by the committee and the traditional Forest school hierarchy (conglin zhi 丛林制). This apparent dual system of authority is further complicated by the presence of outside managers: For example, Huiming has also hired a professional accountant and cultural relics manager, who are part of the clergy. As in most temples I observed in Shanghai, all persons connected with the temple—whether monastics or secular leaders—recognize the undisputed authority of the abbot, as the following example shows.[22]

The temple committee is supposed to hold an official meeting once a month. Based on my observation, the abbot and the department heads meet as a group for a daily lunch, and in all of their conversations it appears that the abbot is the dominant decision maker. Most of the conversations during my 2013 fieldwork were focused on the details of construction sites, materials, and prices. For example, one important new construction during my visit was that of a decorative dragon-shaped ridge on the top of the drum house. The abbot felt that newly imported copper tiles from Japan worked much better than the old glazed tiles, which had started falling down from the roof a few years previously, causing safety issues. The abbot decided to replace all of the roof tiles just as he decided how any of the elements in the temple needed to be replaced or how they should be constructed. During many lunches in which I participated, the temple abbot was indeed the leader, not only making all of the key decisions but also identifying all of the needs in the temple.

Huiming's further conversations with me revealed how pivotal a role an abbot's determined leadership can play in Buddhist revival. He explained to me his vision of promoting Buddhism as well as the sources of his inspiration. He once stood on top of a Buddhist pagoda in Beijing and was surprised to see that the pagoda was used for a nonreligious purpose, housing a monument to a non-Buddhist politician. Since then, he swore to redeem Buddhism one day. The drive for the continuing renovation of the Jing'an Temple has been an important part of fulfilling that personal goal of redemption for the abbot. Drawing a map, he explained to me how the reopened temple was very small in the early 1990s. "The gate was so small that visitors consistently missed the entryway. They had to walk back until they reached Huashan Road. There was a chicken shop on the right side and Jing'an Bank on the other side. No one knew that there was a temple here," he said. As Huiming explained it, because the local government had only returned just over five acres to the temple at that time, it was not possible for it to hold large rituals such as the Ceremony of Saving the Lives of the Water and the Land (Shuilu Fahui 水陆法会).

THE OPPORTUNITY OF TEMPLE EXPANSION FROM URBAN RESTRUCTURING

With the government's 1982 ruling, the Jing'an Temple was reopened. Nevertheless, the temple's monastic leaders were not content with just this, but wanted the temple to be further restored, which included taking back some of the land that had not yet been returned to it. Apart from their determination to use the temple to promote Buddhism, the temple leaders aimed to build a strong reputation for themselves through the restoration, since the achievements and criteria for advancement of monastics in Shanghai is often linked to their ability to carry out successful renovation.

This opportunity for further renovation came in 1995 when the city government started building the number 2 metro line on Nanjing West Road near the temple; to make room for the metro, it planned the demolition of some buildings and the relocation of their residents and businesses. Rather than resist the dismantling of what had once been part of the temple's surrounding neighborhood, Huiming advised city governors and the temple followers to "abide by the government's policy on relocation."[23] He took the "opportunity" raised by the reconfiguration of the temple area to petition the Jing'an Bank and the chicken shop, which bordered the temple, to relocate, enabling the temple to continue its project of "restoration" by regaining more of its original land. However, in order to have the Jing'an Bank and the chicken shop relocated, the temple would have to pay for a large amount of the relocation compensation: The chicken shop had to accept the offer to move out since the owner was just a tenant of the temple, but the bank requested 50 million RMB in compensation, a large amount of money in 1996.

Part of this money was offset when the city decided to build one of the metro exits directly under the temple's drum tower, for which it provided compensation of 6 million RMB to the temple. However, other sources of financing proved more elusive: Neither the Religious Affairs Bureau nor the Shanghai Buddhist Association wanted to get involved in financing the twenty-nine-year-old abbot's visionary scheme because they thought he was too ambitious. The abbot eventually persuaded the bank to agree on a settlement of 31 million RMB, but 25 million RMB were still needed. It seemed impossible to find these funds, but then, finally, when Huiming was at a point of extreme desperation, another Buddhist temple, the Zhenru Temple (Zhenru Si 真如寺), lent the money.[24]

However, the construction was more expensive than originally imagined, so Huiming had to employ an additional strategy to realize his vision: He teamed up with real estate developers to rebuild the temple. In return for their experienced help with planning for the restoration and in lowering construction costs, the developers were given the titles to manage and collect rent from shops on both sides of the temple for twenty-two years. Teaming up with real estate developers to restore the temple challenged the popular stereotype of what is sacred and what is worldly profit making.[25] However, Huiming was convinced that this was the only way to find the resources to finally achieve his aim of restoration. In addition to the funds provided by secular commercial developers, he also held many water and land ceremonies to collect donations from practitioners at large. After each festival, he would preach for twenty minutes, explaining to practitioners his future plans for the temple. In this way, he gained popularity and legitimacy for his large-scale renovation project.

The temple renovation project was very expensive not only because of the high costs of construction, but also due to the demand for land. During the dispute concerning whether the Jing'an Temple should acquire the land from the former Jing'an Bank, there was also debate over the planned relocation of the temple into nearby Jing'an Park. Huiming successfully argued that the Jing'an Temple had been in that exact spot for a thousand years; therefore, the temple should not be relocated anywhere else; rather, businesses should have to relocate so that the temple could function as a glittering jewel in the heart of this commercial district. The Shanghai Buddhist Association also lent its authority to battle the infiltration of further commercial development into the neighborhood. Due to Huiming's ingenuity and perseverance, what could have been the further erosion of the temple's land from the construction of the metro line became the means for the temple to acquire new land and rebuild.

With space for the temple secured, Huiming turned his attention to creating the interior temple, a process that has taken up much of the subsequent two decades. Besides building up a basic infrastructure, Huiming believed that it was important for the temple to present an impressive spectacle to visitors. In the abbot's own words, he wanted to "build a temple which people cannot tear down." As Mr. Gao, the head of the renovation team, explained to me, the design of the Jing'an Temple is based on the style of the Song dynasty.[26] The architectural additions of roof ridges (*jiwe* 脊吻), cornices, and decorative brackets were made from a careful selection of imported Burmese teakwood. When I spotted a picture in Mr. Gao's office of Abbot Huiming standing in a forest, I was told that the picture was taken while the abbot was picking up teak in the Burmese woods. When I asked why the abbot needed to travel all the way to a foreign country to select the wood for the temple's construction, Mr. Gao replied with an expression of surprise on his face as if I had not understood the crucial point that nothing in the temple was put there by accident. From the designs to the materials themselves, everything was specifically chosen by the abbot.

Mr. Gao told me about other memorable structures in the renovated temple: A 3.3-meter peace bell weighing 7.3 tons cast in bronze was erected, and a historic Jing'an Bubble Well (Jing'an Yongquan 静安涌泉) was recovered and constructed below the bell tower, with its head fashioned in a hexagonal shape and made of a single piece of Jinshan 金山 stone.[27] The wall of the well was reconstructed with 666 pieces of granite, with the base stone weighing six thousand kilograms. A Jing'an pagoda was built in the northwest corner of the temple. The design of its upper story was based on that of the pagoda in Beijing that had first inspired Huiming to dedicate himself to the revival of Buddhism many years before. The ornamentation decorating the upper story of the pagoda is made of gold gilt.

When, in a 2015 visit, I heard criticism from a few Chinese scholars regarding the architectural style of Jing'an Temple, saying it was falling into the trap of "luxury Buddhism" (*shehua fojiao* 奢华佛教), a critique they made of the many massive construction projects and ornate decorations of newly renovated temples in the post-Mao period, I wondered how the abbot would respond, especially since there were calls for donations for the construction of the Golden Buddha at the time. The abbot was irritated and refused to respond. About one minute later, he replied, after staring at me, that "Buddhism was once under calamity. Now it is our chance to build up something that will last forever."

Today, many high-ranking staff members of the Jing'an Temple recall the historical decisions to renovate the temple and the manner in which Abbot Huiming made them happen with vision and determination. The abbot had the power to decide to demolish the old buildings and rebuild the temple in Song-style architecture. Although the staff had different opinions about how the temple should look in twentieth-century China, the final renovation was valued as such a big success that other temples followed Jing'an's model in their plans for expansion.

THE REVITALIZATION OF RELIGIOUS AND PHILANTHROPIC ACTIVITIES

Under Huiming's efforts, the temple not only has built up an impressive structure but also has witnessed the revival of monastic, lay, and devotional activities. Although there are still restrictions on religious activities, state-approved religious sites like the Jing'an Temple are important urban spaces for the development of religious rituals, including those that cannot always be depicted by the state as merely "cultural events." There are public Buddhist lectures on Saturdays at the temple, each drawing about two hundred lay participants. Most of those attending are elderly female laypersons who are very conversant with the major Chinese Buddhist sutras. The speakers are mostly faculty members from the Shanghai Buddhist Academy. The two-hour lectures begin with the lay participants reciting the sutras; following this, the speakers pose questions.

Every year on the day of the Chongyang Festival (Chongyang Jie 重阳节), the Jing'an Temple will make and deliver "long-life noodles" (*chang shou mian* 长寿面) to the elderly in the neighboring housing communities in Jing'an District and invite seniors from the city to participate in a long-life noodle banquet in the temple restaurant. Through conversations from the latter part of my fieldwork, I came to realize that the community's elders were the key population the Community Resident Committee (CRC) focused on. The majority of CRC programs were designed for them. When I asked the elders how they felt when they received the noodles from the temple's Dharma masters (*fashi* 法师), they replied that they felt honored and happy. Every year, the Jing'an Temple gives a scholarship to neighborhood students. The CRC also arranges a temple tour for scholarship recipients. Mr. Sun, the party secretary of the CRC, mentioned that there are some neighborhood residents who will volunteer in the temple on the first and fifteenth days of each month in the lunar calendar. Since volunteerism was a practice promoted by the state during the Beijing Olympics in 2008 and Shanghai Expo in 2010, the Jing'an CRC was encouraged to bring this agenda back to their residential community. The Jing'an Temple was seen as a good fit, as residents volunteered in the temple and implemented the practice of volunteerism in the neighborhood. However, I noticed that most of the actual volunteers were young people. When I spoke with

Abbot Huiming, he told me that this was because it was his vision to organize young volunteers, not the neighborhood elders, which showed that Huiming did not always share the views of the local government. He acted on his own vision of what an urban monastery should be.

Not all of the temple's projects of community outreach have met with success, however. In 2012, the abbot tried to develop a print magazine to teach Buddhism to the public, but the Shanghai Buddhist Association stalled on granting permission for the project. The would-be editor of this magazine, Yi, is a female in her late twenties, third-generation Buddhist, a representative in the Political Consultative Conference of the Chinese People (Zhengxie 政协), a key staffer in the local lay association (*jushilin* 居士林), and a lecturer at the university. When I asked Yi the reason for the delay in publication of the magazine, she replied that it was not because of a lack of enthusiasm among the lay volunteers of the magazine, but rather that state policies had not advanced far enough to permit publication. When I asked for the details of the state's disapproval, she only said that the volunteers should focus on what they could do at the moment, which was reorganizing the temple archives. When I asked a similar question of the abbot, he briefly answered that the development of public media is an issue of considerable delicacy.

While the magazine has yet to be published, the temple has attracted a lot of visitors: On Lunar New Year's Eve in 2013, the crowd at the temple was so large that the temple staff was concerned about public safety. The next morning, more than one hundred thousand people visited the temple even after the abbot deliberately raised the ticket price from 40 RMB to 100 RMB in order to control the crowds. It is hard to miss a long queue outside of the temple on Nanjing Road starting from the first day until the fifteenth day of the first lunar month.

While the presence of so many worshippers on important festival days along with its organized activities for laypersons point to the temple's strength as an active religious site, the example of the government's restriction of its proposed publication of a magazine points to the state's continued ambivalence about the temple's religiosity. As the next section explores, much of this ambivalence is negotiated in terms of whether the temple functions as a "cultural" or a "religious" site.

INTERACTION WITH THE LOCAL GOVERNMENT

In the middle of my conversation with CRC party officials one day, a guest dropped in. The Jing'an CRC party secretary and the office director both stood up to receive him and introduced him as a higher official (*lingdao* 领导) to me. When I asked politely for his name and title, he shied away and told me that it was "not convenient" (*bu fangbian* 不方便), meaning that he did not want to or could not say. After he realized the nature of my visit, he scolded the others for speaking with me. One CRC party secretary explained to him that I was introduced by Master Yayun 亚蕴, the provost of the Jing'an Temple, so they were required to receive me. After this official spent more than thirty minutes scolding me on how improperly "we," that is, the Taiwanese diaspora, behave in Shanghai, he shifted the subject back to the relationship between the local government and the temple. He pointed out that there was some coordination between the two sides, adding that it was "reasonable for the monastery to return the favors or conduct some charitable work in the neighborhood since they have caused a lot of inconvenience for their neighbors. The construction of the temple has been going on and on for years. You can see the Yuyuan Road is very small. Can you think about all the pollution and noise and dust and traffic jams caused by this construction?" He was right about one thing: After twenty years, the temple restoration project was still going on.

By contrast, Director Li of the Jing'an Subdistrict Office of the People's Government of Jing'an District (Jing'an Qu Renmin Zhengfu Jing'an Jiedao Banshichu 静安区人民政府静安街道办事处) voiced a very positive view of the revival of the temple. He considered the impact of noise or dust as being very minimal to the local neighborhood and saw the reconstruction of the temple as part of a successful state-planned urban renewal, which initially responded to Deng Xiaoping's call in the late 1980s to build up Shanghai to as large a scale as possible. When I asked Li about the roles of the temple in today's Jing'an District, he replied that it has two functions. The first is that it enriches the urban culture. He explained that he has witnessed that there is always a long queue of devotees waiting to get into the temple during the first and fifteenth days of each month in the lunar calendar. "People come from everywhere to visit the temple," said Li. "The second is the function of charity," he added, noting that the monastery had donated a lot of money not only to the city for charity but also to the Jing'an CRC, especially for the elderly. In Li's eyes, the temple has become a critical institution for the development of the Jing'an commercial zone in terms of contributing to social causes. When I went over the donation list of the Fuhui Charitable Foundation with the foundation director, I discovered that most of the funds were donated to charitable events organized by the government, including local governments, such as scholarships distributed by the Jing'an Subdistrict Office.

Jing'an District has been designated by the district and city governors as a "double advanced" district (shuanggaoqu 双高区) for the twenty-first century. The district governor has vowed to build up not only advanced and high-ranking commercial areas, but also an advanced and high-quality neighborhood. In this context, the refurbished Jing'an Temple carries important cultural symbolism for the district and the city. In the view of officials like Li, who referred positively to the activities of devotees following the ritual calendar, this cultural role is not necessarily separate from the temple's religious functions. However, some of the leading temple monks are more wary of local authorities' desires to promote the temple as a cultural site. The temple's provost once complained to me that most of his day is occupied by accompanying visiting party leaders and governors from all over China on tours of the temple. Indeed, when I looked at his schedule, I could see that he spent more than 90 percent of his time in touring with important guests. He described both district and city governors as utilizing the temple as a "cultural business card."

When I asked how they engaged with the topic of religious "Buddhism" during tours, all of the party secretaries in the CRC insisted that they always introduced the Jing'an Monastery as one of several important cultural sites of the city. In Wang Zongyu's research on the revival of the Dongyue Temple (Dongyue Miao 东岳庙) in Beijing, he pointed out one important statist narrative, a view he shared with Han Xiuzhen: "The process (of recovery) [is] strategic. In order to take over the resources and space released by the state, the local city governors, who are the decision-makers, could not revitalize the temple in the name of 'religion,' which would challenge party ideology. Therefore, they revitalized the temple in the name of revitalizing 'folk culture'" (Wang Zongyu 2014, 331–332). The mayor of Beijing even gave the order that the Dongyue Temple should not be recognized as a religious site. A similar view informs many Shanghai and Jing'an District officials' views of the Jing'an Temple, but, unlike the officials described by Wang in Beijing, many of the local officials I talked to in Shanghai, like Director Li, do not necessarily see the "cultural" and "religious" functions of the temple as mutually exclusive: They perceive the temple as a cultural site preserved in Chinese tradition, with Buddhism (a religion) as a part of that well-recognized tradition. However, there are also limits to how far the state will go in tolerating the promotion of the temple's religious role.

In 2010, before the start of the world expo held in Shanghai, Amrit Shakya, the director of the Nepal pavilion at the expo, was planning for the installation of a holy flame (shenghuo 圣火) from Lumbini, the sacred land where Buddha was born. Shakya requested that the holy flame be temporarily accommodated in the Jing'an Temple between August 23 and September 3, that is, between the time of its arrival in China and the official opening of the Nepal pavilion. The abbot and the temple committee were quite enthusiastic about this form of sacred transnational religious cooperation. They held several preparation meetings in August and included members from the United Front Work Department and the Office of the Director of the Religious Affairs Bureau of Jing'an District. "It was a great honor to be chosen to accommodate the holy flame," Fan, the head of the Cultural Relics Department in the temple said. However, in the end, the temple's hosting of the flame was not approved. When I asked him about the reason for the disapproval, with some disappointment, Fan replied that the municipal authorities thought that hosting the flame would be "too religious."

However, a later incident points to the willingness of the authorities to recognize the "religious" character of the temple, particularly when it enables them to avoid potential dissent. On November 15, 2010, right after I left

Shanghai, there was a large fire in a tall building on Jiaozhou Road in Jing'an District. It was started by human error in repairing electrical connections in the middle of the night. Once the fire started, the city government did not have the capacity to put the blaze out. The building was too tall, and many burned to death without a chance of rescue. The event represented a significant case of institutional failure. The people of the city were shocked by the tragedy, and the community mourned the dead. A sociologist informant, Liu, who is a professor at a local university, said to me, "In order to cover up the number of casualties, the media didn't release an accurate death toll." The anger of the mourning crowds was translated into social action: "More than 10,000 Shanghai residents placed flowers in front of the debris in order to remember the dead. It was a silent but powerful way for the residents to express their feelings," Liu said.

The following year, I discovered that, immediately following the tragedy, Abbot Huiming donated 1 million RMB in the name of the temple to the victims' families. Within six days, the temple also collected another 310,000 RMB from the temple staff and the public. The temple also held Buddhist funeral rituals to mark both the third and fourth periods of seven days (*san qi, si qi* 三七、四七) following the incident. In reviewing the photos of the ceremonies in the temple's yearbook, I found elaborate decorations in the rituals involving colorful paper horses. Those paper horses were burned during the ceremony for victims, marking the first time the temple was permitted to hold a large-scale burning of ritual paper within its courtyard. On December 18, the eve of the fifth seven-day period after the incident, the temple held an "offering sacrifice to protect the departed spirits" (*fang yankou* 放焰口). On the nineteenth, the temple held Buddhist funeral rituals to commemorate the fifth seven-day period of the incident. Dewu 德悟, an elder monk who had led the temple's recovery in the early 1990s, was invited back to officiate the whole ceremony to demonstrate the significance of the event. More than two hundred family members of the victims participated in the ceremony. The commemorative rituals continued until the Lunar New Year in 2011. Not only was the religious service to the dead personal for the victims' families; it was also socially significant for the city residents collectively. The incident of people who died through "injustice" (*wangsi* 枉死) needed to find closure, and this "public" Buddhist funeral ritual offered some comfort to those affected by the tragedy.

By December 14, the party leader from the Jing'an District, the mayor of the district, the district committee chairman, and the district commissioner of the United Front Work Department had visited the temple to express their gratitude to Huiming for how he dealt with the aftermath of the fire incident (*shanhou* 善后). This can be considered tacit permission from the United Front Work Department for what the abbot had been doing. In a later interview with a temple staffer, I learned that, because the temple had offered space to display more than forty photos of the victims for the purposes of commemoration,[28] the city government could legitimately drive out any residents who attempted to send in flowers or stay near the debris area, arguing that, in the temple, there was a designated space for them to express their grief.

When the district mayor and the official of the United Front Work Department visited the temple abbot, it was a gesture of consent and appreciation for the temple's contribution. In the eyes of local Jing'an officials, the comfort of religious rituals had prevented the possible escalation of discontent suggested by the silent protests. In this way, in the minds of the authorities, the temple had effectively integrated itself into the community by offering its religious functions and support. The power relationship between the local government and the temple was proved negotiable and the abbot has gained legitimacy for the temple to be treated as a religious entity over time.

A similar event further illustrates the carefully calibrated reconciliation between the religious and cultural identities of the temple. In 2014, I was informed that the temple had received its second relic of the Buddha (*fo zhi sheli* 佛指舍利), part of his thumb. The temple staff was overjoyed in sharing this information when I met them, and I was granted the chance to pay my respects to the relic in a locked worship room. When I asked why both of the relics were not available to the public, the abbot replied, "We have to keep a low profile." He explained that the temple was extremely privileged to be able to receive the second sacred donation, and it would be wiser to stay low-key about it. However, in 2015 the abbot decided to make the relics available to the public. That summer, they were displayed as cultural relics (*fo zhi shelizhan* 佛指舍利展) in the Jing'an Museum. It was a sensational exhibition among Buddhists. On my entrance into the museum, I ran into a Tzu Chi sister,[29] one of my former informants, at the door. She told me that she was very touched when she paid tribute to the relics. Once I stepped into the exhibition room, I noticed that all of the people in the room, rather than simply gazing at the relics in admiration, as one might expect for a "museum" exhibition, were kneeling and whispering prayers as devotees. The large number of prostrating devotees made the space quite crowded and imbued it with the disorderly feel of a worship site rather than the regulated space of a museum. However, the devotees who tried to donate money could not find the donation box since the event was designed as an exhibition. Some of them just left the money and envelopes on the fence or floor. The guard, a young monk, tried to stop visitors from leaving money, but the people seemed confused about what to do. This event showed that the temple had come further in functioning as a high-profile religious site, but at the same time, the state's insistence on its role as a cultural site was still felt in the designation of the relic hosting as a cultural exhibition. The inability of the devotees to leave offerings points to the continuing ambivalence between the two designations.

Nevertheless, the temple is growing overall and its religious activities are expanding. It is also still undergoing restoration. The staff works closely and energetically with government authorities for the purposes of receiving charity. Religious services, including Buddhist funerals (*foshi* 佛事), the Ceremony of Saving the Lives of the Water and the Land, and the Ceremony of the Bodhisattva Ksitigarbha (Dizang Fahui 地藏法会) are held periodically. I also noticed that there has been an increase in the holding of salvation rites (*chaodu fahui* 超度) and collection of monetary donations for domestic and international disasters, such as the earthquakes in Nepal and Tibet (May 15, 2015) and the chemical explosion in Tianjin 天津 (August 14, 2015). This continuation of commemorative services along with the temple's continued involvement in charitable giving shows how, following the fire incident of 2010, it continues to seek an acceptable religious role for itself in the eyes of the municipal authorities.

Moreover, for the first time, in October 2016, the temple was allowed to conduct a series of religious festivals and water and land ceremonies at the Shanghai Exhibition Center (Shanghai Zhanlan Zhongxin 上海展览中心), a space outside of the temple. In the beginning, the people in charge of the exhibition center refused to lend the space to the temple because they had never worked with a religious community and set up the rule that "everyone who joins the events in the exhibition center has to wear Western-style suits" (*xizhuang* 西装). Abbot Huiming was furious and argued, "I was never asked to

Jing'an Temple on West Nanjing Road, Shanghai, summer 2013. Photo by the author.

wear Western-style suits even when I attended the local people's assembly." In the end, the space rental in the exhibition center was approved because the exhibition center accepted that Buddhist practice is part of Chinese traditional culture. In this way, however, the abbot and the temple, using the rubric of "culture," have found ways not only to expand the range of religious activities in their own temple, but also to spread them further into public space.

STUDYING "TEMPLE AGENCY"

Harry Frankfurt's (1971) definition concerning freedom of action is "acting on a desire with which the agent identifies." How have the agents in my study of the Jing'an Temple reacted to political and economic opportunities and challenges over its thirty years of restoration? I hypothesize that the sources of change are primarily environmental, such as policy changes and neighborhood changes; they force the religious institution to adjust to what is going on around it, economically and politically (Ammerman, Tatom, and Farnsley 1997; Cimino, Mian, and Huang 2013). However, the Buddhist institution is not just forced to change passively. As I have explained in this chapter, the temple is sometimes shaped by government policy; at other times, it acts as the agent that shapes it.

In the Mao era and early post-Mao period, it seems that the Jing'an Temple was mostly shaped by changing policy, with little agency of its own. Yet, beginning from the 1990s, the temple employed the government's policies on urban renewal to gain resources (money and space) and complete its development in cooperation with secular commercial firms. After establishing its legitimacy, the temple worked together with commercial partners to rebuild. Under conditions of neighborhood gentrification, it has created its own niches by which it relates to its population most particularly in its commemoration services for those who were victims of the 2010 fire in the district. Moreover, as the ceremonies at the Shanghai Exhibition Center show, while the temple's religious projects are sometimes restricted by authorities' fear that their religious nature has exceeded a "cultural" function, the temple sometimes is also able to use the label of culture to advance the public visibility of Buddhist religiosity. At each stage, the temple's assertion of agency and influence has been facilitated by the determination, resourcefulness, and political savvy of its abbot.

NOTES

1. This chapter is based on fieldwork I conducted at Jing'an Temple from 2013 to 2016, funded by an RGC General Research Fund (project no. 14609315).

2. For example, the assistant minister of rites for feudal China (*libu shilang* 礼部侍郎) donated the money and rebuilt the main hall of the temple. In 1741, a merchant from She 歙 County donated money to rebuild the whole temple. The same year, a Qing inspector

(*xundao* 巡道) dredged the renowned temple bubble well (*yongquan* 涌泉) and donated twenty-four acres of land to the temple.

3. The Office of Shanghai Local History (Shanghai Shi Difang Zhi 上海市地方志), accessed December 27, 2015, http://www.shtong.gov.cn.

4. The five board members of the Buddhist Nanxiang Rural Experimental School were Master Chisong, then abbot of the Jing'an Temple, Master Baisheng, Zhao Puchu, Mao Xiaotong, and Guheng.

5. A renovation committee was established, and many prominent Buddhist leaders of the Republican era, including Yuanying 园瑛, Chisong 持松, Weifang 苇舫, Qingding 清定, and Zhao Puchu 赵朴初 were among its members. Jing'an Boke 静安博客, Shanghai Jing'an Si 上海静安寺, accessed December 10, 2015, http://www.shjas.org/a/cwgc/gcls/gcls/20150407/2.html.

6. In 1950, the district was named the Jing'an Temple District. In 1951, the district was named Jing'an District. In 1956, the whole district was renovated under urban renewal. In 1961, the district was re-created.

7. I am thankful for the assistance of Dr. Shao Jiade in collecting data from the Republican era for my project.

8. Jing'an Boke 静安博客, Shanghai Jing'an Si 上海静安寺, accessed December 10, 2015, http://www.shjas.org/a/cwgc/gcls/gcls/20150407/2.html.

9. As of 2016, about 108 Buddhist temples have been reopened and more than one thousand new monks and nuns registered in Shanghai.

10. The president and deputy president of the Temple Restoration Committee at the Jing'an Temple in 1984 were Master Zhenchan 真禅 and lay Buddhist Jia Jingsong 贾劲松. Mingyang 明旸 and Jia were the director and vice-director of the Jing'an Temple Restoration Committee at that time.

11. The Jing'an Temple has had a very complicated history regarding its property. The monastery used to generate income through renting out its land during the Qing dynasty and the Republican period. However, the monastery did not receive a property license until 1951. Even before 1945, there were several lawsuits with private individuals regarding the temple property (Jing'an Si Sichan 1947).

12. Other former areas of the temple, such as housing units in the Suiyun 随云 neighborhood, were not returned to the temple but placed under the control of the housing management of the Shanghai BAC. However, the profits generated from the rent of these units now have become income for the Shanghai Buddhist Association.

13. Jing'an District, located in downtown Shanghai, is as small as 7.62 square kilometers but has been at the heart of some of Shanghai's most significant development in the post-Mao period.

14. Office of Shanghai History 上海地方志办公室, accessed September 30, 2015, http://www.shtong.gov.cn. The compilation of this data was completed by Eliot Lee and Cheng Yu Yan in the Department of Cultural and Religious Studies (CRS) at the Chinese University of Hong Kong in November 2015.

15. Director Li, Jing'an Subdistrict Office of the People's Government of Jing'an District, interview with the author, Jing'an Subdistrict Office of the People's Government of Jing'an District, March 14, 2013.

16. There are some exceptions to this trend of not returning: In 2016, I ran into four people from Shanghai and Hong Kong who reported that they have returned to the temple

for the Annual Ceremony of Saving the Lives of the Water and the Land since 1997. The explanation for their loyalty to this particular temple is that this was the temple at which they worshipped with their grandmothers or mothers in the 1950s. However, for many former residents of the neighborhood, it was not convenient to return once their residency had been displaced.

17. The succession of abbots is a complicated issue: In 1915, Abbot Zhengsheng 正生 passed away, with his successor, Qinfang 琴方, also dying in the same year. Liugen 六根 took over the position, but he immediately stirred up suspicion among the gentry concerning his legitimacy and was imprisoned. The Shanghai Administrative Office favored the gentry and granted temple governance to the chair of the Shanghai Buddhist Association and the gentry who cosupervised the temple affairs. In 1922, Yangxi 仰西 promoted the reform of the temple to follow the hierarchy of the Ten Directions Forest school while he was the chair of the Shanghai Buddhist Association. This reform created disputes between the followers of the Ten Directions Forest school and those who preferred the hereditary temple (*zisun pai* 子孙庙) system. Yangxi was later acclaimed as the general representative to supervise Jing'an affairs. In 1923, Liugen was released from jail, and Yangxi appointed Xinru 心如 to be the new abbot. The gentry disapproved of the appointment of Xinru because they supported Zhiwen 志汶 of the Disciple school as successor to the seat. In their complaint, the gentry accused Yangxi of selling land and valuable items from the temple for private purposes. After Xinru resigned, the Shanghai Buddhist Association appointed Jishan 寂山 as the abbot. Zhiwen later returned to the temple with the help of local policemen and appointed himself as the abbot.

18. In 1989, the national BAC first drafted the Pilot Regulation for the Governance of Han Buddhist Temples (Hanchuan Fojiao Simiao Guanli Shixing Banfa 汉传佛教寺庙管理试行办法), which established the temple hierarchy for all Han Chinese Buddhist temples as that of the Ten Directions Forest school.

19. The English translations of monastic titles provided in this chapter are taken from Welch 1967.

20. In this section, all of the data related to the Jing'an Temple before 1990 was collected from the Office of Shanghai History (Shanghai Difang Zhi Bangongshi 上海地方志办公室), accessed February 24, 2016, http://shtong.gov.cn.

21. There were six members of the temple committee in 2015.

22. In this way, it differs from the example of the Kaiyuan Temple provided by Brian Nichols (chapter 4 in this volume), who depicts an ongoing struggle for authority between the Kaiyuan abbot and its Temple Administrative Commission.

23. After the former abbot Zhenchan passed away in 1995, Huiming, then provost, was the highest-ranking monk at the temple and became its "person in charge" (*dangjia* 当家), even though he had not been officially promoted to abbot. Following the further expansion of the temple, he was promoted to abbot.

24. In my research in Shanghai, I found that loans between temples are not uncommon. A timely loan from another temple also assisted in the recovery of the Xiahai 下海 Temple. Wu Rui's (2008, 30) research on the San Guan Tang 三观堂 Temple, another Buddhist temple in Shanghai, illustrates another case.

25. In further investigation in the summer of 2016, I found one more case of a Buddhist institution working closely with a real estate developer.

26. Mr. Gao's name, along with others in this chapter with the exception of the abbot Huiming, is a pseudonym.

27. Jinshan (Golden Mountain) stone (Jinshan *shi* 金山石) is a type of stone that comes exclusively from a mountain of the same name in nearby Suzhou 苏州.

28. With the exception of adherents of Christianity, the victims' families were invited to set up commemoratory spaces within the Jing'an Temple.

29. A lay commissioner from the Shanghai Tzu Chi Foundation.

10

PLACES OF THEIR OWN

Exploring the Dynamics of Religious Diversity in Public Buddhist Temple Space

GARETH FISHER

Like chapter 9 by Huang Weishan, this chapter focuses on Buddhist temples in post-Mao China that have been legally designated by the state as "religious activity sites" (*zongjiao huodong changsuo* 宗教活动场所). While Huang's chapter attends to the complex negotiations between monastic and state agents in the restoration and legalization of these temples, this chapter focuses on nonmonastic actors, namely, lay practitioners and devotees, who occupy these temples' public areas. As the chapter demonstrates, the practices and agendas of these lay practitioners and devotees frequently vary from and are often unknown to both state officials and the monastics themselves who reside in and are often responsible for the administration of these temple sites.

In the post-Mao period, the process by which certain Buddhist temple sites have come to be restored to the sangha has been highly variable. This chapter focuses on two such processes: The first, which I designate the "top-down" approach, reflects partnerships (and sometimes contentions) between well-connected monastics, government officials, and wealthy donors. Huang's chapter on the restoration of the Jing'an Temple represents a good example of this approach, as do many of the temples discussed in chapter 4 by Brian Nichols. Other recently published studies on Buddhist temple restoration in the post-Mao period also largely focus on temples restored through the top-down approach, such as the Nanputuo Temple 南普陀寺 in Xiamen (Ashiwa and Wank 2006), the Bailin Chan Temple 柏林禅寺 in Hebei Province near Shijiazhuang (Yang and Wei 2005; Ji 2007), the Kaiyuan Temple 开元寺 in Quanzhou, Fujian (Nichols 2011 and chapter 4 in this volume), and the Guangji Temple 广济寺 in Beijing (Fisher 2014). I refer to the second process of temple restoration discussed in this chapter as the "bottom-up" approach. This refers to temples and Buddha halls that have been built through the localized, grassroots efforts of nonelite practitioners, that is, practitioners who lack contacts with the state or influential monastics and who, for the most part, lack access to significant funds. Examples of these sites include temples rebuilt by followers of the Venerable Jingkong 净空,[1] which have been organized by ordinary lay practitioners inspired by his teachings (Sun 2010, 94–105; 2011, 505), as well as other smaller temples and Buddha halls. These temples sometimes straddle the line of legality: Some are erected without official recognition from the state in sites that are not designated for religious use, such as commercial office spaces, teahouses, and, particularly in rural areas, restored temple sites that remain unregistered with the state. In many cases, these venues are unknown to official bureaus. In other cases, authorities turn a blind eye. Still other sites, such as the Jingkong temple studied by Sun, are subject to periodic official harassment (Sun 2010, 102–104). Others, however, in spite of the grassroots nature of their construction, are able to make use of formal and informal avenues to gain official permission to operate either as temples with resident monastics, as Buddha halls, or as lay associations.

This chapter compares temples that have been restored following these two processes in terms of the diversity of lay and devotional activities that they foster. It argues that, in spite of the fact that the first type of temple is constructed through a top-down approach and the second through a bottom-up approach, the first type of temple, paradoxically, facilitates the flourishing of far greater religious diversity than the second. This is due to the strong social and religious separation between those involved in the restoration of the temple sites and rank-and-file temple-goers in the top-down type in contrast to their strong connection in the bottom-up type. My argument is based on my ethnographic research into popular Buddhist practices during the first two decades of the twenty-first century. Three sites illustrate these approaches: The first two are exemplary of the top-down approach to Buddhist temple restoration. They are the Guangji Temple, where I conducted ethnographic research extensively from 2002 to 2004 and through shorter return visits in 2007, 2010–2013, 2015, and 2017; and the Bailin Temple, where I conducted ethnographic research in 2010–2013, 2015, and 2017. Representative of the second type of temple is a large temple complex in Jilin Province that refers to itself as a Buddha hall (fotang 佛堂), which I will call the Mingfa Buddha Hall. I conducted research at the Buddha hall in 2011.

A detailed description of the Guangji and Bailin Temples demonstrates how a diverse range of religious actors operates with varying agendas. A depiction of the Mingfa Buddha Hall portrays a religious site constructed by non-elite practitioners, where all activities are focused around the teachings and agenda of the Buddha hall's charismatic lay leader. An analysis of the factors for these differences shows that they relate to the separated nature of temple space and association in the first two temple complexes and their linkage in the third. Through my discussion, I aim to shed light on important questions concerning the nature of Buddhist social association in post-Mao China in comparison with that of other religious groups, more specifically, why Buddhist groups appear to have far fewer underground organizations than their Christian counterparts.

THE GUANGJI TEMPLE

The Guangji Temple, which dates back to the Yuan dynasty, is one of five legally recognized Buddhist religious activity sites within the four ring roads that comprise the centermost part of Beijing. The present-day site of the Guangji Temple was first occupied by a temple for the West Liu village (Xi Liu Cun Si 西刘村寺) constructed during the reign of the Jin dynasty emperor Shizong in the late twelfth century (Xu 2003, 5). This original temple was damaged by warfare at the end of the Mongol Yuan dynasty and then rebuilt by the Ming emperor Xianzong (Xu 2003, 12). Monks were resident in the temple from its beginnings, and during the Qing dynasty and the Republican period, it was used for new ordinations (Xu 2003, 56). By 1949, most religious activities at the Guangji Temple had ceased. In 1953, leaders of the newly formed Buddhist Association of China (BAC) succeeded in reclaiming the temple as a religious site and made it their headquarters (Xu 2003, 46–48). Through most of the Mao era, the temple was closed to public use, open mostly to delegations of visiting Buddhists from overseas. The temple's special status protected it from the worst excesses of the Cultural Revolution, however, and it was one of the first religious sites in China to be restored to religious use following the end of the Cultural Revolution, reportedly at the personal request of Premier Zhou Enlai (Xu 2003, 56). The BAC, which was effectively disbanded with the onset of the Cultural Revolution, resumed its activities at the temple in 1980. The temple once again accepted modest numbers of resident clergy, and clergy and well-connected lay practitioners were allowed access. Nevertheless, the temple remained closed to the general public until the late 1980s, when it abruptly reopened its doors without charging an admission fee.

As the headquarters of the Buddhist Association, the temple houses many important monastic leaders and many of the main offices of the association. The rooms of these eminent monks and the offices are housed entirely in the northernmost of three walled courtyards. The monks in charge of administering the temple proper live on the east and west sides of the temple's central courtyard, where its main public ritual activities take place. The temple's southernmost courtyard (which monks and regular lay practitioners refer to as its "outer courtyard" [waiyuan 外院]) rarely hosts any ritual activities. In general, the temple's monks and the association leaders are rarely seen there except when they quickly exit through the temple to the street outside either on foot or, more often, in cars that they have parked in the courtyard.

In spite of the absence of organized ritual activities, however, from the late 1990s through the early 2010s, this outer courtyard was a vibrant center of lay religious activity, particularly during the temple's Dharma assemblies (fahui 法会),

which are held on the first, eighth, fifteenth, and twenty-third days of the lunar month. During this time, devotees lined up at the courtyard's northernmost shrine to Maitreya (Mile Fo 弥勒佛) to offer incense and pray for blessings and peace before going on to complete a devotional circuit of the temple's central courtyard. Other temple-goers, usually self-defined lay practitioners, participated in interactive discussion groups or listened to the sermons of charismatic lay preachers. The religious content of these discussions and sermons ranged through lessons in ritual etiquette, guides to the correct pronunciation of Buddhist sutras (*jing* 经) and dharanis (*zhou* 咒), and descriptions of how to obtain cures for health ailments through combinations of sutra singing and a correct diet and lifestyle. The preachers' sermons also included warnings of what many of them claimed was a *lack of* or *decline in* moral values in the present-day world as compared to the recent past. Of all of the preachers' activities, it was these moralistic sermons, which were either prearranged or completely spontaneous, that attracted the largest crowds and generated the greatest interest among the laypersons in the courtyard. Preaching mostly to a sympathetic audience, the preachers exemplified this moral decline with what they saw as a rise in greedy (*tanxin* 贪心) and selfish (*sixin* 私心) behavior in Chinese public life and interpreted it as evidence of the world's movement into the Latter Days of the Dharma (*mofa shiqi* 末法时期), a time furthest removed from the teachings of Śākyamuni Buddha. The preachers occasionally distributed their own handouts with guides to sutra singing or essays on interpretations of Buddhist scriptures like the *Lotus Sutra* (*Fahua jing* 法华经) that they themselves had written. Other preachers and other practitioners in the courtyard also distributed bound copies of sutras; video recordings from sermons of famous masters, both lay and monastic; morality books (*shanshu* 善书) on living an upright life in a degenerate age; laminated pictures of buddhas and bodhisattvas; and paper charms designed to protect the wearer from accidents or ill health. The activities of the practitioners who met there, including the preachers, were neither organized nor approved by the monks who administered the temple; for many years, the religious materials they exchanged were entirely unregulated. Indeed, the preachers themselves were sometimes critical of the temple monks and authorized Buddhist institutions within China even as they stood within a space that legally existed because of the power of those institutions.

THE BAILIN CHAN TEMPLE

The Bailin Temple is located in the seat of Zhao County, approximately forty kilometers southeast of Shijiazhuang, the provincial capital of Hebei Province. Its most famous resident was the Zhaozhou Chan Master Congshen (Zhaozhou Congshen Chanshi 赵州从谂禅师), who in the ninth century established an offshoot of the Linji 临济 Chan school. The temple's central pagoda, built in 1330, contains his remains. While the temple contained several halls at various times in its history, only the dilapidated pagoda remained when, in 1987, Dharma Master Jinghui 净慧, then the vice-secretary of the BAC, came to visit with a contingent of Japanese Rinzai (Linji) priests who traced their lineage to Master Congshen. Disappointed to find that so little remained of the original temple where the Zhaozhou monk had practiced, they resolved to fund its restoration. Although Jinghui had no personal connections to the temple, he was moved by the Japanese monks' resolve and made the restoration of the temple his personal project. With both a powerful position within the state-recognized Buddhist Association and an initial source of funds, Jinghui was well positioned to take advantage of the post-Mao Chinese state's new policies on the restoration of religious sites destroyed during the Mao era and its new willingness to look more positively on organized religion if it could be used to promote economic development through tourism.

With both the support of the government and donations from Buddhist practitioners, many of whom were based in Japan or Hong Kong, Jinghui rebuilt all of the original temple halls within just an eleven-year period (Yang and Wei 2005, 63). In 2003, he oversaw the construction of its largest building, the Ten Thousand Buddha Hall (Wan Fo Lou 万佛楼), a seven-story structure containing more than ten thousand gold-plated buddhas (*Fayin* 2003, 48; see also Fisher 2008, 155). A Hebei Buddhist Academy (Hebei Foxueyuan 河北佛学院) was constructed adjacent to the temple grounds in which new monastics could receive a three-year training program in the fundamentals of Chan. Jinghui slowly built up the number of full-time monastics to a total of 150 in 2011 and established a rigorous schedule of meditation three times each day along with normal ritual duties. In 1993, he established a Living Chan Summer Camp (Shenghuochan Xialingying 生活禅夏令营) designed to introduce young adults for one week each year to the basics of Chan philosophy and Buddhist monastic practice (Ji 2006, 2011c). A few of the male campers have gone on to become monks at the temple themselves, while many others have built on their worldly influence to provide economic and political support to the temple and the sangha in China more generally. The temple has also spawned two other monasteries and a nunnery in Shijiazhuang and southern Hebei. The temple's positive reputation as a forward-looking religious institution that attracts young, highly educated, and affluent practitioners and contributes significantly to the local economy earned it a visit from China's then president Jiang Zemin in 2001.

As at the Guangji Temple, it is the Bailin Temple's northernmost end that forms the center of its monastic-led activities. Most of the housing for its monastics is concentrated in its northwestern side, which is also where the academy is located. Most ritual events take place inside the Ten Thousand Buddha Hall, which, with the exception of certain special events, does not admit ordinary devotees (although it allows committed laypersons to attend its evening devotions). Events for the summer camp and other monastic-led events, such as the temple's annual seven-day Repaying Kindness Dharma Assembly (Bao'en Fahui 报恩法会) for laypersons in July (prior to the Hungry Ghost Festival) and meditation retreats during the winter months, are also concentrated around the Ten Thousand Buddha Hall and the halls immediately adjacent to it. When I visited during the time of the summer camps in 2011–2013, the northernmost halls and courtyards of the temple were closed to the general public and used only for the campers. Halls and residence areas on the east and west sides of the temple, which were used to house the campers (and some of the monks), are generally closed to outside visitors. Nevertheless, even during the time of the camp, the southernmost courtyards and halls, including the pagoda commemorating the visit of the Zhaozhou monk, were open to devotees. While the temple initially charged an admission fee to all guests, this was waived in the mid-2000s.

Like other Buddhist sites throughout China, the Bailin Temple fulfills a wide variety of religious and social purposes beyond those led by the temple's monastics. As at the Guangji Temple, many of these functions take place in the public areas of the temple and are largely unrelated to the projects of the temple's monk leaders. The public courtyards of the Bailin Temple do not feature the moralistic sermons of charismatic lay preachers that one could once find in the Guangji Temple. Nor (more curiously) can one find there the large array of unauthorized literature and multimedia materials that are commonly found at the Guangji Temple and many other temples throughout China.[2] Nevertheless, the public courtyards of the Bailin Temple do play host to a rich array of activities: Most of these are devotional in nature. In contrast to Jinghui's emphasis on making the temple into a place for the pursuit of meditative insights and the ethical development of the socially engaged citizen (Yang and Wei 2005, 70; Fisher 2008, 156), the devotees who generally worship at the temple frequently emphasize its efficacious character, that is, its power as a place where worshippers can seek supernatural aid. Much of that perceived efficacy comes from the temple's historical role as the home of the spiritually powerful Zhaozhou monk, whose pagoda receives many offerings each day. However, many devotees I interviewed cited the more recent visit of Jiang Zemin as the strongest evidence of the temple's efficacy. Several told me that the leader of China would never have traveled to an obscure city like theirs if it were not for the magical power of the temple. In this way, the devotees created their own narrative of the president's visit: far from sanctifying the Bailin Temple as a site of Buddhism's compatibility with state policies or its means to improve the economy, the president had confirmed the temple as a powerful site of supernatural efficacy.

Local residents also engage in nonreligious activities at the temple. It often functions as a community social space: Couples frequently use the long benches that line each side of the temple to enjoy time alone together; families bring

Crowds of devotees burn incense in front of the pagoda of the Zhaozhou monk, Master Congshen, at the Bailin Temple, July 2011. Photo by the author.

their children to play in the wide-open spaces of the temple courtyards; a group of senior men gathers on Saturday mornings in the summer months to reminisce and enjoy some shade from the heat. The temple is also a major source of economic opportunity for many local residents. While the regular employees of the temple are generally selected from populations of lay Buddhists outside of the community, local residents take part in many informal activities that connect them to the temple's economy. In addition to the vendors who have official permits to operate vegetarian restaurants and religious merchandise shops within the plaza across from the temple, there are a number of hawkers who line the sidewalk outside the temple selling incense, snacks, and cold drinks. Some local vendors also sell incense within the temple, and others provided photography services up until the mid-2010s, when the ubiquity of camera phones eliminated demand.[3] Tour guides also take visitors around the temple for a fee. The vendors who operate inside the temple are required to have a permit for their activities, though not all have them.

These "tour guides" (*daoyou* 导游) are a noteworthy group at the temple, not only because of their economic activities but also because of their religious ones. Many of the tour guides consider themselves Buddhists and read popular Buddhist manuals extensively in their spare time. They take their responsibilities as teachers of the devotees very seriously: While a typical tour passes along some information about the temple's history, the main focus of the tours is on teaching visiting devotees how to present offerings to the temple's deities in a respectful and efficacious manner. In addition to teaching visitors to the temple about etiquette, some tour guides also pass along moral instruction. The tour guides told me that they sometimes told visitors that the latter's devotional practices would be ineffective if they did not also practice compassionate actions toward others. Sometimes they gave visitors morality books to read free of charge. They also encouraged them to consider becoming vegetarians. Tour guides sometimes formed close relationships with regular devotees and provided them with both counseling and Buddhist-inspired moral instruction for the problems that had brought them to the temple. The religious skills and interests of the tour guides are seldom recognized by the temple's monks, who claim a monopoly on providing spiritual instruction to the devotees, even though they rarely exercise this right. (Most of their Dharma talks are directed to audiences of laypersons, most of whom, like the participants in the Chan camp, are not local.) That the tour guides are legitimate Buddhists is also rejected by the small group of regular laypersons at the temple who insist that real Buddhist followers do not charge money for their services. Yet, for many of the local devotees, the tour guides provide an important spiritual service.

ANALYSIS

The eclectic range of spiritual and social activities in the public courtyards of officially sanctioned religious sites like the Guangji Temple and the Bailin Temple is facilitated by both the separation of physical space at these temples and a social and religious disassociation between the authorities responsible for running the temple on the one hand and many of the lay practitioners and devotees who gather within its spaces on the other. To some extent, the former facilitates the latter: The religious and social activities that take place in the public sections of these temples generally do not interfere with the everyday rituals of the temple monks or with their administrative duties, which take place in other parts of the temples. Preachers in the outer courtyard of the Guangji Temple could also largely complete their sermons out of earshot of the temple monks, whom some of them criticized. Strategically placed gates can divide the Bailin Temple in two when special events such as the Chan camp take place. During these events, large sections of the temple are off-limits to the public, creating within the spaces a social and religious environment that is unique to the event experience. Smaller gates also divide the entrances to individual temple halls in the public areas of the temple. When the monks complete a ritual circuit of the halls each morning, they are separated by these gates from the ritual wanderings of the devotees—though not from their curious gaze. In this way, the devotees become to the monks the masses of sentient beings for whom they chant their devotions, while, to the devotees, the monks, as animated sacred objects, represent the sacred character of the temple, which can function to reinforce their sense of its efficacy. The lack of communication between the two groups prevents any mixing or conflict between their respective religious agendas.

This separation also exists between donors and officials who facilitate the creation of religious sites like the Bailin and Guangji Temples and devotees and lay practitioners who make use of their public areas. Many of the main halls in the Bailin Temple were funded by wealthy donors, many of them overseas Chinese, who are committed to Jinghui's vision of Living Chan but are mostly absent from the temple itself. The Chan summer camp (itself funded mostly by a single donor) focuses on admitting well-educated young people who are interested in Chan philosophy. Many of these campers, as representatives of China's intellectual elite, have gone on to become donors themselves. Their donations are mostly motivated by the desire to support the instruction they received from monks like Jinghui rather than to facilitate the devotional activities that take place in the public areas of the temple. Their physical separation as campers from these devotees facilitates their impression of the Bailin Temple as a place of Chan meditation and instruction rather than a site that facilitates popular devotional activities and the moral education of local businesspersons by the tour guides. This separation often also exists between ordinary temple-goers and visiting officials. The Bailin Temple was cleared for the visit of Jiang Zemin. At the Guangji Temple, the Buddhist Association leaders and religious affairs officials often meet in the northern courtyard of the temple, far away from the preachers or media distributors.

Another source of separation between the monk leaders responsible for administrating the Guangji and Bailin Temples and the devotees and lay practitioners who gather in its public spaces concerns their unconnected patterns of social and religious association. Unlike pastors or priests, who are charged with incorporating lay churchgoers into a congregation under their guidance, the monks I have interviewed at the Guangji and Bailin Temples have typically felt no particular obligations toward the moral education of the laity except in the abstract. On a daily basis, monks mostly occupy themselves with ritual activities, temple upkeep, and administrative tasks. The people whose concerns and needs must be met are other monastics, officials, or, in the case of the Bailin Temple, temple-goers who take part in structured programs like the Chan summer camp and the Repaying Kindness Dharma Assembly. This is not to say that temple-goers themselves eschew contact with the monks: At the Guangji Temple, in spite of some lay preachers' critiques of monks, it was quite common throughout my fieldwork to see monks besieged by laypersons asking for spiritual advice or ritual aid when entering their cars in the courtyard. The monks almost invariably ignored these petitions, and their drivers' horn honking to get the laypersons out of their way was the only recognition of their existence. The monks could ignore these petitioners because they had no social relationships with them; nor was their status or worth defined by the appearance of those relationships. For the most part, the only lay practitioners who enjoy a close relationship with temple monks are those who engage in regular volunteer work (*hufa* 护法 or *yigong* 义工) at the temples,[4] but these represent a minority of temple-goers overall. At both the Guangji and Bailin Temples, regular lay volunteers also isolate themselves from the temple-goers who congregate in the public courtyards. Monks sometimes perform salvation rites (*chaodu* 超度) for the laity or other temple-goers, particularly at the Bailin Temple, but this usually involves only perfunctory interactions between them. This is in sharp contrast to the relationship between lay preachers and their followers at the Guangji Temple and tour guides and their regular clients at the Bailin Temple. A few monks saw themselves as having a moral responsibility to educate a wider range of the laity (see chapter 11 by Travagnin in this volume), but this was far more the exception than the norm.

The social and spatial separation between rank-and-file temple-goers on the one hand and monastic authorities, officials, and donors on the other does not mean there is no contestation between them. During the bulk of my field-work at the Guangji Temple in the early 2000s, there were occasional outbursts of conflict between the temple monks and the lay volunteers who supported them on the one hand and the outer courtyard groups on the other: On one occasion, a monk came out of the inner part of the temple to berate a lay preacher whom he accused of selling her essays for profit; on another occasion, a regular layperson in the outer courtyard made a snide insult to a monk as he swept the courtyard with a broom, causing the latter to attack the former with the broom; the two then entered into a struggle that lay onlookers desperately tried to break up. However, neither incident led to any official attempts to restrict public access to these courtyard areas, even for the laypersons who had been involved in the conflicts. Very often I would be sitting with monks in their quarters when lay volunteers would enter to complain about the distribution of heterodox literature by practitioners in the courtyard. The response of the monks was usually to utter a small grunt of acknowledgment and then continue with whatever they had been doing. In 2006, the temple posted signs banning the preachers and literature distributors, but most of their activities continued unchecked. The courtyard space only started to become significantly restricted beginning in the 2010s when the temple authorities began to use the space for the sale of religious merchandise and when the number of cars they owned began to take up more of the courtyard space. Since the mid-2010s a more concerted effort has been undertaken to curtail the activities of the preachers and regulate the content of the distributed media. At the Bailin Temple, a scuffle between security guards, incense sellers, and devotees provoked the temple authorities to close down the temple for two months in 2009 (see also chapter 4 by Nichols in this volume). It reopened with new rules for the conduct of vendors inside the temple, the initiation of licensing procedures for the tour guides, and a short-lived period of monastic instruction to the guides.

Throughout the period of my fieldwork in the 2010s, however, the public areas of the temple have been active with devotees, tour guides, and other vendors, not all of whom had permits. While the burning of incense and candles has become more strictly regulated, devotional activities have also remained robust.

The occasional conflict between the temple authorities and many of the groups who occupy temple space begs the question of why these authorities allow the groups to gather at all and why, more often than not, they show indifference to their activities even when they result in the creation of a very different kind of social and religious space than those authorities have envisioned. One reason is that public religious activities are part of the traditional landscape of Chinese temples. They function to create Buddhist temples as spaces of "heat and noise" (*renao* 热闹) (Chau 2006, 147–168), alive with religious activity that facilitates an unexamined belief among those who live in and visit the temple that the Dharma is spreading. One monk I interviewed at the Bailin Temple said that providing a space for devotional activities was part of the temple's duty to the Chinese public. In this way, he acknowledged that while, on the one hand, the temple is a "monastery," that is, a place to house monks and facilitate their religious activities, it is also a "temple," that is, a space that caters to a variety of public religious activities, even if those activities need to be separated from those of the monastics for religious and possibly also political reasons. In modern China, both the Republican and Communist states have emphasized the need for temple leaders to act as good citizens and provide services to the public; in the post-Mao period, these services include providing religious spaces for the public as well as facilitating tourism. Ironically, the administrative demands that the modern state places on temple monks also restrict the time that they might spend instructing the devotees and lay practitioners who gather in these spaces. Facilitating devotional activities also provides the temples with a source of revenue (although it is difficult to tell whether, in prominent temples such as the Bailin and Guangji Temples, this source of revenue is very substantial in terms of what they can receive from outside donors and the state). Finally, opening certain areas of their temples to a diverse range of activities also compensates, albeit to a very small extent, for the erosion of non-Buddhist popular religious sites since the beginning of the Mao era and the failure to restore many of those sites in the post-Mao era. By creating a space inside a Buddhist temple for popular religious activities that would have taken place at a variety of religious sites prior to the Communist period, temple authorities also inscribe those activities as Buddhist and subsume them under their authority, even though they have little practical engagement with them.

However, the spatial and social divide between religious activities in the inner and outer courtyards of the Guangji and Bailin Temples reflects a very different sort of arrangement of space and sociality than one might find at a site like the Mingfa Buddha Hall. Here, in spite of the fact that there are no faraway donors, there is little official support, and most of the funding for its impressive temple complex has come from the pockets of ordinary lay practitioners like those who gather in the outer courtyard of the Guangji Temple, one finds far less religious diversity than in the first two sites. This is due to the centering of religious experience around the person of its charismatic leader and the direction of both physical and virtual space toward the making of her own religious projects.

THE MINGFA BUDDHA HALL

I first learned of the Mingfa Buddha Hall in July 2011 during a major Dharma assembly at the Guangji Temple. The leader of the hall, whom I will refer to as Teacher Wang (Wang Laoshi 王老师), enjoyed no relationship with the Guangji Temple monks or the national Buddhist Association that is headquartered at the Guangji Temple. However, her teachings were often shared among the lay practitioners in the temple's outer courtyard, where her virtual presence mingled with that of the flesh-and-blood lay preachers. A Beijing-based follower of Teacher Wang's wheeled a shopping cart into the courtyard filled with dozens of cases that contained DVDs of her sermons. Each case was made up of ten DVDs. These cases were distributed one by one freely to all interested practitioners and included a slip of paper with the follower's phone number, which I contacted. The follower invited me to a two-day series of sermons delivered by Teacher Wang at a teahouse in Beijing, where I had lunch with the teacher. She subsequently invited me for a visit to the Buddha hall itself that August.

Despite its name, the Mingfa Buddha Hall is not just one hall but nine complete buildings, only four of which had been completely constructed during the time of my visit. The main structure of the complex where the Buddha hall's key religious activities take place is a three-story building with many separate rooms including two large halls for religious activities: one for Buddha recitation, morning and evening devotions, and Dharma assemblies, and a second right above it for Teacher Wang's well-attended lectures. The hall also rents small one-story apartments in the local neighborhood to store deceased persons awaiting transportation to the local crematorium. It even rents its own plot of land from which certain vegetables are grown for use in its dining hall. When (and if) the hall is fully constructed, it will boast worship halls to all of the major Buddhist deities. Indeed, there is little to separate this "hall" from a monastery or temple. It even houses a handful of nuns.

The one obvious difference, which accounts for the hall's legal status as a "Buddha hall" (*fotang* 佛堂) rather than a "temple" (*si* 寺), is that its leader is a layperson. Even the resident nuns consider her their leader. Wang was a Buddhist teacher in the main city near the Buddha hall long before it was built. As her following grew larger, it outgrew the makeshift spaces in which she was operating in the city. After many years of fund-raising, Wang's followers gathered together sufficient funds to purchase the plot of land (originally designated as farmland) that houses the present Buddha hall. Teacher Wang used her influence in local and regional Buddhist Associations to secure legal status for the hall as a religious activity site. She herself took up full-time residence at the hall along with several of her followers. The establishment of the hall spread, initially by word of mouth, and lay adherents came, mostly from the surrounding area, but some from hours away, to listen to Teacher Wang's twice-weekly sermons (on Saturday and Sunday afternoons). The contents of the four of Wang's sermons to which I listened in person were virtually identical and relatively simple: They focused on the importance of everyday moral acts toward others, especially kindness to one's family, and the importance of reciting the homage to Amitabha to help improve one's health and to gain rebirth in the Paradise of Western Bliss after one's death. When construction of the temple's three dormitory buildings was completed, arranged along three sides facing the Harmony Hall, it was possible for those coming to listen to the lectures from farther away to stay on Saturday nights so that they could be present for both of the weekend lectures. The hall's dining hall on the first floor of the westernmost dormitory building provides them with meals. Both meals and accommodation are free, paid for only by donations.

After the construction of its initial halls was complete, the Buddha hall began to generate its own literature and multimedia materials, the production of which was paid for by the donations of Teacher Wang's followers. These materials featured transcripts and recordings of Teacher Wang's lectures and testimonies of her followers on how becoming her student had changed their lives. Many of Wang's lectures are also available streaming on the hall's website. These materials have now been distributed to temples throughout Northeast China, including the Guangji Temple in Beijing.

Those who stayed in the Buddha hall for long-term sojourns of a few months often did so because they hoped that it would cure their physical ailments. The Buddha hall's free literature contains testimonies on the effectiveness of this method. As one of these long-term visitors explained to me, days at the hall were spent either reciting homage to Amitabha in the recitation hall or finding ways to help out around the complex, an activity that could help one to earn merit. In Teacher Wang's own examples of earning merit, she often referred to the everyday ethical actions a practitioner should do in being kind to others, most especially members of one's own family, without which, she asserted, the recitation of homage to Amitabha would be ineffective. Nevertheless, the adherents themselves emphasized doing good works in the Buddha hall itself, which included assisting in its construction. With few exceptions, the entire construction of the hall site was completed by lay volunteers, some of whom specialized in construction work. An example of this was the laywoman who was my principal escort during my stay at the hall: From Monday to

Friday, she had a full-time job in commercial construction work. On the weekends, she used her labor and skill to assist on the hall's construction projects, with compensation in merit rather than cash. She was not alone, either: Teams of volunteers worked, sometimes with heavy equipment, all day long and sometimes well into the night on the construction of the Buddha hall's new buildings. They even set up a public address system to relay Teacher Wang's lectures out into the courtyard in front of the Harmony Hall, where the construction of the other buildings was taking place. In this way, as one worker explained to me, the workers could still benefit from the wisdom of her words without having to interrupt their construction efforts. Teacher Wang herself even lent occasional help to the construction, giving credence to its importance as a meritorious activity: Pictures in her office showed her attaching tiles to the roof of one of the new halls with a scarf around her head and neck to protect them from the sun. Another photograph showed her painting blue ceiling tiles that were to be installed on the ceiling of another hall.

ANALYSIS

Several key differences distinguish a site like the Mingfa Buddha Hall from temples like the Guangji and Bailin Temples, which are closer to the center of political and economic power in China: While the temples create both a spatial and social separation between a monastic orthodoxy and public expressions of religiosity, in the Mingfa Buddha Hall the religious site is entirely constructed, funded, and occupied by enthusiastic lay adherents, most of whom would have likely occupied the peripheral spaces of the Guangji and Bailin Temples. The hall does not need to create a space for the public; it is the public.

The physical separation of space that one finds at the Guangji and Bailin Temples is absent at the Mingfa Buddha Hall. The hall has a completely open plan, with no enclosed courtyards. Its design entirely reflects its leader's teachings on Amitabha devotionalism: One enters to find a large reflecting pool (which was still under construction at the time of my visit), designed to simulate those found in descriptions of Amitabha's Pure Land, and a shrine to the bodhisattva Guanyin. At the Guangji and Bailin Temples, the office for visitors is tucked away in the inner courtyards of the temples, and many temple-goers are unaware of its existence. By contrast, at the Mingfa Buddha Hall, a small office is located directly inside the main gates and faces outward to greet the incoming visitors (and to take their donated cash and other items). The office is windowless, and those who staff it sit outside in the summer months. To the right of the office and shrine areas are worship halls intended to showcase a variety of major Buddhist deities. They, too, are not closed off in courtyards but are scattered around the open plan of the site. When one faces the site from the outside, the Harmony Hall looms directly behind the devotional sites. A central pathway leads clearly from the front of the complex to this hall, and the devotees who come to listen to Teacher Wang's sermons stream in from the front gates along this pathway to the hall. The dormitories and dining hall are clustered behind it. There is no restricted area as such, and no gates internally divide any parts of the site. Devotees, lay practitioners, and the resident nuns move back and forth through all sections of the hall. Even Teacher Wang's main office becomes an open, public space at the conclusion of her sermons, as listeners line up to ask for her guidance and receive her blessings.

The open spatial arrangement of the hall is also reflected in the relatively nonhierarchical nature of social association there: In large part because their teacher is a layperson, the divide between laypersons and monastics is less obvious in the Buddha hall than at monasteries like the Guangji and Bailin Temples. Many of Teacher Wang's closest assistants are laypersons rather than nuns, and the nuns at the site take their turns with laypersons in carrying out volunteer work. This is in sharp contrast to the Guangji Temple, where lay volunteers are given duties separate from those of the monks. The daily chanting to Amitabha on the first floor of the Harmony Hall takes place on an ad hoc basis: There is no set schedule and laypersons take turns leading the chanting. The only time during my visit when the religious position of the nuns over the laypersons was acknowledged was during the funeral of one of the hall's lay practitioners. On that occasion, it was essential that one of the nuns recite the prayers beseeching Amitabha to accept the deceased into the Paradise of Western Bliss. Teacher Wang took her place with the other laypersons, who chanted an accompaniment to the nun's prayer as the body of the deceased was carried out of a temporary morgue adjacent to the Buddha hall and onto a crematorium. Monastics and laypersons, as well as women and men, intermingle in the hall's dining hall in contrast to their separation at the Guangji and Bailin Temples. The pictures of Teacher Wang, dressed in a wide-brimmed hat to protect her head from the sun, engaging in painting the ceiling of one temple hall and placing tiles on the roof of another emphasize her connection to her followers, with whom she is working to spread the Dharma.

This apparent nonhierarchical pattern of social association, however, disguises the real distinction in authority and power that occurs at the Buddha hall, that between Wang herself on the one hand and all of the rest of the practitioners and devotees on the other. Wang occupies no politically recognized office at the Buddha hall. As shown previously, in ritual activities also, she can sometimes take on a subordinate position. Yet it is clear to all who attend the Buddha hall that she is its undisputed leader: The hall was constructed in the first place as a platform for her teachings; the roads and paths throughout the hall lead to the central building, from which she delivers her sermons and in which she receives guests. The desire of her followers to communicate with her directly to receive her blessings, a communication that often involves physical contact, speaks to the importance of her personal charisma. Just as Julia Huang (2009) has shown in the case of Cheng Yen, the leader of the Tzu Chi Foundation,

Teacher Wang's authority centers around her person, with whom her followers are intimately connected as she speaks to them and as they physically touch her body, which they believe to contain her magical power of healing. In spite of Wang's own insistence that it is Amitabha who provides blessing, along with individual good works and timely visits to one's doctor, it is clear that her followers believe that Wang herself contains some of this magical power and the closer they are to her presence the more they can partake in it. The center of religious and social authority around the charisma of Teacher Wang is further emphasized by the Buddha hall's use of virtual technology: Teacher Wang's chanting of the homage to Amitabha is played over speakers at every meal in the dining hall and her sermons are broadcast from the Harmony Hall on loudspeakers to the rest of the complex, streamed over the web, and cut onto DVDs that her followers distribute at faraway sites like the outer courtyard of the Guangji Temple. These virtual representations of the master's body and message reimagine the space of the Buddha Hall from an out-of-the-way place in a rural suburb of a medium-sized city to the center of a moral universe.

By contrast, the authority of monastics at temples like the Bailin and Guangji Temples is based on a routinized charisma in the Weberian sense, that is, a charisma based on their status as members of a monastic order founded by the Buddha. On a few occasions, long-term lay volunteers at the Bailin Temple told me stories of miraculous powers exhibited by Jinghui or the temple's present abbot, Minghai 明海. However, the visiting devotees emphasized the power of the temple site itself, which came in part from its status as a monastery but much less from the power of any particular monk. Individual monks were even less known at the Guangji Temple. At both the Bailin and Guangji Temples, lay practitioners and devotees were more likely to form personal relationships with lay preachers or tour guides than with the temple monks. At the Mingfa Buddha Hall, in contrast, there was little obstacle to or even mediation of the intimate personal relationship between Teacher Wang and her followers.

In sites like the Guangji and Bailin Temples, forms of religiosity that are concerned with the magical and efficacious and that center around the personal charisma of religious preachers are subject to the regulation of the religious authorities that control the temple sites. Unconnected to the visions and goals of the temple leaders and the state and lacking any power or authority, temple-goers who listen to the moralizing sermons or everyday ethical advice of charismatic lay preachers or popular tour guides, pray to Buddhist deities for wealth and protection, or try to make a modest living from the sale of religious paraphernalia are always subject to periodic crackdowns or restrictions from their landlords. They are always in danger of losing their space altogether if the temple authorities decide that that space can be put to better use for other purposes, such as sideline economic activities, or if the winds of political change necessitate stricter control over temple practices. In sites like the Mingfa Buddha Hall, by contrast, once securing permission to operate legally (or in some cases even without that permission), apart from the need to pay very min-imal lip service to the state's regulatory categories, grassroots practitioners are free to control their own space. Yet paradoxically the very marginality of lay practitioners and devotees at public religious sites like the Guangji and Bailin Temples facilitates a greater degree of Buddhist religious diversity at those sites: Because none of the lay preachers or devotional groups at the public temples has the authority to erect any permanent structures on the spaces they inhabit, they cannot prevent other voices and religious visions from emerging on those sites to contest their own. As a result, the devotees and lay practitioners who frequent those public spaces are less likely to be drawn toward a single, exclu-sive religious vision or practice than they are at a site like the Mingfa Buddha Hall, where both physical structures and pathways of authority can be created around the teachings of a single leader. In sites like the Buddha hall, ordinary practitioners and devotees are comparatively insulated from the reach of the state and the monastic authorities of the Buddhist Association but also from their ability to level the playing field of popular Buddhist religiosity.

GENERALIZATIONS AND IMPLICATIONS

Religious sites like the Guangji Temple, the Bailin Chan Temple, and the Mingfa Buddha Hall are representative of only a portion of the Buddhist reli-gious scene in China today. Yet they are not isolated cases. In a comparative survey of nine urban Buddhist religious sites in eastern China that I conducted in 2003–2004,[5] I found several that accommodated areas of public religiosity unconnected to the religious projects of the temple's leaders and the state, in-cluding a few that contained popular lay leaders and preachers like those found at the Guangji Temple. One factor that facilitated these public religious spaces included the spatial presence of a large outer or public courtyard, either within the temple itself or in an area just outside of it that neither the authorities inside the temple nor the local state significantly policed. Another factor was the absence of an admission fee into the temple, only a very small one, or one from which lay practitioners with credentials were exempted. Sun's study of the Old Spring Pure Land Temple in Zhejiang Province shows the case of a site similar to that of the Mingfa Buddha Hall, where a popular lay leader has constructed a temple centered on the vision of the Venerable Jingkong, and only his teach-ings are available (Sun 2010, 96–101). The research of Alison Jones (2010) and Dan Smyer Yü (2012) points to the existence of Buddhist groups away from temple spaces in cities like Nanjing and Shanghai: Many of these groups are centered on the religious visions of particular masters, to whom they are often connected through virtual media and who provide set curricula for their followers to master. I have conducted some preliminary research into similar groups in Beijing, one that organizes followers to take part in life rescue (*fangsheng* 放生) activities on weekend mornings at reservoirs in the Beijing municipality and another that is focused on the moral teachings of a Taiwanese-based master whose Beijing followers are organized into small weekly study groups that meet at the homes of practitioners (see also Fisher 2014, 207–208). Some of these Beijing groups, like Teacher Wang's, originally gained their followers by distributing DVDs, books, or advertisements of their public lectures in the outer courtyard of the Guangji Temple. While these groups no doubt represent a growing and important aspect of Buddhist religiosity in contemporary China, their members do not merely leave public religious sites to join them once they have found one that suits them: Some practitioners later leave these master-centered groups, disgruntled by their regimented requirements and frequent requests for funds, and reenter the spiritual marketplace of public religious sites.

Into the second decade of the twenty-first century, public religious spaces like those at the Guangji and Bailin Temples remain important areas of the Buddhist public space in contemporary urban China. Much like the Beijing government's designated zones of protest during the 2008 Olympics, they are facilitated by the state (and in this case religious leaders) but are not discursively controlled by them (see also Fisher 2015). They create room for religious diversity but also keep it contained. I suggest that their existence explains, to a large extent, why Buddhism does not appear to have a phenomenon as significant in size as the unregistered church movement in Chinese Christianity. By both controlling a congregation spatially and leading it discursively, Christian pastors do not create spaces for religious diversity in the way that the leaders of some Buddhist temples do. This allows the pastors and, in the case of the official church, the state, to control their message more effectively, but it also creates a push factor that spurs both ordinary adherents and, in some cases, their pastors to form new churches that are completely separate from state control. In the Buddhist case, this push factor is not as strong, because the expression of religious diversity, even when it is critical of institutional authority, is effectively permitted within legal religious spaces. On the other hand, it is important to recognize that the open spiritual marketplace of these uncontrolled zones of public religiosity also feeds followers into quasi-legal, alternative Buddhist spaces.

NOTES

1. While Jingkong himself has significant influence among Chinese Buddhists worldwide and significant access to funds through his organizations, his influence on mainland Chinese Buddhists is greatest among nonelite practitioners (whether monastic or lay). As Sun's research in Zhejiang and my own fieldwork in Beijing indicate, Jingkong has been at best tolerated and at worst shunned by high-ranking monastics and the state. In the case of the Jingkong temple studied by Sun, no official connections were used. Therefore, and based on the research to which we currently have access, I consider the spread of Jingkong's influence within mainland Chinese Buddhism as an example of nonelite Buddhism.

2. The temple does occasionally circulate its own materials, such as copies of its journal *Chan* 禅, which features essays on Chan practice by prominent monastics and laypersons.

3. The permissibility of these sales is under question: In 2011 and 2012, vendors were permitted mostly unrestricted access to the sidewalk outside the temple, although the incense and drink vendors were not permitted to sell their wares inside the temple. When I visited the temple again in 2013, the temple authorities had forced the vendors to move into the plaza across the street from the temple, in an effort to make the sidewalk less chaotic. However, when I visited in 2015 and 2017, the vendors were back in front of the temple, and several were selling incense inside (albeit somewhat surreptitiously). When I asked the vendors about the reason for the change, some replied that the person responsible for restricting their sales to the plaza was not on duty that day. Others claimed that enforcement had grown lax after 2013 because the authorities appreciated that the vendors depended for their survival on reaching as wide a market as possible and so were turning a blind eye toward their violation of the ban.

4. Meaning upholding or safeguarding the Dharma, *hufa* volunteers are generally long-standing lay practitioners who assist at the temple (including with cleaning, cooking, taking care of monks' robes, and some coordination of visiting devotees on days of Dharma assemblies). *Yigong* is a relatively recent term, used in secular Chinese society, to refer to volunteers in a variety of emerging community service activities (taking care of the elderly, cleaning up the environment, and providing assistance to visitors and tourists). At the Guangji Temple, *yigong* mainly assisted only on the days of major Dharma assemblies, in rituals and with coordinating devotees. They were not always lay practitioners, though some took a strong interest in Buddhist teachings, and generally were known to many of the monks, who were interested in attracting young, well-educated followers (see also Fisher 2014, 34–37).

5. The survey was conducted at temples in the cities of Beijing, Tianjin, Harbin, Changchun, Shenyang, Nanjing, Shanghai, Nanchang, and Guangzhou.

11

CYBERACTIVITIES AND "CIVILIZED" WORSHIP

Assessing Contexts and Modalities of Online Ritual Practices

STEFANIA TRAVAGNIN

CONTEXTS AND CONTESTS

The extended use of advanced technology and media devices by religious organizations has already become a substantial and rapidly increasing phenomenon in mainland China. Today, many major and minor temples own a website, Buddhist monks keep personal and "professional" blogs (including Weibo 微博 accounts), there are several WeChat (Weixin 微信) groups affiliated with religious teachers or groups, and religious images and content are becoming more and more popular in advertising and in movies. Automata are the most recent entries in the contemporary religious mediascape: The robot-monk Xian'er 贤二 was created for the Longquan Temple in late 2015,[1] and just a year later, a calligraphy robot designed to resemble the Chinese philosopher Wang Yangming made his appearance in Guiyang.[2]

This chapter focuses on one specific instance of religion and media in mainland China, online Buddha halls, and analyzes the phenomena of online ritual practices and digital worship that are currently available to Chinese Buddhists.

Examining these phenomena involves engaging with several contexts and areas of contestation. The first context is represented by the legal and political system, in other words, the overall policies on religion implemented by the Chinese government, and the official concern about Chinese attitudes toward religion and religious practice (Leung 2005; Potter 2003; Tong 2010).[3] Since the 1980s, bottom-up initiatives have renovated old Buddhist temples, reinstated traditional community rituals, and reaffirmed the social role of Buddhist communities. At the same time, the regime aims to channel Buddhism's resuscitation

through an ideology of state-led nationalism, characterized by the patriotic slogan "love country, love religion."

Monitoring popular activism has become increasingly challenging in the
twenty-first century, as Buddhist authorities and organizations have expanded
their media presence through an outpouring of blogs, mobile phone–based applications, websites, TV stations, and TV programs. A second important context under investigation is the one of media and thus the recent emergence of
"mediatized" Chinese religions. The new presence of religion in the public domain that we see in China starting from the early 1990s brought religion into
the media world as well, and eventually this intersection between religion and
media empowered religion. Recent studies have shown how religion has
become more present in, for instance, print newspapers, and how terms like
"harmonizing" and "stabilizing" are used in print newspapers to identify the
important social role that religion plays (or should play) today (Yao, Stout, and
Liu 2011). Some scholarly debates also have explained this renewed appearance
of religion as part of a recent "desecularization" in Chinese culture (Yang 2004;
Yao, Stout, and Liu 2011).[4] Although the study of religion and media in China
is still a new and emerging field, the investigation of the presence and influence of the social media in other sectors of Chinese society has produced
quite a substantial scholarship that will help in framing the questions of this
research.[5]

In its analysis of one specific medium, the Internet, tensions between
online and offline religion constitute a third important context of research.[6]
The Internet has become a widespread communication device in China: There
were more than 700 million Internet users in 2016, and it has also become
popular in cultural spheres such as religion. Religion and the Internet in China
has been the subject of several very recent studies. Samuel Lengen stressed that
applications of new media and communication technologies in the context of
religious practice have been read so far mostly in terms of oppression and resistance, and argued that an analytical framework not limited to such a binary
could successfully explain a larger variety of (religious) media production in
China today and could certainly highlight other important dynamics (Lengen
2016). Writing more specifically about Buddhism, André Laliberté has provided an overview of the development of "online Buddhism" in China and
classified and analyzed Buddhist websites that are currently active (Laliberté
2016). Beverley McGuire has demonstrated that the use of blogs by Buddhist
monastics has enriched levels of Dharma communication in China and Taiwan
and at the same time has also affected the media per se by assigning it new
Buddhism-related functions (McGuire 2016).[7] Huang Weishan has conducted
extensive research on the Tzu Chi Foundation's use of WeChat in Shanghai;
her study shows how Buddhists interact in a third (online) space so as to create
an imagined moral community. Huang has argued that WeChat and other
social media have facilitated the creation of a "local networked community" to

connect with a "larger global moral networked community" (Huang 2016). Finally, a recent article by Francesca Tarocco reiterates and expands on Huang's argument, highlighting how, in the urban context, social media has rearticulated the relationships between charismatic clerics and practitioners, bringing those relationships to a new level without undermining offline modes of religious authority (Tarocco 2017). Tarocco's case studies include the "self-claimed 'art-monk'" (Yang 2010), blogger Daoxin 道心 (b.1982; see Tarocco 2017), and the founder of Foguangshan 佛光山, Xingyun 星云 (b. 1927). These monks also feature in Scott Pacey's research on "eminence and edutainment" (Pacey 2016). Using Singhal and Rogers's theory of "education-entertainment," which they define as "the process of purposely designing and implementing a media message to both entertain and educate" (Singhal and Rogers 1999, xii), Pacey has analyzed the emergence of "celebrity monks" and their successful outreach to a wider public via several forms of media, including television programs. Some of these studies, especially those by Huang and Tarocco, have stressed the role of social media in creating and defining new communities, maintaining—if not enhancing—relations among believers and monastics, or highlighted the notion of cyberspace as a "third space" (Huang 2016).[8] Community and space are also key concepts in this chapter.[9] However, this chapter undertakes a different perspective from the sources mentioned by addressing areas of transformation and rupture from the traditional offline Buddhist practice and master-believer relations and not just those of continuity, and considers the impact of online practice on offline sacred sites and the sangha more broadly.

The fourth context in consideration concerns religious rituals—especially Chinese (Buddhist) rituals—namely, how these rituals are filtered and transformed through the medium of the Internet, in other words, how the medium of the Internet not only alters their modes of performance but may also affect their authenticity and efficacy.[10]

Inherent elements and key concepts of these contexts undergo challenges and contestations: Governmental attempts to hijack religious freedom are challenged by the openness of the media presence; the authenticity and efficacy of religious rituals are contested in their online translation and conduct; and relations between offline and online rituals, including the new modalities of counting "merits" that are gained and transferred through online halls, lead to a rethinking of ritual culture in Chinese Buddhism.

This chapter considers these contexts and contestations through three key questions: First, how is overall ritual discourse—and especially traditional Chinese Buddhist ritual discourse—affected and re-formed through the adoption of online ritual devices? Second, how can we classify the setting and modalities of online ritual practices? In other words, is online Buddhist practice a new ritual modality or also (or just) a reflection in the religious domain of the overall adoption of the Internet that is becoming more and more prevalent in contemporary society? Finally, what do online ritual practices reveal about the extent to which Buddhist practices subvert, complement, or strengthen the CCP's patriotic agenda? To answer these questions, this chapter analyzes both the forms of popular online Buddhist ritual practices and the party-state's nationalist ideology about them. It questions the degree to which online ritual practices serve the aims of the CCP; specifically, it reads them in relation to the recent government call for "civilized" (*wenming* 文明) behavior.

ZAIXIAN FOTANG AND WANGSHANG JISI: ONLINE RITUALS VERSUS OFFLINE RITUALS

The Online Buddha Hall (Zaixian Fotang 在线佛堂) and the Online Memorial Worship Site (Wangshang Jisi 网上祭祀) of the Nanputuo Temple comprise the initial and principal case study in the analysis of the phenomenon of online rituals.[11] Nanputuo Temple also has a WeChat account, which was created in 2016 and where other WeChat users, in addition to learning about the history of the temple and activities held there, can perform offerings to buddhas and bodhisattvas (*lifo* 礼佛) as is done in the Online Buddha Hall.

Nanputuo is one of the most important monasteries in twentieth-century China: It was where the monk Taixu[12] implemented his plans for the modern reform of Buddhist institutions, it hosts the well-known Minnan Institute for Buddhist Studies, and it runs one of the most advanced charities managed by Buddhist institutions, the Nanputuo Charity Foundation (Nanputuo Cishan Shiye Jijinhui 南普陀慈善事业基金会).[13]

In Nanputuo's Buddhist cyberspace, visitors perform ritual practices such as copying sutras, reciting liturgies, lighting candles, making offerings, and worshipping deceased members of the family or eminent Buddhist masters of the past. In light of the contexts and contestations outlined in the introduction, this part of the chapter assesses Nanputuo's "online ritual" web pages within the discourse of Chinese (Buddhist) ritual and the overall website of the monastery, while the following section analyzes these cyberactivities within the overall network-domain of online rituality in China.

Visitors to the Online Buddha Hall can virtually open the doors of five "halls" and have access to the main daily liturgy; in so doing, they can perform a total of six different ritual practices. Specifically, the homepage is split into a Buddha Recitation Hall for the recitation of the name of a buddha or bodhisattva; an Offering Hall (Lifo Tang 礼佛堂) for giving virtual offerings to buddhas and bodhisattvas;[14] a Sutra Chanting Hall (Songjing Tang 诵经堂); a Sutra Copying Hall (Chaojing Tang 抄经堂), for copying—or, more accurately, typing— Buddhist scriptures; and a Repentance Hall (Chanhui Tang 忏悔堂). Finally, there is access to videos of the morning and evening devotions that the sangha of Nanputuo perform daily (*zhaomu ke* 朝暮课). The Online Memorial Worship Site provides visitors with the possibility to venerate previous important monks (*xianzu dade* 先祖大德) who distinguished themselves in the history of

Nanputuo and to create and worship tablets of family ancestors. The worship consists of offerings of traditional offline goods such as flowers, candles, and dedication messages in digital form.

The modalities of ritual performance that the Online Buddha Hall and the Online Memorial Worship Site offer lead to the crucial transformation of cardinal pillars in the practice of Chinese Buddhist ritual. This is because, in comparison to offline rituals, the selection of rituals that can be conducted online is more prescribed; there are significant changes in the ritual process; the language and taxonomy of the offline ritual is translated into a new online vocabulary; and, finally, different criteria are used to calculate accumulated merits that reshape the crucial component of the transfer of merits (*huixiang* 回向).[15] Symbolic codes and typical conventions and protocols of the offline ritual appear transformed in the online version; consequently, from the perspective of traditional Chinese ritual, the authenticity and efficacy of the ritual are theoretically compromised, or at least challenged and revalued.

The Offering Hall makes a clear distinction between offline and online Buddhism through proposing a standardization of offerings and recipients of offerings in the latter: The page in fact limits the possible gifts to a fixed set,[16] lists a specific group of buddhas and bodhisattvas to which one can give offerings,[17] and includes a precise dedication formula for the "transfer of merit" that results from the offering. The Buddha Recitation Hall also imposes a permanent array of buddhas and bodhisattvas to be invoked.[18] The Sutra Copying Hall and the Sutra Recitation Hall list sets of canonical and extracanonical scriptures.[19] The Repentance Hall provides visitors with selected figures. In other words, each online hall clearly creates specific ritual paths and boundaries for visitors, so as to define the domain of agency for the online practitioners, as well as decide the forms of Chinese Buddhism (i.e., the relevant buddhas and bodhisattvas) that are available to them for practice.

Modalities, structure, and terminology that have characterized mainstream Chinese Buddhist rituals change substantially with the transfer to the online world. In the Sutra Copying Hall you do not copy (*chao* 抄) but type (*da* 打) texts, and this affects the concept of sutra copying (*chaojing* 抄经), the modalities and rewards of which are explored in several Buddhist scriptures:[20] Simply put, the efficacy of the "sutra writing" is the result of a number of actions and factors that disappear in the "sutra typing" of the online practice.[21] The precise instruction tells the online "scribe" that correctly typed characters will appear in blue, while the wrong ones will be red, in contrast to offline copying, in which one must make sure to correctly trace the copied character. Unlike in the offline version, where one typically writes in the character with ink, in the online version, there is also the possibility of correcting incorrectly copied characters. If a character is too "difficult" to be recognized and typed, then the online scribe can just type Ctrl+Y and move on to the following character, and doing so does not affect the results of the overall practice. Once each line on the first page of the screen has been completed correctly, the visitor can move on to the second page. The typing can also be interrupted and the partial work stored, then resumed at a later moment. Once the text has been fully typed, the online visitor can claim the acquired merit, even if some characters were skipped. Websites promoting the online sutra copying (*wangluo chaojing* 网络抄经) instead of the traditional practice (*chuantong chaojing* 传统抄经) stress that it is the purity of heart-mind (*xin* 心) and the sincere mindfulness that come from typing the sutras that is important, not how the sutras are actually copied. Also, these websites assert that the young generations like to type and that they do not often write anything by hand anymore, a fact that obviously has had an effect on religious practice—and so also on the traditional practice of sutra copying as well. In other words, as the websites themselves point out, by providing the possibility of copying sutras online via type-scribing sutra characters, Buddhism shows itself to be updated and to fit the new era and customs. A very important detail, which the websites stress, is that although the tools of this practice have changed, the efficacy of the practice does not change if it is performed with sincerity.

The online practice of giving offerings (*lifo* 礼佛) presents some differences from the offline version. The giving of offerings is intended as a form of worship that entails a precise ritual etiquette including the intoning of a traditional recitation to accompany the donation, as well as the use of the body (including movements, bows, and prostrations) and the dislocation and relocation of material objects (the purchase, holding, and final delivery of the object).[22] Traditional Chinese civilization is based on respect for etiquette, which then becomes foundational in classical Chinese Buddhism, too. By contrast, the "online offering" involves only a one-click ritual where many of the ritual elements in the offline version are completely deleted, and therefore the efficacy of the ritual is potentially undermined. For instance, according to interviews conducted during my fieldwork from 2012 to 2017, the believer who makes the offering online does not perform any prostrations or other body movements before the actual delivery of the offered object, and there is no transferring of any concrete objects either. The same reasoning can be made for the Online Memorial Worship Site, where, according to my interviews, worship also becomes a one-click ritual and does not involve the usual bodily and material movement that the offline worship would entail.[23]

The online sutra chanting (*songjing* 诵经) and Buddha's name recitation (*nianfo* 念佛) are performed quite similarly to the offline reality. The presence of the recorded recitation in the background re-creates the temple environment. The modality of time counting for the ritual of the name invocation is a new addition, though, and online practitioners can complete the "transfer of merit" after a one-minute recitation. The time counting is based on a recitation that already has been recorded. Therefore, the speed is not controlled by the online visitor and in this respect it is different from offline recitation, where the number of invocations per minute becomes the way to calculate the quality of the practice and amount of gained merit. Time counting seems to be an important factor in the overall online practice since it is also emphasized in the virtual hall for the sutra typing, where visitors are not given a minimum or maximum time for typing the lines of the text, but they can check their typing speed.

Repentance, which is cardinal in Buddhist practice, is somehow neglected by online practitioners, at least according to what is reported on the registry available on the website. An examination of the registry reveals that there is an overall average of 200 registered visitors each day to the online Buddha halls and another few hundred visitors who engage with the worship of ancestors or eminent monks. Specifically, regarding the daily visits to the different online Buddha halls, 130–140 people are active in the hall for the offering to buddhas and bodhisattvas, 20 participate virtually in the sutra chanting, 25 engage in the sutra typing, and 35 practice the online recitation of the Buddha's name. As few as an average of 10 visitors every day enter the online hall for repentance, in contrast to the historically important role of repentance in its offline form.

In contrast, worship of eminent monks and deceased family members is equally popular in online and offline media. One missing element in the online version of these memorials is the portrait or photo of the deceased family members, while the worshipped eminent monks are provided with their photos, so as to form a virtual pagoda whose images repeat (or rewrite) the history of the monastery. A second difference in the offline Buddhist worship of ancestors is that there is very little reference to the bodhisattva Dizang (地藏, Ksitigarbha). Dizang is always present in the offline monastery hall dedicated to the dead, since it is the protection of Dizang that is sought by the living for their deceased relatives, but, as it stands online, the image of Dizang appears only in the background of the home page. At the same time the many pages of worship suggest a visual reproduction of Confucian ancestor worship to replace the usual assemblage of yellow tablets located under the protection and surveillance of Dizang. This online offering is indeed a quite similar representation to the offline worship as defined by Confucians: In front of the tablet with the name of the deceased there are two candles, three incense sticks, and flowers and water (or tea), and these are the offerings that can be made online as well. In a certain sense the online union and synergy of the Buddhist Dizang and Confucian etiquette also correlate with the syncretic nature of daily Chinese ritual practices offline. Similar to the rituals conducted in the other online halls, even in the worship of ancestors or eminent monks the offerings are free of charge for the purpose of letting everyone pay respect to their relatives. However, for the golden lotus ancestor tablet, a formal (but still online) application form is required and the supplicant is charged a onetime fee. Both of these options, as the web page emphasizes, allow worshippers to perform their own worship comfortably from home through a computer and Internet connection; there is no need to make trips to a temple. However, is not pilgrimage to the sacred site an important component of worship ritual? Is the "comfortable" online ritual equally efficacious to the offline and less comfortable one? Does not the mediation of the screen affect the authenticity of the practice? Is online practice an equally sacred replacement for physical sacred space?[24] These questions are addressed in the following section.

In 2013 Nanputuo embarked on a campaign promoting "civilized rituals" (*wenming jisi* 文明祭祀), asking worshippers to avoid the burning of paper money and incense inside the worship hall and other Buddha shrines, and to avoid leaving garbage in the halls.[25] This campaign had been carried out in the past, too, and is in line with official policies that are also applied to parks and other public areas where visitors are asked to be "civilized" (*wenming* 文明). The online rituals fit these policies of "civilized worship"; indeed, according to the website, online rituals offer a "civilized and harmonious worship environment" (*wenming hexie de jisi huanjing* 文明和谐的祭祀环境), which is also environmentally friendly because incense and paper money will not be burned under any circumstance. Again, however, the ritual performance is deprived of a material and symbolic component that is essential from the perspective of traditional Chinese ritual customs: The incense is burned to purify the area, but now the incense fumes are easily replaced with just a two-dimensional image of them. The burning of paper money and the smoke that is sent to reach the other world are also eliminated, and again replaced with a two-dimensional image. Visual culture has been substituted for the performative action, and yet the resulting activity is called "ritual" and its authenticity and efficacy are neither denied nor contested by the website operators.[26]

Online activity also alters the paradigms that are the bases of the offline local Buddhist community and entails a different way for the temple's visitors to relate to the sacred site of the temple and its resident sangha. The offline community relies on monks and nuns who reside in the temple and who answer questions, resolve doubts, listen to concerns, and guide practice, and in this process, devotees build a personal and unique relationship with the resident sangha. Online, those relations are homogenized and their individual character nullified. The online community relies on ready-made instructions found on the screen. It is the screen that functions as a reference point and mediator for the worshippers, and there is no possibility available for online communication with clerics and devotees. The more impersonal connection between the practice and the practitioner in the online halls is ameliorated in part by a sense of identity with a sort of community of visitors through the creation of an online and available registry. The online practitioners are requested to register and open accounts, where their names, ages, genders, addresses, and phone numbers are stored together with the list of all the practices they have conducted (and the merit they have achieved). There is, then, a straightforward way to calculate how many practitioners visit the online halls, the date and time of their visits, and which practices they perform. Interestingly, speaking of communities, not all of the community rituals, which are crucial in Buddhist history and a key feature of the Chinese sense of religiosity, can be performed. Rituals, then, are limited to individual performances that are valued through a quantitative and impersonal counting; interpersonal relations are nullified and the only form of community is the registry. Social media like WeChat or Weibo certainly allows more interaction and exchange online between believers and clerics, as Huang (2016) and Tarocco (2017) have argued; however, these exchanges take place in a virtual space that is different from the offline sacred site. The question of the impact of online practices on the offline sacred site then still remains. The effect of the Internet on traditional ritual practices (especially the absence of some performances) and the rearticulation of the dynamics of religion, space, and place have become key issues in Chinese Buddhism today.

The significance of the online ritual hall and digital worship should also be read within the temple's overall website.[27] On top of the website's main page is a list of the main web pages and sections: news updates, a section on the Nanputuo resident community, a section on the Minnan Institute for Buddhist Studies, a space for the charity foundation, access to the Taixu Library, the *Forum* blog (which lists announcements of various Buddhist ceremonies but does not include interpersonal communications and exchanges), and finally the Online Buddha Hall and Online Memorial Worship Site, which are split into two different pages. The header of the main page, then, summarizes how Nanputuo has to appear according to the Buddhist Association of China and in order to comply with the expectations of the government. Like other Buddhist temples, Nanputuo hosts an institute for educating and training monks and nuns (according to a curriculum decided for the most part by the BAC), serves the community through philanthropic activities, gives access to believers for their ritual practices in a regulated manner, and opens the temple space to religious tourism. Visitors to the Nanputuo website are informed of all the educational, liturgical, and humanitarian activities that are run offline in the temple, and also are allowed to conduct, individually, their own ritual practice online; the first page of the Nanputuo website, then, functions as a link connecting the offline and the online practice. The division of the online practice into two web pages mirrors the structure of the offline temple as well: the Merit Building (Gongde Lou 功德楼), which was built in 2007 as a space for services to the deceased, is outside of the monastic borders and thus separated from the area where devotees participate in offerings to buddhas and chanting. A similar correspondence between the online and offline domains is found in the temple's WeChat account.

ONLINE RITUALS: FREED, CONTROLLED, OR POLITICIZED RELIGIOSITY?

The online Buddha halls and memorial worship site of Nanputuo Monastery are not an isolated case but join a considerable network of online ritual activities in China, Buddhist and otherwise. Many temples, both small and large, and other Buddhist groups have developed online ritual possibilities in the early twenty-first century, and more recently most of them also opened WeChat accounts.[28] A survey of the temples' online ritual halls shows that web pages may appear in different colors but they all reproduce the same base model and probably all use similar software. This homogeneity may be a result of the centralized politics and policies that characterize the Chinese religious landscape. The Chinese web engine Baidu includes a form of "Chinese *Wikipedia*" that has entries for both the online memorials and online rituals and serves as an index of the popularity that Buddhist cyberpractice already has achieved on the mainland. According to the definition of those sites and practices on Baidu, the offering to buddhas that is done online is as authentic and valid as the practice conducted offline in a temple, since it is the practitioner's purity of intent that determines the value of the practice, not the medium that the practice adopts. Baidu also tells us that the practice online just reflects the modernization that has permeated various sectors of Chinese society and Chinese daily life, and it is more "convenient" (*fangbian* 方便) in society today, when everyone may be too busy to find time for visiting a temple. This online practice, then, has been conceptualized and arranged in order to make it easier for Chinese people to conduct their religious rituals.[29] A similar argument is articulated on the web page for the online worship of ancestors, which is also defined as a "convenient" and "civilized" new version of the traditional ritual but one more in line with the busy rhythm of life in China today.[30]

According to Yu Haiqing, media brings at the same time centralization and decentralization of power, and media citizenship undergoes a constant process of identity reconfiguration. Therefore, encouraging (or even simply permitting) online religiosity reshapes religion, community, and the relations between the two (Yu 2008). Guobin Yang analyzes the praxes and modalities of social activism online, in its national and transnational aspects (Yang 2009; see also He 2004; Jongpil 2008). Although I would not conceive of the mediatized religious activity explored in this chapter as a form of social or politically oriented activism, I would not underestimate the form of control that the central government may exert indirectly through these web pages. A possible agenda of the political actors unfolds successfully in four main sectors: reinforcement of national identity; assertion of the "love country, love religion" ideology (which also involves the selection of the proper Chinese Buddhism to practice); weakening of temple roles; and subversion of ritual praxis.

Mediatized rituals, besides fitting into the overall plan of "civilized worship," also dictate *what* constitutes the Chinese Buddhism that believers follow. The selections of buddhas, bodhisattvas, and texts serve this purpose. The Offering Hall is the most visited online hall, Śākyamuni and Amitabha are the most popular buddhas, and Guanyin and Dizang are the most remembered bodhisattvas. The particular emphasis on those two buddhas and two bodhisattvas is in line with offline practices and ritual activities conducted in temples and/or at home. What appears is a traditional sinicized Buddhism, which is in line with the policy of "reviving Chinese civilization" (mostly against the invasion of Western ideas) that the Chinese government has encouraged since the time of Jiang Zemin, and that Xi Jinping restated even more strongly at the Nineteenth National Congress of the CCP (October 2017); in other words, we are simply presented with the online version of the offline officially acceptable Buddhism. For instance, Chinese Buddhism has given special value to four main Mahayana bodhisattvas, namely, Guanyin, Wenshushili 文殊师利, Puxian 普贤, and Dizang, who are said to reside on four sacred mountains in China; those are the bodhisattvas that online followers can worship. Another bodhisattva listed in the Offering Hall is Guan Yu 关羽, who is an interesting figure not just in the Buddhist context but for Chinese religions in general (Cai and Wen 2001; Huang 1967; Zheng 1994). Held in high regard by Confucians, Guan Yu is venerated by Taoists as a god of war who fights demons and by Buddhists as Bodhisattva Sangharama, the protector of the Buddha. Moreover, Guan Yu is a character in many Chinese novels and plays and is thus even more popular among the masses beyond merely the religious sphere. In other words, Guan Yu is Chinese first and Buddhist only second.

Another rather nationalistic tone can be perceived from the page where eminent monks are worshipped: Even here the selection is emblematic. The retrospective construction of Buddhist lineages has been studied extensively, and previous research also shows how inclusion, exclusion, and arrangement of the images of divine figures in a temple hall (whether offline or online) leads to the filtering and reshaping of temple history (see Sharf and Foulk 1993; Travagnin 2018; and chapter 5 by Daniela Campo in this volume). Similarly, the inclusion, exclusion, and arrangement of the images of eminent monks on the online worship page can tell or retell history. For instance, Taixu is present in the online pagoda; while Taixu resided in Nanputuo and was a pivotal figure in the founding of the Minnan Institute for Buddhist Studies, he never became abbot of the Nanputuo Temple. Taixu was also influential as the founder of "Buddhism for the human realm." Buddhism for the human realm was accepted as a socially responsible and engaged form of Buddhism by the Nationalists at first and, after Taixu's death, by the Communists, too. Indeed, since the 1980s, the BAC has adopted its own reading of Buddhism for the human realm as its signature idea and values it as in line with patriotic ideology. Taixu is, in this way, the "patriarch" of the Buddhism approved and promoted by the current government through the BAC; therefore, it is noteworthy that Taixu is remembered—and even venerated—in the online worship hall. This inclusion and veneration indicate that the online site maintains compatibility with the state's agenda for Buddhism.

The financial situation of the monastery can also be affected by the popularization of the online practice. As discussed previously, most of the online offerings do not involve any payment: Incense is not bought at the temple's souvenir shop and there is no request for donations on the web page. Ticket fees for visiting temples and devotees' donations constitute major financial support and independence for the life of the monastic community (see also chapter 4 by Brian Nichols in this volume). A replacement of the offline with the online practice will mean fewer incoming donations from devotees and more dependence on the BAC (i.e., the central government) for funding. In this respect, the emergence of mediatized religions could help to reinforce a "centralization of power," to borrow Yu Haiqing's words, that is, from individual temples to central authorities like the association, which could endanger the temples' agency.

The age of the offline and online followers constitutes another issue worth considering. According to the website of Nanputuo and the details that we find in the visible registry, the online practitioners are youths or young adults, which corresponds to the typical age of Internet consumers. The elder generation does not seem to be attracted to the one-click ritual and continues traditional offline liturgical practice. Nevertheless, if the popularity of online practice increases, it is foreseeable that the number of visits to temples may decrease. This potential scenario may endanger the survival of religious institutions or at least reduce temple visitors to religious tourists only. Such a prospect could change the role that Buddhist monasteries and monastics play in Chinese society offline and could crucially impact the function of monasteries as sacred spaces for religious practice.[31]

The scale of presence of this online religious phenomenon is in line with both the opening of religion since 1980 and the degree of media presence in several sectors of Chinese culture. But why are online halls popular and populated? What are the reasons for resorting to online practice and so possibly dismissing—or not relying only on—offline practice? Discussing the negotiation of religious practice online and offline, scholars tend to see two main reasons for people to participate in online practice: lack of offline centers and teachers nearby and the need to belong to a community and to have an identity when the offline community is not available, which in this case would be identity within the online community (see, for instance, Connelly 2012). However, the case of the Nanputuo Temple does not seem to fit the criteria: The analysis of the available registry of online visitors clearly reveals that, although some of the visitors to online halls are Chinese living overseas, most of them are from Xiamen or other areas where temples and teachers are easily found. During my recent fieldwork in China (summer and autumn 2015) I discussed the phenomenon of online practice with both devotees who perform online rituals and monastics. The interviewed online devotees do see a substantial difference between online ritual performances and offline visits to the temple, and they experienced the latter as a stronger form of practice, given the surrounding sacred space and the presence of a living sangha. Although considered as not equally effective, the online practice is not rejected but carried on in the same way that electronic counters of Buddha's name recitation (*dianzi nianfo jishuqi* 电子念佛计数器) were popular a decade ago.[32] On the other hand, monastics expressed approval as much as concern for the popularity of online rituals: In its favor, they felt that this new modality of practice is indeed a way to attract young people and facilitate practice for Chinese today in their very busy lives. Moreover, monastics pointed out that there are practitioners who prefer to perform their rituals on their own, in a private and not a public space surrounded by a community; for those Buddhists, online rituals represent a valid and preferable alternative. However, they also expressed concern regarding the popularity of this virtual practice because of the absence of the sangha: Lay devotees, the monks argued, need to be mentored and supervised in order to improve their own cultivation; their preoccupation then seemed to be not on the financial survival of the sangha but more on the disappearance of monks and nuns' function as spiritual guides for the devotees.

Xuecheng, chair of the BAC from 2015 to 2018, has written extensively on the use of media and technology in Buddhism. In a recent article published in the Buddhist Association's journal *Fayin* (*Voice of Dharma*), Xuecheng labeled media as "the fourth power" (*disizhong quanli* 第四种权力)[33] and claimed that it is indeed very useful in the present globalized world (Xuecheng 2012).[34] In the same article Xuecheng discussed the history of media development, from the invention of printing to the digital era, in parallel with the history of the development of Western and Eastern civilization (*wenming* 文明). Furthermore, in his Weibo account, Xuecheng celebrated the high number of netizens, one hundred thousand per day, who were chatting with the robot monk Xian'er as an excellent achievement for the Longquan Buddhist community. In a recently published interview Xuecheng stated, "Buddhists and Buddhism accept and welcome all advanced science, and we are paying attention to the development of technology" (Huikong 2016, 254). "This is an Internet age. The development of each industry depends on the Internet. Everything is connected to each other in the same way as the Internet links up different items in total. Isolation is equivalent to weakness. That is why all industries and organizations rely heavily on the Internet, which shows the strength of collective karma. Being connected as one is collective karma. We will be weak if what we Buddhists do only creates individual karma. If we are weak, we will be unable to influence society extensively" (Huikong 2016, 246).

At the same time, however, Xuecheng imposed very strict rules on who among the monks and nuns of the monasteries he supervised could use cell phones and have access to the online world. According to interviews I conducted in Beijing in late 2017, at the Longquan Temple and the Jile Temple, only the small number of clerics who hold specific positions of responsibility were allowed to use cell phones, and they could use them strictly for their missions of religious outreach. Other resident clerics were not allowed to access these

media tools, since it was feared they would bring distraction to their daily cultivation. Again, the usefulness and the dangers in the Buddhist and Buddhists'
adoption of media are both underlined.

Finally, let us return to the question of government concerns about the
practicing of rituals in a "civilized" manner that was mentioned previously in
this chapter. Nanputuo aside, the official government page of numerous cities
encourages the adoption of "civilized rituals" and behavior on the occasion of
important festivities such as the Ullambana Festival (Yulanpen Jie 盂兰盆节)
and the Qingming Festival (Qingming Jie 清明节). For instance, in March
2014, an office of the city government compiled a list of civilized behaviors for
the citizens of Daqing 大庆; the list includes the suggestion that citizens
worship their ancestors in an environmentally friendly manner: Instead of the
traditional burning of incense and paper money, citizens should adopt the
new trend of "civilized rituals," including providing offerings of flowers and
trees, providing memorials within the family household, and relying on online worship. On the occasion of the Qingming Festival in April 2014, the
Civilization Office (Wenming Ban 文明办) of Gucheng 古城 also asked its
local population to perform healthy (*jiankang* 健康) and civilized rituals, such
as online worship, memorials in the family house, and giving offerings such as
flowers; this was requested in order to prevent forest fires, keep the city clean,
and preserve the blue sky in Lijiang 丽江. For the Ullambana in July 2014, the
website of Heshan 鹤山 made a list of suggested civilized rituals and why they
are preferable to the traditional burning of paper money and incense, which
the website depicted as clear signs of "backwardness and ignorance" (*yumei
luohou* 愚昧落后). The civilized rituals include (1) science-friendly rituals (*kexue
jisi* 科学祭祀), which promote scientific awareness vis-à-vis the backward traditional (superstitious) rituals, and list online memorials;[35] (2) environmentally
friendly rituals (*huanbao jisi* 环保祭祀), which promote environmental awareness and exclude burning on streets and rooftops, and any ritual that can
contribute to pollution, may affect people's health, and may damage the
beauty of the rural environment; and (3) safe rituals (*anquan jisi* 安全祭祀),
which exclude rituals that involve dangerous activities that do not abide by fire
regulations. The website of the city of Liangzhou 凉州 added a fourth kind of
civilized ritual, frugal memorials (*jiejian jisi* 节俭祭祀), where extravagance
and waste are forbidden, and the focus is on values such as respect for the
elderly and filial piety. The website of the city of Yutian 玉田 added a fifth
type, green memorials (*lüse jisi* 绿色祭祀), which emphasize an online system
for grave sweeping and online worship and even offer rituals via text message.[36] Mottos such as "civilized memorials for a peaceful Qingming" (*wenming jisi ping'an qingming* 文明祭祀平安清明) can be found on websites and
physical banners around the cities, too. Despite the campaign for a civilized
Qingming, however, some devotees still prefer the traditional practice of
paper burning and grave sweeping because, they argue in various interviews

released on TV, the online and civilized version does not fit Chinese tradition and is not equally effective.[37]

The famous Lama Temple in Beijing also has participated in the campaign for civilized rituals by promoting the "civilized incense offering" (*wenming jingxiang* 文明敬香). As the temple website says, in doing so the Lama Temple shows that it follows the principle of "love country, love religion," fulfills social responsibilities, and has concern for the interests of the community. At the time of this writing, the Lama Temple has not started its own online worship yet, but it calls for the use of good-quality incense in moderation in order to comply with the Buddhist rule of three sticks of incense and the protection of the environment. Calls for civilized practice and use of incense are found written on wooden boards or metal plates on the premises of many monasteries in China. At the same time, shops near major monasteries still sell paper money or gifts to be burned in the traditional way, and some monastics also encourage the ritual burning of them; Zhaojue Temple (Zhaojue Si 昭觉寺) in Chengdu is a good example, with paper or gift money burned in a corner right in front of the temple entrance.

At the recent Nineteenth National Congress of the CCP (October 18–24, 2017), President Xi Jinping expressed his views on the value of *wenming* and the need to accelerate the formation of a system of ecological civilization (*shengtai wenming zhidu tixi* 生态文明制度体系).[38]

MAKING SENSE OF RITUALS ONLINE: BUDDHIST APPROACHES AND THE ONLINE WORLD

Tension between offline and online religion has been articulated often in terms of the binary "sacred" and "profane" and thus in relation to the concepts of religious experience, authority, authenticity, and legitimacy of online practice; the concept of "replication" is also revised when the offline goes online. Whereas the chapter to this point has analyzed the Nanputuo online halls within the Chinese (Buddhist) ritual context, the following paragraphs assess the Nanputuo case within the overall setting of online religion / religion online and read the perceived sacred/profane dualism from a Buddhist perspective. Stephen Jacobs interviewed the designer of the software of a Hindu virtual temple, and the answers he received reflected the daily practice of Hinduism by Hindus as well as foundational tenets of Hindu philosophy. According to the web designer, the Hindu position on reality that everything is illusion should suggest that there is no difference between a physical sacred space and an on-line cyberspace. Then, the web designer argues, "'God is in everything and is omnipresent; we can devote our every action as an act of worship. Why not, then, use the Internet as another venue for worship?'" (N. Iyengar, June 2005, as quoted in Jacobs 2007, 1112). Finally, the web designer does not see the lack of consecration of the virtual temple as a problem, because in-home shrines are not consecrated either but are still considered valid; moreover, the virtual temple is to be conceived as a form of in-home shrine (Jacobs 2007). The legitimacy of the Hindu virtual temple is then assured on the basis of foundational issues of the Hindu tradition.

Something similar can be argued for the virtual halls of Nanputuo or other temples and their legitimacy. One of the key teachings of Mahayana Buddhism (which is the most practiced tradition in East Asia and is the tradition of Nanputuo as well) is the concept of *upāya* (skillful means), according to which modalities of preaching and codes of practice change according to the situation to fit different audiences and circumstances. And if Mahayana can justify killing on the basis of the *upāya* concept, then it can also legitimize online practice as authentic and no less authoritative than offline practice.[39] Mahayana also conceives that samsara and nirvana are not in opposition but can be identified as the same entity; this could provide a different reading of the sacred/profane dualism as well and could solve the question of the authenticity and efficacy of online practice.[40]

When it comes to religious experience and authority, the Internet challenges existing patterns of authority and at the same time creates new ones, and if the dynamics between priest and follower are disrupted, then the synergy between netizen and screen generates another level of experience (Baffelli, Reader, and Staemmler 2011, 20–35). In other words, the online world per se creates new ritual possibilities, based on a different relationship with offline sacred space and the patterns associated with it. The Buddhist religious ritual experience is redefined, whereas the media ritual experience is enhanced.

We can conclude that offline and online practices are not then two realities that collide, but two alternative paths that, in distinct realms of hierarchy and structure, guarantee equal authenticity and authority. From a different perspective, it can be argued that online practice would not exist without an offline referent and that online rituals exist only through reference to the offline religious world. Glenn Young goes a step further and argues that the online and offline worlds are in continuous dialogue and interaction, and the reference that the online makes to the offline seems to suggest a form of dependence of the former on the latter (Young 2013). We may see then a sort of hierarchy, with the offline (still) in a higher position.

BUDDHIST HISTORY AND BUDDHIST RITUAL OVERTURNED

Chinese society is framed within a ritualistic structure. Those rituals maintain relations between this world and the afterlife and preserve harmony and balance in the Chinese universe; therefore, they function as a normative practice. From this perspective, the transformations of ritual discourse in the online world could cause repercussions on the efficacy of the rituals and eventually destabilize the structure of Chinese society. On the other hand, Chinese rituals also appear as a flexible and malleable performance. Indeed, traditional rituals are often altered in their local versions, and the amendments do not affect the validity of the rites. Looked at in this way, online rituals may not be less valid than offline ones: They represent just another variation.

This chapter has specifically analyzed Chinese Buddhist rituals and highlighted two elements as particularly affected in the online translation of Buddhist ritual practice: the sacred and the social space. The liturgical area turns into a computer screen, the sangha's guidance is translated into typed and impersonal instructions, and community rituals disappear completely. Social dynamics and space articulation are erased, but the inner experience of the online practitioner may not be affected and therefore may be equal to the one felt by the offline practitioner. This is also facilitated by the ritualism that the exposure to—and participation in—the Internet process reproduces in cyberspace. In other words, the individual's ritual emotional involvement is not modified. However, it is only via WeChat or Weibo that cyberspace may preserve interactive exchange between clerics and believers, within the restrictions that the online space imposes.

My argument is not that there are not believers going to temples anymore, or that empty sacred sites represent the future for Buddhism in China. In fact, I have witnessed crowds of worshippers in Nanputuo Temple and other temples throughout China, a phenomenon that also is apparent in chapter 4 by Brian Nichols and chapter 10 by Gareth Fisher in this volume. I do not aim to imply that there are neither ritual practices nor other activities at monasteries anymore. I just intend to underline the presence of another *site* for ritual practices, which survives in parallel to the offline one, and I argue that this double siting of ritual practice poses changes and challenges at the present time and possibly will pose challenges in the future to offline community and sacred space.

The Chinese government has intervened in obstructing and then rehabilitating some forms of religion, and the presence of religion in the media might be a clear result and manifestation of these new central policies. At the same time, the phenomenon of mediated and mediatized religion brings in a reconfiguration of the history, structure, and role of temples; reshapes religion in China (and so Chinese religions); and contributes to the writing of a new chapter of the national history of China.

China's State Council issued new regulations on religious affairs in September 2017 that went into effect in February 2018; one of the major points of these new regulations was the need to oversee online religious discussions. In November 2017, it was reiterated clearly that online worship of buddhas and bodhisattvas, as well as memorial worship, should not be accompanied by donations (He 2018). The challenges posed by the Internet and so-called cyberactivities had been the topic of earlier meetings, too, like the Central Religious Work Conference on April 22–23, 2016. Similar arguments were reiterated and proposed again in early July 2018, and later posted in October 2018 on the websites of several temples (including Nanputuo; "Xi Jinping" 2018) among the list of the regulations by which those temples must abide. According to the new regulations, first, the Internet per se is not a problem, but the use of the Internet to propagate messages that contradict or oppose the principles of the party is. Second, online religious activities that are not just the online version of practices existing offline are prohibited; overall, Islam and Christianity, being beliefs that come from the West, are explicitly and specifically targeted in the regulations. The State Administration for Religious Affairs (SARA) also issued a new document on September 11, 2018, banning the online burning of incense and the recitation of liturgies. Nonetheless, one month later, websites of temples like Nanputuo still include the possibility to perform offerings to buddhas and bodhisattvas and so do their WeChat accounts. Moreover, online performances of traditional rituals are still found on the list of the "civilized rituals" mentioned earlier in this chapter.

Therefore, it seems that, up to October 2018, these new regulations restricting online activities have affected mostly Islam and Christianity and nonregistered religious groups; Buddhist temples, on the other hand, have not implemented any considerable changes in their online practice yet. The Buddhist emphasis on patriotism and loyalty to the party, along with Buddhist efforts to promote their religion as acceptably "sinicized," might have prevented the application of the new restrictions.

NOTES

This study is based on research and interviews conducted in China from 2012 to 2017 among communities in Fujian, Zhejiang, Sichuan, and Beijing. The first draft of this chapter was presented in the panel "Chinese Religions Online" at the Association for Asian Studies Annual Meeting in March 2014 and has benefited from the very helpful comments of the panel discussant, Yang Guobin. A revised version was presented at the conference Buddhism after Mao in October 2014, and I am grateful for suggestions that the participants of the meeting, especially Adam Yuet Chau, offered generously. More recently, I am particularly indebted to the numerous exchanges I had with the Animation Center of the Beijing Longquan Monastery (Beijing Longquan Si Dongman Zhongxin 北京龙泉寺动漫中心) and the monk Xianqing 贤清.

1. The figure of Xian'er was created in 2013. In 2014, it became the protagonist of a series of comics and animated cartoons and was later inspiration for the robot. Robot Monk Generation I Xian'er made its first appearance on October 1, 2015; in October 2016, it was replaced with Xian'er Generation II. Xian'er is currently kept at the Longquan Animation Center at the Longquan Temple in Beijing.

2. This robot is part of a Wang Yangming–themed park built in Guiyang.

3. With Deng Xiaoping 邓小平 (1904–1997) we saw the beginning of a change in the official perspective and policies on religion, "a transition from intolerance to conditional religious rights" (Yao, Stout, and Liu 2011, 40). The famous Document no. 19 (Shijiu Hao Wenjian 十九号文件), "The Basic Viewpoint and Policy on the Religious Question during

Our Country's Socialist Period" (Guanyu wo guo shehuizhuyi shiqi zongjiao wenti de jiben guandian he jiben zhengce 关于我国社会主义时期宗教问题的基本观点和基本政策), which was issued in 1982, became a key document for the development of religion in China. It offered a mapping of the religious groups present in China and assured Chinese the right of religious beliefs as long as those beliefs show loyalty and respect for the party and the central government. In the last decade of the twentieth century, Jiang Zemin 江泽民 (b. 1926) contributed to improving the situation even further by delivering positive comments on religion and religious practice (Goossaert and Palmer 2011; Yao, Stout, and Liu 2011). It is usually argued that Deng Xiaoping's new policies represented a transitional phase, since the new opening to religion and the religious was conceived as depending on the continued respect of the government and so of the Chinese Communist Party. However, it was only with Jiang Zemin in the 1990s that the government discussed religion in more directly positive terms and as a potential stabilizing force for the nation (see also chapter 1 by André Laliberté in this volume).

4. Concepts of "secularism," "postsecularism," "secularization," and "desecularization" in China have been subjects of unresolved debates, which are characterized by a lack of general agreement and overall space of contention. Some scholars have talked of "desecularization" (Yang 2004; Yao, Stout, and Liu 2011), some refer to the same time and circumstances in terms of "postsecularism" (Madsen 2009, 2011a, 2011b), and others argue that China never departed from "secularism" (Wang 2002, 2003; Zhao 2010). I thank Ji Zhe for sharing his article "Secularization without Secularism: The Political-Religious Configuration of Post-89 China" (Ji 2015), which offers a review of many of the competing voices in this debate and includes Ji's proposition of "secularization without secularism" as a defining characteristic of the China case.

5. See, for instance, Yu 2008; specifically about the Internet, see Yang Guobin 2009, 2015. Specifically about religion and media in China, see Travagnin 2016b.

6. For scholarship on religion and the Internet, see Campbell 2010 and Hoover and Schofield Clark 2002. More specifically on religion and the Internet in East Asia, see Baffelli, Reader, and Staemmler 2011; Clart 2012; and Dorman and Reader 2007.

7. On Buddhists' blogs, see also Travagnin 2016a.

8. Stewart Hoover refers to virtual online space as "third space," something in between the private and social-professional spheres: "There are many dimensions on which the digital can be located as a unique space between and beyond received polarities. This 'in-betweenness' is, to our way of thinking, basic to the meaning of 'third-ness'" (Hoover and Echchaibi 2012, 9). This concept of "third space" was proposed earlier in other academic fields by scholars such as sociologist Ray Oldenburg (1989).

9. On *communitas,* see Anderson 1983; Campbell 2010. On the role of space and place in religion, and the so-called spatial turn in the study of religion, see, among others, Knott 2010.

10. On ritual in religion, see Asad 1993; Bell 1992, 1997, 1998; and LaFleur 1998. For Chinese rituals, see, for instance, Feuchtwang 1992; Johnson 1995; Reinders 1997, 2015; and Wolf 1974. For ritual in Buddhism, see among others Payne 2004 and Sharf 2005.

11. Online Buddha Hall, accessed October 13, 2018, http://www.nanputuo.com/nptft/; Online Memorial Worship Site, accessed October 13, 2018, http://www.nanputuo.com/nptgdl/.

12. Taixu, a native of Chongde 崇德, Zhejiang Province, became fully ordained at the Tiantong Temple (Tiantong Si 天童寺), Ningbo, in 1907. Taixu was active in Xiamen and

Nanputuo from the mid-1920s, and, most important, he was dean of the Minnan Institute for Buddhist Studies from 1927 to 1933.

13. Among recent studies of Nanputuo, see Ashiwa and Wank 2006 and Wank 2009.

14. This is also available on the temple's WeChat account.

15. This practice generally means "transferring one's accumulated merit to another," and it became interpreted and adopted as a way to transfer (accumulated) merit to buddhas and bodhisattvas, or to a deceased person, or even—especially in the East Asian Mahayana context—to all living beings. Merit is transferred through a formal recitation of verses for the dedication of merit that contains details such as how the merit was generated and who the recipient of that merit is. Merit can be accumulated through a number of activities such as reciting or copying sutras. Philip Clart has discussed the problems in granting "merit" online that religious movements in Taiwan have experienced: "Electronic *shanshu* can fulfil only two of the three basic functions of their print counterparts; the one function not yet available is that of directly generating quantifiable amounts of merit. Therefore, intangible yet quantifiable merit remains for the time being tied to tangible (and equally quantifiable) offline merit products" (Clart 2012, 133–134).

16. The offerings include incense, water, flowers, fruit, and candles.

17. The buddhas listed are Śākyamuni, Amitabha, the Medicine Buddha (Yaoshifo 药师佛), Maitreya (Mile Fo 弥勒佛), and the Eighty-Eight Buddhas (Bashiba fo 八十八佛); the bodhisattvas are the four main Mahayana bodhisattvas worshipped in China (Wenshushili 文殊师利, Puxian 普贤, Guanyin 观音, and Dizang 地藏) and Guan Yu 关羽. The WeChat version includes only Śākyamuni, Amitabha, Guanyin, and Manjusri, but the modes of offering do not differ from what is available on the website.

18. The buddhas include Śākyamuni, Amitabha, and the Medicine Buddha; the bodhisattvas are Guanyin and Dizang.

19. The Sutra Copying Hall includes almost two hundred titles, between texts, dharani, and appellations of buddhas and bodhisattvas; the Sutra Recitation Hall lists almost one hundred texts.

20. See, for instance, *Jingang jing* 金刚经 (*T* no. 8, 235); *Fo shuo dacheng wuliangshou zhuangyan qingjing pingdeng jue jing* 佛说大乘无量寿庄严清净平等觉经 (*T* no. 12, 361); *Chu sanzang jiji* 出三藏记集 (*T* no. 55, 2145).

21. See also *Foguang dacidian* 佛光大辞典, vol. 3, pp. 2949a–2950a; *Bukkyo daijiten* 佛教大辞典, vol. 3, pp. 2567a–2568a.

22. Positions of the body during rituals and actions, like prostrations and bowing, become important because they are symbolic of the vertical hierarchy that characterizes social and religious relations in traditional China (see Reinders 1997, 2015).

23. I do not aim to argue that all worshippers fail to undertake physical prostrations when using the online site; however, Buddhists I interviewed in Fujian, Beijing, Sichuan, and Zhejiang reported this, indicating that it is a widespread phenomenon.

24. Unlike the Christian virtual churches or the Hindu virtual temples, there is no re-creation of the temple layout in this Buddhist online ritual place.

25. The "Promotion of 'Civilized Rituals' in the Merit Hall of Nanputuo Temple in Xiamen," published in October 2013, says,

> In response to the call of the city government to perform civilized rituals, and for facilitating our believers [*xinzhong* 信众] in their memorials for the ancestors in a more convenient way, this temple has deliberated the following: inside the Merit

Hall, where the tablets of the family ancestors are located, you are asked not to conduct activities such as burning incense or candles, using firecrackers, or burning paper money, paper houses, or relics; instead, we encourage reminiscence and worship of the deceased with offerings of flowers, fruit, vegetarian food, and recitations. While performing the rituals, please keep quiet; after the ritual, please put the offered goods into storage; do not litter but keep the environment tidy and clean. We hope this will receive support and cooperation by the believers; thank you for your understanding. (Nanputuo Temple website, accessed October 15, 2018, http:// www.nanputuo.com/nptnews/html/201310/0109530673499.html)

26. Previous studies on "virtual Buddhism" have argued that online ritual activities can hardly be perfect replications of offline practice since online ritual space can host only voice and text, while other senses (smells, incense fumes, etc.) are missing. See Connelly 2012.

27. This refers to the format that the website had until late 2017.

28. See, for instance, Bodhisattva Online (Pusa Zaixian 菩萨在线), accessed October 15, 2018, http://www.pusa123.com; Buddhism in the Human Realm Net (Renjian Fojiao Wang 人间佛教网), accessed October 15, 2018, http://www.365ago.com/fotang/; Universal Buddha's Light Online Buddha Hall (Foguang Puzhao; Zaixian Fotang 佛光普照在线佛堂), accessed September 23, 2014, http://www.360doc.com/content/12/0328/21/7220266_198742565 .shtml; Online Recitation of the Buddha (Zaixian Nianfo 在线念佛), accessed October 15, 2018, http://www.jzfjw.cn/nf/nf.asp. Online halls on Buddhist temples' websites include those at the Fuhui Temple (Fuhui Si 福慧寺), accessed October 15, 2018, http://www.ahfhs .org/fotang/; and the Lotus Chan Temple (Hualian Chan Si 花莲禅寺), accessed October 15, 2018, http://www.lianhuachansi.com/OnlineFuTang.aspx. See Laliberté 2016 for a detailed analysis of Buddhist websites.

29. See "Online Worship of the Buddha," *Wangshang Li Fo* 网上礼佛, accessed October 15, 2018, http://baike.baidu.com/view/4196015.htm.

30. See "Online Worship of the Buddha," *Wangshang Li Fo* 网上礼佛, accessed October 15, 2018, http://baike.baidu.com/view/970812.htm.

31. For more on the possible function of Buddhist monasteries as tourist sites, see chapter 4 by Nichols in this volume.

32. These little objects had a button to click at the time of any recitation of the Buddha's name, and at the end of the day the devotee could see how many times he or she had recited the name of the Buddha; this device enhanced the quantitative rather than the qualitative aspect of the practice. See Heller 2014.

33. Xuecheng is referring to the traditional concept of powers or estates from Christian Europe from the Middle Ages to the French Revolution. The first three powers (or estates) are the clergy, the aristocracy, and the masses. Since the end of the eighteenth century, the media (in the form of news press only at that time) has been defined as a fourth power or estate.

34. This article (see Xuecheng 2012) was posted on the Longquan Temple website as well (accessed October 6, 2018, http://www.longquanzs.org/lqs/hcfs/hcfs/46884.htm) and was indicated to me by monks and volunteers of Longquan as a good piece to really understand Xuecheng's position on the use of media.

35. The propaganda of science versus superstition is then iterated here as well. The present state discourse on rituals resonates with arguments in official campaigns against

superstitious practice that have characterized the People's Republic as much as the previous Republic of China.

36. The online system of grave sweeping is defined as modern, exemplifying another instance of the binary modernity versus tradition in state discourse on religious practice.

37. The Chinese Internet also offers an Online Chinese Memorial Network (Zhongguo Jisi Wang 中国祭祀网), which was inaugurated in 2010, and among various options, it also provides netizens with the possibility of creating a graveyard for the deceased dear to them and making offerings on virtual graves for free. In other words, online worship is a widespread practice that goes beyond the sphere of just Buddhism.

38. In his remarks Xi Jinping listed, among others, the concepts of "material civilization" (*wuzhi wenming* 物质文明), "civilized government" (*zhengzhi wenming* 政治文明), "spiritual civilization" (*jingshen wenming* 精神文明), "civilized society" (*shehui wenming* 社会文明), and "civilized ecology" (*shengtai wenming* 生态文明).

39. Tarocco included similar findings in her article and stated that her informants understood "cyber-Buddhism as a contemporary instantiation of 'skilfulness in means' (*fangbian* 方便)" (Tarocco 2017, 167).

40. More general ritual theories could also be included in this discussion, since some concepts of the theory of "ritual dynamics" such as "ritual transfer" can explain how ritual settings and performances can then be transfused to—and reconstructed in—the digital world, and cyberspace can therefore become an acceptable ritual space (Heidbrink 2007).

REFERENCES

ACMRC (All China Marketing Research Co.). 2010. *The Atlas of Religions in China*. Beijing: National Bureau of Statistics of China.

Adamek, Wendy L. 2007. *The Mystique of Transmission: On an Early Chan History and Its Contexts*. New York: Columbia University Press.

Allès, Élisabeth. 2000. *Musulmans de Chine: Une anthropologie des Hui du Henan*. Paris: EHESS.

Ammerman, Nancy Tatom, and Arthur Emery Farnsley. 1997. *Congregation & Community*. New Brunswick, NJ: Rutgers University Press.

Anālayo bhikkhu. 2013. "The Revival of the Bhikkhunī Order and the Decline of the Sāsana." *Journal of Buddhist Ethics* 20:110–193.

Anderson, Benedict. 1983. *Imagined Communities: Reflections on the Origin and Spread of Nationalism*. London: Verso.

Angelskar, Trine. 2013. "China's Buddhist Diplomacy." NOREF (Norwegian Peacebuilding Resource Centre) Report. http://peacebuilding.no/var/ezflow_site/storage/original /application/280b5bde8e7864209c33d01737fd2db0.pdf. Accessed January 21, 2016.

Asad, Talal. 1993. *Genealogies of Religion: Discipline and Reasons of Power in Christianity and Islam*. Baltimore, MD: Johns Hopkins University Press.

Ashiwa, Yoshiko. 1998. "The Contemporary Cultural Landscape Seen in the Restoration of Bhikkhuni Vinaya." *Journal of Hitotsubashi University* 120:558–585.

———. 2009. "Positioning Religion in Modernity: State and Buddhism in China." In *Making Religion, Making the State: The Politics of Religion in Modern China*, edited by Yoshiko Ashiwa and David L. Wank, pp. 43–73. Stanford, CA: Stanford University Press.

———. 2015. "The Revival of Nun Ordination of the Theravada Tradition in Sri Lanka: A Landscape of the Culture in the Contemporary World." *Hitotsubashi Journal of Social Studies* 46 (1): 19–40.

Ashiwa, Yoshiko, and David L. Wank. 2005. "The Globalization of Chinese Buddhism: Clergy and Devotee Networks in the Twentieth Century." *International Journal of Asian Studies* 2 (2): 217–237.

———. 2006. "The Politics of a Reviving Buddhist Temple in Contemporary China: State, Association and Religion in Southeast China." *Journal of Asian Studies* 65 (2): 337–359.

———. 2009. "Making Religion, Making the State: An Introductory Essay." In *Making Religion, Making the State: The Politics of Religion in Modern China*, edited by Yoshiko Ashiwa and David L. Wank, pp. 43–73. Stanford, CA: Stanford University Press.

————. 2016. "Xiandai Zhongguo fojiao de kuaguo sengsu wangluo: Kuayue minzu guojia de hezuo moshi yu ziyuan liutong" 现代中国佛教的跨国僧俗网络: 跨越民族国家的合作模式与资源流通. In *Ershi shiji Zhongguo fojiao de liangci fuxing* 二十世纪中国佛教的两次复兴, edited by Ji Zhe 汲喆, Daniela Campo 田水晶, and Wang Qiyuan 王启元, pp. 109–132. Shanghai: Fudan daxue chubanshe. Revised version of "The Globalization of Chinese Buddhism: Clergy and Devotee Networks in the Twentieth Century," *International Journal of Asian Studies* 2, no. 2 (2005): 217–237.

Baffelli, Erica, Ian Reader, and Birgit Staemmler, eds. 2011. *Japanese Religions on the Internet.* London: Routledge.

Bandurski, David. 2015. "Meet Mr. 'Hot Phrase.'" *China Media Project.* February 6. Accessed September 25, 2015. http://cmp.hku.hk/2015/02/06/38107/.

Barnett, Robbie. 1994. *Resistance and Reform in Tibet.* Bloomington: Indiana University Press.

Barrett, Timothy H. 2005. "Buddhist Precepts in a Lawless World: Some Comments on the Linhuai Ordination Scandal." In *Going Forth. Visions of Buddhist Vinaya. Essays Presented in Honor of Professor Stanley Weinstein,* edited by William M. Bodiford, pp. 101–123. Honolulu: University of Hawai'i Press.

Bartholomeusz, Tessa J. 1994. *Women under the Bo Tree: Buddhist Nuns in Sri Lanka.* Cambridge: Cambridge University Press.

Bays, Daniel. 2003. "Chinese Protestant Christianity Today." *China Quarterly* 174: 488–504.

Bell, Catherine. 1992. *Ritual Theory, Ritual Practice.* New York: Oxford University Press.

————. 1997. *Ritual: Perspectives and Dimensions.* New York: Oxford University Press.

————. 1998. "Performance." In *Critical Terms for Religious Studies,* edited by Mark Taylor, pp. 205–224. Chicago: Chicago University Press.

Bianchi, Ester. 2001. *The Iron Statue Monastery "Tiexiangsi": A Buddhist Nunnery of Tibetan Tradition in Contemporary China.* Florence: Leo S. Olschki.

————. 2017a. "Subtle Erudition and Compassionate Devotion: Longlian, 'the Most Outstanding *Bhiksuni* in Modern China.'" In *Making Saints in Modern China,* edited by David Ownby, Vincent Goossaert, and Ji Zhe, pp. 272–311. New York: Oxford University Press.

————. 2017b. "Yi Jie Wei Shi 以戒为师: Theory and Practice of Monastic Discipline in Modern and Contemporary Chinese Buddhism." *Studies in Chinese Religions* 3 (2): 111–141.

————. 2017c. "Sino-Tibetan Buddhism: Continuities and Discontinuities. The Case of Nenghai's 能海 Legacy in the Contemporary Era." In *Chinese and Tibetan Esoteric Buddhism,* edited by Yael Bentor and Shahar Meir, pp. 300–318. Leiden: Brill.

————. Forthcoming. "Understanding Jielü 戒律: Resurgence and Reconfiguration of Vinaya-Related Concepts in Modern China." In *Critical Concepts and Methods for the Study of Chinese Religions II: Intellectual History of Key Concepts,* edited by Gregory Scott and Stefania Travagnin. Berlin: De Gruyter.

Bingenheimer, Marcus. 2016. *Island of Guanyin: Mount Putuo and Its Gazetteers.* New York: Oxford University Press.

Birnbaum, Raoul. 2003a. "Buddhist China at the Century's Turn." *China Quarterly* 174:428–450.

————. 2003b. "Master Hongyi Looks Back: A 'Modern Man' Becomes a Monk in Twentieth-Century China." In *Buddhism in the Modern World: Adaptations of an Ancient Tradition,* edited by Steven Heine and Charles S. Prebish, pp. 75–124. New York: Oxford University Press.

———. 2017. "Two Turns in the Life of Master Hongyi, a Buddhist Monk in Twentieth-Century China." In *Making Saints in Modern China,* edited by David Ownby, Vincent Goossaert, and Ji Zhe, pp. 161–208. New York: Oxford University Press.

Bodiford, William M., ed. 2005. *Going Forth. Visions of Buddhist Vinaya. Essays Presented in Honor of Professor Stanley Weinstein.* Honolulu: University of Hawai'i Press.

Borchert, Thomas. 2005. "Of Temples and Tourists: The Effects of the Tourist Economy on a Minority Buddhist Community in Southwest China." In *State, Market, and Religions in Chinese Societies,* edited by Yang Fenggang and Joseph B. Tamney, pp. 87–111. Leiden: Brill.

———. 2009. "A Temple of Their Own? Temple Building, City Development and Local Politics in Southwest China." Paper delivered at the National Meeting of the American Academy of Religion, Montreal, November 7.

Bourdieu, Pierre. 1971. "Genèse et structure du champ religieux." *Revue française de sociologie* 12 (1): 295–334.

Boutonnet, Thomas. 2009. "Vers une 'société harmonieuse' de consommation? Discours et spectacle de l'harmonie sociale dans la construction d'une Chine 'civilisée' (1978–2008)." PhD diss., Université de Lyon, Jean Moulin Lyon 3.

Branigan, Tania. 2012. "Chinese Shrine Seeks Stock-Market Path to Financial Nirvana." *Guardian.* July 5. Accessed February 22, 2018. https://www.theguardian.com/world/2012/jul/05/chinese-shrine-stock-market-nirvana.

Buswell, Robert E. 1992. *The Zen Monastic Experience: Buddhist Practice in Contemporary Korea.* Princeton, NJ: Princeton University Press.

Cabestan, Jean-Pierre. 1994. *Le système politique de la Chine populaire.* Paris: PUF.

———. 2014. *Le système politique chinois. Un nouvel équilibre autoritaire.* Paris: Presses de Sciences Politiques.

Cai Dongzhou 蔡东洲 and Wen Tinghai 文廷海. 2001. *Guan Yu chongbai yanjiu* 关羽崇拜研究. Sichuan: Bashu shushe 巴蜀书社.

Campany, Robert Ford. 1993. "The Real Presence. For Joseph M. Kitagawa." *History of Religions* 32 (3): 233–272.

———. 1996. *Strange Writing. Anomaly Accounts in Early Medieval China.* Albany: State University of New York Press.

Campbell, Heidi A. 2010. *When Religion Meets New Media.* London: Routledge.

Campo, Daniela. 2013. *La construction de la sainteté dans la Chine moderne: La vie du maître bouddhiste Xuyun.* Paris: Les Belles Lettres.

———. 2017. "Chan Master Xuyun: The Embodiment of an Ideal, the Transmission of a Model." In *Making Saints in Modern China,* edited by David Ownby, Vincent Goossaert, and Ji Zhe, pp. 99–136. New York: Oxford University Press.

———. 2017b. "A Different Buddhist Revival: The Promotion of Vinaya (*Jielü* 戒律) in Republican China." *Journal of Global Buddhism* 18:129–154.

———. 2017c. "Imposing the Rules: Reform and Rebellion at Gushan Yongquan Monastery in the 1930s." *Studies in Chinese Religions* 3 (2): 142–174.

Cao Nanlai. 2013. "In the World but Not of the World: Governing Grassroots Christian Charity in China." In *Charities in the Non-Western World: The Development and Regulation of Indigenous and Islamic Charities,* edited by Rajeswary Ampalavanar Brown and Justin Pierce, pp. 187–206. New York: Routledge.

Caple, Jane. 2015. "Faith, Generosity, Knowledge and the Buddhist Gift: Moral Discourses on Chinese Patronage of Tibetan Buddhist Monasteries." *Religion Compass* 9 (11): 462–482.

Carter, James. 2011. *Heart of Buddha, Heart of China. The Life of Tanxu, a Twentieth-Century Monk.* Oxford: Oxford University Press.

Cen Xuelü 岑学吕, ed. 1995. *Xuyun fashi nianpu* 虚云法师年谱. Beijing: Zongjiao wenhua chubanshe.

Chan Sin-wai. 1985. *Buddhism in Late Ch'ing Political Thought.* Boulder, CO: Westview Press.

Chan, Wing-tsit. 1953. *Religious Trends in Modern China.* New York: Columbia University Press.

Chandler, Stuart. 2004. *Establishing a Pure Land on Earth: The Foguang Buddhist Perspective on Modernization and Globalization.* Honolulu: University of Hawai'i Press.

Chang Chia-lan. 2007. "The Modern Legend of Miaoshan: The Development of the Sangha of Vegetarian Nuns in China." In *The Constant and Changing Faces of the Goddess: Goddess Traditions of Asia,* edited by Deepak Shimkhada and Phyllis K. Herman, pp. 246–272. Newcastle upon Tyne: Cambridge Scholars Publishing.

Chang Hao. 1971. *Liang Ch'i-ch'ao and Intellectual Transition in China, 1890–1907.* Cambridge, MA: Harvard University Press.

Charleux, Isabelle. 2015. *Nomads on Pilgrimage. Mongols on Wutaishan (China), 1800–1940.* Leiden: Brill.

Chau, Adam Yuet. 2006. *Miraculous Responses: Doing Popular Religion in Contemporary China.* Stanford, CA: Stanford University Press.

———, ed. 2011a. *Religion in Contemporary China: Revitalization and Innovation.* London: Routledge.

———. 2011b. "Modalities of Doing Religion." In *Chinese Religious Life: Culture, Society, and Politics,* edited by David A. Palmer, Glenn Shive, and Philip Wickeri, pp. 67–84. Oxford: Oxford University Press.

———. 2011c. "Modalities of Doing Religion and Ritual Polytropy: Evaluating the Religious Market Model from the Perspective of Chinese Religious History." *Religion* 41 (4): 547–568.

———. 2012. "Transnational Buddhist Activists in the Era of Empires." In *Religious Internationals in the Modern World,* edited by Abigail Green and Vincent Viaene, pp. 206–229. Basingstoke: Palgrave Macmillan.

———. 2013. "Religious Subjectification: The Practice of Cherishing Written Characters and Being a Ciji (Tzu Chi) Person." In *Chinese Popular Religion: Linking Fieldwork and Theory,* edited by Chang Hsun, pp. 75–113. Taipei: Academia Sinica.

Chen Bing 陈兵 and Deng Zimei 邓子美. 2000. *Ershi shiji zhongguo fojiao* 二十世纪中国佛教. Beijing: Minzu chubanshe.

Chen Guoqiang 陈国强 and Cai Yongzhe 蔡永哲, eds. 1990. *Chongwu renleixue diaocha* 崇武人类学调查. Fujian: Fujian jiaoyu chubanshe.

Chen Huaiyu. 2007. *The Revival of Buddhist Monasticism in Medieval China.* New York: Peter Lang.

Chen Jinguo 陈进国. 2010. "Guanyu Zhongguo zongjiao shengtailun de zhenglun" 关于中国宗教生态论的争论. *Zhongguo minzubao* 中国民族报, July 6.

Chen Xiao 陈霄. 2014. "Beida hou EMBA ban zuigao xuefei jin 90 wan, zhao zhengchuji yishang guanyuan" 北大后EMBA班最高学费近90万, 招正处级以上官员. *China World-wide Net.* July 30. Accessed February 22, 2018. http://china.huanqiu.com /article/ 2014-07/5090830.html.

Chen Xingqiao 陈星桥. 2011. "Yi jie wei shi shao fozhong guifan chuanjie su seng yi: Quanguo hanchuan fojiao guifan chuanjie yantaoban ceji" 以戒为师绍佛种规范传戒肃僧仪—全国汉传佛教规范传戒研讨班侧记. *Fayin* 法音 8:21–26.

Chen Zhenzhen 陳珍珍. 2000. "Tan Fujian de 'fanxing qingxinnü'" 谈福建的 "梵行清信女." *Fayin* 法音1 (185): 63–67.

Cheng, May M. C. 2003. "House Church Movement and Religious Freedom in China." *China: An International Journal* 1 (1): 16–45.

China Corporate Social Responsibility. 2008. "Tzu Chi Foundation Approved to Open Branch in Mainland China." March 3. Accessed February 22, 2018. http://www.chinacsr.com/en/2008/03/03/2136-tzu-chi-foundation-approved-to-open-branch-in-mainland-china/.

China Daily. 2015. "Fangsheng luosi wuran jinghang da yunhe, si luosi dui anbian" 放生螺丝污染京杭大运河，死螺丝堆岸边. *China Daily.* January 13. Accessed February 22, 2018. http://cnews.chinadaily.com.cn/2015-01/13/content_19302534.htm.

China News Net. 2010. "Guangdong chengli fangsheng xiehui, zheng shang zongjiao jie renshi chang 'da'ai'" 广东成立放生协会，政商宗教界人士倡 "大爱." May 22. Accessed February 22, 2018. http://www.chinanews.com/gn/news/2010/05-22/2298262.shtml.

———. 2014. "Guangdong Huizhou juban di ba jie daxing fangsheng jie, gaishan Dongjiang shuizhi huanjing" 广东惠州举办第8届大型放生节 改善东江水质环境. June 6. Accessed October 9, 2018. http://www.chinanews.com/df/2014/06-06/6254140.shtml.

Chiu Tzu-Lung and Ann Heirman. 2014. "The Gurudharmas in Buddhist Nunneries in Mainland China." *Buddhist Studies Review* 31 (2): 241–272.

Chongrou 崇柔. 2013. "Pini shi zhengfa jiuzhu de baozhang" 毗尼是正法久住的保障. February 17, 2011. Accessed October 14, 2018. http://blog.sina.com.cn/s/blog_5f0898c80100q9ho.html.

Chu, William. 2006. "Bodhisattva Precepts in the Ming Society: Factors behind Their Success and Propagation." *Journal of Buddhist Ethics* 13:1–36.

Cimino, Richard P., Nadia A. Mian, and Weishan Huang. 2013. *Ecologies of Faith in New York City.* Bloomington: Indiana University Press.

Clart, Philip. 2012. "Mediums and the New Media: The Impact of Electronic Publishing on Temple and Moral Economies in Taiwanese Popular Religion." *Journal of Sinological Studies* 3:127–141.

Clart, Philip, and Gregory Adam Scott. 2015. *Religious Publishing and Print Culture in Modern China, 1800–2012.* Berlin: De Gruyter.

Cochini, Christian. 2008. *Guide des temples bouddhistes de Chine.* Paris: Les Indes savantes.

Collins, Steven, and Justin McDaniel. 2010. "Buddhist 'Nuns' (*mae chi*) and the Teaching of Pali in Contemporary Thailand." *Modern Asian Studies* 44 (6): 1373–1408.

Connelly, Louise. 2012. "Virtual Buddhism: Buddhist Ritual in Second Life." In *Digital Religion: Understanding Religious Practice in New Media Worlds,* edited by Heidi A. Campbell, pp. 128–135. London: Routledge.

Covell, Ralph R. 2001. "Christianity and China's Minority Nationalities—Faith and Unbelief." In *China and Christianity: Burdened Past, Hopeful Future,* edited by Stephen Uhalley Jr. and Xiaoxin Wu, pp. 271–282. Armonk, NY: M. E. Sharpe.

"Daibiao tuan fu Jing Hu fangwen" 代表团赴京沪访问. 1999. *Xianggang fojiao*, vol. 487.

Dangdai Fojiao Cishan Wang 当代佛教慈善网. 2018. Cibei weihuai jishi zhuren 慈悲为怀济世助人. Accessed October 11, 2018. http://fjcsw.org/.

Dean, Kenneth. 1993. *Taoist Ritual and Popular Cults in Southeast China*. Princeton, NJ: Princeton University Press.

———. 2009. "Further Partings of the Way: The Chinese State and Daoist Ritual Traditions in Contemporary China." In *Making Religion, Making the State: The Politics of Religion in Modern China,* edited by Yoshiko Ashiwa and David L. Wank, pp. 179–210. Stanford, CA: Stanford University Press.

Demiéville, Paul. 1930. "Bosatsukai." In *Dictionnaire encyclopédique du Bouddhisme d'après les sources chinoises et japonaises,* vol. 2, pp. 142–147. Tokyo: Hôbôgirin.

Deng Zimei 邓子美. 1994. *Changgui fojiao yu Zhongguo jindai hua* 常规佛教与中国近代化. Shanghai: Huadong shifan daxue *chubanshe.*

———. 1998. "Ershi shiji zhongguo fojiao zhihui de jiejing: Renjian fojiao lilun de jiangou yu yunzuo" 二十世纪中国佛教智慧的结晶—人间佛教理论的建构与运作. *Fayin* 法音166:3.

Deng Zimei 邓子美 and Wang Jia 王佳. 2008. "Nanputuosi cishan shiye jijinhui yunzuo moshi diaocha" 南普陀寺慈善事业基金会运作模式调查. *Fojiao zai xian* 佛教在线, November 18. Accessed February 22, 2018. http://www.fjnet.com/fjlw/200811/t20081118_92615 .htm.

———. 2012. "Dalu fojiao cishan gongyi zuzhi leixing tanxi" 大陆佛教慈善公益组织类型探悉. In *Jiaoyu zongjiao cishan: Disanjie zongjiao yu cishan shiye luntan wenji* 教育宗教慈善: 第三届宗教与慈善事业论坛文集, edited by Han Wenke and Wei Dedong, pp. 563–579. Lanzhou: Gansu People's Press.

Détienne, Marcel. 1990. *Tracés de fondation*. Louvain: Peeters.

DeVido, Elise A. 2015. "Networks and Bridges: Nuns in the Making of Modern Chinese Buddhism." *Chinese Historical Review* 22 (1): 72–93.

Dikötter, Frank. 2010. *Mao's Great Famine: The History of China's Most Devastating Catastrophe, 1958–1962*. London: Bloomsbury Publishing.

Donglin Charity. 2011. "Xiaofa shengxian yuan, cixue yi shujing" 效法圣贤愿, 刺血以书经. Donglin Charity Net, November 4. Accessed February 22, 2018. http://www .donglincs.com/colL_detail.php?lbid=415&wzid=4033.

Dorman, Benjamin, and Ian Reader, eds. 2007. "Projections and Representations of Religion in Japanese Media." Special issue, *Nova Religio* 3:5–101.

Dreyfus, Georges B. J. 2003. *The Sound of Two Hands Clapping: The Education of a Tibetan Buddhist Monk*. Berkeley: University of California Press.

Duara, Pransenjit. 1991. "Knowledge and Power in the Discourse of Modernity: The Campaigns against Popular Religion in Early Twentieth-Century China." *Journal of Asian Studies* 50:67–84.

———. 1993. *Culture, Power, and the State: Rural North China, 1900–1942*. Stanford, CA: Stanford University Press.

Dudbridge, Glen. (1978) 2004. *The Legend of Miaoshan*. New York: Oxford University Press.

Eng, Irene, and Lin Yi-Min. 2002. "Religious Festivities, Communal Rivalry, and Restructuring of Authority Relations in Rural Chaozhou, Southeast China." *Journal of Asian Studies* 61 (4): 1259–1285.

Ethnic and Religious Affairs. 2014. "Mingsheng Fashi: Fojiao cishan hai you henchang de lu yao zou" 明生法师: 佛教慈善还有很长的路要走. iPhoenix. May 22. Accessed February 22, 2018. http://fo.ifeng.com/guanchajia/detail_2014_05/22/36449378_0.shtml.

Famen Temple. 2011. "Da heshang jianjie" 大和尚简介. Famen Temple. May 23. Accessed February 22, 2018. http://www.famensi.com/xcdhs_content.asp?id=125.

Fan Lizhu 范丽珠. 2005. *Dangdai Zhongguoren zongjiao xinyang de bianqian: Shenzhen minjian zongjiao xintu de tianye yanjiu* 当代中国人宗教信仰的变迁: 深圳民间宗教信徒的田野研究. Taibei: Weibo wenhua 韦伯文化.

———. 2008. "Xiandai zongjiao shi lixing xuanze de ma? Zhiyi zongjiao de lixing xuanze yanjiu fanshi" 现代宗教是理性选择的吗? 质疑宗教的理性选择研究范式. *Shehui* 社会 28 (6): 90–109.

Fan Yinglian 范应莲. 1991. *Wo de enshi Haideng* 我的恩师海灯. Chengdu: Sichuan renmin chubanshe.

Fang Litian 方立天. 2013. *Zhongguo fojiao yu zhongguo* 中国佛教与中国. January 22, 2016. Accessed February 22, 2018. http://www.zgfxy.cn/tjyd/2013/12/18/1417521451.html.

Faqing 法清. 1992. "Minnan caigu de qiyuan he diwei" 闽南菜姑的起源和地位. *Minnan Foxue* 闽南佛学 7.

Fayin 法音. 2003. "Hebei Bailin chansi longzhong juxing Wanfolou luocheng ji foxiang kaiguang zhuangdian fahui" 河北柏林禅寺隆重举行万佛楼落成暨佛像开光法会 September, pp. 47–48.

Feng Lingyuan 冯令源. 2009. *Yindao zongjiao yu shehuizhuyi shehui xiang shiying de lilun yu shijian* 引导宗教与社会主义社会相适应的理论与实践. Beijing: Zhongguo shehui kexue chubanshe.

Feng Yin 奉音. 2008. "Changhui fashi: jianli hongde jiayuan de jingyan ji zuo cishan shiye de kunnan" 常辉法师: 建立弘德家园的经验及做慈善事业的困难. *Fojiao Zaixian* 佛教在线, November 25. Accessed October 12, 2018. http://www.fjnet.com/jjdt/jjdtnr/200811/t20081125_93759.htm.

Feuchtwang, Stephan. 1992. *The Imperial Metaphor*. London: Routledge.

———. 2000. "Religion as Resistance." In *Chinese Society: Change, Conflict and Resistance,* edited by Elizabeth J. Perry and Mark Selden, pp. 161–177. London: Routledge.

Fisher, Gareth. 2008. "The Spiritual Land Rush: Merit and Morality in New Chinese Buddhist Temple Construction." *Journal of Asian Studies* 67 (1): 143–170.

———. 2011a. "In the Footsteps of the Tourists: Buddhist Revival at Museum-Temple Sites in Beijing." *Social Compass* 58 (4): 511–524.

———. 2011b. "Morality Books and the Re-Growth of Lay Buddhism in China." In *Religion in Contemporary China: Tradition and Innovation,* edited by Adam Yuet Chau, pp. 58–80. New York: Routledge Press.

———. 2012. "Religion as Repertoire: Resourcing the Past in a Beijing Buddhist Temple." *Modern China* 38 (3): 346–376.

———. 2014. *From Comrades to Bodhisattvas: Moral Dimensions of Lay Buddhist Practice in Contemporary China*. Honolulu: University of Hawai'i Press.

———. 2015. "The Flexibility of Religion: Buddhist Temples as Multiaspirational Sites in Contemporary Beijing." In *Handbook of Religion and the Asian City: Aspiration and Urbanization in the Twenty-First Century,* edited by Peter van der Veer, pp. 299–314. Berkeley: University of California Press.

———. 2016. "Mapping Textual Difference: Lay Buddhist Textual Communities in the Post-Mao Period." In *Recovering Buddhism in Modern China,* edited by Jan Kiely and J. Brooks Jessup, pp. 257–290. New York: Columbia University Press.

Flower, John. 2004. "A Road Is Made: Roads, Temples, and Historical Memory in Ya'an County, Sichuan." *Journal of Asian Studies* 63 (3): 649–685.

Flower, John, and Pamela Leonard. 1998. "Defining Cultural Life in the Chinese Countryside: The Case of Chuan Zhu Temple." In *Cooperative and Collective in China's Rural*

Development, edited by E. B. Vermeer, Frank N. Pieke, and Woei Lien Chong. Armonk, NY: M.E. Sharpe.

Fojiao tiandi 佛教天地. 2011. *Cishan xinwen* 慈善新闻. Accessed October 3, 2015. www .ebud.net/almsdeed/almsnews/index.html.

Fojiao Zaixian. 2018. Fojiao Zaixian website. Accessed October 30, 2018. http://www.fjnet .com/cssy/default_1.htm.

Foulk, Griffith T. 1993. "Myth, Ritual, and Monastic Practice in Sung Ch'an Buddhism." In *Religion and Society in T'ang and Sung China,* edited by Patricia Buckley Ebrey and Peter N. Gregory, pp. 147–208. Honolulu: University of Hawai'i Press.

———. 1999. "Song Controversies Concerning the 'Separate Transmission' of Ch'an." In *Buddhism in the Sung,* edited by Peter N. Gregory and Daniel A. Getz, pp. 220–294. Honolulu: University of Hawai'i Press.

Frankfurt, Harry. 1971. "Freedom of the Will and the Concept of a Person." *Journal of Philosophy* 68:5–20.

Gentong 根通. 2006. *Zhongguo fojiao cibei jishi de linian yu shijian* 中国佛教慈悲济世的理念 与实践. Proceedings from the conference Shijie fojiao Luntan 世界佛教论坛, Hangzhou, April 13–16.

Gernet, Jacques. 1995. *Buddhism in Chinese Society: An Economic History from the Fifth to the Tenth Centuries.* New York: Columbia University Press.

Getz, Daniel A. 2005. "Popular Religion and Pure Land in Song-Dynasty Tiantai Bodhisattva Precept Ordination Ceremonies." In *Going Forth. Visions of Buddhist Vinaya. Essays Presented in Honor of Professor Stanley Weinstein,* edited by William M. Bodiford, pp. 161–184. Honolulu: University of Hawai'i Press.

Gildow, Douglas. 2014. "The Chinese Buddhist Ritual Field: Common Public Rituals in PRC Monasteries Today." *Journal of Chinese Buddhist Studies* 27:59–127.

———. 2016. "Buddhist Monastic Education: Seminaries, Academia, and the State in Contemporary China." PhD diss., Princeton University.

Gillette, Maris. 2000. *Between Mecca and Beijing: Modernization and Consumption among Urban Chinese Muslims.* Stanford, CA: Stanford University Press.

Gladney, Dru. 1996. *Muslim Chinese: Ethnic Nationalism in the People's Republic.* 2nd ed. Cambridge, MA: Harvard University Asia Center.

Goldfuss, Gabriele. 2001. *Vers un bouddhisme du XXe siècle. Yang Wenhui (1837–1911), réformateur laïque et imprimeur.* Paris: Collège de France—Institut des Hautes Études Chinoises.

Goldstein, Melvyn C. 1998. "The Revival of Monastic Life in Drepung Monastery." In *Buddhism in Contemporary Tibet,* edited by Melvyn C. Goldstein and Matthew T. Kapstein, pp. 15–52. Berkeley: University of California Press.

Goldstein, Melvyn C., and Matthew Kapstein, eds. 1998. *Buddhism in Contemporary Tibet: Religious Revival and Cultural Identity.* Berkeley: University of California Press.

Gong Jun 龚隽 and Lai Yueshan 赖岳山. 2014. "Chonggu Taixu fashi (yinlun): Lun Tai Yi 'Zhongguo di'er lishi dang'anguan' suo zang minguo jiaoyubu dang'anwei zhongxin" 重估太虚法师(引论) 论太以 "中国第二历史档案馆" 所藏民国教育部档案为中心. *Hanyu foxue pinglun* 汉语佛学评论 4:96–178.

Goossaert, Vincent. 2006. "1898: The Beginning of the End for Chinese Religion?" *Journal of Asian Studies* 65:307–335.

———. 2008. "Republican Church Engineering: The National Religious Associations in 1912 China." In *Chinese Religiosities: Afflictions of Modernity and State Formation,* edited by Mayfair Mei-Hui Yang, pp. 209–232. Berkeley: University of California Press.

Goossaert, Vincent, and David Palmer. 2011. *The Religious Question in Modern China*. Chicago: University of Chicago Press.

Goto, Nobuko 後藤延子. 1991. "Shushigaku no seiritsu to bukkyō" 朱子学の成立と仏教. *Jinmon kagaku ronshū* 人文科学論集 25:1–26.

Groner, Paul. 2012. "Ordination and Precepts in the *Platform Sūtra*." In *Readings of the Platform Sūtra*, edited by Morten Schlütter and Stephen T. Teiser, pp. 134–160. New York: Columbia University Press.

Groot, Gerry. 2004. *Managing Transitions: The Chinese Communist Party, United Front Work, Corporatism, and Hegemony*. New York: Routledge.

Guangdong Sheng Fojiao Xiehui 广东省佛教协会. 2017a. "Guangdong sheng fojiao xiehui cishan zhensuo" 广东省佛教协会慈善中医诊所. Accessed October 11, 2018. http://www .gdbuddhism.org/contribution/941.jhtml.

———. 2017b. "Guangdong sheng fojiao xiehui cishan jijinhui" 广东省佛教协会慈善基金会. Accessed October 11, 2018. http://www.gdbuddhism.org/contribution/759 .jhtml.

"Guangzhou shi fodao jiaotu jihui shengtao fangeming fenzi Benhuan" 广州市佛道教徒集会声讨反革命分子本焕. 1958. *Xiandai foxue* 现代佛学 8:3

Guo Shusen 郭树森 and Shi Chunyi 释纯一. 2009. *Zongjiao yu goujian hexie shehui* 宗教与构建和谐社会. Nanchang: Jiangxi renmin chubanshe 江西人民出版社.

Guojia Zongjiao Shiwuju 国家宗教事务局. 2007. "Zongjiao Jiaozhi Renyuan Bei'an Banfa" 宗教教职人员备案办法. Accessed November 1, 2015. www.sara.gov.cn/zcfg/bmgz/2196 .htm.

———. 2010. Ciji Cishan Shiye Jijinhui zai Suzhou juxing guapai dianli 慈济慈善事业基金会在苏州举行挂牌典礼. Accessed October 4, 2015. http://www.sara.gov.cn/ldxx/qxf /ldhd2/5253.htm.

———. 2012. "Guanyu guli he guifan zongjiaojie congshi gongyi cishan huodong de yijian." 关于鼓励和规范宗教界从事公益慈善活动的意见. *Zhongguo zongjiao* 中国宗教, September 7. Accessed August 3, 2015. http://www.chinareligion.cn/zongjiaocishanzhou /zhengcefagui/2012-09-07/1463.html.

Guojia Zongjiao Shiwuju Zongjiao Yanjiu Zhongxin 国家宗教事务局宗教研究中心. 2013. *Cujin zongjiao hexie yantao wenji* 促进宗教和谐研讨文集. Beijing: Zongjiao wenhua chubanshe 宗教文化出版社.

Guojia Zongjiaoju Di Si Si 国家宗教局第四司. 2014. "Wo ju zhaokai nian zongjiao yuanxiao liang ge 'banfa' shishi gongzuo tuijin hui" 我局召开2014年宗教院校两个"办法"实施工作推进会. Accessed October 26, 2018. http://www.daomen.org/t/1759.

"Haideng fashi zhuchi Yunju Shan Zhenru Si" 海灯法师住持云居山真如寺. 1957. *Xiandai foxue* 现代佛学 10:30.

Han Chunli. 2012. "Xuecheng Fashi: chushi shi wei gaizao shijian." *Zhongguo Qingnian dianzibao* (China Youth electronic report) 19. Accessed August 1, 2015; http://www .spark.com.cn/index.php?m=mapdetail&id=162&aid=6908&cid=210&bid=211&did =182&zid=63 (URL no longer functional).

Hargett, James M. 2006. *Stairway to Heaven: A Journey to the Summit of Mount Emei*. Albany: State University of New York Press.

He Chengxiang 何成湘. 1956. "Guowuyuan zongjiao shiwuju juzhang He Chengxiang de zhici" 国务院宗教事务局局长何成湘的致词. *Xiandai foxue* 现代佛学 1:5–6.

He Haiwei 赫海威. 2016. "Zai Longquansi zhao shiye linggan, jishi ni mei zai nali faming weixin" 在龙泉寺找事业灵感，即使你没在那里发明微信. *New York Times* (Chinese), September 8. Accessed October 12, 2018. https://cn.nytimes.com/culture/20160908 /china-longquan-monastery-buddhism-technology/.

He Jianming 何建明. 2018. "Wangluo zongjiao zai Zhongguo de fazhan zhuangkuang he wenti" 网络宗教在中国的发展状况和问题. *Chawang* 察网. Accessed October 15, 2018. http://www.cwzg.cn/politics/201802/40888.html.

He Mingdong 何明栋, ed. 2000. *Xinbian Caoxi tongzhi* 新编曹溪通志. Beijing: Zongjiao wenhua chubanshe.

———, ed. 2002. *Weiyin laoheshang yuanji shi zhounian* 惟因老和尚圆寂十周年. Beijing: Zongjiao wenhua chubanshe.

He Qinglian. 2004. "Media Control in China." *China Rights Forum* 1:11–28.

Heidbrink, Simone. 2007. "Exploring the Religious Frameworks of the Digital Realm: Offline-Online-Offline Transfers of Ritual Performance." *Masaryk University Journal of Law and Technology* 1 (2):175–184.

Heirman, Ann. 1997. "Some Remarks on the Rise of the Bhikṣuṇīsaṃgha and on the Ordination Ceremony for Bhikṣuṇīs according to the Dharmaguptakavinaya." *Journal of the International Association of Buddhist Studies* 20 (2): 33–85.

———. 2001. "Chinese Nuns and Their Ordination in Fifth Century China." *Journal of the International Association of Chinese Studies* 24 (2): 275–304.

———. 2002. *The Discipline in Four Parts: Rules for Nuns According to the Dharmaguptakavinaya.* 3 vols. Delhi: Motilal Banarsidass.

———. 2008. "Where Is the Probationer in the Chinese Buddhist Nunneries?" *Zeitschrift der Deutschen Morgenlandischen Gesellschaft* 158 (1): 105–137.

———. 2011. "Buddhist Nuns: Between Past and Present." *Numen-International Review for the History of Religions* 58:603–631.

Heirman, Ann, and Tzu-Lung Chiu. 2012. "The Gurudharmas in Taiwanese Buddhist Nunneries." *Buddhist Studies Review* 29 (2): 273–300.

Heller, Natasha. 2014. "Buddha in a Box: The Materiality of Recitation in Contemporary Chinese Buddhism." *Material Religion* 10 (3): 294–314.

"Hongyang jiaoguan, zhongxing Tiantai" 弘扬教观, 中兴天台. 2007. *Xianggang fojiao* 香港佛教 567.

Hongyi 弘一. (1933) 2010a. "Fanxing qingxin nü jiangxihui yuanqi" 梵行清信女讲习会缘起. In *Hongyi dashi quanji* 弘一大師全集, edited by Lin Ziqing, vol. 7, p. 626. Fuzhou: Fujian renmin chubanshe.

———. 2010b. "Guanyu nüxing yishuo taolun zhi Zhumo fashi shu" 关于女性异说讨论致竺摩法师书. In *Hongyi dashi quanji* 弘一大師全集, edited by Lin Ziqing, vol. 8, p. 191. Fuzhou: Fujian renmin chubanshe.

———. 2010c. *Hongyi dashi quanji* 弘一大師全集. Edited by Lin Ziqing. 10 vols. Fuzhou: Fujian renmin chubanshe.

Hoover, Stewart M., and Lynn Schofield Clark, eds. 2002. *Practicing Religion in the Age of the Media.* New York: Columbia University Press.

Hoover, Stewart, and Nabil Echchaibi. 2012. "Finding Religion in the Media–Third Spaces of Digital Religion." Working Paper in the Center for Media, Religion, and Culture. University of Colorado.

Horner, Isaline Blew. (1930) 1989. *Women under Primitive Buddhism. Laywomen and Almswomen.* Delhi: Motilal Banarsidass.

Hou Kunhong 侯坤宏. 2012. *Haojie yu chongsheng: Yijiusijiu nian yilai de dalu fojiao* 浩劫与与重生: 一九四九年以来的大陆佛教. Tainan: Miaoxin chubanshe.

Huang Huajie 黄华节. 1967. *Guangong de renge yu shenge* 关公的人格与神格. Taiwan: Shangwu yinshuguan.

Huang, Julia C. 2009. *Charisma and Compassion: Cheng Yen and the Buddhist Tzu Chi Movement.* Cambridge, MA: Harvard University Press.

Huang, Weishan. 2012. "The Bodhisattva Comes Out of the Closet: City, Surveillance, and Doing Religion." *Politics and Religion Journal* 6 (2): 199–216.

———. 2016. "WeChat Together about the Buddha: The Construction of Sacred Space and Religious Community in Shanghai through Social Media." In *Religion and Media in China: Insights and Case Studies from the Mainland, Taiwan and Hong Kong,* edited by Stefania Travagnin, pp. 110–128. London: Routledge.

Hui, Samuel. 2015. "Xi Shifts United Front Policy Away from Taiwan's 'Mainlanders.'" *Want China Times,* September 20.

Huikong 慧空. 2016. *Xuecheng daheshang ceji* 学诚大和尚侧记. Beijing: Zhongguo caifu chubanshe.

Huimin. 2007. "An Inquiry Concerning the Lineage of *Bhikṣuṇī* Ordination." First International Congress on Buddhist Women's Role in the Sangha, Bhikshuni Vinaya and Ordination Lineages with H. H. the Dalai Lama. Accessed February 22, 2018. http://www.congress -on-buddhist-women.org/fileadmin/files/15HuiminBhiksu_01.pdf.

Huiyan 慧严. 2014. "Quanguo fengjing mingshengqu nei Fo Daojiao siguan guanli gongzuo yantaoban zai jing kaiban" 全国风景名胜区内佛道教寺观管理工作研讨班在京开班. Xingtai Buddhism Net 邢台佛教网. Accessed October 25, 2018. http://www.xtfj.org /news/gnxw/2014/0523/11808.html.

Hymes, Robert P. 2002. *Way and Byway: Taoism, Local Religion, and Models of Divinity in Sung and Modern China.* Berkeley: University of California Press.

In Memory of the Venerable Master Hsuan Hua. 1996. Edited by Dharma Realm Buddhist Association Staff, Dharma Realm Buddhist University Staff, Buddhist Texts Translation Society Staff. Burlingame, CA: Buddhist Text Translation Society.

Jacobs, Stephen. 2007. "Virtually Sacred: The Performance of Asynchronous Cyber Rituals in Online Spaces." *Journal of Computer-Mediated Communication* 12:1103–1121.

Jan Yün-hua. 1984. "The Religious Situation and the Studies of Buddhism and Taoism in China: An Incomplete and Imbalanced Picture." *Journal of Chinese Religions* 12:37–64.

Jeavons, Thomas H. 1998. "Identifying Characteristics of 'Religious' Organizations: An Exploratory Proposal." In *Sacred Companies: Organizational Aspects of Religion and Religious Aspects of Organizations,* edited by N. J. Demerath III, Peter Dobkin Hall, Terry Schmitt, and Rhys H. Williams, pp. 79–95. New York: Oxford University Press.

Jessup, J. Brooks. 2012. "Beyond Ideological Conflict: Political Incorporation of Buddhist Youth in the Early PRC." *Frontiers of History in China* 7:551–581.

Ji Zhe 汲喆. 2004. "Buddhism and the State: The New Relationship." *China Perspectives* 55:2–10.

———. 2006. "Non-institutional Religious Re-composition among the Chinese Youth." *Social Compass* 53 (4): 535–549.

———. 2007. "Mémoire reconstituée: Les stratégies mnémoniques dans la reconstruction d'un monastère bouddhique." *Cahiers internationaux de sociologie* 122: 145–164.

———. 2008a. "Secularization as Religious Restructuring: Statist Institutionalization of Chinese Buddhism." In *Chinese Religiosities: Afflictions of Modernity and State Formation*, edited by Mayfair Mei-Hui Yang, pp. 233–260. Berkeley: University of California Press.

———. 2008b. "Ruhe chaoyue jingdian shisuhua lilun? Ping zongjiao shehuixue de sanzhong hou shisuhua lunshu" 如何超越经典世俗化理论?—评宗教社会学的三种后世俗化论述. *Shehuixue yanjiu* 社会学研究 4:55–75.

———. 2009. "Fuxing sanshi nian: dangdai Zhongguo Fojiao de jiben shuju" 复兴三十年: 当代中国佛教的基本数据. *Fojiao guancha* 佛教观察 5:8–15.

———. 2011a. "Buddhism in the Reform-Era China: A Secularised Revival?" In *Religion in Contemporary China: Revitalization and Innovation*, edited by Adam Yuet Chau, pp. 32–52. London: Routledge.

———. 2011b. "Introduction: Le jiao recomposé. L'éducation entre religion et politique dans la modernité chinoise." *Extrême-Orient Extrême Occident* 33:5–34.

———. 2011c. "Religion, jeunesse, et modernité: Le camp d'été, nouvelle pratique rituelle du bouddhisme chinois." *Social Compass* 58 (4): 525–539.

———. 2012. "Chinese Buddhism as a Social Force: Reality and Potential of Thirty Years of Revival." *Chinese Sociological Review* 45 (2): 8–26.

———. 2014. "Buddhist Groups among Chinese Immigrants in France: Three Patterns of Religious Globalization." *Review of Religion and Chinese Society* 1 (2): 212–235.

———. 2015. "Secularization without Secularism: The Political-Religious Configuration of Post-89 China." In *Atheist Secularism and Its Discontents. A Comparative Study of Religion and Communism in Eurasia*, edited by Tam Ngo and Justine Quijada, pp. 92–111. Basingstoke: Palgrave Macmillan.

———. 2016a. "Une journée avec Maître Shi Yongxin. Le Temple Shaolin et sa légende contemporaine." In *Une journée dans une vie, une vie dans une journée: Moines et ascètes aujourd'hui*, edited by Adeline Herrou, pp. 146–74. Paris: Presses Universitaires de France.

———. 2016b. "Buddhist Institutional Innovations." In *Modern Chinese Religion II: 1850– 2015*, edited by Vincent Goossaert, Jan Kiely, and John Lagerwey, pp. 731–766. Leiden: Brill.

———. 2016c. "The Monastic Economy of Buddhism in Contemporary China." Paper presented at the workshop Ateliers d'Anthropologie Comparée du Bouddhisme. École des Hautes Études en Sciences Sociales, Paris, France, April 8.

———. 2016d. *Religion, modernité et temporalité: Une sociologie du bouddhisme chan contemporain*. Paris: CNRS Editions.

———. 2017. "Comrade Zhao Puchu: Bodhisattva under the Red Flag." In *Making Saints in Modern China*, edited by David Ownby, Vincent Goossaert, and Ji Zhe, pp. 312–348. New York: Oxford University Press.

Ji Zhe 汲喆, Daniela Campo 田水晶, and Wang Qiyuan 王启元, eds. 2016. *Ershi shiji zhongguo fojiao de liangci fuxing* 二十世纪中国佛教的两次复兴. Shanghai: Fudan daxue chubanshe.

Ji Zhe and Vincent Goossaert. 2011. "Social Implications of the Buddhist Revival in China." *Social Compass* 58 (4): 32–52.

Jiang Canteng 江灿腾. 2000. *Taiwan dangdai fojiao* 台湾当代佛教. Taibei: Taibei nantian shuju.

Jiangsu Sheng Fojiao Xiehui 江苏省佛教协会. 2012. "Zhongguo foxueyuan Qixiashan fenyuan jianxiao 30 zhounian qingdian zai nanjing juxing" 中国佛学院栖霞山分院建校30 周年庆典在南京举行. *Jiangsu fojiao* 江苏佛教 4:89–90.

Jiequan 界诠. 2010. "Rushi wowen: Huainian Qingzhi laofashi" 如是我闻—怀念青芝老法师. Accessed February 22, 2018. http://blog.sina.com.cn/s/blog_625e84f30100kwir .html.

Jieren 戒忍. 2002. *Miaoshan dashi nianpu* 妙善大师年谱. Beijing: Zhongguo wenlian chubanshe.

Jieren 戒忍, Weihang 惟航, Daoci 道慈, and Jingmin 净旻. 2009. *Miaoshan lao heshang baisui danchen jinian tekan* 妙善老和尚百岁诞辰纪念特刊. Edited by the Buddhist Association of Putuoshan.

Jing'an Si Sichan 静安寺寺产. 1947. *Shanghai Jing'an si sichan yi'an* 上海静安寺寺产一案. City Archives, Shanghai, China Q92–1–498.

Jinghui 净慧, ed. 1990. *Xuyun heshang fahui xubian* 虚云和尚法汇续编. Shijiazhuang: Hebeisheng fojiao xiehui.

Jingyin. 2006. "Buddhism and Economic Reform in Mainland China." In *Chinese Religions in Contemporary Societies,* edited by James Miller, pp. 88–99. Santa Barbara: ABC-CLIO.

Jingyin 净因 and Zhang Qi 张琪. 2008. "Handi fojiao kecheng shezhi diaoyan baogao" 汉地佛教课程设置调研报告. In *Dierjie shijie fojiao luntan wenji* 第二届世界佛教论坛文集, pp. 149–160. Beijing: Zongjiao wenhua chubanshe.

Jiqun 济群. 2013. "Zhi jie de yuanqi ji yiyi" 制戒的缘起及意义. Accessed February 22, 2018. http://www.jiqun.com/dispfile.php?id=5893.

Johnson, David, ed. 1995. *Ritual and Scripture in Chinese Popular Religion: Five Studies.* Berkeley, CA: Institute for East Asian Studies.

Johnson, Ian. 2018. "#MeToo in the Monastery: A Chinese Abbot's Fall Stirs Questions on Buddhism's Path." *New York Times,* September 15. Accessed October 12, 2018. https://www.nytimes.com/2018/09/15/world/asia/metoo-china-monastery.html.

Johnson, Todd M., and Brian J. Grim. 2013. *The World's Religions in Figures: An Introduction to International Religious Demography.* Hoboken, NJ: Wiley-Blackwell.

Jones, Alison D. 2010. "A Modern Religion? The State, the People, and the Remaking of Buddhism in Urban China Today." PhD diss., Harvard University.

———. 2011. "Contemporary Han Chinese Involvement in Tibetan Buddhism: A Case Study from Nanjing." *Social Compass* 58 (4): 540–553.

Jones, Charles B. 1996. "Relations between the Nationalist Government and the Buddhist Association of the Republic of China (BAROC) since 1945." *Journal of Chinese Religions* 24:77–97.

———. 1999. *Buddhism in Taiwan: Religion and the State, 1660–1990.* Honolulu: University of Hawai'i Press.

Jongpil, Chung. 2008. "Comparing Online Activities in China and South Korea: The Internet and the Political Regime." *Asian Survey* 48 (5): 727–751.

Juedeng 觉灯. 2005. *Hanchuan fojiao erbuseng jie chuyi* 汉传佛教二部僧戒刍议. Accessed March 10, 2015. http://www.chinabuddhism.com.cn/a/fayuan/2005/2k05f09.

Jueguang 觉光. 2014. "'Wei Fojiao, wei zhongsheng' de zongjiao ziyou. Xianggang fojiao yu jibenfa 5" "为佛教，为众生" 的宗教自由—香港佛教与基本法. *Xianggang fojiao* 香港佛教 652:41.

Juexing 觉醒, ed. 2007. *Fojiao Lunli yu hexie shehui* 佛教伦理与和谐社会. Beijing: Zongjiao wenhua chubanshe 宗教文化出版社.

Kang Xiaofei. 2009. "Two Temples, Three Religions, and a Tourist Attraction: Contesting Sacred Space on China's Ethnic Frontier." *Modern China* 35 (3): 227–255.

Katz, Paul. 2014. *Religion in China and Its Modern Fate*. Waltham, MA: Brandeis University Press.

Kawanami, Hiroko. 2013. *Renunciation and Empowerment of Buddhist Nuns in Myanmar-Burma: Building a Community of Female Faithful*. Leiden: Brill.

Kiely, Jan, and Brooks Jessup, eds. 2016. *Recovering Buddhism in Modern China*. New York: Columbia University Press.

Kieschnick, John. 2000. "Blood Writing in Chinese Buddhism." *Journal of the International Association of Buddhist Studies* 23 (2): 177–194.

Kindopp, Jason. 2004. "Fragmented Yet Defiant: Protestant Resilience under Chinese Communist Party Rule." In *God and Caesar in China: Policy Implications of Church-State Tensions*, edited by Jason Kindopp and Carol Lee Hamrin, pp. 122–148. Washington, DC: Brookings Institution Press.

Klein, Thoralf, and Christian Meyer, eds. 2011. "Beyond the Market: Exploring the Religious Field in Modern China." Special issue, *Religion* 41 (4).

Knott, Kim. 2010. "Religion, Space and Place: The Spatial Turn in Research and Religion." *Religion and Society: Advances in Research* 1:29–43.

Ko Shu-ling. 2009. "Cross-Strait Talks: SEF, ARATS Ink Three Pacts, Drop One." *Taipei Times*, December 23, p. 1.

Kolås, Ashild. 1996. "Tibetan Nationalism: The Politics of Religion." *Journal of Peace Research* 33:51–66.

Krause, Carsten. 2008. "Interdependenzen zwischen Staat und Buddhismus in der Volksrepublik China." In *Religion und Politik in der Volksrepublik China*, edited by Wiebke Koenig and Karl-Fritz Daiber, pp. 139–168. Würzburg: Ergon-Verlag.

Kuhn, Philip. 1999. *Introduction. Entre passé et présent: Les origines de l'état chinois moderne*, by Pierre-Étienne Will, pp. 11–68. Paris: Éditions de l'École des Hautes Études en Sciences Sociales.

Kuwana, Akiko 桑名晶子. 1994. "Chūgoku Kanan ni okeru furaku-ka no kigen keisei" 中国華南における不落家の起源形成. *Shien* 史苑 55 (1): 28–42.

LaFleur, William R. 1998. "Body." In *Critical Terms for Religious Studies*, edited by Mark Taylor, pp. 36–54. Chicago: University of Chicago Press.

Lai Lei Kuan Rongdao. 2013. "Praying for the Republic: Buddhist Education, Student-Monks, and Citizenship in Modern China (1911–1949)." PhD diss., McGill University.

Lai, Whalen. 1983. "The Transmission Verses of the Ch'an Patriarchs: An Analysis of the Genre's Evolution". *Hanxue yanjiu* (*Chinese Studies*, Taipei) 1 (2): 593–624.

Lai Yonghai 赖永海. 1999. *Zhongguo fojiao wenhua lun* 中国佛教文化论. Beijing: Zhongguo qingnian chubanshe.

Laliberté, André. 2003. "'Love Transcends Borders' or 'Blood Is Thicker than Water'? The Charity Work of the Compassion Relief Foundation in the People's Republic of China." *European Journal of East Asian Studies* 2 (2): 243–261.

———. 2004. *The Politics of Buddhist Organizations in Taiwan 1989–2003. Safeguarding the Faith, Building a Pure Land, Helping the Poor*. London: Routledge.

———. 2005. "'Buddhist for the Human Realm' and Taiwanese Democracy." In *Religious Organizations and Democracy in Contemporary Asia*, edited by Tung-ren Cheng and Deborah Brown, pp. 55–82. Armonk, NY: M. E. Sharpe.

———. 2008. "'Harmonious Society,' 'Peaceful Re-unification,' and the Dilemmas Raised by Taiwanese Charity." In *The Chinese Party-State in the 21st Century*, edited by André Laliberté and Marc Lanteigne, pp. 78–105. London: Routledge.

———. 2009. "Entre désécularisation et resacralisation: Bouddhistes laïcs, temples et organisations philanthropiques en Chine." *Social Compass* 56 (3): 345–361.

———. 2011a. "Buddhist Revival under State Watch." *Journal of Current Chinese Affairs* 40 (2): 107–134.

———. 2011b. "Religion and the State in China: The Limits of Institutionalization." *Journal of Current Chinese Affairs* 40 (2): 3–15.

———. 2012. "Buddhist Charities and China's Social Policy: An Opportunity for Alternate Civility?" *Archives de sciences sociales des religions* 158:95–117.

———. 2013. "The Growth of a Taiwanese Buddhist Association in China: Soft Power and Institutional Learning." *China Information* 27 (1): 81–105.

———. 2015. "The Politicization of Religion by the CCP: A Selective Retrieval." *Asiatische studien/Études asiatiques* 69 (1): 185–211.

———. 2016. "Engaging with a Post-Totalitarian State: Buddhism Online in China." In *Religion and Media in China: Insights and Case Studies from the Mainland, Taiwan and Hong Kong*, edited by Stefania Travagnin, pp. 129–150. London: Routledge.

Lan Jifu 蓝吉富, ed. 2004. *Chanzong quanshu* 禅宗全书, 101 vols. Beijing: Beijing tushuguan chubanshe.

Lang, Graeme, Selina Chan, and Lars Ragvald. 2005. "Temples and the Religious Economy." In *State, Market, and Religions in Chinese Societies*, edited by Fenggang Yang and Joseph B. Tamney, pp. 149–180. Leiden: Brill.

Ledderose, Lothar, and Yongbo Wang. 2014–2015. *Buddhist Stone Sutras in China: Shandong Province*, vols. 1 and 2. Wiesbaden: Harrassowitz Verlag.

Lengen, Samuel. 2016. "Beyond a Conceptual Threshold of Oppression and Resistance: Creativity, Buddhist Mediation, and the Chinese Internet." In *Religion and Media in China: Insights and Case Studies from the Mainland, Taiwan and Hong Kong*, edited by Stefania Travagnin, pp. 19–34. London: Routledge.

Leung, Beatrice. 2005. "China's Religious Freedom Policy: The Art of Managing Religious Activity." *China Quarterly* 184:894–913.

Levine, Sarah, and David N. Gellner. 2005. *Rebuilding Buddhism: The Theravada Movement in Twentieth Century Nepal*. Cambridge, MA: Harvard University Press.

Li Shangquan 李尚全. 2008. "Tansuo dangdai sengjiaoyu de xin moshi" 探索当代僧教育的新模式. *Nanjing Xiaozhuang xueyuan xuebao* 南京晓庄学院学报 2:115–118.

Li Silong. 2013. "The Practice of Buddhist Education in Modern China." *Chinese Studies in History* 46 (3): 59–78.

Li Xiangping 李向平. 2002. "Ershi shiji zhongguo fuojiao de 'geming zouxiang': Jianlun 'renjian fuojiao' sichao de xiandaixing wenti" 二十世纪中国佛教的 '革命走向'—兼论 "人间佛教" 思潮的现代性问题. *Shijie zongjiao yanjiu* 世界宗教研究 3:42–56.

———. 2010. "Zongjiao xinyang de guojia xiangxiangli—jian ping 'zongjiao shengtai lun' sichao" 宗教信仰的国家想象力—兼评 '宗教生态论' 思潮. *Zhongguo minzu bao* 中国民族报, July 27.

Li Yao. 2012. "IPO on Buddhist Mountain Makes Business of Religion." *China Daily*, August 23. Accessed February 22, 2018. http://www.chinadaily.com.cn/china/2012-08/23/content_15699537.htm.

Li Yuzhen 李玉珍. 2007a. "The Ordination System of the Late Imperial China." Paper presented at the First International Congress on Buddhist Women's Role in the sangha, Bhikshuni Vinaya and Ordination Lineages. University of Hamburg, July 18–20.

———. 2007b. "Yunshui bu zhu: Xiaoyun fashi de biqiuni dianfan" 云水不住：晓云法师的比丘尼典范. In *2006 nian Huafan daxue chuangbanren Xiaoyun fashi sixiang xingyi yantaohui ji dishisanjie guoji fojiao jiaoyu wenhua yantaohui huiyi lunwenji* 2006 年华梵大学创办人晓云法师思想行谊研讨会暨第十三届国际佛教教育文化研讨会会议论文集, edited by He Guangyan 何广棪 and Huang Junwei 黄俊威, pp. 11–38. Taibei: Huafandaxue dongfang renwen sixiang yanjiusuo.

———. 2008. "Jietan yange yu funü chujia" 戒坛沿革与妇女出家. In *Zongjiao wenhua yu xingbie lunli guoji xueshu huiyi lunwenji* 宗教文化与性别伦理国际学术会议论文集, pp. 189–224. Taibei: Fajie.

———. 2014. "Ordination into the Sangha and Promulgation of Buddhism: Buddhist Nuns' Identity Formation and Identity Consolidation in Post-War Taiwan." Paper presented for the research project "Vinaya Revival in 20th Century China and Taiwan." CCKF Research Grant, 2015–2018.

Liang Ruoqiao. 2011. "21st Century Monks." *Global Times,* March 29. Accessed February 22, 2018. http://www.globaltimes.cn/content/639025.shtml.

Lijing 理净. 2006. "Dangqian Zhongguo fojiao jiaoyu xianzhuang de fenxi yu sikao" 当前中国佛教教育现状的分析与思考. *Fayuan* 法源 24:46–57.

Lin Benxuan 林本炫. 1994. *Taiwan de zhengjiao chongtu* 台湾的政教冲突. Banqiao: Daoxiang chubanshe.

Lin Huixiang 林惠祥. 1981. "Changzhu niangjia fengsu de qiyuan ji muxi dao fuxi de guodu" 长住娘家风俗的起源及母系到父系的过度. In *Lin Huixiang renleixue lunzhu* 林惠祥人类学论著. Fuzhou: Fujian renmin chubanshe.

Lin Meirong 林美容 and Li Jiakai 李家恺. 2014. "Minnan zhaigu dui minnan fojiao de yingxiang" 闽南斋姑对闽南佛教的影响. *Minzu xuebao* 民族学报 11.

Liu Hongmei 刘红梅. 2008. "Mingmo wenhua jiaorong beijing xia de fojiao jielü fuxing—Yi Lianchi Zhuhong wei zhongxin" 明末文化交融背景下的佛教戒律复兴—以莲池袾宏为中心. *Huaibei meitan shifan xueyuan xuebao* 淮北煤炭师范学院学报 29 (6). Accessed February 22, 2018. http://www.shaolin.org.cn/templates/T_newS_list/index.aspx?nodeid=202&page=ContentPage&contentid=3632.

Liu Shuling 刘舒凌 and Yang Zhe 杨喆. 2014. "Zhongguo Fo, Daojiao jie changdao heli fangsheng de xin fengshang" 中国佛、道教界倡导合理放生的新风尚. *Zhongguo Xinwenwang* 中国新闻网. July 31. Accessed October 10, 2018. http://www.chinanews.com/cul/2014/07-30/6442700.shtml.

Liu Xuanguo 刘选国. 2017. "Pin dengshikou de aixin zhou" 品灯市口的爱心粥. *Gongyi shibao* 公益时报, July 25. Accessed October 12, 2018. http://www.gongyishibao.com/html/zhuanlan/2017/0725/12134.html.

Liu Yandong 刘延东. 2007. "Zai Zhongguo foxueyuan chengli wushi zhounian qingzhu dahui shang de jianghua" 在中国佛学院成立五十周年庆祝大会上的讲话. *Fayin* 法音 1:3–7.

Liu Yuanchun 刘元春. 2002. "Shehui chengshihua fazhan zhong de fojiao xinyang wenti" 社会城市化发展中的佛教信仰问题. *Fayin* 法音11:13–23.

———. 2006. "Fojiao minjian cishan huodong de tedian yu yingxiang: Shanghai 'yaohualu nianfo xiaozu' cishan huodong jishi" 佛教民间慈善活动的特点与影响—上海 "曜华路念佛小组" 慈善活动纪实. *Shijie zongjiao yanjiu* 世界宗教研究 4:135–141.

Loa Lok-sin. 2009. "Taiwan Buddhist Master: 'No Taiwanese.'" *Taipei Times,* March 31, p. 1.

Longlian 隆莲. 1989. "Pusa jieben" 菩萨戒本. In *Zhongguo fojiao* 中国佛教 3:210–216. Shanghai: Dongfang chuban zhongxin.

Longquan zhi sheng 龙泉之声. 2014. "Chuandi zheng nenglian, wobei yi bu ci!" 传递正能量，我辈义不辞! *Longquan zhi sheng* 龙泉之声, August 8. Accessed August 1, 2015. http://forum.longquanzs.mobi/forum.php?mod=viewthread&tid=33352.

Lü Cheng 吕澄. 1950. "Neixueyuan yanjiu gongzuo de zongjie yu jihua" 内学院研究工作的总结与计划. *Xiandai foxue* 现代佛学1:16–18.

———. 1952. "Zhongguo neixueyuan liangnian lai yanjiu gongzuo zongjie baogao" 中国内学院两年来研究工作总结报告. *Xiandai foxue* 现代佛学 4:16–17.

Lu Yunfeng 卢云峰. 2005. "Entrepreneurial Logics and the Evolution of Falun Gong." *Journal for the Scientific Study of Religion* 44 (2): 173–185.

———. 2008. "Chaoyue jidu zongjiao shehuixue—jianlun zongjiao shichang lilun zai huaren shehui de shiyongxing wenti" 超越基督宗教社会学—兼论宗教市场理论在华人社会的适用性问题. *Shehuixue yanjiu* 社会学研究 5:81–97.

Luo Guangwu 罗广武. 2001. *Xin zhongguo zongjiao gongzuo dashi gailan* 新中国宗教工作大事概览. Beijing: Huawen chubanshe.

Ma Bingtao 马炳涛. 2015. "Wanming Zhejiang Tiantaizong yanjiu" 晚明浙江天台宗研究. PhD diss., Xianggang Zhongwen Daxue.

MacInnis, Donald E. 1989. *Religion in China Today: Policy & Practice*. New York: Orbis Books.

Madsen, Richard. 2003. "Catholic Revival during the Reform Era." *China Quarterly* 174:469–487.

———. 2007. *Democracy's Dharma: Religious Renaissance and Political Development in Taiwan*. Berkeley: University of California Press.

———. 2009. "Back to the Future: Pre-Modern Religious Policy in Post-Secular China." March 2. Accessed August 10, 2018. http://www.fpri.org/articles/2009/03/back-future-pre-modern-religious-policy-post-secular-china.

———. 2011a. "Religious Renaissance in China Today." *Journal of Current Chinese Affairs* 2:17–42.

———. 2011b. "Secularism, Religious Change, and Social Conflict in Asia." In *Rethinking Secularism*, edited by Craig Calhoun, Mark Juergensmeyer, and Jonathan Van Antwerpen, pp. 248–269. New York: Oxford University Press.

Magnin, Paul. 1989. "Le bouddhisme en Chine populaire." *Etudes* 370 (2): 249–260.

Mainland Affairs Council (MAC). 2010. *Public Opinion Survey on the Outcome of the Fourth Chiang-Chen Talks (2009–12)*. Accessed February 22, 2018. www.mac.gov.tw/ct.asp?xItem=73045&CtNode=6689&mp=3.

"Making History." 2017. *The Economist* 424 (9054): 36–37.

Makley, Charlene. 2007. *The Violence of Liberation: Gender and Tibetan Buddhist Revival in Post-Mao China*. Berkeley: University of California Press.

"Manasi xian dafo si fojiaotu yonghu zhengfu daibu Benhuan" 玛纳斯县大佛寺佛教徒拥护政府逮捕本焕. 1958. *Xiandai foxue* 现代佛学 10:34.

Manji shinsan dainihon zokuzōkyō 卍新纂大日本续藏经. 1975–1989. Edited by Kawamura Kōshō. 90 vols. Tokyo: Kokusho Kankokai.

Mao Lei 毛磊. 1986. "Zhongguo foxueyuan qingzhu chengli sanshi zhounian" 中国佛学院庆祝成立三十周年. *Renmin ribao* 人民日报, September 15.

McCarthy, Susan K. 2010. "Economic Development and the Buddhist-Industrial Complex of Xishuangbanna." In *Faiths on Display: Religion, Tourism, and the Chinese State*, edited by Tim Oakes and Donald S. Sutton, pp. 157–182. Lanham, MD: Rowman & Littlefield.

———. 2013. "Serving Society, Repurposing the State: Religious Charity and Resistance in China." *China Journal* 70:48–72.

McGuire, Beverley. 2016. "Buddhist Blogs in Mainland China and Taiwan: Discussing a Buddhist Approach to Technology." In *Religion and Media in China: Insights and Case Studies from the Mainland, Taiwan and Hong Kong,* edited by Stefania Travagnin, pp. 151–166. London: Routledge.

McRae, John R. 2005. "Daoxuan's Vision of Jetavana: The Ordination Platform Movement in Medieval Chinese Buddhism." In *Going Forth. Visions of Buddhist Vinaya. Essays Presented in Honor of Professor Stanley Weinstein,* edited by William M. Bodiford, pp. 68–100. Honolulu: University of Hawai'i Press.

Miaoshan laoheshang baisui danchen jinian tekan 妙善老和尚百岁诞辰纪念特刊. 2009. Zhoushan qicai yinwu.

Minghai 明海, Minghan 明憨, and Mingji 明基. 2016. "Jinghui zhanglao de fasi lu" 净慧长老的法嗣录. *Chan* 禅 153:34–60.

Mingshan 茗山. 2002. *Mingshan riji* 茗山日记. Shanghai: Guji chubanshe.

Mingyang 明旸, ed. 1996. *Yuanying fashi nianpu* 圆瑛法师年谱. Beijing: Zongjiao wenhua chubanshe.

MOFA (Ministry of Foreign Affairs). 2014. *Speech by H. E. Xi Jinping President of the People's Republic of China at UNESCO Headquarters,* March 28. Accessed February 22, 2018. http://www.fmprc.gov.cn/mfa_eng/wjdt_665385/zyjh_665391/t1142560.shtml.

Morrison, Elizabeth. 2010. *The Power of Patriarchs. Qisong and Lineage in Chinese Buddhism.* Leiden: Brill.

Moskowitz, Marc L. 2001. *The Haunting Fetus: Abortion, Sexuality, and the Spirit World in Taiwan.* Honolulu: University of Hawai'i Press.

Mu Zhongjian 牟钟鉴. 2006. "Zongjiao wenhua shengtai de zhongguo moshi" 宗教文化生态的中国模式. *Zhongguo minzu bao* 中国民族报, May 16.

———. 2012. "Zongjiao shengtai lun" 宗教生态论. *Shijie zongjiao wenhua* 世界宗教文化 1:1–10.

Munro, Robin. 1989. "Backward toward Liberation." *Chinese Sociology & Anthropology* 21 (4): 3–18.

"Nanhua si quanti sengtu yonghu zhengfu daibu Benhuan" 南华寺全体僧徒拥护政府逮捕本焕. 1958. *Xiandai foxue* 现代佛学 8:31.

"Nanhua si zhuchi Benhuan yuanlai shi ge fangeming fenzi" 南华寺主持本焕原来是个反革命分子. 1958. *Xiandai foxue* 现代佛学 8:30–31.

Nedostup, Rebecca. 2009. *Superstitious Regimes: Religion and the Politics of Chinese Modernity.* Cambridge, MA: Harvard University Asia Center.

Nichols, Brian J. 2011. "History, Material Culture, and Auspicious Events at the Purple Cloud: Buddhist Monasticism at Quanzhou Kaiyuan." PhD diss., Rice University.

———. Forthcoming. "Interrogating Religious Tourism at Buddhist Monasteries in China." In *Buddhist Tourism in Asia: Imagining, Secularizing, and Commodifying the Sacred,* edited by Courtney Bruntz and Brooke Schnedneck, Honolulu: University of Hawai'i Press.

Nyíri, Pál. 2006. *Scenic Spots: Chinese Tourism, the State, and Cultural Authority.* Seattle: University of Washington Press.

———. 2010. *Mobility and Cultural Authority in Contemporary China.* Seattle: University of Washington Press.

Oakes, Timothy. 2005. *Tourism and Modernity in China.* London: Routledge.

Oakes, Timothy, and Donald S. Sutton. 2010. *Faiths on Display: Religion, Tourism, and the Chinese State.* Lanham, MD: Rowman & Littlefield.

Oldenburg, Ray. 1989. *The Great Good Place*. New York: Paragon House.

Ownby, David. 2010. *Falun Gong and the Future of China*. Oxford: Oxford University Press.

Ownby, David, Vincent Goossaert, and Ji Zhe, eds. 2017. *Making Saints in Modern China*. New York: Oxford University Press.

Pacey, Scott. 2016. "Eminence and Edutainment: Xingyun and Daoxin as Television Celebrities." In *Religion and Media in China: Insights and Case Studies from the Mainland, Taiwan and Hong Kong*, edited by Stefania Travagnin, pp. 71–89. London: Routledge.

Palmer, David. 2007. *Qigong Fever: Body, Science, and Utopia in China*. New York: Columbia University Press.

Palmer, David, and Xun Liu. 2012. *Taoism in the Twentieth Century: Between Eternity and Modernity*. Berkeley: University of California Press.

Palmer, David, Glenn Shive, and Philip L. Wickeri, eds. 2011. *Chinese Religious Life*. New York: Oxford University Press.

Parameswaran, Prashanth. 2009. "Restoring the Military Balance in China-Taiwan Relations." *World Politics Review*, September 30. Accessed February 22, 2018. www.worldpolitics review.com/article.aspx?id=4386.

Payne, Richard. 2004. "Ritual." In *Encyclopedia of Buddhism*, edited by Robert Buswell, pp. 723–726. New York: Macmillan.

Penkower, Linda. 2000. "In the Beginning . . . Guanding (561–632) and the Creation of Early Tiantai." *Journal of the International Association for Buddhist Studies* 23 (2): 245–296.

Pew Research Center. 2012. "Table: Religious Composition by Country, by Numbers." In "Religion and Public Life." Accessed February 22, 2018. http://www.pewforum.org /2012/12/18/table-religious-composition-by-country-in-numbers/.

Pittman, Don A. 2001. *Toward a Modern Chinese Buddhism: Taixu's Reforms*. Honolulu: University of Hawai'i Press.

Poon, Shuk-wah. 2011. *Negotiating Religion in Modern China: State and Common People in Guangzhou, 1900–1937*. Hong Kong: Chinese University Press.

Potter, Pitman B. 2003. "Belief in Control: Regulation of Religion in China." *China Quarterly* 174:317–337.

Qin, Wen-jie. 2000. "The Buddhist Revival in Post-Mao China: Women Reconstruct Buddhism on Mt. Emei." PhD diss., Harvard University.

Qiu Shanshan 裘山山. 1997. *Dangdai diyi biqiuni: Longlian fashi zhuan* 当代第一比丘尼—隆莲法师传. Fuzhou: Fujian meishu chubanshe.

Reardon, Chris. 2011. "Ideational Learning and the Paradox of Chinese Catholic Reconciliation." *Journal of Current Chinese Affairs* 40 (2): 43–70.

Reinders, Eric. 1997. "Ritual Topography: Embodiment and Vertical Space in Buddhist Monastic Practice." *History of Religions* 36 (3): 244–264.

———. 2015. *Buddhist and Christian Responses to the Kowtow Problem in China*. London: Bloomsbury.

Ren'ai Charity Foundation. 2009. "Ren'ai xin zhan de boke" 仁爱心栈的博客. February 5. Accessed February 22, 2018. http://blog.sina.com.cn/s/blog_5feb04790100gane.html.

———. 2014. "Ren'ai zai xinjian, Lei Feng zai shenbian" 仁爱在心间, 雷锋在身边. *Ren'ai xin zhan de boke* 仁爱心栈的博客, February 5. Accessed February 22, 2018. http://blog.sina .com.cn/s/blog_5feb04790101qt4x.html.

Robinet, Isabelle. 1997. *Taoism: Growth of a Religion*. Palo Alto, CA: Stanford University Press.

Robson, James. 2010. "Buddhist Sacred Geography." In *Early Chinese Religion*, edited by John Lagerwey and Pengzhi Lü, pp. 1353–1397. Leiden: Brill.

Romberg, Alan. 2010. "2010: The Winter of PRC Discontent." *China Leadership Monitor* 31:1–23.

Ruan Renze 阮仁泽 and Gao Zhennong 高振农, eds. 1992. *Shanghai zongjiao shi* 上海宗教史. Shanghai: Shanghai renmin chubanshe.

Rubinstein, Murray. 1991. *The Protestant Community on Modern Taiwan: Mission, Seminary, and Church*. Armonk, NY: M. E. Sharpe.

Ryan, Chris, and Gu Huimin. 2009. *Tourism in China: Destinations, Cultures and Communities*. London: Routledge.

Sangji Zhaxi (Sangye Tashi) 桑吉扎西. 2005. "Chongqingshi fojiao xiehui longzhong juxing chongqing foxueyuan chengli guapai qingdian yishi" 重庆市佛教协会隆重举行重庆佛学院成立挂牌庆典仪式. *Fayin* 法音 6:46–47.

Sato, Kimihiko 佐藤公彦. 2006. "Ichi hachi kyūgo-nen no Furuta kyōan: Itsuki kyō. Nisshinsensō no kage. misshonarī gaikō no tenkan" 一八九五年 の古田教案: 齋教。日清戦爭の影。ミッショナリー外交の転換. *Ajia. Afurika gengo-gaku kenkyū* アジア。アフリカ言語学研究 72:66–123.

Sawada Mizuho. 1975. 深田瑞穂, *Bukkyō to Chūgoku bungaku* 仏教と中国文学. Tokyo: Kokushokankōkai.

Schak, David. 2011. "Protestantism in China: A Dilemma for the Party-State." *Journal of Current Chinese Affairs* 40 (2): 71–106.

Schipper, Kristofer. 1994. *The Taoist Body*. Berkeley: University of California Press.

Schlütter, Morten. 2008. *How Zen Became Zen: The Dispute over Enlightenment and the Formation of Chan Buddhism in Song-Dynasty China*. Honolulu: University of Hawai'i Press.

Seiwert, Hubert. 1992. "Popular Religious Sects and Southeast China: Sect Connections and the Problem of the Luo Jiao/Bailian Jiao Dichotomy." *Journal of Chinese Religion* 20:33–60.

Seiwert, Hubert, and Ma Xisha. 2003. *Religious Popular Movements and Heterodox Sects in Chinese History*. Leiden: Brill.

Serizawa, Satohiro 芹澤知広. 2012. "Tōnan ajia kakyō kajin shakai ni okeru josei shukke sō ni tsuite no nōto" 東南アジア華僑華人社会における女性出家僧についてのノート総合研究所所報. Accessed December 17, 2017. http://repo.nara-u.ac.jp/modules/xoonips/download .php/AN10403791-20130300-1004.pdf?file_id=6065.

Shakya, Tsering. 1999. *The Dragon in the Land of Snows: A History of Modern Tibet since 1947*. London: Pimlico.

———. 2012. "Self-Immolation, the Changing Language of Protest in Tibet." *Revue d'Etudes Tibétaines* 2 (5): 19–39.

Shanghai Jing'an Si 上海静安寺. 1954. "'Yufojie' de relie qingkuang" "浴佛节" 的热烈情况. *Honghua yuekan* 弘化月刊 156 (May 25): 18.

Shanghai tongzhi 上海通志. 2005. Accessed August 12, 2015. http://www.shtong.gov.cn /node2/node2247/index.html.

Sharf, Robert. 2005. "Ritual." In *Critical Terms for the Study of Buddhism*, edited by Donald S. Lopez, pp. 245–270. Chicago: University of Chicago Press.

Sharf, Robert, and Griffith Foulk. 1993. "On the Ritual Use of Ch'an Portraiture in Medieval China." *Cahiers d'Extrême-Asie* 7:149–219.

Shenghui 圣辉. 2005. *Zhongguo fojiao xiehui wushi nian* 中国佛教协会五十年. Nanjing: Jinling kejingchu.

———. 2013. "Zhongguo meng ye shi fojiao de meng" 中国梦也是佛教的梦. *Xianggang wenhuibao* 香港文汇报. Accessed February 22, 2018. http://bodhi.takungpao.com.hk /sspt/zhiyanzhiyu/2013-05/1635555.html.

Sheng-Yen. 1991. "The Renaissance of *Vinaya* Thought during the Late Ming Dynasty of China." In *Buddhist Ethic and Modern Society. An International Symposium,* edited by Charles Wei-hsun Fu and Sandra A. Wawrytko, pp. 41–54. New York: Greenwood Press.

Shengyin 胜音. 1956. "Zhongguo foxueyuan kaixue dianli de shengkuang" 中国佛学院开学典礼的盛况. *Xiandai foxue* 现代佛学1:8–11.

Shepherd, Robert J. 2013. *Faith in Heritage: Displacement, Development, and Religious Tourism in Contemporary China.* Walnut Creek, CA: Left Coast Press.

Shi Fangfang. 2009. "Evaluation of Visitor Experience at Chinese Buddhist Sites: The Case of Wutai Mountain." In *Tourism in China: Destinations, Cultures and Communities,* edited by Chris Ryan and Huimin Gu, pp. 197–212. London: Routledge.

Shi Yilong 石亦龙. 2009. "Changzhu niangjia yu buluo fujia de bijiao" 长住娘家与不落夫家的比较. Paper presented at Diqijie Haixia Liang'an Minnan Hunqing Wenhua Jie Ji "Minnan Hunqing Wenhua Gaoduan Luntan" Lunwen 第七届海峡两岸闽南婚庆文化节暨 "闽南婚庆文化高端论坛" 论文. Accessed February 22, 2018. http://wenku.baidu .com/view/cd0a6e3367ec102de2bd8959.

Shi Zhengyan 释证严. 1999. *Daai wu guojie* 大爱无国界. Taibei: Fojiao ciji cishan shiye jijinhui 佛教慈济慈善事业基金会.

Shinohara, Koichi. 1999. "From Local History to Universal History: The Construction of the Sung T'ien-t'ai Lineage." In *Buddhism in the Sung,* edited by Peter N. Gregory and Daniel A. Getz, pp. 524–576. Honolulu: University of Hawai'i Press.

Shiu, Henry, and Leah Stokes. 2008. "Buddhist Animal Release Practices: Historic, Environmental, Public Health and Economic Concerns." *Contemporary Buddhism* 9 (2): 181–196.

Singhal, Arvind, and Everett M. Rogers. 1999. *Entertainment-Education: A Communication Strategy for Social Change.* Mahwah, NJ: Lawrence Erlbaum Associates.

Smith, Joanna Handlin. 2009. *The Art of Doing Good: Charity in Late Ming China.* Berkeley: University of California Press.

Smyer Yü, Dan. 2012. *The Spread of Tibetan Buddhism in China: Charisma, Money, Enlightenment.* London: Routledge.

Stark, Rodney, and William Sims Bainbridge. 1987. *A Theory of Religion.* New York: Peter Lang.

Stockard, Janice F. 1992. *Daughters of the Canton Delta: Marriage Patterns and Economic Strategies in South China 1860–1930.* Hong Kong: Hong Kong University Press.

Sun Jiabao 孙家宝. 2012. "Yanjiu zhongxin dang zhibu fu ren'ai cishan jijinhui kaizhan 'xue Lei Feng, xian aixin, zuo gongyi' huodong" 研究中心党支部赴仁爱慈善基金会开展 "学雷锋、献爱心、做公益" 活动. April 11. Accessed August 1, 2015. http://www.sara .gov.cn/zzjg/yjzx/gzdt11/13150.htm.

Sun Yanfei. 2009. "Fighting the Menace of Tourism: When Buddhist Resistance Became Radicalized." Paper delivered at the Annual Meeting of the American Academy of Religion, Montreal, November 7–10.

———. 2010. "Religions in Sociopolitical Context: The Reconfiguration of Religious Ecology in Post-Mao China." PhD diss., University of Chicago.

———. 2011. "The Chinese Buddhist Ecology in Post-Mao China: Contours, Types and Dynamics." *Social Compass* 58 (2): 498–510.

Tainaka, Chizuru 胎中千鶴. 2000. "Nihon tōchi-ki Taiwan no toki kyō ni kansuru ichi shiten" 日本統治期台湾の斎教に関する一視点. *Shien* 史苑 60 (2): 50–72.

Tam Wai Lun 谭伟伦. 2007. *Minjian fojiao yanjiu* 民间佛教研究. Shanghai: Zhonghua shuju.

Tamney, Joseph B. 2005. "Introduction." In *State, Market, and Religions in Chinese Societies*, edited by Yang Fenggang and Joseph B. Tamney, pp. 1–18. Leiden: Brill.

Tang Yuankai. 2012. "Ancient Virtues for the Virtual World: Leading Chinese Buddhist Connects to Followers via the Internet." *Beijing Review*, April 12. Accessed February 22, 2018. http://www.bjreview.com.cn/quotes/txt/2014-05/09/content_446366.htm.

———. 2013. "New Tech Promotes an Old Religion." *China Today*, March 14. Accessed February 22, 2018. http://www.chinatoday.com.cn/english/society/2013-03/14/content_527227.htm.

Tang Yunyun 唐云云. 2014. "Kunming Panlong si shouci bimen xieke kangyi 'shangyehua'" 昆明盘龙寺首次闭门谢客抗议 "商业化." *Zhongguo xinwenwang* 中国新闻网. August 18. Accessed September 17, 2014. http://www.chinanews.com/cul/2014/08-18/6503559.shtml.

Tanxu 倓虚. 1998. *Ying chen huiyilu* 影尘回忆录. Shanghai: Shanghai foxue shuju.

Tao Xiao'ai 陶小爱, Luo Ling 罗玲, Tao Fangfang 陶芳芳, and Li Qi 李琪. 2012. "Shenghui da heshang: Fengxian shi xiuxing, fojiao jingshen yu Lei Feng jingshen xiangtong" 圣辉大和尚:奉献是修行, 佛教精神与雷锋精神相通. *Hunan Fojiao wang* 湖南佛教网, February 28. Accessed October 13, 2018. https://fo.ifeng.com/news/detail_2012_02/28/12834394_0.shtml.

Tarocco, Francesca. 2017. "Technologies of Salvation: (Re)locating Chinese Buddhism in the Digital Age." *Journal of Global Buddhism* 18:155–175.

Terrone, Antonio. 2003. "Householders and Monks: A Study of Treasure Revealers and Their Role in Religious Revival in Contemporary Eastern Tibet." In *Buddhism Beyond the Monastery: Tantric Practices and Their Performers in Tibet and the Himalayas*, edited by Sarah Jacoby and Antonio Terrone, pp. 73–109. Leiden: Brill.

Thornton, Patricia M. 2012. "The New Life of the Party: Party-Building and Social Engineering in Greater Shanghai." *China Journal* 68:58–78.

"Tiantaizong chuanfa dadian" 天台宗传法大典. 2009. *Xianggang fojiao* 香港佛教 585.

Tiezzi, Shannon. 2015. "What Xi's Catchphrases Say About His Priorities for China." *Diplomat*, February 7. Accessed February 22, 2018. http://thediplomat.com/2015/02/what-xis-catchphrases-say-about-his-priorities-for-china/.

Tiguang laoheshang kaishi lu 体光老和尚开示录. 2006. s.l.

Tong, James. 2009. *Revenge of the Forbidden City: The Suppression of the Falungong in China, 1999–2005*. New York: Oxford University Press.

———. 2010. "The New Religious Policy in China: Catching up with Systemic Reforms." *Asian Survey* 5:859–887.

Topley, Marjorie. 1954. "Chinese Women's Vegetarian Houses in Singapore." *Journal of the Malayan Branch of the Royal Asiatic Society* 27 (1): 51–67.

———. 1956. "Chinese Religion and Religious Institutions in Singapore." In *Cantonese Society in Hong Kong and Singapore: Gender, Religion, Medicine and Money*, edited by Jean DeBernardi, pp. 125–174. Hong Kong: Hong Kong University Press.

———. 1975. "Marriage Resistance in Rural Kuangtung." In *Women in Chinese Society*, edited by Margaret Wolf and Roxanne Witke, pp. 67–88. Stanford, CA: Stanford University Press.

Travagnin, Stefania. 2015. "The Impact of Politics on the Minnan Buddhist Institute: Sanmin Zhuyi 三民主义 and Aiguo Zhuyi 爱国主义 in the Context of Sangha Education." *Review of Religion and Chinese Society 2* (1): 21–50.

———. 2016a. "Dingkong—the Blogger Monk in Southern China." In *Figures of Buddhist Modernity in Asia*, edited by Justin McDaniel, Mark Rowe, and Jeffrey Samuels, pp. 170–173. Honolulu: University of Hawai'i Press.

———, ed. 2016b. *Religion and Media in China: Insights and Case Studies from the Mainland, Taiwan and Hong Kong*. London: Routledge.

———. 2018. "Mapping New Systems of Community Networks: Discursive Identity, Cross-Strait Lineage Construction, and Funerary Sacred Space in Taiwanese Buddhism." In *Communities of Memory: Reimagining and Reinventing the Past in East Asian Buddhism*, edited by Mario Poceski, pp. 177–217. Hamburg: Hamburg University Press.

———. Forthcoming. "The Marxist Dimension of Chinese and Taiwanese Buddhism: Mapping Patterns of Interaction between Religion and Politics in the Making of a Buddhist Utopia." In *Buddhist Socialisms in Asia: An Historical Perspective*, edited by Patrice Ladwig. London: Routledge.

Tsai, Lily Lee. 2002. "Cadres, Temple and Lineage Institutions, and Governance in Rural China." *China Journal* 48:1–27.

Tsomo, Karma Lekshe. 1988. *Sakyadhita: Daughters of the Buddha*. New York: Snow Lion Publication.

Tuttle, Gray. 2005. *Tibetan Buddhists in the Making of Modern China*. New York: Columbia University Press.

———. 2010. "The Failure of Ideologies in China's Relations with Tibetans." In *Multi-Nation States in Asia: Accommodation or Resistance*, edited by Jacques Bertrand and André Laliberté, pp. 219–243. Cambridge: Cambridge University Press.

UNESCO. 2011. *World Heritage Convention: China*. Accessed February 22, 2018. http://whc.unesco.org/en/statesparties/cn.

Vidal, Claire. 2014. "Savoir-faire et savoir-être bouddhiques dans la Chine contemporaine. Du court-métrage au pèlerinage du Putuoshan." *Études chinoises* 33 (1): 147–157.

Wang Chao 王超 and Gao Shining 高师宁. 2012. "Zongjiao guanli moshi lunzheng de huigu yu sikao: Cong 'zongjiao wenhua shengtai pingheng lun' shuoqi" 宗教管理模式论争的回顾与思考—从"宗教文化生态平衡论"说起." *Shijie zongjiao yanjiu* 世界宗教研究 5:173–178.

Wang Dong. 2010. "Internationalizing Heritage: UNESCO and China's Longmen's Grottoes." *China Information* 24 (2): 123–147.

Wang Gungwu. 2002. "State and Faith: Secular Values in Asia and the West." In *Critical Views of September 11: Analyses from around the World*, edited by Eric Hershberg and Kevin W. Moore, pp. 224–242. New York: New Press.

———. 2003. "Secular China." *China Report* 39 (3): 305–321.

Wang Hsuan-Li. 2014. "Gushan: The Formation of a Chan Lineage during the Seventeenth Century and Its Spread to Taiwan." PhD diss., Columbia University.

Wang Jia 王佳. 2014. *Zhonguo fojiao he cishan gongyi shiye* 中国宗教和慈善公益事业. Beijing: Zongjiao wehua chubanshe 宗教文化出版社.

Wang Leiquan 王雷泉. 2001. "Zouchu zhongguo fojiao jiaoyu kunjing chuyi" 走出中国佛教教育困境刍议. *Fayin* 法音 10:7–15.

Wang Liansheng 王连胜. (1999) 2012. "Putuo luojiashan zhi" 普陀洛迦山志. Revised unpublished version.

Wang Qifeng 王歧丰. 2014. "Beijing yunju si nanta huifu minguo jiumiao wei quanguo shouli fujian guta" 北京云居寺南塔恢复民国旧貌为全国首例复建古塔. *Chinese News Service* 中国新闻网. Accessed February 22, 2018. http://www.chinanews.com/cul/2014/09 -10/6575049.shtml.

Wang-Toutain, Françoise. 1997. "La voix du Dharma se fait-elle de nouveau entendre en Chine?" In *Renouveaux religieux en Asie*, edited by Catherine Clémentin-Ojha, pp. 61–81. Paris: École Française d'Extrême-Orient.

Wang Zongyu. 王宗昱. 2014. "Beijing Dongyuemiao huifu guochengzhong de wenti" 北京东岳庙恢复过程中的问题. In *Shijiu shiji yilai zhongguo difang daojiao bianqian* 十九世纪以来中国地方道教变迁, edited by Lai Chi Tim 黎志添, pp. 319–339. Hong Kong: Joint Publishing.

Wank, David L. 2009. "Institutionalizing Modern 'Religion' in China's Buddhism: Political Phases of a Local Revival." In *Making Religion, Making the State: The Politics of Religion in Modern China*, edited by Yoshiko Ashiwa and David L. Wank, pp. 126–150. Stanford, CA: Stanford University Press.

Wei Tingting 魏婷婷. 2014. "Minnan 'caigu' shengfen shitong jiqi xinyang shenghuo: Yi Wuzhen 'caigu' wei an" 闽南 "菜姑" 身分认同及其信仰生活—以武镇 "菜姑" 为案. Master's thesis, Overseas Chinese University 华侨大学.

Welch, Holmes. 1961. "Buddhist Organizations in Hong Kong." *Journal of the Hong Kong Branch of the Royal Asiatic Society* 1:98–114.

———. 1963. "Dharma Scrolls and the Succession of Abbots in Chinese Monasteries." *T'oung Pao* 50:93–149.

———. 1967. *The Practice of Chinese Buddhism*. Cambridge, MA: Harvard University Press.

———. 1968. *The Buddhist Revival in China*. Cambridge, MA: Harvard University Press.

———. 1972. *Buddhism under Mao*. Cambridge, MA: Harvard University Press.

Weller, Robert. 2001. *Alternate Civilities: Democracy and Culture in China and Taiwan*. Boulder, CO: Westview.

Weller, Robert, Wu Keping, Fan Lizhu, and Julia Huang. 2017. *Religion and Charity: The Social Life of Goodness in Chinese Societies*. New York: Cambridge University Press.

Wen Jinyu 温金玉. 2006. "Zhongguo dangdai fojiao zhidu jianshe: Yi dalu hanchuan fojiao wei zhongxin" 中国当代佛教制度建设—以大陆汉传佛教为中心. *Foxue yanjiu* 佛学研究 15:144–156.

———. 2010. "Fahai difang: Zhongguo dalu jinnian chuanjie huodong de kaocha" 法海堤防—中国大陆近年传戒活动的考察. *Furen zongjiao yanjiu* 辅仁宗教研究21:1–19.

Wickeri, Philip. 1989. *Seeking the Common Ground: Protestant Christianity, the Three-Self Movement, and China's United Front*. New York: Orbis Books.

Wolf, Arthur. 1974. *Religion and Ritual in Chinese Society*. Stanford, CA: Stanford University Press.

Wong, Cara, Alison McIntosh, and Chris Ryan. 2012. "Buddhism and Tourism Perceptions of the Monastic Community at Pu-tuo-shan, China." *Annals of Tourism Research* 40:213–234.

Wu Jiang. 2008. *Enlightenment in Dispute. The Reinvention of Chan Buddhism in Seventeenth-Century China*. Oxford: Oxford University Press.

Wu Ka-ming. 2011. "Tradition Revival with Socialist Characteristics: Propaganda Storytelling Turned Spiritual Service in Rural Yan'an." *China Journal* 66:101–117.

Wu Keping. 2009. "In Search of Pure Land: Globalization and Buddhist Revival in Contemporary China." Paper presented at the Conference on Religion and Globalization in Asia: Prospects, Patterns and Problems for the 21st Century, sponsored by the Center for the Pacific Rim, University of San Francisco, March 13–14.

Wu Limin 吴立民. 1998. *Chanzong zongpai yuanliu* 禅宗宗派源流. Beijing: Zhongguo shehui kexue chubanshe.

Wu Rui 吴睿. 2008. "Women zhege chaosheng de shidai: Dui dangdai chengshi zongjiao xinyang de renleixue sikao—yi (Shanghai) sanguantang weili" 我们这个朝圣的时代: 对当代城市宗教信仰的人类学思考-以(上海)三观堂为例. Master's thesis, Fudan University.

"Xi Jinping: Yao gaodu zhongshi hulianwang zongjiao wenti" 习近平: 要高度重视互联网宗教问题. *Zhengce Fagui Zhengce Zhidao* 政策法规-政策指导. Accessed October 15, 2018. http://nanputuo.com/policy/info.aspx?channel_id=68&articleid=74874.

Xiamen Fojiao Zaixian 厦门佛教在线. 2011. "Shengting lingdao zhuancheng diaoyan minnan caigu jiaoshi zige rending gongzuo" 省厅领导专程调研闽南菜姑教师资格认定工作. Accessed October 27, 2018. http://www.nanputuo.com/nptnews/html/201110/2122352473499.html.

Xiamenshi Fojiao Xiehui 厦门市佛教协会. *Gazetteer of Xiamen Buddhism*. Unpublished draft.

———. 2006. *Xiamenshi fojiao zhi* 厦门市佛教志. Xiamen: Xiamen daxue chubanshe.

———. 2012. "Xiamenshi fojiao fanxing qingxinnü (caigu) jiaozhi renyuan zige rending banfa (shixing caoan)" 厦门市佛教梵行清信女 (菜姑) 教职人员资格认定办法 (试行草案).

"Xianggang fojiao jie qingzhu Fodan yingqing Foya sheli zhanli dahui" 香港佛教界庆祝佛诞迎请佛牙舍利瞻礼大会. 1999. *Xianggang fojiao*, vol. 469.

Xinhua News. 2009. "Hu Jintao's Speech on Taiwan Draws Positive Comments." January 4. Accessed October 13, 2018. http://www.china.org.cn/china/news/2009-01/04/content_17048229.htm.

Xinhua wang 新华网. 2010. "Changdao ditan shenghuo, ren'ai qianshou zhishu" 倡导低碳生活,仁爱千手植树. *Xinhua wang* 新华网. April 12. Accessed October 13, 2018. http://blog.sina.com.cn/s/blog_489e98b90100hwyz.html.

———. 2013. "Woguo zongjiao jiaozhi renyuan rending bei'an lü da 98%" 我国宗教教职人员认定备案率达 98%. *Xinhua wang* 新华网. December 18. Accessed October 13, 2018. http://www.chinanews.com/gn/2013/12-18/5631312.shtml.

Xirao Jiacuo (Sherab Gyatso) 喜饶嘉错. 1956. "Xirao Jiacuo yuanzhang de kaixue ci" 喜饶嘉错院长的开学词. *Xiandai foxue* 现代佛学 1:4–5.

———. 1957. "Di'erjie quanguo daibiao huiyi bimuci" 第二届全国代表会议闭幕词. *Xiandai foxue* 现代佛学 5:29.

Xu Wei 徐威. 2003. *Guangji si* 广济寺. Beijing: Huawenchubanshe.

Xue Yu 学愚, ed. 2012. *Renjian fojiao yu dangdai lunli* 人间佛教与当代伦理. Hong Kong: Zhonghua shuju.

———. 2015. *Zhongguo fojiao de shehuizhuyi gaizao* 中国佛教的社会主义改造. Hong Kong: Chinese University Press.

Xuecheng 学诚. 1997. "Sengni shoujie gujin tan" 僧尼受戒古今谈. *Fayin* 法音 3:3–12.

———. 2010. "Miaozhan lao heshang sengjiaoyu daigei women de qishi: Zai Miaozhan heshang bainian danchen jinian dafahui shang de zhici" 妙湛老和尚僧教育带给我们的启示—在妙湛和尚百年诞辰纪念大法会上的致辞. Accessed February 22, 2018. http://blog.sina.com.cn/s/blog_489e98b901017ooz.html.

————. 2012. "'Fayin' cong meiti chuanbo kan dongxifang wenming de chayi "法音" 从媒体传播看东西方文明的差异. *Fayin* 法音 4. Accessed February 22, 2018. http://www.longquanzs.org/lqs/hcfs/hcfs/46884.htm.

Xuyun 虚云, ed. 1935. *Zengding fozu daoying* 增订佛祖道影. Xianggang: Xianggang fojing liutongchu yinxing.

————. 1936a. "Xingdengji xu" 星灯集序. *Foxue banyue kan* 125:14–15.

————, ed. 1936b. *Zengjiao Gushan liezu lianfang ji* 增校鼓山列祖联芳集. Fujian: Gushan Yongquan chansi.

Xuyun laoheshang fahui 虚云老和尚法汇. 2005. Beijing: Huangshan shushe. First published as *Xuyun heshang fahui* 虚云和尚法汇. 1953. Xianggang: Xuyun heshang fahui bianyin chu.

Xuyun laoheshang nianpu fahui zengding ben 虚云老和尚年谱法汇增订本. 1997. Taibei: Taiwan Xiuyuan chanyuan yinxing.

Yamabe Nobuyoshi. 2005. "Visionary Repentance and Visionary Ordination in the *Brahmā Net Sūtra.*" In *Going Forth: Visions of Buddhist Vinaya. Essays Presented in Honor of Professor Stanley Weinstein,* edited by William M. Bodiford, pp. 17–39. Honolulu: University of Hawai'i Press.

Yang Der-Ruey 杨德睿. 2010. "Dangdai zhongguo daoshi peixun jiaocheng de tezheng yu yiyi" 当代中国道士培训教程的特征与意义. *Zhongguo nongye daxue xuebao (shehui kexue ban)* 中国农业大学学报 (社会科学版) 27 (1): 29–43.

————. 2011. "From Ritual Skills to Discursive Knowledge: Changing Styles of Taoist Transmission in Shanghai." In *Religion in Contemporary China: Revitalization and Innovation,* edited by Adam Yuet Chau, pp. 81–107. London: Routledge.

————. 2012. "New Agents and New Ethos of Taoism in China Today." *Chinese Sociological Review* 45 (2): 48–64.

————. 2015. "Animal Release: The Dharma Being Staged between Marketplace and Park." *Cultural Diversity in China* 1 (2): 141–163.

Yang Fenggang. 2004. "Between Secularist Ideology and Desecularizing Reality: The Birth and Growth of Religious Research in Communist China." *Sociology of Religion* 65 (2): 101–119.

————. 2006. "The Red, Black, and Gray Markets of Religion in China." *Sociological Quarterly* 47:93–122.

————. 2011. *Religion in China: Survival and Revival under Communist Rule.* Oxford: Oxford University Press.

Yang Fenggang and Wei Dedong. 2005. "The Bailin Buddhist Temple: Thriving under Communism." In *State, Market, and Religions in Chinese Societies,* edited by Yang Fenggang and Joseph B. Tamney, pp. 63–86. Leiden: Brill.

Yang Guang. 2010. "'Art-monk' has his own take on Buddhism." *China Daily.* August 1. Accessed February 18, 2018. http://www.chinadaily.com.cn/china/2010-01/08/content_9285751.htm.

Yang Guobin. 2009. *The Power of the Internet in China: Citizen Activism Online.* New York: Columbia University Press.

————. 2015. *China's Contested Internet.* Copenhagen: NIAS Press.

Yang Jie 杨洁. 2012. "Rang shijie duo yidian ai yu guanhuai" 让世界多一点爱与关怀. *Ren'ai xin zhan de boke* 仁爱心栈的博客. February 5. Accessed February 22, 2018. http://blog.sina.com.cn/s/blog_5feb047901012f6x.html.

Yang Jisheng. 2012. *Tombstone: The Great Chinese Famine, 1958–1962,* translated by Stacy Mosher and Guo Jian. New York: Farrar, Straus and Giroux.

Yang Mayfair Mei-Hui, ed. 2008. *Chinese Religiosities: Afflictions of Modernity and State Formation.* Berkeley: University of California Press.

———. 2011. "Postcoloniality and Religiosity in Modern China: The Disenchantments of Sovereignty." *Theory, Culture & Society* 28 (2): 3–45.

Yao Qingjiang, Daniel A. Stout, and Zhaoxi Liu. 2011. "China's Official Media Portrayal of Religion (1996–2005): Policy Change in a Desecularizing Society." *Journal of Media and Religion* 10:39–50.

Yifa. 2002. *The Origins of Buddhist Monastic Codes in China: An Annotated Translation and Study of the Chanyuan Qinggui.* Honolulu: University of Hawai'i Press.

Yinshun 印顺 and Wang Jia 王佳, eds. 2014. *Zhongguo zongjiao he cishan gongyi shiye* 中国宗教和慈善公益事业. Beijing: Zongjiao wenhua chubanshe.

"You cong yuanfang lai buyilehu 友从远方来不亦乐乎." 2001. *Xianggang fojiao*, vol. 490.

Young, Glenn. 2013. "Reading and Praying Online: The Continuity of Religion Online and Online Religion in Internet Christianity." In *Religion Online: Finding Faith on the Internet,* edited by Lorne L. Dawson and Douglas E. Cowan, pp. 93–105. London: Routledge.

Yu Bin 俞滨. 2003. "'Xiang shiying': Yi lilun chuangxin tuidong shijian chuangxin" "相适应": 以理论创新推动实践创新. *Zhongguo zongjiao* 中国宗教 8:19–27.

Yü, Chün-fang. 1981. *The Renewal of Buddhism in China: Chu-hung and the Late Ming Synthesis.* New York: Columbia University Press.

———. 1992. "P'u-t'o Shan: Pilgrimage and the Creation of the Chinese Potalaka." In *Pilgrims and Sacred Sites in China,* edited by Susan Naqun and Chün-fang Yü, pp. 190–245. Berkeley: University of California Press.

Yu Haiqing. 2008. *Media and Cultural Transformation in China.* London: Routledge.

Yu Lingbo 于凌波. 1995. *Zhongguo jinxiandai fojiao renwuzhi* 中国近现代佛教人物志. Beijing: Zongjiao wenhua chubanshe.

———. 2001. *Kuan-yin: The Chinese Transformation of Avalokitesvara.* New York: Columbia University Press.

———. 2013. *Passing the Light: The Incense Light Community and Buddhist Nuns in Contemporary Taiwan.* Honolulu: University of Hawai'i Press.

Yuan Ke 袁珂. 2012. "Fu guojia zongjiao shiwu ju yanjiu zhongxin dangzhibu dundian diaoyan baogao" 赴国家宗教事务局研究中心党支部蹲点调研报告. *Chuangxian zhengyou wang* 创先争优网. May 11. Accessed February 22, 2018. http://cxzy.people.com.cn/GB/195564/241189/242688/17868804.html.

"Yunmen shan Dajue chansi—zhuanji" 云门山大觉禅寺(专辑). 1988. *Ruyuan wenshi ziliao* 乳源文史资料 7 (October).

Zhang Xueling. 2009. "Buddhism in China." *China Today.* June 19. Accessed February 22, 2018. www.chinatoday.com.cn/ctenglish/se/txt/2009-06/19/content_203310.htm.

Zhang Xuesong 张雪松. 2015. *Fojiao "fayuan zongzu" yanjiu—Zhongguo zongjiao zuzhi moshi tanxi* 佛教 "法缘宗族" 研究—中国宗教组织模式探析. Beijing: Zhongguo renmin daxue chubanshe.

Zhanru 湛如. 2011. "Tigao banxue zhiliang, peiyang hege sengcai" 提高办学质量, 培养合格僧才. *Zhongguo minzu bao* 中国民族报, March 16. Accessed October 13, 2018. http://www.zytzb.gov.cn/tzb2010/S18210/201103/a24827e9d9344d3484581b5e4726da02.shtml.

Zhao Litao. 2010. "Religious Revival and the Emerging Secularism in China." In *State and Secularism: Perspectives from Asia,* edited by Michael Heng Siam-Heng and Ten Chin Liew, pp. 301–317. Singapore: World Scientific.

Zhao Puchu 赵朴初. 1953. "Guanyu Zhongguo fojiao xiehui faqi jingguo he choubei gongzuo de baogao" 关于中国佛教协会发起经过和筹备工作的报告. *Xiandai foxue* 现代佛学 6:4–6.

———. 1996. "Zhongguo foxueyuan sishi nian: Zai qingzhu zhongguo foxueyan chengli sishi zhounian dahui shang de jianghua" 中国佛学院四十年—在庆祝中国佛学院成立四十周年大会上的讲话. *Fayin* 法音11:3–5.

Zhao Xiaohui 赵晓辉 and Tao Junjie 陶俊洁. 2012. "Woguo fojiao mingshan zhengxiang shangshi, qingjing zhi di yinlai shi yu fei?" 我国佛教名山争相上市, 清净之地引来是与非? *Renmin ribao haiwai ban* 人民日报海外版, July 4.

Zheng Shiyou 郑士有. 1994. *Guangong xinyang* 关公信仰. Beijing: Xueyuan chubanshe.

Zheng Weiyi 郑维仪. 2010. "Tracing Tesarā: The Transmission of Buddhist Nuns' Order along the Maritime Silk Road." *Longyang xueshu yanjiu jikan* 龙阳学术研究集刊 5:19–55.

Zhiyan 智炎 and Zongdao 宗道. 2014. "Wuxi Xiangfu chansi Wuxiang zhanglao fangtanlu (xu)" 无锡祥符禅寺无相长老访谈录 (续). *Jiangsu fojiao* 江苏佛教 1:5–15.

Zhongguo Fojiao Xiehui 中国佛教协会. 1986. "Hanyuxi fojiao yuanxiao gongzuo zuotanhui jiyao" 汉语系佛教院校工作座谈会纪要. Accessed February 24, 2019. http://www.chinabuddhism.com.cn/fayin/china/g860820.htm.

———. 1992. "Quanguo hanyuxi fojiao jiaoyu gongzuo zuotanhui jiyao" 全国汉语系佛教教育工作座谈会纪要. *Fayin* 法音 3:7–11.

———. 2009. Fojiao xiehui jiaozhi renyuan zige rending banfa 汉传佛教教职人员资格认定办法. Accessed October 13, 2018. http://www.sara.gov.cn/old/xxgk/zcfg/398605.htm.

———. 2012. "Zhongguo Fojiao Xiehui Jianjie" 中国佛教协会简介. Accessed October 11, 2018. http://www.chinabuddhism.com.cn/js/jj/2012-04-20/869.html.

———. 2014. "Zhongguo Fojiao Xiehui fabu guanyu 'cibei husheng, heli fangsheng'" 中国佛教协会发布关于"慈悲护生, 合理放生"倡议书. *Fojiao zaixian* 佛教在线. July 31. Accessed February 22, 2018. http://news.fjnet.com/jjdt/jjdtnr/201407/t20140730_221273.htm.

———. 2018. Zhongguo Fojiao Xiehui 中国佛教协会. Accessed October 11, 2018. http://www.chinabuddhism.com.cn/index.html.

Zhongguo Fojiao Xiehui Cishan Gongyi Weiyuanhui 中国佛教协会慈善公益委员会. 2012a. *Zhongguo Fojiao Cishan (shangce)* 中国佛教慈善 (上册). Beijing: Zongjiao wenhua chubanshe 宗教文化出版社.

———. 2012b. *Zhongguo Fojiao Cishan (zhongce)* 中国佛教慈善 (中册). Beijing: Zongjiao wenhua chubanshe 宗教文化出版社.

———. 2012c. *Zhongguo Fojiao Cishan (xiace)* 中国佛教慈善 (下册). Beijing: Zongjiao wenhua chubanshe 宗教文化出版社.

———. 2018. Website for Zhongguo Fojiao Xiehui Cishan Gongyi Weiyuanhui 中国佛教协会慈善公益委员会. Accessed October 11, 2018. http://www.zfcs.org/gycs/csxm/.

Zhongguo Foxueyuan 中国佛学院. 2003. "Liang'an dierjie fojiao jiaoyu zuotanhui fojiao jiaoyu zongwuzu zuotan jiyao" 两岸第二届佛教教育座谈会佛教教育总务组座谈纪要. Accessed February 22, 2018. http://www.zgfxy.cn/xscg/xsjl/2011/12/29/090105463.html.

———. 2006. *Zhongguo foxueyuan dashiji* 中国佛学院大事记. Accessed February 22, 2018. http://www.zgfxy.cn/zgfxy50/zgfxy50/xiaoqing/fo50/files/385971.shtml.htm.

———. 2012. "'Wenge' qian bufen xiaoyou minglu" "文革"前部分校友名录. Accessed February 22, 2018. http://www.zgfxy.cn/xyzl/xyml/2012/02/21/125051575.html.

Zhongguo Foxueyuan Zhaosheng Bangongshi 中国佛学院招生办公室. 1994. "Zhongguo foxueyuan 1994 nian zhaosheng jianzhang" 中国佛学院1994年招生简章. *Fayin* 法音 4:18–19.

Zhongguo Gongchandang Zhongyang Weiyuanhui 中国共产党中央委员会. 1982. "Guanyu woguo shehuizhuyi shiqi zongjiao wenti de jiben guandian he jiben zhengce" 关于我国社会主义时期宗教问题的基本观点和基本政策. Guojia Zongjiao Shiwuju 国家宗教事务局. Accessed October 3, 2015. http://sara.gov.cn/gb/zcfg/zc/75352506-2bd0-11da-8858 -93180af1bb1a.html (document no longer available).

Zhonghua Fojiao Xinxiwang 中华佛教信息网. 2005. "Liaoningsheng jingzhoushi cishan zonghui fojiao cishanhui juxing chengli dahui" 辽宁省荆州市慈善总会佛教慈善会举行成立大会. Accessed December 15, 2005. http://news.fjnet.com/jjdt/jjdtnr/t20051215_19039 .htm (document no longer available).

Zhou Minghui 周明慧. 2000. "Yicun yu jiuge: Hui'an chongwu de caigu yu caitang" 依存与纠葛—惠安崇武的菜姑与菜堂. PhD diss., Taiwan Qinghua University.

Zongshun 宗舜. 2012. "Jin liangnian lai dalu fojiao jiaoyu wenti yanjiu pingshu" 近两年来大陆佛教教育问题研究述评. In *Jianwang zhilai: Liang'an foxue jiaoyu yanjiu xiankuang yu fazhan yantaohui lunwen zhuanji* 鉴往知来：两岸佛学教育研究现况与发展研讨会论文专集. Taibei: Zhonghua Foxue Yanjiusuo, pp. 1–19.

ABOUT THE CONTRIBUTORS

ASHIWA YOSHIKO is professor of anthropology and global studies at Hitotsubashi University, Japan. She is coauthor of *The Space of Religion: Temple, State, and Communities of Buddhism in Modern China* (forthcoming) and coeditor of *Making Religion, Making the State: The Politics of Religion in Modern China* (2009), both with David Wank. She has written on religion, art, culture and social values, gender, conflict, and modernity in Sri Lanka, Japan, and elsewhere in Asia.

ESTER BIANCHI is associate professor of Chinese religions and philosophy at the University of Perugia, Italy. Her works include *The Iron Statue Monastery: A Buddhist Nunnery of Tibetan Tradition in Contemporary China* (2001) and *Faxian: Un pellegrino cinese nell'India del V secolo* (2013). Her research looks at Sino-Tibetan Buddhism, Chinese Buddhist monasticism, and the revival of Buddhist monastic discipline in China.

DANIELA CAMPO is *maître de conférences* at Université de Strasbourg, France. She is the author of *La construction de la sainteté dans la Chine moderne: La vie du maître bouddhiste Xuyun* (2013). Her research focuses on the evolution of Chinese Buddhism in twentieth-century China, and especially Buddhist monastic codes, hagiographies, and lineages.

GARETH FISHER is associate professor of religion and anthropology at Syracuse University, New York. He is the author of *From Comrades to Bodhisattvas: Moral Dimensions of Lay Buddhist Practice in Contemporary China* (2014), the first book-length study of Han Chinese Buddhism in post-Mao China. His research interests include the formation of new moralities through organized Buddhism and the cultural politics behind the reconstruction of contemporary Chinese Buddhist temples.

HUANG WEISHAN is assistant professor in the Department of Cultural and Religious Studies at the Chinese University of Hong Kong. She is the coeditor of *Ecologies of Faith in New York City* (2013). Her work focuses on religion and migration, religion and the public sphere, and religion and urbanization. In particular, her research explores the impact of urbanization and religious revival on Mahayana Buddhist communities in contemporary Shanghai.

JI ZHE is professor of sociology at the Institut National des Langues et Civilisations Orientales and director of the Centre d'Études Interdisciplinaires sur le Bouddhisme, France. His recent publications include *Religion, modernité et temporalité: Une sociologie du bouddhisme chan contemporain* (2016) and *Making Saints in Modern China* (coedited with David Ownby and Vincent Goossaert, 2017). His main study areas are Buddhism and the relationship between religion and politics in modern and contemporary China.

ANDRÉ LALIBERTÉ is professor of political studies at the University of Ottawa, Canada. His publications include *Secular States and Religious Diversity* (coedited with Bruce Berman and Rajeev Bhargava, 2016) and *The Politics of Buddhist Organizations in Taiwan* (2004). He has also written on religion and political change in China and Taiwan, and his present research focuses on the outsourcing of social services provision to Buddhist merit societies and foundations.

SUSAN MCCARTHY is professor of political science at Providence College in Rhode Island. She is the author of *Communist Multiculturalism: Ethnic Revival in Southwest China* (2009). Her research focuses on the politics of religion and ethnicity in contemporary China. In particular, she examines how ethnocultural and religious practices facilitate both civic engagement and strategies of unobtrusive resistance.

BRIAN NICHOLS is an associate professor of religious studies in the Department of Humanities at Mount Royal University, Canada. He researches Buddhism in contemporary China with particular focus on the restoration of monastic traditions and the material culture of temple complexes.

STEFANIA TRAVAGNIN is assistant professor and director of the Centre for the Study of Religion and Culture in Asia at the University of Groningen, Netherlands. She is the editor of *Religion and Media in China* (2016). Her research explores Buddhism in China and Taiwan since the late Qing, concepts and methods for the study of Chinese religions, and religious diversity in modern Sichuan.

CLAIRE VIDAL is *maître de conférences* in the Department of Anthropology, Université de Lyon 2 Lumière, France. She received her PhD in ethnology from Université Paris Ouest Nanterre La Défense in 2017, with a thesis entitled "L'île (de) Guanyin: Les facettes sociologiques d'un pèlerinage dans la Chine contemporaine." Her research examines the role of pilgrimages in the revival of Chinese Buddhism.

DAVID WANK is professor of political sciences at Sophia University, Japan. He is the author of *Commodifying Communism: Business, Trust, and Politics in a Chinese City* (1999) and has coedited several volumes. His research looks at sociological questions of state and society in China, the emergence of the market economy, and the revival of Buddhism in China.

INDEX

aiguo aijiao, 63
Amitabha, 47, 283–286, 299, 309
animation, 89–90, 307n1

Bailin (Chan) Temple, 14–15, 43n25,
    99–102, 108, 116, 134, 142, 149n48,
    203, 271–281, 284–288
Baima Temple, 157, 167n32
Baisong Zhenjue, 135, 146
Baita Temple, 97, 119n29
Baojing Jinde, 136–138, 146,
    150nn60–61
Baoshan (Chan) Temple, 185, 203
Baotuo Jiang Temple, 47
Beijing, 10, 13–14, 29, 33, 35, 38–39,
    44n35, 78, 81, 84, 87, 89–92, 97, 102,
    104–109, 111, 118n13, 119n29, 130,
    133–134, 139–140, 147n2, 147n20,
    149n47, 154, 163, 171, 174–175, 181,
    187, 200, 208n5, 209n16, 226, 257,
    259–260, 263, 271, 273, 282–283,
    287–288, 289n5, 302, 304, 307,
    309n23
Benhuan Chengmiao, 130–132, 141, 146,
    148n33
Benmiao Zhiding, 133, 146
biqiu (*bhikṣu*), 147n4, 154, 157, 211
biqiuni (*bhikṣuṇī*), 145, 147n4, 154–155,
    157, 163, 166n14, 166n21, 167n32, 211
blog, 85–86, 90–91, 93, 159, 290–292,
    298, 308n7
blood writing, 93, 106
Buddha hall, 14–15, 227, 271–272,
    275–276, 282–287, 290, 293–294,
    296, 298

Buddha's Light Mountain (Foguangshan),
    37, 39, 44n38, 89, 292
Buddhicization, 211, 214, 216, 224,
    238, 243
Buddhist Academy of China, 13, 73n16,
    155, 171, 173–193, 199, 205, 208n7,
    208n13, 209n17
Buddhist Association of China (BAC),
    1, 4, 7, 10, 12–13, 16n4, 21, 25,
    28–34, 36, 38, 40, 42n10, 43n21,
    43nn23–24, 49, 52–53, 57–58, 64–65,
    77–78, 80–82, 85, 87–89, 91, 95, 97,
    103, 111–114, 116, 118n20, 123–124,
    127, 129–130, 133–135, 140, 144,
    152, 155–157, 159–164, 168nn47–48,
    170n65, 173–187, 190–196, 199, 205,
    211, 213–215, 220–221, 228, 234,
    239, 242, 244nn8–9, 254–255, 257,
    260, 262, 264, 268n12, 269n18, 273,
    275, 285, 295–296, 298, 300–303
Buddhist College of Minnan. *See* Minnan
    Institute for Buddhist Studies
Buddhist governance, 63
Buddhist media, 72n3
Bureau of Religious Affairs.
    See State Administration for
    Religious Affairs

caigu (laynun), 4, 13, 162, 201, 210–242,
    243n1
caitang (laynun hall), 213, 215–231,
    237–238, 240, 242, 245n20, 245n23,
    246n47
Caodong (lineage), 127–128, 130, 142,
    146–148, 256

chan, 11–12, 100, 104, 123–130,
134–135, 140–144, 147n7, 147n11,
148n23, 148n27, 185, 191, 208n14,
274–275, 279, 289n2
Chan genealogy, 125, 127
Chandao Fuben, 146, 148
Changhui, 94
changzhu, 197
chaodu, 217, 266, 280
charisma, 14, 62–63, 123, 131–132, 135,
272, 274, 276, 282, 285–286, 292
charity, 10, 28, 31–41, 42n13, 43nn27–
28, 44n33, 60, 66, 68, 77–81, 83–95,
262, 266, 293, 298; religious charity,
80, 95. *See also* philanthropy
Chen Shuibian (Chen Shui-bian), 36
Chen Zongrong, 102
Chengguan, 125
China dream, 23, 30, 159
Chinese Communist Party (CCP), 9,
21–24, 26–31, 34–41, 42n5, 42n8,
43n22, 44n35, 44n38, 52, 58, 78–79,
82, 98, 174, 176–177, 179–180, 189,
209n16, 212–214, 219, 225–226, 237,
244nn7–8, 293, 300, 304, 308n3
Chongfu Temple, 155, 157, 220
Chongrou, 159
Chongyang Jie, 260
Christianity, 5, 21, 23, 43n3, 43n13,
119n24, 215–216, 218, 247n58,
270n28, 288, 307
chuanfa (dharma transmission), 124–131,
134–136, 138–147, 149, 160; *chuanfa
ji*, 124; *fajuan*, 125; *sishu, fasishu*, 124
Chuanyin, 134, 142, 145, 159, 192
chujia, 72n6, 147n4, 157, 210, 235; *ban
chujia*, 83; *chujiaren*, 157, 210. *See also*
tonsure
Ciguang Hermitage, 231
Ciguang Temple, 228, 231–234, 243,
247n51
City of Ten Thousand Buddhas, 132
Cizhou, 175
clergy, 3, 52, 56, 65, 69–70, 91, 97–99,
101–102, 104, 115–116, 123, 162,
171–172, 192, 211, 217, 238, 242–243,
256, 273, 310n33

Cochini, Christian, 192
commodification (of Buddhism),
16n3, 68–69, 106, 109, 114–117,
118n16
Confucianism, 213; ancestor worship,
296; Confucian etiquette, 296;
Neo-Confucianism, 211–212, 214
conglin, 195, 255–256
cultural heritage, 25, 63, 98, 103–105,
107–110, 234, 243
cultural nexus of power, 63
Cultural Revolution, 2–3, 12–14, 22,
26–27, 37, 46, 51, 55, 57–58, 65,
73n8, 75n26, 108, 123, 129–131,
134–135, 140, 142, 161, 166n17,
168n4, 173–174, 178–179, 192, 208n7,
211–212, 219–223, 225, 227–232,
234, 243, 245n27, 246n42, 251,
253–255, 273
curator, 11, 14, 98, 101–103, 105,
107–111, 115–117
cyberactivity, 290–307
cyberspace, 292–293, 304, 306, 311n40

Dafo Temple, 107
Dajinshan Monastery, 131–132,
148n37
Dalai Lama, 29, 40, 177
Daoxin, 292
Delin, 108, 126, 149n49
Deng Xiaoping, 2, 46, 65, 138, 262
devotee, 9, 14–15, 17n8, 24, 26, 31–32,
40, 45, 47–48, 56, 60, 62, 72n4,
73n11, 75n30, 82, 101, 112–114,
196–197, 210–211, 213, 236, 241,
244n6, 245n17, 262, 265, 271,
274–281, 285–287, 289n4, 297–298,
301–303, 310n32
Dewu, 264
Dixian, 11–12, 124, 126, 133, 135–140,
146, 147n6, 149n51
Dizang (Ksitigarbha), 72n2, 266, 296,
299–300, 309nn16–17
Document no. 19, 2, 307n3
Dongfang Wenjiao Yanjiuyuan, 175
Donglin Charity Merit Association, 93
Dongyue Temple, 263

Emei (Mt.), 69, 72n2, 75n25, 148n25,
    180, 193, 200, 215
emotion, 85, 230, 240, 242–243, 306
erbuseng jie (dual ordination), 12, 152,
    154, 169n56
etatization, 173, 175–176; state-
    corporatism, 176, 199; statist
    institutionalization, 199

fahui (dharma assembly), 47, 83, 107, 266,
    273, 276, 279, 282, 289n4; *shuilu
    fahui*, 257
Falungong, 21, 23, 30–31, 214
famai (dharma/monastic lineage), 11–12,
    123–126, 128–129, 131, 133–136,
    139, 141–144, 160. *See also* Chan
    genealogy
Famen Temple, 81, 97, 99–102, 107, 112,
    193, 204
fangsheng, 10, 78, 92–95, 112, 287
fanxing qingxin nü. See *caigu*
Fayu Temple, 47, 65
Fayuan Temple, 174, 200
Fazun, 175
Fujian, 11, 13, 15, 22, 34, 81, 100,
    103–104, 108, 113, 127, 134, 147n21,
    155, 157, 162, 170n64, 172, 180, 186,
    189, 193, 200–204, 210, 212,
    220–221, 227, 230, 234–235, 271,
    307, 309n23
funeral ritual, 264. *See also chaodu*

Gaomin Monastery, 99, 104, 108, 126,
    130, 135, 149n49
gentry (*shishen*), 252, 255, 269n17;
    gentrification, 252, 267
gift exchange, 68
Great Famine, 208n10
Great Leap Forward, 177, 208n10
Guan Yu, 300, 309n17
Guang'an, 230–231, 246n46
Guangdong Fangsheng Association, 94
Guanghua Temple, 81, 104, 157, 170n64,
    180, 200
Guangji Temple, 14, 133, 140, 147n2,
    147n20, 149n47, 154–155, 271–273,
    275–288, 289n4

Guangxiao Monastery, 130, 148n34
Guankong, 175, 192
Guanyin, 45–49, 51, 53, 55–59, 61,
    63–65, 67, 69, 71, 72n1, 72n3, 72n6,
    73n7, 73nn9–10, 210, 212–213,
    215–217, 223–224, 233, 239–242,
    247n56, 247n65, 247nn67–68,
    248n70, 284, 299–300,
    309nn17–18
Guanzong Monastery, 139, 200
Guifeng Zongmi, 125
guiyi, 16n8
guiyi zheng, 113, 116, 119n29
Guoqing Temple, 180, 200
Gushan, 127, 155

Han Qingjing, 208n5
harmonious society, 23, 30–31, 36, 40,
    56, 79
He Qiyun, 101
Hebei, 14, 31, 44n32, 94, 99, 103,
    106–107, 134, 148n28, 193, 203, 271,
    274–275
Hebei Provincial Buddhist Association, 94
Hong Kong, 11, 23, 25, 27, 33, 35–36, 38,
    44n35, 57, 124, 132–133, 135–143,
    149n43, 149n45, 156, 162, 169n54,
    218, 268n16, 275
Hong Kong Buddhist Association, 38,
    138, 150n63
Hongfa Temple, 32, 148n32, 148n34,
    149n40, 185–186, 194, 204
Hongluo Temple, 98, 106, 109
Hongyi, 157, 167n27, 211, 216–218, 223,
    235, 239, 243, 244nn5–6, 245n15,
    245n23
Hsu Yun Temple, 133
Hu Jintao, 9, 21–23, 27, 31, 35–36,
    38, 56
Huang Chanhua, 191
Huiji Temple, 65
Huiming, 14, 108, 117n6, 251, 255–261,
    264, 266, 269n23, 269n26
Huineng, 185, 208
huixiang, 294
Hunan Province Buddhist Compassion
    Charity Foundation, 87

institutional environment, 49, 60, 62, 66
Internet, 8, 25, 90–91, 94, 150n62,
    291–292, 296, 298, 301–302,
    304–307
Islam, 1, 21, 42n3, 42n13, 74n17, 119n24,
    176, 253, 307

Japan, 2, 21, 28–30, 45, 47, 73n10, 90,
    167n35, 185, 190, 214, 226, 245n23,
    257, 275
Jia Qinglin, 38
Jiang Baohua, 62
Jiang Zemin, 22–23, 27, 35, 275–276,
    279, 300, 308n3
Jiangxi, 93, 104, 128, 130–131, 134, 146,
    148n27, 151n79, 168n47, 189, 202
jianyuan, 140, 255
Jianzhen, 185–186, 204
Jiduan Dingrong, 146, 149n51
Jiechuang Lü Temple, 168n40, 184, 203
jielü (Vinaya, monastic discipline), 83,
    104, 125, 153–168, 172, 191, 196, 198,
    203–204, 209n22, 217, 238, 244n5.
    See also Nanshan lü; pusajie
jielü fuxing (Vinaya resurgence), 153–154,
    158–159, 165n4, 167n27, 170n62
Jiequan, 157, 189–190, 198
Jietai Temple, 109, 118n13
Jilin, 14, 137, 272
Jing'an Temple, 102, 107–109, 111, 202,
    251–271
Jingang Daochang, 175
Jinghai, 191
Jinghui, 100, 108, 127, 131, 134, 141–142,
    145–146, 147n20, 149n39, 149nn47–
    48, 175, 193, 275–276, 279, 286
Jingkong, 272, 287, 288n1
Jinglian Hall, 224–225, 246n34
Jingquan, 137, 146, 150n61
Jiqun, 157, 159, 168n40, 196, 198
Jiuhua (Mt.), 33, 69, 72n2, 75n25,
    193, 201
Juebin, 223, 246n33
Jueguang Qiben (Sik Kok Kwong),
    138–142, 146, 150n64, 150n72
jushi (lay practitioner, layperson,
    laypeople), 4, 9, 14–15, 16n8, 21,

24–26, 31, 37, 42n12, 43n16, 46, 49,
    56, 59, 67–68, 72n3, 73n11, 73n15,
    81, 89, 92, 98, 113–116, 132, 147n4,
    154, 168n35, 178, 197, 208n15,
    210–211, 215, 217, 220, 228, 232–233,
    236, 242–243, 244n8, 245n15,
    260–261, 271–282, 285, 286–287,
    289n2, 289n4. See also devotee; laity
jushilin, 21, 261
Juzan, 192
juzujie (upasaṃpadā, complete ordination),
    154–157

Kaiyuan Temple, 11, 99–100, 102–104,
    107–116, 118nn17–18, 118n20, 201,
    246n46, 269n22, 271
Kang Youwei, 2
karma, 86, 163, 207, 302
Korea, 28–30, 45, 47, 119n28, 140, 223

Laiguo, 126, 130, 149n49
laity, 4, 92, 115–116, 147n4, 159, 279–280
laynun. See caigu
laynun hall, 213, 215–231, 237–238, 240,
    245n20, 245n23, 246n38, 246n47,
    247n62
Lei Feng, 10, 63, 79–80, 86–88, 95
Lian Zhan (Lien Chan), 36, 38
Lianguang Hall, 229–230
Lin Qitai, 81
Lingfeng Ouyi, 149n52
Lingyanshan Temple, 179, 200
Lingyi Jizhao, 145, 148n28
Linji (lineage), 125, 127–128, 130–133,
    141, 145–146, 147n19, 148nn24–25,
    149n38, 218, 227, 274–275
Linji Temple, 107
Liu Feng, 192
liu he, 160, 168n43
Living Chan Summer Camp, 149n48,
    275–276, 279
Longhua Temple, 33, 132–133, 140,
    149n51, 150n72, 203, 252
Longlian, 155–157, 163, 166n21, 166n24,
    167n25, 167nn32–33, 169n56
Longquan Temple, 10, 26, 29, 33, 78–83,
    88–92, 203, 290, 302, 307n1, 310n34

Longxing Temple, 106–107, 109
Lotus Sutra, 191, 274
loving heart congee, 83–86, 93
Lü Cheng, 175, 191, 208n5

Ma Yingjiu (Ma Ying-jeou), 36
Maitreya, 184, 202, 274, 309n17
Medicine Buddha, 309n17
merit (gongde), 15, 31–34, 40, 43n25, 48,
    77–78, 80, 92–95, 111, 114, 136,
    207n2, 224, 283–284, 292, 294–298,
    309n15, 309n25
miaochan xingxue, 2, 171
Miaoci Fayun, 145, 149n45
Miaofalin Hall, 225–226, 246n31,
    246n35
Miaoqing Temple, 223–224, 246n32
Miaoshan (monk), 58, 65, 74n23,
    75nn26–27, 126, 147n18
Miaoshan (divinity), 212, 215, 239–242,
    247n65, 247n68, 248nn69–70
Miaoxin Foyuan, 129–130, 145, 148n29,
    149n39
Miaozhan, 108, 150n73, 195–196,
    220–221, 227, 230–232
Mingfa Buddha Hall, 272, 282, 284,
    286–287
Minghai, 100, 108, 286
Mingkong Weisheng, 129–130
Mingshan, 166n19, 179
Mingxue, 175, 179
Mingyang, 132–133, 140–141, 149n41
Mingzhe, 140–141, 146, 151n74, 175, 192
Mingzhen, 192
Minnan, 13, 210–223, 228–231, 233–241,
    243nn1–2, 244n3, 244n5, 245n15,
    245n20, 247nn52–53, 247n59,
    248n68
Minnan Institute for Buddhist Studies,
    104, 184, 186, 190, 193, 195, 200,
    216, 220–221, 227–228, 230–231,
    233, 244n5, 246n28, 246n33, 293,
    298, 300, 309n12
mixin (superstition), 2, 61, 89, 214, 216,
    247n66
modernization, 46, 75n27, 215, 217, 220,
    245n19, 299

mofa shiqi, 274
morality book (shanshu), 274, 278, 309n15
museumification, 105–107, 109

Nanhua (Chan) Temple, 104, 130,
    132–133, 148n31, 149nn43–44, 180,
    185, 200
Nanputuo Temple, 15, 22, 26, 34, 41,
    104, 108, 118n20, 159, 200, 215, 218,
    220–227, 229–232, 234, 240, 242,
    246n28, 246n46, 246n49, 247n55,
    247n67, 271, 293–294, 297–298,
    300–301, 303–307
Nanshan lü, 125, 153, 155, 157, 244n5
Nanxiang Temple, 252
Nengchan, 140–141, 146
Nenghai, 147n17, 314
Nengshou, 101
nianfo, 99, 113, 295, 302
novice, 147n4, 153–154, 156–158, 162,
    165n7, 165n12, 167n34, 210–211, 221,
    230, 237; shami (śrāmaṇera), 147n14,
    158, 211; shamini (śrāmaṇerī),
    147n14, 211

offering hall, 293–294, 299–300
online Buddhism 291, 294; offline
    practice, 300–301, 305, 310n26;
    online Buddha hall, 290, 293–294,
    296, 298; online Memorial Worship
    Site, 293–295, 298; online practice,
    292, 294–305, 307; online ritual, 290,
    292–293, 297–299, 301–302,
    305–306, 309n24, 310n26; online
    sutra-copying, 293–295, 309n19;
    online worship/digital worship, 15,
    290, 298–300, 303–304, 306
ordination (shoujie, shou juzujie), 4, 12,
    123, 129, 131–135, 140, 142–143,
    147n1, 147n4, 147n15, 149n43,
    152–170, 182, 184, 218, 239, 245n24,
    262, 273; jietan, 153, 162, 164n3,
    169n51; jieti, 160; santan dajie (triple
    platform ordination), 12, 147n4,
    152–157, 162, 165n6, 167n29,
    167nn34–35, 168n47, 169n54, 218
Ouyang Jian, 172, 191, 207n2, 207n5

Panlong Temple, 101–102
Paradise of Western Bliss, 47–48,
    227, 283
patriotism, 190, 207, 237, 307
philanthropy, 3, 10, 23–24, 27, 31–34,
    40–41, 77, 81, 88, 94. See also charity
pilgrimage, 4, 23, 25–26, 40, 42n15,
    45–49, 55–56, 58–59, 63, 70–71,
    73n9, 75n27, 247n67, 296
Political Consultative Conference, 39,
    43n21, 81, 261
probationer (śikṣamāṇā), 154
public servant, 50, 226
Puci, 228, 230–233
Puguang, 228–231, 233
Puji Temple, 47, 64, 65
Pure Land, 47, 88, 92–93, 134, 141, 185,
    191, 224, 284, 287
pusa jie (Bodhisattva precepts), 42n13,
    154, 165n10, 236–237, 247n60
Putuo (Mt.), 11, 26, 45–50, 54–71, 108,
    126, 159, 185–186, 194, 201, 240
Putuoshan xuanyan, 57
Puxian (Samantabhadra), 72n2, 300,
    309n17

Qihuan Jingshe, 172
Qingfu Hall /Qingfu Temple 庆福寺, 227
Qingming Jie, 226, 303
Qixia Temple, 179, 186, 189, 193–194,
    200
Qixian, 148n28
Quanzhou, 11, 34, 99–100, 102–104,
    107–112, 115, 118n18–19, 201,
    204, 210, 214–215, 219, 221,
    234, 236, 243, 245n15, 245n20,
    246n46, 271
quasi-monasticism, 91

reinvention, 3, 8, 12
Religious activity site, 227, 247n58, 271,
    273, 283
Religious Affairs Bureau. See State
    Administration for Religious
    Affairs
religious culture, 62
religious ecology, 5–6

religious field, 49, 51, 55, 58, 66, 70,
    72n2, 73n14
religious market, 5, 119n25
religious professional, 13, 180, 190,
    210–212, 222–239, 243, 247n58,
    247nn62–63
religious revival, 4, 14, 63, 71, 80, 102,
    180, 254
Ren'ai Charity Foundation, 10, 33–34,
    78–79, 85–86
renjian fojiao (Buddhism for the human
    realm), 10, 80, 83, 88, 245n19, 300
repentance hall (chanhui tang), 293–294
revivalist, 11, 14, 98–99, 102–104,
    108–111, 115–117

Śākyamuni, 84
sangha, 9–10, 12–13, 22, 28–29, 59, 88,
    97, 99, 101, 105–107, 111, 116, 139,
    143, 154, 156, 159–164, 171–173,
    176–183, 185–190, 194–196,
    199–200, 202–204, 207, 271, 275,
    292–293, 297, 300–302, 306. See also
    clergy
Sanshi Xuehui, 208n5
Shanghai, 4, 32–34, 41, 46, 48, 84, 97,
    107–110, 118n19, 133, 139–140, 175,
    179, 200, 203, 244n5, 251–257, 260,
    262–264, 266–267, 268n9, 268n13,
    268n16, 269n24, 270n29, 287,
    289n5, 291
Shanghai Buddhist Academy, 180,
    255–256, 260
Shanghai Buddhist Association, 32,
    254–256, 258–259, 261, 268n12,
    269n17
Shenghui, 87, 159–161, 193, 221
Shengyan (Sheng-Yen), 191, 209n23
Shengyi, 132, 145
Sherab Gyatso (Xirao Jiacuo), 156,
    166n23, 174, 177–178
shifang conglin. See conglin
shouzuo, 130
shudi guanli, 183
sijiu (four olds), 2, 203, 246n42
social media, 90–91, 94, 291–292,
    298

Songchun, 175
spiritual technology, 77–78, 85,
    93, 95
State Administration for Religious Affairs
    (SARA), 31, 38, 42n3, 50–57, 64, 66,
    75n26, 78, 97–98, 101–102, 109–110,
    139, 161, 176, 181, 184, 187, 189, 192,
    197, 199, 208n8, 209n20, 226, 234,
    238, 244n8, 258, 305, 307

Taiwan, 9, 16n4, 22–25, 27–30, 35–40,
    42n9, 43n20, 44n35, 44n38, 119n25,
    57, 82, 89, 132, 140, 156, 158,
    162–163, 166n12, 167n35, 168n38,
    169nn54–55, 191–192, 213–214,
    243n2, 244n7, 245n23, 262, 288, 291,
    309n15
Taixu, 10, 34, 88–89, 126, 172–173,
    175–176, 191, 216, 245n19, 246n33,
    253, 293, 298, 300, 308n12
Tanxu, 136–141, 146, 150n55,
    150nn58–59
Tanzhe Temple, 109, 118n13
Taoism, 1, 22, 74nn17–18, 92, 94–95,
    102, 113–115, 117n8, 119nn24–25,
    209n25, 213, 244n10, 253, 300
temple administrative commission, 98,
    101–102, 106–107, 109–110, 112, 115,
    118n13, 118n20, 269n22
temple management, 65, 119n22,
    196
Theravada, 1, 163, 166n16, 169n60,
    170n61, 191, 204
Three Unifiers, 49–50, 63–68, 70,
    75nn27–29
Tianjin, 33, 39, 84, 137, 266, 289n5
Tianning (Chan) Temple, 98, 104–105,
    111, 174, 202
Tiantai (lineage), 11–12, 123–126,
    133–144, 146, 147n10, 150n69,
    166n17, 184, 191, 204
Tiantai (Mt.), 180, 200
Tibet, 25, 29–30, 43n21, 178, 266
Tibetan Buddhism, 1, 22, 29–31, 35,
    42n1, 106n4, 119n28, 147n17, 163,
    174–175, 177–178, 180, 187,
    204, 232

Tiexiang Temple, 155, 162, 163,
    166n18, 166n22, 166n24, 180, 200,
    246n29
Tiguang (Benda Yinxuan), 146, 148n27
tonsure, 3, 123, 129, 134–135, 142, 145,
    147n4, 147n8, 148n25, 149n43, 158,
    167n25, 169n50, 190, 209nn21–22,
    234. See also *chujia*
tourism, 8, 10–11, 16n3, 22–23, 25–27,
    30, 40–41, 47, 49, 56, 58, 61–63,
    68–69, 73n13, 98, 102–107, 112,
    114–117, 275, 281, 298; religious
    tourism, 25–26, 30, 40, 42n15, 62,
    298; tourist site, 3, 11, 47, 69, 97, 99,
    107–109, 111–114, 117; tourist temple,
    97–99, 101–102, 103, 105, 107,
    109, 111, 113, 115–117 , 117n10,
    310n31
Tzu Chi, 38–39, 82, 89, 265, 270n29,
    285, 291

UNESCO, 25–26, 118n19
United Front Work Department, 51–53,
    78, 139, 184, 189, 226, 244n8,
    264–265
upāya, 305

Vietnam, 28, 177
Vinaya. See *jielü*
volunteer, 27, 78–79, 82–86, 91–94, 116,
    260–261, 280, 283–286, 289n4,
    310n34; *hufa*, 132, 280, 289n4; *yigong*,
    82, 280, 289n4; *zhigong*, 82

Wang Enyang, 175
Wang Liansheng, 64–67, 75n28
Wang Lu, 81
wealth circulation, 66–67
WeChat, 89, 91, 94, 290–291, 293,
    298–299, 306–307, 309n14,
    309n17
Weiyin Jinguo, 130, 133
Welch, Holmes, 3, 27, 123, 138, 141–142,
    173
wenming, 56, 290–291, 293, 295, 297,
    299–305, 307, 309n25, 311n38
Wenshu (Manjusri), 72n2, 300, 309n17

Wenshu Temple, 155, 201
World Buddhist Forum, 9, 23, 29, 32, 36, 38, 44nn37–38, 56, 57, 74n22
World Fellowship of Buddhists (WFB), 23, 28–29, 43n19, 138
Wuchang Institute for Buddhist Studies, 172, 194, 202
Wuxiang, 175

Xi Jinping, 9, 21–23, 28, 30, 39, 43n22, 300, 304, 307
Xiamen, 15, 34, 39, 41, 104, 108, 118n20, 200, 210–216, 218–219, 220–221, 223, 226–228, 231–240, 243n2, 244n7, 244n9, 244n13, 245nn16–17, 245n25, 247n52, 247n62, 247n67, 271, 301, 308n12, 309n25
Xian'er, 89–90, 290, 302, 307n1
Xianggang fojiao, 138–139, 141, 150n69
Xianming Nianfa, 146, 150n62
Xiaoyun, 156, 167n25
Xingguang, 157
Xingyang Ciduo, 127, 144
Xingyun (Hsing Yun), 37–39, 44n38, 89, 292
Xiwang Gongcheng, 33
Xuande Shaoyun, 145, 148n28
Xuanhua Dulun, 132, 144
Xuanming Haideng, 145, 149n46
Xuanyang Xingfu, 144, 149n46
Xuecheng, 1, 10, 29, 33–35, 43n21, 78–83, 87–92, 95, 96n1, 134–135, 155–156, 163–164, 170n64, 193, 195, 302, 310nn33–34
Xuedou (Mt.), 184, 202
Xuedou Temple, 184
xueseng (student-monastic, student-monk), 173–175, 177, 179, 185–187, 189–190, 196–198, 205n18, 253
Xuyun, 11–12, 124, 126–135, 138–139, 141–142, 144–149, 168n42

Yang Wenhui, 125, 172–173, 191, 207n2, 215
Yang Zhao, 132
Yanlian, 157
Yanxin Yicheng, 133–134

Yayun, 262
Ye Jun, 175
Ye Xiaowen, 38, 139
Yichao (Benzhao Shengkong), 146, 149n43
Yifa, 104
Yiguandao, 39
Yinkong Changzhen, 131–132, 149n38
Yiran, 157
Yonghe Gong, 97
Yongquan Temple, 127, 147n21, 155, 157, 259, 268n2
Yongxing Niangen, 138–141, 146
Yuanshan, 140, 146
Yuanying, 29, 149n41, 268n5
Yuanzhuo, 157, 170n64
Yuexia, 125
Yufo (Chan) Temple, 32, 97, 150n70, 180, 200, 255
Yulanpen Jie (Ullambana), 303
Yunju (Mt.), 104, 128, 134, 168n47
Yunju Temple, 106–107, 109
Yunmen (lineage), 125, 127–130, 134, 142, 145, 149, 218
Yunmen Temple, 128–130, 134, 149n45, 201
Yunqi Temple, 130
Yuyu, 175

zaijia, 16n8, 168n35. See also *jushi*
Zewu, 231, 234
Zhaijiao, 213–214, 241, 244n11, 244n13, 245n23
Zhang Jingfu, 57, 64, 75n26
Zhang Taiyan, 125
Zhang Zhidong, 2
Zhanru, 43n21, 180, 194, 208n13
Zhanshan Temple, 137, 140–141, 150n58, 151n74, 204
Zhao Puchu, 29, 118n20, 155, 160, 174, 179, 185, 208n7, 268nn4–5
Zhaojue Temple, 304
Zhaozhou Congshen, 274–277
Zhejiang, 10, 23, 34, 45, 51, 55, 58–59, 61–62, 72n5, 74n21, 74n24, 113, 134, 155, 180, 184–185, 189, 200–204,

240, 244n5, 287, 288n1, 308n12, 309n23
Zhengguo, 175, 192
Zhengyan (Cheng Yen), 38, 89, 285
Zhenru Temple, 104, 128, 130–131, 134, 149n46, 168n47, 258

zhike (guest prefect), 130, 149n45, 255–256
Zhina Neixueyuan, 175, 191, 207n5
Zhongfeng Chan Temple, 180, 200
Zhou Enlai, 273
Zhuanfeng, 231
Zongjiao shiwu tiaoli, 183, 306

Printed in the United States
By Bookmasters